W9-BLW-521

Assessing Psychological Trauma and PTSD

ASSESSING PSYCHOLOGICAL TRAUMA AND PTSD

Edited by
JOHN P. WILSON
TERENCE M. KEANE

Foreword by Susan D. Solomon

THE GUILFORD PRESS
New York   London

©1997 The Guilford Press
A Division of Guilford Publications, Inc.
72 Spring Street, New York, NY 10012

Printed in the United States of America

This book is printed on acid-free paper.

Last digit is print number: 9   8   7   6   5   4   3   2

Library of Congress Cataloging-in-Publication Data

Assessing psychological trauma and PTSD / edited by John P.
    Wilson and Terence M. Keane.
        p.   cm.
    Includes bibliographical references and index.
    ISBN 1-57230-162-7
    1. Post-traumatic stress disorder—Diagnosis.
2. Psychodiagnostics.   3. Neuropsychological tests.   I. Wilson,
John P. (John Preston)   II. Keane, Terence Martin.
    [DNLM: 1. Stress Disorders, Post-Traumatic.   WM 170 A846 1997]
    RC552.P67A85   1997
    616.85'21—dc20
    DNLM/DLC
    for Library of Congress   96-30206
                                                                      CIP

Dedication

As this book was being prepared, the war in the former Yugoslavia raged on unrelentingly until 1995. The Balkans War produced a toll of 3.5 million refugees, most of them homeless, amid the death count of over 200,000. Fifty years earlier, World War II created an even larger Holocaust, which devastated Europe and the former Soviet Union. In that same World War, the first atomic bombs destroyed Hiroshima and Nagasaki, killing over 192,000 persons. Twenty years after Hiroshima, the United States entered the Vietnam War, which left nearly 60,000 Americans dead, 300,000 severely injured, and 500,000 with posttraumatic stress disorder (PTSD). After the fall of Saigon in 1975, the Khmer Rouge unleashed a genocide in Cambodia, and once again the Killing Fields left over 1.5 million dead and countless others as homeless refugees. Over a year ago, a terrorist bomb destroyed the Federal Office Building in Oklahoma City. In the carnage were innocent children who were in day care while their parents and others worked in the seemingly safe environment. In addition to these more public events, millions are traumatized each year through domestic violence, child abuse, rape, and hate crimes—their cries too singular or their shame too great to draw attention to their suffering.

To say that we live in an era of trauma and human suffering in the global community is a truism and a tragedy. This book is dedicated to the constructive processes of human rights, efforts toward lasting peace, and the elimination of those human events and acts that threaten the existence of humankind and the rights of the individual. Our knowledge and understanding of trauma and PTSD is an important step in what must become a broader mission for the generations of the future.

Contributors

John Briere, Ph.D., Department of Psychiatry and the Behavioral Sciences, University of Southern California School of Medicine, Los Angeles, California

Juesta M. Caddell, Ph.D., Research Triangle Institute, Research Triangle Park, North Carolina; Department of Psychiatry and Behavioral Sciences, Duke University Medical Center, Durham, North Carolina

Ruth R. DeRosa, M.A. Institute for Behavioral Health, Commack, New York

Steven A. Epstein, M.D., Department of Psychiatry, Georgetown University Medical School, Washington, DC

John A. Fairbank, Ph.D., Research Triangle Institute, Research Triangle Park, North Carolina; Department of Psychiatry and Behavioral Sciences, Duke University Medical Center, Durham, North Carolina

Bonnie L. Green, Ph.D., Department of Psychiatry, Georgetown University Medical School, Washington, DC

B. Kathleen Jordan, Ph.D., Research Triangle Institute, Research Triangle Park, North Carolina; Department of Psychiatry and Behavioral Sciences, Duke University Medical Center, Durham, North Carolina

Danny G. Kaloupek, Ph.D., Department of Veterans Affairs Medical Center, Boston, Massachusetts; Tufts University School of Medicine, Boston, Massachusetts

Terence M. Keane, Ph.D., Department of Veterans Affairs Medical Center, Boston, Massachusetts; Tufts University School of Medicine, Boston, Massachusetts

Rachel Kimerling, M.S., Department of Psychology, University of Georgia, Athens, Georgia

Daniel W. King, Ph.D., Department of Veterans Affairs Medical Center, Boston, Massachusetts; Tufts University School of Medicine, Boston, Massachusetts

Lynda A. King, Ph.D., Department of Veterans Affairs Medical Cetner, Boston, Massachusetts; Tufts University School of Medicine, Boston, Massachusetts

Jeffrey A. Knight, Ph.D., National Center for PTSD — Behavioral Sciences Division, Department of Veterans Affairs Medical Center, Boston, Massachusetts

Janice L. Krupnick, Ph.D., Department of Psychiatry, Georgetown University Medical School, Washington, DC

Robert R. Kurtz, Ph.D., Department of Psychology, Cleveland State University, Cleveland, Ohio

Leslie Lebowitz, Ph.D., National Center for PTSD, Department of Veterans Affairs Medical Center, Boston, Massachusetts

Patti Levin, L.I.C.S.W., Psy.D., The Trauma Center at Human Resource Institute, Brookline, Massachusetts

Spero M. Manson, Ph.D., National Center for American Indian and Alaska Native Mental Health Research, University of Colorado Health Sciences Center, Denver, Colorado

Charles R. Marmar, M.D., Department of Psychiatry, University of California, San Francisco, California; Posttraumatic Stress Disorder Program, Department of Veterans Affairs Medical Center, San Francisco, California

Nada Martinek, Ph.D., Senior Research Assistant, Department of Psychiatry, The University of Queensland, Brisbane, Australia

Thomas J. Metzler, M.A., Department of Psychiatry, University of California, San Francisco, California; PTSD Program, Department of Veterans Affairs Medical Center, San Francisco, California

Kathleen O. Nader, Ph.D., Private Practive, Laguna Hills, California

Elana Newman, Ph.D., Department of Veterans Affairs Medical Center, Boston, Massachusetts; Tufts University School of Medicine, Boston, Massachusetts

Fran H. Norris, Ph.D., Department of Psychology, Georgia State University, Atlanta, Georgia

Scott P. Orr, Ph.D., Harvard Medical School, Boston, Massachusetts; Department of Veterans Affairs Medical Center, Manchester, New Hampshire

Susan M. Orsillo, P.A., Department of Veterans Affairs Medical Center, Boston, Massachusetts; Tufts University School of Medicine, Boston, Massachusetts

Beverley Raphael, M.D., FRANZCP, Department of Psychiatry, The University of Queensland, Brisbane, Australia

Bruce Reis, Ph.D., Department of Psychology, New York University, New York, New York

Jasmin K. Riad, M.A., Department of Psychology, Georgia State University, Atlanta, Georgia

Susan Roth, Ph.D., Department of Psychology—Social and Health Sciences, Duke University, Durham, North Carolina

Julia H. Rowland, Ph.D., Department of Psychiatry, Georgetown University Medical School, Washington, DC

William E. Schlenger, Ph.D., Mental and Behavioral Health Research, Research Triangle Institute, Research Triangle Park, North Carolina; Department of Psychiatry and Behavioral Sciences, Duke University Medical Center, Durham, North Carolina

Marlene Steinberg, M.D., Department of Psychiatry, Yale School of Medicine, New Haven, Connecticut; Private Practice, New Haven, Connecticut, and Northampton, Massachusetts

Frank W. Weathers, Ph.D., Department of Veterans Affairs Medical Center, Boston, Massachusetts; Tufts University School of Medicine, Boston, Massachusetts

Daniel S. Weiss, Ph.D., Department of Psychiatry, Univeristy of California, San Francisco, California; PTSD Program, Department of Veterans Affairs Medical Center, San Francisco, California

John P. Wilson, Ph.D., Department of Psychology, Cleveland State University, Cleveland, Ohio

Jessica Wolfe, Ph.D., National Center for PTSD, Department of Veterans Affairs Medical Center, Boston, Massachusetts; Tufts University School of Medicine, Boston, Massachusetts

Foreword

In drawing together assessment strategies for trauma and post-traumatic stress disorder (PTSD), the editors have provided a valuable and creative stimulus to our knowledge of how to study, prevent, treat, and predict the consequences of exposure to catastrophic and life-threatening situations. By recognizing the need to consider measurement, not only in terms of developing standardized tools, but also in adapting these tools to diverse populations and types of trauma, this work is a unique and comprehensive contribution to assessment. Given the breadth of traumatic events and populations we in our profession are faced with treating and studying, this sensitive approach to measurement is critical.

We all have read innumerable statistics about the rates of trauma and PTSD. By any measure these rates are frightening. We now know that trauma is far from "outside the range of usual human experience" as it was described in DSM-III-R (American Psychiatric Association, 1987). On the contrary, these events seem to happen to the vast majority of people in our society, often repeatedly. And yet these rates that we read about also show a great deal of variability. This variability poses a serious problem for our society. We need to be able to accurately assess the parameters of trauma, establish effective public policy regarding it, and provide the mechanisms for funding the scientific study and the clinical services needed to treat or prevent PTSD. Variability in reported rates can result from many factors, but the most powerful of these is likely to be the measurement tools that are used. And to the extent that our measurement tools are limited, so too is our understanding of the world in which we live, and our ability to improve it.

Epidemiology studies are not the only investigations to require a useful and valid way to measure trauma and PTSD. Clinical studies of the diagnosis, course, comorbidity, and treatment of trauma victims all depend on valid measures of PTSD. And researchers are not the only ones to need these tools. Practitioners in clinical, medical, and legal settings also must know how to identify individuals suffering from the psychological consequences of trauma exposure. And whether we are talking about research or practice, what is valid for one population may not be valid for another. Age, sex, ethnic, and other differences pose major methodological challenges to trauma workers struggling to get a picture of how traumatic events affect the individuals exposed to them. While the diagnostic criteria are fairly clear, victims suffering from PTSD vary in severity, in comorbidity, and in functional impairment. Precipitating stressors also vary in severity, and measurement strategies that require victims to make the link between their symptoms and the traumatic experience that precipitated them may underestimate the extent of traumatic response. The complexity of these issues requires a correspondingly complex approach to trauma and PTSD assessment.

By pulling together some of the foremost experts on PTSD and trauma methodology, the editors demonstrate their understanding of this complexity. Which measure of PTSD is best will vary according to a the trauma professional's purpose and resource constraints. No single measure can definitively determine whether an individual has PTSD. All measures are imperfect and contain errors, suggesting the need for the use of multiple measures of PTSD in situations where accurate diagnosis is critical.

This handbook is all the more valuable for demonstrating the need to look beyond PTSD, since many other negative psychological outcomes can also result from trauma exposure. And regardless of how PTSD is assessed, this handbook also makes clear the need to separately assess exposure to traumatic events. Since the events themselves vary, instrumentation must be sensitive not only to different kinds of victim populations but also to the characteristics of the traumatic experience itself. By offering a comprehensive and detailed overview of available trauma and PTSD instruments, this handbook will help both researchers and practitioners select measures that are best suited to their particular goals and populations.

It is my hope that the rapid proliferation of PTSD instruments that we have witnessed in the past 10 years is coming to an end, and that future research in PTSD assessment will concentrate on refining and validating existing instruments in populations exposed to different types of traumatic events. Through systematic efforts at refinement, our understanding of PTSD will be incrementally enhanced, since the use of standardized measures will allow us to compare the effects of traumatic events across different studies, and to compare the effectiveness of interventions to ameliorate the negative consequences of exposure to these events. This handbook does much to move us in the direction of achieving this goal.

Susan D. Solomon, Ph.D.
*Senior Advisor, Office of Behavioral
and Social Sciences Research,
National Institutes of Health
Member of Board of Directors, International Society
of Traumatic Stress Studies*

REFERENCE

American Psychiatric Association. (1987). *Diagnostic and statistical manual of mental disorders* (3rd ed., rev.). Washington, DC: Author.

Acknowledgments

This book is the culmination of several years of collaboration among the contributors and was designed to provide a standardized reference on the methods, techniques, and clinical procedures for assessing psychological trauma and posttraumatic stress disorder (PTSD). The scope of this work required the assistance of many dedicated persons concerned with the multifaceted nature of psychological trauma. At Cleveland State University, Lynn Viola, the department secretary, provided countless hours of work editing the manuscripts. Special thanks are extended to Joseph (Chris) Bedosky, graduate assistant, without whose persistence, eye for detail, and knowledge of PTSD, this book would not have been completed. Similarly, Sherry Hills, Thomas Malinak, and James Smagola labored to ensure the quality and completeness of each chapter.

We wish also to recognize the staff of the National PTSD Center in Boston for their assistance and research efforts. Finally, thanks are extended to the members of the International Society for Traumatic Stress Studies for their encouragement and endorsement of the project to establish this reference book for the field of traumatology.

Contents

III. Assessing Traumatic Reactions, Dissociation, and Posttraumatic Stress Disorder

Introduction

JOHN P. WILSON

This volume developed out of the recognition that there was a need to fill a void in the standardized references in the field of traumatology, especially in the area of assessing the response to trauma and posttraumatic stress disorder (PTSD). The conceptual, empirical, and psychological advances in the field of traumatic stress studies have made it possible to bring together (in one reference volume) a practical guide for those practitioners, clinicians, and researchers who need to make informed decisions concerning the assessment of traumatic stress responses. The contributors to this volume are among the leaders in the field. Their work has made possible a scientific standardization of methods and techniques to diagnose, assess, and measure traumatic stressor experiences and PTSD symptoms. It is our hope that the use of this volume will ultimately bring to practitioners the possibility of insight and understanding as they work to enable the healing process in victims of trauma.

There are three distinct parts to the organizational structure of this volume. Part I focuses on *conceptual approaches* and *standardized measures* of trauma and PTSD.

In Chapter 1, Fran H. Norris and Jasmin H. Riad present a comprehensive overview of over 20 measures of civilian trauma and PTSD. Practitioners concerned with selecting an appropriate measure of stressors and PTSD should begin here, as this chapter discusses the advantages and limitations of the many self-report measures available. In a similar fashion, John Briere reviews in Chapter 2 standardized assessment procedures for adults who were subjected to abusive experiences as children. Briere highlights the difficulties, that have faced practitioners in the past when trying to make a careful determination of the long-term psychological and psychosocial consequences of childhood abuse. Beyond clinical applications, Chapter 2 will assist those involved in forensic settings, whose litigation centers around questions of sexual abuse and its impact on adult functioning. Part I includes a current review and discussion of physiological assessment techniques for PTSD. In Chapter 3, Scott Orr and Danny Kaloupek report on the step-by-step procedures that can be used to obtain valid physiological techniques for the assessment of PTSD. Of particular importance in Chapter 3 are the research findings that go beyond the limitations of self-report data to demonstrate, with high levels of scientific validity and prediction, the physiological indicators of PTSD. In Chapter 4, Frank Weathers carefully details the logic and psychometric theory which forms the basis for developing measures of trauma and PTSD.

Part II of this volume is devoted to the *assessment of traumatic reactions among victim and survivor populations.* In Chapter 5, William Schlenger and his colleagues present state of the art epidemiological methods for determining PTSD and comorbidity prevalence rates in the general population. Based on the landmark National Vietnam Veterans Readjustment Study (NVVRS) Schlenger and his colleagues have standardized the methods and instruments necessary to carry out this type of survey research. Practitioners concerned with undertaking a research study to accurately determine prevalence rates of PTSD after a trauma or disaster will find Chapter 5 a rich and intelligent guide to carrying out a reliable study.

In Chapters 6 through 9, specific populations of survivors are studied, and measures unique to them are presented in the respective chapters. Among the unique contributions to this book is that of Bonnie L. Green and her colleagues (Chapter 6) who present groundbreaking research on trauma-related disorders in the medical setting. Green and her colleagues demonstrate that life-threatening illness and other diseases can be directly associated with the development of PTSD as well as other psychiatric complications. In Chapter 7, Jessica Wolfe and Rachel Kimerling review the measures and research data on gender issues in the assessment of PTSD. Specific consideration is given to sex differences and their implications for developing appropriate measures of PTSD. Also discussed is the importance of gender-sensitive measures in establishing prevalence rates and accurate differential diagnoses. In Chapter 8, special emphasis on cross-cultural diagnosis of PTSD is examined by Spero Manson, who clearly demonstrates that traumatic reaction must be understood through the lens of one's culture. Furthermore, cultural differences, such as gender differences, have implications for the development of psychological measures and protocols to assess PTSD and other consequences of trauma. These differences also influence the cognitive processing of stressful life events. In Chapter 9, Terence M. Keane and associates present an overview of the measures used to assess military-related PTSD. Since war veterans constitute a large population in the United States as well as other countries, it is not surprising that many of the early scales developed to measure PTSD came from this cohort. This chapter enables the practitioner or researcher to consider a significantly broad choice of validated instruments in work with most military populations or those who are now veterans.

The last three chapters in Part II focus on the assessment of PTSD in children, families, and following traumatic bereavement. In Chapter 10, Kathleen O. Nader reviews and discusses all of the extant measures of PTSD in children. For practitioners especially, this comprehensive chapter organizes a practical discussion of the various measures that have been developed to assess the range of trauma responses manifested by children. The various options for clinicians are presented as to psychometric measures that might be used by practitioners or researchers. In a similar way, Chapter 11 lists and reviews the instruments available to assess traumatic impact to families and highlights some of the difficulties and complexities that practitioners face when attempting to assist traumatized family units. Finally, Part II concludes with an analysis of the interrelationship between traumatic bereavement and PTSD. In Chapter 12, Beverley Raphael and Nada Martinek present the dynamics in which traumatic loss creates special needs for assessment in order to differentiate between normal bereavement, complicated bereavement, and traumatic bereavement associated with traumatic stress syndromes.

In Part III are seven chapters that directly concern *specific techniques for the assessment of traumatic reactions, dissociative tendencies, and PTSD*. Each chapter discusses a specific type of instrumentation or set of procedures to measure posttraumatic reactions and symptoms. Moreover, these chapters contain a range of choices for practitioners, from a short (22-item) Impact of Events Scale—Revised (Weiss & Marmar, Chapter 13) to structured clinical protocols for assessing PTSD (Weiss, Chapter 17) and dissociative phenomena (Steinberg, Chapter 15). Other measures include thematic assessment, which examines cognitive schemata (Roth, Lebowitz, & De Rosa, Chapter 18), and classic projective techniques such as the Rorschach Ink Blot, for which normative data have been established for detecting unconscious manifestations of PTSD (Levin & Reis, Chapter 19). Other important measures for use include the Peritraumatic Dissociative Scale developed by Daniel Weiss and associates (Chapter 14), a powerful 10-item scale with excellent psychometric properties and quick administration. In Chapter 16, Jeffrey A. Knight reviews the neuropsychological assessment of PTSD, an area of particular importance, especially for victims who suffer traumatic brain injury.

Taken together as a set, the three parts of the book provide the reader with readily usable information with direct application to clinical practice, research projects, and educational curricula in colleges and universities. The contributors to this book labored long and with dedication to attempt to make all of the material user friendly and readily understandable so that it can be used to benefit those who suffer from traumatic life events that have injured their sense of well-being.

ASSESSING TRAUMATIC STRESS SYNDROMES: THEORY, STANDARDIZED MEASURES, AND PHYSIOLOGICAL TECHNIQUES

Standardized Self-Report Measures of Civilian Trauma and Posttraumatic Stress Disorder

FRAN H. NORRIS
JASMIN K. RIAD

ORIENTATION, SCOPE, AND ORGANIZATION OF THIS CHAPTER

This chapter reviews 20 standardized self-report measures that are suitable, with some modification, for use with adults by professional or lay interviewers or in paper-and-pencil questionnaires. Each scale is described in terms of its content, number of items, and response formats, and evaluated in terms of the available evidence regarding its reliability and validity. We also describe the population or populations on whom the scale was validated and make recommendations regarding psychometric studies that would be useful. We note strengths and weaknesses but stop short of recommending one scale for all situations. In fact, our assumption is that different scales may be more or less suitable for different purposes in different contexts involving traumatic stress responses.

Because measures of combat-related trauma are described elsewhere in this volume, this chapter focuses on scales that are suitable for studying civilian trauma in clinical or community populations. These populations may include veterans of military service but are not limited to them. The measures described here are those that either have been significant to this field historically or appear quite promising for future research. In deciding which scales warranted inclusion in this chapter, we relied heavily on the published literature and, to a lesser extent, on information gained from networking with investigators working in this area. Given the proliferation of new measures over the past few years, it seems inevitable that news of some promising scales may not have reached us by either means. Nonetheless, we believe that the selected scales comprise a reasonable cross-section of standardized self-report measures available in the field today.

The scales reviewed here fall into two broad categories: five that measure the DSM-IV posttraumatic stress disorder (PTSD) Criterion A, or trauma histories, and 15 that measure DSM-IV PTSD Criteria B–D, or symptom histories. Our chapter is organized accordingly. Researchers and practitioners should plan on selecting one scale from each category to capture the phenomenon of trauma fully and well.

DSM-IV PTSD CRITERION A: ASSESSING TRAUMATIC EVENTS

In this section, we will review five scales that have Criterion A as their sole or primary focus. The scales are the Traumatic Stress Schedule (TSS; Norris, 1990), the Potential Stressful Events Interview (PSEI; Kilpatrick, Resnick, & Freedy, 1991), the Traumatic Events Questionnaire (TEQ; Vrana & Lauterbach, 1994), the Trauma History Questionnaire (THQ; Green, 1995), and the Traumatic Life Events Questionnaire (TLEQ; Kubany, 1995). The last two scales are considered by their authors to be in the experimental phase but appear quite promising for use in future research.

Not included in this chapter are measures that detail the experiences of specific trauma populations, such as adult survivors of child abuse (e.g., Briere, 1992), refugees (Mollica et al., 1995), or victims of natural disasters (e.g., Norris & Kaniasty, 1992). Their exclusion should be taken neither as a criticism nor as a statement that such measures are unimportant. Rather, we excluded them because such instruments almost inevitably need to be tailored to the specific event, population, and context, and thus are difficult to describe or evaluate in a standardized way. The scales described here screen for the occurrence of potentially traumatic events more broadly and are best used to supplement more targeted assessments. For example, we included the TSS in our interviews with victims of Hurricanes Hugo and Andrew, in addition to a fairly lengthy battery assessing specific, hurricane-related experiences. In clinical practice, one of these measures could be used to identify experiences that might subsequently be probed for greater detail in a less structured way.

For each scale, we will note which events are specifically assessed and provide evidence for the scale's reliability and validity, where such data exist. For self-reported trauma histories, reliability evidence has typically taken the form of test–retest correlations. Internal consistency (e.g., Cronbach's alpha) is not applicable to event measures, because the experience of one event does not necessarily imply the experience of another.

Validity is difficult for these scales to establish unequivocally. To the extent face validity may be counted, construct validity has been used most often; that is, checklists of events typically "seem" reasonable. Criterion validity is virtually impossible to establish, because no external standard of accuracy exists. Concurrent validity is sometimes evidenced when similar estimates of trauma prevalence are yielded by different scales (see Resnick, Falsetti, Kilpatrick, & Freedy, in press). In our opinion, content validity could receive much more attention than it has in the development of these scales. Any list of life events, traumatic or otherwise, is a sample representing a larger population of life events. Bruce Dohrenwend (e.g., Dohrenwend, 1974; Dohrenwend, Krasnoff, Askenasy, & Dohrenwend, 1978) must be credited with directing researchers' attention to the fact that decisions made in constructing the list will ultimately determine the kinds of inferences and generalizations that can be made. He raised two basic and related questions: How do we define the events to be sampled? And, what is the population of events from which the sample is to be drawn? Life-event scale developers seldom have described *explicitly* the population of events that the items on their scales purportedly represent. Some consensus among researchers is implicit in these measures: If we exclude the contributions of open-ended or "catchall" items, no trauma scales reviewed here are so broad as to include all events demanding readjustment (e.g., moving to a new place), or even all undesirable life events (e.g., losing a job). Yet, consensus does not appear to have emerged with regard to just where to draw the line between traumatic events and other undesirable events. This is a critical issue for content validity which, like construct validity, is often established more on conceptual than on empirical grounds (Wilson, 1994).

The evaluation of measures of Criterion A has been complicated by the changes that emerged in DSM-IV. In DSM-III-R the definition of trauma was

> an event that is outside the range of usual human experience and that would be markedly distressing to almost anyone, e.g., serious threat to one's life or physical integrity; serious threat or harm to one's children, spouse, or other close relatives and friends; sudden destruction of one's home or community; or seeing another person who has recently been, or is being, seriously injured or killed as the result of an accident or physical violence. (American Psychiatric Association, 1987, p. 250)

In DSM-IV, the definition changed to

> the personal experience of an event that involves actual or threatened death or serious injury, or other threat to one's physical integrity; or witnessing an event that involves death, injury, or a threat to the physical integrity of another person; or learning about unexpected or violent death, serious harm, or threat of death or injury experienced by a family member or other close associate. . . . The person's response to the event must involve intense fear, helplessness, or horror. (American Psychiatric Association, 1994, p. 424)

Whereas the DSM-III-R definition emphasizes the event itself, the DSM-IV definition emphasizes the subjective appraisal of the event.

Traumatic Stress Schedule

The TSS was developed by Fran Norris as a short screening instrument for assessing traumatic stress in the general population. Norris (1990) stated that the format of the scale followed from two basic assumptions: (1) It is important to assess rates of impairment within specific event-defined populations (e.g., crime victims), in addition to assessing those rates within the population at large; and (2) it is important to quantify stressful experiences generically, using descriptors such as life threat, loss, and scope that are not unique to any one event.

In selecting the items for the scale, Norris (1990) had relied on the definition of Criterion A provided in DSM-III-R, in which the defining feature was that events should be beyond the realm of normal human experience. For research purposes, she proposed a more restricted definition of the relevant event population as that involving "violent encounters with nature, technology, or humankind" (p. 1706). She defined a violent event as one that (1) is marked by extreme and/or sudden force, (2) involves an external agent, and (3) is typically capable of arousing intense fear or aversion. The events were selected to provide a reasonable cross-section of this population of events. The scale, as initially published, assessed eight potentially traumatic events: (1) robbery, a theft involving force or threat of force; (2) physical assault; (3) sexual assault, that is, forced, unwanted sexual activity of any kind; (4) loss of a loved one through accident, homicide, or suicide; (5) personal injury or property loss as a result of fire, severe weather, or disaster; (6) being forced to evacuate or otherwise learning of an imminent danger or hazard in the environment; (7) having a motor vehicle accident serious enough to cause injury to one or more passengers; and (8) "some other terrifying or shocking experience."

The original form of this scale was developed as part of an NIMH-sponsored workshop on traumatic stress held in 1988. As part of the proceedings of that workshop, it was published before it was actually used or tested in the field. Ten items were used by Norris (1992); she separated fire from disaster and added serving in combat.

The scale may include several probes that allow for the quantification of generic trauma dimensions. On the basis of a review of the literature, Norris (1990) proposed that six dimensions were most critical to assess: (1) loss (the tangible loss of persons or property), (2) scope (the extent to which persons other than the respondent were affected by the incident), (3) threat to life and physical integrity (including actual physical injury), (4) blame, (5) familiarity, and (6) posttraumatic stress reactions. This last dimension shifted the focus from assessing the characteristics of the stressor to assessing the response to that stressor, with an emphasis on those emotions and cognitions that are tied closely to the event. These four probes are asked separately for each experienced event: (1) being suddenly reminded of it, (2) thinking about it when not meaning to, (3) having nightmares, and (4) avoiding reminiscent situations. The scale originally concluded with five symptom questions that assess symptoms of posttraumatic stress that are not tied to specific events; a sixth was subsequently added to assess anger/irritability. These six nonanchored items can be combined with each anchored set 1–4 to create brief stress measures for each experienced event.

The event portion of this scale has performed well in research on several different samples (see Norris, 1992). Norris and Perilla (1996) reported a test–retest correlation of .88 between English and Spanish versions completed by 53 bilingual volunteers 1 week apart. Estimates of exposure to trauma have been strikingly stable across purposive and random community samples that, as of this writing, have spanned six southeastern cities (Charleston and Greenville, South Carolina; Charlotte, North Carolina; Savannah, Georgia; and Tampa and Miami, Florida). Excluding events that were the focus of these studies, such as Hurricanes Hugo and Andrew, sample frequencies of exposure to one or more traumatic event(s) (using an "ever" time frame) have ranged from 62% to 75%, with an average of 69%. Quite reasonably, higher frequencies (82%) emerged in a study of family members of homicide victims in inner-city Atlanta (M. Thompson, personal communication, March 24, 1995). This scale has been criticized (Resnick et al., in press), rightly we think, for having only a single item of sexual assault (forced, unwanted sexual activity). Another shortcoming is the lack of explicit assessment of childhood physical and sexual abuse. Nonetheless, the TSS has yielded estimates for "any trauma" identical to those obtained by Resnick, Kilpatrick, Dansky, Saunders, and Best (1993) in the National Women's Study (NWS) and much higher than its predecessors, which had relied on a single-item measure of exposure to traumatic events (Breslau, Davis, Andreski, & Peterson, 1991; Helzer, Robins, & McEvoy, 1987).

The symptom portion of this scale is moderately reliable (α = .76) and has yielded estimates of current PTSD for various event samples that are quite similar to those derived by other scales (Resnick et al., 1993; Resnick et al., in press). Nonetheless, the scale has minimal face validity because it is simply too brief to assess all the various ways that PTSD is manifest. For this reason, Norris and Perilla (1996) revised the TSS by dropping the symptom probes and combining it with a revised, 30-item version of the Civilian Mississippi Scale (to be discussed separately).

Potential Stressful Events Interview

A number of measures of trauma and traumatic stress have been developed at the Crime Victims' Research and Treatment Center at the Medical University of South Carolina. The instrument developed for use in the NWS evolved out of the earlier Incident Report Interview, which assesses lifetime history of criminal victimization. The NWS measure evolved into a multifaceted battery now known as the PSEI (Kilpatrick et al., 1991). Four modules of the PSEI are relevant to this chapter: (1) high-magnitude stressors, (2) objective characteristics, (3) subjective reactions, and (4) PTSD. The PTSD module will be described later. The High-Magnitude Stressor section assesses 13 potentially traumatic events: (1) military war zone or combat experience; (2) serious accident in a car, at work, or elsewhere; (3) natural disaster; (4) serious illness, such as cancer or AIDS; (5) childhood sexual abuse; (6) childhood sexual assault; (7) other forced sexual contact; (8) aggravated physical assault (involves a weapon); (9) simple physical assault (no weapon); (10) other situation involving serious injury; (11) other situation involving fear of injury or death; (12) witnessing serious injury or death; and (13) other extraordinarily stressful events. The implicit definition of high-magnitude events is that they potentially involve life threat (rather than external force, see Norris's TSS), as evidenced by the inclusion of serious illness as a qualifying event. This definition is quite in keeping with the definition of PTSD Criterion A as it emerged in DSM-IV. Yet, the sample of events has not expanded much past those that would also be included in the DSM-III-R definition of PTSD Criterion A.

No test–retest data have been reported, but the scale's careful wording increases confidence in its reliability. The scale is behaviorally specific and explicit in its assessment of sexual trauma. These questions are distinguished by a preface that makes it especially clear that the person making the advance could have been a friend or family member, as well as a stranger, and that such experiences can occur anytime in a person's life, even as a child. Using the NWS version of this scale, which differed only slightly from the PSEI, Resnick et al. (1993) found that 69% of the NWS sample had experienced one or more potentially traumatic events. This was the same rate reported by Norris (1992).

The event inventory is supplemented by two interesting sections that provide greater detail about up to three events: first (or only), most recent, and worst. Objective characteristics describe the focal incident in terms of injury to self and others, perceived causation, perception of perpetrator's intent to harm (crime events only), suddenness, expectedness, and warning received. Subjective Reactions is a 15-item measure of responses at the time of the event: feelings of surprise, detachment, panic, embarrassment, shame, disgust. No reliability or validity data have been published on these supplementary modules, but their face validity is high.

Traumatic Events Questionnaire

The TEQ, developed by Scott Vrana and Dean Lauterbach (1994), assesses 11 specific traumatic events: (1) combat; (2) large fires/explosions; (3) serious industrial/farm accidents; (4) sexual assault/rape (forced, unwanted sexual activity); (5) natural disasters; (6) violent crime; (7) adult abusive relationships; (8) physical/sexual child abuse; (9) witnessing someone being mutilated, seriously injured, or violently killed; (10) other life threatening situations; and (11) violent or unexpected death of a loved one. Two nonspecific questions, "other event" and "can't tell," complete the scale. Probes assess dimensions such as life threat and injury after any affirmative response.

Over a 2-week test–retest interval, very high reliability for the total scale was observed (.91) in a sample of 51 students (Lauterbach & Vrana, 1996). In another student sample (n = 440), 84% reported at least one event, which is higher than other rates that have been reported in the literature. Endorsement of "catchall" events was especially high: 30% had some other life-threatening experience, 23% had some other event, and 9% endorsed "can't tell." Specific events also showed high prevalence rates. A particularly striking statistic was that almost half (49%) of Vrana and Lauterbach's (1994) sample reported having experienced a violent or unexpected death of a loved one. This scale defined the event population to include unexpected natural deaths as well as those due to violence from technology or humankind. This expansion is consistent with the present wording of Criterion A in DSM-IV.

Trauma History Questionnaire

The THQ was developed by Bonnie Green and her associates at Georgetown University (Green, 1995). The THQ aims to provide a comprehensive assessment not only of PTSD Criterion A but also of other seriously stressful life events. The scale has 24 items: (1) mugging; (2) robbery—a theft by force; (3) break-in where respondent was present; (4) break-in where respondent was absent; (5) serious accident at work, in a car, or somewhere else; (6) natural disaster where self/loved one is in danger; (7) disaster of human origin where self/loved one is in danger; (8) other serious injury; (9) other situation where self feared being killed or injured; (10) toxin exposure; (11) witnessing serious injury or death; (12) handling bodies; (13) close friend or family member murdered or killed by a drunk driver; (14) had spouse, romantic partner, or child die; (15) self had serious or life-threatening illness; (16) someone close had serious or life-threatening illness, injury, or unexpected death; (17) combat; (18) forced intercourse, oral or anal sex; (19) forced touching of private parts; (20) other unwanted sexual contact; (21) aggravated assault; (22) simple assault; (23) beaten, spanked, or pushed; and (24) any other extraordinarily stressful situation or event. Each event is followed by probes assessing the frequency of the event and the respondent's age at the time of each occurrence. Generic stressor dimensions, such as life threat, are measured by counting relevant events, rather than through the use of probes embedded within events.

Green provided unpublished reliability data collected from 25 female subjects that were tested twice over a 2- to 3- month interval. Excluding the total severe threat index, which received a stability coefficient of only .14, test–retest correlations ranged from .54 for total bereavement to .92 for total crime. Green's take on the population of relevant events is the broadest of all those reviewed here, as this scale includes deaths and illnesses of significant others, even if expected and due to natural causes. This strategy was chosen because, in her research, respondents who provide affirmative responses are interviewed in more detail about their experiences. The scale may be less appropriate than some others reviewed when the investigator's purpose is to estimate the frequency of potentially traumatic events in surveys that do not include a less structured interview component. Two-thirds of the students in her pilot study ($n = 423$) reported that someone close to them had become seriously ill at some time, making the frequency for this one event as high as the total frequency across events obtained using the TSS and PSEI. Whereas the total scale goes beyond the realm of trauma, a number of face-valid measures of traumatic experience are embedded within the larger scale.

Traumatic Life Events Questionnaire

The most recent scale to appear on the scene—the TLEQ—is being developed by Edward Kubany (1995). The scale assesses occurrence of 17 events: (1) natural disaster involving injury or exposure to death; (2) motor vehicle accident involving injury or death; (3) other accident involving injury or death; (4) combat; (5) sudden and unexpected death of a close friend or loved one due to accident, illness, suicide, or murder; (6) mugging or robbing by someone with a weapon; (7) physical assault by an acquaintance or stranger; (8) witnessing someone being attacked or assaulted; (9) being threatened with death or bodily harm; (10) childhood physical abuse; (11) physical abuse from intimate partner; (12) witnessing severe family violence; (13) childhood sexual touching by someone at least 5 years older (probes for force, penetration); (14) childhood sexual touching by someone less than five years older; (15) adulthood unwanted sexual activity (probes for force, penetration); (16) being stalked; and (17) other extremely disturbing or distressing experience. Four additional questions ask if intense fear, helplessness, or horror occurred during any of the 16 events (if yes, the respondent is to indicate which), if the respondent was injured during any of the events (if yes, the respondent is to indicate which), and if any of the events occurred within the last 2 months or 12 months (again, he or she is instructed to indicate which). One final question asks, "Of the events experienced, which event causes you the most distress?"

This scale, although still in the experimental stage, appears very promising. The relevant population is explicitly defined and directly tied to the DSM-IV definition of traumatic events as events involving actual or threatened death or injury. All items are carefully worded. Its present format is suitable for paper-and-pencil (self-) administration but will need some reworking to be suitable for use by lay interviewers. Reliability and validity studies are just now under way, so few data are available at this time. Kubany et al. (in press) administered an earlier 13-item version of the TLEQ to 194 college students in Hawaii. Showing striking consistency, 69% of this sample reported exposure to one or more traumatic events. This was the exact rate found in a survey of 1,000 adults in four southeastern cities (Norris, 1992) and in a representative national sample of women (Resnick et al., 1993).

Summary

Table 1.1 summarizes the descriptions of these five measures of potentially traumatic events. For each scale, the table lists the number of event items included in the scale, the type of data provided, evidence of stability, and the population that the measure was developed on. Evidence of validity was not included, because none of these scales are especially well validated, nor are any apparently especially weak in this regard. The TSS, PSEI, and TLEQ have produced very similar estimates of trauma exposure in different regions of the United States. All in all, these five scales are more alike than different. Each asks about the occurrence of various events and probes affirmative responses for some additional detail. The TSS, TEQ, and TLEQ probe for subjective experiences of life threat and/or injury following any affirmative response. The PSEI takes this approach a step further by recounting in detail the objective and subjective experience of up to three events. One lesson from earlier research has clearly been learned. Not one of these measures used the term "rape." Instead, each referred to unwanted or forced sexual activity. Nonetheless, the attention given to sexual trauma varies. The TSS appears to be the least detailed, the PSEI, the most detailed.

TABLE 1.1. Summary Descriptions of Five Standardized Self-Report Measures of Trauma Exposure

Scale	Number of event items	Data provided	Evidence of stability	Population developed on
Traumatic Stress Schedule	10	Event prevalence and descriptive	T-R (Eng.–Span.) $r = .88$	General/ multicultural
Potential Stressful Events Interview	13	Event prevalence and descriptive	na	Women/ general
Traumatic Events Questionnaire	11	Event prevalence and descriptive	T-R $r = .91$	Under- graduates
Trauma History Questionnaire	24	Event prevalence by type	T-R $r = .54–.92$	Female under- graduates
Traumatic Life Events Questionnaire	17	Event prevalence and descriptive	na	na

Note. na, data not available.

Despite these similarities, the events sampled by each scale differ some-what, reflecting differences, implicit or explicit, in the definitional bound-aries of the relevant population of events. The TSS appears to use the most objective and restricted definition, and the THQ appears to use the broadest definition. Perhaps because of the redefinition of PTSD Criterion A that emerged in DSM-IV, the trend in research seems to be away from assessing events that set the stage for trauma toward incorporating the subjective reac-tion into the specification of the traumatic event itself. The once-defining feature that traumatic events should be beyond the range of normal human experience has clearly faded into the past. On the positive side, these trends show that the field is progressing and being shaped by empirical findings showing that exposure to trauma is not rare and that life threat is inargua-bly the stressor dimension that is most predictive of PTSD Criteria B–D. On the negative side, as criterion events become more psychologized, we may lose the ability to identify the relative contributions of observable environ-mental happenings to the well-being of normal populations.

One issue that requires additional consideration is the use of "catchall" events that compromise specificity. All of the reviewed scales used this tech-nique. The reasoning behind the inclusion of these items is clear. It would be too difficult, costly, and unacceptable to researchers to enumerate every traumatic event that might conceivably occur. Such items also give respon-dents the chance to report experiences that were important to them, which can be informative as well as helpful in building rapport. On the other hand, these items may be tapping into personal crises and failures that are not truly in the domain of traumatic life events.

We recently reviewed the responses to this open-ended question provid-ed by persons who participated in our study of Hurricane Andrew. Of 404 respondents, 36 (9%) reported some other "shocking or terrifying experience" on the TSS. Fourteen people told of events that clearly qualified as traumat-ic, according to DSM-III-R definitions, but these events were not asked about directly (or specifically enough) in other TSS questions (e.g., being on the scene of a bank robbery, train accident, threatened with a gun). Five told of events that should have been picked up by other items (e.g., combat ex-periences) but for some reason were not. For these 19 respondents (roughly half), the item served its purpose: catching other trauma histories not else-where recorded. An additional six people told us about life-threatening or very serious illnesses experienced by themselves (going blind temporarily, surgery) or loved ones (grandfather's cancer) that seem to qualify under DSM-IV PTSD criteria, although they were not in the domain of experiences we were initially attempting to capture with the TSS. Three people mentioned deaths due to natural causes of loved ones, and seven told of other unfor-tunate (husband convicted of murder, son in prison) or unusual (paranor-mal) experiences. Thus roughly 28–44% of the events captured by this item (2–3% of the total sample) would not qualify under more restrictive defini-tions. When reviewing the literature across these scales, it is striking that catchall items seem to have even higher rates of endorsement on longer measures. Compared to 9% of our sample, 23% of Vrana and Lauterbach's sample reported some other event. Even in Green's sample, 14% reported some other event, although the THQ asked about 23 specific events, including serious illnesses of self and others, and deaths of close family members, regardless of cause. When affirmative answers were explored in subsequent interviews, Green found that few of the events qualified as Criterion A events (personal communication, April 12, 1995).

A related issue with these items was highlighted by Vrana and Lauterbach's (1994) finding that a high percentage of TEQ respondents rated the "other event" as their very worst. This finding may reflect an intrinsic bias wherein subjects primarily note an other event *if* it was their subjective worst. Conceivably, all respondents have experienced undesirable changes in their lives, but they do not always bring these to mind. The issue here is again one of content validity. If "traumatic events" and "undesirable events" are synonymous terms, these scales need to be expanded to capture the range of undesirable events that have been important in life-events research more generally (e.g., Dohrenwend et al., 1978). In our opinion, it is better for measures of PTSD Criterion A to focus more specifically on a clearly defined population of events. This is not to say other events are not important in the lives of individuals, but simply that they are beyond the domain of concern for these measures. For example, in our research, we have typically included a scale of normative life events in addition to a scale of traumatic life events (see also Resnick et al., in press). Perhaps this is analogous to developing a scale for anxiety rather than, or in addition to, a scale of depression or generalized distress. To summarize, these catchall questions seem necessary, but the responses they elicit may be seriously compromising the content validity of all of the measures that were reviewed here. Regardless of which scale is selected, the researcher or clinician should probe for content of these events.

Finally, it should be remembered that, as in all areas of research, different scales serve different purposes. The TSS purports to be a brief screen for traumatic stress, whereas the THQ and TLEQ aim to provide comprehensive trauma histories. Explicit or detailed scales of sexual trauma may be less acceptable to researchers outside this field who are seeking to supplement their instruments with a brief measure of traumatic life events. Interviewers in clinical settings, however, clearly require scales that provide as much detail as possible about events and reactions to those events. Sources for obtaining these five measures are provided in the Appendix.

DSM-IV PTSD CRITERIA B-D:
ASSESSING INTRUSION, AVOIDANCE, AND AROUSAL

In this section, we will review 15 scales that purport to measure symptomatic criteria for PTSD or very closely related constructs. We will describe each scale in terms of its length and format, provide some background regarding its development, and evaluate its psychometric properties. Rules for establishing reliability and validity are much better developed for symptom measures than for event measures, which raises the standards by which these symptom scales will be judged. Regarding reliability, it is usually important for symptom measures to establish both internal consistency and stability over time. Validity data for symptom scales usually take the form of criterion validity or construct validity. Sometimes, criterion validity is established in terms of a scale's correlations with more established measures in the field. A PTSD scale should correlate highly—but not too highly—with measures of general psychopathology and should correlate most highly with other measures of posttraumatic stress. Most highly regarded is evidence that the scale can correctly classify subjects into diagnostic groups, determined by some independent criterion. Statistics are usually provided regarding the measure's sensitivity (the proportion of cases correctly classified) and specificity (the proportion of noncases correctly classified). Construct validity is important as well. In this case, validity is usually established by showing that scale scores differ across groups having different objective trauma histories. Sometimes, construct validity is examined by exploring how well the observed factor structure of the scale conforms to theoretical predictions.

The difficulty of creating a measure that is both sensitive and specific to PTSD should not be taken lightly, because the disorder is composed of a broad, if unique, constellation of psychological symptoms. In the tradition of the American Psychiatric Association's DSM, these symptoms are grouped into three criteria. DSM-IV PTSD Criterion B is the reexperiencing of the trauma. Intrusive symptoms, such as thinking about the event when the individual does not intend to, having nightmares or flashbacks, or being suddenly reminded of the event by environmental stimuli, are extremely common experiences following traumatic life events. Criterion C encompasses avoidance, hopelessness, and a numbing of responsiveness to the external world. Often, trauma victims feel estranged from other people and lose interest in things they formerly enjoyed. Criterion D refers to a varied collection of symptoms indicative of increased arousal. Being jumpy, easily startled or hyperalert, having trouble sleeping or concentrating, or feeling easily angered or irritated characterize Criterion D. To satisfy DSM-IV criteria for PTSD, the person must show at least one intrusion symptom, three avoidance symptoms, and two arousal symptoms. Previous research suggests that most victims of potentially traumatic events will show some of these symptoms, but only a minority (6–9%) develop chronic PTSD (e.g., Norris, 1992; Resnick et al., 1993).

The measures that are included fall into four broad, overlapping categories, reflecting different measurement strategies. First, following in the footsteps of earlier measures, such as the Reaction Index (Frederick, 1985a) and the NWS Module PTSD (Kilpatrick, Resnick, Saunders, & Best,

1989), a number of different investigators have recently and independently developed scales that precisely follow the symptom criteria for PTSD as outlined in DSM-III-R or DSM-IV. These measures include the PTSD Symptom Scale (PSS; Foa, Riggs, Dancu, & Rothbaum, 1993), the PTSD-Interview (PTSD-I; Watson, Juba, Manifold, Kucala, & Anderson, 1991), and the Purdue PTSD Scale (Lauterbach & Vrana, 1996). It is not a coincidence that many of these scales have 17 items. The second strategy has been to develop scales that assess symptoms of posttraumatic stress continuously and in a manner less rigidly tied to DSM guidelines. The Mississippi Scale (Keane, Caddell, & Taylor, 1988), the Penn Inventory (Hammarberg, 1992), and Trauma Symptom Inventory (TSI; Briere, 1995) are examples here. The Impact of Event Scale (IES) was described elsewhere in this volume and so will not be included, although this is the group of scales with which it would belong. The third strategy has been to derive PTSD subscales from larger symptom inventories that are commonly used in clinical practice and research. Examples here are the Minnesota Multiphasic Personality Inventory (Keane, Malloy, & Fairbank, 1984) and the Symptom Checklist (SCL-90; Saunders, Arata, & Kilpatrick, 1990; Ursano, Fullerton, Kao, & Bhartiya, 1995) PTSD scales. A fourth strategy has been to develop measures that are tailored to the experiences and culturally relevant outcomes of specific trauma populations, such as refugees. The Harvard Trauma Questionnaire (HTQ; Mollica et al., 1992) is the premiere example of this approach. The remainder of this chapter is organized in accord with this scheme.

Reaction Index

Calvin Frederick's (1985b) Reaction Index (RI) represented one of the earliest attempts to design a standardized measure for the precise purpose of assessing PTSD among victims of civilian trauma. Frederick (1985b) introduced the scale as a checklist, but it was subsequently revised substantially (see Frederick, 1987). The present Form A (adult version) consists of two distinct sections. Items 1–20 constitute the symptoms portion and are answered on a 5-point format (*none of the time* = 0 to *most of the time* = 4). Frederick considers raw scores of 25–39 to be indicative of moderate PTSD, 40–59 severe PTSD, and 60 plus very severe PTSD. Items 21–28 assess the onset and duration of symptoms and help seeking related to the event, and are not included in the previous scores and ratings.

Although the scoring algorithm assumes item equivalence, internal consistency (alpha) of the revised RI has not been documented. An alpha of .60 was reported by Realmuto et al. (1992), but they had used the original yes–no format. The Likert-type scale of the revised version should produce a higher value. Frederick (1987) reported a test–retest coefficient (actually interrater reliability) of .77.

Regarding validity, Frederick (1987) reported high levels of agreement between determinations of caseness based on the RI and those based on the MMPI-PTSD scale and showed that continuous scores on the two scales correlate highly. Frederick (1985a) and Pynoos (1987) report that the adult version correlates highly (.95) with caseness as determined by independent diagnoses, but the validation study itself does not appear to have been published. Frederick (personal communication, May 23, 1995) informed us that the diagnoses were made by himself and two other clinicians, and that "caseness" was defined in terms of behavior, medical charts, and family input when all clinicians agreed 100% of the time. Frederick (personal communication, April 19, 1995) informed us that the scale has been used extensively internationally in such counties as Armenia, Mexico, the Dominican Republic, Egypt, Italy, Norway, Uganda, Australia, and Thailand. There is a child version of this measure that has become widely used and well known (e.g., Pynoos et al., 1987).

National Women's Study PTSD Module

The (NWS) PTSD Module developed by Dean Kilpatrick and colleagues (1989) was revised from the version of the Diagnostic Interview Schedule (DIS) used in the National Vietnam Veterans Readjustment Study (NVVRS). It was designed for use by lay interviewers and was also included in the Crime Victim Center's research on Hurricane Hugo and other natural disasters (Freedy, Kilpatrick, & Resnick, 1993). It has 20 items that span the range of symptoms associated with PTSD. Questions are first answered yes or no. Then, dates of first and last experiences of that symptom are recorded for all affirmative responses. None of the items are anchored to the specific event or events experienced. This characteristic of the scale makes it easy to administer to people with multiple or complex trauma histories. Another advantage of this assessment approach is that the respondent is not required to attribute the symptom to a specific experience, a characteristic for which the original DIS has been criticized (Solomon & Canino, 1990). However, open-ended probes are used to assess symptom content in specific instances. For example, if an individual reports nightmares, he or she is asked what the nightmares are about. The scale has typically been scored to yield dichotomous measures of lifetime and current PTSD rather than to yield a continuous measure of PTSD symptomatology.

Because of the dichotomous nature of the scoring algorithms, the scale's reliability and validity data have both taken the form of kappa coefficients. Resnick et al. (1993) reported that stability over a 1-year interval for lifetime PTSD was adequate (x = .45). Data collected from clinical cases as part of the DSM-IV field trials provided evidence of concurrent validity. Kappa coefficients of agreement between a PTSD diagnosis made on the basis of this module and the Structured Clinical Interview for DSM-III-R (SCID) were .71 for current PTSD and .77 for lifetime PTSD. These analyses also indicated that the NWS Module had high sensitivity for lifetime (.99) and current

(.96) PTSD. However, specificity was somewhat lower
.80 for current PTSD.

PTSD Symptom Scale and Modified PTSD Sympt

PSS-I and PSS-SR

The PSS was developed by Edna Foa and her colleagues (1993) as part of their research program on victims of rape. The PSS assesses the severity over the past 2 weeks of PTSD symptomatology. The scale has 17 items that correspond directly to DSM-III-R criteria (4 reexperiencing, 7 avoidance, 6 arousal). Symptoms are scored on a 4-point scale, from *not at all* to *very much*. The scale comes in two forms: PTSD Symptom Scale Interview (PSS-I), which is suitable for use by lay interviewers, and PTSD Symptom Scale Self-Report (PSS-SR), which can be self-administered.

Foa et al. (1993) provided considerable evidence supporting the reliability and validity of the PSS, based on longitudinal data collected from a sample of rape victims (n = 95). The PSS-SR (α = .91) was slightly more internally consistent than the PSS-I (α = .85). For the interview version, subscale alphas were .69, .65, and .71, whereas for the self-report version, these values were .78, .80, and .82 for reexperiencing, avoidance, and arousal scales, respectively. Test–retest reliability over a 1-month period was .80 for the PSS-I and .74 for the PSS-SR; subscales were also adequately stable, although these values were not as high as correlations for the total scales (.56–.71 for PSS-SR; .55–.77 for PSS-I).

Concurrent validity was evidenced by correlating the PSS-I and PSS-SR with other symptom measures, such as the Beck Depression Inventory (BDI; .72, .80), IES-Intrusion (.56, .81), Rape Aftermath Symptom Test (.67, .81), and the State–Trait Anxiety Inventory—State version (.48, .52). Convergent validity was obtained by comparing results obtained with the PSS with diagnoses obtained using the SCID. Overall, the PSS-I correctly identified the SCID-PTSD status of 94% of the subjects, with a sensitivity of .88 and a specificity of .96. The PSS-SR correctly classified 86% of the study's participants. Specificity (1.0) was considerably stronger than sensitivity (.62) in this case.

MPSS-SR

Riggs, Dancu, Gershuny, Greenberg, and Foa (1992) also used the PSS successfully in a sample that contained victims of physical assaults as well as sexual assaults. Although originally developed for assault victims and worded accordingly, the scale was easily adapted to studying the symptom consequences of other traumatic events (Falsetti, Resnick, Resick, & Kilpatrick, 1993). Falsetti et al. modified the self-report version further so that it elicits both frequency and severity information for each symptom (MPSS-SR); that

respondent first rates how frequently the symptom occurred in the
2 weeks and then rates how distressing that symptom was. Very high
alpha coefficients (.96–.97) have been reported for this version, but it is substantially longer than the Foa et al. original scale.

Overall the PSS compares favorably to other structured measures, especially for use in studies of crime-related trauma. Reliability is excellent,
and validity data surpass those available on other civilian scales. It is short
and easy to use by lay interviewers as well as in self-report form. However,
validity data have largely been generated for one specific trauma
population—female victims of crime; thus, further research assessing the stability and validity of the scale in more heterogenous samples would be useful.

Purdue PTSD Scale—Revised

The Purdue PTSD Scale was developed a number of years ago by Don Hart-
sough and his students at Purdue University (e.g., Wojcik, 1988) but did not
appear often in published works. Dean Lauterbach and Scott Vrana (1996),
also at Purdue, have recently revised and regenerated this scale, making it
a very promising measure for use in heterogeneous populations. The Revised Purdue Scale (PPTSD-R) corresponds closely to DSM-IV criteria and,
like similar scales, has 17 items: 4 reexperiencing, 6 avoidance, and 7 arousal.
Respondents report how often they have experienced each symptom in the
last month on a 5-point scale from *not at all* to *often*. The scale can be scored
either continuously or dichotomously.

Lauterbach and Vrana (1996) described three studies undertaken to assess the reliability and validity of the PPTSD-R. Both women and men were
well represented in all studies. In the first, 440 undergraduates who had experienced a variety of traumatic events were tested once. All subscales appeared internally consistent. Alphas were .91, .84, .79, and .81 for the total,
reexperiencing, avoidance, and arousal scales, respectively. In the second
study, 51 undergraduates were tested twice over a 2-week interval. Test–retest
correlations were .72, .48, .67, and .71, respectively.

As for validity data, the Purdue Scale correlated highly with both the
IES (.66) and the Civilian Mississippi Scale (.50) in the larger sample. These
correlations were stronger than those between the scale and general measures of distress, such as the BDI (.37–.39), providing preliminary support
for convergent and discriminant validity. These relations were examined further by adding a third group of 35 students receiving psychology services
to the sample. Reexperiencing and arousal scores were significantly higher
(1) among persons reporting a traumatic event on the TEQ than among persons not reporting an event, (2) among patients than among nonpatients,
and (3) among patients seeking treatment because of a traumatic event than
among patients seeking treatment for other reasons. However, whereas
avoidance scores differed between patient and nonpatient groups, they did
not differ between trauma and no-trauma groups.

In summary, this scale has a number of excellent features. It was developed for use in heterogeneous samples. As the authors correctly note, very few scales have been developed and validated on a broad cross-section of trauma survivors. In addition, most scales have been developed on samples that were exclusively male (e.g., PTSD-I) or exclusively female (e.g., PSS). In addition to this strength, the scale is internally consistent and correlates with other measures of trauma exposure and outcome in meaningful ways. However, before the scale can be recommended without reservations, two issues must be resolved. One is the lack of stability in the reexperiencing subscale. It is not altogether clear that respondents were thinking about the same event on the two testing occasions, which could deflate test–retest coefficients. This issue is avoided in homogeneous samples, such as used by Foa and colleagues for assessing the stability of the PSS. The second issue is the sensitivity of the avoidance measure. Scores on this subscale did not differ between respondents reporting a traumatic event and respondents who did not. In traumatized populations, Criterion C is satisfied less often than Criteria B or D and therefore has a strong impact on classification (Solomon & Canino, 1990; Norris, 1992; Norris & Perilla, 1996). Additional research that clarifies whether avoidance/numbing scores were overly high among nonvictims or overly low among trauma victims would be useful.

PTSD-Interview

Charles Watson and his colleagues (1991) developed the PTSD-I for use with veteran populations, but the scale could easily be applied to other groups. Like the PSS and Purdue Scale, the PTSD-I closely follows DSM-IV guidelines for assessing PTSD. Seventeen items were generated that reflect PTSD symptoms as outlined in DSM-III-R (or IV). Each question is answered on a 7-point scale, from *no* to *extremely,* or *never* to *always.* The scale can be scored continuously or dichotomously. The authors recommend that any symptom receiving a score of 4 or higher be counted toward PTSD diagnosis but note that users could substitute higher or lower values, depending upon the purpose of the assessment. It was designed to be suitable for use by lay interviewers.

Watson et al. reported that the scale has a test–retest reliability coefficient, over 1 week, of .95. This was tested in a sample of 31 veterans, 30 of whom had been in combat. The scale was also quite internally consistent ($\alpha = .92$).

The scale appears to have substantial validity in veteran populations. Watson et al. (1991) administered the PTSD-I and the Modified DIS-PTSD module (a structured interview) to 53 patients and 8 staff at a VA Medical Center. Although the DIS-PTSD measure has been criticized (Weiss, 1993), the authors noted that the issues pertain to its utility with general population rather than clinical samples. The correlations between PTSD-I items and their DIS counterparts averaged .77. Using the DIS as the standard, the kappa was .84, which is quite high. The PTSD-I showed a sensitivity of .89, a specificity of .94, and an overall hit rate of 92%. Watson et al. (1994) exa-mined the convergent validity of the scale in a sample of 80 help-seeking veterans. Scored continuously, the PTSD-I correlated .84 with the Mississip-pi Scale for Combat-Related PTSD and .79 with the MMPI-PTSD scale; va-lidity coefficients were equal to the Mississippi and superior to the MMPI-PTSD scale. Scored dichotomously, kappa coefficients were .59 and .60. There was about 80% agreement between the PTSD-I and each of the other two scales regarding who or who did not qualify as a case; the three scales' con-cordances with one another did not differ significantly in this case.

The Watson et al. scale originally had 20 items. The first question asked if the interviewee had experienced an unusual or extremely distressful event. By current standards in the field, a single item would not provide an ade-quate assessment of PTSD Criterion A; thus users of this scale would be wise to supplement the PTSD-I with a trauma history or screener. (In later research [e.g., Watson et al., 1994], it appears that the authors may have revised this aspect of the scale so as to provide a list of catastrophic experiences, but this list was not detailed or published.) Two final questions determine whether symptoms have been present for at least 1 month.

All in all, this scale is very promising. It is flexible in scoring and ap-pears to be quite reliable and valid. We did not locate any published studies documenting reliability and validity in nonveteran populations. However, the scale is now being used with a variety of trauma populations, including medical trauma victims, auto accident victims, and women who have been sexually or physically assaulted (Watson, personal communication, April 19, 1995). The scale also has been translated into French and Spanish. Validity studies comparing the sensitivity of this scale to other measures in civilian samples would be useful, as would empirical evidence regarding the cross-language stability of the instrument.

Civilian Mississippi Scale and Revised Civilian Mississippi Scale

Civilian Mississippi Scale

The Mississippi Scale for Combat-Related PTSD (Keane, Caddell, & Taylor, 1988) measures self-reported symptoms of posttraumatic stress in veteran populations. Because of its excellent psychometric characteristics, Terence Keane and other researchers associated with the Veterans Administration subsequently developed a civilian form of the scale. The scale had 35 items when used in the NVVRS. Four items were subsequently added, but no psy-chometric or descriptive data have yet appeared in the literature about this 39-item version. The original 35 items fall into four categories. Three align well with criteria for PTSD: 11 items tap reexperiencing (B), 11 items tap withdrawal and numbing (C), and 8 items measure arousal (D). The fourth category consists of 5 items that tap self-persecution (guilt and suicidality). Whereas the Mississippi Scale for Combat-Related PTSD elicited information about symptoms experienced "since I was in the military," the civilian form elicits frequency of symptoms "in the past." All items are answered on a 5-point scale, but the response format varies, sometimes using "not at all true" to "extremely true," sometimes using "never true" to "always true," sometimes using "never" to "very frequently," sometimes using "never true" to "very frequently true," and sometimes using "not at all true" to "almost always true."

Vreven, Gudanowski, King, and King (1995) presented psychometric data from a sample of 668 civilians who participated in the NVVRS. They found the civilian form of the Mississippi Scale to have high internal consistency (.86), although lower than the combat-related form (.94). Their findings regarding convergent validity were debatable: The Mississippi was only weakly related to the DIS-PTSD measure, but the latter measure has not fared well in validity studies. Correlations were much higher between the Civilian Mississippi and the demoralization index of the Psychiatric Epidemiology Research Interview (PERI; .63). Vreven et al. concluded that there is some uncertainty surrounding the scale's convergent and discriminant validity. Lauterbach, Vrana, King, and King (1995) also found, in a university sample, that the scale correlated more highly with the BDI (.72) and Spielberger Trait Anxiety Scale (.71) than with the IES (.34) or PPTSD-R (.50). In contrast, Hovens and van der Ploeg (1993) reported findings from a study of 53 psychiatric inpatients in the Netherlands: Trauma victims and patients with no trauma differed significantly from one another and to about the same extent on their Minnesota Multiphasic Personality Inventory—Keane PTSD Scale (MMPI-PK) and Civilian Mississippi Scale scores. Patients with and without trauma histories did not differ on SCL-90 scores, suggesting that the difference between groups being tapped by the Mississippi was not merely generalized distress.

Revised Civilian Mississippi Scale

Fran Norris and Julia Perilla (1996) revised the Mississippi in a number of ways, partly to shorten the scale, but also to sharpen its focus on posttraumatic stress. The Revised Civilian Mississippi has 30 items. Twenty-eight were selected from the 39-item form. Two intrusion items were selected from the TSS because they had received high endorsement in previous research with victims of traumatic events (Norris, 1992). The Revised Civilian Mississippi has only 24 items in common with the original 35-item version.

Other changes concerned question formats. As noted earlier, the Keane et al. civilian form elicits frequency of symptoms "in the past." Another reason this scale may act more as a general measure of distress than as a scale of posttraumatic stress is that this wording is not tied very closely to specific trauma experiences. Norris and Perilla therefore argued (see also the discussion of Vreven et al., 1995) that it would be better to elicit feelings surrounding a specific stressful event rather than to refer vaguely to feelings "in the past." They also divided the 30 items into two parts: The first 18 items "anchored" the symptom to a specific event (e.g., "Since the event, unexpected noises make me jump"); the last 12 items did not ("I am able to get emotionally close to others"). Another change they made was to score all items on the same 5-point scale (1 = "not at all true", 5 = "extremely true"). This eases administration considerably when data are being collected by lay interviewers.

Norris and Perilla (1996) developed equivalent Spanish and English versions of the Revised Civilian Mississippi Scale and the TSS, using back translation and centering (Brislin, Lonner, & Thorndike, 1973), and conducted a study to assess the instruments' cross-language stability. Participants were 53 bilingual volunteers who completed paper-and-pencil instruments twice, with a 1-week interval between tests. The TSS was used to determine whether the respondent had had a traumatic event and thus should complete the Mississippi. The questionnaire instructed these 37 respondents to think about that event when answering the 18 questions that referenced the event, for example, *Since the event, unexpected noises make me jump.* Respondents were instructed to choose one if they had had two or more traumatic events. Respondents who had not experienced an event were instructed to skip to the second section, which could be completed even if they had not experienced a qualifying event.

The total scale was reasonably consistent internally, with alphas of .86 and .88 for the English and Spanish versions respectively. The 8-item subscale measuring PTSD Criterion B and the 10-item subscale measuring PTSD Criterion C had adequate internal consistency (α's = .70–.79). The 7-item subscale measuring PTSD Criterion D in the Spanish version had a substantially higher alpha than the same subscale in the English version (.68 vs. .52). Five unassigned items did not appear to be measuring a unified concept (English α = .46, Spanish α = .54). Cross-language stability was excellent (r = .84).

Norris and Perilla (1996) also presented data from a study involving 404 residents of southern Dade County, Florida, all of whom had been victims of Hurricane Andrew 6 months previously. This time, the data for the English (n = 299) and Spanish (n = 94) versions of the Revised Mississippi were provided by different respondents, assigned according to their own language preference. Both versions of the scale were found to have good internal consistency. Spanish alphas were .92, .86, .72, and .80 for the total scale and subscales B, C, and D, respectively. Corresponding English alphas were .88, .84, .64, and .69.

In addition to scoring the scale continuously, these authors developed an algorithm for classifying respondents as meeting or not meeting each criterion. To assess validity, Norris and Perilla reasoned that scores on the Mississippi should be higher among victims reporting life threat or injury than among victims reporting personal loss or property damage *only*. This was, in fact, the case: Victims who reported *neither* life threat *nor* injury (*n* = 78) showed a PTSD rate of 9%. In contrast, victims who reported *either* life threat *or* injury but not both (*n* = 189) showed a PTSD rate of 20%. When *both* threat and injury were present (*n* = 137), the rate of PTSD reached 37%. Highly significant differences were also found in the prevalence of each set of criterion symptoms (subscales B, C, and D).

The Revised Civilian Mississippi differs from the earlier versions in ways that seem to be improvements. The scale is shorter and easier to administer but still reliable and perhaps more sensitive. By combining the scale with an event screener, it is easy to use with heterogenous event samples (Study 1; Norris & Perilla, 1996), as well as with homogenous event samples (Study 2). Research is still needed to assess the scale's convergent and divergent validity.

Penn Inventory for PTSD

The Penn Inventory was developed by Melvyn Hammarberg (1992). The scale has 26 items. Each item is composed of four sentences scored 0–3 that represent different levels (severity or frequency) of a feeling or thought. The respondent selects the sentence that best describes him- or herself. Although initially developed for veterans, there is nothing specific to the military in the wording of scale items.

Hammarberg examined the reliability and validity of the instrument in three phases. The first employed a sample of 83 subjects: 28 inpatient combat veterans diagnosed with PTSD, 24 combat veterans who had previously been diagnosed with PTSD but were now at least 6 months posttreatment, 15 age-matched veterans without PTSD, and 16 age-matched nonveterans without PTSD. The scale was found to be quite reliable both in terms of internal consistency (α = .94) and in terms of stability over a 5-day interval (r = .96). Mean scale scores differed between groups who had PTSD at the time of testing or previously and the groups who did not have PTSD. However, inpatient and posttreatment groups did not differ. Using a score of 35 as the cutpoint, the scale demonstrated a sensitivity of .90 and a specificity of 1.0.

In the second phase, 98 new subjects were selected and assigned to the same four categories: 39 inpatient combat veterans diagnosed with PTSD, 26 combat veterans who had previously been diagnosed with PTSD but were now at least 6-months posttreatment, 17 age-matched veterans without PTSD, and 16 age-matched nonveterans without PTSD. The scale again demonstrated high internal consistency with an alpha of .94. Results of between-group tests replicated the findings of Phase 1: PTSD subjects differed significantly from non-PTSD subjects, but inpatients did not differ from former patients. Again using a cutoff of 35, sensitivity was .98 and specificity was .94, for an overall hit rate of .97.

Hammarberg's (1992) third phase involved a wider range of psychiatric cases, including 39 veteran patients with PTSD, 18 veteran inpatients with a diagnosis other than PTSD, and 19 survivors of an oil-rig disaster, of whom 16 were diagnosed as having PTSD. The non-PTSD groups showed significantly lower means on the Penn Inventory than did groups with PTSD. With respect to the veterans in the sample, the Penn again showed excellent sensitivity (.97), although specificity (.61) was lower this time. The Mississippi Scale was also included in this phase of the study and performed similarly. The overall hit rates of the Penn and Mississippi were .86 and .88, respectively. Both performances seem excellent when it is recalled that the scales were discriminating between different groups of psychiatric patients. With respect to the disaster victims, sensitivity was .94 and specificity was 1.0. The high prevalence of PTSD in this group needs to be kept in mind when interpreting these results. Yet they provide at least preliminary evidence that the scale could function effectively with trauma populations other than combat veterans.

Kutcher, Tremont, Burda, and Mellman (1994) administered the Penn Inventory, Combat Mississippi, and MMPI-2-PTSD (a revised version of the MMPI) scale to 109 inpatient veterans, of whom 54 had been diagnosed as having PTSD. Correlations of the Penn with the other two measures were .78 and .72, respectively, showing good convergent validity. However, as did Hammarberg (1992), these investigators found the Penn to correlate more highly with depressive symptomatology than would be ideal for showing good divergent validity. The BDI's correlation with the Penn (.82) was higher than its correlations with the Mississippi (.65) or the MMPI-2-PTSD scale (.68). Showing a specificity of only .33 in this study, the Penn Inventory was less successful than the Mississippi at discriminating PTSD patients from veterans with other psychiatric diagnoses.

To date, little additional evidence has emerged supporting the Penn's reliability and validity in female or nonveteran samples. However, this is a relatively new scale, and those data may be forthcoming. Another weakness is that the scale would not be easily modified into an interview format. Also of interest would be data clarifying the reading level required for understanding the scale, as it is more complex in format than most others reviewed here. Further research clarifying the scale's specificity is also needed. With these qualifications, the scale appears to be an excellent possibility for research involving paper-and-pencil questionnaires.

Trauma Symptom Checklist-40 and Trauma Symptom Inventory

TSC-40

John Briere and Marsha Runtz (1989) created the Trauma Symptom Checklist (TSC) for use in clinical research with adult survivors of childhood sexual abuse. The TSC originally had 33 items divided into five subscales: anxiety, depression, dissociation, postsexual abuse trauma, and sleep disturbance. Briere and Runtz established that the original scale was adequately reliable, with the exception of the sleep disturbance subscale. The scale was then expanded to improve this subscale and to add a subscale for sexual problems. This version has 40 items. Subjects rate the relevance of each item to their own experience on a 5-point scale from *not at all true* to *very often true.*

Using data collected from a large sample (n = 2,963) of professional women, Elliott and Briere (1992) determined that the TSC-40 has high internal consistency (α = .90). The revision was effective in improving the internal consistency of the sleep disturbance subscale (α = .77). The new scale had an alpha of .73. Elliott and Briere also showed that the scale discriminates between women who have and have not been abused as a child. This difference held strongly for all subscales as well as for the total scale. Similarly, Gold, Milan, Mayall, and Johnson (1994) administered the TSC-40 to 669 female college students, divided into groups with no sexual assault or abuse (n = 438), childhood sexual assault/abuse (n = 96), adulthood sexual assault/abuse (n = 89), and both childhood and adulthood sexual assault/abuse (n = 31). Groups differed in meaningful ways except on the sleep disturbance subscale.

More recently, Demaré and Briere (1995) conducted a validation study in a large sample (n = 1,179) composed of both male (45%) and female (55%) university students. Frequencies of childhood abuse were 49% among female students and 33% among male students. The TSC-40 was approximately as reliable among men (total scale α = .91; subscale α's = .65–.73) as among women (total scale α = .92; subscale α's = .68–.76). Moreover, all tests of differences between students reporting childhood sexual abuse and students not reporting such experiences were significant in both the male and female samples.

TSI

For clinical purposes, or for whenever a longer measure is acceptable, Briere (1995) developed the TSI. The TSI has a total of 100 items, scored on a 4-point scale, and contains 10 clinical scales: Anxious Arousal (AA; 8 items, α = .86), Depression (D; 8 items, α = .91), Anger/Irritability (AI; 9 items, α = .90), Intrusive Experiences (IE; 8 items, α = .89), Defensive Avoidance (DA; 8 items, α = .90), Dissociation (DIS; 9 items, α = .82), Sexual Concerns (SC; 9 items, α = .87), Dysfunctional Sexual Behavior (DSB; 9 items, α = .85), Impaired Self-Reference (ISR; 9 items, α = .88), and Tension Reduction Behavior (TRB; 8 items, α = .74). In addition, the inventory includes three validity scales. The scale can be self-administered by anyone with a fifth-grade reading level or higher. Norms and *T*-scores were derived on the basis of a large mail-survey sample (n = 836) that was approximately representative of the U.S. population in terms of sex, ethnicity, and state of residence.

Briere (1995) provided confirmatory factor analyses as evidence of the inventory's construct validity. Although the factors were highly interrelated, these analyses justify conceptualizing the scale in terms of three higher-order constructs. Four of the scales — IE, DA, DIS, and ISR (34 items total) — may be considered as manifestations of traumatic stress, whereas three of the scales — AI, D, and AA (25 items total) — are best viewed as manifestations of generalized dysphoria. The remaining subscales appear to reflect a third factor, Self, that may be more specific to the experience of sexual trauma and dysfunction. Also to assess construct validity, respondents in the national survey were categorized as having experienced childhood or adulthood disaster or interpersonal violence and compared to respondents who had not experienced trauma. All four trauma types were significantly associated with elevated TSI scores. TSI scales correlated in predictable ways with subscales of the Brief Symptom Inventory (BSI) and IES and, when optimally weighted via discriminant function analysis, they predicted 24 of 26 cases (92%) classified as having PTSD on the basis of BSI and IES scores. PTSD negative cases were correctly classified 91% of the time. Studies that have been conducted with clinical samples have yielded similar results regarding reliability and construct validity (Briere, Elliott, Harris, & Cotman, 1995) but have not yet examined the sensitivity and specificity of TSI scales.

MMPI-PTSD (PK) Scale

A different approach to developing measures of PTSD has been to derive new subscales for symptom inventories that are commonly used in clinical practice. The best known among these empirically (as opposed to rationally) derived measures is the MMPI-PTSD (PK) Scale developed by Terry Keane and colleagues (1984). The scale was modified slightly when the revised version of the MMPI, MMPI-2, was released. The original PK Scale had 49 items, but the MMPI-2 version has 46 (see Lyons & Keane, 1992). The items were selected because they discriminated between veterans who did and did not have diagnoses of PTSD. Items are dichotomous, but the scale provides a continuous measure of symptomatology.

Herman, Weathers, Litz, Joaquim, and Keane (1993) provided strong evidence of scale reliability. In their studies, the alpha was .95, and test–retest reliability, over 2–3 days, was .94.

Notwithstanding its excellent reliability, the validity of the scale has been challenged. Because it draws from available items in the MMPI, the PK Scale does not explicitly measure all PTSD symptoms as defined in DSM-IV. However, Watson, Juba, Anderson, and Manifold (1990) found that the scale correlates highly and equally well with various diagnosed symptoms such as intrusive memories, flashbacks, detachment, arousal, and cognitive interference. These were important data for establishing the scale's validity, because otherwise high scores may have indicated the presence of some, but not necessarily all, criterion symptoms. An area of much debate in the literature has been the determination of the scale value that provides the optimal cutpoint for discriminating cases from noncases. Keane et al. originally suggested a cutpoint of 30, but other investigators subsequently suggested using much lower values (see Watson et al., 1990). Based on a series of psychometric studies (Herman et al., 1993), a score of 23 is currently recommended. This value yielded a sensitivity of .79, and a specificity of .71 in veteran samples.

As far as can be judged from the published literature, the PK Scale has been used primarily with veterans. Reliability and validity data derived from veteran populations need to be viewed with caution when the scale is used with other populations. Nonetheless, there is nothing specific to combat or military experience in the wording of the MMPI items and thus no reason why the scale could not be equally applicable to other groups. Koretsky and Peck (1990) administered the original 49-item MMPI-PTSD scale to 18 subjects diagnosed as having civilian trauma and 27 controls who had a variety of psychiatric conditions. Using a cutoff score of 19, the scale correctly classified 89% of the PTSD cases and 85% of the other cases. The scale performed equally well in a second sample of 15 PTSD patients and 9 other psychiatric cases. It also appears that use of the scale for studying civilian trauma is increasing. For example, Dutton, Hohnecker, Halle, and Burghardt (1994) compared the MMPI-PTSD scores obtained by forensic and clinical samples of battered women. Quite reasonably, both groups were very distressed as measured by the PK Scale: The mean of 22 in the clinical sample approached the currently recommended cutpoint, and the mean of 28 in the forensic sample exceeded it. However, the two groups' means were not different significantly, whereas their IES and SCL-PTSD means were. Neal et al. (1994) examined the convergent validity of the scale in a heterogeneous sample of 70 trauma victims; many subjects had service-related trauma, but others were victims of assaults, accidents, or childhood abuse. The MMPI-PTSD scale correlated highly with Clinician-Administered PTSD Scale (CAPS) measures of endorsed symptoms ($r = .84$) and symptom intensity ($r = .85$), and with the IES (.79). On the other hand, correlations were equally high with a measure of general distress (.82). On the basis of CAPS diagnoses of PTSD, a cutoff score of 21 successfully classified 80% of the cases (sensitivity .83, specificity .79.) The IES performed slightly better in this same study. In Hovens and van der Ploeg's (1993) study of 53 psychiatric inpatients in the Netherlands, trauma victims and patients with no trauma differed significantly from one another on their MMPI-PK scores. These differences were of comparable strength to those found for the Civilian Mississippi Scale and greater than those found for the SCL-90. These two scales were highly correlated ($r = .89$), suggesting high concurrent validity.

Whereas the jury is perhaps still out, pending additional validity studies in civilian samples, to date the MMPI-PTSD scale has not performed more effectively than the much shorter IES in nonveteran populations. Using the PK Scale may therefore make the most sense in settings where the MMPI is administered routinely.

Symptom Checklist 90 PTSD Scales

SCL-PTSD

A similar approach was taken by Ben Saunders and his colleagues at the Crime Victims Research and Treatment Center (1990). The SCL-90 (Derogatis, 1977) is a commonly used 90-item self-report symptom inventory. The 90 items are categorized into nine subscales measuring somatization, depression, anxiety, phobic anxiety, hostility, obsessive–compulsive behavior, paranoid ideation, interpersonal insensitivity, and psychoticism. All items are scored on a 5-point scale (0 = *not at all*, 4 = *extremely*). Using items on the SCL-90-R, Saunders et al. derived a 28-item scale that discriminated between crime victims with and without PTSD. They named this scale the SCL-PTSD, but is now also referred to as the CR-PTSD Scale (Crime Related). It is quite reliable (α = .93).

In the only published validation study located to date, Arata, Saunders, and Kilpatrick (1991) compared the SCL-PTSD scale to the IES. Subjects were 266 women with a history of criminal victimization. The rate of PTSD was 7.5%. Victims with and without PTSD differed significantly and greatly on both the SCL-PTSD and IES scales. The SCL-PTSD scale was only moderately correlated with the IES (.44), suggesting that the two measures might be tapping different aspects of the same phenomenon. Regression analyses confirmed this impression: The SCL scale made a unique contribution to the prediction of caseness over and above the contribution of the IES. The unique contribution of the SCL-PTSD scale was actually somewhat greater than the unique contribution of the IES. Of the 20 cases, the IES correctly classified 17, compared to 15 for the SCL-PTSD. This difference in sensitivity was not statistically significant. Of the 246 noncases, the IES correctly classified 207, compared to 223 for the SCL-PTSD. This difference in specificity was significant, with the SCL appearing superior. These results, although encouraging, need to be viewed with some caution, because the validation sample was not completely independent of the derivation sample. Moreover, generalizability was limited by the restriction of the sample to female crime victims.

Because of the frequent use of the SCL-90, however, the scale can be expected to have widespread use. Dutton, Hohnecker, Halle, and Burghardt (1994) found forensic and clinical samples of battered women to differ significantly on the SCL-PTSD scale, but the difference was no greater than that obtained for the Global Severity Index (GSI) of the SCL-90. The difference was equivalent to that found for the IES-avoidance subscale but smaller than the two groups' difference on the IES-intrusion subscale. In another analysis of battered women (Dutton, Burghardt, Perrin, Chrestman, & Halle, 1994), the SCL-PTSD scale and GSI showed almost identical correlations with various beliefs (e.g., safety, trust, esteem, intimacy) theorized to mediate the effects of criminal victimization.

Like the MMPI-PTSD scale, an advantage of the SCL-PTSD scale is that it can be administered, and often is, without knowledge of trauma history. Also, like the MMPI, the SCL-90 is used in many settings anyway, so the PTSD subscale can be scored at no additional cost. However, until independent validation studies are conducted, its precision as a measure of posttraumatic stress remains uncertain.

SCL-Supplemented PTSD

Robert Ursano and his colleagues at Uniformed Services University of the Health Sciences (USUHS; 1995) also created a PTSD measure for the SCL-90. Theirs was rationally rather than empirically derived; that is, 31 items were selected on their apparent relevance and then assigned to categories B, C, and D. To provide coverage of criterion symptoms that were not well measured, they added 12 items, such as nightmares, feelings of reliving something unpleasant, avoidance, and feeling hyperalert. An advantage of this scale over the Saunders et al. SCL-90-PTSD scale is that DSM guidelines, rather than a cutpoint, can be used to classify respondents as "probable PTSD" or not.

Reliability data were not reported by Ursano et al. (1995). Validity was assessed by comparing results obtained using this scale with results obtained using the MMPI-PTSD scale and a score of 19 as the cutpoint (Ursano, Fullerton, Kao, Bhartiya, & Dinneen, 1992; cited in Ursano et al., 1995). In four community samples of disaster victims, sensitivity averaged 67% and specificity 91%. Overall, 88% were classified correctly. The scale was also related highly to the IES. Given its similar measurement strategy and controversy over optimum cutpoint, the MMPI-PTSD may not have been the best choice as a criterion measure for the purpose of documenting the precision of this scale as a measure of PTSD. Additional reliability and validity studies are therefore still needed before the scale can be recommended without reservation.

Harvard Trauma Questionnaire

The HTQ was developed by Richard Mollica and his colleagues (1992) at the Indochinese Psychiatric Clinic at Harvard. Both traumatic events and symptoms are included in the questionnaire. In the first section, 17 items describe a range of stressors experienced by refugees, such as torture, rape, murder, and lack of food or water. For each item, the respondent notes whether he or she has (1) not experienced, (2) heard about, (3) witnessed, or (4) personally experienced that stressor. The symptom portion consists of 30 items, 16 of which correspond to DSM-IV criteria, and 14 of which tap other aspects of distress as it is expressed in Indochinese culture. Items are scored on a 4-point scale from *not at all* = 1 to *extremely* = 4, and the investigators now recommend scoring the scale as the mean item value (Mollica, personal communication, April 18, 1995). The HTQ is available in

Khmer, Lao, and Vietnamese. Linguistic equivalence was established using back translation and centering.

The HTQ is important to review here because it illustrates an approach to the cross-cultural assessment of trauma and PTSD. The investigators (Mollica et al., 1995) note that it is important to *adapt* rather than merely translate the questionnaire for each trauma population and culture. The "core" PTSD section should be kept equivalent across languages, but the remaining symptom questions should vary so that they are specific and relevant to the culture of respondents. These items should be identified by ethnographic studies, clinical experience, key informants, and healers in the setting of interest (Mollica et al., 1995).

Mollica et al. (1992) examined the reliability and validity of the Cambodian, Lao, and Vietnamese versions of the instrument in a sample of 91 Indochinese refugees, of whom 34 were men and 57 were women, and of whom 55 were Cambodian, 20 Laotian, and 16 Vietnamese. Alpha coefficients were .90 for the stressor portion of the HTQ and .96 for the symptom portion. Test–retest correlations (examined in a subsample consisting of 10 individuals from each nation) were .89 for the stressor portion and .92 for the symptom portion, with a 1-week interval between tests.

To assess criterion validity, research participants were divided into groups on the basis of independent diagnoses. The PTSD group ($n = 65$) showed significantly higher symptom scores than the non-PTSD group ($n = 26$). A cutpoint of 75 (mean item value of 2.5) was found to maximize classification accuracy. Sensitivity was .78, specificity was .65, and the overall hit rate was .75. Evidence of construct validity was the finding that scores on the stressor portion correlated highly with scores on the symptom portion.

These initial studies provided the tools used in a large-scale study (Mollica, Poole, & Tor, in press) involving a random sample of nearly 1,000 Cambodian refugees living in camps along the Thai–Cambodian border. Approximately one-third of the sample had PTSD scores in the clinical range (2.5 plus), and two-thirds had depression scores in the clinical range. Most relevant to the purpose of this chapter were the exceptionally strong relations between traumatic experiences and symptom scores. Rates of PTSD varied from 14% among refugees reporting four or fewer trauma events to 81% among refugees reporting 25 or more trauma events. The relative odds ratio was 38.9 in the most traumatized group. Rates of depression varied from 45% to 93%. In this case, the relative odds ratio was 21.8 in the most traumatized group. These data are instructive in showing that posttraumatic stress symptoms were more specifically associated with the cumulative amount of trauma, whereas depressive symptoms were more pervasive among the refugees.

Summary

Table 1.2 summarizes the information available on these 15 scales. Taken together, they provide a wide array of choices for measuring posttraumatic stress. Some scales adhere closely to DSM-IV criteria; others take a broader sweep. Some are relatively short, whereas others are relatively long. Some take advantage of available clinical data, such as the MMPI or SCL-90; most require additional assessment materials. With only a few exceptions or reservations, all of the scales reviewed here show acceptable reliability and validity, although some test creators have documented these attributes more completely than have others. Undoubtedly, clinician administered interviews will remain the "gold standard" in the field. Yet, as a group, these self-report measures performed well when contrasted directly with them. In Table 1.2, we have reserved the descriptor of "strong" validity for those scales that have shown sensitivity and specificity in clinical samples within studies that have been subjected to peer review. This crude summary may give undue weight to criterion validity at the expense of construct validity, which is excellent among many of the scales whose validity is described only as moderate in Table 1.2. Sources for obtaining these measures are shown in the Appendix.

Historically, the measurement of civilian trauma has lagged behind that related to military trauma. None of the scales reviewed in this chapter were published prior to 1984, and most are much more recent. In fact, recent years have seen a proliferation of measures of posttraumatic stress. The scales reviewed here, although numerous, do no not comprise a complete set. The practice of using scales that lack documented reliability and validity has waned but has not disappeared. This practice can no longer be justified, because a number of very sound measures exist.

This progress in developing reliable and valid self-report measures of PTSD should aid epidemiological and community-based studies immensely over the next few years. We hope researchers in this area will find these summaries to be useful when they are selecting scales appropriate for their own research. Whereas practitioners may usually find clinician-administered measures more suitable, they may nonetheless face occasions where it is not feasible to conduct such labor-intensive and costly assessments. When communities suddenly find themselves in crisis, needs must be assessed on a broader scale so that clinical services can be targeted to where they are needed most. Even in less dramatic times, self-report scales may supplement structured interviews well. For example, because they require less of the clinician's own time and resources, self-report scales could make it easier for clinicians to evaluate the well-being of their clients for longer periods of time after treatment has been terminated. Systematic follow-up procedures could identify individuals at risk for recidivism and in need of additional assessment. They could also generate "real-world" data regarding the long-term utility of different treatment approaches.

Notwithstanding the quality of these measures, we believe there is still room for improvement. Perhaps it is our own bias, but one disappointment in this literature was the lack of attention to diversity in validation samples. Excluding the Revised Civilian Mississippi and the HTQ, little attention was given to potential ethnic or cross-cultural differences in symptom expres-

TABLE 1.2. Summary Descriptions of 15 Standardized Self-Report Measures of Posttraumatic Stress

Scale	How derived	Number of items	Evidence of stability	Evidence of consistency	Validity	Population validated on
Reaction Index	Rationally	20	Interrater $x = .77$	na	Moderate	Male and female trauma victims
NWS Module	Rationally	20	T-R $x = .45$	na	Strong	Women/ general
PSS	Rationally	17	T-R $r = .74-.80$	.85-.91	Strong	Female rape victims
MPSS	Revised PSS	34	na	.96	na	na
Purdue PTSD-R	Rationally	17	T-R $r = .71$	.91	Moderate	Under-graduates
PTSD-Interview	Rationally	20	T-R $r = .95$	.92	Strong	Male veterans
Civilian Mississippi	Revised Combat Mississippi	35	na	.86	Moderate	General
Revised Mississippi	Revised Civilian Mississippi	30	T-R (Eng.–Span.) $r = .84$	.86-.92	Moderate	Multicultural
Penn Inventory	Rationally	26	T-R $r = .96$	.94	Moderate –strong	Male veterans/ disaster victims
TSC-40	Rationally	40	na	.90-.92	Moderate	Male and female abuse survivors
TSI	Rationally	100	na	.74-.90	Moderate –strong	General/ clinical
MMPI-PTSD	Empirically	46	T-R $r = .94$	.95	Strong	Male veterans
SCL-PTSD	Empirically	28	na	.93	Moderate	Female crime victims
SCL-Supplemented PTSD	Rationally	43	na	na	Moderate	Disaster victims/ workers
HTQ-symptoms	Rationally	16 + 14 .	T-R $r = .92$	.96	Moderate –strong	Indochinese refugees

Note. na, data not available.

sion. We concluded this chapter with the HTQ because it illustrates a forward-thinking approach that balances cross-cultural standardization with cultural specificity in developing assessment tools. In our increasingly global and mobile society, cross-cultural equivalence and relevance are extremely important issues for psychometricians to address in future research.

We believe, however, that progress in this area would be served best by efforts to refine and cross-validate the existing measures of PTSD. Can we, if only for awhile, forgo the temptation of generating new, but largely similar, scales? We hope the answer to this question is yes. As measurement becomes more standardized, we can build a database that elucidates the prevalence and nature of PTSD across different populations and events.

APPENDIX: SOURCES FOR OBTAINING STANDARDIZED SELF-REPORT SCALES

Scale and contact person	Mailing address	Telephone
Civilian Mississippi Terence Keane or Frank Weathers	National Center for PTSD, Boston DVA Medical Center, 150 South Huntington Avenue, Boston, MA 02130	(617)232-9500 ext. 4130/4136
Civilian Mississippi — Revised Fran Norris (English) Julia Perilla (Spanish)	Department of Psychology, Georgia State University, University Plaza, Atlanta, GA 30303	(404)651-1607
Harvard Trauma Questionnaire Richard Mollica	Indochinese Psychiatry Clinic, St. Elizabeth's Hospital, 77 Warren Street, Brighton, MA 02135	(617)789-2102
MMPI-PTSD Terence Keane or Frank Weathers	National Center for PTSD, Boston DVA Medical Center, 150 South Huntington Avenue, Boston, MA 02130	(617)232-9500 ext. 4130/4136
NWS PTSD Module Heidi Resnick	Crime Victims Research and Treatment Center, Medical University of South Carolina, 171 Ashley Avenue, Charleston, SC 29425	(803)792-2945
Penn Inventory Melvyn Hammarberg	Department of American Civilization, 301A College Hall, University of Pennsylvania, Philadelphia, PA 19104	(215)898-7365
PTSD Interview Charles Watson	Research and Psychology Services, DVA Medical Center, 4801 North Eighth Street, St. Cloud, MN 56303	(612)252-1670

(cont.)

APPENDIX (cont.)

Scale and contact person	Mailing address	Telephone
PTSD Symptom Scale (PSS) Edna Foa	Medical College of Pennsylvania, Eastern Pennsylvania Psychiatric Institute, 3200 Henry Avenue, Philadelphia, PA 19129	(215)842-4010
PSS — Modified Sherry Falsetti	Crime Victims Research and Treatment Center, Medical University of South Carolina, 171 Ashley Avenue, Charleston, SC 29425	(803)792-2945
Potential Stressful Events Interview Dean Kilpatrick	Crime Victims Research and Treatment Center, Medical University of South Carolina, 171 Ashley Avenue, Charleston, SC 29425	(803)792-2945
Purdue PTSD Scale — Revised Scott Vrana	Department of Psychological Sciences, Purdue University, West Lafayette, IN 47907	(317)494-6977
Reaction Index Calvin Frederick	VA Medical Center, Building 258, Room 118B, Los Angeles, CA 90073	(310)824-3174
SCL-PTSD Ben Saunders	Crime Victims Research and Treatment Center, Medical University of South Carolina, 171 Ashley Avenue, Charleston, SC 29425	(803)792-2945
SCL-Supplemented PTSD Robert Ursano	Department of Psychiatry, Uniformed Services, University of the Health Sciences, 4301 Jones Bridge Road, Bethesda, MD 20814	(301)295-2470
Trauma History Questionnaire Bonnie Green	Department of Psychiatry, Georgetown University, 611 Kober–Cogan Hall, Washington, DC 20007	(202)687-6529

Trauma Symptom Checklist-40 John Briere	Department of Psychiatry, University of Southern California, School of Medicine, Los Angeles, CA 90033	(213)226-5697
Trauma Symptom Inventory John Briere	Department of Psychiatry, University of Southern California, School of Medicine, Los Angeles, CA 90033	(213)226-5697
Traumatic Events Questionnaire Scott Vrana	Department of Psychological Sciences, Purdue University, West Lafayette, IN 47907	(317)494-6977
Traumatic Life Events Questionnaire Edward Kubany	Pacific Center for PTSD, Department of Veterans Affairs, 1132 Bishop Street, Suite 307, Honolulu, HI 96813	(808)566-1650
Traumatic Stress Schedule Fran Norris (English) Julia Perilla (Spanish)	Department of Psychology, Georgia State University, University Plaza, Atlanta, GA 30303	(404)651-1607

REFERENCES

American Psychiatric Association. (1987). *Diagnostic and statistical manual of mental disorders* (3rd ed., rev.). Washington, DC: Author.

American Psychiatric Association. (1994). *Diagnostic and statistical manual of mental disorders* (4th ed.). Washington, DC: Author.

Arata, C., Saunders, B., & Kilpatrick, D. (1991). Concurrent validity of a crime-related post-traumatic stress disorder scale for women with the Symptom Checklist-90-Revised. *Violence and Victims, 6,* 191–199.

Breslau, N., Davis, G., Andreski, P., & Peterson, E. (1991). Traumatic events and post-traumatic stress disorder in an urban population of young adults. *Archives of General Psychiatry, 48,* 216–222.

Briere, J. (1992). *Child abuse trauma: Theory and treatment of the lasting effects.* Newbury Park, CA: Sage.

Briere, J. (1995). *Trauma Symptom Inventory (TSI): Professional manual.* Odessa, FL: Psychological Assessment Resources.

Briere, J., Elliott, D., Harris, K., & Cotman, A. (1995). Trauma Symptom Inventory: Psychometrics and association with childhood and adult victimization in clinical samples. *Journal of Interpersonal Violence, 10,* 387–401.

Briere, J., & Runtz, M. (1989). The Trauma Symptom Checklist (TSC-33): Early data on a new scale. *Journal of Interpersonal Violence, 4,* 151–163.

Brislin, R., Lonner, W., & Thorndike, R. (1973). *Cross-cultural research methods.* New York: Wiley.

Demaré, D., & Briere, J. (1995). *Trauma Symptom Checklist-40: Validation with sexually abused and nonabused university students.* Unpublished manuscript, University of Southern California, Los Angeles.

Derogatis, L. (1977). *SCL-90: Administration, scoring, and procedure manual for the revised version.* Baltimore: John Hopkins University School of Medicine.

Dohrenwend, B. P. (1974). Problems in defining and sampling the relevant population of stressful life events. In B. S. Dohrenwend & B. P. Dohrenwend (Eds.), *Stressful life events: Their nature and effects* (pp. 275–310). New York: Wiley.

Dohrenwend, B. S., Krasnoff, B., Askenasy, A., & Dohrenwend, B. P. (1978). Exemplification of a method for scaling life events: The PERI Life Events Scale. *Journal of Health and Social Behavior, 19,* 205–229.

Dutton, M., Burghardt, K., Perrin, S., Chrestman, K., & Halle, P. (1994). Battered women's cognitive schemata. *Journal of Traumatic Stress, 7,* 237–255.

Dutton, M., Hohnecker, L., Halle, P., & Burghardt, K. (1994). Traumatic responses among battered women who kill. *Journal of Traumatic Stress, 7,* 549–564.

Elliott, D., & Briere, J. (1992). Sexual abuse trauma among professional women: Validating the Trauma Symptom Checklist-40 (TSC-40). *Child Abuse and Neglect, 16,* 391–398.

Falsetti, S., Resnick, H., Resick, P., & Kilpatrick, D. (1993). The Modified PTSD Symptom Scale: A brief self-report measure of posttraumatic stress disorder. *Behavior Therapist, 16,* 161–162.

Foa, E., Riggs, D., Dancu, C., & Rothbaum, B., (1993). Reliability and validity of a brief instrument for assessing post-traumatic stress disorder. *Journal of Traumatic Stress, 6,* 459–474.

Frederick, C. (1985a). Children traumatized by catastrophic situations. In S. Eth & R. Pynoos (Eds.), *Post traumatic stress disorder in children* (pp. 73–99). Washington, DC: American Psychiatric Press.

Frederick, C. (1985b). Selected foci in the spectrum of posttraumatic stress disorders. In S. Murphy & J. Laube (Eds.), *Perspectives on disaster recovery* (pp. 110–130). New York: Appleton-Century Crofts.

Frederick, C. (1987). Psychic trauma in victims of crime and terrorism. In G. VandenBos & B. K. Bryant (Eds.), *Cataclysms, crises, and catastrophes* (pp. 65–108). Washington, DC: American Psychological Association.

Freedy, J., Kilpatrick, D., & Resnick, H. (1993). Natural disasters and mental health: Theory, assessment, and intervention. In R. Allen (Ed.), *Handbook of postdisaster interventions. Journal of Social Behavior and Personality, 8,* 49–104.

Gold, S., Milan, L., Mayall, A., & Johnson, A. (1994). A cross-validation of the Trauma Symptom Checklist: The role of mediating variables. *Journal of Interpersonal Violence, 9,* 12–25.

Green, B. (1995). *Trauma History Questionnaire.* Unpublished instrument and data. (Available from the author)

Hammarberg, M. (1992). Penn Inventory for Posttraumatic Stress Disorder: Psychometric properties. *Psychological Assessment, 4,* 67–76.

Helzer, J., Robins, L., & McEvoy, L. (1987). Post-traumatic stress disorder in the general population: Findings of the Epidemiologic Catchment Area Survey. *New England Journal of Medicine, 317,* 1630–1634.

Herman, D., Weathers, F., Litz, B., Joaquim, S., & Keane, T. (1993, October). *The PK Scale of the MMPI-2: Reliability and validity of the embedded and stand-alone versions.* Paper presented at the annual meeting of the International Society for Traumatic Stress Studies, San Antonio, TX.

Hovens, J., & van der Ploeg, M. (1993). Posttraumatic stress disorder in Dutch psychiatric in-patients. *Journal of Traumatic Stress, 6*, 91–102.

Keane, T. M., Caddell, J. M., & Taylor, K. L. (1988). Mississippi Scale for Combat-Related Posttraumatic Stress Disorder: Three studies in reliability and validity. *Journal of Consulting and Clinical Psychology, 56*, 85–90.

Keane, T., Malloy, P., & Fairbank, J. (1984). Empirical development of an MMPI subscale for the assessment of combat-related post-traumatic stress disorders. *Journal of Consulting and Clinical Psychology, 52*, 888–891.

Kilpatrick, D., Resnick, H., & Freedy, J. (1991). *The Potential Stressful Events Interview.* Unpublished instrument, Medical University of South Carolina, Charleston, South Carolina.

Kilpatrick, D., Resnick, H., Saunders, B., & Best, C. (1989). *The National Women's Study PTSD module.* Unpublished instrument, Medical University of South Carolina, Charleston, South Carolina.

Koretsky, M., & Peck, A. (1990). Validation and cross-validation of the PTSD subscale of the MMPI with civilian trauma victims. *Journal of Clinical Psychology, 46*, 296–300.

Kubany, E. (1995). *The Traumatic Life Events Questionnaire (TLEQ): A brief measure of prior trauma exposure.* Unpublished scale. (Available from the author, Pacific Center for PTSD, Honolulu, Hawaii.)

Kubany, E., Hayes, S., Abueg, F., Manke, F., & Brennan, J., & Stahura, C. (in press). Development and validation of the Trauma-Related Guilt Inventory. *Psychological Assessment.*

Kutcher, G., Tremont, M., Burda, P., & Mellman, T. (1994). *The effectiveness of PTSD self-report measures with an inpatient veteran population.* Paper presented at the annual meeting of the International Society for Traumatic Stress Studies, Chicago, IL.

Lauterbach, D., & Vrana, S. (1996). Three studies on the reliability and validity of a self-report measure of posttraumatic stress disorder. *Assessment, 3*, 17–25.

Lauterbach, D., Vrana, S., King, D., & King, L. (in press). Psychometric properties of the Civilian Version of the Mississippi PTSD Scale. *Journal for Traumatic Stress.*

Lyons, J., & Keane, T. (1992). Keane PTSD Scale: MMPI and MMPI-2 update. *Journal of Traumatic Stress, 5*, 111–117.

Mollica, R., Caspi-Yavin, Y., Bollini, P., Truong, T., Tor, S., & Lavelle, J. (1992). The Harvard Trauma Questionnaire: Validating a cross-cultural instrument for measuring torture, trauma, and posttraumatic stress disorder in Indochinese refugees. *Journal of Nervous and Mental Disease, 180*, 111–116.

Mollica, R., Caspi-Yavin, Y., Lavelle, J., Tor, S., Yang, T., Chan, S., Pham, T., Ryan, A., & de Marneffe, D. (1995). *Manual for the Harvard Trauma Questionnaire.* Brighton, MA: Indochinese Psychiatry Clinic.

Mollica, R., Poole, C., & Tor, S. (in press). Symptoms, functioning, and health functioning in a massively traumatized population: The legacy of the Cambodian tragedy. In B. P. Dohrenwend (Ed.), *Adversity, stress, and psychopathology.* New York: American Psychiatric Association Press.

Neal, L., Busuttil, W., Rollins, J., Herepath, R., Strike, P., & Turnbull, G. (1994). Convergent validity of measures of posttraumatic stress disorder in a mixed military and civilian population. *Journal of Traumatic Stress, 7*, 447–456.

Norris, F. (1990). Screening for traumatic stress: A scale for use in the general population. *Journal of Applied Social Psychology, 20*, 1704–1718.

Norris, F. (1992). Epidemiology of trauma: Frequency and impact of different potentially traumatic events on different demographic groups. *Journal of Consulting and Clinical Psychology, 60*, 409–418.

Norris, F., & Kaniasty, K. (1992). Reliability of delayed self-reports in disaster research. *Journal of Traumatic Stress, 5,* 575–588.

Norris, F., & Perilla, J. (1996). Reliability, validity, and cross-language stability of the Revised Civilian Mississippi Scale for PTSD. *Journal of Traumatic Stress, 9,* 285–298.

Pynoos, R. S., Frederick, C., Nader, K., Arroyo, W., Steinberg, A., Eth, S., Nunez, F., & Fairbanks, L. (1987). Life threat and posttraumatic stress in school-age children. *Archives of General Psychiatry, 44,* 1057–1063.

Realmuto, G., Masten, A., Carole, L., Hubbard, J., Groteluschen, A., & Chhun, B. (1992). Adolescent survivors of massive childhood trauma in Cambodia: Life events and current symptoms. *Journal of Traumatic Stress, 5,* 589–600.

Resnick, H., Falsetti, S., Kilpatrick, D., & Freedy, J. (1996). Assessment of rape and other civilian trauma-related posttraumatic stress disorder: Emphasis on assessment of potentially traumatic events. In T. Miller (Ed.), *Stressful life events* (2nd ed., pp. 235–271). Madison, CT: International Universities Press.

Resnick, H., Kilpatrick, D., Dansky, B., Saunders, B., & Best, C. (1993). Prevalence of civilian trauma and posttraumatic stress disorder in a representative national sample of women. *Journal of Consulting and Clinical Psychology, 61,* 984–991.

Riggs, D., Dancu, C., Gershuny, B., Greenberg, D., & Foa, E. (1992). Anger and posttraumatic stress disorder in female crime victims. *Journal of Traumatic Stress, 5,* 613–626.

Saunders, B., Arata, C., & Kilpatrick, D. (1990). Development of a crime-related posttraumatic stress disorder scale for women with the Symptom Checklist-90 Revised. *Journal of Traumatic Stress, 3,* 439–448.

Solomon, S., & Canino, G. (1990). The appropriateness of DSM-III-R criteria for posttraumatic stress disorder. *Comprehensive Psychiatry, 31,* 227–237.

Ursano, R., Fullerton, C., Kao, T., & Bhartiya, V. (1995). Longitudinal assessment of posttraumatic stress disorder and depression after exposure to traumatic death. *Journal of Nervous and Mental Disease, 183,* 36–42.

Vrana, S., & Lauterbach, D. (1994). Prevalence of traumatic events and post-traumatic psychological symptoms in a nonclinical sample of college students. *Journal of Traumatic Stress, 7,* 289–302.

Vreven, D., Gudanowski, D., King, L., & King, D. (1995). The Civilian Version of the Mississippi PTSD Scale: A psychometric evaluation *Journal of Traumatic Stress, 8,* 91–110.

Watson, C., Juba, M., Anderson, P., & Manifold, V. (1990). What does the Keane et al. PTSD Scale for the MMPI measure? *Journal of Clinical Psychology, 46,* 600–606.

Watson, C., Juba, M., Manifold, V., Kucala, T., & Anderson, P. (1991). The PTSD Interview: Rationale, description, reliability and concurrent validity of a DSM-III based technique. *Journal of Clinical Psychology, 47,* 179–185.

Watson, C., Plemel, D., DeMotts, J., Howard, M., Tuorilla, J., Moog, R., Thomas, D., & Anderson, D. (1994). A comparison of four PTSD measures' convergent validities in Vietnam veterans. *Journal of Traumatic Stress, 7,* 75–82.

Weiss, D. (1993). Structured clinical interview techniques. In J. Wilson & B. Raphael (Eds.), *International handbook of traumatic stress syndromes* (pp. 179–189). New York: Plenum Press.

Wilson, J. (1994). The historical evolution of PTSD diagnostic criteria: From Freud to DSM-IV. *Journal of Traumatic Stress, 7,* 681–689.

Wojcik, E. (1988). Disruption to pre-trauma social support networks considered as a factor in post-traumatic stress reaction (Doctoral dissertation, Purdue University, 1987). *Dissertation Abstracts International, 49,* 246B.

CHAPTER 2

Psychological Assessment of Child Abuse Effects in Adults

JOHN BRIERE

INTRODUCTION AND STATEMENT OF PURPOSE

As a group, adults abused as children exhibit a wide range of psychological and interpersonal problems relative to those without such a history. Although a causal relationship between such difficulties and child abuse cannot be established using the retrospective methodologies common to the field, the extensive replication of findings and a recent meta-analysis (Neumann, Houskamp, Pollock, & Briere, 1996) suggests that childhood maltreatment is, in fact, a significant risk factor for later psychological disorder.

Probably due in part to the psychologically injurious aspects of child abuse, the rates of self-reported child maltreatment in clinical samples are considerably greater than in the general population. For example, the incidence of self-reported sexual abuse histories among women averages around 50% across outpatient, inpatient, and emergency room samples (Briere, 1992b), as opposed to rates of slightly more than half that magnitude in general population samples (Elliott & Briere, 1995; Finkelhor, Hotaling, Lewis, & Smith, 1990; Wyatt, 1985).

Given the frequency with which abuse survivors appear in clinical settings, and, yet, the seeming regularity of their misassessment by standardized measures, the present chapter examines some of the assessment and measurement issues in this area. Among the concerns facing the clinician are (1) the relative accuracy of the client's retrospective abuse report, given recent concerns about "false memories" of abuse; (2) how to systematically assess the specific details and context of the victimization experience, including its type (i.e., sexual, physical, psychological), frequency, duration, the victim's age at abuse onset and offset, and so on, since more severe abuse appears to increase subsequent mental health impairment; and (3) how to accurately assess the specific nature and extent of any abuse-related symptomatology or dysfunction that might be present.

The issue of the validity or truthfulness of a given abuse report has been widely debated of late. Even those questioning a given abuse disclosure, however, typically do not deny the high incidence and potential negative impacts of child abuse. Instead, there may be opinions voiced that a specific abuse allegation is the result of psychopathology, greed, or vindictiveness, or that an evaluator/therapist has intentionally or inadvertently implanted "false memories" of abuse in a client who has no abuse history (Gardner, 1992; Loftus, 1993; Wakefield & Underwager, 1992). Although clinical experience suggests that most reports of long-past abuse are accurate in their major details, a small minority of abuse reports are likely to be significantly distorted or confabulated. Regardless of its frequency, potentially inaccurate reporting of abuse is of real concern and must be considered during the assessment process.

The second issue, the specific nature of a given individual's abuse history, is often explored during an unstructured clinical interview. Such free-form evaluation is subject to error or oversight, however, including the absence of systematic coverage of all abuse-relevant historical material. The last several years have witnessed the development of a number of more structured and comprehensive abuse history measures, each of which are described in this chapter.

The third issue involves the accurate and sensitive assessment of abuse effects. Because the study of child abuse and its impacts is still in its relative infancy, there has been little meaningful focus on the actual psychological evaluation of abuse-specific distress and disorder. In the absence of abuse-relevant assessment procedures, clinicians and researchers have tended to use generic measures of global phenomena such as anxiety, depression, and personality disorder. Unfortunately, as is noted later, such measures may easily overlook or misinterpret specific, abuse-related psychological disturbance.

Child abuse effects may also be difficult to measure adequately because of their pervasiveness. Early abuse may disrupt the parent–child attachment bond (Alexander, 1992); interfere with normal psychological and neurophysiological development (Cole & Putnam, 1992); motivate the development of avoidance strategies that are, in and of themselves, detrimental (Briere, 1996a; Herman, 1992); and generalize or elaborate over time (Gelinas, 1983). The complexity of such effects suggests the need for multiple measures and sources of data in any comprehensive abuse-relevant evaluation.

Among the known effects of child maltreatment are those seen in other forms of trauma, that is, posttraumatic stress (Craine, Henson, Colliver, & MacLean, 1988; Rowan, Foy, Rodriguez, & Ryan, 1994; Saunders, Villeponteaux, Lipovsky, Kilpatrick, & Veronen, 1992) and dissociation (Briere & Runtz, 1990a; Chu & Dill, 1990; DiTomasso & Routh, 1993). In addition to the more common dissociative responses, abuse has been associated with psychogenic amnesia (Briere & Conte, 1993; Elliott & Briere, 1995; Feldman-Summers & Pope, 1994; Herman & Schatzow, 1987; Loftus, Polonsky, & Fullilove, 1994; Williams, 1994) and dissociative identity disorder (Putnam, 1989; Ross, Anderson, Heber, & Norton, 1990).

Also found in some adults abused as children, however, are less trauma-specific symptoms and disorders, such as helplessness, guilt, and low self-esteem (Briere & Runtz, 1990b; Jehu, 1989; Wind & Silvern, 1992), anxiety, depression, and anger (Bifulco, Brown, & Adler, 1991; Elliott & Briere, 1992; Saunders et al., 1992; Yama, Tovey, & Fogas, 1993), and anxiety-mediated responses such as sexual dysfunction (Hunter, 1991; Wyatt, Newcomb, & Riederle, 1993) and somatization (Drossman et al., 1990; Springs & Friedrich, 1992). Abuse survivors are also more likely to engage in drug and alcohol abuse (e.g., Dembo et al., 1989; Singer, Petchers, & Hussey, 1989; Zierler et al., 1991), as well as externalizing behaviors such as compulsive and indiscriminate sexual activity (Alexander & Lupfer, 1987; Wyatt, 1988; Zierler et al., 1991), bingeing or chronic overeating (Connors & Morse, 1993; Waller, 1992), aggression (Pollock et al., 1990), suicidal behavior (e.g., Briere & Runtz, 1986; Brown & Anderson, 1991; de Wilde, Kienhorst, Diekstra, & Wolters, 1992), and self-mutilation (van der Kolk, Perry, & Herman, 1991; Walsh & Rosen, 1988).

Because of the variety of abuse-related responses, psychological assessment can be incomplete if, for example, only a Minnesota Multiphasic Personality Inventory (MMPI), a posttraumatic stress disorder (PTSD) measure, or a test of borderline traits is administered. Instead, a comprehensive assessment of abuse-related difficulties should involve multiple measures that encompass not only the usual tests of anxiety or depression, but also instruments that tap, for example, posttraumatic stress, dissociation, somatization, sexual difficulties, and enduring maladaptive personality traits.

PSYCHOLOGICAL TESTS AND MEASURES USED IN ABUSE EFFECTS RESEARCH AND PRACTICE

To date, most studies of child abuse effects have used research instruments that have not been standardized or normed on the general population, and thus may not be especially helpful in clinical contexts (Briere, in press). In other instances, abuse effects have been tested with standardized, but abuse-nonspecific instruments such as the MMPI, the Millon Clinical Multiaxial Inventory (MCMI), and the Rorschach. Each of these latter measures are examined in this chapter in relative detail, due to their frequent use in the assessment of child abuse survivors. As well, those measures used to assess generic posttraumatic disturbance will be considered as they relate to the evaluation of abuse survivors.

Assessment Issues Relevant to Abuse Survivors

Before specific assessment tools are discussed, several issues relevant to the assessment of abuse survivors should be considered. Although less technical than test psychometrics, these aspects of the testing process are critically important to effective evaluation.

Rapport and Sensitivity

Because most abuse survivors were, almost by definition, maltreated by authority figures, it is not uncommon for former victims to approach the psychological assessment process with fear, distrust, and performance or evaluation concerns. As a result, the clinician must especially strive to provide a manifestly safe and nonjudgmental testing environment, and to approach the issue of childhood maltreatment in a gradual and nonupsetting manner (Armstrong, 1995; Courtois, 1995). The psychological assessor with a brusque, dismissive, or intrusive manner runs the risk of motivating negativistic or avoidant responses in the client, as well as potentially increasing the survivor's scores on dysphoria and stress measures. This dynamic is especially likely to occur if the evaluation includes a structured interview or projective (as opposed to objective) test, since the survivor must interact directly with the evaluator in order to produce test data.

The Role of Avoidance

As noted earlier, chronic child abuse promotes and reinforces the development of avoidance defenses. Unfortunately, this tendency to avoid or attenuate distress may decrease the survivor's response to psychological assessment, in some instances leading to a significant underpresentation of abuse history and abuse effects. Most basically, any assessment technique that requires the abuse survivor to recall abuse-related events is indirectly asking him or her to reexperience those events; a phenomenon that can motivate denial or other cognitive avoidance responses. These responses, in turn, may reduce the extent of abuse history or level of abuse-related symptomatology accessible by psychological tests.

Avoidance also may present in the form of dissociative amnesia, per DSM-IV, in which case the client may have insufficient recall of abuse experiences on measures of childhood maltreatment history. As noted earlier, a number of studies suggest that some instances of childhood sexual and physical abuse may be relatively unavailable to conscious memory for extended periods of time, during which, presumably, the subjects of these studies would deny or underestimate historical events that did, in fact, occur. Although these studies have been criticized for their methodological shortcomings (e.g., Briere, 1992a; Loftus, 1993), the repeated replication of reduced or absent memories of childhood abuse experiences suggests that, in fact, individual self-reports regarding childhood maltreatment may be sub-ject to a nontrivial rate of false negatives.

Avoidance also can affect clients' reports of symptomatology on assess-ment instruments (Epstein, 1993; Friedrich, 1994). Dissociative numbing and defensive avoidance of painful material are both prevalent in survivors of physical and sexual abuse (DiTomasso & Routh, 1993; Chu & Dill, 1990), and both may suppress clients' scores on symptom measures. For example, El-liott and Briere (1994) report on a subsample of children for whom there was compelling evidence of sexual abuse (e.g., unambiguous medical find-ings, photographs taken by the abuser, or abuser confession) but who, nonetheless, both (1) denied that they had been abused, and (2) scored *lower* than control subjects (children without sexual abuse histories) on the Trau-ma Symptom Checklist for Children (TSCC; Briere, 1996). As the authors note, it is likely that these children were using denial and other avoidance strategies to keep from confronting their abuse and its psychological impacts. In the absence of outside corroboration, these children probably would have been judged as nonabused on interview or through psychological testing.

Symptom underreporting, although an important issue in the assessment of abuse survivors, is obviously difficult to identify in any given individual. At present, the practitioner is limited to reliance on validity scales that, for example, index defensiveness or "fake good" responses (e.g., the L and K scales of the MMPI), Positive Impression Management scale of the Personality As-sessment Inventory (PAI; Morey, 1991), Desirability scale of the MCMI, or Response Level scale of the Trauma Symptom Inventory (TSI; Briere, 1995a). Unfortunately, although these validity indicators may point to some cases of underreporting, it is likely that other instances will go unidentified un-less the clinician can detect them during the evaluation interview.

Overreporting, Confabulation, and Malingering

In addition to underreporting, some individuals may overreport or mis-represent abuse histories and/or abuse-related symptomatology. Occasion-ally, inaccurate abuse histories may occur in psychosis or extreme personality disorders. On the other hand, research suggests that borderline personality disorder may be associated with, among other things, severe sexual abuse (e.g., Briere & Zaidi, 1989; Herman, Perry, & van der Kolk, 1989; Ogata et al., 1990), and recent research implicates child abuse in at least some exacer-bated or atypical psychotic presentations (e.g., Ross, Anderson, & Clark, 1994; Briere, Woo, McRae, Foltz, & Sitzman, in press). In addition, there are no data to suggest that more disturbed individuals have a *lower* probability of being abused than other people. As a result, the child abuse reports of psy-chotic or borderline individuals should not be discounted automatically, but, instead, should be evaluated for their credibility in the same manner as any other childhood abuse reports might be considered.

Per the recent concern over "false memories" of abuse, it is also possible for individuals to confabulate abuse memories as a result of the demand characteristics associated with certain memory recovery techniques. Specifically, the inappropriate use of hypnosis, overly directive interventions, or other activities that especially capitalize on suggestion may reduce the accuracy of therapy-associated recollections of abuse (Briere, 1995b; Lindsay, 1994; Enns, McNeilly, Corkery, & Gilbert, 1995). Unfortunately, because not all therapy is good therapy, it also may be necessary on occasion to query the client regarding the nature of previous therapeutic interventions—especially when the reported abuse appears especially unlikely.

Although overreporting is likely to be less frequent than underreporting in nonforensic clinical situations, it is obviously important to identify it when it occurs. Unfortunately, as per underreporting, it is difficult to uncover cases of overreporting through the use of psychological tests. Overreporting of symptomatology, for example, may be detected only in its most gross instances through validity scale scores, such as elevations on the F scale (and F-K) of the MMPI, the Debasement scale of the MCMI, or the Atypical Response scale of the TSI. Similarly, elevated psychosis scores on standardized instruments—if found to represent true psychotic disorder—may suggest that the client is too cognitively disorganized or delusional to respond in valid ways to psychological tests of trauma. Finally, the client whose historical reports or symptom presentation appear especially unlikely (e.g., descriptions of alien abductions, technically impossible abuse scenarios, or especially bizarre symptomatology) obviously is overreporting or confabulating, although even such individuals may have experienced other, actual abuse events and may nevertheless report at least some events or symptoms accurately.

Moderating Phenomena

Another issue in the assessment of abuse survivors is the role of extraneous events in subjects' responses to psychological assessment. Child abuse often occurs in the context of a variety of other potentially detrimental phenomena, including lower socioeconomic status, generalized family disturbance, parental substance abuse, other forms of maltreatment (e.g., concomitant physical or psychological abuse in a sexual abuse victim), and the presence of other upsetting events such as witnessing spousal abuse. As well, the survivor may be suffering from coexisting, but non-abuse-related psychological symptoms or disorders at the time of testing. These factors also may elevate symptom scales, and thus confound what otherwise might be seen as straightforward abuse effects.

In addition, a number of studies indicate that childhood abuse is a significant risk factor for subsequent revictimization as an adult (Runtz, 1987; Wind & Silvern, 1992; Wyatt et al., 1993). As a result, what may appear to be the effects of childhood abuse in a given individual may be, in fact, the impacts of more recent sexual or physical assaults or the exacerbating interaction of child abuse and adult assault. The potential existence of these more proximal events requires that the client's adult history also be taken into account before his or her symptoms can be attributed solely to childhood events.

Given these potential intervening variables, the evaluator can rarely determine exactly which symptoms or difficulties in an adult survivor of abuse are, in fact, directly related to a given instance of abuse. Furthermore, it will almost never be true that psychological testing, alone, can serve as an absolute litmus test for whether abuse has occurred in a given individual (Briere, in press; Courtois, 1995). Instead, such data should be combined with all other available information (including the relevant child abuse literature) to provide hypotheses about what *may* be abuse effects in someone who has reported abuse. Other than in a court of law, however, the ultimate issue is less likely to be "Are these symptoms or dysfunctions directly due to a specific act of child abuse, devoid of all other potential mediating factors," but rather "What is the current symptom status of this individual for whom a child abuse history is known?"

Commonly Used Abuse-Nonspecific Tests

There are several psychological tests that are widely applied to abuse survivors despite their lack of focus on abuse effects. In each case, the assessor must walk the delicate balance between (1) having access to data that, although not abuse-specific, can be valid and useful, yet (2) the potential for such data to underassess or distort abuse effects. By becoming more aware of the strengths and weaknesses of these tests, the evaluator can maximize their helpfulness and lessen their problematic aspects.

MMPI

The MMPI and its successor, the MMPI-2, are extremely popular instruments, and thus have been frequently applied to abuse survivors. The MMPI scores of clinically presenting sexual abuse survivors have been examined in a number of studies, wherein a profile characterized by elevations in scale 4 (Pd) and 8 (Sc) appears to be most prevalent, often followed by lesser elevations on 2 (D), 7 (Pt), and/or 6 (Pa) (e.g., Belkin, Greene, Rodrigue, & Boggs, 1994; Engles, Moisan, & Harris, 1994; Hunter, 1991; Goldwater & Duffy, 1990; Lundberg-Love, Marmion, Ford, Geffner, & Peacock, 1992). The relationship between this 2-point profile and a history of childhood sexual abuse has been documented for some time— for example, Caldwell and O'Hare (1975) noted two decades ago that women with elevated 4–8 profiles often report "a seductive and ambivalent father" and "a high frequency of incest" (p. 94).

Although a body of evidence suggests that sexual abuse survivors in therapy tend to present with a 4–8 MMPI configuration (although see Carlin & Ward, 1992, for other profiles found in sexually abused groups), it is not

clear whether this configuration should be interpreted in the manner suggested by standard interpretive texts. Tsai, Feldman-Summers, and Edgar
(1979) present a common description of those with this profile:

> (a) a history of poor familial relationships; (b) problems stemming from
> early establishment of an attitude of distrust toward the world; (c) poor
> social intelligence and difficulty in becoming emotionally involved with
> others; (d) sexuality seen as a hostile act through which anger is released;
> (e) low self-concept; and (f) a characteristic pattern of choosing men in-
> ferior to themselves in relationships. . . . [and note that] Such features of
> the 4–8 profile in general are consistent with observations made about wom-
> en in therapy who were sexually molested in childhood. (p. 414)

Although there are some obvious similarities between what is known
about clinically presenting abuse survivors and standard 4–8 interpretations,
traditional approaches to MMPI interpretation may be misleading in the
evaluation of abuse-related disturbance. For example, according to Lundberg-
Love et al. (1992),

> Historically, clinically significant elevations on the Pd and Sc scales have
> been interpreted as evidence of sociopathy and schizophrenia, respective-
> ly. Indeed, Scott and Stone (1986) concluded that the results of their test-
> ing indicated that incest survivors possessed a general deviancy from societal
> standards and a tendency to act out in antisocial, immature, and egocen-
> tric ways. (p. 98)

Lundberg-Love et al. note that the sexual abuse survivors in their sample accomplished a 4–8 profile through the differential endorsement of certain Pd and Sc items (as measured by Harris & Lingoes's [1968] subscales)
over others. Specifically, survivors' Scale 4 elevations were due primarily to
endorsement of familial discord and current feelings of alienation, rather
than the authority and social imperturbability Pd items often endorsed by
more antisocial individuals. Similarly, their sexual abuse sample scored
highest on the social alienation and reduced ego-mastery items of Scale 8,
as opposed to the clinical levels of bizarre sensory experiences and emotional
alienation endorsements often found in true schizophrenics. The Lundberg-
Love et al. study supports clinical experience that the MMPI scale scores of
abuse survivors (especially 4 and 8) should be followed up by examination
of the Harris and Lingoes (or other) content subscales to determine the actual meaning of any scale elevation.

It is not only clinical scale interpretation of the MMPI that may suffer
when applied to abuse survivors. Also potentially problematic is the F scale
of this measure, which tends to be endorsed to a greater extent by former
child abuse victims, as well as other trauma survivors (Briere, in press). Elliott (1993), for example, found that psychiatric inpatients with victimization histories had twice the likelihood of invalid MMPI profiles than their

nonvictimized cohorts (30% vs. 15%). It is likely that, for some abused individuals, elevated F scores reflect the tendency for trauma-related dissociative and intrusive symptomatology to produce unusual experiences and chaotic, disorganized internal states. Under such conditions, an elevated F scale may not suggest a "fake bad" response or invalid protocol as much as an accurate portrayal of extreme stress or internal disorganization (Elliott, 1994). Apropos of this issue, the TSI's Atypical Response scale requires a *T*-score of 90 or higher before the client's test is considered to be potentially invalid.

A positive development with regard to the assessment of abuse-related disturbance is the recent inclusion of two PTSD scales in the MMPI-2: the PK (Keane, Malloy, & Fairbank, 1984) and the PS (Schlenger & Kulka, 1989). As noted in other chapters of this volume, the PK and PS scales, although of only moderate predictive validity with reference to true PTSD, are clearly more effective than other MMPI scales in assessing posttraumatic stress. Although little has been done to evaluate the efficacy of these new scales in identifying child abuse trauma, preliminary clinical experience suggests they are helpful in pinpointing some of the symptoms associated with posttraumatic disturbance in victimized populations.

MCMI

The MCMI (Millon, 1983), MCMI-II (Millon, 1987), and MCMI-III (Millon, 1994) are among the most popular of personality tests (Choca, Shanley, & Van Denburg, 1992; Piotrowski & Lubin, 1990). As such, they are widely applied in clinical situations, including in the assessment of abuse survivors. Interestingly, however, only three published references to the MCMI scores of adults abused as children could be found through computerized and manual literature searches. Each of these studies (Bryer, Nelson, Miller, & Krol, 1987; Busby, Glenn, Steggell, & Adamson, 1993; Fisher, Winne, & Ley, 1993) indicate that physical and/or sexual abuse survivors score in the clinical range on a variety of MCMI-I/MCMI-II scales, most typically on the Avoidant, Dependent, Passive–Aggressive, and Borderline personality scales, and the Anxiety, Somatoform, Thought Disorder, Major Depression, and Delusional Disorder syndrome scales.

As per the MMPI, a potential problem associated with interpreting abuse survivors' responses to the MCMI is whether high scores on a given scale indicate that the survivor, in fact, "has" the relevant disorder or personality style. For example, although yet to be tested empirically, clinical experience suggests that adults abused as children who have elevated scores on MCMI scales that involve psychosis (i.e., Thought Disorder and Delusional Disorder) do not necessarily have psychotic symptoms, nor do all of those with a clinical Borderline scale score necessarily have borderline personality disorder. Instead, the psychotic scales are likely to tap the posttraumatic symptoms (especially intrusion and avoidance) and chaotic internal experience of severe abuse survivors, whereas the Borderline scale may be affected by the greater externalization activities and interpersonal difficulties of the severely abused.

In support of the potential misidentification of abuse survivors on the MCMI, Choca et al. (1992) note that individuals with PTSD (a common diagnosis among survivors of extreme childhood abuse, as noted earlier) often score in the clinical range on a variety of MCMI scales. They further note that these scale elevations "do not exclusively identify individuals with PTSD because there may be individuals with other diagnoses who also fit the same pattern of scale elevations" (p. 128). Stated in the reverse, individuals with PTSD are likely to appear to have other psychiatric disorders on the MCMI by virtue of the relevance of other scale items to posttraumatic symptomatology.

With the advent of the MCMI-III, some of the issues associated with the misinterpretation of child abuse survivors' test protocols may be reduced to some extent, since this measure does have a PTSD scale. The latter is loosely tied to DSM-IV criteria, although, like many trauma measures, the symptoms are not anchored to any specific traumatic event, and no time frame is specified for symptom duration. In addition, review of the items of this scale reveals a number of depressive items not directly associated with DSM-IV diagnostic criteria. Results of the MCMI-III validation studies indicate that the MCMI PTSD scale is reliable (α = .89, test–retest = .94) and that it has some validity in the detection of subjects diagnosed with PTSD (Millon, 1994). To the extent that the PTSD scale operates as advertised, it may facilitate the interpretation of abuse survivors' MCMI scores by indicating the presence of posttraumatic stress. In such an instance, although other less relevant scales might also be elevated (e.g., Thought Disorder), the presence of a high PTSD score would alert the examiner to the possibility of alternate explanations for such scale elevations.

Rorschach

In contrast to the MCMI, there are a number of studies of child abuse survivors' Rorschach responses (e.g., Abramson, 1989; Meyers, 1988; Owens, 1984; Nash, Hulsey, Sexton, Harralson, & Lambert, 1993; Saunders, 1991). These studies document several response patterns common to clinical child abuse survivors, most of which parallel classic Rorschach indicators of borderline personality disorder or, more recently, PTSD (Berg, 1983; Saunders, 1991; Sugarman, 1980; van der Kolk & Ducey, 1989). Those Rorschach indicators most frequently present in abuse survivor protocols (using Exner's [1986] system, unless otherwise indicated); appear to be higher color-dominated responses; more blood, anatomy, morbid, and sexual content; greater aggression (per Holt's [1977] scoring system); both more active and more passive movement, as well as more atypical movement responses (per Rappaport, Gil, & Schafer's [1945–1946] system, modified by Saunders, 1991);

greater bodily concerns; more confabulation; and in some cases, a higher Egocentricity Index.

As is true of the other standard measures reviewed here, the Rorschach has both positive and negative qualities with regard to the assessment of former child abuse victims. On one hand, the Rorschach appears to provide an opportunity to avoid the constraints of objective testing, wherein the survivor typically is forced to respond to a specific test item and therefore to a specific minihypothesis regarding the structure of psychological disturbance. Instead, the Rorschach offers a set of relatively free-form stimuli, to which the client may respond in any manner he or she chooses. As a result, the productions of the client are less predetermined and therefore more free to reflect whatever abuse effects might be discoverable by such a method.

On the other hand, the interpretation systems used to classify Rorschach responses (especially non-Exnerian systems) are often theory driven, and thus are subject to whatever level of misinterpretation of abuse effects the underlying theory potentially entails. For example, several of the abuse-related indicators presented earlier can be interpreted as reflective of a psychotic or near-psychotic process, yet the studies from which these indicators were derived included few psychotic individuals. In a similar vein, although some PTSD sufferers revealed apparent signs of thought disorder and/or impaired reality testing in van der Kolk and Ducey's (1989) Rorschach study of war veterans, these indicators "coexisted with an absence of psychotic thinking in clinical interviews, suggesting that the subjects possessed a basically intact reality orientation that was only overwhelmed by intrusive traumatic material in the context of unstructured tests" (Saunders, 1991, p. 50). Thus, naive interpretation of survivor's Rorschach responses may confuse severe abuse-related posttraumatic symptomatology (or more chronic borderline symptoms) with psychosis or psychotic processes.

Summary

This brief review of the MMPI, MCMI, and Rorschach, as they apply to the assessment of child abuse survivors suggests that important and helpful information can be gathered from such measures, but that such instruments may misinterpret abuse-related symptomatology as, instead, evidence of other disorders. This misinterpretation is thought to arise from (1) the pervasiveness of abuse-related symptoms, such that they may peripherally relate to a variety of forms of psychological disturbance; (2) the potential for intrusive, avoidant, hypervigilant, and disorganizing, abuse-related symptomatology to be tapped by measures of psychosis and personality disorder; and (3) the fact that such generic measures were initially developed without reference to abuse-related (or even posttraumatic) phenomena, and thus are unlikely to be sensitive to abuse-related distress per se. On the other hand, these and related measures have been fully standardized, now often include PTSD-specific scales or scoring systems, and allow assessment of a wide range of symptoms—many of which are relevant to abuse survivors.

Abuse-Specific Evaluation

Because adults abused as children present with a variety of relatively specific difficulties, it is appropriate that their evaluation include measures sensitive to abuse-related concerns and symptoms. For this reason, the following section is devoted to those assessment issues most relevant to former child abuse victims. As well, it provides a more detailed analysis of the few psychological tests that specifically tap abuse-relevant symptomatology. It should be reiterated, however, that being an abuse survivor does not, in some mysterious way, preclude one's evaluation with generic psychological tests. Rather, it is likely that psychological assessment of the abuse survivor is most successful when it involves standard psychological measures such as the MMPI-2, MCMI-III, and Rorschach, augmented with one or more abuse-specific measures.

Evaluating Abuse History

As noted by Norris and Riad (Chapter 1, this volume) in a broader context, detailed assessment of abuse-related difficulties must include evaluation of both the circumstances of the abuse and the psychological disturbance potentially arising from it. Unfortunately, most instruments that evaluate traumatic events in adulthood either overlook childhood abuse or merely include it (often without behavioral definition) as one of many traumas that the subject can endorse. There are, however, five scales that specifically examine childhood maltreatment history. These scales vary considerably in terms of the number of forms of abuse or neglect they assess and the amount of abuse-specific detail they offer.

Assessing Environments III, Form SD

The Assessing Environments III (AEIII), Form SD (Rausch & Knutson, 1991) is a revision of the AEIII, first introduced by Berger, Knutson, Mehm, and Perkins in 1988. This scale consists of 170 items, forming six scales: Physical Punishment, Sibling Physical Punishment, Perception of Discipline, Sibling Perception of Punishment, Deserving Punishment, and Sibling Deserving Punishment. The reliability of scales comprising the current version of the AEIII was evaluated in a sample of 421 university students, yielding KR-20 coefficients ranging from .68 to .74 (Rausch & Knutson, 1991).

Advantages of this scale are the inclusion of both the respondent's self-report and his or her report of siblings' maltreatment, thereby allowing a more detailed and complete assessment of the family environment (Rausch & Knutson, 1991). Also helpful is the inclusion of scales that tap subjects' perceptions and attributions regarding their maltreatment, since subjective appraisal of one's victimization is an important predictor of ultimate psychological impact (Spaccarelli, 1994). Disadvantages include the sole focus on physical maltreatment and the absence of specifics regarding the time frame of the maltreatment — data that are necessary to determine conformity to existing operational definitions of physical abuse.

Childhood Trauma Questionnaire

The Childhood Trauma Questionnaire (CTQ; Bernstein et al., 1994) is a 70-item measure that assesses childhood trauma in six areas: physical, sexual, and emotional abuse, physical and emotional neglect, "and related areas of family dysfunction (e.g., substance abuse)" (Bernstein et al., 1994, p. 1133). Items in the CTQ begin with the phrase "When I was growing up," and are rated on 5-point Likert-type scales. Principal components analysis of the CTQ in a sample of 286 substance-dependent patients yielded four factors that subsequently comprised the scales of this measure: physical and emotional abuse, emotional neglect, sexual abuse, and physical neglect. Internal consistency of these factor subscales were moderately high (α's ranging from .79 to .94) and, in a subsample of 40 patients, test–retest correlations ranged from .80 to .83 for an average intertest interval of 3.6 months (Bernstein et al., 1994).

This preliminary measure shows considerable promise, primarily for its brevity of administration, breadth of coverage, and available psychometric data. Potential limitations include the combination of psychological and physical abuse on the same scale (potentially underevaluating the experience of individuals with significant psychological abuse histories, but who were never physically hit), the lack of information regarding the age range for abusive events, and, as the authors note (Bernstein et al., 1994, p. 1136), the absence of specific items regarding characteristics of the maltreatment.

Child Maltreatment Interview Schedule

The Child Maltreatment Interview Schedule (CMIS; Briere, 1992b) is a 46-item measure, with some items branching to a number of subquestions that yield greater detail on a given abuse or neglect experience. The CMIS evaluates the following areas of maltreatment, each limited to events that occurred before age 17: level of parental physical availability (including parents, stepparents, and foster parents, as well as instances of institutional care); parental disorder (i.e., history of psychological treatment, alcoholism or drug abuse); parental psychological availability; psychological abuse, physical abuse, emotional abuse, sexual abuse, ritualistic abuse; and perception of physical and sexual abuse status. For each area, specific questions probe the age of onset, the relationship to the abuser, and the severity of the maltreatment. The Psychological Abuse component of the CMIS is a seven-item scale taken from Briere and Runtz (1988; 1990b), where it has demonstrated moderate internal consistency (α's ranging from .75 to .87). The CMIS is also available in a short form (CMIS-SF; Briere, 1992b) that contains most of the items of the original measure, but with less detail in some areas (e.g., sexual abuse), and no questions in others (e.g., parental physical availability and ritualistic abuse).

The advantages of the CMIS are its inclusion of many types of maltreatment and the considerable detail it provides regarding specifics of the abuse or neglect—in most cases sufficient to determine conformity with existing definitions of abuse. Deficiencies include the absence of test–retest data or any other relevant psychometric information beyond the reliability of the Psychological Abuse subscale.

Childhood Maltreatment Questionnaire

The Childhood Maltreatment Questionnaire (CMQ; Demaré, 1993) focuses extensively on psychological abuse and neglect, although it also includes scales for sexual and physical maltreatment. This questionnaire contains three components: the Psychological Maltreatment Questionnaire (PMQ), the Physical Abuse Questionnaire (PAQ), and the Sexual Abuse Questionnaire (SAQ). The PMQ has 12 scales, each tapping a form of child maltreatment identified as significant in the psychological abuse literature. These include Rejecting, Degrading, Isolating, Corrupting, Denying Emotional Responsiveness, Exploiting (Nonsexual), Verbal Terrorism, Physical Terrorism, Witness to Violence, Unreliable and Inconsistent Care, Controlling and Stifling Independence, and Physical Neglect. The PAQ has a single scale, whereas the SAQ consists of Parental and Nonparental versions. Each CMQ item assesses the frequency of maltreatment behaviors on or before age 17. Initial validation trials, using large samples of university students, suggest that the scales of the CMQ are valid (α's ranging from .76 to .95) and predictive of symptomatology (Demaré & Briere, 1995, 1996).

Strengths of the Child Maltreatment Questionnaire include its inclusion of many forms of abuse and neglect (especially psychological abuse—an area of maltreatment often overlooked by assessment instruments), the relatively comprehensive content coverage for each scale, and the typically high internal consistency found for each. Potentially problematic for some clinical users is the length of the measure, although it does not exceed that found in many other psychological tests. As well, like most others in this area, the scales do not offer sufficient specific information regarding the details of each abuse type.

Traumatic Events Scale

The Traumatic Events Scale (TES; Elliott, 1992) assesses a wide range of childhood and adult traumas. As per those scales reviewed by Norris and Riad

(Chapter 1, this volume), the TES evaluates adult traumas in detail. Of the 30 specific traumas examined by the TES, however, 10 are devoted to childhood traumas, both interpersonal and environmental. Interpersonal traumas include physical abuse, psychological abuse, and sexual abuse, as well as witnessing spouse abuse. Considerable detail is obtained vis-à-vis characteristics of child abuse, including age at first and last incident, relationship to perpetrator, and level of distress about the abuse—both at the time it occurred and currently. Additional details address sexual abuse in particular, such as whether the abuser used threats or force to gain sexual access and whether penetration occurred.

The primary benefits of the TES are its focus on both adult and childhood traumas, the inclusion of items that tap the subjective level of distress associated with each trauma (thereby making it more relevant to DSM-IV trauma criteria), and the extensive detail it gathers regarding characteristics of childhood abuse. As per most other scales in this area, its greatest weakness is the absence of test–retest reliability data.

Summary

The five measures outlined here provide an opportunity for practitioners and researchers to examine child abuse histories in detail and in a structured manner. Given the rigor and attention to detail offered by these scales, it is somewhat surprising that clinicians and investigators have used them relatively infrequently. Part of this problem is no doubt because most of these instruments are relatively new, and few of them are widely known or distributed.

Abuse-Relevant Symptom Measures

Given the recent development of a number of trauma-oriented psychological tests, as described in other chapters of this volume, one might expect that these more specific measures would have clinical relevance to adults abused as children. Unfortunately, most current trauma measures were developed solely for research applications, and thus have insufficient normative or validity data to fully justify their general use as clinical instruments. Furthermore, of these measures, few have been used in the study of abuse survivors. Those tests that have been used in abuse research are described here, albeit as instruments that, upon further development and standardization, may be more widely applied in future clinical settings. Until that point, however, most of these measures must be treated as experimental, and specific clinical conclusions should not be made on their basis alone.

Impact of Event Scale

The items and psychometric properties of the Impact of Event Scale (IES; Horowitz, Wilner, & Alvarez, 1979) are described in other chapters of this volume. As a result, only the association between IES scores and child abuse history is discussed here. Adults abused as children appear to score higher on IES scales than nonabused individuals in a variety of nonclinical samples (e.g., Alexander, 1993; Briere & Elliott, 1996; Elliott & Briere, 1995; Murphy, Kilpatrick, Amick-McMullan, & Veronen, 1988; Runtz, 1991). Elliott and Briere (1995), for example, report that adults with sexual abuse histories in the general population score higher on both the Intrusion and Avoidance scales of the IES.

As noted in other chapters, the IES is popular measure in research on posttraumatic stress. Unfortunately, the lack of normative or standardization data on the IES has reduced its clinical efficacy, since nonnormed tests provide little information regarding the actual clinical significance of a given abuse survivor's score.[1]

Dissociative Experiences Scale

Because the Dissociative Experiences Scale (DES; Bernstein & Putnam, 1986) is the most popular measure of dissociation available (Carlson & Armstrong, 1995), it has been used to study many traumatized populations, including adults abused as children (e.g., Chu & Dill, 1990; Coons, Bowman, Pellow, & Schneider, 1989; DiTomasso & Routh, 1993; Swett & Halpern, 1993). A meta-analysis that included 26 studies of abuse survivors' DES scores found a moderate relationship between childhood physical or sexual abuse and DES scores, suggesting the potential utility of this measure in the assessment of abuse-related trauma (van IJzendoorn & Schuengel, in press).

However, because the DES has not been normed on the general population, it usually is not possible to interpret any given score on this measure. Even the suggested cutpoint for possible Dissociative Identity Disorder (DID) on this measure (e.g., Carlson et al., 1993) should not be seen as definitive, since many individuals scoring above this point do not have DID (Armstrong, 1995). As a result, until general population norms become available, this scale may be most effective clinically as a structured review of dissociative symptomatology, wherein any given item endorsement operates solely as qualitative information regarding a specific dissociative symptom.

Los Angeles Symptom Checklist

The Los Angeles Symptom Checklist (LASC; formerly the Symptom Checklist; Foy, Sipprelle, Rueger, & Carroll, 1984) is a 43-item measure of posttraumatic stress, 17 items of which can be scored dichotomously to generate a diagnosis of PTSD. The full 43 items yield three continuous scales that tap reexperiencing, avoidance, and hyperarousal symptoms, as well as a to-

---

[1]A recent general population study by Briere and Elliott (1996) may ultimately allow normative comparisons.

tal score that reflects general distress and dysphoria. Although this measure has been used primarily in research on combat veterans, several studies have found abuse survivors to have higher LASC scores than those subjects without an abuse history (e.g., Elliott & Briere, 1995; Rowan et al., 1994). In fact, because this measure examines a range of symptoms beyond PTSD per se, it may be especially sensitive to the difficulties of former abuse victims (Briere, in press).

As per the IES, DES, and other similar measures, there are insufficient normative data available to justify the use of the three LASC scales in clinical practice. Although the clinician may use the 17 items as a screen for potential PTSD, the actual diagnosis of this disorder should arise from a diagnostic interview and not on the basis of the LASC alone.

Trauma Symptom Checklist-40

The Trauma Symptom Checklist-40 (TSC-40; Briere & Runtz, 1989; Elliott & Briere, 1992) is a 40-item self-report research measure that evaluates symptomatology in adults arising from childhood or adult traumatic experiences. The TSC-40 is an expanded version of the Trauma Symptom Checklist-33 (TSC-33; Briere & Runtz, 1989). It consists of six subscales (e.g., Anxiety, Dissociation, Sexual Concerns) as well as a total score.

Studies using the TSC-40 indicate that it is a relatively reliable measure (a's typically average around .7 for subscales and around .9 for the full scale). The TSC-40 and TSC-33 have moderate predictive validity with reference to a wide variety of traumatic experiences, including childhood abuse (e.g., Briere & Elliott, 1993; Gold, Milan, Mayall, & Johnson, 1994; Russ, Shearin, Clarkin, Harrison, & Hull, 1993; Wind & Silvern, 1992). The TSC-40 is not appropriate for clinical use, however, since its reliability and normative data, although adequate for research, are generally insufficient for clinical applications.

Trauma Symptom Inventory

The Trauma Symptom Inventory (TSI) is a 100-item instrument that evaluates acute and chronic posttraumatic symptomatology. Each symptom item is rated on a 4-point scale according to its frequency of occurrence over the prior 6 months. Recent research suggests that it is sensitive to the lasting sequelae of childhood abuse (e.g., Briere, 1995a; Briere, Elliott, Harris, & Cotman, 1995; Elliott & Briere, 1995).

The TSI has 3 validity scales and 10 clinical scales, all of which yield normative *T*-scores. There are 12 critical items covering issues such as self-mutilation, suicidality, and potential violence against others. The validity scales of the TSI are Response Level (RL), measuring a general underendorsement response style or a need to appear unusually symptom-free; Atypical Response (ATR), evaluating extreme distress, a general overendorsement response set, or an attempt to appear especially disturbed or dysfunction-al; and Inconsistent Response (INC), measuring unusually inconsistent re-sponses to TSI item-pairs. The 10 clinical scales of the TSI are Anxious Arousal, Depression, Anger/Irritability, Intrusive Experiences, Defensive Avoidance, Sexual Concerns, Dysfunctional Sexual Behavior, Impaired Self-Reference, and Tension-Reduction Behavior. Common 2- and 3-point scale profiles are described in the TSI professional manual (Briere, 1995a). There is also a scoring program available for this instrument (Briere & PAR staff, 1995).

The TSI was standardized on a random sample of 828 adults from the general population and has been separately normed for military personnel based on a sample of 3,659 Navy recruits. Norms are available for four com-binations of sex and age (males and females ages 18–54 and 55 or older). The clinical scales of the TSI are internally consistent (mean α's ranging from .84 to .87 in general population, clinical, university, and military samples) and exhibit reasonable convergent, predictive, and incremental validity. Va-lidity scales covary as expected with validity scales from the MMPI-2 and PAI. In a standardization subsample, TSI scales predicted independently assessed PTSD status in over 90% of cases. In a psychiatric inpatient sample, TSI scales identified 89% of those independently diagnosed with borderline personality disorder.

Advantages of the TSI include the existence of standardized scale *T*-scores based on general population norms, the inclusion of validity scales, and its broad coverage of abuse-relevant symptomatology. Specifically, in-clusion of less PTSD-specific scales such as sexual distress and dysfunction, impaired self-reference, dysphoria, and anger, allows a more comprehen-sive assessment of postabuse difficulties. Weaknesses include its relatively recent development (and thus the need for further exploration of its exter-nal validity), the absence of scales to measure other common abuse seque-lae (e.g., somatization, cognitive distortions, and relationship difficulties), and its circumscribed availability (per American Psychological Association guidelines, the TSI may only be used by those with graduate training in psy-chology or a related field, who have taken course work in the use of psycho-logical tests).

DISCUSSION

This chapter has reviewed some of the major issues associated with the assessment of abuse-related distress and dysfunction. In general, it appears that traditional measures of psychological symptoms and disord-ers are necessary but insufficient to provide a clear and detailed clinical pic-ture of many abuse survivors. Although such measures can provide important information (e.g., regarding trauma-nonspecific conditions such as major depression or psychosis), they may overlook certain symptoms or misinterpret certain abuse effects as evidence of other, less relevant difficulties. Two of these instruments, the MMPI-2 and the MCMI-III, have improved this situation to some extent by providing PTSD-oriented scales, although they appear to cast a wider net than PTSD symptomatology per se. These scales only address one component of abuse-specific symptomatology, however, and thus underestimate the range of potential abuse impacts.

Partially because professional interest in the lasting effects of child abuse is a relatively new phenomenon, only a handful of abuse-relevant tests are available for researchers. Furthermore, clinicians are constrained by the absence of normative data for most of these measures—a minimal requirement for the valid interpretation of most psychological test results. As a result, the clinician is to some extent forced to choose between standardized but insensitive, generic tests, and specific but typically nonstandardized psychological measures in the evaluation of abuse effects. When standardized tests are administered, the clinician must be careful to consider the applicability of standard interpretation approaches to these measures, and the potential availability of trauma-specific subscales. Especially important is the clinician's appreciation of the theory and underlying model of symptom development associated with any given measure, and the extent to which such theory is congruent with what is known about abuse-related psychological dysfunction.

Our growing understanding of the incidence and impacts of childhood abuse far outstrips the measurement technology currently available to assess such phenomena. Given this limitation, and the complexity of childhood maltreatment effects, the practitioner must proceed with all due caution. On the other hand, the evaluator who is well-versed on the abuse-effects literature, and aware of the relative strengths and weaknesses of the tests he or she uses, will find that abuse-relevant assessment approaches can provide valid and important data on the survivor's psychological functioning. This increment in understanding will only increase as more standardized abuse- and trauma-sensitive instruments are developed.

REFERENCES

Abramson, J. T. (1989). The Egocentricity Index: Form color, color form and color ratio, and content in the Rorschach tests of sexually abused adult female inpatients. *Dissertation Abstracts International, 49*(12-A, Pt. 1), 3657.

Alexander, P. C. (1992). Application of attachment theory to the study of sexual abuse. *Journal of Consulting and Clinical Psychology, 60,* 185–195.

Alexander, P. C. (1993). The differential effects of abuse characteristics and attachment in the prediction of long-term effects of sexual abuse. *Journal of Interpersonal Violence, 8,* 346–362.

Alexander, P. C., & Lupfer, S. L. (1987). Family characteristics and long-term consequences associated with sexual abuse. *Archives of Sexual Behavior, 16,* 235–245.

Armstrong, J. (1995). Psychological assessment. In J. L. Spira (Ed.), *Treating dissociative identity disorder.* San Francisco: Jossey-Bass.

Belkin, D. S., Greene, A. F., Rodrigue, J. R., & Boggs, S. R. (1994). Psychopathology and history of sexual abuse. *Journal of Interpersonal Violence, 9,* 535–547.

Berg, M. (1983). Borderline psychopathology as displayed on psychological tests. *Journal of Personality Assessment, 47,* 120–133.

Berger, A. M., Knutson, J. F., Mehm, J. G., & Perkins, K. A. (1988). The self-report of punitive childhood experiences of young adults and adolescents. *Child Abuse and Neglect, 12,* 251–262.

Bernstein, D. P., Fink, L., Handelsman, L., Foote, J., Lovejoy, M., Wenzel, K., Sapareta, E., & Ruggiero, J. (1994). Initial reliability and validity of a new retrospective measure of child abuse and neglect. *American Journal of Psychiatry, 151,* 1132–1136.

Bernstein, E. M., & Putnam, F. W. (1986). Development, reliability, and validity of a dissociation scale. *Journal of Nervous and Mental Disease, 174,* 727–734.

Bifulco, A., Brown, G. W., & Adler, Z. (1991). Early sexual abuse and clinical depression in adult life. *British Journal of Psychiatry, 159,* 115–122.

Briere, J. (1992a). Methodological issues in the study of sexual abuse effects. *Journal of Consulting and Clinical Psychology, 60,* 196–203.

Briere, J. (1992b). *Child abuse trauma: Theory and treatment of the lasting effects.* Newbury Park, CA: Sage.

Briere, J. (1995a). *Trauma Symptom Inventory professional manual.* Odessa, FL: Psychological Assessment Resources.

Briere, J. (1995b). Science versus politics in the delayed memory debate: A commentary. *Counseling Psychologist, 23,* 290–293.

Briere, J. (1996a). A self-trauma model for treating adult survivors of severe child abuse. In J. Briere, L. Berliner, J. Bulkley, C. Jenny, & T. Reid (Eds.), *The APSAC handbook on child maltreatment* (pp. 140–157). Newbury Park, CA: Sage.

Briere, J. (1996b). *Trauma Symptom Checklist for Children (TSCC).* Odessa, FL: Psychological Assessment Resources.

Briere, J. (in press). *Psychological assessment of posttraumatic states in adults.* Washington, DC: American Psychological Association.

Briere, J., & Conte, J. (1993). Self-reported amnesia for abuse in adults molested as children. *Journal of Traumatic Stress, 6,* 21–31.

Briere, J., & Elliott, D. M. (1993). Sexual abuse, family environment, and psychological symptoms: On the validity of statistical control. *Journal of Consulting and Clinical Psychology, 61,* 284–288.

Briere, J., & Elliott, D. M. (1996). *Psychometric characteristics of the Impact of Events Scale in a large normative sample.* Unpublished manuscript, University of Southern California School of Medicine, Los Angeles, CA.

Briere, J., Elliott, D. M., Harris, K., & Cotman, A. (1995). Trauma Symptom Inventory: Psychometrics and association with childhood and adult trauma in clinical samples. *Journal of Interpersonal Violence, 10,* 387–401.

Briere, J., & PAR staff. (1995). *Computer scoring system for the Trauma Symptom Inventory (TSI)* [Computer program]. Odessa, FL: Psychological Assessment Resources.

Briere, J., & Runtz, M. (1986). Suicidal thoughts and behaviors in former sexual abuse victims. *Canadian Journal of Behavioral Science, 18,* 413–423.

Briere, J., & Runtz, M. (1988). Symptomatology associated with childhood sexual victimization in a nonclinical adult sample. *Child Abuse and Neglect, 12,* 51–59.

Briere, J., & Runtz, M. (1989). The Trauma Symptom Checklist (TSC-33): Early data on a new scale. *Journal of Interpersonal Violence, 4,* 151–163.

Briere, J., & Runtz, M. (1990a). Augmenting Hopkins SCL scales to measure dissociative symptoms: Data from two nonclinical samples. *Journal of Personality Assessment, 55,* 376–379.

Briere, J., & Runtz, M. (1990b). Differential adult symptomatology associated with three types of child abuse histories. *Child Abuse and Neglect, 14,* 357–364.

Briere, J., Woo, R., McRae, B., Foltz, J., & Sitzman, R. (in press). Lifetime victimization history, demographics, and clinical status in female psychiatric emergency room patients. *Journal of Nervous and Mental Disease.*

Briere, J., & Zaidi, L. Y. (1989). Sexual abuse histories and sequelae in female psychiatric emergency room patients. *American Journal of Psychiatry, 146,* 1602–1606.

Brown, G. R., & Anderson, B. (1991). Psychiatric morbidity in adult inpatients with childhood histories of sexual and physical abuse. *American Journal of Psychiatry, 148,* 55–61.

Bryer, J. B., Nelson, B. A., Miller, J. B., & Krol, P. A. (1987). Childhood sexual and physical abuse as factors in adult psychiatric illness. *American Journal of Psychiatry, 144,* 1426–1430.

Busby, D. M., Glenn, E., Steggell, G. L., & Adamson, D. W. (1993). Treatment issues for survivors of physical and sexual abuse. *Journal of Marital and Family Therapy, 19,* 377–391.

Caldwell, A. B., & O'Hare, C. (1975). *A handbook of MMPI personality types.* Santa Monica, CA: Clinical Psychological Services.

Carlin, A. S., & Ward, N. G. (1992). Subtypes of psychiatric inpatient women who have been sexually abused. *Journal of Nervous and Mental Disease, 180,* 392–397.

Carlson, E. B., & Armstrong, J. (1995). The diagnosis and assessment of dissociative disorders. In S. J. Lynn & J. L. Rhue (Eds.), *Dissociation: Theoretical, clinical, and research perspectives* (pp. 159–174). New York: Guilford Press.

Carlson, E. B., Putnam, F. W., Ross, C. A., Torem, M., Coons, P., Dill, D., Lowenstein, R. J., & Braun, B. G. (1993). Validity of the Dissociative Experiences Scale in screening for multiple personality disorder: A multicenter study. *American Journal of Psychiatry, 150,* 1030–1036.

Choca, J. P., Shanley, L. A., & Van Denburg, E. (1992). *Interpretative guide to the Millon Clinical Multiaxial Inventory.* Washington, DC: American Psychological Association.

Chu, J. A., & Dill, D. L. (1990). Dissociative symptoms in relation to childhood physical and sexual abuse. *American Journal of Psychiatry, 147,* 887–892.

Cole, P. M., & Putnam, F. W. (1992). Effect of incest on self and social functioning: A developmental psychopathology perspective. *Journal of Consulting and Clinical Psychology, 60,* 174–184.

Connors, M. E., & Morse, W. (1993). Sexual abuse and eating disorders: A review. *International Journal of Eating Disorders, 13,* 1–11.

Coons, P. M., Bowman, E. S., Pellow, T. A., & Schneider, P. (1989). Post-traumatic aspects of the treatment of sexual abuse and incest. *Psychiatric Clinics of North America, 12,* 325–335.

Courtois, C. (1995). Assessment and diagnosis. In C. Classen (Ed.), *Treating women molested in childhood.* San Francisco: Jossey-Bass.

Craine, L. S., Henson, C. H., Colliver, J. A., & MacLean, D. G. (1988). Prevalence of a history of sexual abuse among female psychiatric patients in a state hospital system. *Hospital and Community Psychiatry, 39,* 300–304.

Demaré, D. (1993). *The Childhood Maltreatment Questionnaire.* Unpublished manuscript, University of Manitoba, Winnipeg, Canada.

Demaré, D., & Briere, J. (1995, August). *Trauma Symptom Checklist-40: Validation with sexually abused and nonabused university students.* Paper presented at the annual meeting of the American Psychological Association, New York, NY.

Demaré, D., & Briere, J. (1996). *Validation of the Trauma Symptom Inventory with abused and nonabused university students.* Unpublished manuscript, University of Manitoba, Winnipeg, Canada.

Dembo, R., Williams, L., LaVoie, L., Berry, E., Getreu, A., Wish, E., Schnieder, J., & Washburn, M. (1989). Physical abuse, sexual victimization, and drug use: Replication of a structural analysis among a new sample of high risk youths. *Violence and Victims, 4,* 121–138.

de Wilde, E. J., Kienhorst, I. C., Diekstra, R. F., & Wolters, W. H. (1992). The relationship between adolescent suicidal behavior and life events in childhood and adolescence. *American Journal of Psychiatry, 149,* 45–51.

DiTomasso, M. J., & Routh, D. K. (1993). Recall of abuse in childhood and three measures of dissociation. *Child Abuse and Neglect, 17,* 477–485.

Drossman, D. A., Lesserman, J., Nachman, G., Li, Z., Gluck, H., Toomey, T. C., & Mitchell, C. M. (1990). Sexual and physical abuse in women with functional or organic gastrointestinal disorders. *Annals of Internal Medicine, 113,* 828–833.

Elliott, D. M. (1992). *Traumatic Events Survey.* Unpublished psychological test. Los Angeles: Harbor–UCLA Medical Center.

Elliott, D. M. (1993, November). *Assessing the psychological impact of recent violence in an inpatient setting.* Paper presented at the meeting of the International Society for Traumatic Stress Studies, San Antonio, TX.

Elliott, D. M. (1994). Assessing adult victims of interpersonal violence. In J. Briere (Ed.), *Assessing and treating victims of violence* (New Directions for Mental Health Services series, MHS No. 64, pp. 5–16). San Francisco: Jossey-Bass.

Elliott, D. M., & Briere, J. (1992). Sexual abuse trauma among professional women: Validating the Trauma Symptom Checklist-40 (TSC-40). *Child Abuse and Neglect, 16,* 391–398.

Elliott, D. M., & Briere, J. (1994). Forensic sexual abuse evaluations of older children: Disclosures and symptomatology. *Behavioral Sciences and the Law, 12,* 261–277.

Elliott, D. M., & Briere, J. (1995). Symptomatology associated with delayed recall of sexual abuse. *Journal of Traumatic Stress, 8,* 629–647.

Engles, M. L., Moisan, D., & Harris, R. (1994). MMPI indices of childhood trauma among 110 female outpatients. *Journal of Personality Assessment, 63,* 135–147.

Enns, C. Z., McNeilly, C. L., Corkery, J. M., & Gilbert, M. S. (1995). The debate about delayed memories of child sexual abuse: A feminist perspective. *The Counseling Psychologist, 23,* 181–279.

Epstein, R. S. (1993). Avoidant symptoms cloaking the diagnosis of PTSD in patients with severe accidental injury. *Journal of Traumatic Stress, 6,* 451–458.

Exner, J. E. (1986). *The Rorschach: A comprehensive system* (2nd ed.). New York: Wiley.

Feldman-Summers, S., & Pope, K. S. (1994). The experience of "forgetting" childhood abuse: A national survey of psychologists. *Journal of Consulting and Clinical Psychology, 62,* 636–639.

Finkelhor, D., Hotaling, G., Lewis, I. A., & Smith, C. (1989). Sexual abuse and its relationship to later sexual satisfaction, marital status, religion, and attitudes. *Journal of Interpersonal Violence, 4,* 279–399.

Fisher, P. M., Winne, P. H., & Ley, R. G. (1993). Group therapy for adult women survivors of child sexual abuse: Differentiation of completers versus dropouts. *Psychotherapy, 30,* 616–624.

Foy, D. W., Sipprelle, R. C., Rueger, D. B., & Carroll, E. M. (1984). Etiology of post-traumatic stress syndrome in Vietnam veterans: Analysis of premilitary, military, and combat exposure influences. *Journal of Consulting and Clinical Psychology, 52,* 79–87.

Friedrich, W. N. (1994). Assessing children for the effects of sexual victimization. In J. Briere (Ed.), *Assessing and treating victims of violence* (New Directions for Mental Health Services series, MHS No. 64, pp. 17–27). San Francisco: Jossey-Bass.

Gardner, R. (1992). *True and false accusations of child sexual abuse.* Cresskill, NJ: Creative Therapeutics.

Gelinas, D. J. (1983). The persisting negative effects of incest. *Psychiatry, 46,* 312–332.

Gold, S. R., Milan, L. D., Mayall, A., & Johnson, A. E. (1994). A cross-validation study of the Trauma Symptom Checklist: The role of mediating variables. *Journal of interpersonal Violence, 9,* 12–26.

Goldwater, L., & Duffy, J. F. (1990). Use of the MMPI to uncover histories of child-hood abuse in adult female psychiatric patients. *Journal of Clinical Psychology, 46,* 392–398.

Harris, R., & Lingoes, J. (1968). *Subscales for the Minnesota Multiphasic Personality Inventory* [mimeographed materials]. Department of Psychology, University of Michigan.

Herman, J. L. (1992). *Trauma and recovery: The aftermath of violence—from domestic abuse to political terror.* New York: Basic Books.

Herman, J. L., Perry, C., & van der Kolk, B. A. (1989). Childhood trauma in border-line personality disorder. *American Journal of Psychiatry, 146,* 490–494.

Herman, J. L., & Schatzow, E. (1987). Recovery and verification of memories of child-hood sexual trauma. Psychoanalytic Psychology, 4, 1–14.

Holt, R. R. (1977). A method for assessing primary process manifestations and their control in Rorschach responses. In M. A. Rickers-Ovsiankina (Ed.), *Rorschach psychology* (2nd ed., pp. 375–420). Huntington, NY: Krieger.

Horowitz, M. D., Wilner, N., & Alvarez, W. (1979). Impacts of Event Scale: A measure of subjective stress. *Psychosomatic Medicine, 41,* 209–218.

Hunter, J. A. (1991). A comparison of the psychosocial maladjustment of adult males and females sexually molested as children. *Journal of Interpersonal Violence, 6,* 205–217.

Jehu, D. (1989). *Beyond sexual abuse: Therapy with women who were childhood victims.* Chichester, UK: Wiley.

Keane, T. M., Malloy, P. F., & Fairbank, J. A. (1984). Empirical development of an MMPI subscale for the assessment of combat-related posttraumatic stress disorder. *Journal of Consulting and Clinical Psychology, 52,* 888–891.

Lindsay, D. S. (1994). Contextualizing and clarifying criticisms of memory work [Special Issue]. The recovered memory/false memory debate. *Consciousness and Cognition: An International Journal, 3,* 426–437.

Loftus, E. F. (1993). The reality of repressed memories. *American Psychologist, 48,* 518–537.

Loftus, E. F., Polonsky, S., & Fullilove, M. T. (1994). Memories of childhood sexual abuse: Remembering and repressing. *Psychology of Women Quarterly, 18,* 67–84.

Lundberg-Love, P. K., Marmion, S., Ford, K., Geffner, R., & Peacock, L. (1992). The long-term consequences of childhood incestuous victimization upon adult wom-en's psychological symptomatology. *Journal of Child Sexual Abuse, 1,* 81–102.

Meyers, J. (1988). The Rorschach as a tool for understanding the dynamics of women with histories of incest. In H. D. Lerner & P. M. Lerner (Eds.), *Primitive mental states and the Rorschach* (pp. 203–228). Madison, CT: International Universities Press.

Millon, T. (1983). *Millon Clinical Multiaxial Inventory Manual.* Minneapolis: Interpretive Scoring System.

Millon, T. (1987). *Manual for the MCMI-II* (2nd ed.). Minneapolis: National Computer Systems.

Millon, T. (1994). *Manual for the MCMI-III.* Minneapolis: National Computer Systems.

Morey, L. C. (1991). *Personality Assessment Inventory: Professional manual.* Odessa, FL: Psychological Assessment Resources.

Murphy, S. M., Kilpatrick, D. G., Amick-McMullan, A., & Veronen, L. J. (1988). Current psychological functioning of child sexual assault survivors: A community study. *Journal of Interpersonal Violence, 3,* 55–79.

Nash, M. R., Hulsey, T. L., Sexton, M. C., Harralson, T. L., & Lambert, W. (1993). Long-term sequelae of childhood sexual abuse: Perceived family environment, psychopathology, and dissociation. *Journal of Consulting and Clinical Psychology, 61,* 276–283.

Neumann, D. A., Houskamp, B. M., Pollock, V. E., & Briere, J. (1996). The long-term sequelae of childhood sexual abuse in women: A meta-analytic review. *Child Maltreatment, 1,* 6–16.

Ogata, S. N., Silk, K. R., Goodrich, S., Lohr, N. E., Westen, D., & Hill, E. M. (1990). Childhood sexual and physical abuse in adult patients with borderline personality disorder. *American Journal of Psychiatry, 147,* 1008–1013.

Owens, T. H. (1984). Personality traits of female psychotherapy patients with a history of incest: A research note. *Journal of Personality Assessment, 48,* 606–608.

Piotrowski, C., & Lubin, B. (1990). Assessment practices of health psychologists: Survey of APA Division 38 clinicians. *Professional Psychology: Research and Practice, 21,* 99–106.

Pollock, V. E., Briere, J., Schneider, L., Knop, J., Mednick, S. A., & Goodwin, D. W. (1990). Childhood antecedents of antisocial behavior: Parental alcoholism and physical abusiveness. *American Journal of Psychiatry, 147,* 1290–1293.

Putnam, F. W. (1989). *Diagnosis and treatment of multiple personality disorder.* New York: Guilford Press.

Rappaport, D., Gil, M., & Schafer, R. (1945–1946). *Diagnostic psychological testing: The theory, statistical evaluation, and diagnostic application of a battery of tests* (Vols. 1–2). Chicago: Year Book Publishers.

Rausch, K., & Knutson, J. F. (1991). The self-report of personal punitive childhood experiences and those of siblings. *Child Abuse and Neglect, 15,* 29–36.

Ross, C. A., Anderson, G., & Clark, P. (1994). Childhood abuse and the positive symptoms of schizophrenia. *Hospital and Community Psychiatry, 45,* 489–491.

Ross, C. A., Anderson, G., Heber, S., & Norton, G. (1990). Dissociation and abuse among multiple personality patients, prostitutes, and exotic dancers. *Hospital and Community Psychiatry, 41,* 328–330.

Rowan, A. B., Foy, D. W., Rodriguez, N., & Ryan, S. (1994). Posttraumatic stress disorder in a clinical sample of adults sexually abused as children. *Child Abuse and Neglect, 18,* 51–61.

Runtz, M. R. (1987). *The psychosocial adjustment of women who were sexually and physically abused during childhood and early adulthood: A focus on revictimization.* Unpublished Master's thesis, University of Manitoba, Winnipeg, Canada.

Runtz, M. R. (1991). *The influence of coping strategies and social support on recovery from child abuse.* Unpublished doctoral dissertation, University of Manitoba, Winnipeg, Canada.

Russ, M. J., Shearin, E. N., Clarkin, J. F., Harrison, K., & Hull, J. W. (1993). Subtypes of self-injurious patients with borderline personality disorder. *American Journal of Psychiatry, 150,* 1869–1871.

Saunders, B. E., Villeponteaux, L. A., Lipovsky, J. A., Kilpatrick, D. G., & Veronen, L. J. (1992). Child sexual assault as a risk factor for mental disorders among women: A community survey. *Journal of Interpersonal Violence, 7,* 189–204.

Saunders, E. A. (1991). Rorschach indicators of chronic childhood sexual abuse in female borderline patients. *Bulletin of the Menninger Clinic, 55,* 48–71.

Schlenger, W., & Kulka, R. A. (1989). *PTSD scale development for the MMPI-2.* Research Triangle Park, NC: Research Triangle Park Institute.

Scott, R. L., & Stone, D. A. (1986). MMPI measures of psychological disturbance in adolescent and adult victims of father–daughter incest. *Journal of Consulting and Clinical Psychology, 42,* 251–259.

Singer, M. I., Petchers, M. K., & Hussey, D. (1989). The relationship between sexual abuse and substance abuse among psychiatrically hospitalized adolescents. *Child Abuse and Neglect, 13,* 319–325.

Spaccarelli, S. (1994). Stress, appraisal, and coping in child sexual abuse: A theoretical and empirical review. *Psychological Bulletin, 116,* 340–362.

Springs, F. E., & Friedrich, W. N. (1992). Health risk behaviors and medical sequelae of childhood sexual abuse. *Mayo Clinic Proceedings, 67,* 527–532.

Sugarman, A. (1980). The borderline personality organization as manifested on psychological tests. In J. S. Kwawer, H. D. Lerner, P. M. Lerner, & A. Sugarman (Eds.), *Borderline phenomena and the Rorschach* (pp. 39–57). New York: International Universities Press.

Swett, C., & Halpern, M. (1993). Reported history of physical and sexual abuse in relation to dissociation and other symptomatology in women psychiatric inpatients. *Journal of Interpersonal Violence, 8,* 545–555.

Tsai, M., Feldman-Summers, S., & Edgar, M. (1979). Childhood molestation: Variables related to differential impacts on psychosexual functioning in adult women. *Journal of Abnormal Psychology, 88,* 407–417.

van der Kolk, B. A., & Ducey, C. (1989). Clinical implications of the Rorschach in post-traumatic stress disorder. In B. A. van der Kolk (Ed.), *Post-traumatic stress disorder: Psychological and biological sequelae* (pp. 29–42). Washington, DC: American Psychiatric Press.

van der Kolk, B. A., Perry, J. C., & Herman, J. L. (1991). Childhood origins of self-destructive behavior. *American Journal of Psychiatry, 146,* 490–494.

van IJzendoorn, M. H., & Schuengel, C. (in press). The measurement of dissociation in normal and clinical populations: Meta-analytic validation of the Dissociative Experiences Scale (DES). *Clinical Psychology Review.*

Wakefield, H., & Underwager, R. (1992). Uncovering memories of alleged sexual abuse: The therapists who do it. *Issues in Child Abuse Accusations, 4,* 197–213.

Waller, G. (1992). Sexual abuse and bulimic symptoms in eating disorders: Do family interaction and self-esteem explain the links? *International Journal of Eating Disorders, 12,* 235–240.

Walsh, B. W., & Rosen, P. (1988). *Self-mutilation: Theory, research, and treatment.* New York: Guilford Press.

Williams, L. M. (1994). Recall of childhood trauma: A prospective study of women's memories of child sexual abuse. *Journal of Consulting and Clinical Psychology, 62,* 1167–1176.

Wind, T. W., & Silvern, L. E. (1992). Type and extent of child abuse as predictors of adult functioning. *Journal of Family Violence, 7,* 261–281.

Wyatt, G. E. (1985). The sexual abuse of Afro-American and white American women in childhood. *Child Abuse and Neglect, 9,* 231–240.

Wyatt, G. E. (1988). The relationship between child sexual abuse and adolescent sexual functioning in Afro-American and White American women. *Annals of the New York Academy of Sciences, 528,* 111–122.

Wyatt, G. E., Newcomb, M. D., & Riederle, M. H. (1993). *Sexual abuse and consensual sex: Women's developmental patterns and outcomes.* Newbury Park, CA: Sage.

Yama, M. F., Tovey, S. L., & Fogas, B. S. (1993). Childhood family environment and sexual abuse as predictors of anxiety and depression in adult women. *American Journal of Orthopsychiatry, 63,* 136–141.

Zierler, S., Feingold, L., Laufer, D., Velentgas, P., et al. (1991). Adult survivors of childhood sexual abuse and subsequent risk of HIV infection. *American Journal of Public Health, 81,* 572–575.

CHAPTER 3

Psychophysiological Assessment of Posttraumatic Stress Disorder

SCOTT P. ORR
DANNY G. KALOUPEK

INTRODUCTION

There is a substantial and growing literature aimed at providing a psychobiological characterization of posttraumatic stress disorder (PTSD). Much of this literature is based on research that has used psychophysiological measures and techniques to assess various features of the disorder as specified in the *Diagnostic and Statistical Manual of Mental Disorders,* fourth edition (DSM-IV; American Psychiatric Association, 1994). The results have provided a consistent picture of greater physiological reactivity to depictions of the traumatic event (DSM-IV symptom B.5) in individuals with PTSD compared to individuals who experienced similar events but did not develop PTSD. Similarly, psychophysiological studies of the startle response have provided laboratory evidence consistent with the symptom of exaggerated startle (DSM-IV symptom D.5).

Despite the successful application of psychophysiological method to the study of posttraumatic adjustment, little has been written about the practical aspects of using these measures and methods for the diagnosis, evaluation, and treatment of PTSD. Typical discussions of the technology and methods for psychophysiological research are likely to appear intimidating to the nonexpert. Descriptions of technical concerns such as analog-to-digital converters, signal averaging, band-pass filters, and time constants make for laborious, if not discouraging, reading. In the past, equipping and maintaining a state-of-the-art psychophysiological laboratory also has been expensive and time consuming. Fortunately, personal computers and integrated circuitry have had a dramatic impact on the field of psychophysiology by reducing costs and easing the burden of psychophysiological data management and summarization. It is no longer necessary for an individual to have a high level of expertise in psychophysiological technology and methods, and extensive financial resources in order to take advantage of the benefits offered by psychophysiological assessment.

The present chapter aims to provide a brief, nontechnical overview of psychophysiological methodology and findings in PTSD. In so doing, it discusses some potential applications, limitations, and adaptations of psychophysiological measurement. We hope that this will encourage individuals to seriously consider the value of this methodology in both clinical and research contexts.

OVERVIEW OF PSYCHOPHYSIOLOGICAL EVIDENCE IN RELATION TO TRAUMA AND PTSD

Challenge Tasks

One of the most consistent findings is that of heightened psychophysiological reactivity to cues reminiscent of the traumatic event in individuals diagnosed with PTSD (for reviews see McFall, Murburg, Roszell, & Veith, 1989; Orr, 1994; Prins, Kaloupek, & Keane, 1995; Shalev & Rogel-Fuchs, 1993). A number of these studies have presented standardized audiovisual cues to combat veterans. Typically, combat sounds, such as mortar explosions or gunfire, and pictures of combat situations have produced larger physiological responses, including heart rate (HR), blood pressure, electrodermal activity, and forehead electromyogram (EMG) in veterans with PTSD compared to those without PTSD (Blanchard, Kolb, Pallmeyer, & Gerardi, 1982; Blanchard, Kolb, Gerardi, Ryan, & Pallmeyer, 1986; Blanchard, Kolb, Taylor, & Wittrock, 1989; Dobbs & Wilson, 1960; Malloy, Fairbank, & Keane, 1983; McFall, Murburg, Ko, & Veith, 1990; Pallmeyer, Blanchard, & Kolb, 1986). Standardized combat-related words have also produced larger skin conductance (SC) responses in combat veterans with PTSD compared to combat veterans with other psychiatric disorders (McNally et al., 1987). Other studies using individually tailored imagery scripts have reported larger SC, HR, and facial EMG (lateral frontalis) responses during recollection of trauma-related experiences in individuals with PTSD compared to those without PTSD. This trauma-specific reactivity has been found with Vietnam, World War II, and Korean War combat veterans (Orr, Pitman, Lasko, & Herz, 1993; Pitman, Orr, Forgue, de Jong, & Claiborn, 1987; Pitman et al., 1990), as well as with victims of civilian traumatic events (Shalev, Orr, & Pitman, 1993; Blanchard, Hickling, Taylor, Loos, & Gerardi, 1994; Blanchard et al., in press). A large, multisite study combined the standardized audiovisual and script-driven imagery procedures in an examination of combat-related PTSD in 1,328 Vietnam War veterans (Keane et al., 1996). Results of this study replicated findings of heightened physiological reactivity in combat veterans with PTSD but found the magnitude of the effects, while highly significant, to be somewhat smaller than previously observed.

Whether the trauma-relevant cues used in these studies were standardized or idiographic, the critical element appears to be activation of the memory network in which the traumatic event is encoded. Once a memory is activated, emotions that are associatively linked with it also become activated along with their accompanying physiological responses. Interestingly, physiological reactivity to trauma-related cues was moved from the category of arousal symptoms in the DSM-III-R to the category of reexperiencing symptoms in the DSM-IV (PTSD criterion B.5). This change is of conceptual significance, because it recognizes physiological reactivity as a measure of the degree to which an event is emotionally reexperienced, rather than as a pathological symptom per se.

The body of evidence outlined here supports the idea that physiological responses can provide an index of the emotional experience associated with the memory of the traumatic event. An extension of this idea is that the presence (or absence) of clinical pathology can be inferred from reactivity to trauma-related cues. Several investigators (Blanchard, Kolb, & Prins, 1991; Malloy et al., 1983; Orr et al., 1993; Pitman et al., 1987; Shalev et al., 1993) have attempted to use such physiological reactivity as a marker for PTSD. These diagnostic applications have produced sensitivity values in the range of 60–90% and specificity values of 80–100%.

Startle

Exaggerated startle is another PTSD symptom that has been investigated by means of psychophysiological measures and methods. The original inclusion of exaggerated startle as an arousal symptom of PTSD was based on clinical impression rather than empirical evidence. As with the other arousal symptoms of PTSD, it is generally presumed that the exaggerated startle response was not present prior to the traumatic event. Thus, it is a potential marker for the disorder.

The startle response is characterized by a pattern of muscular reflexes, including eyeblink, that is produced by any intense stimulus with a sudden and unexpected onset. It is mediated by simple brainstem neural circuitry (Davis, 1984) but can be modulated by the emotional state of the organism. For example, negative emotional imagery (Cook, Hawk, Davis, & Stevenson, 1991; Vrana & Lang, 1990), slides with aversive contents (Bradley, Cuthbert, & Lang, 1990, 1993; Cook, Davis, Hawk, Spence, & Gautier, 1992; Vrana, Spence, & Lang, 1988), threat of electric shock (Grillon, Ameli, Foot, & Davis, 1993), and noxious odors (Miltner, Matjak, Braun, Diekmann, & Brody, 1994) have been shown to increase startle magnitude.

There is laboratory evidence indicating larger magnitude eyeblink EMG startle responses to intense auditory stimuli in individuals with PTSD compared to individuals without PTSD (Butler et al. 1990; Morgan, Grillon, Southwick, Davis, & Charney, 1995; Orr, Lasko, Shalev, & Pitman, 1995; Shalev, Orr, Peri, Schreiber, & Pitman, 1992a). However, not all individuals with

PTSD show a measurable elevation of startle response (Butler et al., 1990; Morgan et al., 1991; Ornitz & Pynoos, 1989), which is consistent with the fact that the symptom of exaggerated startle is not necessary for conferring the diagnosis of PTSD. Although the magnitude of the eyeblink startle response tends to differ between PTSD and normal individuals, the rate of its habituation does not. Individuals with PTSD are just as effective in learning to suppress the muscular component of startle to repetitive stimuli as individuals without PTSD (Orr et al., 1995; Ross et al., 1989; Shalev et al., 1992a).

Defensive Response and Habituation

The magnitudes of autonomic responses to repeated presentations of intense (i.e., loud) stimuli have also been found to be greater in individuals with PTSD. Specifically, they produce larger HR responses and show a slower rate of decline of SC response magnitude compared to individuals without PTSD (Orr et al., 1995; Paige, Reid, Allen, & Newton, 1990; Shalev et al., 1992a). Findings in identical twins indicate that there are strong genetic determinants for both HR (Boomsma & Gabrielli, 1985; Carroll, Hewitt, Last, Turner, & Sims, 1985; Ditto, 1993; Kotchoubei, 1987) and SC (Lykken, Iacono, Haroian, McGue, & Bouchard, 1988) response and habituation. This suggests the possibility that the greater HR reactivity and slower decline of SC responses may reflect a constitutional risk factor rather than a consequence of trauma.

It is important to note that heightened psychophysiological reactivity to intense auditory stimuli is not unique to PTSD; individuals with other types of anxiety also show increased reactivity. For example, studies of generalized anxiety disorder (GAD), agoraphobia, social phobia (Lader, 1967; Lader & Wing, 1964), and panic disorder (Roth, Ehlers, Taylor, Margraf, & Agras, 1990) have also observed a slower decline in SC responses to repeated presentations of intense auditory stimuli compared to nonanxious subjects. Grillon, Ameli, Goddard, Woods, and Davis (1994) have reported larger eyeblink startle responses in panic disorder patients, most notably when they are exposed to threat of an aversive stimulus, but no difference in the rate of eyeblink response habituation, compared to nonanxious individuals.

Indicators of Persistent Arousal

A chronic, stress-related disorder such as PTSD might be expected to produce long-term alterations of basal sympathetic activity that would be manifested as, for example, persistent increases in blood pressure and HR levels. Such alterations could have serious health consequences, including increased risk of hypertension and cardiovascular disease (Blanchard, 1990). With respect to PTSD, inferences about basal psychophysiological levels have typically been made from data collected within studies involving trauma-related challenge tasks. Physiological levels are recorded for some period while individuals sit quietly prior to exposure to trauma-related stimuli. The findings from these procedures have been mixed. Some studies have reported elevated HR and blood pressure levels at rest in PTSD subjects compared to non-PTSD controls (for a review see Blanchard, 1990), whereas a number of other studies have not (Blanchard, Hickling, Taylor, Loos, & Gerardi, 1994, 1996; McFall et al., 1990; Orr et al., 1993; Pitman et al., 1990; Shalev et al., 1993).

It seems clear that definitive conclusions regarding physiological levels associated with PTSD cannot be drawn from data collected prior to a challenge procedure. As noted by Prins et al. (1995), the higher physiological readings (e.g., HR) may be the result of entering a psychologically threatening situation rather than reflecting a biologically stable elevation in autonomic activation. Thus, anxiety generated by anticipation of the trauma-related stimuli can explain the observed elevations in resting psychophysiological levels within the challenge study context. One way to address this possibility is to collect physiological data during a laboratory session when subjects know that they will not discuss or be exposed to trauma-related stimuli. This approach was taken by McFall, Veith, and Murburg (1992) who found comparable HR and blood pressure levels at rest for combat veterans with PTSD and those without PTSD in a study in which the veterans were not anticipating exposure to trauma-related cues.

Differences in HR and blood pressure levels, recorded manually by a triage nurse, also have been found in a retrospective examination of the medical records of Vietnam War combat veterans with PTSD who were seeking medical or psychiatric help at a VA hospital compared with help-seeking Vietnam Era veterans without PTSD (Gerardi, Keane, Cahoon, & Klauminizer, 1994). The investigators suggest that seeking medical care may be sufficient to activate memories related to prior trauma in individuals with PTSD and thereby produce anticipatory arousal. In this sense, their explanation for the results is consistent with that given here for elevated baseline physiological levels in laboratory studies of reactivity to trauma-related cues.

Electrical Activity of the Brain

In recent years, there has been a substantial increase in the measurement of electrophysiological brain activity as a means of assessing information processing in relation to psychopathological conditions. For example, event-related potentials (ERPs) have been explored for their use as markers of genetic risk for disorders such as schizophrenia and alcoholism (for discussions see Cloninger, 1990; Friedman, 1990; Simons & Miles, 1990). Paige et al. (1990) examined the early sensory components of the ERP waveform in combat veterans with PTSD using an augmentation–reduction paradigm. Individuals were presented with a series of 500-ms-duration tones with intensities ranging from 74 to 104 dB. Paige et al. reported that PTSD veterans demonstrated a decrease in P200 amplitude in response to increasing tone intensities (reduction), a pattern opposite to that found in non-PTSD veterans (augmentation). The authors suggested that this finding reflects an elevated central nervous system sensitivity in PTSD, and an attempt by the cortex to reduce stimulation. McFarlane, Weber, and Clark (1993) measured ERPs during presentations of frequent, infrequent, and distractor tones to examine the later stages of stimulus processing in PTSD. Individuals with PTSD, relative to controls, demonstrated a longer latency N200 and attenuated P300 to the infrequently presented and distractor tones, suggesting that participants with PTSD had more difficulty discriminating these stimuli. McFarlane et al. interpreted these findings as a reflection of the disturbed concentration found in PTSD.

Other studies have used more general indicators of brain wave activity to show lateralized differences related to PTSD. A recent study (Schiffer, Teicher, & Papanicolaou, 1995) examined evoked potentials to a series of clicks during neutral imagery and recollection of painful childhood events in individuals with and without a history of childhood trauma. They reported evoked potentials indicative of greater activity in the right versus left hemisphere during recollection of the painful childhood events in the traumatized group. McCaffrey, Lorig, Pendrey, McCutcheon, and Garrett (1993) measured electroencephalographic (EEG) alpha and theta activity following exposure to a variety of pleasant and unpleasant odors. Vietnam veterans with PTSD showed a larger relative increase in alpha activity of the left versus right hemisphere compared to veterans without PTSD when they were exposed to an odor such as that of burning hair. McCaffrey et al. point out that this could be due to increased activity in an emotional processing area of the right hemisphere or reduced arousal in the left hemisphere. Although these findings (Schiffer et al., 1995; McCaffrey et al., 1993) are not conclusive, they are consistent with speculation that the right hemisphere plays an important role in the processing of emotional memories. Interestingly, the results of these studies are congruent with evidence from positron emission tomography (PET) of individuals with PTSD showing increased activity in right-sided limbic and paralimbic areas during imagery of past traumatic events (Rauch et al., 1995).

Treatment Outcome Indicators

The use of psychophysiological measurement for assessing treatment progress and outcome is a relatively unexplored area in PTSD, with only a few published reports to date. In a case report of combat-related PTSD treated with imaginal flooding, Keane and Kaloupek (1982) demonstrated that improvement was associated with a reduction in HR response magnitude during recollection of the trauma. Shalev et al. (1992b) found psychophysiological responses during trauma-related imagery to be sensitive to psychiatric improvement following a systematic desensitization procedure. Finally, Boudewyns and Hyer (1990) reported that a reduction in SC response magnitude during trauma-related imagery following treatment was associated with a relatively higher "adjustment" score at 3 months posttreatment.

PSYCHOPHYSIOLOGICAL METHODS AND TECHNIQUES OF ASSESSING TRAUMATIC IMPACT

This section briefly outlines features of psychophysiological paradigms that have been used to study PTSD. The reader is referred to the respective publications for detailed descriptions of methodology. It is strongly recommended that individuals who plan to integrate psychophysiological recording into their assessment of PTSD familiarize themselves with the relevant published work before launching the effort.

Reactivity to Trauma-Related Cues

Audiovisual Stimuli

This method of assessment involves the presentation of standardized stimuli such as light flashes, combat sounds (mortar explosions or gunfire), and pictures of combat situations, while psychophysiological responses are recorded (e.g., Blanchard et al., 1986; Dobbs & Wilson, 1960; Malloy, Fairbank, & Keane, 1983; McFall et al., 1990). The intensity level of the auditory stimuli may be varied within the procedure, beginning at a low level of sound or trauma-relevant content and increasing to progressively higher levels. Standardized neutral stimuli (e.g., music or slides depicting outdoor scenes) that are not related to the trauma provide a comparison for assessing physiological reactivity specific to trauma-relevant content.

Reactivity to the various stimuli can be derived as difference scores between periods with different content. For example, if trauma-related stimuli are interspersed with neutral stimuli (e.g., music), a response score can be computed by subtracting the physiological level during presentation of the neutral stimulus from that recorded during presentation of the trauma-related stimulus. This difference score represents the individual's relative reactivity to the two stimuli. A positive value would indicate greater reactivity to the trauma-related stimulus. Scores of this sort have the advantage of removing individual differences in baseline physiological levels and nonspecific reactivity that reflect extraneous biological or psychological influences.

The use of standardized stimuli to assess psychophysiological reactivity allows maximal control to be exercised over the selection and presentation of the stimuli. Furthermore, each individual's reactivity is measured to the same set of cues. Thus, differences in physiological reactivity are more readily attributable to individual differences in the emotional relevance of the stimuli. A limitation of the use of standardized stimuli, especially in studies of emotion, is that the selected stimuli may not match a particular individual's unique experience(s). This could result in less than optimal activation of the target emotion(s).

Script-Driven Imagery

This method is derived from the imagery procedure developed by Lang and his colleagues for the study of fear and phobias (Cook, Melamed, Cuthbert, McNeil, & Lang, 1988; Lang, Levin, Miller, & Kozak, 1983; Levin, Cook, & Lang, 1982; McNeil, Vrana, Melamed, Cuthbert, & Lang, 1993). As noted earlier, several studies have used script-driven imagery to study psychophysiological reactivity in PTSD; details of the methodology can be found in Pitman et al. (1987) and Orr et al. (1993).

Briefly, the procedure involves preparing various scripts that portray actual or hypothetical experiences of the persons being assessed, including the two most stressful trauma-related experiences they can recall. Other experiences may include stressful lifetime experiences not related to the trauma, positive experiences, or neutral experiences, depending on the most relevant comparison for the question at hand. A written description of each personal experience is reviewed and edited to produce a script of about 30 seconds' duration, composed in the second person, present tense. Standard scripts portraying various hypothetical experiences are also included and provide a means for comparing responses to stimuli that are the same for all individuals within or between studies. Scripts are recorded in a neutral voice for playback in the laboratory while psychophysiological activity is measured. Individuals are instructed to listen carefully during the playing of each script and imagine them as vividly as possible. The reading and imagining of each script is followed by a period of relaxation after which several self-reports are made on Likert-type scales. A response score is calculated for each physiologically dependent variable, separately for each script, by subtracting the preceding baseline period value from the value during imagery.

An important feature of the script-driven imagery method is its flexibility. Scripts can be tailored to capture an individual's unique experience of a traumatic event and can also be used to assess emotional reactivity to most any traumatic event. For example, a Vietnam War veteran whose job was handling dead bodies in a morgue might be unresponsive to standard combat-related sights and sounds but highly reactive to a script describing the experience of working in a morgue. The potential limitations of this method include its reliance on the subject's ability to recall the events in question and willingness to comply with instructions to vividly imagine the experiences. Failure of recall or compliance can result in an underestimate of an individual's emotional reactivity.

Reactivity to High-Intensity Stimuli

The Startle Response

Generating and measuring the human startle response is relatively simple. It is usually accomplished by exposing individuals to stimuli that have an appropriate combination of (high) intensity and (sudden) onset, and then quantifying the magnitude of muscular or autonomic reactivity they produce. Acoustical stimuli, either brief bursts of white noise or pure tones, with intensities ranging from 85 to 116 dB, are commonly used for generating startle responses in the laboratory. Studies of startle responses in humans commonly use eyeblink (*orbicularis oculi*) EMG as the measure of startle.

One approach to the assessment of startle responses in PTSD involves recording eyeblink EMG responses to very brief (40 ms) presentations of white noise with intensities that vary across trials (Butler et al., 1990). This method allows for an examination of the effect of intensity on response magnitude within individuals as well as between diagnostic groups. There are statistical benefits of this within-subjects approach, and it may require fewer participants than designs that use fixed stimulus intensities. On the other hand, the possibility of carryover effects from one intensity to another makes interpretation of the results more complex.

The Defense Response and Habituation

A second approach to studying psychophysiological reactivity to high-intensity stimuli has used multiple presentations of the same stimulus, most often a 95-dB, 500-ms, pure tone with 0-ms rise and fall times (e.g., Orr et al., 1995; Shalev et al., 1992a). Heart rate and SC responses to the stimulus presentations have been measured, in addition to eyeblink EMG; these measures have provided indices of autonomic reactivity to high-intensity stimuli. It is important to note that these studies have used stimuli with longer durations than studies focusing exclusively on EMG startle (e.g., Butler et al., 1990). High-intensity stimuli of a long duration might be expected to produce a defense response in addition to startle. Response scores for each trial are computed by subtracting the mean level immediately preceding tone onset from the maximum increase in level within a prespecified window following the tone. Because there are differences in the latencies of response onsets, the window is longer for autonomic (1–4 seconds) than for eyeblink (20–200 ms) responses.

An advantage to the use of a single intensity level is that it allows for an examination of the rate of decline of response magnitude across trials (i.e., habituation). The rate of habituation reflects an individual's ability to learn not to respond to repetitive stimuli, essentially to ignore irrelevant information. As noted earlier, the rate of electrodermal habituation has been found to be slower in clinically anxious, compared to nonanxious, individuals.

Assessing Persistent Arousal

Very few studies of PTSD have assessed basal psychophysiological levels outside of a context that includes exposure to trauma-related cues. Consequently, any observed elevations in resting or baseline physiology can be explained as the result of anticipatory anxiety about the forthcoming stressor. One strategy for circumventing this problem is to collect basal physiology during a time when individuals are not anticipating a confrontation with reminders of their traumatic experience (e.g., McFall et al., 1992). An alternative approach would be to assess basal physiology by means of ambulatory monitoring methods. This has the advantage of obtaining physiological measures under relatively natural conditions, which may provide a more accurate representation of normal basal activity. Data could be obtained over a 24- or 48-hour period using recording devices such as the Holter Monitor or Vitalog MC-2. This would also allow for an examination of the rhythmic cycles (e.g., circadian) that characterize many physiological variables.

Electrophysiological Assessment of Information Processing

Electrophysiological research in PTSD has included measurement of alpha activity in the EEG, ERPs, and evoked potentials. ERPs are obtained from the electroencephalographic scalp potentials that are generated by presentations of discrete stimuli (such as tones). The characteristic waveforms usually become apparent only when averaged over multiple trials. These waveforms are analyzed in terms of the amplitude and latency of characteristic components that are designated by their positive or negative electrical potential and the timing of their onset after stimulus presentations. For example, N200 refers to a negative-going response 200 ms after the stimulus, whereas P300 refers to a positive response at about 300 ms. The component responses represent different aspects of sensory and information processing that occur when anticipating or responding to discrete internal and external events. For example, the N100 component appears to be sensitive to variations in attention, whereas the P300 component has been shown to be sensitive to the meaningfulness of a stimulus for a given task. Electrophysiological activity can also be used to assess the impact of emotional cues on information processing. As noted earlier, Schiffer et al. (1995) generated evoked potentials by presenting a series of brief clicks (86 dB, 3 per second) while individuals engaged in recollections related to either a traumatic or neutral experience. Inferences about emotional activity were made by comparing relative response differences between the left and right hemispheres.

Assessing Treatment Progress or Outcome

Any of the methods discussed here could potentially be used to assess whether therapy produces measurable changes in physiological reactivity. Very simply, reactivity to trauma-related cues or startle responses could be assessed prior to, and then following, an intervention to determine the degree of changes associated with treatment. As an example, a report on three cases of PTSD by Shalev et al. (1992b) describes the use of script-driven imagery for evaluating treatment success. Physiological reactivity (HR, SC, and EMG) to scripts describing trauma-related events (among others) was measured before and after a desensitization procedure. The pattern of changes in psychophysiological reactivity demonstrated the method's sensitivity to improvement as well as its potential for revealing partial improvement. In their study of direct therapeutic exposure in Vietnam War combat veterans, Boudewyns and Hyer (1990) created 5-minute tapes for veterans based on their most stressful experience in Vietnam. Physiological reactivity (HR, SC, and EMG) was measured while the veterans listened to three presentations of the tape. Response scores for each tape presentation were calculated by subtracting the highest 1-minute mean value from the lowest 1-minute mean value of the preceding baseline. The relative changes in these physiological response scores before and after treatment provide measures of the change in emotional reactivity that can be used to estimate treatment efficacy and make comparisons between different treatment conditions.

A BASIC PRIMER ON PSYCHOPHYSIOLOGICAL MEASURES AND TECHNIQUES

Background

Professionals who are interested in using psychophysiology in their research or clinical practice must be willing to commit some time and effort to acquiring the requisite knowledge of physiology, biomedical equipment, and computers. A conceptual grasp of the systems and methods is essential, even if true technical understanding and mastery are not. As we note later, expert consultation and assistance is valuable, if not essential, when planning for, collecting, and interpreting psychophysiological data. However, engaging a consultant and making use of his or her advice increases the need for knowledge rather than diminishing it.

The next section is intended to provide the reader with a brief overview of some of the measurement and interpretational issues that need to be addressed when considering the use of psychophysiological assessment. An edited volume by Cacioppo and Tassinary (1990) provides an excellent detailed and up-to-date discussion of theory, methodology, and analysis of psychophysiological processes.

Resting and Prestimulus Physiological Levels

Most psychophysiological investigations assess resting levels at the beginning of the procedure as a reference point for comparison with subsequent values.

It is also common to obtain additional baseline values from rest periods at points throughout the procedure as a means of tracking shifts in tonic arousal. A decision must be made regarding the optimal amount of time for stabilization and collection of initial resting level data. In a review of studies that collected resting HR levels, Hastrup (1986) noted a negative correlation between HR level and duration of the rest period, indicating that shorter rest periods yielded higher HR levels. From this review, it appears that about 15 minutes should be allowed for initial stabilization before assessing basal HR level. However, compromises are inevitable; rest periods that are too long may result in boredom (even sleep) or restlessness, whereas rest periods that are too short will not allow sufficient time for physiological stabilization.

Periodic sampling of baseline values is important for determining general physiological trends or to provide reference values for calculating the magnitude of responses (e.g., to trauma-relevant stimuli). Physiological levels can change over time, especially when a variety of stimuli are being presented. Consequently, if one is interested in measuring the response to a specific stimulus, it is desirable to obtain baseline or comparison values that precede and are proximal to the target stimulus. Reasonable estimates of baseline levels may be obtained from relatively brief periods of time if the individual is sitting quietly and is not extremely anxious. For example, the studies of trauma-related imagery discussed earlier collected baseline data for 30 seconds prior to each script and allowed 1–3 minutes between trials. Depending on the protocol and type of stimuli being used, as well as the particular measure(s) being recorded, more or less time between stimulus presentations may be needed to allow for stabilization.

How Many Measures?

The most frequently used indices of emotional arousal in psychophysiological studies of PTSD have been measures of peripheral autonomic activity (i.e., HR, SC, and blood pressure). As noted earlier, several studies have also used facial EMG to assess emotional reactivity, and a few studies have recorded ERPs in order to evaluate cognitive processing in PTSD. Although the selection of measures should be determined by the conceptual and theoretical issues to be addressed, there are practical considerations as well. Practical considerations will include such issues as the measure's historical usages and popularity, amount of technical expertise required for data collection and interpretation, and expense and availability of instrumentation.

There is ample evidence that measures are differentially sensitive to emotional and psychological states and behaviors. It is important to recognize that one measure cannot simply be substituted for another. Fowles (1980), in particular, has explored some of the differential value of HR and SC as psychophysiological indicators. For example, HR will better index responding associated with active avoidance behavior, whereas SC will better index active inhibition. Although HR and SC can provide useful indices of general arousal, they do not necessarily inform about its valence (i.e., whether it is positive or negative). Measures of facial EMG activity are particularly good at providing information about the valence of the emotional arousal (for a review, see Fridlund & Izard, 1983). For example, an increase in zygomaticus major activity (the muscle group involved in smiling) is characteristic of a pleasant emotional experience, whereas increased corrugator activity (the muscle group involved in frowning) has been found to accompany a depressed mood (Sirota & Schwartz, 1982). Corrugator EMG is especially useful for discriminating between positively and negatively valenced emotions.

Finally, it is important to recognize that there are often differences between individuals in the relative degree to which responses appear in one system versus another (for discussion, see Stern & Sison, 1990). For example, exposure to a generic stressor such as mental arithmetic may produce an increase in HR and SC levels for some individuals, whereas other individuals will show change in one system but not the other, and still others may show small or no changes at all. Measurement of only a single system greatly increases the likelihood that reactivity will be underestimated or missed completely in individuals who happen to be more responsive in another system.

The Measurement of Psychophysiological Activity

Cardiovascular

Heart rate and blood pressure are probably the most commonly used cardiovascular measures. Heart rate can be obtained very simply by counting the number of beats (e.g., via radial pulse) or in a more complicated way by recording the electrocardiogram (ECG) and precisely measuring the time between successive R-wave peaks either directly or by means of a cardiotachometer. Blood pressure can be recorded either manually or by means of an automated cuff placed on an arm or finger. A recent innovation in psychophysiological recording allows for continuous recording of blood pressure and HR from a finger cuff. Heart rate is typically expressed in beats per minute (bpm), whereas, interbeat interval (or heart period) is expressed in milliseconds (ms); blood pressure is expressed in millimeters of mercury (mm Hg). The rate of sampling and level of precision required for obtaining HR and blood pressure data will be determined by the manner in which the signals are recorded (e.g., from the raw ECG or from a cardiotachometer), as well as by the issues being addressed. For example, if one is interested in assessing resting level, samples might be obtained a few times per minute over an extended period of time from several minutes to hours. However, if the objective is to evaluate responsivity to a brief stimulus, the recording interval would be relatively short; for HR it would be desirable to capture each successive beat during the stimulus presentation as well as for a short period immediately before, and perhaps after, the stimulus is presented.

Electrodermal

Perhaps the most widely studied response system has been that of electrodermal activity, including measures of skin resistance, conductance, and potential. Even though the electrodermal system serves a thermoregulatory function and is influenced by such factors as ambient temperature and humidity, when these factors are controlled, there is a high correlation between sympathetic activity and SC responses (Wallin, 1981). As noted by Lang, Bradley, and Cuthbert (1990), "Conductance change is a near-direct measure of general sympathetic nervous system activity" (p. 383). This specificity makes SC an especially useful measure for assessing emotional arousal. Skin conductance is recorded by maintaining a very small constant voltage between two electrodes and measuring the variations in current that result from sweat gland activity. Conductance increases when the sweat ducts fill, membrane permeability changes, and sweat diffuses into the skin (Edelberg, 1972). Skin conductance is usually recorded from the fingers or palm of the nondominant hand through metal or silver/silver chloride electrodes. When using "wet" electrodes, it is important to use a paste that approximates the salinity of sweat (see Fowles et al., 1981) and not an electrolytic paste, such as that used for ECG, EEG, and EMG recording.

Electromyographic

Muscle activity can be recorded through small surface electrodes placed over the muscle(s) of interest. Accurate location of the electrodes is very important so as to maximize detection of activity of the muscle group of interest and minimize that associated with nearby muscles. A discussion of the technical aspects of EMG recording and description of where to position electrodes for specific muscle groups of the face and body can be found in Cacioppo, Tassinary, and Fridlund (1990). Careful consideration should be given to selection of muscle sites and adhering to recommended procedures for electrode placement. For example, measuring "frontalis" EMG by locating electrodes over each eye (e.g., Andreassi, 1980, p. 155), a common practice in biofeedback applications, is at variance with the placements recommended by Cacioppo and associates and is likely to be highly susceptible to nonselective muscle activity. Recording EMG activity requires equipment that can amplify the microvolt signals and provide filtering of the raw signal so as to include the primary frequencies associated with muscle activity. It is usually desirable to rectify (make positive) and "smooth" the raw EMG so that the signal more clearly reflects meaningful changes and is less sensitive to momentary fluctuations. Proper abrading of the recording site, so as to reduce skin resistance, and the use of an electrolytic paste, which further reduces resistance, are essential to the quality of the EMG recordings.

Electrocortical

Electrocortical activity is measured by placing electrodes on the scalp at strategic locations and then amplifying and filtering the microvolt signals so that they are easily discriminated from background noise and retain the desired information. Electrodes are commonly attached via a cap (much like a bathing cap) that positions and holds them at the correct locations on the head. The number of electrodes may range from as few as 10 to over 100, depending on the particular application. Electrodes are also placed near the eyes so that vertical and horizontal eye movements can be detected. Movement of the eyes can introduce artifact into the EEG record; consequently, data from trials that include significant movement are often eliminated from analyses. Personal computers have revolutionized EEG research; they can be programmed to handle nearly all data management and scoring tasks. As computers become more powerful, new methods of assessing and depicting brain activity are becoming available, such as topographical maps that produce pictures to concisely represent a composite of brain electrical activity. However, the technology remains rather sophisticated, data management can be time consuming, and many of the scoring and interpretational issues are complex.

Factors That Can Influence the Quality of Psychophysiological Recordings

Compliance with Protocol Demands

Any psychophysiological protocol requires that participants understand and adhere to a particular set of demands. The complexity of these demands will be determined by the nature of the protocol task and the physiological measures being obtained. Validity and interpretability of the psychophysiologic data will be significantly influenced by the degree of compliance with protocol demands. Even simple tasks, such as listening to a series of tones, will require that individuals sit quietly and keep their eyes open. These modest requirements may be challenging for an individual who is very anxious or not well rested. Complex tasks may also make significant demands on the physical and cognitive abilities of an individual, such as understanding and remembering a set of instructions, concentrating and focusing attention, discriminating among different types of stimuli, or staying invested in a task when there are a few hundred trials. Of particular importance to trauma-related assessment are the emotional demands of the task. It may be very difficult for an individual to remain engaged in a procedure that produces significant emotional discomfort, as when exposed to reminders of a traumatic event. Individuals may try to reduce distress by averting their gaze from a visual stimulus or distracting themselves when they are supposed to be vividly recalling an upsetting experience. Emotional distress may cause an increase in motor activity such as fidgeting. The increased motor activity can elevate physiological activity, which can influence the determination of physiological reactivity to a particular stimulus.

Occasional deviations from a protocol are inevitable, and although such deviations cannot be completely eliminated, an effort can be made to identify them and assess their impact. It is important to have some means for monitoring individuals as they go through the assessment protocol. A closed-circuit video system can be used to observe gross body movements or to verify that an individual is complying with task demands. The testing situation also offers a unique opportunity for observing an individual during exposure to trauma-related cues; thus, it is advantageous to have some means by which the individual can be unobtrusively observed. Although failure to comply with task demands, such as viewing or vividly recalling trauma-related materials, may reduce the interpretability of the psychophysiological data, such noncompliance may be clinically informative.

Pharmacological Agents

Physiological levels and responses can be strongly influenced by a variety of substances, including prescribed and nonprescribed drugs, alcohol, caffeine, and nicotine. For example, beta blocking agents that are commonly prescribed for hypertension can reduce cardiovascular activity level and attenuate reactivity (e.g., Fredrikson et al., 1985). The anticholinergic drugs that are commonly used to treat depression can produce a substantial elevation in resting HR level. Unfortunately, it is not always possible to perform psychophysiological testing on individuals in a medication-free state. On occasion, testing may be coordinated with a change in medications and can be performed once the individual has been removed from the current medication(s) and prior to beginning the new drug regimen. Little is known about the impact of many of the medications on psychophysiological responding; consequently, it may not be possible to estimate responses in the unmedicated state. In some instances, it may be possible to use physiological measures that are not influenced by a particular medication. For example, Fredrikson et al. observed that measures of cardiovascular activity and reactivity were influenced by a beta blocker, whereas SC level and reactivity were not. As a matter of course, medications should be noted, so that the information is available for subsequent consideration.

Nicotine, caffeine, and alcohol are commonly used substances that can influence physiological systems. Unfortunately, they do not have uniform influences across physiological systems, and the impact of withdrawal can be as problematic as that of consumption (e.g., Hughes, 1993; Lane & Williams, 1985; Lyvers & Miyata, 1993; Perkins, Epstein, Jennings, & Stiller, 1986; Ratliff-Crain, O'Keefe, & Baum, 1989). It is a common practice to ask individuals to abstain from using nicotine or caffeine for some period (often 30 minutes or more) prior to testing. However, some individuals may find that the period of abstinence produces discomfort, and it is difficult to know how this will influence the test results. Estimates of an individual's typical daily consumption of nicotine, caffeine (coffee and soda), and alcohol should be obtained prior to testing.

POTENTIAL APPLICATIONS
OF PSYCHOPHYSIOLOGY

Diagnosis

The current standard means for conferring a diagnosis of PTSD is to compare symptoms reported by an individual with the criteria set forth for PTSD in the DSM-IV (American Psychiatric Association, 1994). Consequently, diagnostic accuracy is heavily dependent on the reliability and validity of the self-reported symptoms. There are a number of reasons for exercising caution when considering individuals' appraisal and description of their cognitive, emotional, and behavioral experiences. A clear discussion of the elements and complexity of this issue as they pertain to the reporting of physical symptoms is provided by Pennebaker (1983). He notes that symptom awareness is influenced by a variety of internal and external cues, as well as the way in which the cues are perceived. As a means of maximizing diagnostic accuracy, Keane and colleagues (Lyons, Gerardi, Wolfe, & Keane, 1988; Litz, Penk, Gerardi, & Keane, 1992) have argued for a multimethod approach that incorporates information obtained from clinical interview, psychometrics, and psychophysiological assessment. This allows the diagnostician to consider the degree of convergence or divergence across multiple sources of information. Psychophysiological assessment is unique among these informational sources in that it provides data that are not solely dependent on the accuracy of self-reported experiences.

Psychophysiological measures of reactivity to trauma-related cues have been found to provide good discrimination of PTSD from non-PTSD cases identified on the basis of a structured clinical interview. Furthermore, this appears to hold true even when individuals attempt to hide or exaggerate their responses (Gerardi, Blanchard, & Kolb, 1989; Orr & Pitman, 1993). The encouraging results obtained from psychophysiological testing suggest that reactivity to trauma-related cues can provide information that will assist in making diagnostic decisions and assessing treatment outcome in relation to diagnostic status. Recently, Pitman and Orr (1993) also have discussed the potential value of including psychophysiological assessment as part of forensic psychiatric evaluations.

Despite the frequent replication of differential psychophysiological response to trauma cues, in some studies, as many as 40% of patients with PTSD do not show the expected elevation in reactivity. In fact, Prins et al. (1995) highlight a trend across studies that indicates better performance in identifying individuals who do not qualify for an interview-based PTSD diagnosis than in identifying those who do qualify for the diagnosis. The fact that roughly one-third to one-quarter of individuals diagnosed with PTSD based on DSM criteria are physiologically nonreactive raises an important issue regarding the proper boundaries for PTSD diagnoses. At present it is impossible to determine whether self-report and interviewer-based procedures are overly inclusive or whether psychophysiological reactivity as a diagnostic requirement is overly exclusive. The reality is that neither assessment technique provides an error-free measure of PTSD, and the diagnostician is advised to look for convergent information from a variety of sources as a means of overcoming the limitations of each individual approach.

Assessing Specific Symptoms

Physiological reactivity to internal or external cues that are related to the traumatic event is just one of the five possible reexperiencing symptoms listed in the DSM-IV. Consequently, it is possible to obtain a diagnosis of PTSD without the presence of psychophysiological reactivity as a reported symptom or demonstrated response. A conservative approach to interpreting objectively documented psychophysiological reactivity would be to confine inferences to the presence of DSM-IV, criterion B.5. As we will discuss later, this does not imply that the subjective report of reactivity is identical to a psychophysiological demonstration. In fact, the time may have come to consider the need for more concrete evidence for establishing symptom presence.

The presence or absence of an exaggerated startle response (DSM-IV, criterion D.5) can also be substantiated from psychophysiological assessment. Given that most anyone will startle under the right conditions, the diagnostic question is whether a given individual shows an exaggerated startle response. Addressing this question by means of self-report requires the use of comparative information that must be provided by the individual being evaluated and the diagnostician. Obviously, the frames of reference for such comparisons can vary widely. Measuring startle in terms of psychophysiological reactivity to intense stimuli offers a more standardized means for making comparisons.

Treatment Process and Outcome

To date, the application of psychophysiological methods to treatment-related issues in PTSD is relatively unexplored; there are only a few published studies and case reports. Furthermore, this work has focused on only one use of psychophysiology (i.e., assessing treatment outcome). The change in physiological reactivity to trauma-related cues before treatment and following treatment can provide a useful index of clinical improvement. For example, it can be used to compare the relative efficacies of one therapy to another, or to help determine whether a therapy has had the desired effect for a given client.

Psychophysiology may also prove useful for predicting the clinical course of PTSD. An early study by Meakins and Wilson (1918) exposed soldiers diagnosed with "irritable heart" (probably PTSD) and healthy subjects to bright flashes and blank pistol discharges while pulse rate and respiration were monitored. Of the individuals diagnosed with "irritable heart," those who showed the larger physiological responses were the ones who were subsequently unable to return to duty. To our knowledge, there are no published studies that have used psychophysiological measures for predicting treatment outcome in PTSD. A study of obsessive–compulsive disorder has shown that peak HR response can be used to predict the amount of posttreatment fear reduction (Kozak, Foa, & Steketee, 1988). Research is needed to determine whether there might be a similar relationship between physiological reactivity and treatment outcome for PTSD.

Exposure-based therapeutic techniques such as imaginal flooding or desensitization have as one of their goals the reduction of emotional distress. The amount of distress experienced while recalling a particular experience during therapy is often assessed by asking the client to provide a rating such as the number of "subjective units of distress" (SUDs). Progress over the course of a therapy session is evaluated by having the client provide periodic SUDs ratings to track the within-session reduction in distress that is considered necessary for good therapeutic outcome (see Foa & Kozak, 1986). In addition to self-reported distress, it is possible, even using relatively primitive recording equipment, to continuously monitor physiological arousal for the same purpose.

Changes in physiological arousal could be used by the therapist for determining how best to proceed in a particular session or between sessions. For example, a gradual decrease in physiological arousal might be taken as an indication that a given experience is becoming less distressing for the client. However, a precipitous decrease in arousal might indicate that the client has disengaged from the task, perhaps because it has become overwhelming (but see Rachman & Whittal, 1989). A gradual increase in physiological arousal could indicate that a client is becoming emotionally engaged in the therapeutic task or, if prolonged, it might suggest that the particular therapeutic approach was not having the desired effect.

Conceptual Insights: PTSD versus Other Disorders

The previous discussion focuses on some of the practical applications of psychophysiological assessment. In addition, psychophysiological data can provide valuable conceptual information regarding the nature of PTSD. For example, the heightened physiological reactivity to trauma-related stimuli observed in PTSD is similar to that observed in simple phobia (Cook et al., 1988; McNeil et al., 1993). Simple phobics show larger HR and SC responses during imagery of their phobic objects compared to other anxious groups with less specific fears, such as agoraphobia. Patients with agoraphobia have been found to be physiologically unresponsive during imagery of their fear-related contexts (Cook et al., 1988; Zander & McNally, 1988). In PTSD the heightened physiological reactivity seems to be quite specific to cues associated with the traumatizing event. Individuals with PTSD are no more reactive to non-trauma-related stressors such as mental arithmetic than are individuals without PTSD (Blanchard et al., 1982, 1986, 1989; Pallmeyer et al., 1986).

An important factor in determining or modulating physiological reactivity across various anxiety disorders appears to be the specificity of the fear. In terms of Lang's (1985) bioinformational theory of emotion, the memory networks associated with specific fears, may be more readily or strongly activated than less specific fears because the external cues used to trigger the fear are more closely matched with its internal representation. Thus, both PTSD and simple phobia would appear to have fear networks that are highly specific and thereby easily activated. Whereas the specificity of responses to trauma-related cues suggests a similarity with simple phobia, the findings of slower habituation of SC responses to intense auditory stimuli (Orr et al., 1995; Shalev et al., 1992a) suggest a similarity with disorders characterized by more diffuse forms of anxiety. Interestingly, the one reported study (Lader, 1967) that included a group of individuals with simple phobia reported that they did not differ from nonanxious individuals in their rate of SC habituation. Also, as noted earlier, both PTSD and panic disorder have been found to be associated with an elevated eyeblink startle response. Finally, the reduced P300 amplitude observed in PTSD (McFarlane et al., 1993) has also been observed for other disorders, including depression (Bruder et al., 1995), suggesting that these disorders may share particular cognitive impairments. Taken together, these psychophysiological studies provide information that may be important in shaping the conceptualization of PTSD as an anxiety disorder and some of the features that it shares with other disorders.

LIMITATIONS IN THE USE OF PSYCHOPHYSIOLOGY

Conceptual Limitations of Psychophysiological Measures

Psychophysiological assessment sometimes has an exaggerated image as a truly objective means for detecting an individual's psychological or emotional state. Although psychophysiological measures and methods can provide unique information, they are not inherently more valid or more objective than typical assessment methods involving self-report or interviews. It is usually necessary to interpret psychophysiological information in the context of evidence collected via these other assessment methods. Because it is common for psychophysiological assessments to provide ambiguous evidence about diagnostic status or psychological state, just as other methods do, there is often no choice but to rely on convergence from multiple sources of evidence.

Simulation and Dissimulation of Responses

There is limited available evidence on the issue of faking in the context of the psychophysiology of PTSD. A study by Gerardi, Blanchard, and Kolb (1989) suggests that veterans with PTSD were unable to significantly alter their responses during a second test session when instructed to do so. Veterans without PTSD were able to increase their physiological reactivity so as not to differ from the PTSD group on the simple measures. However, when a previously used HR cutoff score was combined with baseline HR level, a high level of correct classification was obtained. Orr and Pitman (1993) instructed a group of veterans without PTSD to try to increase their reactivity during trauma-related imagery so as to appear as though they had PTSD. A discriminant function based on SC and corrugator EMG responses accurately classified 16 of the 16 veterans when not trying to simulate PTSD, and 12 of the 16 veterans when they were simulating PTSD. Interestingly, the simulating veterans were able to produce HR responses as large as those of individuals with PTSD, suggesting that HR responses may be more susceptible to simulation.

Imperfect Covariation between Self-Report and Psychophysiology

It is important to recognize that the PTSD diagnosis is presently based on subjective information that is not necessarily comparable to information recorded directly from physiological systems. Self-reported physiological activity and emotional experience often do not correlate well with measured physiological responses. For example, research on autonomic perception and response covariation (e.g., Eifert & Wilson, 1991; Spinhoven, Onstein, Sterk, & le Haen-Versteijinen, 1993; Tyrer, Lee, & Alexander, 1980) makes it clear that self-reports of psychophysiological reactivity are not interchangeable with observations or recordings of such activity.

Lang (1985) has noted that correlations between self-reported fear and psychophysiological arousal seldom account for more than 10% of the variance. The lack of convergence between self-reported experiences and measured physiological activity raises important questions about the underlying processes that determine them and their validity and primacy for assessing emotional experiences. Lack of convergence between self-reported emotion and physiological measures can be problematic when the goal is to arrive at a formal diagnosis, but it nonetheless offers potentially valuable information for case conceptualization. For example, large physiological reactivity during recollection of an experience that an individual says is not troublesome may indicate that there are residual emotional issues that the individual is unaware of or not reporting. On the other hand, the absence of clear physiological arousal during recollection of an experience that an individual says is highly distressing may indicate that some emotional resolution has occurred, but that cognitive appraisal of the experience needs to be addressed.

Individual Biological Influences

Individual differences that can influence psychophysiological reactivity arise from characteristics such as age, sex, race, menstrual cycle, and physical fitness level. Their relationship to sustained and reactive features of autonomic activity has been established in studies employing psychophysiological methods; quantification of this information is highly encouraged. There are few examples from the trauma literature that directly demonstrate the impact of these factors, however one study by Shalev et al. (1993) did find that female participants with PTSD demonstrated 33% greater physiological responding to their trauma script than males with PTSD. More examples such as this can be expected as the literature on the psychophysiology of trauma develops.

Appropriateness of Trauma Cue Presentations

The final influence to be noted as a potential explanation for imperfect association between psychophysiological responding and PTSD diagnosis is cue adequacy. A question that must be asked each time a trauma-related psychophysiological challenge is administered is how well the challenge material matches the individual's traumatic event. In this respect, there may be an advantage to idiographic approaches to trauma cue selection. Although standardized presentations benefit from uniformity and their potential for allowing tight experimental control, they suffer the disadvantage of variable degree of correspondence with individual experience. Idiographic presentations may be designed to closely approximate the internal (memory) representations of the traumatic experience and thereby improve the validity of assessment.

Implications for Future Research and Clinical Practice

Reliance on self-report as the means for establishing a formal PTSD diagnosis (e.g., via DSM-IV) is consistent with the standards for most mental disorders and is practical in terms of applicability. However, it may be time to consider refining the criteria for PTSD to incorporate less subjective evidence. In particular, we propose that the accumulated findings from studies using trauma-relevant challenge tasks are substantial enough to justify a greater role for direct psychophysiological evidence in the diagnostic determination.

As context for this proposal, it is noteworthy that PTSD is rather unique among the diagnostic categories for mental disorders in that it requires specification of the experience that is presumed to have caused the symptoms to develop. Although this requirement can be cumbersome and precipitate diagnostic ambiguities, it also can be viewed as a positive reflection of the knowledge base on which the diagnostic criteria for PTSD have developed. Which is to say, if we knew (and could reach consensus) on the experiential causes of depression or schizophrenia, this information would likely be included as part of the diagnostic criteria for these disorders, too.

The idea that PTSD has somewhat more advanced diagnostic standards than is typical of mental disorders opens the way for further refinements, presumably to be based on empirical evidence. The consistent and robust demonstration of differential physiological reactivity to trauma-related cues by individuals with a PTSD diagnosis stands as a prime candidate for incorporation into the formal definition of the disorder. Relocation of the DSM symptom concerned with physiological reactivity to trauma cues from the Arousal category to the Reexperiencing category (B.5) as part of the DSM-IV was a change in this direction. However, although the DSM-IV captures the emphasis on evocation of emotion-related physiological reactions, it still allows the evidence to remain subjective. This latitude seems unnecessary, given the accumulation of psychophysiological findings and, as we have noted earlier, the increased availability of inexpensive and easy-to-use physiological recording devices. Furthermore, there is already a necessarily subjective symptom option in Category B that refers to "intense psychological distress" upon exposure to trauma cues (B.4), but which is otherwise identical in content to B.5. Given the fact that only one B symptom is required for the PTSD diagnosis, these symptoms are redundant as subjective complaints.

An alternative approach might be to separate the inherently subjective symptoms in the Category B (B.1–B.4) from the potentially empirical demonstration of physiological reactivity (B.5). Consistency with the current diagnostic standard could be maintained by requiring one symptom from the B.1–B.4 group or concrete psychophysiological evidence consistent with B.5. Among the advantages of this approach is that it preserves the possibility that some individuals who may be unable to report meaningfully on their subjective state (e.g., young children, stroke victims) still have a means for providing evidence of reexperiencing.

In conclusion, there are some points implied by this proposal that should be clarified. First, this is a call for a limited application of psychophysiological techniques to document a symptom. It does not make physiological reactivity either necessary or sufficient as an indicator of PTSD status. Although we are inclined to believe that evidence will eventually support psychophysiological reactivity as a necessary feature of the disorder, this possibility remains to be demonstrated. By the same token, the body of evidence concerning psychophysiological reactivity in relation to the various anxiety disorders makes it doubtful that such reactivity by itself will be a unique index of PTSD. Second, exaggerated startle response (D.5) is another symptom that may eventually warrant the requirement of concrete physiological demonstration. However, the evidentiary base for this change is not as well developed as that for physiological reactivity. Third, this proposal is not intended as an endorsement of the taxonomic approach of DSM to PTSD diagnosis. Rather, it recognizes the important role that DSM plays in providing standardization for the study and treatment of the disorder, given our limited knowledge (and theory) about it. We offer this suggestion as a step toward making the standardization a bit more rigorous.

REFERENCES

American Psychiatric Association. (1994). *Diagnostic and statistical manual of mental disorders* (4th ed.). Washington, DC: Author.

Andreassi, J. L. (1980). *Psychophysiology: Human behavior and physiological response.* New York: Oxford University Press.

Blanchard, E. B. (1990). Elevated basal levels of cardiovascular responses in Vietnam veterans with PTSD: A health problem in the making? *Journal of Anxiety Disorders, 4,* 233–237.

Blanchard, E. B., Hickling, E. J., Buckley, T. C., Taylor, A. E., Vollmer, A., & Loos, W. R. (1996). The psychophysiology of motor vehicle accident related posttraumatic stress disorder: Replication and extension. *Journal of Consulting and Clinical Psychology, 64,* 742–751.

Blanchard, E. B., Hickling, E. J., Taylor, A. E., Loos, W. R., & Gerardi, R. J. (1994). The psychophysiology of motor vehicle accident related posttraumatic stress disorder. *Behavior Therapy, 25,* 453–467.

Blanchard, E. B., Kolb, L. C., Gerardi, R. J., Ryan, P., & Pallmeyer, T. P. (1986). Cardiac response to relevant stimuli as an adjunctive tool for diagnosing post-traumatic stress disorder in Vietnam veterans. *Behavior Therapy, 17,* 592–606.

Blanchard, E. B., Kolb, L. C., Pallmeyer, T. P., & Gerardi, R. J. (1982). A psychophysiological study of post-traumatic stress disorder in Vietnam veterans. *Psychiatric Quarterly, 54,* 220–229.

Blanchard, E. B., Kolb, L. C., & Prins, A. (1991). Psychophysiological responses in the diagnosis of posttraumatic stress disorder in Vietnam veterans. *Journal of Nervous and Mental Diseases, 179,* 97–101.

Blanchard, E. B., Kolb, L. C., Taylor, A. E., & Wittrock, D. A. (1989). Cardiac response to relevant stimuli as an adjunct in diagnosing post-traumatic stress disorder: Replication and extension. *Behavior Therapy, 20,* 535–543.

Boomsma, D. I., & Gabrielli, W. F., Jr. (1985). Behavioral genetic approaches to psychophysiological data. *Psychophysiology, 22,* 249–260.

Boudewyns, P. A., & Hyer, L. (1990). Physiological response to combat memories and preliminary treatment outcome in Vietnam veteran PTSD patients with direct therapeutic exposure. *Behavior Therapy, 21,* 63–87.

Bradley, M. M., Cuthbert, B. N., & Lang, P. J. (1990). Startle reflex modification: Emotion or attention? *Psychophysiology, 27,* 513–522.

Bradley, M. M., Cuthbert, B. N., & Lang, P. J. (1993). Pictures as prepulse: Attention and emotion in startle modification. *Psychophysiology, 30,* 541–545.

Bruder, G. E., Tenke, C. E., Stewart, J. W., Towey, J. P., Leite, P., Voglmaier, M., & Quitkin, F. M. (1995). Brain event-related potentials to complex tones in depressed patients: Relations to perceptual asymmetry and clinical features. *Psychophysiology, 32,* 373–381.

Butler, R. W., Braff, D. L., Rausch, J. L., Jenkins, M. A., Sprock, J., & Geyer, M. A. (1990). Physiological evidence of exaggerated startle response in a subgroup of Vietnam veterans with combat-related PTSD. *American Journal of Psychiatry, 147,* 1308–1312.

Cacioppo, J. T., & Tassinary, L. G. (1990). *Principles of psychophysiology: Physical, social, and inferential elements.* New York: Cambridge University Press.

Cacioppo, J. T., Tassinary, L. G., & Fridlund, A. J. (1990). The skeletomotor system. In J. T. Cacioppo & L. G. Tassinary (Eds.), *Principles of psychophysiology: Physical, social, and inferential elements* (pp. 325–384). New York: Cambridge University Press.

Carroll, D., Hewitt, J. K., Last, K. A., Turner, J. R., & Sims, J. (1985). A twin study of cardiac reactivity and its relationship to parental blood pressure. *Physiology and Behavior, 34,* 103–106.

Cloninger, R. F. (1990). Event-related potentials in populations at genetic risk: Genetic principles and research strategies. In J. W. Rohrbaugh, R. Parasuraman, & R. Johnson, Jr. (Eds.), *Event-related brain potentials: Basic issues and applications* (pp. 333–342). New York: Oxford University Press.

Cook, E. W., Davis, T. L., Hawk, L. W., Spence, E. L., & Gautier, C. H. (1992). Fearfulness and startle potentiation during aversive visual stimuli. *Psychophysiology, 29,* 633–645.

Cook, E. W., Hawk, L. W., Davis, T. L., & Stevenson, V. E. (1991). Affective individual differences and startle reflex modulation. *Journal of Abnormal Psychology, 100,* 5–13.

Cook, E. W., III, Melamed, B. G., Cuthbert, B. N., McNeil, D. W., & Lang, P. J. (1988). Emotional imagery and the differential diagnosis of anxiety. *Journal of Consulting and Clinical Psychology, 56,* 734–740.

Davis, M. (1984). The mammalian startle response. In R. C. Eaton (Ed.), *Neural mechanisms of startle* (pp. 287–351). New York: Plenum Press.

Ditto, B. (1993). Familial influences on heart rate, blood pressure, and self-report anxiety responses to stress: Results from 100 twin pairs. *Psychophysiology, 30,* 635–645.

Dobbs, D., & Wilson, W. P. (1960). Observations on the persistence of war neurosis. *Diseases of the Nervous System, 21,* 686–691.

Edelberg, R. (1972). Electrical activity of the skin: Its measurement and uses in psychophysiology. In N. S. Greenfield & R. A. Sternbach (Eds.), *Handbook of psychophysiology* (pp. 367–418). New York: Holt, Rinehart & Winston.

Eifert, G. H., & Wilson, P. H. (1991). The triple response approach to assessment: A conceptual and methodological reappraisal. *Behaviour Research and Therapy, 29,* 283–292.

Foa, E. B., & Kozak, M. J. (1986). Emotional processing of fear: Exposure to corrective information. *Psychological Bulletin, 99,* 20–35.

Fowles, D. C. (1980). The three-arousal model: Implications of Gray's two-factor learning theory for heart rate, electrodermal activity, and psychopathy. *Psychophysiology, 17,* 87–104.

Fowles, D. C., Christie, M. J., Edelberg, R., Grings, W. W., Lykken, D. T., & Venables, P. H. (1981). Publication recommendations for electrodermal measurements. *Psychophysiology, 18,* 232–239.

Fredrikson, M., Danielssons, T., Engel, B. T., Frisk-Holmberg, M., Strom, G., & Sundin, O. (1985). Autonomic nervous system function and essential hypertension: Individual response specificity with and without beta-adrenergic blockade. *Psychophysiology, 22,* 167–174.

Fridlund, A. J., & Izard, C. E. (1983). Electromyographic studies of facial expressions of emotion and patterns of emotions. In J. T. Cacioppo & R. E. Petty (Eds.), *Social psychophysiology: A sourcebook* (pp. 243–286). New York: Guilford Press.

Friedman, D. (1990). Event-related potentials in populations at genetic risk: A methodological review. In J. W. Rohrbaugh, R. Parasuraman, & R. Johnson, Jr. (Eds.), *Event-related brain potentials: Basic issues and applications* (pp. 310–332). New York: Oxford University Press.

Gerardi, R. J., Blanchard, E. B., Kolb, L. C. (1989). Ability of Vietnam veterans to dissimulate a psychophysiological assessment for post-traumatic stress disorder. *Behavior Therapy, 20,* 229–243.

Gerardi, R. J., Keane, T. M., Cahoon, B. J., & Klauminizer, G. W. (1994). An *in vivo* assessment of physiological arousal in posttraumatic stress disorder. *Journal of Abnormal Psychology, 103,* 825–827.

Grillon, C., Ameli, R., Foot, M., & Davis, M. (1993). Fear-potentiated startle: Relationship to the level of state/trait anxiety in healthy subjects. *Biological Psychiatry, 33,* 566–574.

Grillon C., Ameli R., Goddard A., Woods, S. W., & Davis M. (1994). Baseline and fear potentiated startle in panic disorder patients. *Biological Psychiatry, 34,* 431–439.

Hastrup, J. L. (1986). Duration of initial heart rate assessment in psychophysiology: Current practices and implications. *Psychophysiology, 23,* 15–18.

Hughes, J. R. (1993). Possible effects of smoke-free inpatient units on psychiatric diagnosis and treatment. *Journal of Clinical Psychiatry, 54,* 109–114.

Keane, T. M., & Kaloupek, D. G. (1982). Imaginal flooding in the treatment of a post-traumatic stress disorder. *Journal of Consulting and Clinical Psychology, 50,* 138–140.

Keane, T. M., Kolb, L. C., Kaloupek, D. G., Orr, S. P., Thomas, R. G., Hsieh, F., & Lavori, P. (1996). *Utility of psychophysiological measurement in the diagnosis and treatment of post-traumatic stress disorder: Results of a Department of Veterans Affairs Cooperative Study.* Manuscript submitted for publication.

Kotchoubei, B. I. (1987). Human orienting reaction: The role of genetic and environmental factors in the variability of evoked potentials and autonomic components. *Activitas Nervosa Superior, 29,* 103–108.

Kozak, M. J., Foa, E. B., & Steketee, G. (1988). Process and outcome of exposure treatment with obsessive–compulsives: Psychophysiological indicators of emotional processing. *Behavior Therapy, 19,* 157–169.

Lader, M. H. (1967). Palmar skin conductance measures in anxiety and phobic states. *Journal of Psychosomatic Research, 11,* 271–281.

Lader, M. H., & Wing, L. (1964). Habituation of the psycho-galvanic reflex in patients with anxiety states and in normal subjects. *Journal of Neurology, Neurosurgery, and Psychiatry, 27,* 210.

Lane, J. D., & Williams, R. B. (1985). Caffeine affects cardiovascular response to stress. *Psychophysiology, 22,* 648–655.

Lang, P. J. (1985). The cognitive psychophysiology of emotion: Fear and anxiety. In A. Tuma & J. Maser (Eds.), *Anxiety and the anxiety disorders* (pp. 131–170). Hillsdale, NJ: Erlbaum.

Lang, P. J., Bradley, M. M., & Cuthbert, B. N. (1990). Emotion, attention, and the startle reflex. *Psychological Review, 97,* 377–395.

Lang, P. J., Levin, D. N., Miller, G. A., & Kozak, M. J. (1983). Fear behavior, fear imagery, and the psychophysiology of emotion: The problem of affective-response integration. *Journal of Abnormal Psychology, 92,* 276–306.

Levin, D. N., Cook, E. W., & Lang, P. J. (1982). Fear imagery and fear behavior: Psychophysiological analysis of clients receiving treatment for anxiety disorders. *Psychophysiology, 19,* 571–572.

Litz, B. T., Penk, W. E., Gerardi, R. J., & Keane, T. M. (1992). Assessment of posttraumatic stress disorder. In P. A. Saigh (Ed.), *Posttraumatic stress disorder: A behavioral approach to assessment and treatment* (pp. 50–84). Boston, MA: Allyn & Bacon.

Lykken, D. T., Iacono, W. G., Haroian, K., McGue, M., & Bouchard, T. J. (1988). Habituation of the skin conductance responses to strong stimuli: A twin study. *Psychophysiology, 25,* 4–15.

Lyons, J. A., Gerardi, R. J., Wolfe, J., & Keane, T. M. (1988). Multidimensional assessment of combat-related PTSD: Phenomenological, psychometric, and psychophysiological considerations. *Journal of Traumatic Stress, 1,* 373–394.

Lyvers, M., & Miyata, Y. (1993). Effects of cigarette smoking on electrodermal orienting reflexes to stimulus change and stimulus significance. *Psychophysiology, 30,* 231–236.

Malloy, P. F., Fairbank, J. A., & Keane, T. M. (1983). Validation of a multimethod assessment of posttraumatic stress disorders in Vietnam veterans. *Journal of Consulting and Clinical Psychology, 51,* 488–494.

McCaffrey, R. J., Lorig, T. S., Pendrey, D. L., McCutcheon, N. B., & Garrett, J. C. (1993). Odor-induced EEG changes in PTSD Vietnam veterans. *Journal of Traumatic Stress, 6,* 213–224.

McFall, M. E., Murburg, M. M., Ko, G. N., & Veith, R. C. (1990). Autonomic responses to stress in Vietnam combat veterans with posttraumatic stress disorder. *Biological Psychiatry, 27,* 1165–1175.

McFall, M. E., Murburg, M. M., Roszell, D. K., & Veith, R. C. (1989). Psychophysiologic and neuroendocrine findings in posttraumatic stress disorder: A review of theory and research. *Journal of Anxiety Disorders, 3,* 243–257.

McFall, M. E., Veith, R. C., & Murburg, M. M. (1992). Basal sympathoadrenal function in posttraumatic distress disorder. *Biological Psychiatry, 31,* 1050–1056.

McFarlane, A. C., Weber, D. L., & Clark, C. R. (1993). Abnormal stimulus processing in posttraumatic stress disorder. *Biological Psychiatry, 34,* 311–320.

McNally, R. J., Luedke, D. L., Besyner, J. K., Peterson, R. A., Bohm, K., & Lips, O. J. (1987). Sensitivity to stress-relevant stimuli in posttraumatic stress disorder. *Journal of Anxiety Disorders, 1,* 105–116.

McNeil, D. W., Vrana, S. R., Melamed, B. G., Cuthbert, B. N., & Lang, P. J. (1993). Emotional imagery in simple and social phobia: Fear versus anxiety. *Journal of Abnormal Psychology, 102,* 212–225.

Meakins, J. C., & Wilson, R. M. (1918). The effect of certain sensory stimulations on respiratory and heart rate in cases of so-called "irritable heart." *Heart: A Journal for the Study of the Circulation, 7,* 17–22.

Miltner, W., Matjak, M., Braun, C., Diekmann, H., & Brody, S. (1994). Emotional qualities of odors and their influence on the startle reflex in humans. *Psychophysiology, 31,* 107–110.

Morgan, C. A., Grillon, C., Southwick, S. M., Davis, M., & Charney, D. S. (1996). Exaggerated acoustic startle reflex in Gulf War veterans with posttraumatic stress disorder. *American Journal of Psychiatry, 153,* 64–68.

Morgan, C. A., Southwick, S. M., Grillon, C., Davis, M., Ouillette, V., & Charney, D. S. (1991). Yohimbine potentiates startle reflex in humans. *American Psychiatric Association 144th Annual Meeting, New Research Abstracts* (p. 127). Washington, DC: American Psychiatric Association.

Ornitz, E. M., & Pynoos, R. S. (1989). Startle modulation in children with posttraumatic stress disorder. *American Journal of Psychiatry, 146,* 866–870.

Orr, S. P. (1994). An overview of psychophysiological studies of PTSD. *PTSD Research Quarterly, 5,* 1–7.

Orr, S. P., Lasko, N. B., Shalev, A. Y., & Pitman, R. K. (1995). Physiologic responses to loud tones in Vietnam veterans with posttraumatic stress disorder. *Journal of Abnormal Psychology, 104,* 75–82.

Orr, S. P., & Pitman, R. K. (1993). Psychophysiologic assessment of attempts to simulate posttraumatic stress disorder. *Biological Psychiatry, 33,* 127–129.

Orr, S. P., Pitman, R. K., Lasko, N. B., & Herz, L. R. (1993). Psychophysiologic assessment of posttraumatic stress disorder imagery in World War II and Korean Combat Veterans. *Journal of Abnormal Psychology, 102,* 152–159.

Paige, S. R., Reid, G. M., Allen, M. G., & Newton, J. E. O. (1990). Psychophysiological correlates of posttraumatic stress disorder in Vietnam veterans. *Biological Psychiatry, 27,* 419–430.

Pallmeyer, T. P., Blanchard, E. B., & Kolb, L. C. (1986). The psychophysiology of combat-induced post-traumatic stress disorder in Vietnam veterans. *Behaviour Research and Therapy, 24,* 645–652.

Pennebaker, J. W. (1983). Physical symptoms and sensations: Psychological causes and correlates. In J. T. Cacioppo & R. E. Petty (Eds.), *Social psychophysiology: A sourcebook* (pp. 543–564). New York: Guilford Press.

Perkins, K. A., Epstein, L. H., Jennings, J. R., & Stiller, R. (1986). The cardiovascular effects of nicotine during stress. *Psychopharmacology, 90,* 373–378.

Pitman, R. K., & Orr, S. P. (1993). Psychophysiologic testing for post-traumatic stress disorder: Forensic psychiatric application. *Bulletin of the American Academy of Psychiatry and Law, 21,* 37–52.

Pitman, R. K., Orr, S. P., Forgue, D. F., Altman, B., de Jong, J. B., & Herz, L. R. (1990). Psychophysiologic responses to combat imagery of Vietnam veterans with posttraumatic stress disorder versus other anxiety disorders. *Journal of Abnormal Psychology, 99,* 49–54.

Pitman, R. K., Orr, S. P., Forgue, D. F., de Jong, J. B., & Claiborn, J. M. (1987). Psychophysiologic assessment of posttraumatic stress disorder imagery in Vietnam combat veterans. *Archives of General Psychiatry, 44,* 970–975.

Prins, A., Kaloupek, D. G., & Keane, T. M. (1995). Psychophysiological evidence for autonomic arousal and startle in traumatized adult populations. In M. J. Friedman, D. Charney, & A. Deutch (Eds.), *Neurobiological and clinical consequences of stress: From normal adaption to PTSD* (pp. 291–314). New York: Raven.

Rachman, S., & Whittal, M. (1989). Fast, slow, and sudden reductions in fear. *Behaviour Research and Therapy, 27,* 613–620.

Ratliff-Crain, J., O'Keefe, M. K., & Baum, A. (1989). Cardiovascular reactivity, mood, and task performance in deprived and nondeprived coffee drinkers. *Health Psychology, 8,* 427–447.

Rauch, S. L., van der Kolk, B. A., Fisler, R. E., Alpert, N. M., Orr, S. P., Savage, C. R., Fishman, A. J., Jenike, M. A., & Pitman, R. K. (1996). A symptom provocation study of posttraumatic stress disorder using positron emission tomography and scipt-driven imagery. *Archives of General Psychiatry, 53,* 380–387.

Ross, R. J., Ball, W. A., Cohen, M. E., Silver, S. M., Morrison, A. R., & Dinges, D. F. (1989). Habituation of the startle reflex in posttraumatic stress disorder. *Journal of Neuropsychiatry, 1,* 305–307.

Roth, W. T., Ehlers, A., Taylor, C. B., Margraf, J., & Agras, W. S. (1990). Skin conductance habituation in panic disorder patients. *Biological Psychiatry, 27*, 1231–1243.

Schiffer, F., Teicher, M. H., & Papanicolaou, A. C. (1995). Evoked potential evidence for right brain activity during the recall of traumatic memories. *Journal of Neuropsychiatry and Clinical Neurosciences, 7*, 169–175.

Shalev, A. Y., Orr, S. P., Peri, P., Schreiber, S., & Pitman, R. K. (1992a). Physiologic responses to loud tones in Israeli post-traumatic stress disorder patients. *Archives of General Psychiatry, 49*, 870–875.

Shalev, A. Y., Orr, S. P., & Pitman, R. K. (1992b). Psychophysiologic response during script-driven imagery as an outcome measure in posttraumatic stress disorder. *Journal of Clinical Psychiatry, 53*, 324–326.

Shalev, A. Y., Orr, S. P., & Pitman, R. K. (1993). Psychophysiologic assessment of traumatic imagery in Israeli civilian post-traumatic stress disorder patients. *American Journal of Psychiatry, 150*, 620–624.

Shalev, A. Y., & Rogel-Fuchs, Y. (1993). Psychophysiology of the posttraumatic stress disorder: From sulfur fumes to behavioral genetics. *Psychosomatic Medicine, 55*, 413–423.

Simons, R. F., & Miles, M. A. (1990). Nonfamilial strategies for the identification of subjects at risk for severe psychopathology: Issues of reliability in the assessment of event-related potential and other marker variables. In J. W. Rohrbaugh, R. Parasuraman, & R. Johnson, Jr. (Eds.), *Event-related brain potentials: Basic issues and applications* (pp. 343–363). New York: Oxford University Press.

Sirota, A. D., & Schwartz, G. E. (1982). Facial muscle patterning and lateralization during elation and depression imagery. *Journal of Abnormal Psychology, 91*, 25–34.

Spinhoven, P., Onstein, E. J., Sterk, P. J., & le Haen-Versteijnen, D. (1993). Discordance between symptom and physiological criteria for the hyperventilation syndrome. *Journal of Psychosomatic Research, 37*, 281–289.

Stern, R. M., & Sison, C. E. (1990). Response patterning. In J. T. Cacioppo & L. G. Tassinary (Eds.), *Principles of psychophysiology: Physical, social, and inferential elements* (pp. 193–215). New York: Cambridge University Press.

Tyrer, P., Lee, I., & Alexander, J. (1980). Awareness of cardiac function in anxious, phobic, and hypochondriacal patients. *Psychological Medicine, 10*, 171–174.

Vrana, S. R., & Lang, P. J. (1990). Fear imagery and the startle probe reflex. *Journal of Abnormal Psychology, 99*, 189–197.

Vrana, S. R., Spence, E. L., & Lang, P. J. (1988). The startle probe response: A new measure of emotion? *Journal of Abnormal Psychology, 97*, 487–491.

Wallin, B. G. (1981). Sympathetic nerve activity underlying electrodermal and cardiovascular reactions in man. *Psychophysiology, 18*, 470–476.

Zander, J. R., & McNally, R. J. (1988). Bio-informational processing in agoraphobia. *Behaviour Research and Therapy, 26*(5), 421–429.

CHAPTER 4

Psychometric Theory in the Development of Posttraumatic Stress Disorder Assessment Tools

FRANK W. WEATHERS
TERENCE M. KEANE
LYNDA A. KING
DANIEL W. KING

INTRODUCTION

In the last 15 years, scientific research on posttraumatic stress disorder (PTSD) has increased dramatically, yielding a wealth of knowledge regarding the clinical phenomenology, etiology, and treatment of this complicated, intractable disorder. Clearly the recognition of PTSD as a formal diagnostic entity in the third edition of the *Diagnostic and Statistical Manual of Mental Disorders* (DSM-III; American Psychiatric Association, 1980) provided considerable impetus for this extraordinary volume of research, but perhaps the most important catalyst has been the development of reliable and valid measures for assessing the core and associated symptoms of PTSD. The pivotal role of psychometrically sound assessment tools in PTSD research was underscored in the National Vietnam Veterans Readjustment Study (NVVRS; Kulka et al., 1990), the most extensive epidemiological study of PTSD ever conducted. According to Kulka et al., when the contract for the NVVRS was awarded in 1984, no validated measures of PTSD were yet available. Consequently, prior to conducting the main survey component of the study, the investigators were compelled to conduct a preliminary validation study in which various candidate measures were evaluated for their ability to distinguish PTSD cases from noncases. Several measures proved useful for this purpose and provided the means for achieving the primary research goal of estimating the prevalence of PTSD in combat veterans and matched controls.

Since then, the situation has changed substantially. The development and evaluation of standardized PTSD measures has become one of the most productive areas of research in the field of traumatic stress, and a wide variety of measures is now available, including questionnaires, structured interviews, and physiological protocols (for a recent review see Newman, Kaloupek, & Keane, 1996). Most of these measures enjoy at least some empirical support, and several, such as the Impact of Event Scale (IES; Horowitz, Wilner, & Alvarez, 1979), the Mississippi Scale for Combat-Related PTSD (Mississippi Scale; Keane, Caddell, & Taylor, 1988), the PK scale of the Minnesota Multiphasic Personality Inventory (MMPI) and MMPI-2 (Keane, Malloy, & Fairbank, 1984; Lyons & Keane, 1992), and the PTSD module of the Structured Clinical Interview for DSM-III-R (SCID; Spitzer, Williams, Gibbon, & First, 1990) have been examined extensively on diverse populations in a variety of settings. Given this abundance of instruments and a rapidly expanding empirical literature, researchers and clinicians can now choose instruments tailored to their particular assessment needs. Furthermore, they can increase their confidence in assessment decisions by relying on converging information obtained from multiple measures in an assessment battery, an approach that has been strongly advocated in the assessment of PTSD (Keane, Wolfe, & Taylor, 1987; Kulka et al., 1990).

The primary purpose of this chapter is to help readers become informed consumers of the burgeoning literature on the psychometric evaluation of PTSD assessment tools. It is intended primarily for those who wish to draw on this literature as a guide for selecting appropriate instruments for their particular assessment needs. Toward that end, we outline the key issues, principles, and techniques involved in developing and evaluating psychological assessment instruments, illustrating them with examples drawn from empirical work on a variety of PTSD measures. The chapter is divided into four sections. First, we describe a number of issues regarding scale construction and protocol development. Second, we discuss the concept of reliability from the perspective of classical test theory. Third, we discuss the concept of validity. Finally, we describe contemporary psychometric approaches, including generalizability theory, confirmatory factor analysis, and item response theory.

It is important to recognize that many of the concepts described in this chapter overlap with each other and that distinctions among them are not always clear-cut. For example, referring to the distinctions among content-related, criterion-related, and construct-related categories of validity, the *Standards for Educational and Psychological Testing* (1985) advises:

> The use of the category labels does not imply that there are distinct types of validity or that a specific validation strategy is best for each specific inference or test use. Rigorous distinctions between the categories are not possible. Evidence identified usually with the criterion-related or content-related categories, for example is relevant also to the construct-related category. (p. 9)

Under some circumstances the distinction between reliability and validity can also be blurred. For example, internal consistency statistics, usually interpreted as reflecting reliability across items on a scale, can also be seen as evidence of construct validity, in that a high degree of homogeneity among a set of items suggests they are measuring a single construct. Also, a study comparing PTSD diagnoses derived from a structured interview administered by lay interviewers versus experienced clinicians could be seen as a measure of test–retest reliability or as a measure of criterion-related validity, with the clinician's diagnosis as the standard against which the lay interviewer's ratings are compared. Despite the overlap, a broad distinction between reliability and validity and the further distinctions among the three categories of validity are meaningful and useful. In general, the two central concerns in the psychometric evaluation of an assessment instrument are the extent to which scores are free from measurement error (reliability) and the extent to which empirical evidence can be produced to demonstrate that the instrument measures what it purports to measure (validity).

Space constraints permit only the most general introduction to psychometric theory. Readers who plan to conduct research on existing PTSD measures or who are interested in developing new measures can find more in-depth discussions of the topics covered in this chapter in introductory texts such as Anastasi (1988), Crocker and Algina (1986), Cronbach (1990), and Suen (1990); in classic texts such as Gulliksen (1950), Lord and Novick (1968), and Nunnally (1978); and in the many works cited throughout the chapter. In addition, the *Standards for Educational and Psychological Testing,* cited earlier, is an essential reference for anyone involved in psychometric research, offering explicit, authoritative recommendations regarding the development, evaluation, and use of psychometric instruments. Finally, readers are encouraged to consult a recent special issue of the journal *Psychological Assessment* devoted to methods for increasing the psychometric integrity of psychological assessment instruments. This special issue makes an important contribution to the literature, with articles that (1) provide exhaustive coverage of topics such as content validity (Haynes, Richard, & Kubany, 1995); (2) discuss psychometric issues involved in assessment areas such as projectives (Weiner, 1995) and neuropsychology (Prigatano, Parsons, & Bortz, 1995); and (3) discuss psychometric issues involved in assessing special populations such as couples (Kashy & Snyder, 1995), substance abusers (Carroll, 1995), minorities (Okazaki & Sue, 1995), and the elderly (La Rue & Markee, 1995).

ISSUES IN SCALE CONSTRUCTION AND PROTOCOL DEVELOPMENT

Developing an effective psychological assessment instrument is a complex, painstaking, and iterative process. There is no single recipe that can be followed, no set of necessary and sufficient steps that invariably produces the desired result. Rather, the creation of a useful scale requires expertise in the content area to be assessed, familiarity with the merits and shortcomings of various response formats, and a thorough understanding of the statistical concepts and procedures for establishing reliability and validity. It demands considerable ingenuity, careful trial and revision, and the accumulation of an extensive empirical database across a wide range of settings, populations, and assessment tasks.

Although different authors vary in terms of the number and sequence of the stages they identify in the test construction process, there is consensus about the major steps involved. For the purposes of this chapter we will consider five such stages: (1) specifying the purpose of the instrument, (2) defining the construct, (3) designing the instrument, (4) pilot testing and revising, and (5) establishing reliability and validity for the final version. In this section, we discuss the first four stages of the process. The remaining sections of the chapter are concerned with the conceptual issues and statistical techniques for accomplishing the last stage.

Specifying the Purpose of the Instrument

Before work on actually creating a new PTSD instrument can begin, it is essential to determine how it will be used. Identifying the major purposes for the instrument shapes the design of the instrument and enhances the likelihood that it will perform satisfactorily when it reaches final form. Most PTSD assessment instruments are designed to accomplish several assessment tasks, although some are better suited than others for certain applications. For example, questionnaires are simple to administer and yield information about overall severity of PTSD symptoms, but are not widely accepted in the role of diagnostic criterion or "gold standard." As in other areas of psychopathology, the most common "gold standard" in research on PTSD is a clinical diagnosis made on the basis of a structured interview. In a similar vein, physiological assessment procedures can provide direct evidence regarding reactivity to reminders of a trauma, but do not provide data regarding other PTSD symptoms.

Identifying the Assessment Tasks

Some of the most common reasons for developing a PTSD assessment tool are as follows:

1. *To obtain a continuous measure of the severity of the disorder.* Continuous measures provide relatively fine-grained information about PTSD symptom severity. Because they are capable of detecting subtle changes in symptom

status over time, they serve well as outcome measures. They are also useful in correlational analyses for testing hypotheses about PTSD in relationship to other constructs. All PTSD questionnaires and many structured interviews yield continuous scores. In addition, physiological measures yield continuous measures of reactivity in one or more response channels (e.g., heart rate, skin conductance, blood pressure), although it is more difficult to make the case that these are continuous measures of PTSD per se.

2. *To determine current and lifetime diagnostic status.* In many types of clinical research, including case-control, epidemiological, and treatment outcome studies, participants are classified as PTSD or non-PTSD. Accurate determination of PTSD "caseness" in these designs depends on the use of diagnostic instruments that yield present or absent decisions based on clear inclusion and exclusion criteria. PTSD diagnostic status is most often assessed with a structured interview. However, any continuous measure of PTSD, including questionnaires and physiological measures, can also serve as a dichotomous measure simply by selecting an appropriate cutoff score and dividing the sample into cases (scoring above the cutoff) and noncases (scoring below the cutoff).

3. *To assess distinct dimensions of symptom severity.* On most PTSD instruments, symptom severity is assessed as a single dimension, such as frequency or subjective distress. Items on the Clinician-Administered PTSD Scale (CAPS; Blake et al., 1990), however, were designed to assess the separate dimensions of frequency and intensity, with intensity ratings based on the additional dimensions of duration, subjective distress, and functional impairment.

4. *To assess associated features of PTSD.* A number of instruments, including the CAPS and questionnaires such as the Mississippi Scale, the Penn Inventory (Hammarberg, 1992), the Trauma Symptom Inventory (TSI; Briere, 1995), and the Los Angeles Symptom Checklist (LASC; King, King, Leskin, & Foy, 1995) include items to tap associated features of PTSD, including guilt, depression, substance abuse, and impairment of social and occupational functioning.

5. *To assess a range of stress response syndromes.* The DSM-IV symptoms of PTSD are widely acknowledged as encompassing some of the most significant sequelae of traumatic life events. Nonetheless, some clinical investigators, arguing that these symptoms do not adequately capture the full range of posttraumatic adjustment problems, have promoted the recognition of a spectrum of stress disorders, including acute stress disorder, PTSD, and complex PTSD. The TSI is an excellent example of an instrument designed specifically to assess the clinical phenomenology of all of these posttraumatic syndromes.

6. *To assess response bias.* As in other areas of psychopathology, the evaluation of response bias has been a central concern in the assessment of PTSD. Response bias may stem from efforts to minimize or exaggerate symptom severity, from carelessness, or from confusion or misinterpretation of test

items. Most PTSD measures are quite face valid, meaning the content they are intended to assess is obvious to respondents, making it easy to deliberately distort responses in a particular direction. For example, Lyons, Caddell, Pittman, Rawls, and Perrin (1994) found that the Mississippi Scale scores of combat veterans with PTSD were indistinguishable from those of three control groups without PTSD, who were instructed to respond as if they had the disorder. This suggests that it is relatively easy for respondents to shape their answers to create a desired impression, and in the absence of additional information regarding the validity of responses, such distortion would be impossible to detect. Currently, few PTSD measures include items to assess response bias. The PK scale, when scored from the full MMPI or MMPI-2, can be interpreted in the context of the validity scale profile. Also, the TSI contains three scales to evaluate different aspects of response bias. The CAPS, the only interview to address this issue, assesses response validity at the item level and as a global rating that takes into account the entire interview. Unfortunately, these ratings, especially at the item level, are very difficult to make reliably (Weathers & Litz, 1994).

7. *To assess PTSD in the context of existing instruments.* PTSD scales have been developed from existing measures of psychopathology, including the PK scale and the crime-related (CR-PTSD; Saunders, Arata, & Kilpatrick, 1990) and war-zone-related (WZ-PTSD; Weathers et al., 1996) PTSD scales of the Symptom Checklist 90 — Revised (SCL-90-R; Derogatis, 1983). Using these measures brings the additional benefits of the parent instrument, such as the assessment of response validity and the assessment of comorbid problems such as depression, anxiety, and substance abuse. The availability of these measures also permits the assessment of PTSD in archival data sets collected before the existence of instruments developed specifically for PTSD.

8. *To quantify some directly observable PTSD-relevant behavior.* This is the primary goal both in the development of physiological assessment procedures (e.g., Malloy, Fairbank, & Keane, 1983; Pitman, Orr, Forgue, de Jong, & Claiborn, 1987) and in the development of protocols assessing other aspects of PTSD, such as emotional numbing (Litz, 1992) and intimacy deficits (Weathers et al., 1995).

Identifying the Target Populations

Another critical aspect of specifying the purpose of a PTSD assessment tool is to identify the populations in which it will be used. Much of the early research on PTSD assessment instruments was conducted on combat veterans, and both the PK scale and the Mississippi Scale, were originally developed specifically for this population. For the Mississippi Scale, this choice of populations dictated item content, with many items referring directly to experiences in the military. The use of veterans also undoubtedly influenced the MMPI items included in the PK scale. Although there is some evidence that the PK scale is useful in civilian trauma populations (e.g., Koretzky &

Peck, 1990), indicating some generalizability of content, other items likely would have emerged had the scale been developed in a population of rape victims, for example.

The importance of specifying the target population is illustrated by recent efforts to develop PTSD scales on the SCL-90-R (Derogatis, 1983). In developing the CR-PTSD scale, Saunders et al. (1990) identified 28 SCL-90-R items that differentiated crime victims with and without PTSD. Weathers et al. (1996) employed the same methodology in a sample of combat veterans, but found that only 11 of the 25 items on their WZ-PTSD scale overlapped with items on the CR-PTSD scale. The influence of the target population can sometimes be more qualitative and subtle, and requires experience with a given population and extensive pilot testing. For example, in our work with male combat veterans, we have found that in evaluating subjective distress, even slight changes in the phrasing of probe questions can evoke very different responses. Specifically, descriptors such as "upset" and "afraid" (How *upset [afraid]* did you feel?) tend to elicit lower levels of endorsement relative to "distress or discomfort" or "bothered" (How much *distress* or *discomfort* did you feel? How much did it *bother* you?).

Increasingly, test developers have created instruments that would measure PTSD in any population and have begun to validate and norm their instruments in diverse groups of trauma survivors. Recent examples of such measures include the Penn Inventory, the civilian version of the Mississippi Scale (Keane et al., 1988; Vreven, Gudanowski, King, & King, 1995), and the TSI. This approach should promote standardization of PTSD assessment and lead to an evaluation of the common aspects of PTSD resulting from any type of traumatic life event. Two population specifications that will likely remain important for instrument construction are the distinction between children and adults, and the distinction between victims of single or circumscribed traumatic events and victims of chronic interpersonal trauma. Each of these distinctions has implications for the format and content of test items.

Defining the Construct

Defining the construct to be measured and determining appropriate item content is another crucial step in the development of a PTSD assessment tool. Inadequate specification of the construct could result in the exclusion of items measuring core features of PTSD or the inclusion of items tapping irrelevant content. Either of these undesired outcomes could result in misleading correlations between PTSD and other constructs, or in diagnostic inaccuracies that could, in turn, affect prevalence estimates or formation of distinct groups for case control research. Unfortunately, PTSD has proven to be a difficult construct to define, and there is continued debate regarding the appropriate boundaries of the syndrome and its relationship to other disorders and other hypothesized sequelae of traumatic life events.

The formal diagnostic criteria for PTSD, first introduced in the DSM-III in 1980, constitute the most widely accepted and frequently invoked operational definition of the disorder. The advantage of this definition is that it is a consensus standard reflecting the most current clinically and empirically informed conceptualization of PTSD. The disadvantage is that the diagnostic criteria, and thus the construct, have evolved considerably as more information about the disorder has become available. Some notable changes from the DSM-III to the DSM-IV (American Psychiatric Association, 1994) include (1) redefining the stressor criterion; (2) adding a distinct hyperarousal symptom cluster; (3) combining numbing and avoidance symptoms into the same cluster; (4) dividing cued "symptom intensification" into cued physiological arousal and psychological distress; (5) adding avoidance of thoughts and feelings; (6) dropping guilt and nonspecific memory impairment, but adding memory impairment related to the trauma; (7) adding "sense of a foreshortened future," based primarily on research with traumatized children, and qualifying several criteria to reflect alternative symptom expression in children; and (8) adding the requirement that the syndrome cause significant distress or impairment in social or occupational functioning.

These changes in the diagnostic criteria reflect the difficulties in identifying and articulating the core symptoms of PTSD. Undoubtedly these criteria will continue to evolve, posing a moving target for developers of PTSD assessment tools. In addition, several other factors extend and blur the boundaries of PTSD, further complicating efforts to derive an explicit operational definition. First, PTSD has consistently been found to be associated with high rates of comorbid syndromes, including depression, anxiety, substance abuse, and dissociation (e.g., Kulka et al., 1990; Orsillo et al., 1996). The reasons for this comorbidity are not clear, but it has prompted some investigators to challenge the assumption that PTSD is a distinct diagnostic entity. Even those who view PTSD as a unique disorder have raised questions regarding its appropriate placement in the current psychiatric taxonomy. Davidson and Foa (1991), for example, recently reviewed clinical and laboratory findings variously supporting the classification of PTSD as an anxiety disorder, as a dissociative disorder, or as part of a new etiologically based category of stress disorders.

Second, some clinical researchers have contended that the current diagnostic criteria for PTSD do not adequately represent the full range of posttraumatic symptomatology, especially in victims of chronic interpersonal trauma such as physical and sexual abuse or spouse battering. For example, arguing for a broader conceptualization of posttraumatic sequelae, Herman (1992) has promoted the recognition of a diagnostic category that she labels "complex PTSD," which includes symptom clusters such as affective dysregulation, dissociation, and self-destructive behaviors. Third, emphasizing the impact of traumatic events on core beliefs about the self and the world, constructivist models of traumatic stress (e.g., Janoff-Bulman, 1992; McCann & Pearlman, 1990) have expanded the domain of posttraumatic problems beyond the realm of PTSD symptoms per se. All of these issues reflect the controversy and ambiguity currently surrounding the PTSD construct and speak to the practical difficulty test developers face in deriving an unambiguous definition of the disorder as the basis of a useful assessment tool.

Most structured PTSD interviews, such as the PTSD module of the SCID, are based on the DSM-III-R (and now DSM-IV) conceptualization of PTSD and follow the diagnostic criteria closely. The CAPS also follows the DSM criteria, but includes additional questions assessing social and occupational impairment and associated features such as guilt and dissociation. Among PTSD questionnaires, however, there is considerably more variability in how the construct is defined, and thus greater diversity in item content. The IES, developed prior to the availability of formal diagnostic criteria, was based on clinical observations of individuals suffering from what Horowitz et al. (1979) termed "stress response syndromes." Items were written to assess what were then viewed as the two primary symptom clusters developing in response to stressful life events, intrusions and avoidance, so the IES does not assess hyperarousal symptoms.

The Mississippi Scale, developed for use in combat veterans, was based primarily on the DSM-III diagnostic criteria for PTSD, but Keane et al. (1988) included items tapping associated features of combat-related PTSD, including depression, substance abuse, and impairment in social and occupational functioning. The Penn Inventory was based on DSM-III and DSM-III-R criteria, but also includes items assessing identity confusion, spirituality, and goal-directed behavior. The TSI, easily the most comprehensive of all current questionnaires, was designed to encompass a broad spectrum of posttraumatic symptomatology, including the core symptoms of PTSD as well as a variety of symptoms associated with complex PTSD and acute stress disorder. Finally, like the structured interviews, some PTSD questionnaires such as the PTSD Symptom Scale (PSS; Foa, Riggs, Dancu, & Rothbaum, 1993) and the PTSD Checklist (PCL; Weathers, Litz, Herman, Huska, & Keane, 1993) are based directly on the DSM diagnostic criteria.

The PTSD construct undoubtedly will continue to evolve, as a result, we hope, of accumulation of scientific evidence supporting the inclusion or exclusion of various phenomena. New measures will emerge and existing measures will require periodic revision. As advances are made, it will remain incumbent on PTSD test developers to explicate and defend precise definitions of the construct as they conceptualize it. It should be noted that clear definitions of the construct are less central in the development of empirically derived measures, such as the PK scale and the PTSD scales of the SCL-90-R, in that items on these scales are selected only for their ability to discriminate those with and without PTSD. Nonetheless, the significance of the definition of the construct is implicit in terms of how PTSD and non-PTSD groups are defined, since some PTSD measure, with its attendant definition, must be employed to determine caseness.

Designing the Instrument

After specifying the purpose and defining the construct to be measured, the next stage in developing a PTSD assessment tool is designing the new instrument. The steps involved in designing a scale vary depending on whether the scale is rationally derived or empirically derived. As noted earlier, empirically derived PTSD instruments consist of items on existing scales that statistically differentiate PTSD cases and noncases. In contrast, rationally derived instruments consist of new items based on clinical observation and theoretical conceptualizations of the construct being measured. Since it involves the creation of new items, developing rationally derived instruments is a much more elaborate process. In general, designing the instrument entails five tasks.

Determining the Length of the Scale

The first task in designing a rationally derived measure is to determine the overall length of the scale and approximately how many items will be devoted to each aspect of the construct. Also, test developers must decide whether response bias will be addressed, either by reversing some proportion of items or by including additional items specifically for that purpose. Most rationally derived PTSD scales contain fewer than 40 items and do not include items to evaluate response bias. For example, the Mississippi Scale consists of 35 items and addresses the issue of response bias only through the inclusion of reversed items (e.g., "I still enjoy doing many things I used to enjoy"). A notable exception is the TSI, a 100-item instrument yielding 10 clinical scales and 3 validity scales. For empirically derived scales, this task consists simply of determining the number of items to retain. In developing the PK scale, Keane et al. (1984) identified 49 MMPI items that differentiated veterans with and without PTSD at $p < .001$, and retained these items on the final scale. This task can be more difficult, however. In developing the WZ-PTSD scale of the SCL-90-R, Weathers et al. (1996) found significant differences between PTSD and non-PTSD groups on nearly every item on the SCL-90-R. In order to reduce the number of items on the final scale, they decided to employ a more stringent statistical criterion, retaining 25 items that offered the greatest discrimination between the groups.

Selecting an Item Format

The second task is to select an item format. For rationally derived questionnaires, this involves designing both the item-stem and response-option formats. Most PTSD questionnaires employ a Likert-type format, with items consisting of brief statements assessing PTSD symptoms and a response continuum (typically a 5-point scale) indicating level of endorsement or agreement, frequency or severity of symptoms, or degree of subjective distress. Most questionnaires employ a single response option format for all items. The IES, for example, assesses symptom frequency on a 4-point scale ranging from "not at all" to "often." Similarly, the PCL assesses subjective distress on a 5-point scale ranging from "not at all" to "extremely." In contrast, the Mississippi Scale contains items assessing symptom frequency ("If something happens that reminds me of the military, I become very distressed and upset," with five response options ranging from "never" to "very frequently"), as well as items assessing symptom endorsement ("No one understands how I feel, not even my family," with response options ranging from "not at all true" to "extremely true"). A notable exception to the Likert-type format is the Penn Inventory, which is modeled after the Beck Depression Inventory (BDI; Beck, Ward, Mendelson, Mock, & Erbaugh, 1961) and consists of items comprising four graded statements reflecting increasing levels of psychopathology.

For PTSD interviews, the typical item format consists of one or more standard prompt questions and a rating scale to evaluate symptom severity. The SCID-PTSD module, for example, consists of single prompt questions for each symptom and a three severity rating options, "absent," "subthreshold," and "present," although these ratings are typically treated as dichotomous (present–absent) judgments. Several recently developed interviews, including the PTSD Interview (PTSD-I; Watson, Juba, Manifold, Kucala, & Anderson, 1991) and the Structured Interview for PTSD (SI-PTSD; Davidson, Smith, & Kudler, 1989), provide a broader continuum of rating options and yield both continuous and dichotomous scores, both for individual items and for the disorder. Employing the most elaborate item format of any PTSD interview, the CAPS assesses the frequency and intensity of symptoms separately by means of initial and follow-up prompt questions and behaviorally anchored 5-point rating scales.

Developing an Item Pool

For rationally derived PTSD scales, the next task is to create items to assess the various aspects of the construct. This task requires considerable expertise in the clinical phenomenology of the disorder and is usually based on clinical observation and descriptions of trauma-related symptoms in the literature. For questionnaires, test developers typically create many more items than they plan to incorporate into the final form of the instrument, eliminating items through pilot testing and review. Apart from their correspondence with key aspects of the construct, what are some of the desirable characteristics of items on questionnaire measures of psychopathology? Holden and Fekken (1990) recently addressed this question in an intriguing investigation. Drawing on extensive analysis of items on the Basic Personality Inventory (BPI; Jackson, 1976) they suggested that good items (1) are free from negatives and absolutes, (2) can be answered quickly, (3) include undisguised contents and inquire about pathological or unusual content when appropriate, (4) emphasize general behavior tendencies, and (5) contain comparisons to other people or include statements by other people.

Reviewing and Revising Items

Once the initial item pool is created, items should be reviewed by experts in PTSD. Items should be evaluated in terms of their match to the symptoms being assessed, and in terms of readability, degree of ambiguity, and redundancy with other items. Feedback from the review process serves as the basis for revising or eliminating items from the pool. For example, in developing the Mississippi Scale, Keane et al. (1988) began with a pool of 200 items, which they eventually reduced to the 35 items on the final scale through a process of expert review. Similarly, in developing the TSI, Briere (1995) began with a pool 182 items, reducing it to the 100 items on the final scale through a combination of expert review and preliminary item analyses on a sample of respondents.

Specifying the Protocol

The final task in designing a PTSD assessment tool is to specify the protocol for administering and scoring the instrument. The protocol should include instructions for the clinician, specifying the target populations, standard testing conditions, procedures for administration, explicit scoring rules, and guidelines for interpreting scores. It should also include instructions to respondents, explaining the format and describing or illustrating appropriate responses. For questionnaires, the protocol is typically straightforward, with administration involving only a few brief instructions to respondents, and scoring consisting of simply summing the items to obtain a total score. For interviews the protocol can be more elaborate and less structured. For example, interviewers may need to clarify prompt questions ad lib, or they may need to determine whether to skip out of a section, or to inquire about lifetime symptom status. Scoring interviews may also be more complicated, particularly if an interview yields both continuous and dichotomous diagnostic scores.

Pilot Testing and Revising the Instrument

After the initial item pool has been created and reviewed, and the protocol has been specified, the instrument should be pilot tested on a sample of respondents from the target population. The purpose of such pilot testing is to conduct preliminary statistical analyses of individual items, and to obtain additional qualitative feedback about item content. The techniques for this process are described here. This information is then used to further revise items or to eliminate additional items as the scale nears its final form.

Once the final form has been reached, test developers set about exploring its reliability and validity.

ESTABLISHING RELIABILITY AND VALIDITY

Reliability

In general, reliability refers to the consistency of test scores over repeated measurements. If a test is reliable, it means that respondents achieve the same or nearly the same score each time they are evaluated. However, all psychological assessment procedures are unreliable to some extent, meaning they entail some degree of measurement error, so observed scores for a group of respondents are never exactly reproducible upon retesting. The classical test theory approach to reliability (Crocker & Algina, 1986; Gulliksen, 1950; Lord & Novick, 1968) is based on a simple formula depicting this point:

$$X = T + E$$

From this perspective, an observed test score (X) is viewed as the sum of two components, a respondent's true score (T), and an error component (E). True scores have been variously defined and interpreted but, in general, reflect a respondent's actual standing on the attribute being measured. Measurement errors may be either systematic or random. Systematic errors, such as a tendency to use the extreme ends of a rating scale to exaggerate or minimize symptom severity, are relatively constant across repeated measurements. Although they reflect inaccuracies, systematic errors do not contribute to inconsistency in observed scores and thus do not reduce reliability. In contrast, random errors fluctuate across repeated measurements and thus play an important role in the reliability of an assessment instrument. Random errors can arise from a number of sources, including lapses in concentration, fluctuations in mood, carelessness, adoption of a random response set, variability in interpretation of ambiguously worded items, or variability in responses due to characteristics of the examiner (e.g., age, gender, ethnicity).

Classical test theory makes three key assumptions about random errors. Across a large number of observations, random errors are assumed to have a mean of zero ($M_E = 0$), to be uncorrelated with true scores ($r_{TE} = 0$), and to be uncorrelated with errors on other testing occasions ($r_{E1E2} = 0$). It can then be shown that

$$s^2_X = s^2_T + s^2_E$$

This formula indicates that observed score variance consists of true score variance and error variance. For reliable tests, error variance is minimal, and thus most of the variability in observed scores is attributable to genuine differences among respondents.

Classical test theory defines the "reliability coefficient" as the correlation between observed scores on parallel tests. Two tests are considered parallel if they yield the same true scores and have equal error variances. Drawing on these definitions and the assumptions about random errors, it can be shown that

$$r_{X1X2} = s^2_T / s^2_X$$

That is, the "reliability coefficient," defined as the correlation between two parallel tests, is equivalent to the ratio of true score variance to observed score variance. Thus, the correlation coefficient can range from 0 (if observed scores are completely random and consist only of error variance) to 1 (if observed scores are completely free from measurement error and consist only of true score variance).

Several procedures have been developed for obtaining estimates of reliability (Crocker & Algina, 1986). Some procedures involve administering two tests. The alternate forms method requires constructing two comparable forms of a test and administering both within a very short time span. The reliability coefficient obtained by correlating scores on the two forms is called the "coefficient of equivalence." The test–retest method involves administering the same instrument twice, with some reasonable time period between administrations, and the resulting reliability coefficient is called the "coefficient of stability," or simply the "test–retest reliability coefficient."

Other procedures permit reliability estimates from a single test administration. The split-half method involves dividing the items on an instrument in half, correlating the scores from the two half-tests, then using the Spearman–Brown formula to calculate the projected reliability for the whole test. The general form of the Spearman–Brown formula, which can be used to estimate reliability following any change in the length of a test, is

$$r_{SB} = k r_{XX} / [1 + (k - 1) r_{XX}]$$

where r_{SB} is the reliability of the altered test, r_{XX} is the reliability of the original test, and k is a factor indicating how much longer ($k > 1$) or shorter ($k < 1$) the new test will be. So, if the correlation between the two halves of a test were .60, the projected reliability coefficient for the full test would be $2(.60)/[1 + (.60)] = .75$. The main problem with the split-half approach is that there are many ways to divide the test items in half, and each division could yield a different reliability coefficient. For that reason, test developers rely on measures of internal consistency instead, most commonly Cronbach's alpha (Cronbach, 1951). Coefficient alpha reflects item homogeneity, or the degree to which items are intercorrelated, and can be interpreted as the mean of all possible split-half reliability coefficients.

Another useful index of measurement error is the standard error of measurement, which can be used to construct confidence intervals around observed scores for individual respondents. The formula for the standard error of measurement is

$$s_E = s_X \sqrt{1 - r_{XX}}$$

where s_X is the standard deviation of observed scores, and r_{XX} is the reliability coefficient. The general form of the 95% confidence interval (CI) for an observed score is $X \pm 1.96\, s_E$. So, for example, if a respondent obtained a score of 50 on a test with $s_X = 10$ and $r_{XX} = .84$, then $s_E = 4$ and the 95% CI would be (with rounding) 50 ± 8. Thus, there is a 95% probability that the interval from 42–58 contains the respondent's true score.

It is important that all reliability coefficients be reported and interpreted with reference to the specific procedures used to estimate them, since each procedure takes into account different sources of error. The test–retest method takes into account variability due to changes in respondents and changes in the testing conditions, but not variability due to items. In contrast, internal consistency and split-half methods primarily take into account variability due to item content. The alternate forms method also takes into account variability due to items, but if the interval between administrations of the two forms is sufficiently long, it may also be affected by the same sources of variability as the test–retest method. Generalizability theory (to be described) makes these design considerations explicit and provides a much more flexible framework for conceptualizing and evaluating potential sources of measurement error.

The measures of reliability described thus far are appropriate for assessment measures that yield continuous scores. Different techniques for estimating reliability are needed when the scores of interest are dichotomous, such as present–absent diagnostic decisions. One approach is to calculate the percentage of agreement between two raters by counting the number of times both agree that the diagnosis is either present or absent and dividing by the total number of respondents. The problem with this approach is that it fails to take into account the fact that a certain amount of agreement would be expected by chance. The kappa statistic (Cohen, 1960) was developed to overcome this limitation. The formula for kappa is

$$\kappa = (P_o - P_c) / (1 - P_c)$$

where P_o is the proportion of observed agreement, and P_c is the proportion of agreement due to chance. As this formula indicates, kappa provides an index of chance-corrected agreement. A kappa of 0 does not mean that there is no agreement, only that the agreement does not exceed the level expected by chance. A kappa of 1 indicates perfect agreement. There is some disagreement among investigators as to how large a kappa is needed to reflect a satisfactory level of reliability. Fleiss (1981) addressed this issue, describing kappas from .40 to .60 as fair, kappas from .60 to .75 as good, and kappas above .75 as excellent.

In the evaluation of PTSD measures, the two most commonly reported forms of reliability are test–retest reliability and coefficient alpha. A crucial consideration in estimating test–retest reliability is the duration of the interval between administrations of an instrument. The interval must be long enough to reduce memory and practice effects, but brief enough so that scores are not greatly affected by genuine changes in PTSD symptom severity. In most instances, investigators have selected intervals ranging from a few days to a week. Another commonly employed strategy, useful for identifying poor items on a scale, is to examine the correlations of individual items with the total score, and to examine the changes in alpha that result from removing one item at a time.

In the original report on the Mississippi Scale, for example, Keane et al. (1988) found a test–retest reliability of .97 at a 1-week interval and an alpha of .94. Examining individual items, they found that item-total correlations ranged from .23 to .73 with a mean of .58. Similarly, for the Penn Inventory, Hammarberg (1992) found a test–retest reliability of .96 at approximately a 5-day interval, an alpha of .94, and item-total correlations ranging from .43 to .90, with a mean of .75. Excellent reliability has also been found for PTSD interviews. For example, Weathers et al. (1992) administered the CAPS twice with independent clinicians at a 2- to 3-day interval. Test–retest reliability for CAPS total severity scores ranged from .90 to .98 across three different rater pairs, and alphas ranged from .85 to .87 for the three PTSD symptom clusters, with an alpha of .94 for all 17 symptoms. Using the CAPS as a diagnostic instrument, they found a kappa of .89 for the optimal diagnostic scoring rule.

Similar findings have been reported for many other PTSD measures, indicating that it is possible to reliably assess PTSD symptom severity and diagnostic status. One unfortunate aspect of the growing literature on the reliability of PTSD assessment tools is that investigators almost never report standard errors of measurement. This is a regrettable lapse, since these would provide a useful tool for interpreting individual scores, particularly when cutoff scores are employed for diagnostic decision making. If a respondent scores just above or just below a suggested cutoff, it would be helpful to employ a confidence interval in determining caseness. Finally, although reliability is important, validity is of even greater concern. The next section describes various methods for evaluating different types of validity and illustrates their application to various PTSD instruments.

Validity

"Validity" is a general term referring to the scope and quality of evidence supporting the inferences, interpretations, classifications, decisions, or predictions made on the basis of test scores. According to the *Standards for Educational and Psychological Testing* (1985):

> Validity is the most important consideration in test evaluation. The concept refers to the appropriateness, meaningfulness, and usefulness of the specific inferences made from test scores. Test validation is the process of accumulating evidence to support such inferences. A variety of inferences may be made from scores produced by a given test, and there are many ways of accumulating evidence to support any particular inference. Validity, however, is a unitary concept. Although evidence may be accumulated in many ways, validity always refers to the degree to which that evidence supports the inferences that are made from the scores. The inferences regarding specific uses of a test are validated, not the test itself. (p. 9)

Three different types of validity are usually considered: content validity, criterion-related validity, and construct validity.

Content Validity

"Content validity" refers to the extent to which items or stimuli on a psychological assessment instrument measure key aspects of the construct being evaluated. As discussed earlier, consideration of item content is primarily relevant for rationally derived instruments and is less of a consideration for empirically derived instruments. Haynes et al. (1995) recently presented a detailed conceptual analysis of content validity and provided an exhaustive set of practical guidelines for establishing content validity for a wide variety of assessment instruments and tasks. They describe more fully many of the procedures outlined earlier in the chapter in the sections on specifying the purpose of the instrument, defining the construct, and designing the instrument. Identifying more than a dozen potentially relevant steps in the content validation process, they emphasize the iterative, sequential nature of developing a quality assessment tool. Furthermore, they highlight the indispensable role of expert judgment in generating and revising items, and in determining the extent to which the item pool provides sufficient coverage for all important facets of the construct to be measured.

Criterion-Related Validity

"Criterion-related validity" refers to the ability of a measure to accurately predict some outcome variable of interest. When the predictor and the criterion are assessed simultaneously, this is referred to as "concurrent validity," and when the criterion is assessed at some point in the future, this is referred to as "predictive validity." In research on PTSD assessment tools, the most common application of criterion-related validity is in the evaluation of diagnostic utility, or the ability of a measure to predict diagnostic status. A central concern in establishing criterion-related validity is the question of how best to define the criterion. Although other procedures for establishing caseness have been proposed (e.g., Kulka et al., 1990; Spitzer, 1983), the criterion or so-called "gold standard" most often employed in PTSD research is a diagnosis based on a structured clinical interview.

A typical investigation of the diagnostic utility of a PTSD questionnaire, for example, involves (1) administering the questionnaire and a structured diagnostic interview to a sample of respondents, (2) diagnosing each respondent as PTSD or non-PTSD on the basis of the interview, (3) selecting a cutoff score on the questionnaire and dichotomizing the sample into test positives (scoring at or above the cutoff) or test negatives (scoring below the cutoff) on the basis of the structured interview, and (4) constructing a 2 × 2 table to compare the questionnaire to the diagnosis. As shown in Figure 4.1, four outcomes are possible in this procedure, two involving agreement between the test and the diagnosis, and two involving disagreement or classification errors. In terms of agreement, respondents with a positive diagnosis and a positive test are called "true positives," and those with a negative diagnosis and a negative test are called "true negatives." In terms of disagreement or errors, respondents with a negative diagnosis but a positive test are called "false positives," and those with a positive diagnosis but a negative test are called "false negatives."

Figure 4.1 also provides definitions of various indices of diagnostic utility, including (1) sensitivity (the probability of a positive test, given a posi-

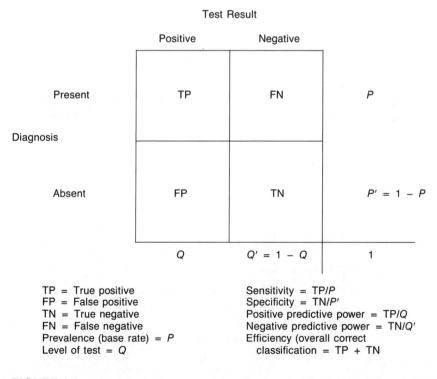

FIGURE 4.1. Definition of key terms in evaluating the diagnostic utility of a PTSD instrument. Based on Kessel and Zimmerman (1993) and Kraemer (1992).

tive diagnosis); (2) specificity (the probability of a negative test, given a negative diagnosis); (3) positive predictive power (the probability of a positive diagnosis, given a positive test); (4) negative predictive power (the probability of a negative diagnosis, given a negative test); and (5) efficiency or overall correct classification (the probability that the test and the diagnosis agree). The diagnostic utility for all possible cutoff scores on a questionnaire can be evaluated by constructing separate 2 × 2 tables and calculating these various probabilities.

Across the range of possible cutoff scores, there is a trade-off between sensitivity and specificity, with lenient scores having higher sensitivity but lower specificity, and stringent scores having lower sensitivity but higher specificity. This relationship can be depicted by plotting sensitivity against specificity for each possible cutoff score, which results in a Receiver Operating Characteristic (ROC) curve (see Kraemer, 1992). Figure 4.2 compares the ROC curves for three PTSD instruments. The ROC curve for the Mississippi Scale extends nearest the ideal test point in the upper-right corner, indicating that across a range of cutoffs, it is the best predictor of a PTSD diagnosis.

Although measures of test performance such as sensitivity, specificity, and efficiency, depict the relationship between test and diagnosis, Kraemer

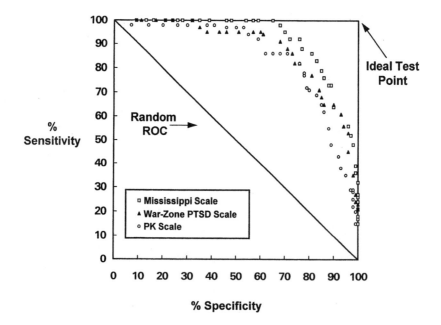

FIGURE 4.2. Receiver Operating Characteristic (ROC) curves for the Mississippi Scale, PK scale, and WZ-PTSD scale. From Weathers et al. (1996). Copyright 1996 by Plenum Press. Reprinted by permission.

(1992) has shown that they are ambiguous indicators of diagnostic utility, because they are uncalibrated and do not take into account chance agreement between test and diagnosis. She proposed the use of weighted kappa coefficients as indicators of the quality of sensitivity [$\varkappa(1)$], specificity [$\varkappa(0)$], and efficiency [$\varkappa(.5)$]. The measures of test quality are calibrated such that a value of 0 represents chance agreement, and a value of 1 represents perfect agreement.

Plotting the quality of sensitivity against the quality of specificity results in the Quality Receiver Operating Characteristic (QROC) curve, which permits ready identification of the optimally sensitive, specific, and efficient cutoffs. Figure 4.3 compares the QROC curves for the same three PTSD instruments shown in Figure 4.2. The QROC curves are a one-to-one remapping of the ROC curves that permits straightforward identification of the optimally sensitive, specific, and efficient cutoffs. These various cutoff scores are useful for different assessment tasks. Optimally sensitive cutoffs are useful for screening, optimally specific cutoffs are useful for making definitive diagnoses, and optimally efficient cutoffs, which are the cutoffs most often reported in the literature, are useful for differential diagnosis. Figure 4.3 shows that the Mississippi Scale outperforms the other instruments with respect to the quality of sensitivity, specificity, and efficiency.

Construct Validity

Construct validity is the most encompassing category of validity, and it can be argued that all types of validity evidence are relevant for construct validity (Cronbach & Meehl, 1955; *Standards for Educational and Psychological Testing,* 1985). "Construct validity" refers to the extent to which a pattern of evidence exists supporting the interpretation of a test as a measure of some underlying attribute. The accumulation of relevant evidence must be guided by an explicit theory in which the construct to be measured is defined and its hypothesized relationships with other constructs are made explicit.

Test developers may draw on a number of different sources of evidence in the construct validation of an assessment instrument. An important source of evidence is the pattern of correlations between the instrument and measures of other constructs. Ideally, the instrument should correlate strongly with other measures of the same construct (convergent validity) and should correlate weakly with measures of other constructs (discriminant validity). Campbell and Fiske (1959) provided an elegant framework for evaluating convergent and discriminant validity, which they referred to as the multitrait–mulitmethod matrix. In this approach, each of several distinct constructs is measured by each of several methods, and the resulting correlation matrix is examined to determine if correlations between different measures of the same construct exceed those between measures of different constructs. For example, in an effort to evaluate the construct validity of the CAPS, Weathers et al. (1992) assessed each of four constructs (PTSD, depression, anxiety, and

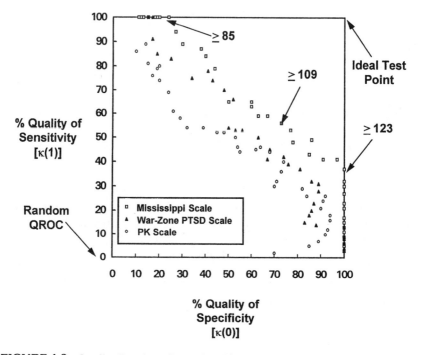

FIGURE 4.3. Quality Receiver Operating Characteristic (QROC) curves for the Mississippi Scale, PK scale, and WZ-PTSD scale. From Weathers et al. (1996). Copyright 1996 by Plenum Press. Reprinted by permission.

antisocial personality disorder) using three different methods (structured interview, dedicated questionnaire, and MMPI scale). They found that the resulting pattern of correlations generally conformed to predictions. The CAPS correlated strongly with other measures of PTSD, correlated moderately with measures of depression and anxiety, and correlated weakly with measures of antisocial personality.

Other sources of evidence for construct validity include (1) evidence for content validity, especially expert judgment regarding the appropriateness of items for the construct being measured; (2) the internal consistency of items, which may be taken as evidence that the instrument is measuring a single construct; (3) factor analysis, which may reveal theoretically meaningful dimensions underlying test scores (to be discussed); (4) differences in test scores among groups hypothesized to vary in the underlying construct; and (5) changes in test scores as a result of treatment or some other intervention hypothesized to directly influence respondents' standing on the construct.

CONTEMPORARY APPROACHES

Generalizability Theory

Generalizability theory (G theory) was developed by Cronbach and his colleagues (Cronbach, Gleser, Nanda, & Rajaratnam, 1972; see also Brennan, 1983; Shavelson & Webb, 1991) in order to address the ambiguities and limitations of the classical-test-theory approach to reliability. Like classical test theory, G theory is concerned with the replicability of scores across repeated measurements, but G theory replaces the classical-test-theory concept of a true score with the concept of a universe score. As Cronbach et al. (1972) explain:

> A behavioral measurement is a sample from the collection of measurements that might have been made, and interest attaches to the obtained score only because it is representative of the whole collection or *universe*. If the decision maker could, he would measure the person exhaustively and take the average over all the measurements. Educators and psychologists have traditionally referred to the average reached via exhaustive measurement as "the true score" for the person. We speak instead of a *universe score*. This emphasizes that the investigator is making an inference from a sample of observed data, and also that there is more than one universe to which he might generalize. . . . "The universe score is estimated to be 75" is without meaning until we answer the question, "Which universe?" This ambiguity is concealed in the statement "The estimated true score is 75," for no one thinks to inquire, "Which truth?" (pp. 18–19)

Thus, from a G-theory perspective, investigators must explicitly describe what Cronbach et al. refer to as the universe of admissible observations, or the entire set of observations that they would be willing to accept as interchangeable for a given assessment task. They can then determine the extent to which respondents' scores from a single observation generalize to their universe scores.

G theory is based on an analysis of variance (ANOVA) framework. Different conditions or facets of measurement, which represent potential sources of error, are employed as factors in an experimental design, and the proportion of variance attributable to each facet is estimated through the techniques of ANOVA. In classical test theory, only one facet at a time can be considered. Test–retest reliability, for example, is concerned primarily with the facet of occasions. Similarly, internal consistency is concerned primarily with the facet of items. A significant advantage of G theory is that multiple facets of observation can be represented in the same design, and there are few restrictions on the type of facets that can be examined. This permits much more elaborate experimental designs and allows for the estimation of variance due to the interaction of two or more facets.

G theory distinguishes between G studies and D studies. In G (generalizability) studies, multiple facets are included in an experimental design in order to identify as many significant sources of variability in test scores as possible. Data from a comprehensive G study can then be put to use in designing a D (decision) study, in which some decision or conclusion about respondents will be reached on the basis of test scores. Although the emphasis in G theory is on the estimation of variance components attributable to respondents or to one or more facets of observation, G coefficients, analogous to reliability coefficients in classical test theory, can be calculated for a variety of different D studies.

G theory also distinguishes between relative and absolute decisions, and different G coefficients are calculated for each type of decision. "Relative decisions" refer to situations in which test scores are used to indicate a respondent's relative standing in a distribution, such as when the correlation between two different measures is explored. "Absolute decisions" refer to situations in which test scores are used to indicate a respondent's status with respect to a fixed standard, such as on a driver's license examination. In contrast, classical test theory reliability coefficients only apply to relative decisions.

To date, investigators have not applied G theory in developing PTSD assessment tools. This is unfortunate, given the power and flexibility of this approach. In the following example we illustrate the application of G theory to the development of a physiological assessment protocol measuring physiological and psychological reactivity to slides and sounds depicting combat scenes. The data for this example are fictitious, but are based on data taken from the physiological protocol in use at our PTSD clinic. Table 4.1 presents the results of a two-facet G study. In this design, 20 respondents observed six slides on each of two occasions. As shown in Table 4.1, nearly half of the variance in observed scores was universe score variance (i.e., variance attributable to persons). Variance attributable to occasions and slides was negligible, as was variance attributable to the persons-by-occasions and occasions-by-slides interactions. However, the persons-by-slides interaction

TABLE 4.1. Estimated Variance Components for Psychophysiological Protocol Data

Source of variation	df	Mean squares	Estimated variance component	% Total variance
Persons (p)	19	80.29	5.8941	47
Occasions (o)	1	40.92	0.2582	2
Slides (s)	5	17.37	0.1303	1
po	19	5.42	0.3183	3
ps	95	7.66	2.0697	17
os	5	8.02	0.2253	2
pos, e	95	3.52	3.5156	28

accounted for 17% of the variance, suggesting that individual respondents reacted differently to different slides. A relatively large residual variance component (28%) was also found, suggesting the presence of a significant amount of unmeasured or random error in the observed scores.

Table 4.2 presents the projection of the G-study data in Table 4.1 to four possible D-study designs, based on calculations analogous to the Spearman–Brown formula. The first column simply repeats the variance components from the G study. The last two rows in the first column provide the relative and absolute G coefficients (.50 and .47) for generalizing from a single slide on a single occasion. The next four columns show the impact of increasing number of slides from one to four or eight and increasing the number of occasions from one to two. For example, the second column presents the projected generalizability for a D study in which respondents watch four slides on one occasion. A substantial increase in generalizability is observed for this design, up to .77 for relative decisions and .74 for absolute decision.

Confirmatory Factor Analysis

Underlying the psychometric work on PTSD is the idea that PTSD is a hypothetical construct that is reflected in observed behaviors, including responses to assessment devices. One way of representing this notion is by means of factor analysis, a multivariate statistical procedure that can be used to identify the constructs or latent variables that appear to account for observed responses. The responses may be from a collection of items on a test or a collection of scores in a battery of tests. Viewing factor analysis from this perspective, one can think of the observed scores as being regressed on

TABLE 4.2. Alternative Decision Studies for Psychophysiological Protocol

Source of variation	G study $N_o = 1$ $N_s = 1$	Alternative D studies $N_o = 1$ $N_s = 4$	$N_o = 1$ $N_s = 8$	$N_o = 2$ $N_s = 4$	$N_o = 2$ $N_s = 8$
Persons (p)	5.8941	5.8941	5.8941	5.8941	5.8941
Occasions (o)	0.2582	0.2582	0.2582	0.1291	0.1291
Slides (s)	0.1303	0.0326	0.0163	0.0326	0.0163
po	0.3183	0.3183	0.3183	0.1591	0.1591
ps	2.0697	0.5174	0.2587	0.5174	0.2587
os	0.2253	0.0563	0.0282	0.0282	0.0141
pos, e	3.5156	0.8789	0.4394	0.4394	0.2197
Error variances					
Relative	5.9035	1.7146	1.0164	1.1160	0.6376
Absolute	6.5174	2.0617	1.3191	1.3059	0.7971
Generalizability coefficients					
Relative	.50	.77	.85	.84	.90
Absolute	.47	.74	.82	.82	.88

factors in a series of multiple regression equations, one for each of the items (or tests). Each equation takes this general form:

$$Y_{ji} = b_{Y1}F_{j1} + b_{Y2}F_{j2} + \ldots + b_{Ym}F_{jm} + e_{ji}$$

Here, let us consider each dependent variable (Y_{ji}) to be a score for person j on item i; the independent variables ($F_{j1}, F_{j2}, \ldots, F_{jm}$) are factor scores for person j; the regression weights ($b_{Y1}, b_{Y2}, \ldots, b_{Ym}$) are what are called the "factor loadings"; and e_{ji} symbolizes a residual uniqueness or error in prediction.

If, for example, there are 35 items (as on the Mississippi Scale), there will be 35 such equations, and each item score for an individual is a weighted sum of that person's standing on the factors, plus residual. As in any multiple regression procedure, the direction of influence is from the independent variables to the dependent variable. Thus, factor analysis highlights the idea that the factors or hypothetical constructs are responsible for the observed scores on the items. A large value for b would indicate that the latent variable has an important influence on an observed item score; conversely, a small value for this regression weight or factor loading would indicate that the latent variable does not seem to account for the observed score. In computing a factor-analytic solution for an observed data set, one is interested in the matrix of values for the factor loadings (the weights for the regressions of all items on the factors), a matrix depicting how the factors relate to one another, and possibly a matrix of residuals. Details on the computations of elements in these matrices may be found in many sources, including Harman (1976), Gorsuch (1983), and Loehlin (1992).

Historically, the more common factor-analytic strategy has been the unrestricted or exploratory approach. Using this approach, the factor analyst allows the data to determine the solution; that is, the data determine the values of the loadings of each item on each factor, frequently the number of factors, and under certain circumstances the extent to which factors intercorrelate with one another. The goal is to empirically discover the hypothetical constructs that are responsible for the observed pattern of relationships among the items. Sizes of loadings on the various resulting factors are examined; the content of items that load highest on each factor is evaluated; and the usual criterion for the adequacy of the exploratory solution is its interpretability vis-à-vis some a priori or post hoc conceptualization of the constructs.

Recently, emphasis has been given to what is called restricted or confirmatory factor analysis, in which features of the factor solution are hypothesized or specified beforehand. Based on a theoretical or conceptual framework, the factor analyst specifies the number of factors proposed to be responsible for the relationships within the data set. Furthermore, items are designated to load on particular factors; typically, each item is specified to load on only one factor to facilitate interpretation of the solution (Anderson & Gerbing, 1988). Factors may or may not be allowed to correlate, depending upon the theory guiding the understanding of the constructs. The factor analyst also has control over how the residuals are to be treated; in most circumstances, they should not be permitted to covary. The adequacy of the hypothesized factor solution is evaluated by comparing a matrix of relationships among observed item scores, usually a variance–covariance matrix, with one that is derived using the hypothesized factor solution. Descriptions of the algorithms for estimating parameters for the hypothesized solution and for computing the reproduced matrix can be found in works by Joreskog and Sorbom (1979), Bollen (1989), and Loehlin (1992).

An important aspect of any hypothesized factor solution is that there be fewer parameter estimates (factor loadings, factor variances and covariances, and residuals) in the hypothesized solution than there are variances and covariances among the observed variables. When items are specified to load on only one factor, they are obviously specified not to load on the other factors, suggesting a series of potentially disconfirmable propositions about the underlying structure of the data. As Mulaik and James (1995) pointed out, the larger the difference between the number of parameter estimates and the number of variances and covariances among the observed variables (i.e., the more degrees of freedom), the greater the potential for disconfirming a model. "Good models" are those with a strong potential to be disconfirmed (many degrees of freedom) but for which the accompanying data do not support disconfirmation.

In the end, a discrepancy index serves as a basis of evaluation of a hypothesized solution. This index is a weighted sum of squared deviations of the reproduced associations from the observed associations. Ideally, the discrepancy value should be a minimum, as this outcome would indicate "close fit" or that the hypothesized constructs are likely responsible for the observed scores. Large discrepancy values suggest the possibility of an alternative representation of the factor structure. When the observed scores are continuous and multivariate normally distributed, and when either maximum likelihood or generalized least-squares estimation is used, the distribution of the discrepancy statistic takes on a known form, that of noncentral chi-square, with degrees of freedom equal to the difference between the number of parameter estimates in the hypothesized factor-analytic model and the number of variances and covariances among the observed variables. Low values of chi-square, relative to the degrees of freedom, suggest endorsement of the hypothesized factor structure. Discussion of the nature of the noncentral chi-square and its implications for evaluation of model–data fit is provided by Browne and Cudeck (1993).

Due to certain problems with the chi-square statistic as an indicator of model–data fit (Bentler & Bonett, 1980), many other fit indices have been developed in recent years. For overviews of the various indices, see Chapter 4 of Joreskog and Sorbom's (1993) SIMPLIS guide and the review by Hu and Bentler (1995).

A psychometric study by King and King (1994) illustrates the application of confirmatory factor analysis to PTSD assessment. The data were responses to the 35-item Mississippi Scale from 2,272 Vietnam theater and era veterans who participated in the NVVRS (Kulka et al., 1990). Consistent with Bagozzi and Heatherton's (1994) total disaggregation conceptualization of a multifaceted construct, PTSD was proposed as a second-order umbrella factor that subsumed four symptom categories or first-order factors, namely Reexperiencing and Situational Avoidance, Withdrawal and Numbing, Arousal and Lack of Control, and Guilt and Suicidality. Each of these first-order factors, in turn, was postulated to account for the responses to Mississippi Scale items, with content judged to reflect that symptom category. Residuals were specified to be uncorrelated. The hypothesized structure is depicted in Figure 4.4, where arrows indicate direction of influence. Because the data were considered ordinal and judged not multivariate normally distributed, a matrix of polychoric correlations was analyzed using weighted least-squares estimation (Browne, 1984).

To appraise the viability of the hypothesized structure, King and King (1994) employed sequential chi-square difference testing of hierarchically nested factor models. This process involves the systematic inspection of outcomes when several reasonable and increasingly restrictive models are fit to the data and compared with one another. One of the models is the hypothesized structure. Initially, they fit a four-factor first-order solution, each factor coinciding with a symptom category and allowing all four factors to covary (see Figure 4.5). This model is a multidimensional representation of PTSD in that it lacks the global organizing PTSD second-order factor that is ap-

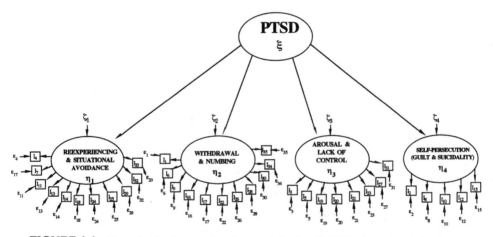

FIGURE 4.4. Hypothesized second-order model using LISREL (Joreskog & Sorbom, 1993) notation. I_j = Mississippi Scale item number. Reproduced by special permission of the Publisher, Psychological Assessment Resources, Inc., Odessa, FL 33556, from *Assessment*, Vol. 1, No. 3. Copyright 1994 by PAR, Inc. Further reproduction is prohibited without permission from PAR, Inc.

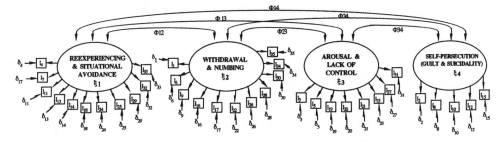

FIGURE 4.5. Four-factor first-order model, using LISREL (Joreskog & Sorbom, 1993) notation. I_j = Mississippi Scale item number. Reproduced by special permission of the Publisher, Psychological Assessment Resources, Inc., Odessa, FL 33556, from *Assessment*, Vol. 1, No. 3. Copyright 1994 by PAR, Inc. Further reproduction is prohibited without permission from PAR, Inc.

parent in the hypothesized model. Next, they fit the hypothesized second-order model (Figure 4.4). Finally, they fit a single-factor first-order solution, with all items loading on a unitary PTSD factor (see Figure 4.6).

Table 4.3 summarizes the confirmatory factor-analytic findings. Of particular interest are the values associated with the chi-square difference tests (labeled Dc^2). In a series of hierarchically nested models, the difference in two chi-square statistics is distributed as chi-square with the degrees of freedom equal to the difference in the degrees of freedom associated with each model (Steiger, Shapiro, & Browne, 1985). Therefore, the tests of the significance of the difference between chi-squares (again, the columns under Dc^2) provide a mechanism for judging the competing models and assessing

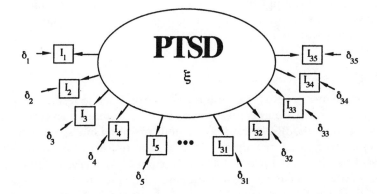

FIGURE 4.6. Single-factor first-order model, using LISREL (Joreskog & Sorbom, 1993) notation. I_j = Mississippi Scale item number. Reproduced by special permission of the Publisher, Psychological Assessment Resources, Inc., Odessa, FL 33556, from *Assessment*, Vol. 1, No. 3. Copyright 1994 by PAR, Inc. Further reproduction is prohibited without permission from PAR, Inc.

TABLE 4.3. Chi-Square Difference Tests of Competing Models of Mississippi Scale Structure

Model	c^2	df	Dc^2	df	p
Four-factor first-order	1,023.27	554			
Single-factor second-order	1,024.35	556	1.08	2	.58
Single-factor first-order	1,051.41	560	28.14	4	< .001

Note. Findings are from King and King (1994).

whether the hypothesized model is most appropriate, given the data. As shown in Table 4.3, the first two models, the four-factor first-order solution and the single-factor second-order solution, were comparable in fit ($p = .58$). But the single-factor first-order solution differed from the other two (for both, $p < .001$). Hence, the hypothesized single-factor second-order solution is superior to the four-factor first-order solution because it achieves like fit with two fewer parameters being estimated. Moreover, the hypothesized structure appears superior to the single-factor first-order solution because the reduction in the number of parameter estimates in the latter model (four) produces unacceptable damage to fit. This is indicated by the large chi-square difference relative to the associated degrees of freedom.

In summary, confirmatory factor analysis enhances theory testing and development by allowing the researcher to statistically evaluate the soundness of a hypothesized factor structure. In addition, the parameter estimates that result are efficient, meaning that their standard errors are as small as they can be and therefore are presumably better approximations of the true parameter values. Also, the available statistical software packages furnish a wealth of detailed information regarding how models might be improved. Morris, Bergan, and Fulginiti (1991) offer interesting commentary on the use of confirmatory factor analysis versus exploratory factor analysis in clinical assessment research.

Item Response Theory

Item response theory (IRT) is a contemporary approach to test development and evaluation that has tended to supplant classical test theory in recent years. Like factor analysis, IRT presupposes that an individual's standing on a hypothetical construct or latent variable can predict how that person responds to an item on a psychometric instrument. Whereas the mathematical foundation for factor analysis is linear regression, the form of the relationship in IRT is that of a curvilinear probability function, portraying what is called an "item characteristic curve." In its early stage of development, the mathematical expression was the cumulative normal ogive, an S-shaped curve framed by an X axis representing scores or standing on the hypothetical construct or attribute of interest, and a Y axis representing the probability of responding to a binary or dichotomous ("correct"/"incorrect") item in the keyed direction. As the theory was developed further, the normal ogive was replaced by a more mathematically tractable, logistic function (Birnbaum, 1968). The specific form of this function is governed by up to three parameters or item characteristics: (1) the item discrimination index, a reflection of how well the item distinguishes between those low and those high on the attribute, where low and high are determined by (2) an item difficulty or threshold level, the point on the attribute continuum at which the probability of choosing one response option over another is .50, and (3) a guessing parameter, the probability of guessing correctly or responding in the keyed direction when the person actually possesses little or none of the attribute. One advantage of IRT over classical test theory is that the estimates of these characteristics are not dependent upon the makeup of the sample upon which they are computed.

A researcher using IRT must first select the particular model that is most suited to the measure, with concern for item type, the dimensionality of the construct, and which blend or mixture of the possible item characteristics are needed to best capture the nature of the construct. The basic IRT model for simple, dichotomous items has been expanded to accommodate other forms of items. Masters and Wright (1984) and Thissen and Steinberg (1986) present details on the various available models, their relationships to one another, and applications, and excellent introductory presentations of the foundations of IRT are provided by Hulin, Drasgow, and Parsons (1983) and Hambleton, Swaminathan, and Rogers (1991).

Of particular interest here are items with multiple, graded response options, such as the Likert-type scales used for the Mississippi Scale, CAPS, PSS, LASC, and other PTSD assessment instruments. One IRT approach for such item types is Samejima's (1969) graded response model, which was employed by King, King, Fairbank, Schlenger, and Surface (1993) to study the items comprising the Mississippi Scale, with data again drawn from the NVVRS. Using one discrimination parameter and $k - 1$ difficulty parameters (where k equals the number of options on the response scale), the graded response model provides for k operating characteristics. These are like item characteristic curves for each response option, each depicting the probability that an individual will select that option as a function of his or her standing on the attribute. An example from the King et al. findings, operating characteristics for Mississippi Scale Item 6 ("I am able to get emotionally close to others"), is presented as Figure 4.7. As can be seen, for this item, optimal probabilities of the five possible responses are well distributed across the range of the attribute continuum. In addition, only those individuals who are quite high on the PTSD dimension have a reasonable probability of endorsing the "never" option.

More important, IRT applications supply a plot of an item's reliability in the form of an item information curve, depicting the amount of information or precision of measurement (*Y* axis) across the range of possible attri-

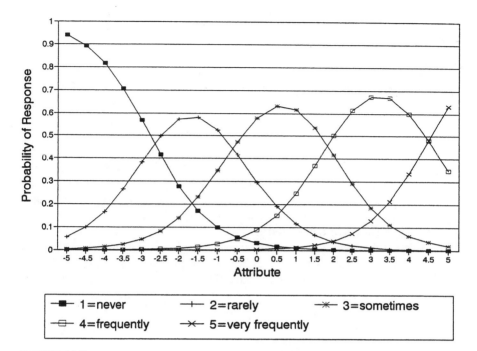

FIGURE 4.7. Operating characteristics for Mississippi Scale Item 6. Adapted from King, King, Fairbank, Schlenger, and Surface (1993, p. 462). Copyright 1994 by the American Psychological Association. Adapted by permission.

bute scores (X axis). The item information curve can be interpreted as item reliability since, for a given position on the attribute continuum, the square root of its inverse is the standard error of measurement. For example, as King et al. (1993) noted, and as demonstrated in Figure 4.8, Mississippi Scale Item 8 ("... I wish I were dead") is highly accurate or precise in discriminating among persons very high on the PTSD dimension, compared to Item 24 ("I fall asleep easily at night"), which provides moderate information or precision across a broad attribute range. A similar test information function may also be derived to portray how the full collection of items performs across the range of attribute positions.

In addition to supplying estimates of item parameters, item characteristic curves, item information functions, and the test information function—all of which assist in understanding the items as indicators of the construct— IRT also generates maximum likelihood estimates of individuals' scores. An important point is that these scores are item invariant. In other words, it is possible to administer different and varying numbers of items drawn from a common content bank to two or more individuals and derive scores that share the same attribute scale. In fact, one of the more valuable applications of IRT has been the implementation of individual computerized adaptive testing, in which an examinee is administered only as many items as are neces-

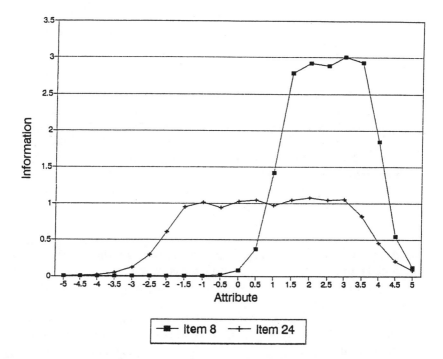

FIGURE 4.8. Item information functions for Mississippi Scale Items 8 and 24. Adapted from King, King, Fairbank, Schlenger, and Surface (1993, pp. 465–466). Copyright 1994 by the American Psychological Association. Adapted by permission.

sary to determine his or her standing on an attribute at some predetermined level of precision. Largely used, to date, in cognitive assessment (primarily aptitude tests for admission to college and professional programs), computer-administered, individually tailored tests appear to have great potential for affective measurement as well, such as the assessment of PTSD and other diagnostic entities. Wainer (1991) offers an excellent edited volume on computerized adaptive testing.

We previously stated that IRT-based item characteristics are sample invariant; that is, the discrimination, difficulty, and guessing parameters should be the same, regardless of the sample used to estimate them. Therefore, if one discovers that parameter estimates are not the same from population to population, then the possibility of differential item functioning or item bias arises. In PTSD research, for example, differential item functioning across groups might suggest that the item in question has different meanings for the groups, and hence that PTSD may not be manifest in a consistent manner across trauma populations. Another application of differential item functioning techniques is for equating test items across language translations. To the extent that equivalent item characteristics can be documented, one has more confidence in comparable PTSD measurement across language groups, thereby enhancing the potential validity of cross-cultural research. King et al. (1993) give further specifics on the implications of IRT for PTSD assessment.

SUMMARY AND CONCLUSIONS

In the last 15 years, extraordinary progress has been made in the development of reliable and valid PTSD assessment tools. The field of PTSD assessment has rapidly evolved from the situation in the early 1980s, when no measures of any kind existed, to the present situation, in which more than two-dozen questionnaires, interviews, and physiological protocols are available for a wide variety of assessment tasks. These instruments meet the practical needs of clinicians who require psychometrically sound tools for diagnosing and assessing individuals with PTSD and monitoring their progress in treatment. Perhaps even more important, they have also greatly facilitated empirical research regarding the clinical phenomenology and basic psychopathological processes involved in the response to traumatic life events.

In developing and evaluating new PTSD assessment instruments, investigators have generally followed the psychometric principles and techniques outlined in this chapter. We identified five basic stages, each involving multiple tasks. These stages include specifying the purpose of the instrument, defining the construct, designing the instrument, pilot testing and revising, and establishing reliability and validity. Throughout the entire process there is considerable interplay between creative input, based on a clear conceptualization of PTSD, and empirical feedback, based on rigorous investigation of the statistical properties of the instrument. To date, much of the statistical evaluation of PTSD instruments has been based on the methods of classical test theory. The contemporary approaches we described, including generalizability theory, confirmatory factor analysis, and item response theory, should greatly enhance the revision of existing instruments and the development of new, more sophisticated PTSD measures.

Although much progress has been made, there are several issues that still need to be addressed. First, with few exceptions, most PTSD assessment instruments are quite face valid and do not include items to assess response bias. This leaves them subject to deliberate distortion of responses, which can markedly reduce their usefulness. PTSD is not unique in this respect; most self-report measures of other types of psychopathology suffer from the same limitation. Nonetheless, the detection and quantification of response bias is an important area that deserves consideration by PTSD test developers. Second, many PTSD instruments were developed in a particular trauma population, such as combat veterans or rape victims, and have not been evaluated across populations. This creates a confounding of instrument and population that limits direct comparisons of PTSD symptomatology resulting from different types of trauma. A related concern is that many PTSD instruments were initially developed on relatively small samples of convenience, and few have been normed on large, representative samples. It will be important in the future to adopt a standard battery of PTSD instruments that can be used across different traumatized populations, and to develop adequate norms for each measure.

Third, much more work is needed on the validation of existing PTSD instruments. For example, although there is ample evidence supporting the convergent validity of various PTSD measures, little has been documented regarding discriminant validity; that is, test developers often report robust correlations between different measures of PTSD, but they typically fail to report the equally necessary weak correlations between measures of PTSD and measures of other constructs. Such evidence is crucial for demonstrating that scores on PTSD scales reflect "PTSD-ness" and are not better conceptualized as measures of anxiety or depression, for example, or as measures of global distress. Finally, as the PTSD construct evolves and as the database on existing instruments accumulates, it will become necessary to revise specific items or even entire measures to address empirically identified weaknesses and thereby enhance reliability and validity. Such revisions, such as the recent revision of the MMPI, can be unsettling for clinicians and researcher alike, but they are essential for continued progress in the field.

REFERENCES

American Psychiatric Association. (1980). *Diagnostic and statistical manual of mental disorders* (3rd ed.). Washington, DC: Author.

American Psychiatric Association. (1994). *Diagnostic and statistical manual of mental disorders* (4th ed.). Washington, DC: Author.

Anastasi, A. (1988). *Psychological testing* (6th ed.). New York: Macmillan.

Anderson, J. C., & Gerbing, D. W. (1988). Structural equation modeling in practice: A review and recommended two-step approach. *Psychological Bulletin, 103*, 411–423.

Bagozzi, R. P., & Heatherton, T. F. (1994). A general approach to representing multifaceted personality constructs: Application to state self-esteem. *Structural Equation Modeling: A Multidisciplinary Journal, 1*, 35–67.

Beck, A. T., Ward, C. H., Mendelson, M., Mock, J. E., & Erbaugh, J. K. (1961). An inventory for measuring depression. *Archives of General Psychiatry, 4*, 561–571.

Bentler, P. M., & Bonett, D. G. (1980). Significance tests and goodness of fit in the analysis of covariance structures. *Psychological Bulletin, 88*, 588–606.

Birnbaum, A. (1968). Some latent trait models and their uses in inferring an examinee's ability. In F. M. Lord & M. R. Novick (Eds.), *Statistical theories of mental test scores* (Part 5, pp. 397–474). Reading, MA: Addison-Wesley.

Blake, D. D., Weathers, F. W., Nagy, L. M., Kaloupek, D. G., Klauminzer, G., Charney, D. S., & Keane, T. M. (1990). A clinician rating scale for assessing current and lifetime PTSD: The CAPS-1. *Behavior Therapist, 13*, 187–188.

Bollen, K. A. (1989). *Structural equations with latent variables.* New York: Wiley.

Brennan, R. L. (1983). *Elements of generalizability theory.* Iowa City: American College Testing Program.

Briere, J. (1995). *Trauma Symptom Inventory (TSI) professional manual.* Odessa, FL: Psychological Assessment Resources.

Browne, M. W. (1984). Asymptotic distribution free methods in analysis of covariance structures. *British Journal of Mathematical and Statistical Psychology, 37,* 62–83.

Browne, M. W., & Cudeck, R. (1993). Alternative ways of assessing model fit. In K. A. Bollen & J. S. Long (Eds.), *Testing structural equation models* (pp. 136–162). Newbury Park, CA: Sage.

Campbell, D. T., & Fiske, D. W. (1959). Convergent and discriminant validation by the multitrait–multimethod matrix. *Psychological Bulletin, 56,* 81–105.

Carroll, K. M. (1995). Methodological issues and problems in the assessment of substance abuse. *Psychological Assessment, 7,* 349–358.

Cohen, J. (1960). A coefficient of agreement for nominal scales. *Educational and Psychological Measurement, 20,* 37–46.

Crocker, L., & Algina, J. (1986). *Introduction to classical and modern test theory.* New York: Holt, Rinehart & Winston.

Cronbach, L. J. (1951). Coefficient alpha and the internal structure of tests. *Psychometrika, 16,* 297–334.

Cronbach, L. J. (1990). *Essentials of psychological testing.* New York: HarperCollins.

Cronbach, L. J., Gleser, G. C., Nanda, H., & Rajaratnam, N. (1972). *The dependability of behavioral measurements: Theory of generalizability for scores and profiles.* New York: Wiley.

Cronbach, L. J., & Meehl, P. E. (1955). Construct validity in psychological tests. *Psychological Bulletin, 52,* 281–302.

Davidson, J. R. T., & Foa, E. B. (1991). Diagnostic issues in posttraumatic stress disorder: Considerations for the DSM-IV. *Journal of Abnormal Psychology, 100,* 346–355.

Davidson, J. R. T., Smith, R. D., & Kudler, H. S. (1989). Validity and reliability of the DSM-III criteria for post-traumatic stress disorder: Experience with a structured interview. *Journal of Nervous and Mental Disease, 177,* 336–341.

Derogatis, L. R. (1983). *SCL-90-R: Administration, scoring, and procedures manual—II.* Towson, MD: Clinical Psychometric Research.

Fleiss, J. L. (1981). *Statistical methods for rates and proportions.* New York: Wiley.

Foa, E. B., Riggs, D. S., Dancu, C. V., & Rothbaum, B. O. (1993). Reliability and validity of a brief instrument for assessing post-traumatic stress disorder. *Journal of Traumatic Stress, 6,* 459–473.

Gorsuch, R. L. (1983). *Factor analysis* (2nd ed.). Philadelphia: Saunders.

Gulliksen, H. (1950). *Theory of mental tests.* Hillsdale, NJ: Erlbaum.

Hambleton, R. K., Swaminathan, H., & Rogers, H. K. (1991). *Fundamentals of item response theory.* Newbury Park, CA: Sage.

Hammarberg, M. (1992). Penn Inventory for Posttraumatic Stress Disorder: Psychometric properties. *Psychological Assessment, 4,* 67–76.

Harman, H. H. (1976). *Modern factor analysis* (3rd ed., rev.). Chicago: University of Chicago Press.

Haynes, S. N., Richard, D. C. S., & Kubany, E. S. (1995). Content validity in psychological assessment: A functional approach to concepts and methods. *Psychological Assessment, 7,* 238–247.

Herman, J. L. (1992). *Trauma and recovery.* New York: Basic Books.

Holden, R. R., & Fekken, G. C. (1990). Structured psychopathological test item characteristics and validity. *Psychological Assessment, 2,* 35–40.

Horowitz, M. J., Wilner, N., & Alvarez, W. (1979). Impact of Event Scale: A measure of subjective stress. *Psychosomatic Medicine, 41,* 209–218.

Hu, L., & Bentler, P. M. (1995). Evaluating model fit. In R. H. Hoyle (Ed.), *Structural equation modeling: Concepts, issues, and applications* (Part 5, pp. 76–100). Thousand Oaks, CA: Sage.

Hulin, C. L., Drasgow, F., & Parsons, C. K. (1983). *Item response theory: Application to psychological measurement.* Homewood, IL: Dow Jones-Irwin.

Jackson, D. N. (1976). *The Basic Personality Inventory.* Port Huron, MI: Research Psychologists Press.

Janoff-Bulman, R. (1992). *Shattered assumptions: Towards a new psychology of trauma.* New York: Free Press.

Joreskog, K. G., & Sorbom, D. (1979). *Advances in factor analysis and structural equation models.* Lanham, MD: University Press of America.

Joreskog, K. G., & Sorbom, D. (1993). *LISREL 8: Structural equation modeling with the SIMPLIS command language.* Hillsdale, NJ: Erlbaum.

Kashy, D. A., & Snyder, D. K. (1995). Measurement and data analytic issues in couples research. *Psychological Assessment, 7,* 338–348.

Keane, T. M., Caddell, J. M., & Taylor, K. L. (1988). Mississippi Scale for Combat-Related Post-Traumatic Stress Disorder: Three studies in reliability and validity. *Journal of Consulting and Clinical Psychology, 56,* 85–90.

Keane, T. M., Malloy, P. F., & Fairbank, J. A. (1984). Empirical development of an MMPI subscale for the assessment of combat-related posttraumatic stress disorder. *Journal of Consulting and Clinical Psychology, 52,* 888–891.

Keane, T. M., Wolfe, J., & Taylor, K. L. (1987). Post-traumatic stress disorder: Evidence for diagnostic validity and methods of psychological assessment. *Journal of Clinical Psychology, 43,* 32–43.

Kessel, J. B., & Zimmerman, M. (1993). Reporting errors in studies of the diagnostic performance of self-administered questionnaires: Extent of the problem, recommendations for standardized presentation of results, and implications for the peer review process. *Psychological Assessment, 5,* 395–399.

King, D. W., King, L. A., Fairbank, J. A., Schlenger, W. E., & Surface, C. R. (1993). Enhancing the precision of the Mississippi Scale for Combat-Related Post-Traumatic Stress Disorder: An application of item response theory. *Psychological Assessment, 5,* 457–471.

King, D. W., King, L. A., Leskin, G., & Foy, D. W. (1995). The Los Angeles Symptom Checklist: A self-report measure of post-traumatic stress disorder. *Assessment, 2,* 1–17.

King, L. A., & King, D. W. (1994). Latent structure of the Mississippi Scale for Combat-Related Post-traumatic Stress Disorder: Exploratory and higher-order confirmatory factor analyses. *Assessment, 1,* 275–291.

Koretzky, M. B., & Peck, A. H. (1990). Validation and cross-validation of the PTSD Subscale of the MMPI with civilian trauma victims. *Journal of Clinical Psychology, 46,* 296–300.

Kraemer, H. C. (1992). *Evaluating medical tests: Objective and quantitative guidelines.* Newbury Park, CA: Sage.

Kulka, R. A., Schlenger, W. E., Fairbank, J. A., Hough, R. L., Jordan, B. K., Marmar,

C. R., & Weiss, D. S. (1990). *Trauma and the Vietnam War generation: Report on the findings from the National Vietnam Veterans Readjustment Study.* New York: Brunner/Mazel.

La Rue, A., & Markee, T. (1995). Clinical assessment research with older adults. *Psychological Assessment, 7,* 376–386.

Litz, B. T. (1992). Emotional numbing in combat-related post-traumatic stress disorder: A critical review and reformulation. *Clinical Psychology Review, 12,* 417–432.

Loehlin, J. C. (1992). *Latent variable models: An introduction to factor, path, and structural analysis* (2nd ed.). Hillsdale, NJ: Erlbaum.

Lord, F. M., & Novick, M. R. (1968). *Statistical theories of mental test scores.* Reading, MA: Addison-Wesley.

Lyons, J. A., Caddell, J. M., Pittman, R. L., Rawls, R., & Perrin, S. (1994). The potential for faking on the Mississippi Scale for Combat-Related PTSD. *Journal of Traumatic Stress, 7,* 441–445.

Lyons, J. A., & Keane, T. M. (1992). Keane PTSD Scale: MMPI and MMPI-2 update. *Journal of Traumatic Stress, 5,* 111–117.

Malloy, P. F., Fairbank, J. A., & Keane T. M. (1983). Validation of a multimethod assessment of posttraumatic stress disorders in Vietnam veterans. *Journal of Consulting and Clinical Psychology, 51,* 488–494.

Masters, G. N., & Wright, B. D. (1984). The essential process in a family of measurement models. *Psychometrika, 49,* 529–544.

McCann, I. L., & Pearlman, L. A. (1990). *Psychological trauma and the adult survivor: Theory, therapy, and transformation.* New York: Brunner/Mazel.

Morris, R. J., Bergan, J. R., & Fulginiti, J. V. (1991). Structural equation modeling in clinical assessment research with children. *Journal of Consulting and Clinical Psychology, 59,* 371–379.

Mulaik, S. A., & James, L. R. (1995). Objectivity and reasoning in science and structural equation modeling. In R. H. Hoyle (Ed.), *Structural equation modeling: Concepts, issues, and applications* (Part 7, pp. 118–138). Thousand Oaks, CA: Sage.

Newman, E., Kaloupek, D. G., & Keane, T. M. (1996). Assessment of posttraumatic stress disorder in clinical and research settings. In B. A. van der Kolk, A. C. McFarlane, & L. Weisaeth (Eds.), *Traumatic stress: The effects of overwhelming experiences on mind, body, and society* (pp. 242–275). New York: Guilford Press.

Nunnally, J. C. (1978). *Psychometric theory* (2nd ed.). New York: McGraw-Hill.

Okazaki, S., & Sue, S. (1995). Methodological issues in assessment research with ethnic minorities. *Psychological Assessment, 7,* 367–375.

Orsillo, S., Weathers, F. W., Litz, B. T., Steinberg, H. R., Huska, J. A., & Keane, T. M. (1996). Current and lifetime psychiatric disorders among veterans with warzone-related post-traumatic stress disorder. *Journal of Nervous and Mental Disease, 184,* 307–313.

Pitman, R. K., Orr, S. P., Forgue, D. F., de Jong, J. B., & Claiborn, J. M. (1987). Psychophysiologic assessment of posttraumatic stress disorder imagery in Vietnam combat veterans. *Archives of General Psychiatry, 44,* 970–975.

Prigatano, G. P., Parsons, O. A., & Bortz, J. J. (1995). Methodological considerations in clinical neuropsychological research: 17 years later. *Psychological Assessment, 7,* 396–403.

Samejima, F. (1969). Estimation of latent ability using a response pattern of graded scores. *Psychometric Monograph No. 17, 34*(4, Pt. 2).

Saunders, B. E., Arata, C. M., & Kilpatrick, D. G. (1990). Development of a crime-related posttraumatic stress disorder scale for women within the Symptom Checklist-90—Revised. *Journal of Traumatic Stress, 3,* 439–448.

Shavelson, R. J., & Webb, N. M. (1991). *Generalizability theory: A primer.* Newbury Park, CA: Sage.

Spitzer, R. L. (1983). Psychiatric diagnosis: Are clinicians still necessary? *Comprehensive Psychiatry, 24,* 399–411.

Spitzer, R. L., Williams, J. B. W., Gibbon, M., & First, M. B. (1990). *Structured Clinical Interview for DSM-III-R.* Washington, DC: American Psychiatric Association Press.

Standards for educational and psychological testing. (1985). Washington, DC: American Psychological Association.

Steiger, J. H., Shapiro, A., & Browne, M. W. (1985). On the multivariate asymptotic distribution of sequential chi-square statistics. *Psychometrika, 50,* 253–263.

Suen, H. K. (1990). *Principles of test theories.* Hillsdale, NJ: Erlbaum.

Thissen, D., & Steinberg, L. (1986). A taxonomy of item response models. *Psychometrika, 51,* 567–577.

Vreven, D. L., Gudanowski, D. M., King, L. A., & King, D. W. (1995). The civilian version of the Mississippi PTSD Scale: A psychometric evaluation. *Journal of Traumatic Stress, 8,* 91–109.

Wainer, H. (1991). *Computerized adaptive testing: A primer.* Hillsdale, NJ: Erlbaum.

Watson, C. G., Juba, M. P., Manifold, V., Kucala, T., & Anderson, P. E. D. (1991). The PTSD Interview: Rationale, description, reliability, and concurrent validity of a DSM-III-based technique. *Journal of Clinical Psychology, 47,* 179–188.

Weathers, F. W., Blake, D. D., Krinsley, K. E., Haddad, W. H., Huska, J. A., & Keane, T. M. (1992, November). *The Clinician-Administered PTSD Scale: Reliability and construct validity.* Paper presented at the annual meeting of the Association for Advancement of Behavior Therapy, Boston, MA.

Weathers, F. W., Haddad, W. P., Litz, B. T., Keane, T. M., Palmieri, P. A., & Steinberg, H. S. (1995, November). *Intimacy in war-zone-related PTSD: Cognitive and affective responses to simulated interpersonal situations.* Paper presented at the annual meeting of the Association for Advancement of Behavior Therapy, Washington, DC.

Weathers, F. W., & Litz, B. T. (1994). Psychometric properties of the Clinician-Administered PTSD Scale-Form 1 (CAPS-1). *PTSD Research Quarterly, 5,* 2–6.

Weathers, F. W., Litz, B. T., Herman, D. S., Huska, J. A., & Keane, T. M. (1993, October). *The PTSD Checklist (PCL): Reliability, validity, and diagnostic utility.* Paper presented at the annual meeting of the International Society for Traumatic Stress Studies, San Antonio, TX.

Weathers, F. W., Litz, B. T., Herman, D. S., Keane, T. M., Steinberg, H. R., Huska, J. A., & Kraemer, H. C. (1996). The utility of the SCL-90-R for the diagnosis of war-zone-related PTSD. *Journal of Traumatic Stress, 9,* 111–128.

Weiner, I. B. (1995). Methodological considerations in Rorschach research. *Psychological Assessment, 7,* 330–337.

ASSESSING TRAUMATIC REACTIONS AMONG VICTIM AND SURVIVOR POPULATIONS

CHAPTER 5

Epidemiological Methods for Assessing Trauma and Posttraumatic Stress Disorder

WILLIAM E. SCHLENGER
JOHN A. FAIRBANK
B. KATHLEEN JORDAN
JUESTA M. CADDELL

INTRODUCTION

Since the inclusion in DSM-III (American Psychiatric Association, 1980) of a specific, operational definition of the posttraumatic stress disorder (PTSD) syndrome, there has been a rapid accumulation of knowledge about the epidemiology of the disorder (see Wilson & Raphael, 1993). This accumulation has been based on findings from a number of major epidemiological studies of PTSD resulting from a variety of exposures, including the combat experiences of Vietnam veterans (e.g., Kulka et al., 1990), criminal victimization (e.g., Kilpatrick, Saunders, Veronen, Best, & Von, 1987), exposure to natural disasters (e.g., Norris, 1992), and so on. We have reviewed this literature in more detail elsewhere (Fairbank, Schlenger, Caddell, & Woods, 1993; Fairbank, Schlenger, Saigh, & Davidson, 1995).

The purpose of this chapter is to describe some of the important conceptual and practical issues involved in conducting epidemiological studies of PTSD. By *epidemiological* studies, we mean studies aimed at assessing the prevalence and/or incidence of PTSD in specific population groups, assessing the relationship of PTSD to other psychiatric disorders, and identifying risk and other etiological factors for the development of PTSD.

We focus here on issues germane to *community* studies, rather than *clinical* studies. Community epidemiological studies are aimed at assessing specific exposures and/or disorders among a specified population, regardless of whether individuals have sought treatment or otherwise come to the attention of the treatment system. Consequently, community studies involve the study of samples selected for reasons other than their exposure or disease status. Instead, samples for such studies should be selected to be *representative* of the specific population or subgroup to which inference is to be made (e.g., Vietnam veterans, crime victims, incest survivors).

We focus here on community studies for several reasons. First, many of the important issues involved in conducting clinical studies are addressed in other chapters in this volume (e.g., Green, Epstein, Krupnick, & Rowland, Chapter 6). Second, although clinical studies are extremely valuable for improving our understanding of those who seek treatment for PTSD and for designing systems of care that can deliver effective treatment to them, such studies contain an inherent bias that limits their utility for enhancing our understanding of the basic epidemiology of PTSD. That bias arises from the well-established fact (e.g., see Shapiro et al., 1984) that only a relatively small portion of those who meet the diagnostic criteria for a specific psychiatric disorder seek treatment for it. The impact of the biases introduced by this self-selection of treatment-seeking populations cannot be *definitively* determined (since the bias cannot be studied in the context of a randomized experiment), which limits the contribution that clinical studies can make to our understanding of the basic epidemiology of psychiatric disorders.

Third, it is also true that not everyone who seeks treatment for a given disorder actually has that disorder. With PTSD, issues of secondary gain (e.g., malingering) are sometimes important among those seeking treatment, and represent another source of potential bias. Furthermore, although many of those exposed to trauma may experience symptoms of PTSD, not all will develop the full syndrome (Weiss et al., 1992).

We will focus in this chapter on two important issues that must be addressed in all community epidemiological studies of PTSD: (1) measurement of exposure, and (2) case identification. By *measurement of exposure,* we mean: How do we determine *whether* a given individual has been exposed to an event that fulfills Criterion A of the DSM-IV (American Psychiatric Association, 1994) diagnostic criteria for PTSD (i.e., a bona fide traumatic event), and how much of an exposure has the individual received? By *case identification* we mean: How can we tell whether a given individual meets the diagnostic criteria for PTSD, and therefore should be considered to be a "case"? Operationally, we define a "case" to be a person who experiences a pattern of symptoms that satisfies the DSM-IV criteria for PTSD.

In both instances, our goal is to increase the *internal validity* (Cook & Campbell, 1979) of the research. This is important because classification errors in either exposure or case identification introduce bias and therefore reduce the internal validity of case versus noncase comparisons, which are the heart of epidemiological studies. Such biases can spuriously inflate important relationships, or mask them, leading to inaccurate conclusions about prevalence, risk factors, and so on.

Although we focus here on issues of internal validity, we also recognize the importance of *external* validity in epidemiological studies of PTSD. We have discussed some of the issues of external validity in such studies elsewhere (Kulka & Schlenger, 1993; Kulka et al., 1991; Fairbank, Jordan, & Schlenger, 1996), focusing primarily on the importance of representative sampling methods.

ASSESSMENT OF EXPOSURE TO TRAUMA

It is tautological that anyone who meets the criteria for the diagnosis of PTSD has been exposed to one or more "extreme events." It is also true, however, that not everyone who has been exposed to an extreme event develops PTSD. As a result, assessment of exposure is an important component of the internal validity of epidemiological studies of PTSD, and critical to the examination of etiology.

Assessment of exposure in community epidemiological studies of PTSD to date has typically relied on *retrospective self-reports* in the context of a survey interview. That is, most studies have involved structured survey interviews that included questions about various major categories of extreme events to which one might have been exposed in the past (e.g., "Have you ever been . . . ?"). A follow-up set of questions concerning the details of the exposure is posed to those who indicate having had a given exposure. The interview is typically conducted by a trained survey interviewer who has experience conducting structured interviews but has no clinical expertise and no advanced training or experience in trauma or its assessment.

For example, exposure to extreme events was assessed comprehensively in the National Vietnam Veterans Readjustment Study (NVVRS; Kulka et al., 1990). Since the NVVRS focused on combat-related PTSD, the survey interview included a comprehensive set of over 100 questions about the veteran's experience while he or she was in Vietnam. These items addressed specific experiences that may have been stressful (e.g., "How often were you under enemy fire?" "How often did you experience hand-to-hand combat?"). Using factor analysis, this set of items was combined into specific indices assessing major types of war-zone stressor exposure (four types for men, six for women), all of which showed good internal consistency reliability (median coefficient α = .873). These specific indices were then combined into an overall exposure index that was used to divide Vietnam veterans into high versus low/moderate war zone stress exposure groups for analytic purposes.

Additionally, although the NVVRS was focused on war-zone trauma, Vietnam veterans could have been exposed to other kinds of trauma that could have produced PTSD both before and after their Vietnam experience. Therefore, the NVVRS interview included questions about other extreme events to which they may have been exposed.

The assessment of noncombat exposures began by focusing the respondent on "unusual events that are extraordinarily stressful—things that do not happen to most people, but when they do they can be frightening, upsetting, or distressing to almost anyone." The interviewer then went through a list of major categories of such exposures (e.g., serious accidents; natural disasters such as tornado, flood, major earthquake; physical assault, torture, rape, abuse, mugging; seeing someone who was mutilated, seriously injured, or violently killed) and asked the respondent to indicate whether he or she had ever been exposed to each. Then, for each category for which the respondent indicated an exposure, the interviewer asked a structured set of questions about the details of the event (e.g., "Was the person involved directly?" "Was the event bloody or grotesque?" "Was the person in real danger of being seriously injured or killed?"). This information was later reviewed and coded into whether each event was or was not likely to meet the definition of Criterion A for PTSD.

To provide a context for participants, the section of the interview that addressed noncombat exposures followed immediately after a set of questions about "stressful life events" (e.g., significant illness, loss of job, divorce, natural death of family member) that participants may have experienced. The rationale for doing so was that if the inquiry was first focused on lower magnitude stressors, and then shifted to higher magnitude stressors ("Now I'd like to talk with you about . . . "), the likelihood of "false positive" responses to the extreme events assessment would be reduced. This was a concern because of anecdotal experiences during the pilot phase of the NVVRS that suggested that participants may have trouble distinguishing everyday stressors from the kinds of "extreme events" that satisfy the PTSD exposure criterion (Criterion A). The NVVRS assessment package was subsequently extended to cover more fully noncombat trauma by Jordan, Schlenger, Fairbank, and Caddell (1995) for use in The Women Inmates Health Study, a study of the prevalence of psychiatric disorders among women felons entering prison in North Carolina.

Reviewing the details of the NVVRS stressor exposure assessment serves to underline an important point: Stressor exposure is a multidimensional construct; that is, there are many different kinds of stressors to which a person may be exposed, and multiple important aspects of each exposure that should be assessed (e.g., frequency, severity). Comprehensive assessment of exposure requires specific inquiry about each type of stressor, assessment of qualitative aspects of the exposures that are reported, and assessment of the frequency and intensity of each type of exposure. In addition, beginning by assessing lower magnitude stressors ("stressful life events") may help clarify for respondents the meaning of questions about high-magnitude stressors and thereby contribute to improved validity of the assessment.

A second example of assessing exposure in the context of a community epidemiological study comes from the work of Dean Kilpatrick, Heidi Resnick, and their colleagues (Kilpatrick et al., 1987; Resnick, Kilpatrick, Dansky, Saunders, & Best, 1993). On the basis of experiences gained through conducting a series of epidemiological studies focusing on noncombat events (particularly sexual assaults), these investigators have developed the Trauma Assessment for Adults (TAA; Resnick, Best, Freedy, Kilpatrick, & Falsetti, 1993), a structured assessment of exposure to extreme events that is available in both interview and self-administered formats. Resnick, Falsetti, Kilpatrick, and Freedy (1996) emphasize a number of important considerations in the assessment of exposure to extreme events, including:

1. Begin by providing a context for the assessment by explaining the nature of extreme events, so that the intent of the specific questions will be clearer and focus the respondent's attention on the kinds of events of interest.
2. Include behaviorally specific, operational questions (e.g., asking a series of detailed questions about specific sex acts, such as "Has anyone ever made you have anal sex by force or threat of harm?" rather than a global question such as "Have you ever been sexually assaulted?").
3. Assess the broad range of potential events to which respondents may have been exposed.
4. Include assessment of qualitative aspects of the exposure (i.e., details of what happened and the ways in which the event was threatening).
5. Establish the traditional psychometric properties (reliability and validity) of the assessment.

The TAA is a brief version of the more comprehensive Potential Stressful Events Interview (PSE; Kilpatrick, Resnick, & Freedy, 1991), which was developed for use in the DSM-IV PTSD field trial. This trial was conducted to collect information to address specific issues being considered by the committee that drafted the PTSD criteria for inclusion in DSM-IV (American Psychiatric Association, 1994). The PSE includes sections assessing low magnitude stressors, high-magnitude stressors, and objective and subjective characteristics of reported high-magnitude stressors.

As is always the case, the level of detail provided by the PSE has a price—it is time-consuming to administer. In the context of community epidemiological research, in which exposure is one of multiple important constructs being measured, there is always a trade-off between the scientifically desirable level of detail and the costs (in terms of fiscal resources, respondent burden, etc.) associated with collecting those details. The TAA represents a compromise between the fine detail provided by the PSE (which may be more feasible to use in clinical settings) and the practical demands of community epidemiological studies.

Similarly, Norris (1990, 1992) developed the Traumatic Stress Schedule (TSS; see Norris & Riad, Chapter 1, this volume) to assess exposure to nine categories of extreme events (and one specific event—Hurricane Hugo) for use in an epidemiological study of exposure to trauma in four cities in the southeastern United States. The TSS assesses lifetime and past-year exposure to these event categories, and also includes a five-item stress symptom measure that does not require the respondent to link his or her symptoms to a specific extreme event.

A final example that demonstrates a somewhat different approach to assessing exposure comes from an important longitudinal study of a cohort of young adults enrolled in a large HMO conducted by Breslau and her colleagues (Breslau, Davis, Andreski, & Peterson, 1991; Breslau, Davis, & Andreski, 1995). The cohort was assessed in 1989, and again in 1992, for exposure to extreme events and for the presence of PTSD and other psychiatric disorders.

The exposure assessment used by Breslau and her colleagues is more open-ended than the others, in that it begins with a global question about exposure to "terrible experiences" that cites a series of examples ("things like being attacked or raped, being in a fire or flood or bad traffic accident, being threatened with a weapon, or watching someone being badly injured or killed"). Those answering "no" are probed about whether they ever experienced a "great shock because something like that happened to someone close to you," which is another type of potential extreme event. Those answering "yes" to the original question are asked to describe the "worst" such event in their lives, which is coded into specific categories (e.g., combat, rape, physical assault, etc.), and then probed for "anything else like this" and then for "any other terrible or shocking experience." As a result, the assessment results in a description of up to three such events.

The above represent examples from current practice of state-of-the-art assessment in the context of community epidemiological studies, and demonstrate many of the important principles in such assessment. The most important weakness that all of the examples share is that they are *retrospective* methods, usually covering substantial recall periods (e.g., "Have you ever in your life . . . ?"). This limitation is inherent in self-report methods of assessing exposure to trauma, and is problematic because it allows for potential confounding of *reaction* to an exposure with *description of* that exposure. In addition, Bromet and Dew (1995) note that cross-sectional, retrospective studies are subject to biases from selective mortality that might result from the exposure, nonresponse bias in which nonexposed individuals may be not motivated and those exposed too preoccupied (or angry) to participate, and interviewer bias resulting from the fact that interviewers cannot be blinded to exposure status.

It is important to remember that misclassifications of exposure can occur in both directions—that is, both false positives and false negatives are possible. As an example of a false positive, one subject in the NVVRS reported during the survey interview that he served five tours in Vietnam and was exposed to heavy combat during each. His military record, however, showed that he spent most of his relatively brief stay in the military in a military prison in Norfolk, Virginia.

Conversely, findings from a study of documented child sexual abuse victims demonstrate that false negatives are also a potential problem. Williams (1994a) interviewed in adulthood 129 women who had been treated for sexual victimization during childhood (on average about 17 years prior to the interview). When interviewed, 38% of the sample did not report the documented incident, even when the interviewer described to them the specific details. Although there may be a variety of interpretations of why these events were not "remembered" (Loftus, Garry, & Feldman, 1994; Williams, 1994b), it is clear that simply asking someone about exposures does not guarantee accurate assessment.

Confidence in self-reports of exposure can be increased, however, in several ways. First, confidence would be increased if those reports can be shown to correspond with independent measures of exposure. For example, the NVVRS team was able to demonstrate good correspondence between the NVVRS self-report measures of exposure and exposure-related information in veterans' military records (Kulka et al., 1990)—for example, those whose military record indicated that they had received the Purple Heart were much more likely to be classified as high-stress exposure based on self-report than those who did not, and those whose record indicated that they had a "tactical" military occupational specialty (MOS) were classified as higher exposure than those with nontactical MOS's, and so on.

It is important to remember, however, that independent sources of exposure information often do not provide *definitive* indicators of exposure. Anyone who has ever worked with official records—be they clinical case records, military service records, school records, police records, and so on—recognizes that such records are subject to errors of both omission and commission. Nevertheless, such records can be an important source of corroboration, in the *construct* (rather than *criterion*) validity sense.

Second, confidence in self-reports can be increased by having multiple assessments over time, each of which focuses on a discrete and more limited time period. The multiple assessment approach is a characteristic of prospective, longitudinal studies, of which Breslau's study of the young adult cohort (Breslau et al., 1995) is an excellent example. Use of multiple assessments helps to control for reporting errors associated with compression of time. This phenomenon, referred to as "telescoping," occurs when an event is remembered as occurring more recently than it actually did (Sudman & Bradburn, 1973). Telescoping threatens the internal validity of epidemiological studies of PTSD by potentially increasing reports of exposure (i.e., creating "false-positive" exposure reports). In addition, prospective, longitudinal studies provide an excellent vehicle for methodological studies of the validity of exposure assessment.

PTSD CASE IDENTIFICATION

A second important assessment issue in community epidemiological studies is case identification. One of the most challenging scientific issues in such studies is how one determines who is a "case" and who is not. In clinical studies, patients assessed because they are seeking treatment come to the assessment with certain problems, or symptoms, and a "story" to tell (e.g., "I'm here because . . . "). Diagnostic interviews in clinical settings, therefore, often begin with questions such as "Can you tell me why you are here?", "How I can help you?", and so on. In community studies, however, the subject has *not* come to the assessment for the purpose of telling a story. On the contrary, the assessor has approached the subject for the purpose of *learning* his or her story but does not have a "presenting problem" from which to start the assessment process.

We focus here on case identification as a *binary* decision — that is, each subject is classified as a "case" or "not a case" — since this is the epidemiological tradition. We recognize, however, that for many psychiatric disorders, including PTSD, there are subthreshold, or subclinical, phenomena that are of interest — that is, people who exhibit some clinically significant symptoms of the syndrome, but not enough symptoms to meet the letter of the DSM definition. Weiss et al. (1992) discuss this phenomenon in more detail and present estimates of the prevalence of "partial PTSD" for Vietnam veterans (also see Weiss, Chapter 17).

Similarly, although we limit our focus here to identification of cases of PTSD, epidemiological studies of people exposed to a variety of extreme events have demonstrated that (1) PTSD is often accompanied by comorbid psychiatric disorders, including depressive and substance-use disorders (see Fairbank et al., 1993, 1995), and (2) other psychiatric disorders, including borderline personality disorder and the dissociative disorders, have been shown to be related to traumatic exposure (see Herman, Perry, & van der Kolk, 1989; Zanarini, Gunderson, Marino, Schwartz, & Frankenburg, 1989; or Jordan, Schlenger, Caddell, & Fairbank, 1996). Thus, although we focus here on PTSD as an example, investigators designing epidemiological studies of traumatic exposure will likely want to assess for a broader range of trauma-related and comorbid disorders.

There are at least four major categories into which existing PTSD case identification methods for use in epidemiological studies can be divided, based on the underlying approach taken. These categories are:

1. Survey interview approaches
2. Semistructured clinical interview approaches
3. Psychometric approaches
4. Psychobiological approaches

More detailed descriptions of specific measures, instruments, and methods reflecting these approaches and their psychometric and other properties can be found in various other chapters in this book. In addition, there are research design features that can facilitate case identification. These various approaches are described in the following sections.

The Survey Interview Approach

The survey interview approach to case identification is based on the premise that people can reliably report their experience of specific psychiatric symptoms if the symptoms are briefly described to them in a survey interview setting. Consequently, survey interview approaches use fully structured interviews in which the interviewer simply reads the prescribed questions (e.g., "Have you ever experienced . . . ?") and records the responses, with no interpretation and no unstructured probing. Interviewers in this approach are trained in survey interview techniques, but need have no clinical training with respect to the phenomenology of PTSD.

The most widely used example of the survey interview approach is the Diagnostic Interview Schedule (DIS; Robins, Helzer, Croughan, & Ratcliff, 1981), a fully structured survey interview developed for use in community epidemiological studies, specifically for the National Institute of Mental Health's (NIMH) Epidemiologic Catchment Area (ECA) program (Regier et al., 1984). The DIS is based on the survey interview approach and supports diagnosis of a variety of specific psychiatric disorders as defined in DSM-III, including PTSD. More recently, using the DIS as the starting point, the World Health Organization has developed the Composite International Diagnostic Interview (CIDI; Robins, Wing, Wittchen, & Helzer, 1988) to incorporate changes in diagnostic criteria reflected in ICD-10 and DSM-IV. Additionally, a version that assesses psychiatric disorders in children and adolescents — the Diagnostic Interview Schedule for Children (DISC; Costello, Kalas, Kessler, & Klaric, 1982) — has been developed.

Empirical examinations of the psychometric properties of the DIS have generally shown it to be reliable (e.g., Helzer et al., 1985), but have raised important questions about its validity. For example, Anthony et al. (1985) showed that for most disorders, diagnoses based on the DIS agreed poorly with diagnoses made by clinicians based on a semistructured clinical interview. Similarly, although the DIS-PTSD module was found in the NVVRS Preliminary Validation Study (Schlenger et al., 1992) to correspond reasonably well with diagnoses based on structured clinical interview in a sample of Vietnam veterans undergoing treatment, Kulka et al. (1991) found it to have very poor sensitivity when used to assess a community sample of Vietnam veterans. Kilpatrick et al. (1994), however, used a modified version of the DIS designed to overcome the kinds of problems experienced in the NVVRS in the DSM-IV field trial and found better correspondence with PTSD diagnoses based on structured clinical interview in a mixed clinical and community sample.

The Clinical Interview Approach

The clinical interview approach shares the survey interview approach's focus on specific symptoms, but differs in at least two ways. First, the interview is conducted by an experienced clinician. Use of trained, experienced clinicians allows the integration of information gained through observation of the respondent during the interview rather than relying concretely on what the respondent said (e.g., the respondent denied experiencing "emotional numbing" but remained affectless throughout the interview, even when describing extreme combat events).

Second, the interview is semistructured—that is, it includes specific questions about all of the symptoms of interest, but the interviewer is encouraged to probe for more information where appropriate. Elicitation of additional information about symptoms through the use of follow-up probes (e.g., "Can you tell me more about that?", "What was that like for you?") increases the validity of the symptom assessment. For example, in the NVVRS Preliminary Validation Study (Schlenger et al., 1992), we noticed that patients often responded affirmatively to symptom questions in survey interviews, but when probed, the experience they described may have been a psychiatric symptom but often was not the one described in the original question. Experiences such as these suggest that the constructs embodied in the symptoms that comprise the DSM-IV definitions of psychiatric disorders may be difficult for many people to recognize on the basis of brief, survey interview questions, which underlines the importance of the role of clinical judgment in valid case identification.

The first semistructured clinical interview to support diagnosis of PTSD was the Structured Clinical Interview for DSM-III-R (SCID; Spitzer, Williams, Gibbon, & First, 1992). The PTSD module of the SCID was developed by the NVVRS research team and incorporated into Form NP-V of the SCID. Since it was developed for use in a study of combat-related PTSD, it focused largely on the kinds of extreme events that are associated with war-zone situations. All PTSD symptoms are assessed, including lifetime ("Have you ever had this symptom?") and current ("Do you have this symptom now?").

Subsequently, other clinical interview protocols have been developed. These include the Clinician Administered PTSD Scale (CAPS; Blake et al., 1995) and the Structured Interview for PTSD (SI-PTSD; Davidson, Smith, & Kudler, 1989). The CAPS has the advantage of including frequency and severity ratings for each symptom (as opposed to the present–absent indicator of the SCID), while the SI-PTSD includes ratings of severity.

Recently, interviews that may be thought of as hybrids of the survey and clinical interview approaches have been developed. For example, Angold, Cox, Prendergast, Rutter, and Simonoff (1992) have developed the Child and Adolescent Psychiatric Assessment (CAPA) to assess psychiatric disorder in children and adolescents. The CAPA is designed to be used by "lay" (i.e., nonclinical) interviewers, but its use involves extensive training of those interviewers in the meaning of psychiatric symptoms. This training provides interviewers with a basis to make certain judgments about whether the symptom that a subject describes is or is not the symptom to which the question refers. This approach retains the cost-efficiencies associated with the use of lay interviewers, but may enhance the accuracy of symptom assessment. Other diagnostic measures for use with children are described by Nader in Chapter 10.

The Psychometric Approach

Both the survey interview and clinical interview approaches to case identification may be described as *rational*, in that they are structured by the symptoms that comprise the DSM definition of PTSD, and impose the DSM decision rules (e.g., at least one B Criterion symptom, three or more C Criterion symptoms, etc.). Subjects are judged to be cases only if their reported symptom pattern conforms strictly to the DSM definition. In other words, using these approaches, one decides if a subject is a case by inquiring about the specific symptoms of PTSD, and then following the DSM definition of caseness.

The other two major approaches share a fundamentally different conceptualization of the problem of case identification, an approach that is better described as *empirical* than *rational*. Both are based on the psychometric tradition of empirical validity, in which "tests" measuring specific "traits" (or "constructs") are derived by comparing the responses to sets of standardized stimuli of people who have the trait to the responses of those who do not. Items that discriminate between the known groups are incorporated into the test, and those that do not are not.

In what we refer to as the psychometric approach, "stimuli"—be they symptom descriptions, statements with which the subject is asked to agree or disagree, and so on—are presented to the subject, and his or her responses are recorded. Psychometric instruments are typically presented in a self-report format (i.e., the subject reads the items and records responses without the intervention of an interviewer). There is an increasing body of evidence suggesting that "sensitive" information is more likely to be revealed in self-report settings than interview settings (e.g., see Turner, Lessler, & Gfroerer, 1992), which may be an advantage for this method in assessing for PTSD.

Probably the best known example of the psychometric approach to PTSD case identifications is the Mississippi Scale for Combat-Related PTSD (Keane, Caddell, & Taylor, 1988). The Mississippi Scale consists of 35 items with 5-point, Likert-style response categories. The scale was created from a pool of potential items developed by a group of clinicians experienced in treating Vietnam veterans with PTSD to represent broadly the kinds of complaints voiced by veterans with PTSD. From this pool, those that were shown empirically to discriminate combat veterans with PTSD from those without were included in the scale. To reduce the potential impact of response set, 10 of the items are phrased in the negative direction (i.e., the low end of the scale is associated with PTSD). The Mississippi Scale has been shown to be reliable and strongly related to the clinical diagnosis of PTSD (Keane et al., 1988; Kulka et al., 1991). For the NVVRS, a "civilian" version of the Mississippi scale was created that appears to have promise for assessing noncombat PTSD (Vreven, Gudanowski, King, & King, 1995).

Another excellent example of the psychometric approach to PTSD case identification is the PTSD scale of the Minnesota Multiphasic Personality Inventory (MMPI; Keane, Malloy, & Fairbank, 1984). Using groups of combat veterans with and without PTSD, a set of 49 MMPI items was identified that significantly discriminated the groups. This scale has also been shown to be both reliable and strongly related to clinical diagnosis, and has been carried into the new MMPI-2 (Butcher, Dahlstrom, Graham, Tellegen, & Kaemmer, 1989) as research scale PK. In addition, scale PS of the MMPI-2 represents an extension of the original scale, and includes the original Keane scale items that cross-validated in the NVVRS sample, plus a number of new items that were incorporated into MMPI-2 that were found in the NVVRS to discriminate between Vietnam veterans with PTSD and those without.

Psychobiological Approaches

Psychobiological approaches are another step removed from the potential problems associated with relying on self-report. These approaches involve identifying psychobiological correlates of PTSD — that is, reliable psychobiological differences between PTSD cases and noncases. If such differences exist, they would represent potentially a more "objective" method for identifying PTSD cases. Potential psychobiological correlates that have been studied to date have included both psychophysiological and neurobiological measures — psychophysiological reactivity in response to presentations of trauma-related stimuli (e.g., slides depicting combat scenes) and imagery, and urinary cortisol levels. (Psychophysiological approaches are described in more detail by Orr & Kaloupek, Chapter 3.)

Studies of physiological reactivity associated with trauma exposure have a long history, dating back as far as World War I, when veterans with "shell-shock" were shown to demonstrate greater increases in heart rate and respiration than did control subjects in response to laboratory presentations of combat-related stimuli (Meakins & Wilson, 1918). Over the years, these findings have been extended to veterans of other wars as well (Blanchard, Kolb, Gerardi, Ryan, & Pallmeyer, 1986; Blanchard, Kolb, Pallmeyer, & Gerardi, 1982; McFall, Murburg, Roszell, & Veith, 1989; Malloy, Fairbank, & Keane, 1983; Pitman & Orr, 1993). Skin conductance, heart rate, electromyogram, and blood pressure measures have typically been found, either alone or in combination, to discriminate reliably PTSD cases from noncases among combat-exposed veterans. Tomarken (1995) has recently summarized important issues with respect to the psychometric properties of psychophysiological measures.

Although this considerable body of research indicates the significant potential of psychophysiological techniques for the assessment of PTSD, these studies have been conducted almost exclusively with war veterans who have multiple exposures to traumatic events and chronic symptomatology. Recently, however, Shalev, Orr, and Pitman (1993) found that PTSD cases could be reliably discriminated from noncases among Israeli civilians exposed to noncombat trauma. These findings, if replicated, suggest that measuring psychophysiological responses to trauma-related imagery may be an effective assessment tool for PTSD related to a variety of traumatic exposures.

Although psychophysiological measures may seem difficult to "fake," is this, in fact, the case? This issue has not been intensively studied to date, but the results of a study conducted by Gerardi, Blanchard, and Kolb (1989), in which the ability of non-PTSD veterans to "fake" increased physiological reactivity in response to combat stimuli was studied, serve as an important caveat. Findings indicated that although the baseline levels of physiological reactivity of PTSD veterans were significantly higher than those of non-PTSD veterans, there were no differences in the responses to combat stimuli of PTSD veterans and non-PTSD veterans attempting to fake PTSD.

Finally, there are substantial issues surrounding the feasibility of using psychophysiological approaches, particularly in the context of community studies. The cost of equipment, the expertise necessary to conduct the assessment, and the requirements for a controlled environment would, in most cases, be prohibitive in such studies. Thus, although promising, the role of psychophysiological assessment in PTSD case identification in epidemiological studies is probably limited at present.

More recently, studies have also begun to identify neurobiological correlates of PTSD that may be useful in case identification. For example, Yehuda and her colleagues (Yehuda et al., 1990) found significantly lower mean 24-hour urinary cortisol levels in combat veterans with PTSD than in age-comparable, nonpsychiatric controls. Subsequently, Yehuda et al. (1995) found that Holocaust survivors with PTSD had lower mean 24-hour urinary cortisol levels than a comparison group of Holocaust survivors without PTSD and another comparison group of sociodemographically matched controls who were not exposed to the Holocaust. These latter findings strengthen the specificity of the relationship between urinary cortisol and PTSD, suggesting that this relationship may eventually be useful in PTSD case identification.

Research Design-Based Approaches

Judicious selection of assessment techniques and instruments is not the only way to improve case identification in epidemiological studies. The ability to identify cases can be influenced by research design features as well. Traditionally, cohort studies are designed so that all subjects undergo the same assessment procedure. When the disorder of interest is relatively rare, however — that is, when most people in the cohort *do not* have the disorder — alternative designs may be both more efficient and effective.

For example, Kulka et al. (1991) note that the findings of seven major community epidemiological studies of the prevalence of PTSD among Vietnam veterans had prevalence estimates ranging from 13% to 17%. In other words, more than 80% of the veterans who participated in these studies did *not* have PTSD. Comprehensive PTSD case identification, however, is resource intensive, and expending those resources on subjects who very likely do not have PTSD is inefficient.

One solution to this dilemma is the two-stage design (see Dohrenwend, 1989). In two-stage designs, all subjects are first assessed with a brief screening instrument that has been shown to be related to the specific diagnosis being studied. This allows the investigators to divide the cohort into "likely cases" and "likely noncases." Then at the second stage, *all* of those who screen positive (i.e., the likely cases) and a *subsample* of the negatives (i.e., the likely noncases) are selected for a more comprehensive assessment.

By including in the second stage all of the apparent cases, the statistical power for risk factor and other analyses is increased, and a basis for estimating the sample-specific false-positive screening rate is established (i.e., what proportion of the "likely cases" identified by the screening are ultimately determined to be noncases?). Additionally, by including a subsample of the screen negatives, an empirical basis for estimating the sample-specific false negative screening rate is established (i.e., what proportion of the "likely noncases" are ultimately determined to be PTSD cases?). Because the second-stage sample is a probability sample, second-stage findings can be weighted back to formulate unbiased prevalence estimates for the original cohort, corrected for the observed screening bias.

As an example of how this approach can be implemented, subjects in the NVVRS (Kulka et al., 1990) were screened at the first stage with the Mississippi Scale. All veterans who scored over the specified cutoff of 89, which was selected to emphasize sensitivity over specificity (i.e., to increase the likelihood that all of the true PTSD cases in the sample screened positive, and were therefore included in the second stage), were then included in the Clinical Examination sample, along with a subset of those who screened negative. Participants in the Clinical Examination underwent a comprehensive, multimeasure PTSD assessment, which served as the basis for the NVVRS composite PTSD diagnosis (details of this procedure are provided in Schlenger et al., 1992).

Thus, there are a variety of ways to improve case identification in community epidemiological studies. Although there are varying opinions as to which method is "best," one fact is clear: No single existing method is "perfect"—that is, none provides a true "gold standard" for PTSD diagnosis. Spitzer (1983) recommends the LEAD standard (Longitudinal, Expert, and All Data), which emphasizes assessment by trained clinicians using multiple sources of information. The NVVRS research team (Schlenger et al., 1992) extended this to the CAMMI standard—Comprehensive Assessment of Multimethod–Multisource Information. The CAMMI standard emphasizes the integration of information from multiple methods and multiple sources into case identification algorithms.

The point is that in the absence of a definitive biological marker that can be measured with absolute reliability, PTSD case identification must rely on less-than-perfect assessment measures. That is, although there are a number of "good" measures of PTSD, none is "perfect." Consequently, given the importance of valid case identification to internal validity, the use of multiple measures that employ varying methodologies and data sources is recommended. Relying on multiple measures, and requiring multiple positive indications for an individual to be classified as a case, is feasible even in community studies, and increases confidence in the diagnosis.

ETHICAL CONSIDERATIONS

Assessment of traumatic exposure and PTSD diagnosis involves focusing the attention of subjects on experiences and symptoms that are likely to have been — and may continue to be — painful. This fact leads to concerns related to the protection of human subjects: Is participation in such assessments "harmful" to subjects, and what safeguards are prudent to guard against any potential negative consequences?

Based on our experiences in conducting a variety of epidemiological studies of PTSD, we believe that participation in such assessments is not "harmful" in any meaningful sense. Although a minority of participants will experience an observable emotional reaction to the assessment (e.g., may become tearful when describing details of an exposure) and may experience some distress, that experience is not in and of itself damaging. Nevertheless, in our view, investigators conducting community epidemiological studies of PTSD should be aware that some participants may experience distress; inform all potential participants in advance of that possibility; train interviewers to manage emotional responsivity in participants, and provide them support in doing so; and arrange in advance a professional referral network for participants who request referral.

As an example of how these mandates can be implemented, even in the context of a national survey, NVVRS survey interviews were conducted by experienced survey interviewers who were trained to administer the interview in a 10-day training session. In addition to covering the mechanics of the interview process, the training also focused on issues related to respecting the rights of research participants (e.g., voluntary participation, informed consent, confidentiality) and interviewer "sensitivity." In this component of the training, which was provided by a team of experienced clinicians expert in diagnosing and treating PTSD in combat veterans, trainers helped interviewers identify the parts of the interview that were most likely to evoke emotional responses. In addition, training focused on how to recognize cues that indicate emotional reactivity, and how to *manage* such reactivity when it occurred. It is important to train survey interviewers to recognize and maintain appropriate role boundaries such that they do not make the error of attempting to provide "counseling" or other interventions that are beyond their professional competence.

In addition to this training, we established support networks for participants *and for interviewers*. To support participants, interviewers always carried with them a list of local mental health treatment resources (e.g., Vet Centers, community mental health centers) in the event that the participant requested information. In addition, interviewers were trained to report to the clinical training team anything "unusual" that occurred during their contacts with participants (e.g., during an interview, during a phone call in which the interviewer was trying to set up an interview). Clinicians would then discuss the facts of the case with the interviewer, and they would together decide on a course of action (e.g., the clinician might call the participant to make a referral). Furthermore, NVVRS participants were followed up by phone about a week after their interview and asked specifically about its impact on them, if any. During these calls, referral assistance was offered to all who requested it. In fact, the number of interviews in which participants were distressed was small, and no reactions were severe.

We also implemented a support network for interviewers, in recognition of the fact that these interviews could be stressful both for participants and for interviewers. In addition to their special training, interviewers had access to clinical backup at all times (i.e., there was always a clinician whom they could call). In addition, we held periodic conference calls of small groups of interviewers with members of the clinical team to provide peer support, discuss specific problems, and allow interviewers to benefit from the experiences of their colleagues.

Safeguarding the privacy of the respondent during the assessment process is also a challenging aspect of community epidemiological research. Interviews in community studies are typically conducted in the participant's home, with family members and others also present. Precautions must be taken to protect the confidentiality of the participant's answers by conducting the interview out of the hearing range of others in the residence. Issues of privacy are particularly important for potentially vulnerable populations, such as children and adolescents, who could be placed at risk if their answers to sensitive questions (e.g., questions about substance use and abuse, sexual behavior) were overheard.

Several recent technological advances in survey methods show considerable promise for enhancing the privacy of respondents in community studies of sensitive behaviors. Such advances include new computer technologies in which laptop computers "read" (prerecorded) interview questions to respondents wearing headphones, and the interviewee responds by pressing the appropriate key on the computer's keyboard. This technology, referred to as audio computer-assisted self-interviewing (A-CASI), has already been applied to several standardized assessment instruments, including the DISC.

SUMMARY

Assessment of exposure and case identification are two corner-stones of the internal validity of community epidemiological studies of PTSD. Inaccurate assessment of either can lead to unwarranted conclusions about PTSD incidence and prevalence, about its relationship to other disorders, and its risk factors, all of which can detract from treatment and prevention efforts.

Assessment of exposure is complicated by the fact that there are many kinds of exposures that can lead to PTSD, and individuals can have multiple exposures of varying frequency and intensity. Most studies have assessed exposure via one-time survey interviews, although documented misclassifications associated with self-reports of exposure underscore the importance of independent corroboration. Although existing instruments have moved the field forward, it is clear that periodic assessment of exposure in the context of prospective, longitudinal studies represents an important advance, and that independent corroboration should always be sought where feasible.

Case identification in community studies is complicated by the lack of a "presenting problem" to serve as a starting point for assessment. Instruments based on a variety of underlying approaches to diagnostic decision making have been developed that have acceptable psychometric properties. Nevertheless, none represents a true "gold standard." In the absence of such a standard, confidence in case identification can be improved by using *multiple* assessments that can provide an empirical basis for a "best estimate" diagnosis, and through design features that focus assessment resources on people who are likely to be cases of, or at risk for, PTSD.

Community epidemiological studies of PTSD involve some special ethical considerations. Investigators conducting such studies should train interviewers and other staff in the details of human subjects' protection, including voluntary participation, informed consent, and confidentiality. In addition, interviewers and others who have direct contact with research participants should be prepared in advance to identify and manage emotional reactivity on the part of some study participants. Investigators should plan for networks to support both participants and interviewers.

One important implication of this is that competent conduct of community epidemiological studies of PTSD requires skills from a variety of disciplines. Consequently, such studies are best conducted by multidisciplinary teams of investigators that can bring the full range of skills and expertise — for example, psychological, sociological, statistical, methodological, logistical — to bear. Assembling such multidisciplinary teams, and fielding the large-scale data collection efforts that these studies require, is both expensive and time consuming.

Finally, although the field has advanced rapidly since the official designation in 1980 of PTSD as a specific psychiatric disorder, many basic epidemiological questions remain unanswered. For PTSD related to some types of traumatic exposure (e.g., combat, rape), questions of prevalence and comorbidity have been relatively well studied, but for other exposures, basic questions remain. Across the board, however, important issues of etiology remain unresolved. Addressing these questions comprehensively will require large-scale, prospective, cohort studies conducted by multidisciplinary teams of investigators using multiple measures of exposure and multiple case identification measures.

ACKNOWLEDGMENTS

Preparation of this chapter was supported in part by Grant No. MH45797 from the National Institute of Mental Health.

REFERENCES

American Psychiatric Association. (1980). *Diagnostic and statistical manual of mental disorders* (3rd ed.). Washington, DC: Author.

American Psychiatric Association. (1994). *Diagnostic and statistical manual of mental disorders* (4th ed.). Washington, DC: Author.

Angold, A., Cox, A., Prendergast, M., Rutter, M., & Simonoff, E. (1992). *The Child and Adolescent Psychiatric Assessment (CAPA)*. Unpublished instrument, Developmental Epidemiology Program, Duke University, Durham, NC.

Anthony, J. C., Folstein, M., Romanoski, A. J., Von Korff, M. R., Nestadt, G. R., Chalal, R., Merchant, A., Brown, C. H., Shapiro, S., Kramer, M., & Gruenberg, E. M. (1985). Comparison of the lay Diagnostic Interview Schedule and a standardized psychiatric diagnosis. *Archives of General Psychiatry, 42,* 667–676.

Blake, D. D., Weathers, F. W., Nagy, L. M., Kaloupek, D. G., Gusman, F. D., Charney, D. S., & Keane, T. M. (1995). The development of a clinician-administered PTSD scale. *Journal of Traumatic Stress, 8,* 75–90.

Blanchard, E. B., Kolb, L. C., Gerardi, R. J., Ryan, P., & Pallmeyer, T. P. (1986). Cardiac response to relevant stimuli as an adjunctive tool for diagnosing post-traumatic stress disorder in Vietnam veterans. *Behavior Therapy, 17,* 592–606.

Blanchard, E. B., Kolb, L. C., Pallmeyer, T. P., & Gerardi, R. J. (1982). A psychophysiological study of post-traumatic stress disorder in Vietnam veterans. *Psychiatric Quarterly, 54,* 220–229.

Breslau, N., Davis, G. C., Andreski, P., & Peterson, E. (1991). Traumatic events and post-traumatic stress disorder in an urban population of young adults. *Archives of General Psychiatry, 48,* 216–222.

Breslau, N., Davis, G. C., & Andreski, P. (1995). Risk factors for PTSD-related traumatic events: A prospective analysis. *American Journal of Psychiatry, 152,* 529–535.

Bromet, E., & Dew, M. A. (1995). Review of psychiatric epidemiologic research on disasters. *Epidemiologic Reviews, 17,* 113–119.

Butcher, J. N., Dahlstrom, W. G., Graham, J. R., Tellegen, A., & Kaemmer, B. (1989). *Minnesota Multiphasic Personality Inventory-2 (MMPI-2): Manual for administration and scoring*. Minneapolis: University of Minnesota Press.

Cook, T. D., & Campbell, D. T. (1979). *Quasi-experimentation*. Boston: Houghton Mifflin.

Costello, A. J., Edelbrock, C. S., Kalas, R., Kessler, M. D., & Klaric, S. H. (1982). *The National Institute of Mental Health Diagnostic Interview for Children (DISC)*. Rockville, MD: National Institute of Mental Health.

Davidson, H., Smith, R., & Kudler, H. (1989). Validity and reliability of the DSM-III criteria for posttraumatic stress disorder: Experience with a structured interview. *Journal of Nervous and Mental Disease, 177*, 336–341.

Dohrenwend, B. P. (1989). The problem of validity in field studies of psychological disorders revisited. In L. N. Robins (Ed.), *Validity of psychiatric diagnosis*. New York: Raven Press.

Fairbank, J. A., Jordan, B. K., & Schlenger, W. E. (1996). Designing and implementing epidemiologic studies. In E. B. Carlson (Ed.), *Trauma research methodology*. Lutherville, MD: Sidran Press.

Fairbank, J. A., Schlenger, W. E., Caddell, J. M., & Woods, M. G. (1993). Post-traumatic stress disorder. In P. B. Sutker & H. E. Adams (Eds.), *Comprehensive handbook of psychopathology*. New York: Plenum Press.

Fairbank, J. A., Schlenger, W. E., Saigh, P. A., & Davidson, J. R. T. (1995). An epidemiologic profile of post-traumatic stress disorder: Prevalence, comorbidity, and risk factors. In M. J. Friedman, D. S. Charney, & A. Y. Deutch, (Eds.), *Neurobiological and clinical consequences of stress: From normal adaptation to PTSD*. New York: Raven Press.

Gerardi, R. F., Blanchard, E. B., & Kolb, L. C. (1989). Ability of Vietnam veterans to dissimulate a psychophysiological assessment for post-traumatic stress disorder. *Behavior Therapy, 20*, 229–243.

Helzer, J. E., Robins, L. N., McEvoy, L. T., Spitznagel, E. L., Stoltzman, R. K., Farmer, A., & Brockington, I. F. (1985). A comparison of clinical and Diagnostic Interview Schedule diagnoses. *Archives of General Psychiatry, 42*, 657–666.

Herman, J. J., Perry, J. C., & van der Kolk, B. A. (1989). Childhood trauma in borderline personality disorder. *American Journal of Psychiatry, 146*, 490–495.

Jordan, B. K., Schlenger, W. E., Caddell, J. M., & Fairbank, J. A. (in press). Etiologic factors in the development of borderline personality disorder in a sample of convicted women felons. In M. C. Zanarini (Ed.), *The role of sexual abuse in borderline personality disorder*. Washington, DC: American Psychiatric Press.

Jordan, B. K., Schlenger, W. E., Fairbank, J. A., & Caddell, J. M. (1996). Prevalence of psychiatric disorders among incarcerated women, II: Convicted felons entering prison. *Archives of General Psychiatry, 53*, 513–519.

Keane, T. M., Caddell, J. M., & Taylor, K. L. (1988). Mississippi scale for combat-related post-traumatic stress disorder: Three studies in reliability and validity. *Journal of Consulting and Clinical Psychology, 56*, 85–90.

Keane, T. M., Malloy, P. F., & Fairbank, J. A. (1984). The empirical development of an MMPI subscale for the assessment of combat-related posttraumatic stress disorder. *Journal of Consulting and Clinical Psychology, 52*, 888–891.

Kilpatrick, D. G., Resnick, H. S., & Freedy, J. R. (1991). *The Potential Stressful Events interview*. Unpublished instrument, Crime Victims Research and Treatment Center, Department of Psychiatry, Medical University of South Carolina, Charleston, SC.

Kilpatrick, D. G., Resnick, H. S., Freedy, J. R., Pelcovitz, D., Resick, P., Roth, S., & van der Kolk, B . (1994). The posttraumatic stress disorder field trial: emphasis on criterion A and overall PTSD diagnosis. In T. A. Widiger (Ed.), *DSM-IV sourcebook* (Vol, 5). Washington, DC: American Psychiatric Press.

Kilpatrick, D. G., Saunders, B. E., Veronen, L. J., Best, C. L., & Von, J. M. (1987). Criminal victimization: Lifetime prevalence, reporting to police, and psychological impact. *Crime and Delinquency, 33,* 479–489.

Kulka, R. A., & Schlenger, W. E. (1993). Survey research and field designs for the study of posttraumatic stress disorder. In J. P. Wilson & B. Raphael (Eds.), *International handbook of traumatic stress syndromes.* New York: Plenum Press.

Kulka, R. A., Schlenger, W. E., Fairbank, J. A., Hough, R. L., Jordan, B. K., Marmar, C. R., & Weiss, D. S. (1990). *Trauma and the Vietnam War generation: Report of findings from the National Vietnam Veterans Readjustment Study.* New York: Brunner/Mazel.

Kulka, R. A., Schlenger, W. E., Fairbank, J. A., Hough, R. L., Jordan, B. K., Marmar, C. R., & Weiss, D. S. (1991). Assessment of posttraumatic stress disorder in the community: prospects and pitfalls from recent studies of Vietnam veterans. *Psychological Assessment, 3,* 547–560.

Loftus, E. F., Garry, M., & Feldman, J. (1994). Forgetting sexual trauma: What does it mean when 38% forget? *Journal of Consulting and Clinical Psychology, 62,* 1177–1181.

McFall, M. E., Murburg, M., Roszell, D. K., & Veith, R. C. (1989). Psychophysiologic and neuroendocrine findings in posttraumatic stress disorder: A review of theory and research. *Journal of Anxiety Disorders, 3,* 243–257.

Malloy, P. F., Fairbank, J. A., & Keane, T. M. (1983). Validation of a multimethod assessment of posttraumatic stress disorder. *Journal of Consulting and Clinical Psychology, 51,* 488–494.

Meakins, J. C., & Wilson, R. M. (1918). The effect of certain sensory stimulations on respiratory and heart rate in cases of so-called "irritable heart." *Heart, 7,* 17–22.

Norris, F. H. (1990). Screening for traumatic stress: A scale for use in the general population. *Journal of Applied Social Psychology, 20,* 1704–1718.

Norris, F. H. (1992). Epidemiology of trauma: Frequency and impact of different potentially traumatic events on different demographic subgroups. *Journal of Consulting and Clinical Psychology, 60,* 409–418.

Pitman, R. K., & Orr, S. P. (1993). Psychophysiologic testing for post-traumatic stress disorder: Forensic psychiatric application. *Bulletin of the American Academy of Psychiatry and the Law, 21,* 37–52.

Regier, D. A., Myers, J. K., Kramer, M., Robins, L. N., Blazer, D. G., Hough, R. L., Eaton, W. W., & Locke, B. Z. (1984). The NIMH Epidemiologic Catchment Area Program: Historical context, major objectives, and study population characteristics. *Archives of General Psychiatry, 41,* 934–941.

Resnick, H. S., Best, C. L., Freedy, J. R., Kilpatrick, D. G., & Falsetti, S. A. (1993). *Trauma assessment for adults.* Unpublished interview protocol, Crime Victims Research and Treatment Center, Department of Psychiatry, Medical University of South Carolina, Charleston, SC.

Resnick, H. S., Falsetti, S. A., Kilpatrick, D. G., & Freedy, J. R. (1996). Assessment of rape and other civilian trauma-related post-traumatic stress disorder: Emphasis on assessment of potentially traumatic events. In T. W. Miller (Ed.), *Stressful life events* (2nd ed.). New York: International Universities Press.

Resnick, H. S., Kilpatrick, D. G., Dansky, B. S., Saunders, B. E., & Best, C. L. (1993). Prevalence of civilian trauma and posttraumatic stress disorder in a representative national sample of women. *Journal of Consulting and Clinical Psychology, 61,* 984–991.

Robins, L. N., Helzer, J. E., Croughan, J., & Ratcliff, K. S. (1981). National Institute of Mental Health Diagnostic Interview Schedule: Its history, characteristics, and validity. *Archives of General Psychiatry, 38,* 381–389.

Robins, L. N., Wing, J., Wittchen, H. U., & Helzer, J. E. (1988). The Composite International Diagnostic Interview: An epidemiologic instrument suitable for use in conjunction with different diagnostic systems and in different cultures. *Archives of General Psychiatry, 45,* 1069–1077.

Schlenger, W. E., Kulka, R. A., Fairbank, J. A., Hough, R. L., Jordan, B. K., Marmar, C. R., & Weiss, D. S. (1992). The prevalence of post-traumatic stress disorder in the Vietnam generation: A multimethod, multisource assessment of psychiatric disorder. *Journal of Traumatic Stress, 5,* 333–363.

Shalev, A. Y., Orr, S. P., & Pitman, R. K. (1993). Psychophysiologic assessment of traumatic imagery in Israeli civilian patients with posttraumatic stress disorder. *American Journal of Psychiatry, 150,* 620–624.

Shapiro, S., Skinner, E. A., Kessler, L. G., Von Korff, M., German, P. S., Tishler, G. L., Leaf, P. J., Benham, L., Cottler, L., & Regier, D. A. (1984). Utilization of health and mental health services: Three epidemiologic catchment area sites. *Archives of General Psychiatry, 41,* 971–978.

Spitzer, R. L. (1983). Psychiatric diagnosis: Are clinicians still necessary? *Comprehensive Psychiatry, 24,* 399–411.

Spitzer, R. L., Williams, J. B. W., Gibbon, M., & First, M. B. (1992). The Structured Clinical Interview for DSM-III-R (SCID): I. History, rationale, and description. *Archives of General Psychiatry, 49,* 624–629.

Sudman, S., & Bradburn, N. (1973). Effects of time and memory factors on response in surveys. *Journal of the American Statistical Association, 68,* 805–815.

Tomarken, A. J. (1995). A psychometric perspective on psychophysiological measures. *Psychological Assessment, 7,* 387–395.

Turner, C. F., Lessler, J. T., & Gfroerer, J. C. (Eds.). (1992). *Survey measurement of drug use: Methodological studies.* Washington, DC: U. S. Government Printing Office.

Vreven, D. L., Gudanowski, D. M., King, L. A., & King, D. W. (1995). The civilian version of the Mississippi PTSD scale: A psychometric evaluation. *Journal of Traumatic Stress, 8,* 91–109.

Weiss, D. S., Marmar, C. R., Schlenger, W. E., Fairbank, J. A., Jordan, B. K., Hough, R. L., & Kulka, R. A. (1992). The prevalence of lifetime and partial post-traumatic stress disorder in Vietnam theater veterans. *Journal of Traumatic Stress, 5,* 364–376.

Williams, L. M. (1994a). Recall of childhood trauma: A prospective study of women's memories of child sexual abuse. *Journal of Consulting and Clinical Psychology, 62,* 1167–1176.

Williams, L. M. (1994b). What does it mean to forget child sexual abuse? A reply to Loftus, Garry, and Feldman (1994). *Journal of Consulting and Clinical Psychology, 62,* 1182–1186.

Wilson, J. P., & Raphael, B. (Eds.). (1993). *International handbook of traumatic stress syndromes.* New York: Plenum Press.

Yehuda, R., Kahana, B., Binder-Byrnes, K., Southwick, S. M., Mason, J. W., & Giller, E. L. (1995). Low urinary cortisol excretion in Holocaust survivors with post-traumatic stress disorder. *American Journal of Psychiatry, 152,* 982–986.

Yehuda, R., Southwick, S. M., Nussbaum, G., Wahby, V., Giller, E. L., & Mason, J. W. (1990). Low urinary cortisol excretion in patients with posttraumatic stress disorder. *Journal of Nervous and Mental Disease, 178,* 366–369.

Zanarini, M. C., Gunderson, J. G., Marino, M. F., Schwartz, E. O., & Frankenburg, F. R. (1989). Childhood experiences of borderline patients. *Comprehensive Psychiatry, 30,* 18–25.

CHAPTER 6

Trauma and Medical Illness: Assessing Trauma-Related Disorders in Medical Settings

BONNIE L. GREEN
STEVEN A. EPSTEIN
JANICE L. KRUPNICK
JULIA H. ROWLAND

INTRODUCTION

In this chapter we address trauma and posttraumatic stress disorder (PTSD) in the context of medical settings. Two major aspects of this topic are covered. The first addresses medical illnesses that might serve as stressors for the development of PTSD, with a focus on life-threatening illness. We discuss assessment of PTSD in this context, including how life-threatening illness fits the A (stressor) criterion and how PTSD may manifest somewhat differently in patients with life-threatening illness. Second, we focus on trauma as an *instigator* for medical outcomes. In this discussion we address high-risk behavior, medical symptoms and somatization, and medical utilization associated with prior trauma exposure. This section includes issues related to screening for trauma in medical populations and guidelines for dealing with somatizing patients.

MEDICAL ILLNESS AS A PTSD STRESSOR EVENT

Physical Injury

A fairly substantial literature now documents that PTSD can develop following accidental injury. For example, several studies have documented the course of PTSD following burn injuries. Roca, Spence, and Munster (1992) diagnosed PTSD (via the Structured Clinical Interview for DSM [SCID]) in 7% of hospitalized burn survivors at discharge; this increased to 22% at

4-month follow-up. Likewise, Perry, Difede, Musngi, Frances, and Jacobsberg (1992) found an increase in PTSD among burn victims (also assessed using the SCID), from 35% at 2 months to 45% at 12 months. In a small sample of survivors of serious accidental injury who presented at a shock-trauma center, Epstein (1993) found that 40% of patients met full criteria for PTSD by psychiatric interview during the 9-month follow-up period. In this study, one-third of the individuals with PTSD showed delayed (2–3 months) onset. These studies indicate that PTSD can result from accidental injury, a traditional PTSD stressor (Criterion A), in that individuals have been exposed to an external event in the past, even if the effects are lingering. The damage can be assessed in a short period, and once the person is treated, the actual threat subsides. This type of event has more in common with combat and disaster than it does with life-threatening medical illness.

Life-Threatening Illness

Interest in life-threatening illness as a potential PTSD stressor has expanded in recent years. A handful of researchers has begun or reported studies to examine PTSD secondary to medical illness. Most of these have been in the context of individuals' experience with cancer or myocardial infarction. A few have looked at specific trauma related to medical intervention as a cause of PTSD.

Cancer

Interest in the psychiatric impact of cancer has been an active area of research interest and funding. One of the primary reasons for this is the growing number of cancer survivors (estimated at over 8 million in the United States alone, 5 million of whom were diagnosed more than 5 years ago). For some cancers (e.g., Hodgkin's disease, testicular cancer, childhood leukemia), the vast majority of individuals treated will be cured of their illness. Most patients will live for extended periods of time with their disease. To achieve these advances, however, treatments have become more aggressive, lengthy, and toxic. As a consequence, in the last two decades, cancer has become a chronic illness for many survivors.

A number of studies have shown that receiving a diagnosis of cancer causes significant psychological distress. Derogatis et al. (1983) found that 47% of a cross-section of cancer patients met criteria for a psychiatric disorder in comparison with 12–13% estimated for the general population (Myers et al., Tischler, 1984). Cella and Tross (1986) found that 60 male Hodgkin's disease survivors showed lower motivation for intimacy and higher avoidant thinking about illness (both symptoms of PTSD) than a comparison group of 20 physically healthy men. Advanced disease stage was associated with the highest risk for psychological distress and psychosocial disruption during the first 2 years after treatment. In a subsequent study, Cella, Mahon, and Donovan (1990) gave the Impact of Event Scale (IES) to 40 patients within 30 days of a *recurrence* of cancer. They found marked elevations on both intrusion and avoidance subscales, with 43% of the sample exceeding the clinical cutoff score for intrusive symptoms and 80% exceeding the cutoff for avoidant symptoms. These levels of stress-related symptomatology are comparable to those for individuals who present with more traditional trauma-induced disorders. Women who had experienced a prior recurrence tended to exhibit fewer avoidance symptoms than those for whom this was a first recurrence, and 78% of patients felt that their initial diagnosis of cancer was *less* distressing than news of a recurrence; only 8% reported the reverse. The threat to life may be perceived as increased at this time for patients who are aware that the odds of survival are often dramatically reduced when a recurrence is diagnosed.

Despite recognition of the potentially traumatic impact of a cancer diagnosis, only recently have researchers systematically examined cancer survivors for the incidence of PTSD. Alter and colleagues (1992) examined the incidence of PTSD in three patient groups who were an average of about 5 years posttreatment: adolescent survivors of cancer ($n = 20$), their mothers ($n = 20$), and adult breast cancer survivors ($n = 27$). As part of the multicenter DSM-IV field trial for PTSD, this was the only site examining medical illness as a stressor event. Subjects were assessed using the PTSD module of the SCID, the Diagnostic Interview Schedule (DIS), and several self-report measures. For adult survivors, the authors reported *lifetime* and *current* prevalence rates of cancer-related PTSD of 22% and 4%, respectively (Alter et al., 1996). Mothers were found to have lifetime rates of 54% and current rates of 25% (Pelcovitz et al., 1996). Adolescent survivors had lifetime and current rates of 54% and 33%, respectively (Alter et al., 1992). No differences were found related to time since treatment or, interestingly, to stage of illness (e.g., early vs. advanced breast cancer).

Stuber, Christakis, Houskamp, and Kazak (1996) reported data on 64 pediatric cancer survivors between the ages of 7 and 19 who had been off of treatment for at least 2 years, and their parents. Parents and children completed the PTSD Reaction Index (Adult and Child versions, respectively). This instrument showed that 13% of patients, 40% of mothers, and 33% of fathers scored in the "severe" range (> 13) on the Reaction Index. Their self-report data suggested that for many children, the memories that lingered after treatment were of the procedures themselves (e.g., bone-marrow biopsies, spinal taps, etc.) rather than their life-threatening condition. Similar to Alter et al.'s (1992) data, they found no difference in Reaction Index scores by time since treatment ended, suggesting that the problem may be a chronic one. Their data provided evidence for PTSD, but the diagnosis was not assessed using a diagnostic interview.

In a recent study conducted by the authors (Green et al., 1996), we examined the incidence of PTSD in women 4 to 12 months posttreatment for early-stage breast cancer. All women completed an extensive battery of self-report instruments and were then interviewed using the SCID for DSM-III-R, including the PTSD module. Data on 160 women ranging in age from 26 to 75 years ($M = 53$) showed that, at some time after their diagnosis of breast cancer, 36% of the women had experienced recurrent, intrusive recollections or ruminations, 8% met full PTSD diagnostic criteria for numbing/avoidance, and 27% met hyperarousal criteria. At the time of interview, 20% reported current intrusive recollections or ruminations, 4% met numbing/avoidance criteria, and 11% met criteria for hyperarousal. Only 5% of the women met full criteria for lifetime (postdiagnosis) cancer-related PTSD, whereas 2.5% met current criteria. Thus, the incidence of cancer-related PTSD was very low in this population. Another 4% of the sample might be conceptualized as meeting criteria for "subsyndromal PTSD," that is, meeting intrusive and arousal criteria but having only two (rather than three) avoidance symptoms. Thus, about 9% of the sample was highly symptomatic, and up to 20% of the sample had intrusion, two avoidance symptoms, *or* two arousal symptoms. These findings are very similar to those reported by Cordova et al. (1995) using the IES and a screen for PTSD symptoms. They estimated that 5–10% of breast cancer survivors would likely meet DSM-IV criteria for PTSD.

Risk for PTSD decreased with age, consistent with a model that cancer in younger women is more unexpected, and hence life-threatening, than in older women. Indeed, in premenopausal women, the disease itself does actually seem to be more aggressive (Spinelli et al., 1995). We had also hypothesized that women undergoing longer and more intense treatment for their disease might be at greater risk for PTSD. However, no differences were found by type of surgery or whether a woman went on to receive adjuvant chemotherapy, although there was some confound to the latter, as younger women were more likely to receive chemotherapy.

Taken as a whole, current studies in this area, although still sparse, suggest that although PTSD can occur as a function of diagnosis and treatment of cancer in adults, it may affect only a small number of selected patients. The higher rates of PTSD symptomatology in pediatric cancer survivors and our younger sample indicate that age may be an important risk factor and may also put individuals at risk for chronic problems. Furthermore, parents seem to be at particular risk when their *child* has cancer. These studies also demonstrate that although age at time of treatment may be a risk factor, treatment *recency* is not, suggesting that symptoms, when they occur, appear soon after illness and do not subside quickly, but if untreated, may be relatively persistent over time

Myocardial Infarction

A number of studies have been conducted on the association between myocardial infarction (MI) and PTSD symptoms. In an early report, Kutz and colleagues (Kutz, Garb, & David, 1988) presented four case studies of patients

exhibiting PTSD post-MI. Later, they examined PTSD symptoms in 100 patients 6- to 18-months (average 14-months) post-MI (Kutz, Shabtai, Solomon,
Neumann, & David, 1994) using a self-report questionnaire for PTSD symptoms (Solomon, 1989). They found "probable" chronic PTSD in 16% of their
sample and "probable" acute PTSD (lasting less than 6 months and not present
at time of evaluation) in 9% of the sample, yielding a 25% lifetime risk. In
19 (76%) of the subjects with chronic PTSD, the disorder appeared within
3 months of their MI. The appearance of symptoms was found to be related
to ethnic background, prior traumatic experiences, and anticipation of disability following illness. Prior MI, cardiac-related hospitalization, and prior
PTSD of noncardiac origin increased risk of MI-related PTSD, as did greater anticipation of subsequent MI-caused disability. The strong association
between concern over disability and PTSD prompted the researchers to suggest that denial or only mild apprehension at the time of MI may be adaptive in the long term. They also found that PTSD may play a central role
in the tendency to seek emergency medical help in this population. Almost
half (47%) of patients who reported repeated visits to emergency settings
for "feeling another heart attack" met symptom criteria for PTSD, as opposed
to 20% of those who did not utilize emergency medical services. One might
speculate that hyperarousal precipitated these physical symptoms in some
individuals.

Doerfler, Pbert and DeCosimo (1994) assessed 50 men 6 to 12 months
following hospitalization for first MI ($n = 27$) or coronary artery bypass graph
(CABG) surgery ($n = 23$). Using DSM-III-R criteria applied to an algorithm
of information gathered on self-report, 4 patients (8%) met full criteria for
PTSD. These authors noted that self-reported anxiety, depression, and anger
correlated strongly with PTSD symptoms. Although they cautioned that corroboration using interview data was warranted, they concluded that PTSD
may represent an unrecognized problem for some men who sustain an MI
or undergo CABG surgery.

In a third study, van Driel and Op den Velde (1995) conducted a psychiatric evaluation of 23 consecutively admitted patients 1–2 weeks after admission for first MI. The SCID-III-R PTSD module was used to assess the
presence of PTSD symptoms related to the MI, as well as lifetime PTSD associated with other events. In addition, information was collected about life
history, social situation, prior traumatic experiences, and subjective perception of the MI. Eighteen survivors were interviewed again 22–26 months later.
About half the subjects reported perceived life threat, anxiety, or helplessness post-MI. However, only one subject met criteria for acute stress disorder (DSM-IV) during admission. On follow-up, *none* of the subjects met criteria
for PTSD at 2 years. One subject who initially experienced an acute stress
disorder had sufficient symptoms during the first year to warrant a diagnosis of partial PTSD at follow-up.

In summary, studies examining MI-related PTSD also suggest that only a small number of adults may be at potential risk for this disorder. As noted earlier, however, a somewhat higher number of patients may experience sub-syndromal levels of symptomatology. Furthermore, although rates of PTSD associated with life-threatening illness are too low to warrant routine screening for the disorder, MI may represent a special case. Clinical data suggest that denial in the early period post-MI may be important for recovery. Thus, patients who experience acute emotional distress in this period are not only more likely to develop later PTSD, but may also be at greater risk for poor recovery or death from their disease, and receive further evaluation.

Other Medical Trauma/Illnesses

Another set of studies have looked at the role of unexpected and traumatic medical procedures on incidence of PTSD. Shalev, Schreiber, Galai, and Melmed (1993) presented four case studies in which other medical illness and/or treatment procedures produced symptoms of PTSD. Each of these involved acute and traumatizing events (arrest and recovery during cardiac catheterization; emergency craniotomy; recurrent resuscitation for MI; complicated tonsillectomy in a woman with a history of panic disorder) that occurred suddenly or following what had been thought to be easily tolerated or benign events, and in which there was a clear discrepancy between physical healing and psychological recovery. Chemtob and Herriott (1994) reported a case of PTSD in a 24-year-old woman following severe Guillain–Barré syndrome. These reports highlight the importance of addressing the emotional consequences of medical events that are atypical or unexpected in the course of treating the illness, whether it is a cancer that occurs "off time" in the young, or a routine procedure gone awry.

ASSESSMENT ISSUES ASSOCIATED WITH LIFE-THREATENING ILLNESS AND PTSD

Life-Threatening Illness as a "Criterion A" Stressor

The definition of a traumatic event that may lead to the diagnosis of PTSD, and acute stress disorder as well, in the DSM-IV (American Psychiatric Association, 1994) requires that the person has "experienced, witnessed, or was confronted with an event or events that involved *actual or threatened death* or serious injury, or a *threat to the physical integrity* of self or others" (p. 427, emphasis added). This definition also requires that the person's response involve intense fear, helplessness, or horror. Thus, the definition of the stressor, threatened death and/or threat to physical integrity, clearly could include life-threatening illness as a potential stressor event for PTSD. Although this was theoretically true in DSM-III-R (American Psychiatric Association,

1987), life-threatening illness is explicitly named in the DSM-IV text accompanying the PTSD diagnosis. Until very recently, however, little empirical data actually existed to address whether life-threatening illness indeed produced PTSD at any notable level.

There are two fundamental ways in which life-threatening illness is different from more traditional stressors. First, the threat from such events is not from the external environment, as in events such as disasters, rape, combat, and automobile accidents. Rather, it arises internally, so that the threat and the individual cannot be separated. This fact may make the experience qualitatively different from one in which the threat arises from the outside. Second, once a person has been treated for the illness and survived, the ongoing stressor may not be the memory of the past event, but rather the threat that in the future the illness may recur, or be exacerbated, with death resulting. Conceptualized this way, the threat is not primarily in the past, but in the future. With the exception of such illnesses as MI, seizure disorder, or acute leukemia, in which the acute onset may *also* be life-threatening, the immediate "death encounter" in the majority of life-threatening illnesses is not experienced in the initial episode but, rather, looms ahead. This type of threat is more vague than the moment of immediately imminent death that one might experience with a tornado, a mugging, or a rape. However, certain aspects of treatment for these illnesses (e.g., surgery) may be stressful in their own right, and may even be perceived as a "death encounter."

Prior to beginning our studies of breast cancer survivors, we noted that the "threat" associated with cancer is primarily the *information* that one has the disease. In this sense, the diagnosis of cancer is similar to learning that one has been exposed to radioactive or toxic chemical contamination (Green, Lindy, & Grace, 1994). The "stressor" in these cases is the information that one has been exposed, or has cancer or heart damage, which is learned after the fact. We labeled this an "information stressor" in the case of individuals exposed to radioactive contamination (Green et al., 1994). The threat for these individuals was in the future (i.e., they were worried that they might develop cancer, or might pass on genetic abnormalities to their children, etc.). These differences in the nature and source of threat have important diagnostic implications. Specifically, the intrusive images/thoughts about the threat may not be actual recollections of the event(s), such as the precise moment of receiving the news that one has cancer or has been exposed to deadly chemicals, but more future-oriented ruminations about possible recurrence, manifestation of physical problems, or death. We next address this distinction with our research data on breast cancer survivors. Davidson, Fleming, and Baum (1986) addressed a similar issue in residents exposed to radioactivity following the nuclear leak at Three Mile Island (TMI). The future threat in that situation produced chronic stress symptoms, including high levels of intrusive thoughts and avoidance of reminders, lasting up to 5 years. However, although these situations clearly produced chronic stress responses

(Davidson et al., 1986; Green et al., 1994), there was little evidence that they produced PTSD. They also may be only partial analogs for cancer or myocardial infarction, in which the probability of future death is much higher.

In summary, cancer and other life-threatening illnesses may be qualitatively different, in a psychological sense, from more traditional PTSD stressor events in a number of ways. These include the fact that the threat is internal rather than external, and that it is ongoing, chronic, and future oriented. Thus, the focus of the survivor is on the future rather than the past. On the other hand, many aspects overlap as well; for example, the news about having a potentially deadly illness can be sudden and unexpected, the treatment may be traumatic, and many of the mental/emotional processes for avoiding and integrating the experiences are likely similar. The anxiety and arousal associated with the information, and certainly with some of the associated procedures, may be quite similar as well, along with the disruption in relationships brought on by the knowledge that one has had an experience that others may not be able to understand or find equally frightening.

Assessing PTSD following Life-Threatening Illness

One general concern in assessing psychological symptoms or disorders in a medical population is the differentiation between symptoms characteristic of the stress response and those typically produced by the illness or treatment. For example, pain related to surgery can cause sleeplessness and irritability. Radiotherapy and chemotherapy cause fatigue and lethargy in many cases, as well as depressed mood. Difficulty concentrating can result from a variety of treatments and medications. As with the diagnosis of other psychiatric disorders in persons with medical illnesses, it may be difficult to identify the source of the symptom. Thus, in the case of PTSD following medical illness events, the differential diagnosis is not only between PTSD and other psychiatric disorders, but also between PTSD and the medical conditions that have served as the source of stress.

A second concern regarding assessment of PTSD in this context relates to potential differences in *intrusive thinking*. As noted, we assessed PTSD via the SCID for DSM-III-R (from which we can also derive DSM-IV symptoms and diagnoses). Although about one-third of our subjects reported intrusive thinking, for some the content of the images and thoughts was *ruminative* and future oriented, rather than a *recollection* of past events. Most of these women reported thinking constantly and involuntarily about the fact that they had this potentially deadly disease. Other women had actual recollections, such as picturing the doctor telling them that their biopsy showed a malignancy, or being wheeled into surgery. Of the 8 women with PTSD, 5 had recollections, and 3 had only intrusive ruminations. This distinction applied to dreaming as well (e.g., dreaming that mother and sister had cancer vs. dreaming about the details of breast surgery).

With regard to the *denial/numbing symptoms,* life-threatening illness poses particular problems for the symptom of a sense of a "foreshortened future." To begin with, this symptom has not been well defined in adults. In our cancer population, the SCID question "Has (the trauma) changed the way you think about the future?" nearly always elicited a positive response. Yet, for the most part, the changes reported seemed to indicate appropriate and healthy adaptation (e.g., enjoying the present more since the future is not guaranteed, putting one's affairs in order, talking to children about one's will). We did not count these types of responses as indications of a pathological sense of foreshortened future. We only counted this symptom if the woman felt she were going to die soon (since this was unlikely in this good-prognosis group) or, if she could not think about the future in terms of more than a few weeks or months. Rather than scoring a different way of thinking about the future as pathological in these cancer patients, we viewed the general reevaluation of mortality/longevity, and associated behaviors and feelings, as appropriate and adaptive.

With regard to the *arousal symptom* of hypervigilance, we found that it took a different form in our cancer survivors than in survivors of other types of traumas. Rather than being hyperalert to their surroundings, these individuals became hyperalert to their physical health and any bodily changes that might signal that the cancer was recurring. Thus, this symptom may resemble hypochondriasis in a medically ill population. For example, subjects with this symptom reported examining themselves for additional lumps, sometimes many times a day, or far more often than would be appropriate for routine monitoring. They also looked for, and became concerned about, discoloration, bumps, moles, indentations, and so forth, that could mean a recurrence of the breast cancer or a metastasis to other sites. They did *not* report being hypervigilant about the environment or their safety, as one finds in survivors of other events.

TRAUMA AS AN ETIOLOGICAL FACTOR IN MEDICAL OUTCOMES

In this second part of our chapter, we review issues and studies related to medical illness as a trauma *outcome,* addressing the association between prior exposure to traumatic events and subsequent negative health behaviors, somatizing, and health care utilization. In these cases, patients present in medical settings with physical problems and complaints that may have a traumatic etiology, although we would like to be clear that we are not suggesting that physical symptoms following trauma have *only* psychological origins. Many traumatic events are or can be associated with physical injury, and there may be physical damage or dysfunction present, even if these are not easily detectable. Later we propose a model of factors that contribute to somatizing outcomes following trauma events.

Trauma and High-Risk Health Behavior

The relationship between trauma and vulnerability to high-risk health behavior has become a particularly salient issue in recent years as researchers have attempted to understand risk factors for the development of HIV and AIDS. A small, but growing, body of evidence suggests that assessment of trauma may be particularly important in youths who have been assaulted and/or abused, since they may be particularly prone to engage in practices that place them at high risk of contracting HIV. Cunningham, Stiffman, Dore, and Earls (1994) interviewed adolescent and young-adult patients of public health clinics in 10 cities. They found that a history of physical abuse, sexual abuse, or rape was related to engaging in a variety of HIV-risk behaviors and to a continuation or increase in the total number of these behaviors between adolescence and young adulthood. After controlling for gender and race, these investigators found the following:

1. Having been raped did not significantly contribute to HIV-risk behavior during adolescence, but did contribute by young adulthood.
2. Having been beaten was significantly associated with engaging in more HIV-risk behaviors during adolescence and young adulthood.
3. Having been sexually abused, in and of itself, did not significantly increase the likelihood of HIV-risk behavior, but, when it occurred in combination with other forms of abuse (e.g., physical abuse), it became an important determinant of risk behavior.
4. Having experienced more than one type of abuse (vs. experiencing no abuse) contributed significantly to mean number of HIV-related risk behaviors during adolescence and young adulthood.

This study also delineated the types of risky behaviors most prevalent for each trauma group. For example, after controlling for race, they found that male subjects who had been raped were three times as likely as those who had not been raped to engage in homosexual activity during adolescence and young adulthood. A history of abuse of any type was associated with a fourfold increase in the likelihood that a female would not always use (or have her partners use) condoms as a young adult. The odds of choosing risky sexual partners increased by 1.2–1.3 for abused youth in general, and by 2.5 for young adult males in particular. Youths who had been beaten, raped, or sexually abused were also at increased risk for engaging in prostitution (odds ratio = 1.3–9.0) and for using injectable drugs (odds ratio = 1.4–10.3).

It has also been found that men who reported a history of childhood sexual abuse had a twofold increase in prevalence of HIV infection compared to nonabused men. In a sample of HIV-symptomatic patients, 65% reported a history of sexual and/or physical abuse (Allers & Benjack, 1991). Stiffman, Dore, Earls, and Cunningham (1992), exploring the influence that mental health problems during adolescence might have on AIDS-related risk behaviors in young adults, found an association between PTSD and other disorders typically seen subsequent to trauma, such as depression, anxiety and substance abuse, and higher incidence of risk behaviors. Rotheram-Borus, Koopman, and Bradley (1989) found odds of 5.9 that youths with symptoms of PTSD would use intravenous drugs.

Allers, Benjack, White, and Rousey (1993) suggested some pathways through which individuals who were sexually traumatized in childhood might become adolescents and adults at high risk for HIV infection. They noted that survivors often lack feelings of self-worth and communication skills needed to set and maintain appropriate limits with sexual partners. The tendency of sexually abused individuals toward reenactments and, hence, revictimization, often includes involvement with others who may threaten harm, making it that much more difficult to insist on safer sex practices. Courtois (1979) has identified an increased level of impulsive sexual behavior as a long-term consequence of child sexual abuse, and this pattern often increases the number of sexual encounters and sexual partners, behavior known to increase risk of infection. Kalinski, Rubinson, Lawrance, and Levy (1990) argued that the adolescent who has been sexually abused is often too focused on present survival to be very concerned about future health. Furthermore, those who are severely depressed may be demonstrating passive suicidal behavior, seeing HIV as a way to end their struggle.

Thus, empirical evidence supports the hypothesis that individuals with a history of exposure to trauma, particularly rape, sexual abuse, and/or physical abuse, are at unusually high risk for life-threatening disorders and illnesses, including drug abuse and HIV infection. Although the studies reviewed have focused largely on the impact of early trauma on later risk for HIV exposure, it is clear that this is only one of many adverse health outcomes to which this group is vulnerable. Others include accidents related to risk taking and drug and alcohol use; cancers associated with smoking, alcohol, or early sexual activity; mental illness; and suicide. That these outcomes may be largely preventable in adolescents and young adults should raise both alarm and hope, the latter if intervention efforts can be targeted at these vulnerable groups to forestall their becoming prey to these conditions.

In addition to HIV studies, studies of disaster and war have also shown an association between traumatic exposure and negative health behaviors. For example, following the Buffalo Creek disaster, survivors showed increased alcohol use, cigarette smoking, and use of prescription drugs (Gleser, Green, & Winget, 1981). Lebanon War veterans with PTSD were shown to engage in more frequent adverse health practices (e.g., cigarette smoking and alcohol use) than veterans without PTSD (Shalev, Bleich, & Ursano, 1990; Solomon, 1988).

Trauma and Somatizing Symptoms/Disorders

Negative Perceptions of Health Status in Traumatized Populations

Since perception of health predicts utilization of health care practitioners and facilities, the relationship between traumatic exposure and negative perceptions of health status is of high interest. Investigators who have studied this relationship have found that a range of trauma experiences are associated with adverse health reports. In most cases, investigators have relied on self-reports of health, which can be influenced by psychological state as well as by organic dysfunction.

In the National Vietnam Veterans Readjustment Study, both male and female veterans with high war-zone exposure reported more health problems and poorer health in general than did Vietnam Era veterans (those serving outside of Vietnam during the same period) or civilians (Kulka et al., 1990). In a study comparing Vietnam Era to combat veterans (Centers for Disease Control, 1988), it was found that combat veterans were almost twice as likely as their noncombat counterparts to assess their health as only "fair" or "poor." They also were significantly more likely than the noncombat veterans to report a wide variety of medical problems. Wolfe, Schnurr, Brown, and Furey (1994) also found a relationship between extent of war-zone exposure and negative health reports among Vietnam veteran nurses; importantly, subsequent analysis suggested that it was the presence of PTSD rather than exposure per se that predicted this relationship.

Sexual assault and sexual abuse have similarly been associated with negative health perceptions. Kimerling and Calhoun (1994) evaluated somatic symptoms and treatment seeking among women during the year immediately following a sexual assault. When compared to a matched comparison group, women who had experienced this trauma reported elevated levels of somatic complaints. As the year progressed, somatic symptoms diminished but medical health care seeking remained elevated. Thus, there appears to be prospective evidence supporting increased levels of somatic symptoms and treatment seeking after sexual assault. Waigandt, Wallace, Phelps, and Miller (1990) had similar results, finding that women who had been sexually assaulted reported more current illness symptoms 2 years after the assault than a matched comparison group. As in the Kimerling and Calhoun study, a distinction between somatized and organ-based medical symptoms could not be made, because there were no independent medical evaluations during the course of the study.

In a comparison of individuals who had been held hostage in a terrorist hijacking versus nonabducted family members, ex-hostages reported significantly higher rates of severe headaches, intestinal problems, rheumatic pains and difficulties, and skin and stomach problems 6–9 years after they were released from captivity (van der Ploeg & Kleijn, 1989). In the case of both traumatic bereavement and floods, intensity and duration of exposure predicted subsequent reports of health problems (Bartone, Ursano, Wright, & Ingraham, 1989; Hovanitz, 1993). In many of these reports, the extent to which subsequent physical complaints reflect actual diagnosable organ damage versus psychological distress remains unclear.

It is also important to consider that persons with adult traumatic exposure are at risk for PTSD, a disorder that in itself may be associated with poor health outcomes and somatization. Indeed, Friedman and Schnurr (1995) observed that PTSD is an important mediator through which trauma may be related to negative physical health outcomes. Somatization after traumas such as war and natural disaster has been reported in numerous studies dating back to the 1940s (for a general discussion and references, see Rundell, Ursano, Holloway, & Silberman 1989). Recent, well-controlled studies have also addressed this issue. For example, Lebanon War veterans with PTSD were found to have higher rates of medical symptom reporting than combat veterans without PTSD, although the two groups had comparable medical morbidity, as determined by objective evaluation (Shalev et al., 1990). The authors did not report on the presence of comorbid or pretrauma psychiatric disorders, so the relative contribution of trauma and resultant PTSD to the subsequent development of somatization cannot be accurately assessed. Solomon (1988) studied Lebanon War veterans 1, 2, and 3 years after the war. She found that veterans with combat stress reaction and those with PTSD had higher rates of somatic complaints at all three time assessments.

Wolfe et al. (1994) studied 109 female veterans of the Vietnam War. The authors found that degree of traumatic exposure and PTSD were predictors of reports of negative outcomes, as measured by self-reports of health problems. Regression analyses determined that effects of traumatic exposure on perceived health were partially mediated by increases in PTSD after exposure. The authors noted three primary factors that may account for this association: (1) PTSD has been associated with disorders such as depression and anxiety, and persons with these disorders have a heightened tendency to somatize; (2) PTSD symptoms, such as hyperarousal and numbing, may lead to increased risk of cardiovascular and gastrointestinal disturbances; (3) and heightened perceptions of autonomic changes that may occur in PTSD may also explain increased levels of symptom experience and reporting.

In a general population study using data from the Los Angeles site of the National Institute of Mental Health Epidemiologic Catchment Area project, Golding (1994) examined the association between lifetime sexual assault history and lifetime somatic symptoms in 1,610 randomly selected women, 299 of whom reported a lifetime history of sexual assault. Women who had a history of sexual assault were found to have not only poorer health perceptions, but also more functional limitations and a greater frequency of both medically explained and unexplained symptoms. Physical symptoms pertained to a wide range of organ systems, a finding that is inconsistent with the theory that sexual assault should be associated specifically with reproductive or sexual symptoms. As the author noted, it is difficult to determine a causal relationship between assault and somatic symptoms. In the subset of women who reported at least five lifetime unexplained symptoms, sexual assault occurred before the first symptom for 57%, at about the same time for 2%, and after the first symptom for 42%.

Golding (1994) outlined a number of possible reasons for an association between sexual assault and long-term physical health and somatic symptoms, suggesting that (1) stressful life events in general may be associated with poor physical health; (2) sexual assault may lead to other stressful life events (e.g., the breakup of a relationship); (3) stress may impair immune functioning; (4) stressors may be associated with detrimental changes in health-related behaviors (e.g., substance abuse); (5) psychological distress may be associated with functional health limitations; and (6) sexual assault may increase attention to bodily symptoms. For many persons who have experienced sexual and physical assault, the interaction of the trauma(s) with additional risk factors such as other stressors, comorbid psychiatric conditions, constitutional vulnerability, and poor social support may provide the most comprehensive explanation for somatization, poor health status, and increased utilization of health services.

Trauma Histories in Medical or Psychiatric Populations

Somatization has been defined as "a tendency to experience and communicate somatic distress and symptoms unaccounted for by pathological findings, to attribute them to physical illness, and to seek medical help for them" (Lipowski, 1988, p. 1358). Recent research on somatization has highlighted early factors that contribute to the development of somatizing behavior, including genetics and the experience of illness in childhood. Subsequent life events including childhood and adult trauma, as well as other stressors, appear to place a person at higher risk for adult somatization. In addition, somatization in an adult or child should always trigger evaluation for other frequent, concomitant psychiatric disorders such as depression, anxiety, dissociation, and substance dependence. It is critical to appreciate that multiple factors (including individual factors, social context, and acute precipitants) may contribute to somatization when one is reviewing the relationship between trauma history and somatization (see Table 6.1).

An excellent example of research addressing the multiple factors that may contribute to somatization is the South London Somatization Study (Craig, Boardman, Mills, Daly-Jones, & Drake, 1993). As part of this 2-year longitudinal study, the authors assessed childhood experiences of somatizers, that is, persons with an emotional disorder who presented with unexplained physical symptoms to a primary care practitioner. A logistic regression model showed that adult somatization was best modeled by childhood "lack of care," that is, periods of neglect or abuse as measured by a

TABLE 6.1. Contributors to Somatization

Individual factors
  Genetics/neurophysiology/temperament
  Childhood trauma (e.g., physical or sexual abuse)
  Physical injury due to a traumatic event
  Personal experiences with illness
  Illness cognitions (e.g., body consciousness, illness worry, somatic attributional
    style)

Social/contextual factors
  Parent or sibling illness
  Parent or sibling somatization
  Early childhood chaotic environment
  Reinforcing factors (i.e., secondary gain)
  Cultural factors
  Social support

Precipitating factors
  Acute life stressors (e.g., loss, trauma)
  Acute psychiatric illness (e.g., depression, anxiety)
  Personal or familial medical illness, particularly if serious

---

structured interview, *plus* the experience of childhood illness. Ideally, such a model needs to be applied to a validation cohort to determine its generalizability to other populations.

There are a number of somatizing disorders in DSM-IV, with varying degrees of presence of organic physical pathology and different symptom patterns (see Table 6.2). Although it is often difficult clinically to differentiate among these psychiatric disorders (e.g., determining whether chronic fatigue syndrome should be classified as "psychological factors affecting medical condition" or as a somatoform disorder), it is useful to discuss these disorders separately.

Psychological Factors Affecting Medical Condition. When medical evaluation reveals the presence of a physical disorder, but psychological factors adversely affect the physical disorder, the appropriate DSM-IV diagnosis is "psychological factors affecting medical condition." Although this category was considered a mental disorder in its own right in DSM-III-R, in DSM-IV it is only an "other condition that may be a focus of clinical attention." Diagnostic criteria include (1) the presence of a general medical condition, and (2) psychological factors that adversely affect the general medical condition. Although psychological factors may affect medical conditions in a number of ways (e.g., denial of the need for surgery), maladaptive health behaviors and stress-related physiological responses have been shown to be highly prevalent in persons with a history of child abuse.

Maladaptive health behaviors that may affect a general medical condition include overeating in a person with obesity; lack of exercise in a per-

TABLE 6.2. The Somatizing Disorders (DSM-IV)

Diagnosis	DSM-IV classification	Clinical presentation	Demographic and epidemiological features
Psychological factors affecting medical condition	"Other conditions that may be a focus of clinical attention" (i.e., not a DSM-IV mental disorder)	General medical condition adversely affected by specific psychological or behavioral factors (e.g., stress-related exacerbation of ulcer; unsafe sex).	Occurs at all ages. Highly prevalent. ?Male–female ratio.
Somatization disorder	Somatoform disorder	Polysymptomatic. Recurrent and chronic. "Sickly" by history.	Younger age. Female predominance. Rare in general population, but more common in primary care.
Conversion disorder	Somatoform disorder	Monosymptomatic. Mostly acute. Simulates neurological disease.	Female predominance. Younger age. Rare in general population, more common in medical settings.
Pain disorder	Somatoform disorder	Psychological factors have an important role in pain syndrome.	Prevalent. Female predominance for some conditions. Any age.
Hypochondriasis	Somatoform disorder	Disease concern or preoccupation.	Male–female ratio equal. 5–10% incidence in primary care. Middle or older age. Previous physical disease.
Factitious disorder	Factitious disorder	Intentional production or feigning of physical signs or symptoms in order to assume the sick role.	Rare. ?Male predominance. Adult age.

son with heart disease; cigarette smoking, particularly in a person with lung disease; and unsafe sex (for anyone). General medical disorders that may be affected by stress-related physiological responses include irritable bowel syndrome (IBS), esophageal motility disorders, hypertension, and asthma. Among these disorders, trauma history has been studied only among the gastrointestinal disorders. For example, Walker, Katon, Roy-Byrne, Jemelka, and Russo (1993) found that patients with IBS had significantly higher rates of sexual victimization than patients with inflammatory bowel disease, a disorder for which the relationship to stress is less clear than with IBS. As the authors noted, the effects of sexual victimization could not be separated from other risk factors or from psychiatric comorbidity, since lifetime psychiatric disorder rates were significantly higher in persons with IBS. In addition, this study examined medical *patients* with IBS, for whom rates of psychiatric disorder and abuse are likely to be higher than those seen in either a community sample or the general population of persons with IBS. Thus, as is the case with similar disorders such as chronic pain, health care seekers have higher rates of psychological distress and morbidity than non-health-care seekers.

Drossman et al. (1990) found similar results in a university-based gastroenterology practice. In their study, which the authors acknowledged was limited by referral bias, lack of use of standardized interview or questionnaire, and lack of assessment of comorbid psychiatric disorders, higher rates of sexual and physical abuse were found in women with functional, as opposed to organic, gastrointestinal disorders. In this study, the most common functional disorders were IBS, chronic abdominal pain, and nonulcer dyspepsia. The most common organic disorders were Crohn's disease, peptic ulcer disease, and ulcerative colitis.[1]

In an earlier uncontrolled study that also did not use well-validated measures, Eisendrath, Way, Ostroff, and Johanson (1986) found that the presence of four factors helped to differentiate persons with psychogenic abdominal pain from persons with inflammatory bowel disease or general medical–surgical problems: past history of somatization; the presence of a symptom model (a significant other with prominent physical symptoms); prominent guilt; and a history of physical abuse by either a parent or spouse.

Somatoform Disorders. Somatoform disorders are disorders in which there are physical symptoms or signs that are not fully explained by a general medical condition. These disorders include somatization disorder, conversion disorder, pain disorder, and hypochondriasis. Loewenstein (1990) has extensively reviewed recent and historical literature regarding the association

---

[1]The distinction between functional and organic can be difficult to make. Although there may be pathophysiological processes underlying "functional" disorders, the term "organic" is often used to refer to disorders for which there are clearly pathological (tissue) abnormalities (e.g., a visible ulcer in a person with peptic ulcer disease).

between somatoform disorders and childhood abuse. In general, persons with somatoform disorders have been found to have elevated rates of childhood abuse. Specific aspects of this association, with attention to recent well-controlled studies and methodological issues, are presented here.

1. *Somatization disorder.* Somatization disorder is diagnosed when a person has a history of eight or more unexplained physical complaints, beginning before the age of 30, and occurring over a period of several years. Persons with somatization disorder often have chaotic and stressful childhoods and adulthoods, with unstable families and considerable psychosocial stress. For example, Morrison (1989a) reported that 55% of 60 women with somatization disorder had a history of molestation (unwanted sexual contact with or without intercourse) compared to only 16% of 31 women with a primary affective disorder. Similarly, adult survivors of sexual abuse have been found to have elevated rates of somatization disorder. Pribor and Dinwiddie (1992) reported a lifetime prevalence rate of 14% in adult survivors of incest, compared to the general population prevalence of less than 1%. Despite these findings, Morrison (1989b) has questioned the etiological significance of a history of sexual abuse in the development of somatization disorder. In his study, Morrison found that among persons with somatization disorder, a history of molestation was not associated with different types or levels of symptoms than those seen in a person without such a history. However, he addressed only gross symptomatology among a group of women currently in psychiatric treatment. It should be noted that obtaining an abuse history is essential to guiding the course of psychotherapy with a person with somatization disorder, even if symptom profiles cannot be specifically associated with the type or pattern of abuse.

2. *Conversion disorder.* Prior to the abandonment of the seduction theory, Freud had linked conversion to unwanted early childhood sexual experiences. In the current DSM-IV diagnostic scheme, conversion disorder is diagnosed when a person manifests neurological deficits presumably associated with psychological factors (specifically, because the initiation or exacerbation of a deficit is preceded by conflicts or other stressors) for which neurological evaluation does not find an explanatory cause. Persons with conversion disorder may have a motor symptom or deficit, sensory symptom or deficit, seizures or convulsions, or a mixed presentation. A history of sexual and/or physical abuse has been found to be common in persons with pseudoseizures, the only conversion disorder in which trauma has been systematically evaluated. Loewenstein (1990) reviewed a number of early reports that linked pseudoseizures to abuse, but these are largely case reports. In a recent study that utilized a comparison group, Alper, Devinsky, Perrine, Vazques, and Luciano (1993) found a of a history of sexual or physical abuse of 32% in persons with nonepileptic seizures, as opposed to only 9% in a comparison group of persons with complex partial epilepsy. However, a standard abuse instrument was not used, the interviewer was apparently not

blinded to subjects' medical and psychiatric history, and there were significantly more women in the nonepileptic seizure group than in the complex partial epilepsy group.

Dissociative disorder, although not classified as a somatoform disorder, is conceptually and historically related to conversion. In addition, dissociation is a symptom that is included in the list of possible symptoms that meet criteria for somatization in DSM-IV somatization disorder. Walker, Katon, Neraas, Jemelka, and Massoth (1992) found that women with chronic pelvic pain had elevated levels of dissociation as measured by the Dissociative Experiences Scale (Carlson & Putnam, 1993), as compared to a group of women without chronic pelvic pain. Women with chronic pelvic pain were also significantly more likely to have experienced childhood abuse, including severe childhood sexual abuse. Thus, it appears that women with chronic pelvic pain should be assessed for histories of abuse and comorbid psychiatric symptomatology, including dissociative experiences. Pribor, Yutzy, Dean, and Wetzel (1993) evaluated 99 female psychiatric outpatients who had a history of somatic complaints. They found strong associations among abuse history, dissociation, and somatization disorder, indicating that among persons presenting for psychiatric treatment, the presence of one of these problems should trigger careful assessment of the other two.

PTSD symptoms may also manifest as somatization symptoms. Lindy, Green, and Grace (1992) reported four cases of somatic reenactment, defined as "a repetitive set of physical symptoms . . . that contain a somatic repetition of the trauma itself" (p. 180), in which reenactments manifest as somatization. In one case they described, a 48-year-old woman presented for treatment for persistent urinary urgency without dysuria, a condition that had developed 3 months following a devastating supper club fire. A full-scale genitourinary workup was negative, but during subsequent psychotherapy she remembered that some moments before the fire broke out, two friends had asked her if she wanted to join them in the lavatory. The patient, in retrospect, became aware of sensing her bladder, and, finding that there was no urgency, had said "no" to her friends. These friends died in the fire because of their geographical location in the building (i.e., the rest room) and were found only days later. Understanding the symptom as traumatic reenactment ushered in a period of intense guilt, grief, and mourning, and ultimately the alleviation of the physical symptom.

3. *Pain disorder.* Pain disorder is a term new to DSM-IV that replaces the DSM-III-R diagnosis somatoform pain disorder. There are two types of pain disorder: pain disorder associated with psychological factors, for which psychological factors are believed to have the major role in the etiology of the pain complaint; and pain disorder associated with both psychological factors and a general medical condition, for which both psychological factors and a general medical condition (e.g., arthritis) are judged to have etiological importance. It is difficult to reliably determine the *relative* contributions of medical and psychological factor, but there have been

reports of increased frequency of sexual and physical abuse in the histories of persons without any known organic pathology to explain the pain complaint. Rapkin, Kames, Darke, Stampler, and Nakiloff (1990) found an association between childhood physical abuse and adult pain syndromes, while Kuch, Evans, Watson, and Bukela (1991) and Muse (1986) found a link between motor vehicle accident involvement and development of chronic pain. As noted by Walker et al. (1988), studies of the association between childhood sexual abuse and chronic pain have been hampered by methodological limitations such as small sample size, absence of controls, and use of nonstandardized interview instruments. Another methodological limitation seen in this area of research has been the failure to control for the presence of psychosocial variables that may confound the determination of the role of abuse in symptomatology. For example, Domino and Haber (1987), comparing headache sufferers with and without abuse histories, did not report on other stressful life experiences or other measures of current psychiatric disorder or psychological distress. Thus, it is important when reviewing findings in this area to assess carefully for methodological limitations and interpret results cautiously.

In one well-designed study, Walker et al. (1988) found that 64% of 25 women with chronic pelvic pain had experienced sexual abuse prior to the age of 14, as compared to 23% of 30 women who were being evaluated for infertility or bilateral tubal ligation. In addition, 48% (as compared to 13% of the controls) had experienced sexual abuse after age 14. This study assessed persons with both types of DSM-IV pain disorder: Approximately half of the chronic pelvic pain patients had demonstrable findings on laparoscopy, whereas half did not. There were no differences on any of the psychosocial measures (which included abuse history and psychiatric diagnoses) between the groups. Furthermore, the chronic pelvic pain group and the comparison group had comparable degrees of pathology as determined by laparoscopy. Thus, it seems that psychosocial variables contribute greatly to the tendency to have the experience of chronic pain, *even in the presence of demonstrable physical diagnostic findings.* Therefore, the physician must learn to explore psychosocial variables in chronic pain, whether or not the evaluation reveals any underlying pathology. It is also important to realize that for women with chronic pelvic pain, the absence of findings on laparoscopy does not necessarily indicate absence of somatic etiology. To address this problem, Reiter, Shakerin, Gambone, and Milburn (1991) studied a group of women with chronic pelvic pain, all of whom had negative laparoscopies. Women with presumed somatic etiologies for their pain (e.g., irritable bowel syndrome, abdominal wall myofascial pain) had a lower prevalence of sexual trauma than those without a somatic etiology.

Despite the reported association between childhood abuse and the experience of chronic pelvic pain, the reason for the association is not known (Rosenthal, 1993). First, childhood sexual abuse may lead to other sequelae such as psychiatric symptoms and disorders. Second, both sexual and physical abuse may lead to chronic pelvic pain. Third, childhood sexual and physical abuse may lead to other factors that themselves place a person at risk for chronic pelvic pain (e.g., having an abusive *adult* relationship). Finally, childhood sexual and physical abuse often occur in families with other risk factors for the development of somatization (e.g., losses, divorce, emotional abuse, and alcoholism). Thus, as we have seen with other somatizing disorders, it is critical that the clinician assesses multiple variables when evaluating a person with unexplained pain and a history of abuse.

4. *Hypochondriasis.* The final common somatoform disorder is hypochondriasis, which is diagnosed when a person is preoccupied with fears of having, or is convinced that he or she has, a serious disease (e.g., AIDS or cancer) despite negative medical findings and reassurance. As is true for the other somatoform disorders, these persons often have significant psychiatric comorbidity (e.g., depression, panic disorder, and obsessive–compulsive disorder). Loewenstein (1990) reviewed early studies of hypochondriasis, concluding that childhood sexual abuse or physical abuse was not commonly found in patients with hypochondriasis. However, in a study published subsequent to this review, Barsky, Wool, Barnett, and Cleary (1994) found that adults diagnosed with DSM-III-R hypochondriasis recalled more childhood trauma than nonhypochondriacal patients. Specifically, persons with hypochondriasis, in comparison with control subjects, reported more traumatic sexual contact (29% vs. 7%), physical violence (32% vs. 7%), and major parental upheaval (29% vs. 9%) before the age of 17.

Factitious Disorder. Factitious disorder is diagnosed when a person intentionally produces or feigns signs or symptoms of an illness. A repetitive pattern of such acts, involving multiple unexplained symptoms and medical encounters over years, has been ineptly termed Munchausen syndrome, after Baron Karl Friedrich Hieronymus von Munchausen, an 18th-century gentleman who traveled extensively and embellished the details of his life. This extreme form of somatization is quite rare, so the literature consists of only case reports or case series. Many authors have commented on the prevalence of childhood abuse in these extremely disturbed individuals (e.g., Eisendrath, 1989; Feldman & Ford, 1994; Foulks & Houck, 1993). Persons who make themselves ill often appear to be reenacting an abusive relationship as they attempt to gain control over puzzled doctors, even as they abuse their own bodies. Once the ruse is discovered, doctors caring for such patients are tempted to terminate treatment abruptly and angrily, thus perpetuating the abusive cycle. A nonconfrontational approach is preferred (Stern, 1980). For example, Eisendrath (1989) reported a case of a woman who had repeatedly injected herself with urine in order to induce a systemic infection. The psychiatric consultant discovered that she felt guilty about a sexual relationship with her boyfriend and an incestuous relationship she had as an adolescent. Rather than confront the patient, the consultant interpreted that she might feel the need to punish herself because of her guilt feelings.

Munchausen syndrome by proxy (factitious disorder by proxy, a criterion set provided for further study in DSM-IV) is a disorder in which a person produces or feigns symptoms or signs in *another* person. Typically the perpetrator is the mother and the victim is a young child. Clearly, this behavior constitutes a severe form of child abuse. In addition, it is important to assess the perpetrator for comorbid psychiatric disorders including Munchausen syndrome and current stressors. As with Munchausen syndrome, the perpetrator him- or herself often has a personal history of child abuse. Finally, other members of the family need to be assessed for present and prior abuse (Feldman & Ford, 1994).

HEALTH CARE UTILIZATION

Recent studies suggest that individuals who have been exposed to trauma are high users of health care services. Given our previous discussion, this association is not at all surprising. Indeed, increased usage of medical services has been found in studies of battered women and survivors of criminal victimization (including sexual assault), sexual abuse, natural disasters, concentration camps, and prisoner-of-war situations.

In Koss, Woodruff, and Koss's (1990) study of more than 2,000 female health maintenance organization patients, it was found that 57% of their sample had experienced crime victimization (rape, physical assault, and noncontact crime), including 21% who had experienced a completed rape. Exploring the long-term consequences of criminal victimization, these investigators (Koss, Koss, & Woodruff, 1991) determined that severely victimized women, in contrast to nonvictims, reported more distress and made twice as many physician visits in the year following their trauma. Crime victims had outpatient health care costs that were 2.5 times greater than nonvictimized individuals. The investigators found an increase of 15–24% in victims' *nonpsychiatric* physician visits during the year following victimization versus less than a 2% change in such visits among nonvictims. The increase in utilization seemed to be an enduring phenomenon as well. During 3 years of follow-up, victims' physician visits never returned to their preexposure levels.

Using data from the Los Angeles Epidemiologic Catchment Area (ECA) study, Golding, Stein, Siegel, Burnam, and Sorenson (1988) also documented a link between sexual assault and increased use of both mental health and medical services. Among this sample of randomly selected community residents, respondents with a history of sexual assault were nearly twice as likely as those who had never been assaulted to have used mental health services in the 6 months prior to the interview and were also significantly more likely to report a physical health problem. Those who had been victimized were approximately one-third more likely than nonvictims to report a physician visit in the preceding 6 months. Interestingly, individuals who lacked health care insurance were found to be especially likely to consult medical providers.

A number of other studies also point to increased utilization of medical resources in women who have experienced sexual assault or abuse. Waigandt et al. (1990) found that sexual assault victims reported a significantly greater number of doctor visits than a matched control group for 2 years following their attacks. Kimerling and Calhoun (1994) followed a group of recently raped women prospectively for 1 year and found them to have significantly higher medical, but not psychiatric, utilization than a matched control group. Differences were evident by 4 months postassault and persisted throughout the follow-up period. In Norris, Kaniasty, and Scheer's (1990) comparison of men and women who had been exposed to violent crime versus adults who had experienced property crimes, medical utilization was significantly higher among those who had been physically assaulted. Furthermore, it was determined (Koss et al., 1991) that the most powerful predictor of physician visits and outpatient costs among their criminally victimized sample was severity: The greater the severity of criminal victimization, the lower the level of current perceived health status, and the higher the number of physician visits and outpatient medical costs.

Bergman and Brismar (1991) compared medical records of battered women to records of a matched control group for 10 years preceding and 5 years following the battering. Results showed that, in addition to the hospital admissions relating directly to their assaults, the battered women had a significantly higher number than controls of admission rates for nontraumatic surgical disorders, gynecological disorders, induced abortion, medical disorders, and suicide attempts.

Studies of concentration camp survivors (Eitinger, 1973) have shown that survivors have more periods of illness, longer leaves due to illness, and more frequent and enduring hospitalizations than a group of controls. Similarly, in a study of medical utilization following the trauma of prisoner-of-war (POW) captivity, a National Academy of Sciences investigation (Page, 1992) found that World War II and Korean War former POWs had significantly higher rates of hospital admissions, nutritional problems, tuberculosis, various infectious and parasitic diseases, and cardiovascular and gastrointestinal diseases than veterans who had not been POWs.

Finally, increased medical utilization has also been documented in association with exposure to natural disasters. Hospital referrals more than doubled following the Bristol, England flood of 1968 (Bennet, 1968), with depth of flooding clearly predicting subsequent use of medical services. The 1974 Brisbane, Australia flood was followed by an increased number of visits made to health care practitioners, a finding that was particularly evident among males. A comparison of the 7 months preceding and the 7 months following the Mount St. Helen's eruption in 1980 indicated no significant increase in hospital admissions, but there was a significant increase in emergency room visits (Adams & Adams, 1984).

In summary, the relationship between exposure to trauma and increased risky health behaviors and practices, increased negative subjective ratings of physical and mental health, and increased utilization of health care services has been well documented. Such exposure bodes poorly not only for our citizens' health but also for an economy already severely strained by health care expenditures.

ASSESSMENT ISSUES RELATED TO MEDICAL OUTCOMES OF TRAUMA

The findings just described have important implications for assessment. Clearly, individuals who have been traumatized are more likely to be seen in health care settings than their nonexposed counterparts. Furthermore, they are more likely to be seen in primary care or medical emergency settings than in the mental health sector. Thus, as Kamerow, Pincus, and Macdonald (1986) suggest, the primary care setting is a potentially useful place in which to identify and assess trauma victims, which should increase the likelihood that they will receive appropriate care. Such identification can help medical providers better understand the full nature of patients' difficulties and anticipate reactions to particular procedures.

Given the relatively high prevalence of trauma survivors in medical settings, primary care providers should be trained to identify trauma exposure in their patients. Taking a trauma history should be an integral part of medical history taking, particularly in persons who somatize, dissociate, have high distress, and use excessive health care resources. In light of the high-risk health behaviors frequently engaged in by traumatized youth, routine trauma screening in the evaluation of children and adolescents, particularly those with the problems just identified, or with behavior problems, is particularly important. Such screening should also be a component of any public health effort to target substance abuse and HIV-risk as well as other detrimental health behaviors.

Although it is tempting to suggest that one or two general questions could be used by busy physicians to do a quick screening in these settings, this approach has a number of drawbacks. First, words such as "rape," "abuse," and so on, result in underreporting, as individuals may be reluctant to label as abusive those acts committed by known others such as parents or boyfriends (Resnick, Falsetti, Kilpatrick, & Freedy, in press). Rather, detailed questions about specific behaviors are required to learn whether certain of these experiences have occurred (Resnick et al., in press). Furthermore, individuals/patients will not necessarily volunteer information about specific events to open-ended questions ("Has anything terrible, frightening, etc., ever happened to you?"), or respond to a list of possible examples with events *not* on the list. Again, this suggests the importance of asking about each important event. The most efficient strategy would be to employ one of the self-report measures reviewed by Norris and Riad (Chapter 1, this volume), or others (e.g., Kriegler et al., 1992; Mac Ian & Pearlman, 1992), to query for a *range* of events. Self-report inquiry requires no physician time (it can be included in an intake packet, although it may be appropriate to have the patient put the survey information into a sealed envelope upon completion). The physician would have the option of reviewing the report, of asking the patient whether he or she wanted to discuss anything reported, or of asking additional questions about the events reported to get a clinical sense of their potential connection, psychologically or temporally, with the physical complaints/condition for which the patient has sought help. Self-report measures may be more *comfortable* for the physician, who may not be completely at ease inquiring about specific details of past abuse, especially in the sexual arena. Self-report may be more comfortable for the patient as well, as the questionnaire may "break the ice" in terms of talking about sensitive or difficult areas.

We highly recommend giving an event inventory as a screening device since open-ended questions such as those in the Diagnostic Interview Schedule have been shown to turn up lower rates of lifetime trauma exposure (e.g., 40%: Breslau, Davis, Andreski, & Peterson, 1991) compared to more detailed/specific screening (e.g., 62% [men] and 51% [women]: Kessler, Sonnega, Bromet, Hughes, & Nelson, 1995; 69%: Norris, 1992; and 69%: Resnick, Kilpatrick, Dansky, Saunders, & Best, 1993) in representative community samples. Furthermore, questionnaires or interviews with detailed questions in a specific area turn up much higher rates in that area (e.g., 27% experiencing sexual assault: Resnick et al., 1993) than instruments with only one screening question (e.g., 4% sexual assault: Norris, 1992) in general population samples. Thus, omnibus trauma-screening questions are likely to miss important events. Clearly, there is a need to balance time and efficiency with appropriateness and usefulness. Particularly in populations in which trauma is likely to be more common, and more likely to be playing a role in symptoms and behavior, a longer screen would be more appropriate. Examples of such populations would be high-risk adolescents, patients with disorders or treatment courses that have been shown to be linked with traumatic exposure, such as irritable bowel syndrome or pelvic pain (and their treatments), or in patients who have multiple and/or chronic somatic complaints with unclear etiology.

If using a longer instrument is not possible and a physician wants to include a few trauma-history questions in his or her screening, we recommend inclusive questions that do not label the behavior with such terms as "rape" and "abuse" (Resnick et al., in press). We also urge separate questions for sexual trauma, physical trauma (including examples of parents and spouse as perpetrators), serious accident, serious illness, and combat.

Since it can be seen that the specific details of the questions are very important (Norris & Riad, Chapter 1, this volume; Resnick et al., in press), it is not best left to physicians or investigators to design their own instrument. Furthermore, questions that are poorly designed may in some cases be worse than not asking about trauma at all, if they discourage reporting of emotionally salient experiences. Discussing trauma with patients, especially interpersonal events such as childhood abuse, date rape, or battery, requires some degree of skill on the part of the practitioner. Mental health training during medical school and residency should, we hope, include instruction and experience in discussing sensitive topics with patients in a helpful and empathic manner. Often the most devastating aspect of early trauma is that others did not protect the person from the trauma/abuse, or they denied or minimized the importance of what was reported. To repeat this in a medical setting would be counterproductive at best.

For physicians inquiring about trauma, a clear follow-up plan or procedure needs to be in place when significant trauma *is* recognized. One option is for the physician to schedule a subsequent follow-up visit within a short time frame to explore and evaluate the traumatic exposure and its impact on symptoms and course of treatment. This procedure may result in a mental health consultation or referral, or in a short course of psychotherapy with the primary care physician. The physician who does not feel qualified to conduct such sessions would appropriately recommend a consultation with, or referral to, a mental health professional. Such links/networks and plans need to be in place prior to screening.

Mental health practitioners also need to be reminded of the importance of inquiring about past traumatic exposure and recent stressors, in addition to the now more common practice of assessing for comorbid psychiatric disorders, in persons who present with somatizing symptoms. When somatization has been identified, further extensive psychosocial assessment is warranted. The patient should never be told that a symptom is "all in your head," rather that, as is true for all of us, stress can affect bodily symptoms. There should ensue a careful behavioral assessment for circumstances that contribute to the symptom, and there should be an evaluation for coexisting mental disorders such as anxiety, depression, PTSD, dissociation, and chemical dependence. The mental health practitioner should collaborate closely with a survivor's primary care practitioner to encourage appropriate medical practice in the treatment of somatizers: regularly scheduled frequent visits (to discourage urgent or emergency symptoms), care provision by one provider whenever possible, invasive evaluations and tests only when indicated by *objective* medical findings, and hospitalization only when absolutely necessary. For persons with somatization disorder, such principles have been shown to decrease health care utilization and costs without adversely affecting patient outcomes and satisfaction (Smith, Monson, & Ray, 1986). For detailed discussion of the management of somatization, see, for example, Foulks and Houck (1993).

It is particularly important that a history of abuse, if present, be identified by the primary care physician, since a pattern of abusive relationships may be repeated in the doctor–patient relationship. Persons with somatization disorder are generally extremely frustrating for the physician, who is often tempted to reenact with the patient a pattern from early childhood: abandonment ("I can't treat you anymore"); anger (yelling at the patient); abuse (administering painful procedures to "teach" the patient the consequences of persistent, dramatic physical complaints). Thus, close collaboration between mental health and the primary care practitioners is essential to providing appropriate care for these persons.

In conclusion, assessment of trauma in medical settings is an underappreciated but important aspect of medical history taking. Medical practitioners should be attuned to the psychological sequelae of traumatic medical illnesses and events such as cancer diagnosis and treatment. Equally important is the recognition of the role that trauma history may play in the development and exacerbation of medical symptoms, health care utilization, and high-risk behavior. Screening for trauma can lead to more sensitive and appropriate care for such patients than might otherwise be available. These recommendations highlight the need for carefully worded but brief, standardized screening instruments, with training regarding how to do follow-up questioning, and how best to consult with, or refer to, mental health colleagues. Mental health practitioners will need to take the lead in guiding medical colleagues not only in the area of assessment but also in subsequent collaborative efforts to help the survivor to address the impact of trauma on the body and the use of health services.

REFERENCES

Abrahams, M. J., Price, J., Whitlock, F. A., & Williams, G. (1976). The Brisbane Floods, January 1974: Their impact on health. *Medical Journal of Australia, 2,* 936–939.

Adams, P. R., & Adams, G. R. (1984). Mount St. Helens ashfall: Evidence for a disaster stress reaction. *American Psychologist, 39,* 252–260.

Allers, C. T., & Benjack, K. J. (1991). Connections between childhood abuse and HIV infection. *Journal of Counseling and Development, 71,* 14–17.

Allers, C. T., Benjack, K. J., White, J., & Rousey, J. T. (1993). HIV vulnerability and the adult survivor of childhood sexual abuse. *Child Abuse and Neglect, 17,* 291–298.

Alper, K., Devinsky, O., Perrine, K., Vazques, B., & Luciano, D. (1993). Nonepileptic seizures and childhood sexual and physical abuse. *Neurology, 43,* 1950–1953.

Alter, C. L., Pelcovitz, D., Axelrod, A., Goldenberg, B., Harris, H., Meyers, B., Grobois, B., Mandel, F., Septimus, A., & Kaplan, S. (1996). The identification of PTSD in cancer survivors. *Psychosomatics, 37*(2), 137–143.

Alter, C. L., Pelcovitz, D., Axelrod, A., Goldenberg, B., Septimus, A., Harris, H., Meyers, B., Grobois, B., & Kaplan, S. (1992, October). *The identification of PTSD in cancer survivors.* Paper presented at the 39th meeting of the Academy of Psychosomatic Medicine, San Diego, CA.

American Psychiatric Association. (1987). *Diagnostic and statistical manual of mental disorders* (3rd ed., rev.). Washington, DC: Author.

American Psychiatric Association. (1994). *Diagnostic and statistical manual of mental disorders* (4th ed.). Washington, DC: Author.

Barsky, A. J., Wool, C., Barnett, M. C., & Cleary, P. D. (1994). Histories of childhood trauma in adult hypochondriacal patients. *American Journal of Psychiatry, 151,* 397–401.

Bartone, P. T., Ursano, R. J., Wright, K. M., & Ingraham, L. H. (1989). The impact of a military air disaster on the health of assistance workers. *Journal of Nervous and Mental Disease, 177,* 317–328.

Beebe, G. W. (1975). Follow-up studies of World War II and Korean War prisoners: II. Morbidity, disability, and maladjustments. *American Journal of Epidemiology, 101,* 400–422.

Bennet, G. (1968). Bristol floods 1968: Controlled survey of effects on health of local community disaster. *British Medical Journal, 3,* 454–458.

Bergman, B., & Brismar, B. (1991). A 5-year follow-up study of 117 battered women. *American Journal of Public Health, 81,* 1486–1489.

Breslau, N., Davis, G. C., Andreski, P., & Peterson, E. (1991). Traumatic events and posttraumatic stress disorder in an urban population of young adults. *Archives of General Psychiatry, 48,* 216–222.

Carlson, E. B., & Putnam, F. W. (1993). An update on the Dissociative Experiences Scale. *Dissociation, 6*(1), 16–27.

Cella, D. F., Mahon, S. M., & Donovan, M. (1990). Cancer recurrence as a traumatic event. *Behavioral Medicine, 16,* 15–22.

Cella, D. F., & Tross, S. (1986). Psychological adjustment to survival from Hodgkin's disease. *Journal of Consulting and Clinical Psychology, 54*(5), 616–622.

Centers for Disease Control. (1988). Health status of Vietnam veterans: II. Physical health. *Journal of the American Medical Association, 259,* 2708–2714.

Chemtob, C., & Herriott, M. (1994). Post-traumatic stress disorder as a sequela of Guillaine-Barre syndrome. *Journal of Traumatic Stress, 7*(4), 705–711.

Cordova, M. J., Andrykowski, M. A., Kenady, D. E., McGrath, P. C., Sloan, D. A., & Redd, W. H. (1995). Frequency and correlayes of posttraumatic-stress-disorder-like symptoms after treatment for breast cancer. *Journal of Consulting and Clinical Psychology, 63*(6), 981–986.

Courtois, C. (1979). The incest experience and its aftermath. *Victimology: An International Journal, 4,* 337–347.

Craig, T. K. J., Boardman, A. P., Mills, K., Daly-Jones, O., & Drake, H. (1993). The South London Somatisation Study: Longitudinal course and the influence of early life experiences. *British Journal of Psychiatry, 163,* 579–588.

Cunningham, R. M., Stiffman, A. R., Dore, P., & Earls, F. (1994). The association of physical and sexual abuse with HIV risk behaviors in adolescence and young adulthood: Implications for public health. *Child Abuse and Neglect, 18,* 233–245.

Davidson, L. M., & Baum, A. (1986). Chronic stress and posttraumatic stress disorders. *Journal of Consulting and Clinical Psychology, 54*(3), 303–308.

Davidson, L. M., Fleming, I., & Baum, A. (1986). Post-traumatic stress as a function of chronic stress and toxic exposure. In C. Figley (Ed.), *Trauma and its wake* (Vol. 2, pp. 57–77). New York: Brunner/Mazel.

Derogatis, L. R., Morrow, G. R., Fetting, J., Penman, D., Piasetsky, S., Schmale, A. M., Henrichs, M., & Carniche, C. L. M., Jr. (1983). The prevalence of psychiatric disorders among cancer patients. *Journal of American Medical Association, 249,* 751–757.

Doerfler, L. A., Pbert, L., & DeCosimo, D. (1994). Symptoms of posttraumatic stress disorder following myocardial infarction and coronary artery bypass surgery. *General Hospital Psychiatry, 16,* 193–199.

Domino, J. V., & Haber, J. D. (1987). Prior physical and sexual abuse in women with chronic headache: Clinical correlates. *Headache, 27,* 310–314.

Drossman, D. A., Lesserman, J., Nachman, G., Zhiming, L., Gluck, H., Toomey, T. C., & Mitchell, C. M. (1990). Sexual and physical abuse in women with functional or organic gastrointestinal disorders. *Annals of Internal Medicine, 113,* 828–833.

Eisendrath, S. J. (1989). Factitious physical disorder: Treatment without confrontation. *Psychosomatics, 30*(4), 383–387.

Eisendrath, S. J., Way, L. W., Ostroff, J. W., & Johanson, C. A. (1986). Identification of psychogenic abdominal pain. *Psychosomatics, 27*(10), 705–712.

Eitinger, L. (1973). A follow-up study of the Norwegian concentration camp survivors' mortality and morbidity. *Israel Annals of Psychiatry and Related Disciplines, 11,* 199–209.

Epstein, R. S. (1993). Avoidant symptoms cloaking the diagnosis of PTSD in patients with severe accidental injury. *Journal of Traumatic Stress, 6*(4), 451–458.

Feldman, M. D., & Ford, C. V. (1994). *Patient or pretender: Inside the strange world of factitious disorders.* New York: Wiley.

Foulks, D. G., & Houck, C. A. (1993). Somatoform disorders, factitious disorders, and malingering. In A. Stoudemire & B. S. Fogel (Eds.), *Psychiatric care of the medical patient* (pp. 267–288). New York: Oxford University Press.

Friedman, M. J., & Schnurr, P. P. (1995). The relationship between trauma, posttraumatic stress disorder, and physical health. In M. J. Friedman, D. S. Charney, & A. Y. Deutch (Eds.), *Neurobiological and clinical consequences of stress: From normal adaptation to PTSD* (pp. 507–524). Philadelphia: Lippincott-Raven.

Gleser, G. C., Green, B. L., & Winget, C. N. (1981). *Prolonged psychosocial effects of disaster: A study of Buffalo Creek.* New York: Academic Press.

Golding, J. M. (1994). Sexual assault history and physical health in randomly selected Los Angeles women. *Health Psychology, 13*(2), 130–138.

Golding, J. M., Stein, J. A., Siegel, J. M., Burnam, M. A., & Sorenson, S. B. (1988). Sexual assault history and use of health and mental health. *American Journal of Community Psychology, 16,* 625–644.

Green, B. L., Lindy, J. D., & Grace, M. C. (1994). Psychological effects of toxic contamination. In R. J. Ursano, B. G. McCaughey, & C. S. Fullerton (Eds.), *Individual and community responses to trauma and disaster* (pp. 154–176). Cambridge, UK: Cambridge University Press.

Green, B. L., Rowland, J. H., Krupnick, J. L., Epstein, S. E., Stockton, P., Stern, N. M., Spertus, I. L., & Steakley, C. (1996). *Posttraumatic stress disorder in women with breast cancer: Prevalence and phenomenology.* Manuscript submitted for publication.

Hovanitz, C. A. (1993). Physical health risks associated with aftermath of disaster: Basic paths of influence and their implications for prevention intervention. *Journal of Social Behavior, 8,* 213–254.

Kalinski, E. M., Rubinson, L., Lawrance, L., & Levy, S. R. (1990). AIDS, runaways, and self-efficacy. *Family and Community Health, 13,* 65–72.

Kamerow, D. B., Pincus, H. A., & Mac Donald, D. I. (1968). Alcohol abuse, other drug abuse and mental disorders in medical practice: Prevalence, costs, recognition, and treatment. *Journal of the American Medical Association, 255,* 2054–2057.

Kessler, R. C., Sonnega, A., Bromet, E., Hughes, M., & Nelson, C. B. (1995). Posttraumatic stress disorder in the National Comorbidity Survey. *Archives of General Psychiatry, 52,* 1048–1060.

Kimerling, R., & Calhoun, K. S. (1994). Somatic symptoms, social support and treatment seeking among sexual assault victims. *Journal of Consulting and Clinical Psychology, 62*(2), 333–340.

Koss, M. P., Koss, P. G., & Woodruff, J. (1991). Deleterious effects of criminal victimization on women's health and medical utilization. *Archives of Internal Medicine, 151,* 342–347.

Koss, M. P., Woodruff, W. J., & Koss, P. G. (1990). Relation of criminal victimization to health perceptions among women medical patients. *Journal of Consulting and Clinical Psychology, 58,* 147–152.

Kriegler, J. A., Blake, D. D., Schnurr, P., Bremner, J. D., Zaidi, L. Y., & Krinsley, K. (1992, October). *The Early Trauma Interview.* Boston: National Center for Posttraumatic Stress Disorder.

Kuch, K., Evans, R. J., Watson, P. C., & Bukela, C. (1991). Road vehicle accidents and phobias in 60 patients with fibromyalgia. *Journal of Anxiety Disorders, 5,* 273–280.

Kulka, R. A., Schlenger, W. E., Fairbank, J. A., Hough, R. L., Jordan, B. K., Marmar, C. R., & Weiss, D. S. (1990). *Trauma and the Vietnam War generation.* New York: Brunner/Mazel.

Kutz, I., Garb, R., & David, D. (1988). Post-traumatic stress disorder following myocardial infarction. *General Hospital Psychiatry, 10,* 169–176.

Kutz, I., Shabtai, H., Solomon, Z., Neumann, M., & David, D. (1994). Post-traumatic stress disorder in myocardial infarction patients: Prevalence study. *Israeli Journal of Psychiatry and Related Science, 31*(1), 48–56.

Lindy, J. D., Green, B. L., & Grace, M. (1992). Somatic reenactment in the treatment of posttraumatic stress disorder. *Psychotherapy and Psychosomatics, 57,* 180–186.

Lipowski, Z. J. (1988). Somatization: The concept and its clinical application. *American Journal of Psychiatry, 145,* 1358–1368.

Loewenstein, R. J. (1990). Somatoform disorders in victims of incest and child abuse. In R .P. Kluft (Ed.), *Incest-related syndromes of adult psychopathology* (pp. 75–107). Washington, DC: American Psychiatric Press.

Mac Ian, P. S., & Pearlman, L. A. (1992). Development and use of the TSI Life Event Questionnaire. *Treating Abuse Today: The International Newsjournal of Abuse, Survivorship and Therapy, 2*(1), 9–11.

Morrison, J. (1989a). Childhood sexual histories of women with somatization disorder. *American Journal of Psychiatry, 146,* 239–241.

Morrison, J. (1989b). Childhood molestation reported by women with somatization disorder. *Annals of Clinical Psychiatry, 1,* 25–32.

Muse, M. (1986). Stress-related, posttraumatic chronic pain syndrome: Behavioral treatment approach. *Pain, 25,* 389–394.

Myers, J., Weissman, M. M., Tischler, G. L., Holzer, C. E., Leaf, P. J., Orvaschel, H., Anthony, J. C., Boyd, J. H., Burke, J. D., Kramer, M., & Stoltzman, R. (1984). Six-month prevalence of psychiatric disorders in three communities. *Archives of General Psychiatry, 41,* 959–967.

Norris, F. H. (1992). Epidemiology of trauma: Frequency and impact of different potentially traumatic events on different demographic groups. *Journal of Consulting and Clinical Psychology, 60,* 409–418

Norris, F. H., Kaniasty, K. A., & Scheer, D. A. (1990). Use of mental health services among victims of crime: Frequency, correlates, and subsequent recovery. *Journal of Consulting and Clinical Psychology, 58,* 538–547.

Page, W. F. (1992). *The health of former prisoners of war.* Washington, DC: National Academy Press.

Pelcovitz, D., Goldenberg, B., Kaplan, S., Weinblatt, M., Mandel, F., Meyers, B., & Vinciguerra, V. (1996). Posttraumatic stress disorder in mothers of children with cancer. *Psychosomatics, 37,* 116–126.

Perry, S., Difede, J., Musngi, G., Frances, A. J., & Jacobsberg, L. (1992). Predictors of posttraumatic stress disorder after burn injury. *American Journal of Psychiatry, 149,* 931–935.

Pribor, E. F., & Dinwiddie, S. H. (1992). Psychiatric correlates of incest in childhood. *American Journal of Psychiatry, 149,* 52–56.

Pribor, E. F., Yutzy, S. H., Dean, J. T., & Wetzel, R. D. (1993). Briquet's syndrome, dissociation, and abuse. *American Journal of Psychiatry, 150,* 1507–1511.

Rapkin, A. J., Kames, L. D., Darke, L. L., Stampler, F. M., & Nakiloff, B. D. (1990). History of physical and sexual abuse in women with chronic pelvic pain. *Obstetrics and Gynecology, 76,* 92–96.

Reiter, R. C., Shakerin, L. R., Gambone, J. C., & Milburn, A. K. (1991). Correlation between sexual abuse and somatization in women with somatic and nonsomatic chronic pelvic pain. *American Journal of Obstetrics and Gynecology, 165,* 104–109.

Resnick, H. S., Falsetti, S. A., Kilpatrick, D. G., & Freedy, J. R. (in press). Assessment of rape and other civilian trauma-related posttraumatic stress disorder: Emphasis on assessment of potentially traumatic events. In T. W. Miller (Ed.), *Clinical disorders and stressful life events.* Madison, CT: International Universities Press.

Resnick, H. S., Kilpatrick, D. G., Dansky, B. S., Saunders, B. E., & Best, C. L. (1993). Prevalence of civilian trauma and posttraumatic stress disorder in a representative sample of women. *Journal of Consulting and Clinical Psychology, 61,* 984–991.

Roca, R. P., Spence, R. J., & Munster, A. M. (1992). Posttraumatic adaptation and distress among adult burn survivors. *American Journal of Psychiatry, 149,* 1234–1238.

Rosenthal, R. H. (1993). Psychology of chronic pelvic pain. *Obstetrics and Gynecology Clinics of North America, 20*(4), 627–642.

Rotheram-Borus, M. J., Koopman, C., & Bradley, J. S. (1989). Barriers to successful AIDS prevention programs with runaway youth. In J. D. Woodruff, D. Doherty, & J. G. Athey (Eds.), *Troubled adolescents and HIV infection* (pp. 37–55). Washington, DC: Child and Adolescent Service System Program Technical Assistance Center, Georgetown University Child Development Center.

Rundell, J. R., Ursano, R. J., Holloway, H. C., & Silberman, E. K. (1989). Psychiatric responses to trauma. *Hospital and Community Psychiatry, 40*(1), 68–74.

Shalev, A., Bleich, A., & Ursano, R. J. (1990). Posttraumatic stress disorder: Somatic comorbidity and effort tolerance. *Psychosomatics, 31,* 197–203.

Shalev, A., Schreiber, S., Galai, T., & Melmed, R. N. (1993). Post-traumatic stress disorder following medical events. *British Journal of Clinical Psychology, 32,* 247–253.

Smith, G. R., Monson, R. A., & Ray, D. C. (1986). Psychiatric consultation in somatization disorder. *New England Journal of Medicine, 314,* 1407–1413.

Solomon, Z. (1988). Somatic complaints, stress reaction, and posttraumatic stress disorder: A three-year follow-up study. *Behavioral Medicine, 14*(4), 179–185.

Spinelli, C., Ricci, E., Berti, P., Viacava, P., Campani, D., Cicchetti, D., Rossi, G., & Miccoli, P. (1995). Relationship between five-year survival and age at diagnosis in breast cancer: Multivariate analysis. *Breast Disease, 8,* 209–216.

Stern, T. A. (1980). Munchausen's syndrome revisited. *Psychosomatics, 21*(4), 329–336.

Stiffman, A. R., Dore, P., Earls, F., & Cunningham, R. (1992). The influence of mental health problems on AIDS-related risk behaviors in young adults. *Journal of Nervous and Mental Disease, 180,* 314–320.

Stuber, M., Christakis, D., Houskamp, B., & Kazak, A. E. (1996). Posttraumatic symptoms in childhood leukemia survivors and their parents. *Psychosomatics, 37,* 254–261.

Stuber, M. L., Meeske, K., Gonzalez, S., Houskamp, B., & Pynoos, R. (1994). Posttraumatic stress after childhood cancer. I: The role of appraisal. *Psycho-Oncology, 3,* 305–312.

van der Ploeg, H. M., & Kleijn, W. C. (1989). Being held hostage in the Netherlands: A study of long-term aftereffects. *Journal of Traumatic Stress, 2,* 153–169.

van Driel, R. C., & Op den Velde, W. (1995). Myocardial infarction and post-traumatic stress disorder. *Journal of Traumatic Stress, 8*(1), 151–159.

Waigandt, A., Wallace, D. L., Phelps, L., & Miller, D. A. (1990). The impact of sexual assault on physical health status. *Journal of Traumatic Stress, 3*(1), 93–102.

Walker, E. A., Katon, W. J., Hansom, J., Harrop-Griffiths, J., Holm, L., Jones, M. L., Hickok, L., & Jemelka, R. P. (1992). Medical and psychiatric symptoms in women with childhood sexual abuse. *Psychosomatic Medicine, 54,* 658–664.

Walker, E. A., Katon, W., Harrop-Griffiths, J., Holm, L., Russo, J., & Hickok, L. R. (1988). Relationship of chronic pelvic pain to psychiatric diagnoses and childhood sexual abuse. *American Journal of Psychiatry, 145,* 75–80.

Walker, E. A., Katon, W. J., Neraas, K., Jemelka, R. P., & Massoth, D. (1992). Dissociation in women with chronic pelvic pain. *American Journal of Psychiatry, 149,* 534–537.

Walker, E. A., Katon, W. J., Roy-Byrne, P. P., Jemelka, R. P., & Russo, J. (1993). Histories of sexual victimization in patients with irritable bowel syndrome or inflammatory bowel disease. *American Journal of Psychiatry, 150,* 1502–1506.

Wolfe, J., Schnurr, P. P., Brown, P. J., & Furey, J. (1994). Posttraumatic stress disorder and war-zone exposure as correlates of perceived health in female Vietnam War veterans. *Journal of Consulting and Clinical Psychology, 62*(6), 1235–1240.

CHAPTER 7

Gender Issues in the Assessment of Posttraumatic Stress Disorder

JESSICA WOLFE
RACHEL KIMERLING

INTRODUCTION

The study of posttraumatic stress disorder (PTSD) has expanded considerably to include the effects of trauma on different populations. In recent years, females, in particular, have received increasing attention in terms of their distinctive exposure to certain types of trauma (e.g., sexual assault, domestic abuse) and their particular response to severe stress. To date, the construct of PTSD has been extensively formulated around the experiences of male combat veterans while the manifestations of traumatic stress in females have been approached in a comparative fashion. Some research has suggested that females are distinctly vulnerable to adverse reactions or stress disorders following stressor exposure, while other studies have alluded to findings that PTSD symptomatology appears more severe in females than males (Breslau, Davis, Andreski, & Peterson, 1991). Few empirical studies to date, however, have investigated differential outcome following exposure to similarly stressful events in males and females, and there are limited data addressing mechanisms or factors that might explicate why females appear more susceptible to this anxiety disorder. Finally, problems with existing instrumentation may influence findings to the degree that format or content do not identify salient concerns for females. Gender-based findings of differential risk factors in PTSD or its severity suggest that significant gaps exist in current conceptualizations of this disorder. We suggest that the construct of PTSD be reevaluated to include symptoms and characteristics of both genders.

This chapter begins by reviewing portions of the extant literature on prevalence, etiology, and diagnostic characterizations associated with PTSD in females. We consider probable effects of stressor exposure in terms of developmental stages for females, exploring how both exposure and response set may vary across points in the lifespan. Next, we review the relationship of PTSD in females to various functional correlates and domains (e.g., disposition, affect regulation, reporting style, psychosocial functioning, revictimization, perceptions of physical health, and overall psychiatric comorbidity) and discuss associations and findings as they apply differentially to females. Then, basic parameters of existing PTSD assessment methodologies are considered, with an emphasis on salient constructs and specialized diagnostic issues in the evaluation of female PTSD. The chapter concludes by suggesting a model whereby the interaction between gender and PTSD is viewed as a complex, multidimensional topic in need of further scientific study. We recommend a number of areas in which additional study and research can contribute significantly to refining current understanding of gender issues in the assessment and diagnosis of PTSD. These inquiries can advance the understanding of normative responses to trauma across genders, avoiding the bias inherent in focusing on one category of experiences. On a practical level, these efforts can enhance diagnostic efforts and help refine treatment interventions that focus on both symptom remediation and improved functional well-being.

GENDER AND PREVALENCE

Studies Comparing Males and Females

Adult Community Studies

Of the few studies directly comparing the prevalence of PTSD between women and men, some preliminary differences have emerged. Breslau and colleagues (Breslau et al., 1991; Breslau & Davis, 1992) used the Diagnostic Interview Schedule (DIS; Spitzer, 1981; Robins, Helzer, Croughan, & Ratcliffe, 1981) to study a large urban sample ($n = 1,007$) of male and female health maintenance organization (HMO) members ages 21–30. They found that 39% ($n = 394$) of the combined sample described exposure to an event consistent with a traumatic stressor. Of individual respondents, nearly 24% met DSM-III-R criteria for PTSD (American Psychiatric Association, 1987), yielding a lifetime sample prevalence of 9.2%. Nearly 57% ($n = 53$) of those with the disorder were classified as "chronic," defined in this instance as symptom duration of greater than 1 year. Several important findings emerge from these data. First, PTSD chronicity was associated with a variety of factors, including greater symptom severity, increased likelihood of a comorbid anxiety or affective disorder, and more medical problems. Second, the PTSD diagnosis was linked to certain respondent characteristics, notably female gender: Women were four times more likely than men to develop chronic, but not nonchronic, forms of PTSD following Criterion A stressor exposure. Other

PTSD "risk" factors were defined as early separation from parents, a positive family history of anxiety disorders or antisocial personality, preexisting anxiety or depression in the proband, and "neurotic style." No gender differences emerged for the development of PTSD following specific types of exposure apart from the aftermath of rape, where approximately 80% of the sample met criteria for the disorder. However, analyses did not address differential rates of gender-linked exposure or any comparisons in the willingness of men versus women to report PTSD symptoms associated with particular experiences. Study results may also have been affected by the tendency of the DIS to underestimate rates of PTSD (Weiss, 1993).

Cottler, Compton, Mager, Spitznagel, and Janca (1992) utilized the St. Louis-area sample from the National Institute of Mental Health's Epidemiologic Catchment Area (ECA) study to explore PTSD rates and their relationship to substance abuse in men and women. The authors used the DIS and DSM-III criteria (American Psychiatric Association, 1980) to evaluate a relatively ethnically diverse sample of young and middle-aged men and women. Results indicated that female gender and cocaine or opiate use were the two strongest predictors of both exposure to a traumatic stressor and the subsequent development of PTSD. Significant first-order correlations were obtained for younger age, Caucasian race, antisocial personality (ASP) diagnosis, and depression; however, no gender interactions were found among outcomes. Similar to the work by Breslau et al. (1991; Breslau & Davis, 1992), Cottler et al. (1992) based PTSD prevalence estimates on the most common traumatic life events, a method that potentially limits knowledge about the broader variety of stressor events. In addition, neither rape nor sexual assault—typically very strong predictors of PTSD in women—were distinctively classified, possibly constraining results of interactions among gender, event prevalence, and their sequelae.

Norris (1992) employed more rigorous diagnostic and stressor definitions to characterize traumatic exposure and PTSD in a large sample ($n = 1,000$) of men and women. Using an ethnically diverse, urban Southern U.S. data set of various age groups, the author classified numerous stressor events into broader categories encompassing violence, hazard/natural disaster, or accidental occurrences. Norris then obtained continuous measures of global distress and PTSD symptomatology, as opposed to earlier studies that relied exclusively on dichotomous classifications. Findings revealed gender differences in both traumatic exposure and associated traumatic stress. Women were more likely to have suffered sexual assault, whereas men were at greater risk for motor vehicle accidents, physical assault, and combat exposure, experiences producing higher overall exposure rates for males. In addition, a number of significant interactions pertaining to gender, event typology, and distress emerged. First, rape yielded the highest rates of PTSD, although stated rates (14%) were lower than those found by other authors (Resnick, Kilpatrick, Dansky, Saunders, & Best, 1993). Second, although failing to reach statistical significance, women demonstrated a trend for higher rates of PTSD. Third, among participants with criminal victimization, women were significantly more likely to meet PTSD criteria than men. Thus, these data suggest a differential gender risk for stressor exposure as well as for the subsequent development of PTSD. This study also reported differential risk by gender for the development of PTSD symptoms when exposure was controlled. However, these comparisons rest on the assumption that there is little qualitative difference among rape, sexual assault, and other forms of victimization.

In summary, most studies reviewed were not well controlled for differing rates of gender-linked exposure. Accordingly, it is possible that the high rates of sexual assault in women and the extremely high rates of PTSD in sexual assault survivors contribute to the appearance that female gender is a risk factor for PTSD. Also, although female gender emerged as a risk factor for the development of PTSD symptoms, the majority of these studies did not statistically control for gender effects (i.e., analyzing risk factors separately by gender). Since there are data showing that the PTSD diagnosis or PTSD chronicity have different prevalences with respect to gender, it remains important to compile data that directly compare differential, gender-based prevalence rates in terms of risk factors for PTSD. This issue could be effectively explored by examining data in conjunction with findings from studies of special populations that have experienced a specific stressor (e.g., war veterans). Similarly, knowledge of PTSD risk factors appropriate to women should be examined among studies of female populations.

Other potential methodological or assessment issues in these prevalence studies relate to instrumentation and subject response characteristics, specifically, the finding that the definition of Criterion A stressor events fluctuated across studies. The inclusion of rape and sexual assault as Criterion A events, for example, was inconsistent. Similarly, certain diagnostic instruments are less valid and reliable for identifying PTSD (e.g., standard administration of the DIS). Moreover, the potential reporting differences in men's and women's ability or willingness to describe traumatic events using various evaluation formats (e.g. interview, self-report) have not been studied. Gender-role socialization may contribute to the individual's impression of the acceptability of either reporting victimization experiences or psychological distress related to such experiences. All of these issues represent methodological concerns that could substantially impact outcome findings.

Special Populations

Disasters. The relevance of gender as a factor in outcome following natural or technological disasters is equivocal, although some authors have shown an association between female gender and poorer recovery (e.g., Burger, 1992; Steinglass & Gerrity, 1990). Realmuto, Wagner, and Bartholow

(1991), for example, evaluated a community 13 months after its exposure to a technological disaster and found that PTSD was significantly more common among females overall. Positively diagnosed individuals also were more likely to be older and to have histories of prior psychiatric problems. In another study involving two communities exposed to a severe natural disaster, female gender was again associated with higher rates of PTSD, although PTSD for the total sample decreased over time at 4- and 16-month follow-ups (Steinglass & Gerrity, 1990). Thus, there is preliminary information suggesting poorer postdisaster recovery in females in community samples when event characteristics are relatively stable.

War Veterans. The National Vietnam Veterans Readjustment Study (NVVRS) offers some of the most comprehensive data on the long-term functioning of male and female veterans following war exposure (Kulka et al., 1988, 1990). Secondary analyses by Weiss et al. (1992) found surprisingly few differences in PTSD lifetime prevalence between men and women: Male Vietnam theater veterans demonstrated a lifetime PTSD rate of 30.9%, whereas that of female theater counterparts was 26%. Lifetime rates for partial PTSD also were comparable: Just over 22% of men met partial PTSD criteria compared to 21.2% of women. Thus, although current diagnostic rates were disparate (15.2% for men, 8.7% for women), the likelihood of having had the disorder at some point following the war was similar. However, these analyses do not consider differences in PTSD base rates or interactions of gender by stressor type (Wolfe, Brown, Furey, & Levin, 1993a).

These data raise questions about whether certain precursors or postwar factors influence the subsequent expression of men's and women's traumatic stress syndromes in some unique way. NVVRS data on comorbidity and physical health, although not definitively resolving these questions, offer clues about possible answers. For example, although rates of comorbid, lifetime depression in male veterans with PTSD are high, female veterans in the NVVRS had appreciably higher rates of both lifetime and current depressive syndromes (42% lifetime, 23% current depression; Kulka et al., 1990). Furthermore, although theater veterans with high war-zone stress consistently reported more postwar health problems than theater cohorts with lower war-zone exposure, there is preliminary evidence that women's health complaints surpassed those of men (Wolfe & Young, 1993; Wolfe, Brown, & Kelley, 1993; Wolfe, Proctor, & Skinner, 1994c; Wolfe, Proctor, Sullivan, & Duncan Davis, 1995). Thus, although fewer women than men currently met PTSD criteria, there appear to be pre- and postwar factors that are distinctively associated with PTSD in female veterans or that interact with specific dimensions of women's war-zone experiences. Analyses of these data may illuminate factors associated with PTSD outcomes and links between these processes and gender status.

Homelessness. Recently, several authors have found that female veterans, like their male counterparts, comprise noteworthy subsets among the homeless in this country (Leda, Rosenheck, & Gallup, 1992). Like homeless male veterans, homeless women suffer from substantial comorbid depression and psychosocial dysfunction. Furthermore, homeless female veterans may be at greater risk than men for major psychiatric illness, although they are less likely to have had that illness diagnosed (Leda et al., 1992). North and Smith (1992) used the DIS and found higher rates of PTSD among women than Leda et al., with rates of PTSD diagnoses and PTSD symptoms exceeding those of men. In addition, both women and men had a high incidence of comorbid, lifetime psychiatric illness. Nearly three-fourths of men and women alike had PTSD diagnoses that preceded homelessness, suggesting that the homeless population in general is at considerable risk for psychosocial difficulties.

PTSD and Children. Only a few epidemiological studies have examined the topics of gender and PTSD in children. Cappelleri, Eckenrode, and Powers (1993) reviewed child abuse data from 19 U.S. states and found that age, family income, and ethnicity were risk factors for the occurrence of both sexual and physical childhood abuse. Consistent with other studies (e.g., Rose, 1991), female gender emerged as a strong risk factor for sexual, but not physical, abuse. Livingston, Lawson, and Jones (1993) studied 43 girls and boys ages 6–15 who were prior victims of sexual or physical abuse by a parent or parenting figure. Using a well-validated child assessment instrument (Diagnostic Interview for Childhood Adjustment—Revised; DICA-R; Herjanic & Reich, 1982), they found that a PTSD diagnosis was best predicted by the total number of stressors plus abuse, rather than by the type of child abuse per se, a finding not typical in samples limited to girls. In a 14-year longitudinal study of older adolescents, Reinherz, Giaconia, Lefkowitz, Pakiz, and Frost (1993) found that numerous teenagers met criteria for a lifetime DSM-III-R Axis I disorder, with substance abuse among the most common, and PTSD and obsessive–compulsive disorder the least frequent, diagnoses. Still, gender differences were found for three Axis I disorders—major depression, PTSD, and alcohol abuse/dependence—with female gender significantly associated with the first two. Using a sample of young adults, Fischer (1992) evaluated college students and determined that among child abuse victims, women were significantly more likely than men to have suffered incest. Furthermore, heterosexual forms of abuse were far more common in girls than boys. Unlike their male counterparts, women's attributions about the childhood event were less likely to evidence blame for the perpetrator. Finally, childhood sexual abuse was a significant predictor of subsequent teenage or adult sexual abuse for women, suggesting that earlier traumatic exposure is a factor in the adult exposure–outcome relationship. Still, distinctions between extrafamilial and familial forms of abuse and the relationship to PTSD require further study.

Data on gender and PTSD in childhood are also available from studies of natural disasters. Shannon, Lonigan, Finch, and Taylor (1994) assessed cohorts of children after exposure to a destructive hurricane and found wide variation in PTSD symptom rates based on race, gender, and age: Girls and younger children were each at greater risk for the disorder. The authors also found variations in symptoms between girls and boys: Girls were more likely than boys to report problems with emotional processing and affective reactivity posttrauma, suggesting that PTSD may be associated with female gender or, alternatively, related to the reporting or experiencing of emotional distress following exposure. In studies involving survivors of the Buffalo Creek Dam collapse, Green et al. (1991) studied children ages 2–15 and determined that 37% of the children met diagnostic criteria for PTSD 2-years postevent. Consistent with Shannon et al.'s (1994) findings, investigators confirmed that girls reported more symptoms of distress than boys, although younger girls and boys in general had the fewest symptoms. When models predicting PTSD were derived, experiences of life threat, female gender, younger age, and parental psychopathology (e.g., depression), were significantly associated with the PTSD diagnosis. These findings are similar to those obtained in young adults (e.g., Breslau et al., 1991; Resnick, Kilpatrick, Best, & Kramer, 1992), and suggest that characteristics of both the event and the environment distinctively influence gender-linked outcomes.

The relationship of PTSD and gender in children may be associated with reporting characteristics. At least one study (Pillitteri, Seidl, Smith, & Stanton, 1992) examined the effects of both the victim's and abusing parent's gender on subsequent event reporting by medical personnel and found that, although parental gender was *not* a factor in abuse documentation, emergency room personnel were significantly less likely to report abuse when the child was female. Also, reporting was decreased when the family was viewed as middle- (vs. lower- or upper-) socioeconomic class.

In summary, prevalence data in special populations suggest that rates of PTSD in women are appreciable, often exceeding levels found in men. Methodological issues (e.g., failure to account for multiple stressor exposures, differential impact ascribed to exposure categories), however, may currently limit the reliability of these findings. It is increasingly clear that assessment of both respondent characteristics (e.g., social desirability, response styles, test formats) and the social context (e.g., family status; relationship to perpetrator) are needed to help elucidate etiologies associated with gender differences, especially those involving sequelae of childhood trauma.

Studies of Women

Sexual and Physical Assault

A growing number of studies of PTSD in women have addressed the effects of particular stressors, notably rape and sexual assault. One of the most comprehensive studies to date used random digit dialing to obtain a national probability sample of 4,008 American women (85.2% White, 11.6% Black; Resnick et al., 1993). Data were weighted by age and race to approximate the 1989 distribution of these characteristics among U.S. women. Using telephone interviews, women were queried about PTSD using the PTSD assessment module from the National Women's Study (NWS; Kilpatrick, Resnick, Saunders, & Best, 1989) which offered a number of methodological improvements: Histories of traumatic events were queried in greater detail for possible Criterion A events, and symptom measures were expanded for congruence with DSM-III-R criteria (NVVRS; Kulka et al., 1990). Also, DIS exclusionary criteria that had previously diminished the instrument's sensitivity for PTSD were deleted (see Resnick et al., 1992). These advances led to important findings on rates of current and lifetime exposure and trauma in women. First, the lifetime rate for exposure to trauma was 69%, with 36% of women reporting exposure to sexual or aggravated assault, or the homicide of a close friend or family member. Thus, severe personal assault or loss were common. Second, the sample's prevalence for lifetime PTSD was 12.3%, 4.6% of whom had the disorder within the past 6 months. Consistent with previous findings, rates of PTSD were appreciably higher for survivors of crime- versus noncrime-related traumas (26% vs. 9%). As shown earlier (e.g., Cohen & Roth, 1987), experiences involving direct threat to life or the receipt of physical injury emerged as the strongest risk factors for PTSD.

A growing number of studies confirm that initial rates of PTSD following *completed sexual assault* (i.e., rape) are inordinately high (> 90%), a finding confirmed in numerous female samples (Foa, 1994; Foa & Riggs, 1993; Hanson, 1990; Kilpatrick et al., 1989; Kramer & Green, 1991; Resick, 1993; Rothbaum, Foa, Riggs, Murdock, & Walsh, 1992). Despite the clearly traumatic effects of these assaults, recent research offers important data on patterns of recovery and adjustment. By 3-months postassault, initial PTSD rates are likely to decrease by as much as half (e.g., 47%), suggesting that rapid recovery occurs for a subset of survivors in the early postassault period (Rothbaum et al., 1992). Although assessment methods and research into these mechanisms are still evolving, a range of premorbid factors appears to influence psychological outcome. Resnick et al. (1992) assessed 295 female crime victims aged 18 and older for their precrime psychiatric status, level of crime stress, and subsequent PTSD. The authors found that high crime stress (defined as perceived threat to life, actual injury, or completed rape) was more strongly associated with a PTSD diagnosis than low crime stress exposure (35% vs. 13%). Although precrime psychiatric status was not associated with high crime *exposure,* a significant interaction was found among crime stress level, precrime depression, and PTSD: PTSD was greatest in women in the high crime group with preexisting histories of depression. Thus, at least for women, there is preliminary evidence that preexisting affective status impacts adaptation following subsequent trauma exposure, with depression in particular contributing to the risk for developing PTSD.

Battering and Domestic Violence

The deleterious effects of domestic abuse in women have been well studied and confirmed. Walker (1991) documented high rates of PTSD in women exposed to spousal or partner abuse, and West, Fernandez, Hillard, Schoof, and Parks (1990), using interviews and rating scales, found that 37% of women in a local battered women's shelter met criteria for major depression at the time of assessment. Of note, 47% of the sample met criteria for PTSD, confirming the strong association between domestic abuse and posttraumatic stress. Similar to outcome models of rape, certain components of domestic violence appear to contribute to the prediction of PTSD. Degree/extent of abuse, level of subjective distress, perceived life threat, and overall event severity, for example, all predict negative outcomes following battering (e.g., Browne, 1993; Houskamp & Foy, 1991; Kemp, Rawlings, & Green, 1991). To the degree that women are more widely subjected to these experiences, female gender could appear to constitute an increased risk for PTSD outcomes.

Childhood Sexual Abuse

There is considerable consensus that childhood sexual and physical abuse in females, primarily incest, is widely associated with a propensity for revictimization and the diagnosis of PTSD in adulthood (Albach & Everaerd, 1992; Chu, 1992; Kendall-Tackett, Williams, & Finkelhor, 1993; O'Neill & Gupta, 1991). Several investigators have found that as many as 73% of female childhood abuse survivors meet criteria for PTSD at some point, although onset is often delayed. Also, severe forms of female child sexual abuse have been strongly linked to a number of comorbid psychiatric conditions, particularly depression and substance abuse (e.g., Hanson, 1990). Briere and Runtz (1987) sampled 391 women using the DIS and a structured interview, and found that one-third of the sample reported sexual abuse or molestation before the age of 18. These individuals were more likely than nonvictims to meet lifetime criteria for depression, phobia, obsessive–compulsive disorder, and sexual disturbances, with depression the most strongly associated with childhood abuse.

Clinical Samples

The majority of PTSD studies involving clinical samples to date have involved males, typically treatment-seeking Vietnam combat veterans (e.g., McFall, Mackay, & Donovan, 1991, 1992; Foy & Card, 1987; Mueserk, Yarnold, & Foy, 1991; Zaidi & Foy, 1994). In other settings, Rose (1991) studied a sample of persistently mentally ill individuals and found that gender was related to certain types of earlier abuse, notably childhood sexual abuse in females. Briere and Runtz (1987) found that nearly 44% of female clients at a mental health crisis center reported childhood sexual victimization. These histories were strongly associated with more symptoms of dissociation, anxiety, rage, sleep disturbance, substance abuse, suicidality, and revictimization. Gordon (1990) found that certain demographic characteristics were specific to female (but not male) adult childhood sexual abuse survivors, defined as occurring before age 18. Women were substantially more likely to have been younger and assaulted by a family member or relative rather than a non-relative. In contrast, male victims were typically older and closer in age to the perpetrator of the assault. Perpetrators for both genders were overwhelmingly male, a finding confirmed by large-scale studies of sexual assault victims (e.g., National Victim Center [NVC], 1992). The clear impact of these characteristics, however, (i.e., younger age, perpetrator familiarity) on longer range outcome is not known at this time.

Preclinical Studies

Animal studies have used tests of learned helplessness, sensitization, startle, seizure potential, and olfactory threshold to offer provocative preclinical data on gender and traumatization. Some preclinical studies with rats found gender differences in vulnerability to exogenous hazardous chemicals (e.g., Bell, Miller, & Schwartz, 1992; Matthews, Dixon, Herr, & Tilson, 1990); in one study, for example, female rats were more sensitive to hippocampal damage after exposure to an organophosphate flame retardant (tris[2-chloro-ethyl]phosphate; TRCP) than were males. Based on these data, Tilson, Veronesi, McLamb, and Matthews (1990) administered a single dose of TRCP to female rats and found that females experienced a range of adverse events including acute seizures, permanent damage to hippocampal neurons, and persistent impairment in the acquisition of a spatial memory task. Several authors (e.g., Bell et al., 1992; van der Kolk & Saporta, 1993) have conjectured that these data provide compelling support for kindling or sensitization etiologies of traumatization. These models propose that acquired sensitization is linked to the development of the autonomic hyperreactivity observed in both multiple chemical sensitivity syndrome (MCS) and PTSD (Friedman, 1991; Friedman, 1994b). One possible explanation is that hormonal differences account for much of the variability in certain response parameters (e.g., changes in seizure threshold following administration of convulsants such as TRCP). Some investigators (e.g., Newmark & Penry, 1980) have demonstrated that estrogen, but not testosterone, lowers seizure thresholds and other reactions across various species. Similarly, findings showing that ovariectomies produce little change in the sensitization of adult female rats, compared to increased sensitization in males following gonadectomies (Robinson & Becker, 1986), has led some authors to conclude that the presence of male hormones constitutes a kind of neuroendocrine "buffer" for certain stressors, potentially mitigating sensitization after exposure to novel, aversive stimuli.

The preliminary nature of these investigations, as well as their focus to date on only limited classes of exposure, suggests that far more research is needed to understand the complexities of neuroendocrine status as it relates to behavioral exposure, reactivity, and trauma based on gender. Optimally, such research would illustrate both individual and interactive effects of hormones, including bidirectional effects (e.g., the neuroprotective impact of progesterone during the menstrual cycle in regulating epilepsy). Thus, information is needed on how hormones can serve protective versus irritative functions to improve understanding of the biology of gender and its links to behavioral response (Friedman, 1991, 1994a; Murburg, Ashleigh, Hommer, & Veith, 1994a; Murburg, McFall, & Veith, 1994b; van der Kolk & Saporta, 1993; Yehuda et al., 1994).

In summary, extant studies of PTSD in women have outlined a number of critical predictor variables, including the range of traumatic events most prevalent in women, salient event characteristics that increase the risk of PTSD, and other susceptibility factors. Specific exposure dimensions include the threat to life, injury, completed rape, and prolonged duration of stressor exposure. The association of these characteristics with high rates of exposure may contribute to the greater prevalence of PTSD in women. Whether a differential vulnerability for PTSD in women relates to underlying or intrinsic characteristics (e.g., hormonal or genetic diatheses) as opposed to external factors remains unclear. Little research to date has addressed differential rates of multiple trauma in males and females or levels of PTSD symptoms following multiple rather than single events. When examined in conjunction with data regarding early childhood victimization, this gap in the conceptualization of traumatic exposure underlines the importance of including within the PTSD construct the experiences of multiply victimized individuals as well as the investigation of mechanisms by which such experiences contribute to PTSD vulnerability and chronicity across gender.

ANTECEDENTS AND CORRELATES OF PTSD IN FEMALES

Developmental and Behavioral Precursors

Early family environment is increasingly thought to play a role in the development and progression of trauma symptoms in females. Nash, Hulsey, Sexton, Harralson, and Lambert (1993) studied adult psychopathology in 105 abused and nonabused women to assess the relationship of childhood abuse experiences to later symptoms and found that although early sexual abuse influenced the development of somatic symptoms and schema distortions, the presence of a dysfunctional family environment (e.g., substance abuse in parents, pronounced emotional neglect, witnessing domestic stress/violence) was a stronger predictor of severe psychiatric distress, including dissociation. Often characterized as more subtle forms of "environmental" deprivation, early neglect and abuse thus appear to impact development significantly in some girls from the outset. A growing number of studies show that young girls' exposure to these dysfunctional family environments is strongly associated with a wide range of trauma *spectrum* disorders, only a portion of which are PTSD (Graziano, 1992). In these instances, marked psychosocial, affective, and behavioral disturbances are common, although their manifestations vary widely by individual and developmental stage.

The most telling sequelae of disturbed home settings in girls include serious problems with shame, guilt, stigmatization, and self-blame (Moscarello, 1992). Certain cognitive problems (e.g., highly biased or negative self-attributions) also figure prominently in young girls suffering interpersonally based trauma. Fischer (1992) found that young female abuse survivors were substantially less likely than male survivors to attribute blame to the perpetrator and more apt to blame themselves, showing confusion over what constituted bona fide abuse and assaultive behavior by others. These attributions have often been associated with subsequent development of even more serious affective and behavioral problems, for example, dysphoria, depression, shame, guilt, and social isolation. Beyond the adverse impact of these symptoms, the emergence of severe depression and guilt is likely to increase the risk for revictimization by disrupting social mastery and positive, active coping.

Engel et al. (1993) have provided comparative data on the effects of early childhood abuse following adult trauma. The authors assessed the effect of male and female veterans' premilitary (childhood) trauma on adjustment to military/war-zone stressors and found that, although men described more combat exposure, women reported higher rates of premilitary childhood abuse and associated psychiatric problems. Furthermore, gender significantly modified the impact of premilitary childhood abuse on war-related PTSD symptomatology. With differences in psychiatric history and combat levels controlled, women (but not men) with prior childhood abuse had significantly more PTSD symptomatology than either men or women without these backgrounds. However, it is unclear to what degree this interaction stems from differences in traumatic military experiences among women and men (e.g., sexual harassment or assault for women, injury or life threat for men) or from a particular interaction with gender-linked characteristics of earlier abuse (e. g., sexual vs. physical). Still, there appear to be complex relationships among gender, early trauma experiences, and adult outcomes.

Major Symptom Correlates and Related Functional Domains

Affective Disorders

Major depression and dysthymia continue to be recognized as among the most common comorbid features of PTSD in both male and female trauma survivors. Similar to substance abuse, it is often difficult to determine whether depression following trauma constitutes an independent disorder, or whether affective symptoms are primarily a correlate of the posttrauma syndrome. This dilemma is compounded by the fact that many comorbid features of PTSD (e.g., substance abuse) are highly represented in depressive disorders (see Kofoed, Friedman, & Peck, 1993). In a study of female alcoholics, researchers documented extensive incest histories. Furthermore, those with comorbid depression were significantly more likely to meet criteria for PTSD than counterparts who were not clinically depressed (Kovach, 1986). Recent biological evidence suggests that it may be possible to distinguish primary depression from depression associated with PTSD. Murburg et al. (1994b) were able to differentiate PTSD patients with comorbid depression from individuals with primary major depression by using a number of sympathoadrenal neurobiological measures. Expanded use of these paradigms with other samples is likely to clarify the contribution of gender to diagnostic distinctions.

Borderline Personality Disorder

The diagnosis of borderline personality disorder (BPD) shows considerable overlap with PTSD in both etiology and symptom expression, especially among women. To date, women typically constitute about 75% of individuals diagnosed with BPD and researchers estimate that 80% of individuals with BPD have notable childhood trauma (e.g., childhood physical or sexual abuse; Gunderson, Zanarini, & Kisiel, 1991). These estimates involve samples that are largely female, however, and rates are considerably lower when men are included (Goldman, D'Angelo, DeMaso, & Mezzacappa, 1992). Up to one-third of borderline individuals also meet criteria for PTSD (Gunderson, & Sabo, 1993; Blank, 1994). In addition, childhood trauma both with and without accompanying borderline symptomatology seems to confer a greater likelihood of experiencing adult trauma as well as the development of PTSD (Albach & Everaerd, 1992; Bremner, Southwick, Johnson, Yehuda, & Charney, 1993; O'Neill & Gupta, 1991).

The distinction between BPD and PTSD is often complicated, especially in cases of chronic traumatic stress. Numerous features—affective instability, dissociation, impulsivity, self-injurious behavior, severe disruptions in relationships—are common in both disorders and in women with either childhood or adult trauma (Blank, 1994; Landecker, 1992). To date, the literature suggests preliminary methods for differentiating the two disorders, by detailing the trauma history with respect to the onset of symptoms. Since the diagnosis of BPD connotes notable characterological problems, for example, it is conceivable that histories of relatively healthy relationships and stable functioning prior to stressor exposure support a diagnosis of PTSD. This distinction is likely to be exceedingly difficult when the stressor occurs early in childhood and effects are pervasive throughout personality and emotional development (Herman, Perry, & van der Kolk, 1989).

Herman (1992) has argued that the current construct of PTSD is based largely on research studying highly circumscribed, single events (e.g., combat, rape, natural disaster). Thus, it ignores the probable impact of earlier or more chronic exposure on outcome. As indicated in this chapter, females appear to be at greater risk for serious revictimization across the lifespan. Accordingly, current PTSD conceptualizations may not adequately capture the spectrum of female stressor exposure and posttrauma responses, contributing to misdiagnosis of primary borderline personality. This phenomenon is likely to be compounded by elements of clinician bias, which show that professionals more readily ascribe Axis II disorders and BPD in particular to women than men (Adler, 1990; Becker, 1994).

Recent reconceptualizations of BPD have been offered in attempts to lessen inaccurate and potentially pejorative aspects of diagnostic labeling. These models view early family environment and traumatic experiences in an etiological framework whereby borderline symptomatology reflects formerly adaptive responses to multiple, recurrent, and chronic stressors (Arntz, 1994; Landecker, 1992). Despite these advances, the phenomenological and etiological overlap between PTSD and BPD requires further investigation in several areas. For example, childhood sexual and physical abuse tend to occur within distinctive family environments (Finkelhor & Baron, 1986); yet abuse and family environment each have been shown to independently predict PTSD symptomatology (Weaver & Clum, 1993). Whether symptoms of BPD result from chronic childhood trauma in the presence of more disturbed — versus relatively more functional — family environments remains unclear. Also lacking is an understanding of differences between BPD patients who report abuse and those who do not. If such differences exist, it is possible that two subtypes of the disorder exist, one reflecting predominantly posttrauma symptomatology and the other reflecting more characterological dimensions (Gunderson & Sabo, 1993). Rates and correlates of these subtypes and their relationship to gender, chronic early trauma, and sex-role socialization warrant more explication.

Substance Abuse

Substance abuse has been widely observed in both men and women diagnosed with PTSD (e.g., Brown & Wolfe, 1994; Keane, Caddell, Martin, Zimering, & Fairbank, 1983; Kofoed et al., 1993; Kulka et al., 1990). However, like depression, causal relationships are difficult to ascertain (e.g., Keane & Wolfe, 1990). Of the few studies comparing men and women, Recupero, Brown, Stout, Wolfe, and Morello (1994), found that 59% of carefully diagnosed substance-abuse patients confirmed experiences of trauma across the lifespan. Moreover, 40% reported continuing to experience extreme distress from the event in the past year. Twenty-five percent of participants overall met diagnostic criteria for PTSD. Among these, however, women reported more trauma across the lifespan and were significantly more likely than men to meet PTSD criteria at the time of substance-abuse treatment. Still, possible differential severity of trauma was not statistically controlled. Thus, gender differences may have emerged because women had more frequent or severe trauma exposure. Cottler et al. (1992) used data from the St. Louis Epidemiologic Catchment Area (ECA) Survey to assess the prevalence of PTSD in substance abusers. Sixteen percent of respondents described exposure to a DSM Criterion A event. When other variables were statistically controlled, female gender and use of either cocaine or opiates significantly predicted a PTSD diagnosis. Given the magnitude of substance-abuse problems in society generally, the relationship of these conditions to traumatization and gender (or gender experiences) are areas for further study.

Dissociation

Dissociation is a moderately common correlate of severe trauma (Putnam, 1989). Although some research suggests that dissociative experiences are relatively frequent in the general population (Vanderlinden, Van Dyck, Vandereycken, & Vertommen, 1993), dissociation has been most widely documented within highly distressed clinical samples (Chu & Dill, 1990; Saxe et al., 1993, 1994; Spiegel & Cardeña, 1991; Classen, Koopman, & Spiegel, 1993), with women represented more than men (Saxe et al., 1993, 1994). The presence of dissociative tendencies at the point of trauma, however, now appears to have particular significance. Marmar et al. (1994) and others (e.g., Koopman, Classen, & Spiegel, 1994) found that dissociation during exposure constituted a significant predictor of poorer outcome (i.e., chronic PTSD), a finding substantiated in at least one study of female childhood incest survivors (Albach & Everaerd, 1992). Thus, numerous experiential factors reported by women may impact trauma outcome.

Eating Disorders

Several authors have concluded that victimization in females, particularly sexual assault, may be related to the emergence of eating disorders, including anorexia, bulimia, and body dysmorphia (e.g., Root, 1991). Similar to other disorders, however, the exact nature of this association remains unclear and may vary depending on certain characteristics, for example, explicit avoidance/aversion to trauma cues versus alterations in satiety secondary to neurochemically based mood disturbances. Regardless, current rates of eating problems among females in the general population and the mortality associated with this disturbance confirm that the interface between eating disturbances and PTSD is critically important for a variety of health reasons.

Attributional Style

Cognitive attributions about traumatic events are commonly associated with the nature of trauma outcomes in women and men (see Chapter 18, this volume, Roth, Lebowitz, & DeRosa). For women, preexisting beliefs about the significance of interpersonal relationships are frequently impacted. Gidycz and Koss (1991) examined the contribution of cognitive attributions to posttrauma outcomes in a large sample of college-aged women. Taking into consideration certain robust predictors (e.g., preexisting mental health history, assault-related degree of force), the authors found that alterations in certain aspects of cognitive style contributed to additional outcome variance: Cognitive attributions about oneself, others, and the world, for example, differentiated the stress responses of abused female versus male children. Hunter, Goodwin, and Wilson (1992) studied similar constructs in age-stratified groups of sexually abused boys and girls. Although children in general did not show marked self-blame, results showed an association between female gender and the tendency to attribute causal implications to oneself.

Individuals exposed to trauma often experience social alienation stemming from a perception that they have been rendered permanently different (Herman, 1992). In women, stigmatization and alienation frequently emerge when the victim or members of her social network ascribe blame, presumably in an effort to make sense of the event. In rape in particular, survivors often describe feeling permanently "marked." Such perceptions of social stigma can be readily reaffirmed by reduced interpersonal contact (Jones et al., 1984): When social withdrawal occurs, for example, opportunities for positive reframing become significantly reduced, increasing the likelihood that faulty attributions are entrenched.

Other Functional Domains

Social Support

Social support is critical in the assessment of posttrauma functioning. Social support has been widely theorized to buffer the deleterious effects of stress (Cohen & Wills, 1985), in some cases preventing chronic PTSD. Although pretrauma support is influential in determining subsequent social support, factors such as gender and the type of trauma also can create obstacles for obtaining posttrauma support from the community and family. In this section, we review important sources of support for individuals exposed to trauma, highlighting areas of particular significance for women.

In relationships with both family and friends, the manifestations of PTSD symptoms often erode existing support systems. Research with male Vietnam War veterans shows that symptoms of emotional numbing, increased irritability, and angry outbursts (or rage) significantly affect marital discord, substantially decreasing a partner's support (Herndon & Law, 1985). Individuals in the larger social network often respond to the trauma survivor's reluctance to disclose aspects of the trauma with feelings of estrangement or even resentment. Although it has not yet been empirically studied (see Harkness,

1993), this effect may be more pronounced with female trauma survivors, in whom symptoms of unpredictable, rageful outbursts are considered surprising, socially undesirable, inconsistent with role, and less deserving of external validation (Herman, 1992). Still, the family remains an important source of support for the trauma survivor (Figley, 1985; Mitchell, 1991; Resick, 1981), particularly for women. In many cases, the family helps shape the immediate environment, particularly if vocational role and family tradition emphasize this involvement. Consequently, the ability of the family to support a female survivor can have considerable impact. Educating family members about the process of coping with trauma is likely to improve the quality of support, although further study of the specific applicability of this to women with PTSD is needed.

The survivor's family may also suffer a wide range of posttrauma consequences as a result of their concern for the woman. The rage of male partners toward the perpetrator or the uncontrollability of the event can temporarily impede the ability to offer support. Also affected are family members who themselves experience secondary traumatization, possibly to the point of developing PTSD symptoms (Figley, 1985). In these cases, the female survivor may feel compelled to resume a prior caregiver role at the expense of her own psychosocial needs (Wolfe, Mori, & Krygeris, 1994a).

Although much of the attention paid by clinicians to social support focuses on the immediate social network, support from the survivor's community is also critical in facilitating adjustment. In cases of sexual and physical assault, the perpetrator is frequently a friend or partner (National Victim Center, 1992). Thus, a former source of intimate support has evolved rapidly into a threat. On a broader scale, previously available social networks can be disrupted, especially if the assailant is popular with others. In domestic violence in particular, support can be eroded by social and cultural pressures to maintain the integrity of the marital or family structure. Similarly, in work-based sexual harassment, contact with supportive individuals may be lost when a woman must leave her place of work to protect herself from continued contact with the perpetrator. All of these experiences are likely to impact the development of symptoms.

It is possible that stigmatization occurs more often with female trauma survivors, especially in cases of sexual assault or marital violence in which the perpetrator is known. These victims, in particular, appear highly sensitive to implicit social schemas (e.g., rape myths) that convey responsibility on the part of the survivor, intensifying feelings of social detachment (Calhoun & Atkeson, 1991; Lebowitz & Roth, 1994; Roth & Lebowitz, 1988). In such cases, support groups offer unique opportunities for improving social comparisons and the quality of social support.

Health Status

The stress literature points strongly to an association between stressor exposure and increased reporting of physical symptoms and poor health in survivors. Decreased immunocompetence has been found using a variety of laboratory and *in vivo* stressors as well as a variety of self-report health measures (for reviews, see Ader & Cohen, 1993; Cohen & Williamson, 1991; Kiecolt-Glaser & Glaser, 1987). Reports of poor health are especially pronounced in women who describe exposure to high-magnitude events such as physical assault, criminal victimization (Koss, Woodruff, & Koss, 1991; Randall, 1990), and sexual assault (Kimerling & Calhoun, 1994; Waigandt, Wallace, Phelps, & Miller, 1990).

Nearly all studies examining the relationship between reports of stressor exposure and health status have documented poor global health perceptions or increased reports of physical symptoms in traumatized women when compared to matched normal control subjects. Waigandt et al. (1990) found that female victims reported significantly more illnesses postassault than nonvictims, and twice as many reproductive physiology symptoms measured by the Cornell Medical Index (CMI; Bartone, Ursano, Wright, & Ingraham, 1989). Koss et al. (1991) replicated these results, showing marked elevations on all CMI subscales except for dermatological and opthalmological problems. Randall (1990) noted increases in self-reported health problems, including chronic headaches, abdominal pain, sexual dysfunction, and recurrent vaginal infection among women with repeated physical abuse by a partner.

To date, one prospective, longitudinal study has investigated the health status of women with trauma (Kimerling & Calhoun, 1994). A group of female sexual assault victims and an age-matched comparison group were repeatedly assessed by clinicians starting from 2 weeks postassault until 1 year postincident. The authors found that sexual assault victims reported significantly more somatic symptoms than did nonvictimized women. Furthermore, survivors rated their problems as more severe. Despite a trend showing that the frequency and severity of physical symptoms declined over the year, a number of health problems remained constant, including headaches, allergies, skin problems, nausea, and gynecological problems. Thus, initial and continuing health problems separated women with sexual trauma from those without these experiences.

Numerous investigators have found increments in heterogeneous physical symptoms of male veterans with PTSD compared to matched cohorts without the disorder (e.g., Kulka et al., 1990; Litz, Keane, Fisher, Marx, & Monaco, 1992; Shalev, Bleich, & Ursano, 1990; Solomon, 1988; Stretch, 1991). Similar associations have been observed among American female military personnel (Wolfe et al., 1994b; Wolfe, Schnurr, Brown, & Furey, 1994d). Wolfe et al. (1994d) found that female veterans with PTSD reported significantly more cardiovascular, gastrointestinal, gynecological, dermatological, opthalmological, and pain symptoms than women without this diagnosis. Few studies, however, have compared the posttrauma health status of men and women directly, an important opportunity for tests of gender-linked issues.

The documented association between reported poorer health following trauma exposure or traumatic stress is important, particularly in light of emerging evidence that stress reactions substantially mediate the relationship between the exposure to trauma and resulting health concerns. Wolfe et al. (1994d) used demographic variables and health status before Vietnam as covariates and found separate, robust effects of both war-zone exposure and PTSD when each variable was entered simultaneously into a model. However, when PTSD and exposure were controlled for each other, PTSD most strongly predicted poor health, substantially reducing the association between war-zone exposure and health. This effect suggests a mediating role for PTSD in the association between exposure and perceived health. Friedman and Schnurr (1995) reanalyzed these data using pathanalytic techniques to determine how much of the trauma–health relationship was direct, that is, not accounted for by the association between trauma and PTSD. For health perceptions, 56% of the total effect of exposure was mediated by PTSD (standardized path coefficient $= -.295; p < .001$); for number of current health problems, only the indirect effects of exposure reached statistical significance, with PTSD mediating 76% of the effect of exposure (standardized path coefficient $= .326; p < .001$). These empirical findings are among the first to suggest that the intensity of individual stress reactions influences the development of adverse changes in health status, at least in female veterans.

In conclusion, studies of symptoms associated with trauma exposure and PTSD in women show significant disturbances in posttrauma recovery related to reported health status, eating disorders, substance abuse, depression, and disrupted social and family functioning. In some cases, these difficulties seem distinctive for women. Accordingly, these symptoms are areas for careful clinical assessment. To the extent that associated symptoms impact primary symptoms of PTSD, they may contribute significantly to chronicity in this disorder.

ASSESSMENT METHODS AND APPROACHES

Conceptual Overview

Based on the findings reviewed here, it is clear that the evaluation of life trauma in women requires a multidimensional approach, particularly when trauma has transpired in childhood. Empirical data clearly highlight the need to assess more than the commonly recognized dimensions of event type, frequency, and overall severity (Resnick, 1992; Riggs, Cascardi, Hearst, & Foa, 1993; Cascardi, Riggs, Hearst-Ikeda, & Foa, 1996). In addition, research demonstrates that individual attributions about stressor causality and etiology have critical effects on both immediate and long-term outcome, as do factors such as self-esteem, self-schema, worldview, trust, social standing, and relational capacity (Wilson, 1994; Wind & Silvern, 1992). Thus, clinicians are urged to go beyond the primary DSM-IV symptom criteria when assessing a survivor's posttrauma adjustment and outcome. This orientation is supported by numerous studies on the effects of trauma exposure on women. Various investigators (e.g., Draucker, 1993; Finkelhor & Browne, 1986; Hazzard, 1993) have documented the influence of trauma-related attributions and cognitions (e.g., self- blame/stigmatization, betrayal, powerlessness) in sexually traumatized women and found effects that often exceed traditional symptom expectations. These findings suggest that alterations in the preceding domains have a profound impact on functional outcome in a number of ways, ranging from self-esteem and self-efficacy to mood and interactional style (Hazzard, 1993).

Age is an important factor to consider in the design of assessment protocols. In younger women and girls, disturbances in the preceding domains are commonly associated with affective distress or depression (Nolen-Hoeksema & Girgus, 1994). Although clinical depression may remit in women, findings from research increasingly suggest that effects of depression and associated adaptation play an important (though poorly understood) role in subsequent adult PTSD (Breslau & Davis, 1992; Gidycz & Koss, 1991; Resnick et al., 1993). Thus, the clinician is advised to carefully explore childhood stressor antecedents, accompanying cognitive and behavioral changes, and affective sequelae, even in the absence of etiological models.

Assessing Primary and Associated Features

One of the more challenging issues in assessing PTSD in women relates to definition of the stressor. Although there are excellent instruments for evaluating normative symptom criteria (e.g., the Structured Clinical Interview for DSM-III-R [SCID]; Spitzer, Williams, & Gibbon, 1986; Spitzer, Williams, Gibbon, & First, 1990; and the Clinician-Administered PTSD Scale; [CAPS]; Blake et al., 1990), delineation of Criterion A may remain problematic. Fortunately, several checklist and interview formats are available that help facilitate identification of a range of stressors, for example, the Evaluation of Lifetime Stressors Interview (ELS; Krinsley et al., 1994), the PTSD Symptom Scale (PSS; Foa, Riggs, Dancu, & Rothbaum, 1993), the Women's Military Stress Interview (WMSI; Rosenheck & Wolfe, 1994), and the Life Stressor Checklist (LSC; Wolfe, Kimerling, & Brown, 1993c; see Appendix). Most of these instruments specify high-magnitude events that are easily recognized (e.g., criminal victimization, natural disaster). Events linked to developmental or psychosocial disruptions, however, often are more difficult to elicit despite their importance for female survivors (e.g., permanent separation from a child, abortion). Instruments such as the LSC, which review broader developmental experiences, may help with defining lifespan events (Wolfe et al., 1993c).

Often, when trauma has occurred in the context of an ongoing relationship, stressors may not be readily recognized for their abusive potential. In these instances, the semantics in inquiring about such events have paramount importance. Several community surveys have found that many women do not spontaneously endorse sexual assault or rape when interviewers use these terms and the event has been perpetrated by someone familiar (National

Victim Center, 1992). These studies strongly suggest that behavioral descriptors and queries are needed, for example, "Have you ever been forced, or threatened with force, to have sex against your will? By sex, we mean penetration of the vagina, anus, or mouth, by a penis or other object." Use of this type of inquiry has produced notable increases in reported assaults in a variety of samples.

Recently enacted changes in the DSM-III-R and DSM-IV (American Psychiatric Association, 1987, 1994) diagnostic criteria for PTSD also are likely to have implications for assessing women. Specifically, the incorporation of *witnessing* a traumatic event as a Criterion A event is likely to broaden the range of applicable exposures over the lifespan. When observation of trauma transpires in domestic, caretaking, or vocational settings, this criterion refinement may add ecological validity to the stressors encountered by women, improving both accuracy of detection and diagnosis. Although few empirical data are currently available, women's witnessing of trauma may have distinctive implications for diagnosis and treatment. Wolfe, Brown, and Kelley (1993b) evaluated severe stressors encountered by male and female veterans during their Persian Gulf War deployment and found differences among gender, exposure typology, and PTSD symptomatology. Women were significantly more likely to show an association between generalized clinical distress or PTSD symptoms and the *observation of trauma* involving others, whereas men were more impacted by specific military events (e.g., anticipating or being put on rocket/SCUD alert). In addition, women's (but not men's) PTSD symptomatology at 1-year postdeployment was linked to particular postmilitary life events, for example, subsequent witnessing of a serious accident or injuries involving others (Wolfe & Young, 1993).

The definition of "symptom patterns" requires comparable specificity and sensitivity at the psychometric and clinician levels. The SCID (Spitzer et al., 1986, 1990) and DIS (Helzer & Robins, 1988; von Korff & Anthony, 1982) each provide reliable diagnostic data for Axis I diagnoses and contain specific modules for determining the presence or absence of PTSD (Weiss, 1993). These instruments are limited in part, however, by a reliance on dichotomous classification schemas. In contrast, structured interviews such as the CAPS (Blake et al., 1990), which has excellent psychometric properties, offer continuous measures of all primary PTSD criteria and associated features, enabling assessment of both frequency and severity/intensity dimensions. Other scales such as the PSS (Foa et al., 1993), the PTSD Checklist (PCL; Weathers, Litz, Huska, & Keane, 1991), the Impact of Event Scale (IES; Horowitz, Wilner, & Alvarez, 1979), the Impact of Event Scale-Revised (IES-R; Weiss, Marmar, Metzler, & Ronfeldt, 1995), and the Mississippi Scale for Combat-Related (or Civilian) PTSD (Keane, Caddell, & Taylor, 1988), to name a few, can be used either in interview or self-report formats and possess good to excellent psychometric validity and reliability. The reader is referred to companion chapters in this volume for more detailed discussion of these procedures.

Detailed, careful delineation of symptomatology is especially important when there is repeated victimization or marked symptom chronicity (e.g., following incest or long-term battering). Instruments such as the Trauma Symptom Checklist (TSC; Bagley, 1991) appear to have the ability to differentiate consequences of briefer trauma exposure from sequelae of longer term abuse. Particular attention should also be paid to Axis II disorders, especially borderline personality, in which sequelae of more severe trauma histories are likely to be represented (Gunderson & Sabo, 1993). The SCID II (Spitzer et al., 1986) and structured interviews for complex PTSD (Herman, 1992) are recommended for delineating complicated components of chronic or untreated severe stress disorders.

Social Support

To date, no standardized measures of social support specifically meet the needs of trauma survivors. Although there are a number of social support measures with reasonable psychometric properties, for example, the Social Adjustment Scale (SAS; Paykel, Prusoff, & Uhlenhuth, 1971; Paykel, Weismann, & Prusoff, 1978) and the Social Support Questionnaire (SSQ; Sarason, Levine, Basham, & Sarason, 1983), there are no comparative norms for trauma victims. Hence, assessment of social support might be augmented by using an unstructured interview that focuses on perceptions and status of the woman's relationships with a range of significant individuals (e.g., friends, family, community; McCann & Pearlman, 1990). In particular, reports of support availability, helpfulness, and change should be carefully assessed. When a traumatic stressor has substantially altered a relationship (e.g., through separation or death), it is critical to examine the spectrum of effects on the woman and on those in her immediate network. A single mother, for example, may turn increasingly to a child for support, altering boundaries and demands on the family's operational structure. When trauma occurs in the work or community setting, a woman may be forced to leave existing relationships, losing esteem and support derived from important relationships with colleagues and friends. In all of these cases, the clinician is strongly advised to assess the functional impact of these losses and to evaluate the feasibility of other potential replacement sources.

Psychophysiology

Psychophysiological assessment of the stress response remains one of the more useful methods for assessing posttrauma functional change, because it permits the collection of objective, empirically reliable data along with subjective reports. To date, however, the vast majority of psychophysiological research in PTSD has been conducted with male veterans with combat-related PTSD. These data compellingly demonstrate pronounced psychophysiological reactivity to trauma-relevant stimuli in numerous male

PTSD populations (Gerardi, Keane, Cahoon, & Klauminzer, 1994). However, the relative paucity of data regarding physiological reactivity in women and noncombat PTSD leaves the significance of physiological assessments in these populations as partly unknown (but see Shalev, Orr, & Pitman, 1993). Still, psychophysiological assessment's wide utility in traumatized men suggests considerable promise for this methodology with women. Here we review current methods of psychophysiological assessment in terms of strengths and limitations for assessing women and discuss evidence for gender differences in the psychophysiological response to severe stress.

Current research emphasizes the importance of measuring physiological arousal across multiple channels, typically heart rate (HR), systolic blood pressure (SBP), diastolic blood pressure (DBP), skin conductance (SC), facial electromyogram (EMG), and subjective units of distress (SUDS). Existing theoretical models and empirical data from men recommend the use of similar multimodal assessments in women for determining autonomic parameters in which women are impacted by traumatic stress. Extant literature on physiological response, ranging from nonclinical samples to laboratory stresses, indicate preliminary gender differences in certain parameters. Males, for example, tend to display higher vascular responses (i.e., SBP and DBP) to the presentation of acute behavioral stressors such as mathematical tasks, public speaking, and Stroop color-naming tasks; women, conversely, show more pronounced cardiac (i.e., HR) responsivity to similar tasks (Allen, Stoney, Owens, & Matthews, 1993; Stoney, Davis, & Matthews, 1987; Stoney, Matthews, McDonald, & Johnson, 1988). Menopausal status may also be an additional consideration when assessing women. Postmenopausal women appear to show vascular as well as cardiac reactivity secondary to declining levels of estrogens, suggesting that hormonal status is a significant factor in women's psychophysiological responsivity (Matthews, 1992). Two popular paradigms for psychophysiological assessment of PTSD include the measurement of baseline physiological states followed by the presentation of (standardized) trauma-relevant stimuli and the use of ideographic or self-generated trauma cues. Although use of a standardized technique typically affords greater stimulus control within and across samples, the ideographic technique may be particularly appropriate for female PTSD populations, given the diversity and breadth of stressor exposure and the unusually high degree of personal familiarity with assault perpetrators (Kimerling, Wolfe, Schnurr, Clum, & Chrestman, 1994). This hypothesis awaits empirical validation.

Given preliminary data, physiological reactivity to trauma stimuli appears to be an important indicator of PTSD status and PTSD severity in women. Shalev et al. (1993) assessed physiological reactivity in a small sample of men ($n = 9$) and women ($n = 4$) with PTSD and found that women exhibited psychophysiological responses that were 33% higher on average than male participants on all assessed physiological domains (i.e., HR, SC, facial EMG). Severity of PTSD symptoms, however, were not analyzed. Hence, it is not yet known whether autonomic differences correlate with PTSD severity in women.

Additional Domains

Investigations into the psychobiology of PTSD are likely to have growing utility. Numerous investigators have begun to delineate disturbances of the hypothalamic–pituitary–adrenal axis (HPA) that appear to be specific to PTSD (e.g., Everly, 1993; Murburg et al., 1994a; Murburg et al., 1994b; Yehuda et al., 1994). In women, these alterations may have antecedents in traumatic childhood experiences. Trickett and Putnam (1993) hypothesized that childhood PTSD in females substantially impacts critical neuroendocrine and biological processes specific to pubertal development (e.g., suppression or acceleration of menses). When linked with disruptions in behavioral, psychosocial, and affective domains, these phenomena may adversely affect capabilities for adapting to later trauma sequelae. As behavioral, developmental, and biological findings are integrated, more will be learned about the role of sex characteristics in these outcomes.

As noted earlier, the diversity of health domains affected in the posttrauma period suggests that it is helpful to assess health status along numerous dimensions, including current and past physical status, number of physician-diagnosed disorders, range of health systems affected, number of health symptoms, and degree and type of functional impairment. Also, the relationship or concordance between subjective and objective reporting is likely to be important. A number of health measures are available for these purposes, some of which have been used extensively in a variety of medical and psychiatric groups (e.g., Pennebaker Inventory of Limbid Languidness [PILL; Pennebaker, 1982]; Cornell Medical Index [CMI; Bartone et al., 1989]) and a range of comparative data are available. Reported changes in *functional* health status are especially useful, since they afford the opportunity to compare functional capacities with subjective distress and perceived impairment. Widely validated brief instruments such as the Short Form-36 (SF-36; Ware & Sherbourne, 1992) are useful for this purpose.

Finally, anger and rage constitute important areas for evaluation of PTSD in women. Although widely thought to be primarily problematic in men, rage and associated behavioral disturbances may be more common than anticipated in a subset of traumatized women, particularly those with childhood abuse (Adshead, 1994; Kendall-Tackett et al., 1993). Preliminary descriptive data suggest that these problems involve both self-injurious and outwardly destructive behavior that, if not properly evaluated, leads to serious misdiagnosis and imprecision in treatment.

In conclusion, existing instrumentation has considerable potential for the thorough and valid assessment of PTSD and associated symptoms in women. Still needed are guidelines for the practical use of these instruments with women (e.g., delineation of multiple traumas) along with empirical data on the sensitivity of these instruments across gender and any potential for gender bias. At present, the CAPS is one of the most comprehensive and reliable instruments available for the measurement of PTSD. For women who are multiply victimized, however, the current structure of such event-focused instruments may make broad-based inquiry and the linkage of various events to diverse symptom patterns especially challenging. Still, the need for this approach is clear.

At least two types of gender bias in instrumentation may exist. First, bias may be content related. The wording and choice of events and symptoms queried may be more reflective of the experience of one gender (Wolfe et al., 1993a). Second, statistical bias may exist; that is, measures may differ by gender in their sensitivity for detecting symptoms or in their predictive power. To date, no empirical PTSD study has addressed this issue. Research in this area is essential for future investigations seeking to validate correlates of gender, rather than method variance, as a factor associated with vulnerability in traumatic stress.

FUTURE DIRECTIONS

Existing literature suggests several possible gender differences in exposure to trauma, PTSD symptoms, and risk factors. These differences can be ascribed to a variety of complex methodological, biological, social, and environmental factors. Consequently, more research is needed to delineate the range and impact of these factors. In particular, rigorous research should examine components of measurement and design — as well as psychological factors — as they relate to gender. In this section, we consider existing data in these areas and highlight a number of research directions for dealing with gender-fair diagnostic measurement of PTSD phenomena, as well as the spectrum of gender-linked biological and social factors that are likely to influence the evolution of this disorder.

On the surface, empirical data preliminarily suggest that the prevalence of PTSD is increased in women under certain conditions. The majority of studies reaching this conclusion use female samples and emphasize two sets of critical but related findings: (1) the existence of greatly elevated rates of rape and sexual assault among females in the United States, and (2) the highly deleterious impact of this type of trauma (e.g., Rothbaum et al., 1992). Careful circumspection of these data suggest, therefore, that event prevalence will be one important factor to consider in any conclusion that female gender is a "risk" factor for PTSD (Resick, 1993).

In contrast to studies of women, investigations comparing PTSD prevalences between men and women yield more equivocal results. Men appear to show an enhanced risk for lifetime exposure to traumatic stressors (e.g., Norris, 1992), whereas female gender has been preliminarily linked to greater PTSD chronicity (Breslau et al., 1991; Kessler, Sonnega, Bromet, Hughes, &

Nelson, 1995). Current conceptualizations of gender may contribute to these assumptions such that, when exposure frequency, severity, and chronicity are taken into account, apparent gender differences could change. Events such as sexual assault and domestic violence are far more prevalent in women than men. Consequently, study designs that employ more robust assessment of exposure parameters (e.g., contact with violence, perceptions of life threat, duration of trauma) are likely to improve analyses of the effect of these experiences. Also, broader assessment designs might optimally tap a wider range of exposure and outcome domains. Based on data reviewed in this chapter, there is good evidence that these domains should include, at a minimum, the total number of traumatic events, duration of exposure (e.g., episodic vs. chronic), and severity of exposure across certain dimensions (e.g., life-threatening vs. non-life-threatening, moderate vs. severe). In particular, measures of stressor exposure should pay increased attention to distinctive stressor experiences across gender. In this vein, the evaluation of role-related, social/contextual, and symbolic or connotative factors associated with prominent stressors for women are likely to be important. If implemented, this type of approach could also facilitate consideration of extant PTSD threshold models that predict the emergence of traumatic stress when certain individual tolerances are exceeded (Houskamp & Foy, 1991; Kulka et al., 1990; Wilson, 1994; Wilson & Krauss, 1985; Wilson, Smith, & Johnson, 1985; Wolfe & Keane, 1993).

Other assessment issues pertain to the context, content, and format of evaluations, in particular, the rationale employed in assessment design, test selection, and test construction. Many currently available psychometric tests for PTSD were developed largely in the context of the experiences of male combat veterans. Hence, questions concerning generalizability can be raised. There is also some empirical evidence to suggest that the testing situation itself can be impacted by factors such as the gender and orientation of the diagnosing practitioner. Several studies have found that medical practitioners diagnose clinical depression more often in women than men, regardless of actual diagnostic status (e.g., Potts, Burnam, & Wells, 1991). This finding is upheld even when depression severity and demographic characteristics are controlled, suggesting that illness intensity is not the only variable to influence diagnostic impressions. In PTSD, judgments about chronicity might also be influenced by certain factors. At this time, it remains unclear whether findings of higher rates of chronic PTSD in women reflect problems in understanding the manifestations of PTSD in this population, in which failure to improve is attributed to gender status.

Some respondent characteristics are likely to influence the interpretation of gender role in PTSD outcomes. Although little is currently known about effects and patterns of disclosure of trauma, recent research from related fields (e.g., health services research) suggest that distinctive gender differences in reporting styles exist. Women, for example, typically endorse more physical and emotional symptoms than do men and also report greater symptom severity (Verbrugge, 1983, 1985). This finding appears to apply (at least preliminarily) to female children as well (Roberts, Andrews, Lewinsohn, & Hops, 1990). Although this finding may suggest overreporting of symptoms in women, it is possible that these data belie actual differences in the physical and psychological status of women and men. It is possible, for example, that gender-role socialization impacts an individual's willingness or ability to disclosure trauma exposure or PTSD symptoms. This difference could then be construed as a male tendency to suppress symptom experiences rather than female overreporting. At the present time, there are essentially no data exploring the relationship of gender to trauma reporting or trauma-symptom disclosure, although several studies are currently underway (e.g., Prins, Hearst-Ikeda, Wilson, & Wolfe, 1995). Clearly, more research is required to determine if gender is associated with the reporting or detection of PTSD and whether either group differs in its approach to identifying or disclosing actual experiences (see Lisak, 1994).

One problem on a conceptual level is the relative paucity of testable hypotheses as to how female gender is conceptualized as a "risk" factor for PTSD. Clearly, childhood sexual abuse has been prominently associated with a spectrum of debilitating disorders, including chronic PTSD (Briere & Runtz, 1987; Polusny & Follette, 1995), and prevalence studies confirm that this abuse is vastly overrepresented in women. Yet, apart from increased exposure to certain forms of trauma and violence in women, no specific gender correlates have been defined that permit empirical testing of a vulnerability construct for this disorder. Similarly, no PTSD study that we are aware of has proposed any comprehensive or operational model involving gender that explicitly specifies parameters associated with women's differential risk. Such studies, which are ongoing in research on depression, benefit strongly from the integrated consideration of psychosocial and biological factors (e.g., Nolen-Hoeksema & Girgus, 1994). Consequently, these models might offer useful avenues for empirical tests of the role of gender in PTSD.

In the absence of empirical tests, models elucidating the role of gender in depression may offer preliminary evidence for a possible female "diathesis" in PTSD. These studies emphasize the adverse impact of disturbed family environments (particularly disturbed mother–child interactions and sexual abuse) in the genesis of depressive conditions in young girls as well as the effects of depression on subsequent psychological development. The data are consonant with the general psychiatric literature which, to date, has found higher rates of numerous depressive disorders in women (e.g., Goldman & Ravid, 1980; Nolen-Hoeksema, 1987; Strickland, 1989; Weissman & Klerman, 1977, 1985; Weissman, Leaf, Holzer, Meyers, & Tischler, 1984). Preliminary data from some PTSD studies (e.g., Resnick et al., 1992) have recently suggested that preexisting depression in adult female trauma victims adversely influences outcome following adult sexual assault, specifically the development of PTSD. If findings of greater preexisting depression in women with adult PTSD are eventually confirmed, it is possible that depression, rather than *female gender* per se, will constitute one factor linked to vulnerability for traumatization following stressor exposure. Clearly, research on this topic will need to address the range of possible antecedent effects that link early psychosocial domains, developmental phenomena, and family background to the establishment of clinical depression, as well as the complex psychological and biological pathways through which clinical affective disturbance mediates traumatic response.

The intricate interaction between more general stress and PTSD may also provide data on the relationship of gender to this disorder. Similar to catastrophic stress, research demonstrates that daily stressors are capable of impacting well-being in a variety of ways. Verbrugge (1985), for example, found that recurrent exposure to daily, negative life events reliably affected women's mood states, along with altering reports of physical well-being, coping, and behavioral repertoires (e.g., the decision to seek medical care). It is possible, therefore, that seemingly routine stressors impact women distinctively (e.g., greater distress in response to perceived competition between social and vocational roles, job discrimination, and fluctuations in social support; Verbrugge, 1989). Lack of economic and social advantage also may distinctively impact coping abilities in women, especially their ability to carry out activities associated with critical caretaking or domestic roles. To what extent this interrelationship extends to the domain of traumatic stressors and, additionally, whether such an interaction differs between men and women, is still unknown.

Clearly, the interplay among gender, personal characteristics, and the content and context of trauma exposure is exceedingly complex. Considerable work is needed to evaluate which domains—or their subsets—are associated with the acquisition or, more critically, the progression of traumatic stress syndromes. Existing diagnostic methods offer a strong footing from which empirical efforts can proceed. These methods suggest that development of increasingly refined but empirically valid and reliable measures of event impact and response characteristics will help substantially in illustrating how gender is linked to trauma outcome. Just as important, these advances can improve our clinical abilities to detect traumatic stress, as well as our appreciation for the most appropriate treatment methods. Continued progress in the development of "ecologically" valid measures and more functional or operational definitions of gender—whether psychological, social, behavioral, or biological—are all areas for future contributions.

APPENDIX: LIFE STRESSOR CHECKLIST—REVISED[1]

Jessica Wolfe, Rachel Kimerling,
Pamela Brown, Kelly Chrestman, and Karen Levin

1. **Have you ever been in a serious disaster (for example, a massive earthquake, hurricane, tornado, fire, explosion)?** **YES NO**
   a. How old were you when this first began? _____ b. when it ended? _____
   c. At the time of the event did you believe that *you or someone else* could be *killed* or seriously *harmed* ? **YES NO**
   d. At the time of the event did you experience feelings of *intense helplessness, fear, or horror?* **YES NO**
   e. How upsetting was the event at the time?

	1	2	3	4	5
	not at all		moderately		extremely

   f. How much has it affected your life in the past year?

	1	2	3	4	5
	not at all		moderately		extremely

2. **Have you ever seen a serious accident (for example, a bad car wreck or an on-the-job accident)?** **YES NO**
   a. How old were you when this first began? _____ b. when it ended? _____
   c. At the time of the event did you believe that *you or someone else* could be *killed* or seriously *harmed* ? **YES NO**
   d. At the time of the event did you experience feelings of *intense helplessness, fear, or horror?* **YES NO**
   e. How upsetting was the event at the time?

	1	2	3	4	5
	not at all		moderately		extremely

   f. How much has it affected your life in the past year?

	1	2	3	4	5
	not at all		moderately		extremely

3. **Have you ever had a very serious accident or accident-related injury (for example, a bad car wreck or an on-the-job accident)?** **YES NO**
   a. How old were you when this first began? _____ b. when it ended? _____
   c. At the time of the event did you believe that *you or someone else* could be *killed* or seriously *harmed* ? **YES NO**
   d. At the time of the event did you experience feelings of *intense helplessness, fear, or horror?* **YES NO**

---

[1]Scoring instructions and normative data for the Life Stressor Checklist—Revised (LSCL-R) are available from Wolfe at the Women's Health Sciences Division, National Center for PTSD, upon request and receipt of a data sharing agreement. As this instrument is currently undergoing psychometric refinement, we ask that those using the LSCL-R share their raw data with us to further these efforts. We are very interested in facilitating the use of the LSCL-R in different populations. Consequently, we will provide consultation, normative data, updated test versions, and scoring instructions to those who are willing to sign a data sharing agreement. This instrument is designed to elicit material that may be disturbing or disruptive for some individuals. Accordingly, we would caution against use of the LSCL-R in settings where a trained clinician is not readily available for debriefing or consultation/referral.

e. How upsetting was the event at the time?

	1	2	3	4	5
	not at all		**moderately**		**extremely**

f. How much has it affected your life in the past year?

	1	2	3	4	5
	not at all		**moderately**		**extremely**

4. Was a close family member ever sent to jail?   **YES NO**

a. How old were you when this first began? _____ b. when it ended? _____

c. At the time of the event did you believe that *you or someone else* could be *killed* or seriously *harmed* ?   YES NO

d. At the time of the event did you experience feelings of *intense helplessness, fear, or horror?*   YES NO

e. How upsetting was the event at the time?

	1	2	3	4	5
	not at all		**moderately**		**extremely**

f. How much has it affected your life in the past year?

	1	2	3	4	5
	not at all		**moderately**		**extremely**

5. Have you ever been sent to jail?   **YES NO**

a. How old were you when this first began? _____ b. when it ended? _____

c. At the time of the event did you believe that *you or someone else* could be *killed* or seriously *harmed* ?   YES NO

d. At the time of the event did you experience feelings of *intense helplessness, fear, or horror?*   YES NO

e. How upsetting was the event at the time?

	1	2	3	4	5
	not at all		**moderately**		**extremely**

f. How much has it affected your life in the past year?

	1	2	3	4	5
	not at all		**moderately**		**extremely**

6. Were you ever put in foster care or put up for adoption?   **YES NO**

a. How old were you when this first began? _____ b. when it ended? _____

c. At the time of the event did you believe that *you or someone else* could be *killed* or seriously *harmed* ?   YES NO

d. At the time of the event did you experience feelings of *intense helplessness, fear, or horror?*   YES NO

e. How upsetting was the event at the time?

	1	2	3	4	5
	not at all		**moderately**		**extremely**

f. How much has it affected your life in the past year?

	1	2	3	4	5
	not at all		**moderately**		**extremely**

7. Did your parents ever separate or divorce while you were living with them?   **YES NO**

a. How old were you when this first began? _____ b. when it ended? _____

c. At the time of the event did you believe that *you or someone else* could be *killed* or seriously *harmed* ?   YES NO

d. At the time of the event did you experience feelings of *intense helplessness, fear, or horror?*   YES NO

e. How upsetting was the event at the time?

	1	2	3	4	5
	not at all		moderately		extremely

f. How much has it affected your life in the past year?

	1	2	3	4	5
	not at all		moderately		extremely

8. Have you ever been separated or divorced?　　　　　　　**YES NO**

a. How old were you when this first began? _____ b. when it ended? _____

c. At the time of the event did you believe that *you or someone else* could be *killed* or seriously *harmed*?　　　　　　**YES NO**

d. At the time of the event did you experience feelings of *intense helplessness, fear, or horror*?　　　　　　　**YES NO**

e. How upsetting was the event at the time?

	1	2	3	4	5
	not at all		moderately		extremely

f. How much has it affected your life in the past year?

	1	2	3	4	5
	not at all		moderately		extremely

9. Have you ever had serious money problems (for example, not enough money for food or place to live)?　　　**YES NO**

a. How old were you when this first began? _____ b. when it ended? _____

c. At the time of the event did you believe that *you or someone else* could be *killed* or seriously *harmed*?　　　　　　**YES NO**

d. At the time of the event did you experience feelings of *intense helplessness, fear, or horror*?　　　　　　　**YES NO**

e. How upsetting was the event at the time?

	1	2	3	4	5
	not at all		moderately		extremely

f. How much has it affected your life in the past year?

	1	2	3	4	5
	not at all		moderately		extremely

10. Have you ever had a very serious physical or mental illness (for example, cancer, heart attack, serious operation, felt like killing yourself, hospitalized because of nerve problems)?　　**YES NO**

a. How old were you when this first began? _____ b. when it ended? _____

c. At the time of the event did you believe that *you or someone else* could be *killed* or seriously *harmed*?　　　　　　**YES NO**

d. At the time of the event did you experience feelings of *intense helplessness, fear, or horror*?　　　　　　　**YES NO**

e. How upsetting was the event at the time?

	1	2	3	4	5
	not at all		moderately		extremely

f. How much has it affected your life in the past year?

	1	2	3	4	5
	not at all		moderately		extremely

11. Have you ever been emotionally abused or neglected (for example, being frequently shamed, embarrassed, ignored, or repeatedly told that you were "no good")?　　　　**YES NO**

a. How old were you when this first began? _____ b. when it ended? _____

c. At the time of the event did you believe that *you or someone else* could be **killed** or seriously **harmed**? YES NO

d. At the time of the event did you experience feelings of *intense helplessness, fear, or horror?* YES NO

e. How upsetting was the event at the time?	1	2	3	4	5
	not at all		moderately		extremely

f. How much has it affected your life in the past year?	1	2	3	4	5
	not at all		moderately		extremely

12. Have you ever been physically neglected (for example, not fed, not properly clothed, or left to take care of yourself when you were too young or ill)? YES NO

a. How old were you when this first began? _____ b. when it ended? _____

c. At the time of the event did you believe that *you or someone else* could be **killed** or seriously **harmed**? YES NO

d. At the time of the event did you experience feelings of *intense helplessness, fear, or horror?* YES NO

e. How upsetting was the event at the time?	1	2	3	4	5
	not at all		moderately		extremely

f. How much has it affected your life in the past year?	1	2	3	4	5
	not at all		moderately		extremely

13. <u>WOMEN ONLY</u>: Have you ever had an abortion or miscarriage (lost your baby)? YES NO

a. How old were you when this first began? _____ b. when it ended? _____

c. At the time of the event did you believe that *you or someone else* could be **killed** or seriously **harmed**? YES NO

d. At the time of the event did you experience feelings of *intense helplessness, fear, or horror?* YES NO

e. How upsetting was the event at the time?	1	2	3	4	5
	not at all		moderately		extremely

f. How much has it affected your life in the past year?	1	2	3	4	5
	not at all		moderately		extremely

14. Have you ever been separated from your child against your will (for example, the loss of custody or visitation or kidnapping)? YES NO

a. How old were you when this first began? _____ b. when it ended? _____

c. At the time of the event did you believe that *you or someone else* could be **killed** or seriously **harmed**? YES NO

d. At the time of the event did you experience feelings of *intense helplessness, fear, or horror?* YES NO

e. How upsetting was the event at the time?	1	2	3	4	5
	not at all		moderately		extremely

f. How much has it affected your life in the past year?	1	2	3	4	5
	not at all		moderately		extremely

15. Has a baby or child of yours ever had a severe physical or mental handicap (for example, mentally retarded, birth defects, can't hear, see, walk)? **YES NO**

    a. How old were you when this first began? _____ b. when it ended? _____

    c. At the time of the event did you believe that *you or someone else* could be *killed* or seriously *harmed*? **YES NO**

    d. At the time of the event did you experience feelings of *intense helplessness, fear, or horror?* **YES NO**

e. How upsetting was the event at the time?	1	2	3	4	5
	not at all		**moderately**		**extremely**
f. How much has it affected your life in the past year?	1	2	3	4	5
	not at all		**moderately**		**extremely**

16. Have you ever been responsible for taking care of someone close to you (not your child) who had a severe physical or mental handicap (for example, cancer, stroke, Alzheimer's disease, AIDS, felt like killing him/herself, hospitalized because of nerve problems, can't hear, see, walk)? **YES NO**

    a. How old were you when this first began? _____ b. when it ended? _____

    c. At the time of the event did you believe that *you or someone else* could be *killed* or seriously *harmed*? **YES NO**

    d. At the time of the event did you experience feelings of *intense helplessness, fear, or horror?* **YES NO**

e. How upsetting was the event at the time?	1	2	3	4	5
	not at all		**moderately**		**extremely**
f. How much has it affected your life in the past year?	1	2	3	4	5
	not at all		**moderately**		**extremely**

17. Has someone close to you died suddenly or unexpectedly (for example, an accident, sudden heart attack, murder or suicide)? **YES NO**

    a. How old were you when this first began? _____ b. when it ended? _____

    c. At the time of the event did you believe that *you or someone else* could be *killed* or seriously *harmed*? **YES NO**

    d. At the time of the event did you experience feelings of *intense helplessness, fear, or horror?* **YES NO**

e. How upsetting was the event at the time?	1	2	3	4	5
	not at all		**moderately**		**extremely**
f. How much has it affected your life in the past year?	1	2	3	4	5
	not at all		**moderately**		**extremely**

18. Has someone close to you died (do not include those who died suddenly or unexpectedly)? **YES NO**

    a. How old were you when this first began? _____ b. when it ended? _____

    c. At the time of the event did you believe that *you or someone else* could be *killed* or seriously *harmed*? **YES NO**

  d. At the time of the event did you experience feelings of *intense*
     helplessness, fear, or horror?   YES NO
  e. How upsetting was the event at   **1**   **2**   **3**   **4**   **5**
     the time?   **not at all**   **moderately**   **extremely**
  f. How much has it affected your   **1**   **2**   **3**   **4**   **5**
     life in the past year?   **not at all**   **moderately**   **extremely**

**19. When you were young (before age 16), did you ever see violence
between family members (for example, hitting, kicking, slapping,
punching)?**   **YES NO**
  a. How old were you when this first began? _____ b. when it ended? _____
  c. At the time of the event did you believe that *you or someone else*
     could be *killed* or seriously *harmed*?   YES NO
  d. At the time of the event did you experience feelings of *intense*
     helplessness, fear, or horror?   YES NO
  e. How upsetting was the event at   **1**   **2**   **3**   **4**   **5**
     the time?   **not at all**   **moderately**   **extremely**
  f. How much has it affected your   **1**   **2**   **3**   **4**   **5**
     life in the past year?   **not at all**   **moderately**   **extremely**

20. Have you ever seen a robbery, mugging, or attack taking place?   **YES NO**
  a. How old were you when this first began? _____ b. when it ended? _____
  c. At the time of the event did you believe that *you or someone else*
     could be *killed* or seriously *harmed*?   YES NO
  d. At the time of the event did you experience feelings of *intense*
     helplessness, fear, or horror?   YES NO
  e. How upsetting was the event at   **1**   **2**   **3**   **4**   **5**
     the time?   **not at all**   **moderately**   **extremely**
  f. How much has it affected your   **1**   **2**   **3**   **4**   **5**
     life in the past year?   **not at all**   **moderately**   **extremely**

**21. Have you ever been robbed, mugged, or physically attacked
(not sexually) by someone you did not know?**   **YES NO**
  a. How old were you when this first began? _____ b. when it ended? _____
  c. At the time of the event did you believe that *you or someone else*
     could be *killed* or seriously *harmed*?   YES NO
  d. At the time of the event did you experience feelings of *intense*
     helplessness, fear, or horror?   YES NO
  e. How upsetting was the event at   **1**   **2**   **3**   **4**   **5**
     the time?   **not at all**   **moderately**   **extremely**
  f. How much has it affected your   **1**   **2**   **3**   **4**   **5**
     life in the past year?   **not at all**   **moderately**   **extremely**

22. *Before age 16,* **were you ever abused or physically attacked (not
sexually) by someone you knew (for example, a parent, boyfriend,
or husband hit, slapped, choked, burned, or beat you up)?**   **YES NO**
  a. How old were you when this first began? _____ b. when it ended? _____

c. At the time of the event did you believe that *you or someone else* could be *killed* or seriously *harmed*? YES NO

d. At the time of the event did you experience feelings of *intense helplessness, fear, or horror?* YES NO

e. How upsetting was the event at the time?

	1	2	3	4	5
	not at all		moderately		extremely

f. How much has it affected your life in the past year?

	1	2	3	4	5
	not at all		moderately		extremely

23. *After age 16,* **were you ever abused or physically attacked (not sexually) by someone you knew (for example, a parent, boyfriend, or husband hit, slapped, choked, burned, or beat you up)?** **YES NO**

a. How old were you when this first began? _____ b. when it ended? _____

c. At the time of the event did you believe that *you or someone else* could be *killed* or seriously *harmed*? YES NO

d. At the time of the event did you experience feelings of *intense helplessness, fear, or horror?* YES NO

e. How upsetting was the event at the time?

	1	2	3	4	5
	not at all		moderately		extremely

f. How much has it affected your life in the past year?

	1	2	3	4	5
	not at all		moderately		extremely

24. **Have you ever been bothered or harassed by sexual remarks, jokes, or demands for sexual favors by someone** *at work or school* **(for example, a coworker, a boss, a customer, another student, a teacher)?** **YES NO**

a. How old were you when this first began? _____ b. when it ended? _____

c. At the time of the event did you believe that *you or someone else* could be *killed* or seriously *harmed*? YES NO

d. At the time of the event did you experience feelings of *intense helplessness, fear, or horror?* YES NO

e. How upsetting was the event at the time?

	1	2	3	4	5
	not at all		moderately		extremely

f. How much has it affected your life in the past year?

	1	2	3	4	5
	not at all		moderately		extremely

25. *Before age 16,* **were you ever** *touched* **or made to** *touch someone else* **in a** *sexual way* **because he/she forced you in some way or threatened to harm you if you didn't?** **YES NO**

a. How old were you when this first began? _____ b. when it ended? _____

c. At the time of the event did you believe that *you or someone else* could be *killed* or seriously *harmed*? YES NO

d. At the time of the event did you experience feelings of *intense helplessness, fear, or horror?* YES NO

e. How upsetting was the event at the time?

	1	2	3	4	5
	not at all		moderately		extremely

f. How much has it affected your life in the past year?

1	2	3	4	5
not at all		moderately		extremely

26. *After age 16,* were you ever *touched* or made to *touch someone else* in a *sexual way* because he/she forced you in some way or threatened to harm you if you didn't?　**YES NO**

a. How old were you when this first began? _____ b. when it ended? _____

c. At the time of the event did you believe that *you or someone else* could be *killed* or seriously *harmed*?　**YES NO**

d. At the time of the event did you experience feelings of *intense helplessness, fear, or horror*?　**YES NO**

e. How upsetting was the event at the time?

1	2	3	4	5
not at all		moderately		extremely

f. How much has it affected your life in the past year?

1	2	3	4	5
not at all		moderately		extremely

27. *Before age 16,* did you ever have sex (oral, anal, genital) when you didn't want to because someone forced you in some way or threatened to harm you if you didn't?　**YES NO**

a. How old were you when this first began? _____ b. when it ended? _____

c. At the time of the event did you believe that *you or someone else* could be *killed* or seriously *harmed*?　**YES NO**

d. At the time of the event did you experience feelings of *intense helplessness, fear, or horror*?　**YES NO**

e. How upsetting was the event at the time?

1	2	3	4	5
not at all		moderately		extremely

f. How much has it affected your life in the past year?

1	2	3	4	5
not at all		moderately		extremely

28. *After age 16,* did you ever have sex (oral, anal, genital) when you didn't want to because someone forced you in some way or threatened to harm you if you didn't?　**YES NO**

a. How old were you when this first began? _____ b. when it ended? _____

c. At the time of the event did you believe that *you or someone else* could be *killed* or seriously *harmed*?　**YES NO**

d. At the time of the event did you experience feelings of *intense helplessness, fear, or horror*?　**YES NO**

e. How upsetting was the event at the time?

1	2	3	4	5
not at all		moderately		extremely

f. How much has it affected your life in the past year?

1	2	3	4	5
not at all		moderately		extremely

29. Are there any events we did not include that you would like to mention?　**YES NO**

What was the event? _____

a. How old were you when this first began? _____ b. when it ended? _____
c. At the time of the event did you believe that *you or someone else*
could be *killed* or seriously *harmed*?   YES NO
d. At the time of the event did you experience feelings of *intense*
helplessness, fear, or horror?   YES NO
e. How upsetting was the event at   1   2   3   4   5
the time?   **not at all   moderately   extremely**
f. How much has it affected your   1   2   3   4   5
life in the past year?   **not at all   moderately   extremely**

30. Have any of the events mentioned above ever happened to someone
close to you so that even though you didn't see or experience the
event yourself, you were seriously disturbed by it?   **YES NO**
What was the event? _____

_____

a. How old were you when this first began? _____ b. when it ended? _____
c. At the time of the event did you believe that *you or someone else*
could be *killed* or seriously *harmed*?   YES NO
d. At the time of the event did you experience feelings of *intense*
helplessness, fear, or horror?   YES NO
e. How upsetting was the event at   1   2   3   4   5
the time?   **not at all   moderately   extremely**
f. How much has it affected your   1   2   3   4   5
life in the past year?   **not at all   moderately   extremely**

ACKNOWLEDGMENTS

This work was supported by research grants from the Department of Veterans Affairs Medical Research Service and Health Services Research and Development Service. We thank Marlana Sullivan, Jennifer Duncan Davis, and Paige Crosby Ouimette, Ph.D., for their critical comments and invaluable assistance in preparing the manuscript.

REFERENCES

Ader, R., & Cohen, N. (1993). Psychoneuroimmunology: Conditioning and stress. *Annual Review of Psychology, 44*, 53–85.
Adler, D. A. (1990). Clinicians' practices in personality assessment: Does gender influence the use of DSM-III Axis II? *Comprehensive Psychiatry, 31*, 125–133.
Adshead, G. (1994). Damage: Trauma and violence in a sample of women referred to a forensic service. *Behavioral Sciences and the Law, 12*, 235–249.
Albach, F., & Everaerd, W. (1992). Posttraumatic stress symptoms in victims of childhood incest. 2nd European Conference on Traumatic Stress. *Psychotherapy and Psychosomatics, 57*, 143–151.

Allen, M. T., Stoney, C. T., Owens, J. F., & Matthews, K. A. (1993). Hemodynamic adjustment to laboratory stress: The influence of gender and personality. *Psychosomatic Medicine, 55,* 505–517.

American Psychiatric Association. (1980). *The diagnostic and statistical manual of mental disorders* (3rd ed.). Washington, DC: Author.

American Psychiatric Association. (1987). *The diagnostic and statistical manual of mental disorders* (3rd ed., rev.). Washington, DC: Author.

American Psychiatric Association. (1994). *The diagnostic and statistical manual of mental disorders* (4th ed.). Washington, DC: Author.

Arntz, A. (1994). Treatment of borderline personality disorder: A challenge for cognitive behavioral therapy. *Behavior Research and Therapy, 32,* 419–430.

Bagley, C. (1991). The prevalence and mental health sequels of child abuse in a community sample of women aged 18 to 27. *Canadian Journal of Community Mental Health, 10,* 103–116.

Bartone, P. T., Ursano, R. J., Wright, K. M., & Ingraham, L. H. (1989). The impact of military air disaster on the health of assistance workers. *Journal of Nervous and Mental Disease, 177,* 317–328.

Becker, D. (1994). Sex bias in the diagnosis of borderline personality disorder and posttraumatic stress disorder. *Professional Psychology: Research and Practice, 25,* 55–61.

Bell, I. R., Miller, C. S., & Schwartz, G. E. (1992). An olfactory–limbic model of multiple chemical sensitivity: Possible relationships to kindling and affective spectrum disorders. *Biological Psychiatry, 32,* 218–242.

Blake, D., Weathers, F., Nagy, L., Kaloupek, D., Klauminzer, G., Charney, D., & Keane, T. M. (1990). *Clinician-Administered PTSD Scale.* Unpublished scale, National Center for PTSD, Boston.

Blank, A. (1994, June). Clinical detection, diagnosis and differential diagnosis of PTSD. *Psychiatric Clinics of North America,* pp. 359–383.

Bremner, J. D., Southwick, S. M., Johnson, D. R., Yehuda, R., & Charney, D. S. (1993). Childhood physical abuse and combat-related posttraumatic stress disorder in Vietnam veterans. *American Journal of Psychiatry, 150,* 235–239.

Breslau, N., & Davis, G. C. (1992). Posttraumatic stress disorder in an urban population of young adults: Risk factors for chronicity. *American Journal of Psychiatry, 149,* 671–675.

Breslau, N., Davis, G. C., Andreski, P., & Peterson, E. (1991). Traumatic events and posttraumatic stress disorder in an urban population of young adults. *Archives of General Psychiatry, 48,* 216–222.

Briere, J., & Runtz, M. (1987). Post sexual abuse trauma: Data and implications for clinical practice. *Journal of Interpersonal Violence, 2,* 367–379.

Brown, P. J., & Wolfe, J. (1994). Substance abuse and post-traumatic stress disorder comorbidity. *Drug and Alcohol Dependence, 36,* 51–59.

Browne, A. (1993). Violence against women by male partners: Prevalence, outcomes, and policy implications. *American Psychologist, 48,* 1077–1087.

Burger, L. (1992). *Coping with repetitive natural disasters: A study of the Ladysmith floods.* (Tech. Rep. No. 26). Pretoria: University of South Africa, Psychology Department.

Calhoun, K. S., & Atkeson, B. M. (Eds.). (1991). *Psychology practitioner guidebooks.* New York: Pergamon Press.

Cappelleri, J. C., Eckenrode, J., & Powers, J. L. (1993). The epidemiology of child abuse: Findings from the Second National Incidence and Prevalence Study of Child Abuse and Neglect. *American Journal of Public Health, 83,* 1622–1624.

Cascardi, M., Riggs, D., Hearst-Ikeda, D., & Foa, E. (1996). Objective ratings of assault safety as predictors of PTSD. *Journal of Interpersonal Violence, 11,* 65–78.

Chu, J. A. (1992). The revictimization of adult women with histories of childhood abuse. *Journal of Psychotherapy Practice and Research, 1,* 259–269.

Chu, J. A., & Dill, D. L. (1990). Dissociation in relation to childhood physical and sexual abuse. *American Journal of Psychiatry, 147,* 887–892.

Classen, C., Koopman, C., & Spiegel, D. (1993). Trauma and dissociation. *Bulletin of the Menninger Clinic, 157,* 178–194.

Cohen, L. J., & Roth, S. (1987). The psychological aftermath of rape: Long-term effects and individual differences in recovery. *Journal of Social and Clinical Psychology, 5,* 525–534.

Cohen, S., & Williamson, G. M. (1991). Stress and infectious disease in humans. *Psychological Bulletin, 109,* 5–24.

Cohen, S., & Wills, T. A. (1985). Stress, social support, and the buffering hypothesis. *Psychological Bulletin, 96,* 310–357.

Cottler, L. B., Compton, W. M., Mager, D., Spitznagel, E. L., & Janca, A. (1992). Posttraumatic stress disorder among substance users from the general population. *American Journal of Psychiatry, 149,* 664–670.

Draucker, C. B. (1993). Childhood sexual abuse: Sources of trauma. *Issues in Mental Health Nursing, 14,* 249–262.

Engel, C. C., Engel, A. L., Campbell, S. J., McFall, M. E., Russo, J., & Katon, W. (1993). Posttraumatic stress disorders symptoms and precombat sexual and physical abuse in Desert Storm veterans. *Journal of Nervous and Mental Disease, 181,* 683–688.

Everly, G. S., Jr. (1993). Neurophysiological considerations in the treatment of posttraumatic stress disorder: A neurocognitive perspective. In J. W. Wilson & B. Raphael (Eds.), *International handbook of traumatic stress syndromes* (pp. 795–802). New York: Plenum Press.

Figley, C. R. (1985). From victim to survivor: Social responsibility in the wake of catastrophe. In C. R. Figley (Ed.), *Trauma and its wake: The study and treatment of posttraumatic stress disorder* (pp. 398–415). New York: Brunner/Mazel.

Finkelhor, D., & Baron, L. (1986). Risk factors for child sexual abuse. *Journal of Interpersonal Violence, 1,* 43–71.

Finkelhor, D., & Browne, A. (1986). The traumatic impact of child sexual abuse: A conceptualization. *American Journal of Orthopsychiatry, 55,* 530–541.

Fischer, G. J. (1992). Gender differences in college student sexual abuse victims and their offenders. *Annals of Sex Research, 5,* 215–226.

Foa, E. B. (1994, July). *Psychopathology and treatment of PTSD in rape victims.* Invited Address at the American Psychological Society Convention, Washington, DC.

Foa, E. B., & Riggs, D. S. (1993). Posttraumatic stress disorder and rape. In J. Oldham, M. B. Riba, & A. Tasman (Eds.), *American Psychiatric Press Review of Psychiatry* (Vol. 12, pp. 273–303). Washington, DC: American Psychiatric Press.

Foa, E. B., Riggs, D. S., Dancu, C. V., & Rothbaum, B. O. (1993). Reliability and validity of a brief instrument for assessing post-traumatic stress disorder. *Journal of Traumatic Stress, 6,* 459–473.

Foy, D. W., & Card, J. J. (1987). Combat-related posttraumatic stress disorder etiology: Replicated findings in a national sample of Vietnam era men. *Journal of Clinical Psychology, 43,* 28–31.

Friedman, M. J. (1991). Biological approaches to the diagnosis and treatment of posttraumatic stress disorder. *Journal of Traumatic Stress, 4,* 67–91.

Friedman, M. J. (1994a). Afterword. In M. M. Murburg (Ed.), *Catecholamine function in posttraumatic stress disorder: Emerging concepts* (pp. 343–356). Washington, DC: American Psychiatric Press.

Friedman, M. J. (1994b). Neurobiological sensitization models of post-traumatic stress disorder: Their possible relevance to multiple chemical sensitivity syndrome. *Toxicology and Industrial Health, 10,* 449–462.

Friedman, M. J., & Schnurr, P. P. (1995). The relationship between PTSD, trauma, and physical health outcomes. In M. J. Friedman, D. S. Charney, & A. Y. Deutch (Eds.), *Neurobiological and clinical consequences of stress: From normal adaptation to PTSD* (pp. 507–524). New York: Raven Press.

Gerardi, R. J., Keane, T. M., Cahoon, B. J., & Klauminzer, G. W. (1994). An *in vivo* assessment of physiological arousal in posttraumatic stress disorder. *Journal of Abnormal Psychology, 103,* 825–827.

Gidycz, C. A., & Koss, M. P. (1991). Predictors of long-term sexual assault trauma among a national sample of victimized college women. *Violence and Victims, 6,* 175–190.

Goldman, S. J., D'Angelo, E. J., DeMaso, D. R., & Mezzacappa, E. (1992). Physical and sexual abuse histories among children with borderline personality disorder. *American Journal of Psychiatry, 149,* 1723–1726.

Goldman, N., & Ravid, R. (1980). Community surveys: Sex differences in mental illness. In M. Guttentag, S. Salasin, & D. Belle (Eds.), *The mental health of women.* New York: Academic Press.

Gordon, M. (1990). Males and females as victims of childhood sexual abuse: An examination of gender effects. *Journal of Family Violence, 5,* 321–332.

Graziano, R. (1992). Treating women incest survivors: A bridge between "cumulative trauma" and "post-traumatic stress." *Social Work in Health Care, 17,* 69–85.

Green, B. L., Korol, M., Grace, M. C., Vary, M. G., Leonard, A. C., Gleser, G. C., & Smitson-Cohen, S. (1991). Children and disaster: Age, gender, and parental effects on PTSD symptoms. *Journal of the American Academy of Child and Adolescent Psychiatry, 30,* 945–951.

Gunderson, J. G., & Sabo, A. N. (1993). The phenomenological and conceptual interface between borderline personality disorder and PTSD. *American Journal of Psychiatry, 150,* 19–27.

Gunderson, J. G., Zanarini, M. C., & Kisiel, C. L. (1991). Borderline personality disorder: A review of the data on DSM-III-R descriptions. *Journal of Personality Disorders, 5,* 967–975.

Hanson, R. K. (1990). The psychological impact of sexual assault on women and children: A review. *Annals of Sex Research, 3,* 187–232.

Harkness, L. L. (1993). Transgenerational transmission of war-related trauma. In J. W. Wilson & B. Raphael (Eds.), *International handbook of traumatic stress syndromes* (pp. 635–643). New York: Plenum Press.

Hazzard, A. (1993). Trauma-related beliefs as mediators of sexual abuse impact in adult women survivors: A pilot study. *Journal of Child Sexual Abuse, 2,* 55–69.

Helzer, J. E., & Robins, L. N. (1988). The Diagnostic Interview Schedule: Its development, evolution, and use. *Social Psychiatry and Psychiatric Epidemiology, 23,* 6–16.

Herjanic, B., & Reich, W. (1982). Development of a structured psychiatric interview for children: Agreement between child and parent on individual symptoms. *Journal of Abnormal Child Psychology, 10,* 307–324.

Herman, J. L. (1992). Complex PTSD: A syndrome in survivors of prolonged and repeated trauma. *Journal of Traumatic Stress, 5,* 377–391.

Herman, J. L., Perry, J. C., & van der Kolk, B. A. (1989). Childhood trauma in border-line personality disorder. *American Journal of Psychiatry, 146,* 490–495.

Herndon, A. D., & Law, J. G. (1985). Posttraumatic stress and the family: A multimethod approach to counseling. In C. R. Figley (Ed.), *Trauma and its wake* (pp. 264–279). New York: Brunner/Mazel.

Horowitz, M., Wilner, N., & Alvarez, W. (1979). Impact of Event Scale: A measure of subjective stress. *Psychosomatic Medicine, 41,* 209–218.

Houskamp, B. M., & Foy, D. W. (1991). The assessment of posttraumatic stress dis-order in battered women. *Journal of Interpersonal Violence, 6,* 367–375.

Hunter, J. A., Goodwin, D. W., & Wilson, R. J. (1992). Attributions of blame in child sexual abuse victims: An analysis of age and gender influences. *Journal of Child Sexual Abuse, 1,* 75–89.

Jones, E. E., Farina, A., Hastorf, A. H., Marcus, H., Miller, D. T., & Scott R. A. (1984). *Social stigma: The psychology of marked relationships.* New York: Freeman.

Keane, T. M., Caddell, J. M., Martin, B. W., Zimering, R. T., & Fairbank, J. A. (1983). Substance abuse among Vietnam Veterans with post-traumatic stress disorders. *Bulletin of the Society of Psychologists in the Addictive Behaviors, 2,* 117–122.

Keane, T. M., Caddell, J. M., Taylor, K. L. (1988). Mississippi Scale for Combat-Related Posttraumatic Stress Disorder: Three studies in reliability and validity. *Journal of Consulting and Clinical Psychology, 56,* 85–90.

Keane, T. K., & Wolfe, J. (1990). Comorbidity in post-traumatic stress disorder: An analysis of community and clinical studies. Research findings [Special Issue]. *Journal of Applied Social Psychology, 20,* 1776–1788.

Kemp, A., Rawlings, E. I., & Green, B. L. (1991). Post-traumatic stress disorder (PTSD) in battered women: A shelter sample. *Journal of Traumatic Stress, 4,* 137–148.

Kendall-Tackett, K. A., Williams, L. M., & Finkelhor, D. (1993). Impact of sexual abuse on children: A review and synthesis of recent empirical studies. *Psychological Bulletin, 113,* 164–180.

Kessler, R. C., Sonnega, A., Bromet, E., Hughes, M., & Nelson, C. B. (1995). Posttrau-matic stress disorder in the national comorbidity survey. *Archives of General Psychiatry, 52,* 1048–1060.

Kiecolt-Glaser, J. K., & Glaser, R. (1987). Psychosocial moderators of immune func-tion. *Annals of Behavioral Medicine, 9,* 16–20.

Kilpatrick, D. G., Resnick, H. S., Saunders, B. E., & Best, C. L. (1989). *The National Women's Study PTSD Module.* Charleston: Crime Victims Research and Treatment Center, Department of Psychiatry and Behavioral Sciences, Medical University of South Carolina.

Kimerling, R. E., & Calhoun, K. S. (1994). Somatic symptoms, social support, and treat-ment seeking among sexual assault victims. *Journal of Consulting and Clinical Psychology, 62,* 333–340.

Kimerling, R. E., Wolfe, J., Schnurr, P. P., Clum, G. A., & Chrestman, K. (1994, May). *Differential effects of lifetime stressors and social support on physical health in women.* Paper presented at the American Psychological Association Conference on Wom-en's Health, Washington, DC.

Kofoed, L., Friedman, M. J., & Peck, R. (1993). Alcoholism and drug abuse in patients with PTSD. Contemporary topics in drug dependence and alcoholism [Special Issue]. *Psychiatric Quarterly, 64,* 151–171.

Koopman, C., Classen, C., & Spiegel, D. A. (1994). Predictors of posttraumatic stress symptoms among survivors of the Oakland/Berkeley Calif., firestorm. *American Journal of Psychiatry, 151,* 888–894.

Koss, M. P., Woodruff, W. J., & Koss, P. G. (1991). Criminal victimization among primary care medical patients: Prevalence, incidence, and physician usage. *Behavioral Sciences and the Law, 9,* 85–96.

Kovach, J. A. (1986). Incest as a treatment issue for alcoholic women. *Alcoholism Treatment Quarterly, 3,* 1–15.

Kramer, T. L., & Green, B. L. (1991). Posttraumatic stress disorder as an early response to sexual assault. *Journal of Interpersonal Violence, 6,* 160–173.

Krinsley, K. E., Weathers, F. W., Vielhauer, M. J., Newman, E., Walker E. A., Young, L. S., & Kimerling, R. (1994). *Evaluation of Lifetime Stressors (ELS)—Interview.* Boston: National Center for PTSD, Behavioral Sciences Division, Boston VA Medical Center.

Kulka, R. A., Schlenger, W. E., Fairbank, J. A., Hough, R. L., Jordan, B. K., Marmar, C. R., & Weiss, D. S. (1988). *National Vietnam Veterans Readjustment Study (NVVRS).* Research Triangle Park, NC: Research Triangle Institute.

Kulka, R. A., Schlenger, W. E., Fairbank, J. A., Hough, R. L., Jordan, B. K., Marmar, C. R., & Weiss, D. S. (1990). *Trauma and the Vietnam War generation.* New York: Brunner/Mazel.

Landecker, H. (1992). The role of childhood sexual trauma in the etiology of borderline personality disorder: Considerations for diagnosis and treatment. *Psychotherapy, 29,* 234–242.

Lebowitz, L., & Roth, S. (1994). I felt like a slut—The cultural context and women's response to being raped. *Journal of Traumatic Stress, 7,* 363–390.

Leda, C., Rosenheck, R., & Gallup, P. (1992). Mental illness among homeless female veterans. *Hospital and Community Psychiatry, 43,* 1026–1028.

Lisak, D. (1994). The psychological impact of sexual abuse: Content analysis of interviews with male survivors. *Journal of Traumatic Stress, 7,* 525–548.

Litz, B. T., Keane, T. K., Fisher, L., Marx, B., & Monaco, V. (1992). Physical health complaints in combat-related post-traumatic stress disorder: A preliminary report. *Journal of Traumatic Stress, 5,* 131–141.

Livingston, R., Lawson, L., & Jones, J. G. (1993). Predictors of self-reported psychopathology in children abused repeatedly by a parent. *Journal of the American Academy of Child and Adolescent Psychiatry, 32,* 948–953.

Marmar, C. R., Weiss, D. S., Schlenger, W. E., Fairbank, J. A., Jordan, B. K., Kulka, R. A., & Hough, R. L. (1994). Peritraumatic dissociation and post-traumatic stress in male Vietnam theater veterans. *American Journal of Psychiatry, 151,* 902–907.

Matthews, H. B., Dixon, D., Herr, D. W., & Tilson, H. A. (1990). Subchronic toxicity studies indicate that ris(2-chloroethyl)phosphate administration results in lesions in the rat hippocampus. *Toxicology and Industrial Health, 6,* 1–15.

Matthews, K. A. (1992). Myths and realities of the menopause. *Psychosomatic Medicine, 54,* 1–9.

McCann, L. I., & Pearlman, L. A. (1990). *Psychological trauma and the adult survivor: Theory, therapy and transformation.* New York: Brunner/Mazel.

McFall, M. E., Mackay, P. W., & Donovan, D. M. (1991). Combat-related PTSD and psychosocial adjustment problems among substance abusing veterans. *Journal of Nervous and Mental Diseases, 179,* 33–38.

McFall, M. E., Mackay, P. W., & Donovan, D. M. (1992). Combat-related posttraumatic stress disorder and severity of substance abuse in Vietnam Veterans. *Journal of the Studies on Alcohol, 53,* 357–363.

Mitchell, M. E. (1991). A family approach and network implications of therapy for victims of violence as applied in a case of rape. *Journal of Family Psychotherapy, 2,* 1–13.

Moscarello, R. (1992). Victims and violence: Aspects of the "victim-to-patient" process in women. *Canadian Journal of Psychiatry, 37,* 497–502.

Mueserk, T., Yarnold, P. R., & Foy, D. W. (1991). Statistical analysis for single-case designs: Evaluating outcome of imaginal exposure treatment of chronic PTSD. *Behavioral Modification, 15,* 134–155.

Murburg, M. M., Ashleigh, E. A., Hommer, D. W., & Veith, R. C. (1994a). Biology of catecholaminergic systems and their relevance to PTSD. In M. M. Murburg (Ed.), *Catecholamine function in posttraumatic stress disorder: Emerging concepts* (pp. 3–16). Washington, DC: American Psychiatric Press.

Murburg, M. M., McFall, M. E., & Veith, R. C. (1994b). Basal sympathoadrenal function in patients with PTSD and depression. In M. M. Murburg (Ed.), *Catecholamine function in posttraumatic stress disorder: Emerging concepts* (pp. 175–188). Washington, DC: American Psychiatric Press.

Nash, M. R., Hulsey, T. L., Sexton, M. C., Harralson, T. L., & Lambert, W. (1993). Long-term sequelae of childhood sexual abuse: Perceived family environment, psychopathology, and dissociation. *Journal of Consulting and Clinical Psychology, 61,* 276–283.

National Victim Center. (1992). *Rape in America: A report to the nation.* Arlington, VA: Author.

Newmark, M. E., & Penry, J. K. (1980). Catamenial epilepsy: A review. *Epilepsia, 21,* 281–300.

Nolen-Hoeksema, S. (1987). Sex differences in unipolar depression: Evidence and theory. *Psychological Bulletin, 101,* 259–282.

Nolen-Hoeksema, S., & Girgus, J. S. (1994). The emergence of gender differences in depression during adolescence. *Psychological Bulletin, 115,* 424–443.

Norris, F. H. (1992). Epidemiology of trauma: Frequency and impact of different potentially traumatic events on different demographic groups. *Journal of Consulting and Clinical Psychology, 60,* 409–418.

North, C. S., & Smith, E. M. (1992). Posttraumatic stress disorder among homeless men and women. *Hospital and Community Psychiatry, 43,* 1010–1016.

O'Neill, K., & Gupta, K. (1991). Post-traumatic stress disorder in women who were victims of childhood sexual abuse. *Irish Journal of Psychological Medicine, 8,* 124–127.

Paykel, E. S., Prusoff, B. A., & Uhlenhuth, E. H. (1971). Scaling of life events. *Archives of General Psychiatry, 25,* 340–347.

Paykel, E. S., Weissman, M. M., & Prusoff, B. A. (1978). Social maladjustment and severity of depression. *Comprehensive Psychiatry, 19,* 121–128.

Pennebaker, J. W. (1982). *The psychology of physical symptoms.* New York: Springer-Verlag.

Pillitteri, A., Seidl, A., Smith, C., & Stanton, M. (1992). Parent gender, victim gender, and family socioeconomic level influences on the potential reporting by nurses of physical child abuse. *Issues in Comprehensive Pediatric Nursing, 15,* 239–247.

Polusny, M. A., & Follette, V. M. (1995). Long-term correlates of child sexual abuse: Theory and review of the empirical literature. *Applied and Preventive Psychology, 4,* 143–166.

Potts, M. K., Burnam, M. A., & Wells, K. B. (1991). Gender differences in depression detection: A comparison of clinician diagnosis and standardized assessment. *Psychological Assessment, 3,* 609–615.

Prins, A., Hearst-Ikeda, D., Wilson, K., & Wolfe, J. (1995). *Development and validation of a trauma-specific self-concealment scale.* Unpublished manuscript.

Putnam, F. W. (1989). Pierre Janet and modern views of dissociation. *Journal of Traumatic Stress, 2,* 413–429.

Randall, T. (1990). Domestic violence begets other problems of which physicians must be aware to be effective. *Journal of the American Medical Association, 264,* 940–943.

Realmuto, G. M., Wagner, N., & Bartholow, J. (1991). The Williams pipeline disaster: A controlled study of a technological accident. *Journal of Traumatic Stress, 4,* 469–479.

Recupero, P. R., Brown, P. J., Stout, R., Wolfe, J., & Morello, S. (1994, May). *Traumatic exposure and PTSD symptomatology among substance abusers.* Paper presented at the annual meeting of the American Psychiatric Association, Philadelphia, PA.

Reinherz, H. Z., Giaconia, R. M., Lefkowitz, E. S., Pakiz, B., & Frost, A. K. (1993). Prevalence of psychiatric disorders in a community population of older adolescents. *Journal of the American Academy of Child and Adolescent Psychiatry, 32,* 369–377.

Resick, P. A. (1981, March). *Family support to victims of rape: An intervening variable for recovery?* Paper presented at the annual meeting of the Association for Women in Psychotherapy, Boston, MA.

Resick, P. A. (1993). The psychological impact of rape: Rape [Special Section]. *Journal of Interpersonal Violence, 8,* 223–255.

Resnick, H. S., Kilpatrick, D. G., Best, C. L., & Kramer, T. L. (1992). Vulnerability–stress factors in development of posttraumatic stress disorder. *Journal of Nervous and Mental Disease, 180,* 424–430.

Resnick, H. S., Kilpatrick, D. G., Dansky, B. S., Saunders, B. E., & Best, C. L. (1993). Prevalence of civilian trauma and posttraumatic stress disorder in a representative national sample of women. *Journal of Consulting and Clinical Psychology, 61,* 984–991.

Riggs, D. S., Cascardi, M. B., Hearst, D., & Foa, E. B. (1993, November). Assault characteristics and early symptoms as predictors of assault related post-traumatic stress disorder. In D. S. Riggs (Chair), *Factors predictive of post-traumatic stress disorder: An examination of individual trauma and symptom characteristics.* Symposium conducted at the annual meeting of the Association for Advancement of Behavior Therapy, Atlanta, GA.

Roberts, R. E., Andrews, J. A., Lewinsohn, P. M., & Hops, H. (1990). Assessment of depression in adolescents using the Center for Epidemiologic Studies Depression Scale. *Psychological Assessment, 2,* 122–128.

Robins, L. N., Helzer, J. E., Croughan, J. L., & Ratcliffe, K. S. (1981). National Institute of Mental Health diagnostic interview schedule: Its history, characteristics, and validity. *Archives of General Psychiatry, 38,* 381–389.

Robinson, T. E., & Becker, J. B. (1986). Enduring changes in brain and behavior produced by chronic amphetamine administration: A review and evaluation of animal models of amphetamine psychosis. *Brain Research Review, 11,* 157–198.

Root, M. P. (1991). Persistent, disordered eating as a gender-specific post-traumatic stress response to sexual assault. Psychotherapy with victims [Special Issue]. *Psychotherapy, 28,* 96–102.

Rose, S. M. (1991). Acknowledging abuse backgrounds of intensive case management clients. *Community Mental Health Journal, 27,* 255–263.

Rosenheck, R., & Wolfe, J. (1994). *Military Stress Inventory for Women-R.* Boston: National Center for PTSD, Boston VA Medical Center.

Roth, S., & Lebowitz, L. (1988). The experience of sexual trauma. *Journal of Traumatic Stress, 1,* 79–107.

Rothbaum, B. O., Foa, E. B., Riggs, D. S., Murdock, T., & Walsh, W. (1992). A prospective examination of post-traumatic stress disorder in rape victims. *Journal of Traumatic Stress, 5,* 455–475.

Sarason, I. G., Levine, H. M., Basham, R. B., & Sarason, B. R. (1983). Assessing the social support: The Social Support Questionnaire. *Journal of Personality and Social Psychology, 44,* 127–139.

Saxe, G. N., Chinman, G., Berkowitz, R., Hull, K., Lieberg, G., Schwartz, J., & van der Kolk, B. A. (1994). Somatization in patients with dissociative disorders. *American Journal of Psychiatry, 151,* 1329–1334.

Saxe, G. N., van der Kolk, B. A., Berkowitz, R., Chinman, G., Hall, K., Lieberg, G., & Schwartz, J. (1993). Dissociative disorders in psychiatric inpatients. *American Journal of Psychiatry, 150,* 1037–1042.

Shalev, A., Bleich, A., & Ursano, R. J. (1990). Posttraumatic stress disorder: Somatic comorbidity and effort tolerance. *Psychosomatics, 31,* 197–203.

Shalev, A. Y., Orr, S. P., & Pitman, R. K. (1993). Psychophysiologic assessment of traumatic imagery in Israeli civilian patients with posttraumatic stress disorder. *American Journal of Psychiatry, 150,* 620–624.

Shannon, M. P., Lonigan, C. J., Finch, A. J., & Taylor, C. M. (1994). Children exposed to disaster: I. Epidemiology of post-traumatic symptoms and symptom profiles. *Journal of the American Academy of Child and Adolescent Psychiatry, 33,* 80–93.

Solomon, Z. (1988). Somatic complaints, stress reactions, and posttraumatic stress disorder: A three-year follow-up study. *Behavioral Medicine, 14,* 179–185.

Spiegel, D., & Cardeña, E. (1991). Disintegrated experience: The dissociative disorders revisited. Diagnoses, dimensions, and DSM-IV: The science of classification [Special Issue]. *Journal of Abnormal Psychology, 100,* 366–378.

Spitzer, R. (1981). *NIMH Diagnostic Interview Schedule, Version 3.* Rockville, MD: National Institute of Mental Health. Public Health Service.

Spitzer, R. L., Williams, J. B. W., & Gibbon, M. (1986). *Instruction manual for the Structured Clinical Interview for DSM-III-R.* New York: Biometrics Research Department, New York State Psychiatric Institute.

Spitzer, R. L., Williams, J. B. W., Gibbon, M., & First, M. B. (1990). *Structured Clinical Interview for DSM-III-R, non-patient edition (SCID-NP, Version 1.0).* Washington, DC: American Psychiatric Press.

Steinglass, P., & Gerrity, E. (1990). Natural disasters and post-traumatic stress disorder: Short-term versus long-term recovery in two disaster-affected communities. Traumatic stress: New perspectives in theory, measurement, and research: II. Research findings [Special Issue]. *Journal of Applied Social Psychology, 20,* 1746–1765.

Stoney, C. M., Davis, M. C., & Matthews, K. A. (1987). Sex differences in physiological responses to stress and in coronary heart disease: A causal link? *Psychophysiology, 24,* 127–131.

Stoney, C. M., Matthews, K. A., McDonald, R. H., & Johnson, C. A. (1988). Sex differences in lipid, lipoprotein, cardiovascular, and neuroendocrine responses to acute stress. *Psychophysiology, 25,* 645–656.

Stretch, R. H. (1991). Psychosocial readjustment of Canadian Vietnam Veterans. *Journal of Consulting and Clinical Psychology, 59,* 188–189.

Strickland, B. R. (1989, April). *Gender differences in depression.* Paper presented at the meeting of the Boulder Symposium on Clinical Psychology: Depression (as part of the Milton E. Lipetz Memorial Lecture series), Boulder, CO.

Tilson, H. A., Veronesi, B., McLamb, R. L., & Matthews, H. B. (1990). Acute exposure to tris(2-chloroethyl)phosphate produces hippocampal neuronal loss and impairs learning in rats. *Toxicology and Applied Pharmacology, 106,* 254–269.

Trickett, P. K., & Putnam, F. W. (1993). Impact of child sexual abuse on females:

Toward a developmental, psychobiological integration. *Psychological Science, 4,* 81–87.

van der Kolk, B. A., & Saporta, J. (1993). Biological responses to psychic trauma. In J. P. Wilson & B. Raphael (Eds.), *International handbook of traumatic stress syndromes* (pp. 25–34). New York: Plenum Press.

Vanderlinden, J., Van Dyck, R., Vandereycken, W., & Vertommen, H. (1993). Dissociation and traumatic experiences in the general population of the Netherlands. *Hospital and Community Psychiatry, 44,* 786–788.

Verbrugge, L. M. (1983). Multiple roles and physical health of women and men. *Journal of Health and Social Behavior, 24,* 16–30.

Verbrugge, L. M. (1985). Gender and health: An update on hypotheses and evidence. *Journal of Health and Social Behavior, 26,* 156–182.

Verbrugge, L. M. (1989). The twain meet: Empirical explanations of sex differences in health and mortality. *Journal of Health and Social Behavior, 30,* 282–304.

von Korff, M. R., & Anthony, J. C. (1982). The NIMH Diagnostic Interview Schedule modified to record current mental health status. *Journal of Affective Disorders, 4,* 365–371.

Waigandt, A., Wallace, D. L., Phelps, L., & Miller, D. A. (1990). The impact of sexual assault on physical health status. *Journal of Traumatic Stress, 3,* 93–102.

Walker, L. E. (1991). Post-traumatic stress disorder in women: Diagnosis and treatment of battered women syndrome. Psychotherapy with victims [Special Issue]. *Psychotherapy, 28,* 21–29.

Ware, J. E., & Sherbourne, C. D. (1992). The MOS 36-item short-form health survey (SF-36). *Medical Care, 30,* 473–483.

Weathers, F. W., Litz, B. T., Huska, J. A., & Keane, T. M. (1991). *The PTSD Checklist (PCL).* Boston: National Center for PTSD, Boston VA Medical Center.

Weaver, T. L., & Clum, G. A. (1993). Early family environments and traumatic experiences associated with borderline personality disorder. *Journal of Consulting and Clinical Psychology, 61,* 1068–1075.

Weiss, D. S. (1993). Structured clinical interview techniques. In J. W. Wilson & B. Raphael (Eds.), *International handbook of traumatic stress syndromes* (pp. 165–178). New York: Plenum Press.

Weiss, D. S., Marmar, C. R., Metzler, T. J., & Ronfeldt, H. (1995). Predicting symptomatic distress in emergency services personnel. *Journal of Clinical and Counseling Psychology, 63,* 361–368.

Weiss, D. S., Marmar, C. R., Schlenger, W. E., Fairbank, J. A., Jordan, B. K., & Kulka, R. A. (1992). The prevalence of lifetime and partial post-traumatic stress disorder in Vietnam theater veterans. *Journal of Traumatic Stress, 5,* 365–376.

Weissman, M. M., & Klerman, G. L. (1977). Gender and depression. *Trends in Neurosciences, 8,* 416–420.

Weissman, M. M., & Klerman, G. L. (1985). Sex differences in the epidemiology of depression. *Archives of General Psychiatry, 34,* 98–111.

Weissman, M. M., Leaf, P. J., Holzer, C. E., Meyers, J. K., & Tischler, G. L. (1984). The epidemiology of depression: An update on sex differences in rates. *Journal of Affective Disorders, 7,* 179–188.

West, C. G., Fernandez, A., Hillard, J. R., Schoof, M., & Parks, J. (1990). Psychiatric disorders of abused women at a shelter. *Psychiatric Quarterly, 61,* 295–301.

Wilson, J. P. (1994). The need for an integrative theory of post-traumatic stress disorder. In M. B. Williams & J. F. Sommer, Jr. (Eds.), *Handbook of post-traumatic therapy* (pp. 3–18). Westport, CT: Greenwood Press.

Wilson, J. P., & Krauss, G. E. (1985). Predicting post-traumatic stress disorders among Vietnam veterans. In W. E. Kelly (Ed.), *Posttraumatic stress disorder and the war veterans patient* (pp. 102–147). New York: Brunner/Mazel.

Wilson, J. P., Smith, W. K., & Johnson, S. K. (1985). A comparative analysis of PTSD among various survivor groups. In C. R. Figley (Ed.), *Trauma and its wake: Traumatic stress theory, research, and intervention* (pp. 142–172). New York: Brunner/Mazel.

Wind, T. W., & Silvern, L. E. (1992). Type and extent of child abuse as predictors of adult functioning. *Journal of Family Violence, 7*, 261–281.

Wolfe, J., Brown, P. J., Furey, J., & Levin, K. (1993a). Development of a war-time stressor scale for women (WMSS). *Psychological Assessment: A Journal of Consulting and Clinical Psychology, 5*, 330–335.

Wolfe, J., Brown, P. J., & Kelley, J. M. (1993b). Reassessing war stress: Exposure and the Persian Gulf War. *Journal of Social Issues, 49*, 15–31.

Wolfe, J., & Keane, T. M. (1993). New perspectives in the assessment and diagnosis of combat-related posttraumatic stress disorder. In J. W. Wilson & B. Raphael (Eds.), *International handbook of traumatic stress syndromes* (pp. 165–178). New York: Plenum Press.

Wolfe, J., Kimerling, R., & Brown, P. (1993c). *The Life Stressor Checklist.* Boston: National Center for PTSD, Boston VA Medical Center.

Wolfe, J., Mori, D., & Krygeris, S. (1994a). Treating trauma in special populations: Lessons from women veterans. *Psychotherapy, 31*, 87–93.

Wolfe, J., Proctor, P. P., Brown, P., Kimerling, R., Duncan, J., Sullivan, M., Chrestman, K., & White, R. F. (1994b, May). *Relationship of physical health and post-traumatic stress disorder in young adult women.* Poster presented at the Annual Meeting of the American Psychological Association, Washington, DC.

Wolfe, J., Proctor, S. P., & Skinner, K. (1994c, April). *Impact of war stress and medical concerns on the use of health care resources by returned Persian Gulf War veterans.* Poster presented at the Department of Veterans Affairs meeting, Washington, DC.

Wolfe, J., Proctor, S. P., Sullivan, M., & Duncan Davis, J. (1995, March). *Post-traumatic stress and physical health: Does gender play a role?* Poster presented at the 3rd Annual Research Day, Consolidated Department of Psychiatry at Harvard Medical School, Boston, MA.

Wolfe, J., Schnurr, P. P., Brown, P. J., & Furey, J. (1994d). War-zone exposure and PTSD as correlates of perceived health in female Vietnam veterans. *Journal of Consulting and Clinical Psychology, 62*, 1235–1240.

Wolfe, J., & Young, B. (1993, November). The relationship of gender to symptom reporting following trauma. In T. Klass (Chair), *Gender issues in anxiety disorders.* Symposium conducted at the annual meeting of the Association for Advancement of Behavior Therapy, Atlanta, GA.

Yehuda, R., Giller, E. L., Southwick, S. M., Kahana, B., Boisoneau, D., Ma, X., & Mason, J. W. (1994). Relationship between catecholamine excretion and PTSD symptoms in Vietnam combat veterans and Holocaust survivors. In M. M. Murburg (Ed.), *Catecholamine function in posttraumatic stress disorder: Emerging concepts* (pp. 203–220). Washington, DC: American Psychiatric Press.

Zaidi, L. Y., & Foy, D. W. (1994). Childhood abuse experiences and combat-related PTSD. *Journal of Traumatic Stress, 7*, 33–42.

CHAPTER 8

Cross-Cultural and Multiethnic Assessment of Trauma

SPERO M. MANSON

INTRODUCTION

Recent issuance of the fourth edition of the *Diagnostic and Statistical Manual of Mental Disorders* (DSM-IV; American Psychiatric Association, 1994) marks a dramatically new level of acknowledgment of the role of culture in shaping the symptoms, expression, and course of major mental illness. Whereas prior editions only referred in passing to such matters, for example, with respect to schizophrenia and other psychotic disorders, the present one specifically includes three types of information related to considerations of this nature. These encompass (1) a systematic discussion of cultural variations in the clinical presentation of each DSM-IV disorder; (2) a glossary of frequently encountered idioms of distress, referred to as "culture-bound syndromes"; and (3) an outline to assist the clinician in formulating the cultural dimensions of an individual case. With respect to the first element, the quality and depth of DSM-IV's discussion of culture varies significantly across the disorders. Nonetheless, the mood and anxiety disorders are among those that benefited most from this subsequent revision, especially posttraumatic stress disorder (PTSD). Yet much more remains to be done, and awaits careful work by clinicians and researchers alike that will extend our understanding of the nature, recognition, and meaning of trauma, as well as its representation as PTSD among different cultures.

The present chapter suggests ways to pursue this work. It begins with a brief review of the relevant clinical and epidemiological literature. However, this review does not, as often is the case, exhaustively inventory published studies considered cross-cultural in the broadest sense of the term, that is, simply, inquiries conducted among populations other than White, middle-class America. Rather, the emphasis is instead on the far fewer studies that yield insight into the actual cultural dynamics—for example, values, cognitive-interpretive processes, social structure, and person–environment relationships—underpinning apparent differences in the experience of trauma and its psychiatric sequelae. The discussion next turns to assessment methods, which range from self-administered reports to structured and semi-structured diagnostic protocols. Unfortunately, very little is known about the performance of these tools when applied to populations that are culturally distinct from those among whom said methods were developed initially. Ongoing studies promise to address this gap in regard to the psychometric properties of standard measures as well as innovative adaptations thereof. Thus, preliminary results are described to illustrate the logic behind these efforts and the fruitful directions that are emerging. The chapter closes with a detailed examination of one of the exciting new features, at least for the topic at hand, of the DSM-IV: Appendix I: Outline for Cultural Formulation. It briefly chronicles the development of this clinical procedure, summarizes the underlying epistemological bases, and highlights the structured inquiry that flows from the use of the outline. A case example is presented to illustrate the powerful difference that a cultural formulation of this nature can make to the comprehensive diagnosis and treatment of individuals suffering from PTSD.

TRAUMA AND PTSD ACROSS ETHNICITY AND CULTURE

Recent publications, although widely divergent in their emphases, provide, in combination, a detailed overview of current knowledge with respect to trauma and PTSD in various ethnic groups and cultures. Marsella, Friedman, and Spain (1993) offer a useful orientation for those new to this literature. Topic-specific reviews include the clinical assessment of ethnic minority Vietnam War veterans (Penk & Allen, 1991), clinical and epidemiological findings among refugees (Friedman & Jaranson, 1993), as well as treatment and preventive interventions directed to natural disaster victims in other countries (de Girolamo, 1993). A new volume entitled *Ethnocultural Variation in Trauma and PTSD* (Marsella, Friedman, Gerrity, & Scurfield, 1996), based on the proceedings of an NIMH- and Department of Veterans Affairs-sponsored conference, represents the most complete coverage of this subject to date.

Risk of PTSD and the Meaning of Trauma

This work reveals that certain populations or subgroups, namely, refugees, immigrants, veterans, concentration camp survivors, and other victims of torture, are at high risk of trauma and, by extension, PTSD. Ethnic minorities as well as people from other nations figure prominently in these findings. One consequently might leap to the conclusion that culture is central to their added risk. As will be discussed in a moment, it may contribute in a number of ways to vulnerability, or protection, as the case may be. But, at present, the evidence suggests that the greater visibility of ethnically and culturally diverse victims in these studies is due more to their differential exposure to precipitating stressors than to factors intrinsic to the cultural milieus within which they live.

Consider the following. Kulka et al. (1990), in the National Vietnam Veterans Readjustment Study (NVVRS), report the point prevalence of PTSD among White veterans as 15%, African American veterans as 19%, and Hispanic veterans as 28%. Controlling for differential exposure to war-zone trauma—often a function of military occupational status, which has been shown to vary by socioeconomic status and ethnicity—the differences disappeared between Whites and African Americans and were dramatically reduced between Whites and Hispanics. Other studies indicate that a history of substance abuse (Carter, 1982; Jordan et al., 1991) increases the frequency of exposure to adverse circumstances (e.g., domestic violence, vehicular accidents, homicide), which in turn elevates risk of PTSD. Greater rates of substance abuse are known to be significantly associated with lower socioeconomic status as well as membership in certain ethnic groups. Thus, risk of PTSD distributes unevenly across the social structure as a consequence of substance abuse, indirectly, at best, due to ethnic or cultural factors. Finally, early life stressors also have been shown to contribute substantially to added risk of PTSD (Breslau, Davis, Andreski, & Peterson, 1991). Here, too, socioeconomic status and ethnicity are tightly interwoven, increasing exposure to the requisite antecedents of PTSD and confounding causal attributions that may invoke cultural explanations.

None of this argues against the importance of ethnicity and culture in regard to risk of PTSD. The field just has not thought critically about the matter or struggled much beyond a static conceptualization of either as independent variables to be accounted for in epidemiological and clinical study designs. This is despite intriguing observations that suggest a richness of possibilities.

One possibility is embodied in Parson's (1985) assertion that ethnic minority veterans of the Vietnam War face a "tripartite adaptational dilemma." Such veterans, in his view, must successfully resolve a series of demands posed by bicultural identity, institutional racism, and residual stress upon which war trauma is layered. Failure to do so, according to Parson, increases these individuals' risk of PTSD and related disorders. Penk and Allen (1991) and Marsella et al. (1993) echo this same theme in their attempt to explain apparent ethnic differences in rates of psychiatric illness. Let us explore more deeply the roots of this dilemma.

Numerous accounts by ethnic minority veterans reveal that they were torn among conflicting perspectives on their presence in Vietnam and role in the war. They were required to help subjugate non-White people on behalf of a country that many themselves experienced as racist and colonial.

Furthermore, veterans of American Indian, Alaska Native, Japanese American, and Native Hawaiian descent reported that the Vietnamese not only looked like them, but their families, friends, and neighbors as well. Killing became a very personal matter, not easily compartmentalized or distanced.

Institutional racism was evident in all branches of the military, from the small number of ethnic minorities represented in the officers' ranks, to fewer recommendations for medals. Racial stereotypes contributed to certain combat assignments. For example, the classic belief that American Indians—by virtue of their closeness to nature, a modern-day twist on Rousseau's "Noble Savage"—possess special prowess as scouts and hunters led to their frequent duty as points on patrol or long-range reconnaissance teams, thereby placing them at added risk of injury or death (Barse, 1994; Holm, 1994; Silver, 1994).

Finally, many ethnic minority veterans of the Vietnam War already were exposed to other, chronic adversities that may amplify the stress induced by war-related trauma. More frequent personal losses due to increased mortality, whether of natural or human origin, in their home communities reduced these veterans' coping resources as well as exacerbated their psychological vulnerability. Limited educational and employment opportunities further compound this risk by narrowing the avenues of escape from otherwise oppressive circumstances. And histories of enforced dependence embodied in various governmental programs encourage learned helplessness, thus diminishing the availability of effective responses to new stressors.

Another possibility lies within the interpretive frameworks and activities that culture provides as part of its "meaning-making" function. Among the Navajo, for instance, the concept of *sa' a naghai bik'e hozhq*, or simply *hozq*, is

> the central idea in Navajo religious thinking. But it is not something that occurs only in ritual song and prayer, it is referred to frequently in everyday speech. A Navajo uses this concept to express his happiness, his health, the beauty of his land, and the harmony of his relations with others. It is used in reminding people to be careful and deliberate, and when he says good-bye to someone leaving, he will say *hozhqqgo naninnaa doo* "may you walk or go about according to *hozhq*." (Witherspoon, 1977, p. 47)

Sa' a naghai bik'e hozhq encompasses the notions of connectedness, reciprocity, balance, and completeness that underlie contextually oriented views of human health and well-being (Farella, 1984; Moos, 1979; Sandner, 1979; Stokols, 1991), which are likely to be more common among certain ethnic groups and cultural populations than others. As noted, the Navajo devote considerable time and effort to its maintenance. Traumatic experiences of various kinds—some familiar, some not to non-Navajos—disrupt this sense of coherence: killing another human, contact with the dead or dying, physical injury attributed to witchcraft. Thus, combat posed an additional fear for Navajo Vietnam veterans beyond that anticipated by their peers; the sites of horrific vehicular accidents generally elicit greater anxiety and avoidance among Navajo than non-Navajo people. Imagine, then, how the definition of trauma, the degree to which events are acknowledged as traumatic, and the fear or horror associated with them may be shaped by culture and, thus, increase or reduce risk of PTSD.

There often are, as one might expect, cultural mechanisms for redressing the imbalance resulting from events of this nature. In the case of the Navajo, they are found in elaborate ceremonials such as the Enemy Way or Beauty Way (Kluckhohn & Leighton, 1974). These rituals employ the symbolic reenactment of solutions codified through legend, transmitted by song and prayer. Consequently, Navajo soldiers as they are about to go off to war, and again immediately upon their return, ideally should participate in an Enemy Way ceremony. Occurring prior to combat, it serves a protective function, explicitly recognizing that what the individual soon will undergo is out of the ordinary and beyond normal expectations of how a Navajo should live life. After combat, the ceremonial acts as a means of spiritually "decontaminating" the individual, restoring the balance that may have been either disrupted or threatened by killing and death. Moreover, by virtue of the widespread, active involvement of kith and kin, the Enemy Way ceremony serves to reintegrate the veteran into the social fabric of the community, thus reaffirming individual as well as collective identity. Lack of access to such ceremonials — perhaps because of economics, familial dysfunction, or seasonal timing — may actually lower the probability of successful coping with subsequent trauma and increase risk of PTSD.

Yet another possibility springs from the culturally defined relationship between a person and the world around him or her. On March 24, 1989, the *Exxon Valdez* struck a reef and spilled over 11 million gallons of oil into the previously pristine Prince William Sound. The impacts were enormous, affecting flora, fauna, and humans alike. Subsequent study of these consequences revealed that residents of communities physically touched by the oil spill were at greater risk of major depression, generalized anxiety, and PTSD than those that were not (Palinkas, Downs, Petterson, & Russell, 1993). Significant differences were evident as well between Native and non-Native residents of the same villages, with the former exhibiting consistently higher rates of all three psychiatric disorders. Controlling for differential experience of prespill trauma reduced, but did not eliminate, these disparities. Ethnographic research conducted in tandem with the social impact assessment suggested at least one reason, firmly rooted in the cultural ways of the Native inhabitants.

Subsistence activities — the taking of game, fishing, harvesting mollusks, and gathering edible plants or berries — were widely practiced by Native as well as non-Native residents of the affected communities. The oil spill seriously disrupted local subsistence efforts, forcing greater dependence on more costly market foodstuffs, with dramatic fiscal consequences for all concerned. But the subsequent interruption of subsistence activities had an even more dramatic impact among the Natives. They, unlike their non-Native counterparts, experienced subsistence as a process of enculturation. As grandfathers, fathers, and grandsons hunt or fish, and as grandmothers, mothers, and granddaughters gather, stories are shared about the creation, peoples' places in the world, the significance of the land, and special features thereof. These stories, and their reaffirmation through the manner in which subsistence proceeds, transmit core elements of the culture from one generation to the next. Their disruption, threatened by the spill, occasioned widespread fear and anxiety as to the continuity of long-held traditions, indeed the future of the culture. Further analyses of the data indicated differences in the prevalence of psychiatric disorders among Native respondents that varied in terms of their degree of participation in subsistence activities and strength of cultural identity, lending additional credence to this interpretation.

The challenge before us, then, is to anticipate the role of cultural factors such as these in the stress process, to identify the possible differences that they may make, and to operationalize measures that can be employed to determine their particular contribution to increased or decreased risk of trauma and PTSD.

Symbols, Ritual Structure, and Therapeutic Process

Returning to the literature at large, considerable attention also has been given to the interaction of cultural factors and therapeutic process in regard to trauma and PTSD. This line of inquiry has, however, engendered many more studies with a frankly cultural focus than other areas of emphasis. Truly exciting work has emerged, progressing well beyond now time-worn assertions that clinician and intervention must accommodate this aspect of the patient's presentation, absent a critical analysis of relevant dynamics and concrete suggestions for appropriate treatment leverage. The efforts in question range from thoughtful adaptations, even revisions of Western-oriented psychotherapeutic techniques, to the role of indigenous forms of healing.

Lee and Lu (1989), for example, highlight functional and dysfunctional coping strategies among Asian immigrants and Southeast Asian refugees, describing several culturally informed principles, based on their experience, for treating those who suffer from PTSD. They specifically reference successful accommodations of crisis intervention methods, supportive and behavioral therapy, and even psychopharmacological care to the cultural expectations of these individuals. Others furnish similarly valuable insights (e.g., Jaranson, 1990; Mollica & Lavelle, 1988; Mollica et al., 1992; Rosser, 1986; Westermeyer, 1989). Kinzie and his colleagues provide the longest standing, continuous series of observations in this regard (Boehnlein, 1987a, 1987b; Kinzie, 1985; 1989; Kinzie & Fleck, 1987; Kinzie, Tran, Breckenridge, & Bloom, 1980; Kinzie & Leung, 1989; Kinzie, Frederickson, Ben, Fleck, & Karls, 1984).

Parson's (1985, 1990) approach to treating PTSD among African American veterans, which he refers to as "posttraumatic psychocultural therapy," represents more than the adaptation of biomedically oriented intervention. It entails detailed, explicit work on specific ethnic and cultural dimensions viewed as central to the patient. He cautiously probes the experiential worlds of African American veterans with respect to the history of slavery and Eurocentric attitudes as each may link to and exacerbate combat-related trauma. These connections then become points for intervention, providing him quicker, deeper entry into the trauma. Parson characterizes the operating tenets of this approach in terms of 10 basic principles that distinguish it from other forms of psychotherapy. Many of these principles address directly the ethnic and cultural influences that surfaced in the prior discussion of risk.

A point even further along this continuum is illustrated by increasing attempts to incorporate indigenous healers and their therapeutic methods into institutionally based treatment programs. Krippner and Colodzin (1989) review efforts specific to the treatment of PTSD among Vietnam veterans, which comprise the vast majority of such examples. According to them, participation enabled American Indian and Asian American veterans to "regain power," "cleanse themselves," and "decrease shame, guilt, and rage." Scurfield (1996) offers a detailed account of the addition of a sweat lodge, spiritual leader, and attendance of powwows to the treatment regimen of an inpatient VA-PTSD program. His careful description reveals important, practical lessons from this bid to address the special needs of American Indian patients. However, more light is shed on programmatic issues than on therapeutic elements of the activities themselves.

The latter is best exemplified by Wilson's (1988, 1989; Silver & Wilson, 1990) analyses of the sweat lodge purification ritual (*Inipi Onikare*), once a Northern Plains phenomenon, but now widely practiced in many American Indian communities. This cultural practice is regarded as a

> serious and sacred occasion in which spiritual insights, personal growth, and physical and emotional healing may take place. The purpose of purification is experienced on numerous levels of awareness, including the physical, psychological, social, and spiritual. (Wilson, 1988, p. 44)

Many symbolic aspects of the physical construction of the sweat lodge and the various objects are part of the ritual (Brown, 1971). Of more direct relevance here are the psychological effects attributed to the ritual process. The process includes a physically close circular arrangement of participants to increase unity and bonding, individual prayers involving culturally appropriate forms of self-disclosure of social concerns and needs, as well as needs and concerns of others, and the "opening" of the Four Doors through a cycle of prayers (actual opening of the sweat lodge door with a change in heat and light conditions), which is controlled by the medicine person, who works to lead the group to see more fully the symbolic nature of the ritual as a paradigm of life's central struggles. The juxtaposition of darkness and light may then take on deeper symbolic values as the paradigms of life versus death; insight versus ignorance; growth versus stagnation; hope versus despair; relief versus suffering; renewal versus stasis; connection versus separation; communality versus aloneness, and will versus stagnation. (Wilson, 1988, p. 54)

Wilson (1989) illuminates the psychobiological aspects of altered states of consciousness that commonly have been observed and measured during the ritual and of the shifts in hemispheric dominance of the brain that are part of the altered states of consciousness commonly produced by ritual participation. Other aspects of the ritual are designed to promote a sense of continuity of the community and the continuity of the individual in the culture. The conclusion of the ritual typically is accompanied by a number of positive psychological outcomes, including a sense of emotional release and a feeling of renewal as well as inner strength.

Similar symbolism and processes are evident in the Navajo ceremonials mentioned earlier and in the Peyote Service of the Native American Church (Aberle, 1966; Calabrese, 1994), which also figures importantly in the attempt by many American Indians to cope with traumatic experiences, combat-related or otherwise. Each of these cultural practices is characterized by metaphors of healing, rebirth, and the dawning of a new day: models for spiritual transformation reminiscent of what Wallace (1966) referred to as "religious identity renewal." Available as well are self-symbols that facilitate reflexivity: the ability to analyze objectively one's own life and life in general. Yet another important element is the socially constructed nature of contemplation linked to altered states of consciousness. This aspect of the process focuses attention on the ceremonial environment, preventing a completely personal visionary experience, and thus ties the participant to the goals implicit in the structure of the ritual.

For many people, participation in church and related religious activities may serve similar purposes and offer comparable benefits. This has been particularly well documented for African Americans (Dressler, 1985, 1987; Maypole & Anderson, 1987; Neighbors, 1990; Neighbors, Jackson, Bowman, & Gurin, 1983). The point, for us, however, is that such processes are inextricably bound up with culture, which provides the core symbols, ritual activities that operationalize therapeutic structures, and roles for the participants.

Unfortunately, the topic that occupies the remainder of this chapter—specifically, the cross-cultural and multiethnic assessment of trauma and PTSD—has received little attention (Allodi, 1991; Manson et al., 1996; Marsella et al., 1993). The field slowly is growing aware of the influence of culture and ethnicity on assessment process (Mollica et al., 1992; Westermeyer & Wahmemholm, 1989). Some concern has been expressed in regard to the manner of clinical inquiry, characterized largely in terms of "cultural sensitivity." This is an important dimension of assessment, and, historically, a common theme in the cross-cultural literature with respect to other forms of psychopathology. However, equally fundamental issues have been almost unrecognized and remain unexamined.

THE CHALLENGE OF ASSESSMENT IN CULTURAL CONTEXT

The Difference Culture Makes

Culture may place differential emphasis on particular symptoms, assign unique attributions to the intensity of their experience as well as expression, and shape the general tone of emotional life to which a person should aspire. Thus, distinguishing among mood, symptom, and disorder, which are presumed to vary along a continuum, is not as simple as it might seem (Kleinman & Good, 1985). Although there is little empirical evidence to this effect, current diagnostic operations assume that such experiences are unidimensional, linear, and additive in nature, not unlike a ruler. The cross-cultural literature suggests that the "markers" on the ruler may vary from one group to another akin to the difference between metric and nonmetric systems of measurement. Not only may the scale of measurement differ in terms of minimal unit(s) (e.g., millimeter vs. 1/32 inch), but the significant categories of aggregation may not correspond as well (e.g., centimeter and meter vs. inch, foot, and yard). Assessing the degree to which subjective conditions such as trauma, dysphoria, anxiety, hyperarousal, and avoidance are present in cross-cultural settings, then, is not straightforward, as elegantly demonstrated by McNabb (1990b) in his article on determining the accuracy and meaning of self-reported "satisfaction" among the Eskimo and by Iwata, Okuyama, Kawakami, and Saito (1989) in their report on the Japanese use of Center for Epidemiological Studies—Depression (CES-D) scale values.

Assume that ways are developed to translate from one "ruler" to another, by no means an easy task, even in the simplest form of the problem. This accomplishment does not take into account the normative uncertainty of psychiatric ratings (Chance, 1963; Good & Good, 1986; Guarnaccia, Good, & Kleinman, 1990; Jenkins, 1988; Manson, Shore, & Bloom, 1985; Murphy & Hughes, 1965; Robins, 1989). Specifically, the threshold at which "normal" is demarcated from "abnormal" may vary by gender, ethnicity, and cultural group. For example, the persistently higher prevalence of *symptoms* of depressed mood and anxiety reported among females than males and among Puerto Ricans than White, middle-class Americans (Guarnaccia et al., 1990) may represent culturally patterned variations in the experiential levels of these phenomena and not necessarily higher rates of *disorder*. Consequently, such normative differences imply different "cutoff points" for distinguishing common, unremarkable episodes of mood from those that are unusual and noteworthy. Current DSM debate over the number of symptoms required to meet Criterion C (persistent avoidance or psychic numbing) for PTSD reflects an analogous struggle to establish a viable "cutoff point."

The DSM, however, employs more than just intensity or severity in rendering such judgments. Duration often figures into the diagnostic calculus, for example, 2 weeks of persistent dysphoria to meet criterion for major depressive episode or 1 month for PTSD. Nevertheless, the same logic applies. For example, among the Hopi, sadness and worry are so common and widespread that periods of 1 month or more may be required to reach a level of significance for the individual *and* fellow community members equivalent to that presupposed by the DSM (Manson et al., 1985). Even then, it appears as if duration is but a "proxy" measure of functional impairment. The sadness or worry experienced by a Hopi person becomes a concern when he or she begins to fail to meet deeply ingrained social expectations.

Capturing and Employing Cultural Knowledge

Issues of this nature long have been debated, typically under the rubric of the "emic/etic" distinction, an analogy drawn from descriptive linguistics that attempts to capture the important differences between "insider" and "outsider" views of phenomena and their meaning. There are clear methodological implications of this distinction, especially for highly structured forms of inquiries such as surveys and diagnostic protocols (Bravo, Canino, Rubio-Stepic, Woodbury-Farina, 1991; Freidenberg, Mulvihill, & Caraballo, 1993; Kleinman, 1980; Manson, 1995; McNabb, 1990a; Rogler, 1989). The *American Indian Vietnam Veteran Project* (AIVVP), a study conducted by the National Center for American Indian and Alaska Native Mental Health Research (NCAIANMHR), provides several relevant illustrations.

A central goal of the AIVVP is to conduct a culturally sensitive epidemiological and clinical study that parallels the NVVRS (Manson et al., 1996). The ensuing effort recognizes the importance of standardized comparison as well as possible cultural-bias in the original survey instruments, which were designed largely for administration to White, African American, and Hispanic Vietnam veterans. Unfortunately, this dual concern with replication and cultural validity is problematic, as noted by the foregoing discussion.

Although standardized instruments provide a means for comparison across subgroups or populations, they possess significant deficiencies when employed cross-culturally, especially in light of language differences. Even when respondents from another culture speak English, the use of standardized instruments remains potentially problematic for several reasons.

First, questions that appear in standardized instruments may be *incomprehensible* to members of different ethnocultural groups. For example, among some AIVVP respondents, a question that asks about "feeling as if you were going mad" was interpreted as a question about anger rather than about one's sanity.

Second, some questions may be *unacceptable* to respondents from another culture. For example, asking whether an American Indian respondent has ever abused peyote, a powerful Indian medicine, must be approached with care and respect. It should not simply be included in a list of questions about other types of potentially abused drugs.

Third, some questions may prove *irrelevant* cross-culturally. Consider, for example, a typical query about social support: "About how often have you visited with friends at their homes during the past month? (*Do not count relatives.*)" Especially within reservation communities, the extent and importance of kin-based relationships dictate that most friends are relatives, and that friends frequently are referred to in familial terms. Indeed, within this setting, a friend who is not a relative has little meaning or relevance to the notion of social support.

Finally, other questions may either pose *incomplete* answers or fail to consider local equivalents. For example, an interview of Indian veterans' service utilization patterns that asks extensively about state and Department of Veterans Affairs health services, but ignores the Indian Health Service, tribal programs, or even traditional healing options, has disregarded critical elements in the local service ecology. Likewise, questions that inquire as to whether the respondent has told a health care professional about a particular problem, as an index of help-seeking behavior and subsequent criterion threshold — but not a traditional healer — has overlooked an important local equivalent that carries similar implications for severity of an illness.

Failure to attend to the potential incomprehensibility, inappropriateness, irrelevance, and incompleteness of the questions posed by standardized instruments when used cross-culturally may have serious consequences. Misclassification, by confounding false-positive and false-negative attributions, can easily occur. *Unexamined,* the use of standardized instruments with American Indians, and other ethnic and cultural groups, can lead to significant under- as well as overreporting of symptoms and syndromes, rendering the diagnosis equivocal and comparisons with other groups tenuous (Penk & Allen, 1991).

Under congressional mandate to replicate the NVVRS, the NCAIANMHR was required to employ the instruments from that study, which included the Diagnostic Interview Schedule (later replaced by the Composite International Diagnostic Interview) and the Structured Clinical Interview for Diagnosis. However, in the interests of cultural validity, certain methods were implemented to examine explicitly the capacities and limitations of these instruments. Specifically, two approaches were adopted.

The first approach addressed the form and content of the instruments themselves. Here, a method known as focus group interviews was used to obtain direct comment on and suggested revisions of the comprehensibility, acceptability, relevance, and completeness of interview items and areas of inquiry. In the AIVVP, one or two facilitators convened small groups of 4–10 participants from among tribal members at each of the reservation communities that comprised the study sites. Each group met for eight to ten 2-hour sessions over a 2-month period. Participants were recruited from segments of the local communities, namely, Vietnam veterans, relatives of Vietnam veterans, service providers working with Vietnam veterans, and tribal elders. Each had a unique and important perspective on the area of concern. The focus groups were run on a classroom-like model, but reversed, with the participants as teachers and the facilitators as students. Participants were presented with the original NVVRS instrumentation and were systematically asked a series of questions designed to elicit their reactions to the items and suggestions for improvement. These questions included the following:

> "What does this question mean to me?"
> "Is the intended meaning easily understood?"
> "How would I ask this question of someone else?"
> "Might I encounter resistance in obtaining an answer to this question?"
> "How could I rephrase the question to reduce such resistance?"

The lessons taught by these focus groups were wide ranging. However, the implications for assessing the validity of the interview are relatively straightforward. The general notion of war-related trauma as capable of adversely affecting soldiers, a central tenet of PTSD, clearly resonated with local understandings. Moreover, focus group respondents had little difficulty recognizing many, if not most, of the specific symptoms of PTSD as the result of combat-related trauma. Stories of disturbed sleep, intrusive memories, avoidance, hypervigilance, isolation, and other such symptoms abounded.

Yet, despite this finding, it also became evident that certain items and constellations of symptoms were problematic in these communities. Several of these are conveyed within the opening examples of this section. The research team labored arduously to identify such items, to articulate alternatives, to understand the implications that subsequent modifications might pose for issues of comparability, and to devise creative means for informing the instrumentation along such lines. The modifications can be summarized as changes in question wording, length and construction, specificity, and question probes, which entailed offering alternative phrases. For example, based on focus group comment, it became apparent that the standard question in the Composite International Diagnostic Interview (CIDI) with respect to foreshortened future was poorly understood by local tribal members. They suggested the following alternatives, which were incorporated into the interview protocol and asked immediately after the original item:

> "After or since this experience, did you begin to live from day to day?"
> "After or since this experience, did you begin to think you would die early?"

When these two items were included in the diagnostic algorithm as additional possibilities for fulfilling Criterion C, the lifetime prevalence of CIDI-defined PTSD increased from 38.8% to 46.9%. Moreover, concordance between the CIDI and the SCID, which was administered independently by a clinician, improved substantially, from a kappa of .63 to a kappa of .80. Clearly, relevant cultural knowledge can be elicited, incorporated into the assessment process, and may make an important difference in diagnostic and epidemiological outcomes.

The second approach pursued in this study is the addition of context and depth through key informant interviews with veterans, family members, and the community at large, and through anthropological techniques such as participant observation. Particular emphasis has been given to the familial, community, and historical contexts within which the postwar experiences of American Indian Vietnam veterans have unfolded. Understanding these contexts better enables one to assess phenomena beyond symptoms, and functional impairment in particular, which is vitally important to both diagnosis and treatment.

PTSD has enormous impact on a wide spectrum of activities of daily living. There may be, however, major differences among victims across cultures in regard to the degree of such impact within certain domains. For example, interviews in the early phases of the AIVVP repeatedly underscored the devastating consequences that social isolation, avoidance, and psychic numbing—hallmark symptoms of this disorder—have for American Indian veterans' interpersonal relationships, notably with family and clan. Stories often were told by mothers, sisters, and wives of the community's deep respect for their warriors, a status that is honored. Yet, virtually in the same breath, they voiced their frustration, despair, and fear, for these men proved to be distancing, unconnected, and unpredictable. Caught in a dilemma—obliged to defer to and seek counsel from these latter-day warriors, yet unable to relate to them in expected ways—family members find themselves at a loss: the same kind of loss the veterans experience in regard to their own social displacement. The salience of this appears to be much greater for them than for their White counterparts, whose alienation from more nuclear families is unlikely to pose as widespread a disruption of personal identity. Conversely, in Indian communities, higher education and steady employment are more rare and contribute less to male identity than is the case in non-Indian communities. Hence, the inability, due to PTSD, to hold a job or continue formal education is far less impairing among members of the former. Differences of this nature underscore the importance of ascertaining the broader social and cultural contexts that illuminate the impact of disorder on the individual, family, and community.

DSM-IV AND THE CULTURAL FORMULATION: DISCOVERING CONTEXT

Culturally Informed Diagnosis

The need for diagnostic formulations that better capture the complexity of culture, especially in the context of clinical conditions, is not a new revelation (e.g., Strauss, 1991). In this respect, high priority repeatedly has been given, although not previously realized, to the improvement of diagnostic practice by incorporating a cultural dimension in the assessment process (Fabrega, 1987; Good & Good, 1986; Hughes, 1985; Kleinman, 1988a). DSM-IV, for the first time, represents a serious attempt to enact such improvement. This effort was fueled by mounting evidence that clinicians must attend to the patient's personal perspective, to his or her cultural identity, to cultural factors surrounding a patient's illness, to the influence of cultural factors on social environment and functioning, and to intercultural elements of the clinician–patient relationship (Guarnaccia, in press; Jones & Thorne, 1987; Kleinman, 1988b; Kleinman & Lin, 1981).

The move to address these matters began in 1991 with the formation of the NIMH-sponsored Culture and Diagnosis Group, of which I was a member. The history of their labors is chronicled elsewhere (Mezzich, 1995). The idea for a cultural formulation emerged from discussions of the need to add a cultural dimension to the DSM's multiaxial assessment schema. After further deliberation, the NIMH Group concluded that such an approach would not adequately serve the needs of a cultural formulation, which is more complicated and requires greater organizational flexibility. Consequently, a new schema was developed, building upon the five domains indicated earlier. The NIMH Group on Culture and Diagnosis presented this method, for which it had coined the term "Cultural Formulation Guidelines," to the American Psychiatric Association's (APA) DSM-IV Task Force. The Task Force responded positively, but required pilot testing that subsequently was undertaken by the group, focusing on the four major U.S. ethnic minority populations: African Americans, American Indians, Asian Americans, and Hispanics. The results demonstrated the utility of the guidelines; the APA Task Force accepted the NIMH Group's recommendations and included the guidelines as Appendix I of the DSM-IV.

The DSM-IV Outline for Cultural Formulation is as follows:

> The following outline for cultural formulation is meant to supplement the multiaxial diagnostic assessment and to address difficulties that may be encountered in applying DSM-IV criteria in a multicultural environment. The cultural formulation provides a systematic review of the individual's cultural background, the role of the cultural context in the expression and evaluation of symptoms and dysfunction, and the effect that cultural difference may have on the relationship between the individual and the clinician.
>
> As indicated in the introduction to the manual . . . , it is important that the clinician take into account the individual's ethnic and cultural context in the evaluation of each of the DSM-IV axes. In addition, the cultural formulation suggested below provides an opportunity to describe systematically the individual's cultural and social reference group and ways in which cultural context is relevant to clinical care. The clinician may provide a narrative summary for each of the following categories:
>
> **Cultural identity of the individual.** Note the individual's ethnic or cul-

tural reference groups. For immigrants and ethnic minorities, note separately the degree of involvement with both the culture of origin and the host
culture (where applicable). Also note language abilities, use, and preferences (including multilingualism).

Cultural explanation of the individual's illness. The following may be
identified: the predominant idioms of distress through which symptoms
or the need for social support are communicated (e.g., "nerves," possess-
ing spirits, somatic complaints, inexplicable misfortune), the meaning and
perceived severity of the individual's symptoms in relation to norms of the
cultural reference group, any local illness category used by the individual's family and community to identify the condition (see "Glossary of Culture-
Bound Syndromes"), the perceived causes or explanatory models that the
individual and the reference group use to explain the illness, and current
preferences for and past experiences with professional and popular sources
of care.

**Cultural factors related to psychosocial environment and levels of func-
tioning.** Note culturally relevant interpretations of social stressors, available social supports, and levels of functioning and disability. This would
include stresses in the local social environment and the role of religion
and kin networks in providing emotional, instrumental, and informational support.

**Cultural elements of the relationship between the individual and clini-
cian.** Indicate differences in culture and social status between the individual
and the clinician and problems that these differences may cause in diagnosis and treatment (e.g., difficulty in communicating in the individual's
first language, in eliciting symptoms or understanding their cultural significance, in negotiating an appropriate relationship or level of intimacy,
in determining whether a behavior is normative or pathological).

Overall cultural assessment for diagnosis and care. The formulation concludes with a discussion of how cultural considerations specifically influence
comprehensive diagnosis and care. (American Psychiatric Association, 1994,
pp. 843–844)

The APA Task Force did not support the inclusion of the exemplar cases
developed by the NIMH Group, which were intended to illustrate the application of the guidelines. Consequently, the NIMH Culture and Diagnosis
Group is producing *Introduction to the Cultural Formulation,* a short instructional manual, and a *Cultural Casebook,* which will demonstrate the use of the
guidelines across socially and culturally diverse circumstances.

As noted at the outset of this chapter, the DSM-IV includes as well cultural considerations that appear in text specific to the major disorders. This
new information was developed and negotiated by the NIMH Culture and
Diagnosis Group in much the same way as the Outline for Cultural Formulation. With respect to PTSD, the relevant text reads:

Individuals who have recently emigrated from areas of considerable social unrest and civil conflict may have elevated rates of Posttraumatic Stress
Disorder. Such individuals may be especially reluctant to divulge ex-

periences of torture and trauma due to their vulnerable political immigrant status. Specific assessments of traumatic experiences and concomitant symptoms are need for such individuals. (American Psychiatric Association, 1994, p. 426)

DSM-IV, of course, introduced a new diagnostic category, acute distress disorder, which is pertinent to this discussion. It was added to describe acute reactions to extreme stress, defined in the same way as Criterion A for PTSD, but differs in terms of duration (lasting from 2 days to 4 weeks) with onset no more than 4 weeks after occurrence of the stressor. Here, too, DSM-IV alerts the clinician to possible cultural variation:

Although some events are likely to be universally experienced as traumatic, the severity and pattern of response may be modulated by cultural differences in the implications of loss. There may also be culturally prescribed coping behaviors that are characteristic of particular cultures. For example, dissociative symptoms may be a more prominent part of the acute stress response in cultures in which such behaviors are sanctioned. For further discussion of cultural factors related to traumatic events, see p. 426. (American Psychiatric Association, 1994, p. 430)

Combined, these admonitions anticipate, in an extremely brief fashion, some of the concerns raised earlier. But how does one use this new element to augment the assessment process?

The Wounded Spirit: A Cultural Formulation of PTSD

The cultural formulation is intended to augment, not replace, a careful clinical history. The following case depicts one way in which this procedure can enrich the diagnostic endeavor and provide important insights into the patient's condition and subsequent care.

Clinical History

Patient Identification. J. is a 45-year-old Indian male, married, the father of four sons and three daughters, ages 8 to 20. He, his wife, and five of their children live in a small, rural community on a large reservation in Arizona. His wife has a part-time job in a tribal human services program and sells craft items, which she makes. J. is sporadically employed as a manual laborer. The family maintains some sheep and, during summer months, relocates to a seasonal camp. J. served as a Marine Corps infantry squad leader in Vietnam during 1968–1969. He most recently was seen on an outpatient basis through the Gallup-based VA medical program, where he participates in an all-Indian PTSD support group.

History of Present Illness and Treatment. J. acknowledges alcoholism among two of his four brothers and his father's likely history of PTSD. His father is a World War II combat veteran who served in the Pacific Theater. The onset of J.'s symptoms occurred in early 1969, while he was in Vietnam. He spent most of his tour in the bush, on patrol, conducting ambushes involving heavy combat. J. reported some racial discrimination, notably being called "Chief," always expected to serve as point on patrols because he is Indian, and several near brushes with death when he was mistaken for the enemy by his fellow infantrymen. He suffered from serious shrapnel injuries to the chest; right arm; and hand, of which he recovered only partial use.

That year J. experienced intrusive thoughts almost daily, became hypervigilant, and began to exhibit a range of avoidant symptoms. He felt alienated from others and gradually withdrew from extended social contact. J.'s affect became more restricted; he struggled to avoid thinking about traumatic events. The possibility of dying at any time preoccupied him. His sleep was seriously disturbed; J. reported distressing dreams, often awakening drenched in sweat. He became noticeably irritated, often angry. Sudden flashbacks of combat were common and unpredictable.

Whereas J. previously had drunk alcohol in binge-like fashion, in 1969, while recovering from his wounds, he began to drink heavily on a daily basis. This abated somewhat once he returned home. From 1970 through 1990, his drinking remained highly problematic, characterized by frequent multiday binges, with intermittent periods of sobriety. J. reports numerous occasions on which he had lost consciousness while drinking. He denied more than experimental use of marijuana and cocaine. From 1970 through 1990 he was arrested repeatedly for assault, public intoxication, and D.W.I.

On at least five separate occasions, between 1975 and 1990, J. was treated through tribal outpatient programs for alcohol dependence. In 1990, shortly after the death of his father due to a heart attack, and after his wife threatened to leave him, he entered an Indian-operated, residential alcohol-treatment program in a distant city. That program linked J. with the local VA Medical Center, where he was evaluated extensively, determined to be suffering from PTSD, and, after completing treatment for his alcoholism, transferred to an inpatient unit specializing in the treatment of combat trauma. After attending 1 month of the 12-week course, J. left the program against medical advice, sober, but still experiencing significant PTSD symptoms. He returned to the reservation. Some months later, through local outreach, J. learned of the Gallup support group, which he attended off and on—except during summers—for 2 years. J. has remained sober, but periodically experiences difficulty sleeping, flashbacks, and bursts of anger—albeit less frequently than before. He continues to feel "on guard," and "a little uneasy" around people. J. still has dreams of his dead soldier companions, in which they summon him to join them. But he knows that he cannot. He occasionally hears his father voice "speaking Indian" to him, which is more comforting than fearful, but nonetheless troublesome.

Social and Developmental History. J. was born in an Indian Health Service hospital on his reservation; there were no complications during delivery.

He grew up in a small, rural community with his parents and seven siblings — of which he is the second oldest — living in a housing cluster that included his maternal grandparents and two maternal aunts and their immediate families. J. experimented with alcohol on several occasions during his early teens but reported no serious consequences. He attended boarding school some distance from his home. J. disliked school, describing it as "very difficult" and the teachers as "harsh." Upon further inquiry, he reported frequent and severe beatings by school staff with a belt for being disobedient, like many of the other boys. J. quit midway through his junior year in high school to "help out at home." Eighteen months later, like his father and two uncles before him, he enlisted in the Marines. He married in 1971, shortly after his return to the United States and honorable discharge from the military. J. and his wife established a household near her parents, approximately 70 miles from his natal home, where they continue to reside. He recently began taking GED classes at the tribal community college, works seasonally in construction, and plans to seek vocational training.

Family History. Several male members on both sides of J.'s family have obvious alcohol problems, including two younger siblings. His father, as noted earlier, also appeared to suffer from PTSD, be plagued by nightmares, display unpredictable irritation, and avoid certain activities. J.'s father, previously alcohol dependent as well, had been sober for the 20 years prior to his death.

Course and Outcome. Faced with his father's death, possible divorce by his wife, and loss of his children, J. confronted his alcohol dependence and successfully completed residential treatment. This treatment environment enabled him to examine his use of alcohol as it related to his military experience, one of the first times that he reported talking about the latter outside of his circle of "drinking buddies," virtually all of whom were themselves Indian Vietnam combat veterans. J.'s participation in the VA-PTSD treatment program occurred soon after. However, being the only Indian in the program, greater intensity of intervention and protracted absence from family led to his early departure. J. remains open to counseling for his combat-related trauma and, as noted, has attended a local VA support group.

Diagnostic Formulation

Axis I: 309.81 Posttraumatic Stress Disorder, Chronic
303.90 Alcohol Dependence with Physiological Dependence, Sustained Partial Remission

Axis II: Undetermined

Axis III: 959.4 Injury, hand

Axis IV: Current:
Marital difficulties, moderate Residual grief for loss of father, mild

Past:
    Combat-related trauma, extreme
    Marital difficulties, extreme
    Unemployment, extreme
    Childhood physical abuse, moderate
    Poverty, moderate
    Racial discrimination, moderate
Axis V: Highest past year: GAF = 75
        Current: GAF = 80

Cultural Formulation

This is a complex presentation of an American Indian patient with multiple problems: combat-related trauma, alcohol dependence, a history of childhood physical abuse, and bereavement. Accurate assessment and treatment of his long-term PTSD symptoms initially were precluded by the focus on his alcoholism, which was inevitable, given the particular array of services available in his community and a lack of awareness of PTSD in general. Once his alcohol abuse was controlled, J. sought appropriate guidance and treatment for his trauma-related symptoms, first from the VA and subsequently from traditional cultural resources. J.'s bicultural identity allowed him to be open to different modalities of help, but it also presented challenges for both Indian and non-Indian providers to understand fully his needs and resources. The restricted nature of culturally prescribed mourning practices in his tribe, coupled with severe drinking at the time of his father's death, may have contributed to still unresolved grief.

Cultural Identity. J. is a full-blooded (4/4's quantum) and an enrolled member of a Southwestern American Indian tribe residing largely in Arizona; both of his parents also are tribal members, as are his wife and children.

He speaks and understands English moderately well. J. is fluent in his native language, speaking it most of the time in his home setting among family and friends. The children also are conversant in his native language, but generally more adept than he in English, which is predominant in school and among their peers.

On his mother's side, J. is a descendant of a family of medicine people, hand-tremblers (diagnosticians) among the women and singers (healers) among the men. Consequently, there have been expectations that he would play a leadership role in the cultural and spiritual life of the community. Boarding school interrupted J.'s participation in some of the important aspects of local ceremonial life, but his mother's family worked hard to include him in critical events.

J.'s severe and frequent physical punishment at boarding school was related to issues of identity. He was beaten regularly by non-Indian staff for speaking his native language, for wearing his hair long, and for running away on a number of occasions—all home to his family. J., afraid of ridicule and harassment, attributes his reluctance to share the cultural aspects of his personal background with fellow infantry men to this experience.

Except for military service, and treatment-related absences, J. has lived on the reservation all of his life. The boarding school that he attended was located on a reservation, but more than 100 miles from his home community. During childhood, J. was involved in tribal ceremonial life, orchestrated by his mother's family through clan affiliations. He is a member of the Native American Church, as was his father. J. has begun to take an active part in powwows, prompted by his recent joining of a local gourd society— originally a southern plains phenomenon that has diffused to many other tribes. A gourd society is a men's group comprised of military veterans that serves to honor warriors, provide mutual support, and dances together in public celebrations.

J. is moderately bicultural. Regular interaction with non-Indians has been limited to school, the military, and human service contacts (e.g., the VA and Indian Health Service [IHS]). Although mildly uncomfortable in non-Indian settings, J.'s military experience provided him with important social skills for transitioning to and from majority environments.

Cultural Considerations of Patient's Illness. The pattern of symptoms presented by J. is widely acknowledged as a real problem in his community, although it has no consistently specific label in local terms. Until recently, tribal members had never heard of PTSD, but now have, and sometimes refer to it as the "wounded spirit." J.'s culture typically employs etiological rather than descriptive categories to refer to illness. Here, the consequences of being a warrior and participating in combat have long been recognized. Indeed, a ceremony has evolved to prevent as well as treat the underlying causes of these consequences.

There is considerable cultural shaping of J.'s problem drinking and subsequent alcohol dependence. Talking about the traumas that J. experienced poses various risks for him and fellow Indian veterans, risks that are psychologically, historically, and culturally constructed. Few contexts are relatively free from these risks in their community. One of them, however, is group drinking, most often with other veterans. Recognition of the risks of talking and the culturally ascribed role of alcohol as excusing such talk helps to explain, at one level, why J. maintained a lifestyle of heavy drinking for 20 years after his return from Vietnam. The resurrection of the agony, fear, guilt, sorrow, and horror associated with combat is done while being "blanked out," to use the local term. Veterans have no memory of what transpires when they were drinking, what they talked about, whether they wept, or who fought. It is this ability of alcohol—to enable one to disclose intimate details about "Nam," and yet, at the same time, forget it, even for a brief moment—that many Indian veterans cite as the most important reason for their drinking.

J.'s hearing his father's voice years following the death is not considered by his tribal community to be out of the ordinary. However, it is uncommon to talk openly about these experiences or to dwell at much length on the death of a loved one. Either pose, a serious risk to the individual and to those around him. Thus, J., who was not able to participate in the brief, intense period of ritual mourning at the time of his father's death, but now is capable of doing so, finds few cultural avenues open to him to resolve this enormous sense of loss.

As noted earlier, J. attends a VA-sponsored support group comprised entirely of all Indian Vietnam veterans. This group functions as an important substitute for the circle of "Indian drinking buddies" from whom J. separated as a part of his successful alcohol treatment. The regular summer hiatus in his attendance relates to familial responsibilities, namely sheepherding at summer camps and powwow activities, which bridge his absences from the support group. The same-ethnicity composition of the VA support group proved to be important to J. His discomfort with the brief PTSD inpatient experience stemmed from different styles of disclosure, expectations in regard to reflexivity, and therapeutic group membership defined exclusively on the basis of status as a combat veteran.

Until 1991, J. had participated sporadically in the Native American Church. His reimmersion in it, and now steady involvement, provides an understanding of the forces that led to his drinking, ongoing reinforcement of the decision to remain sober, and encouragement to continue positive life changes. The roadman who leads the services that J. regularly attends is himself a Vietnam combat veteran. Thus, much of the symbolism contained in the ritual structure (e.g., an altar shaped as a combat-V; Marine flag upon which the staff, eagle feather fan, and sage are placed) are relevant to this other dimension of J.'s identity.

J. feels that he is ready to benefit from the major tribal ceremonial intended to bless and purify its warriors. His family is busily preparing for that event, which is quite costly and labor intensive.

Cultural Factors Related to Psychosocial Environment and Levels of Functioning. Steady employment opportunities are rare in J.'s community. Thus, he has chosen to attend community college to complete his GED and prepare for vocational training. This is not easy, but is made possible by the shared resources (food, money, transportation) of the large extended family with whom he resides. Work is sporadic for him, but he readily seeks odd jobs.

J. received active encouragement from family and the community as he began to work seriously on sobriety and recovery from war trauma. Introduced through Native American Church contacts, members of a local gourd society sought him out and invited him to join them. He did and participates in their activities with increasing frequency.

As a consequence of this support, J. just entered a physical rehabilitation program at VA center, which has helped him to cope better with the handicap posed by his injured hand. Previously, the mere mention of this disability sent him into a hostile rage, with a lengthy tirade—not entirely unfounded—about the poor quality and insensitivity of medical care.

J. has begun to visualize social and economic stability in his future. Although challenges remain, notably the successful resolution of remaining PTSD symptoms, his overall functioning has improved and is expected to continue to do so.

Cultural Elements of the Clinician–Patient Relationship. Upon presentation at the Gallup VA outpatient medical program, J. already had some experience with majority behavioral health services. The primary providers at the program were non-Indian, but experienced in working with veterans from J.'s tribe. Hence, after reviewing his case, they recommended the all-Indian support group, which has worked well. Moreover, his positive experience with these providers increased J.'s respect for their abilities and has led him to seek periodic counseling from them in an adjunctive fashion. This counseling has focused on cognitive-behavioral strategies for managing his anger and on recognizing situations that consistently prove to be problematic for him. Neither they nor he discuss underlying causes in this regard, but focus instead on changing the overt behaviors and how J. thinks about them. J. and his providers have talked about his upcoming ceremonial, for which the latter have voiced support.

Overall Cultural Assessment. J.'s residential alcohol treatment proved effective because it separated J. from his "Indian drinking buddies," addressed issues specific to Native Americans, and allowed him to acknowledge possible links between his problems with alcohol and combat trauma. J.'s initial reticence to seek help from local cultural resources may have been compounded by significant insults to his ethnic identity—early on during boarding school and later in the military—thereby confusing his sense of self. His brief tenure in the PTSD inpatient program underscored the severity of his symptomatology, its relationship to Vietnam, and commonality among combat veterans. However, the alien nature of that treatment experience also emphasized the need for something different, more familiar, which J. initially found in the Indian Vietnam veteran support group.

J.'s comfort with this support group enabled him to explore more deeply, in a culturally appropriate fashion, his combat trauma, and also awakened him to the physical abuse he suffered in boarding school: something shared with many of these veterans. A sense of ethnic pride emerged from the bonding that ensued; moreover, he felt able to seek more narrowly defined help from non-Indian providers at the Gallup VA program. These gains facilitated his joining a local gourd society, which further reinforced feelings of belonging, connection, and dignity as a warrior.

Cultural values surrounding family and a large, extended kin network have kept important resources in place for J., even during times when he severely tested those commitments. He now is drawing upon them as he pursues significant self-improvement.

Involvement in the Native American Church has helped J. to struggle effectively with the reasons for his drinking, to continue self-reflection, and to maintain a life plan. That the roadman also is a Vietnam War veteran encourages further attention to shared traumatic experiences and the ways in which one may seek to escape their memory.

J. has a great deal of work before him. His PTSD symptoms are impairing. He looks hopefully to the tribal ceremonial to assist with the resolution of their cause. Continued work with VA counselors, the support group, and the gourd society may have long-term benefits along these lines as well. Perhaps most difficult is the residual grief over the death of his father. The options within his culture by which to process these feelings are less clear.

CONCLUSION

This chapter has attempted to reframe the focus, for the researcher and clinician, on issues of ethnicity and culture in the assessment of trauma and PTSD. Cries for reliable and valid methods abound, often leading us to consider issues of survey techniques, symptom frequencies, psychometric properties, underlying dimensional structures, definitions of impairment, measures of ethnic identity, and the like. All are important, and with sufficient time, effort, and resources, can be resolved within the current limits of our understanding of ethnicity and culture.

The biggest challenge facing us, however, is to revisit our assumptions along these lines, to explore new ways of eliciting the specialized knowledge and experiences that such concepts represent, and to develop useful, practical means for employing that knowledge to better inform clinical work and research. Not, in my experience, easy tasks, or ones truly valued, despite protestations otherwise. The questions raised are often provocative and defy easy solution. As a colleague once said to me, "These are interesting issues, but they slow things down." He is correct. Yet it is an exciting challenge that can, if undertaken seriously, invigorate one's own efforts and expand theoretical as well as programmatic understanding of trauma and PTSD, with great potential benefit for the individuals, families, and communities who, after all, suffer the consequences.

ACKNOWLEDGMENTS

The preparation of this chapter was supported in part by NIMH R01 MH42473-09 and K02 MH00833-05. I gratefully acknowledge insights shared by my colleagues, particularly Drs. Jan Beals, Theresa O'Nell, and Candace Fleming. As always, special thanks and appreciation to the American Indian Vietnam combat veterans and their families, who continue to give so much of themselves for fellow veterans.

REFERENCES

Aberle, D. F. (1966). *The Peyote Religion among the Navaho.* Chicago: University of Chicago Press.

Allodi, F. (1991). Assessment and treatment of torture victims: A critical review. *Journal of Nervous and Mental Disease, 179,* 4–11.

American Psychiatric Association. (1994). *Diagnostic and statistical manual of mental disorders* (4th ed.). Washington, DC: Author.

Barse, H. (1994). American Indian veterans and families. *American Indian and Alaska Native Mental Health Research, 6*(1), 39–47.

Boehnlein, J. (1987a). Clinical relevance of grief and mourning among Cambodian refugees. *Social Science and Medicine, 25,* 765–772.

Boehnlein, J. (1987b). Culture and society in post-traumatic stress disorder: Implications for psychotherapy. *American Journal of Psychotherapy, 41,* 519–530.

Bravo, M., Canino, G. J., Rubio-Stepic, M., & Woodbury-Farina, M. (1991). A cross-cultural adaptation of a psychiatric epidemiologic instrument: The Diagnostic Interview Schedule's adaptation in Puerto Rico. *Culture, Medicine and Psychiatry, 15,* 275–295.

Breslau, N., Davis, G., Andreski, P., & Peterson, E. (1991). Traumatic events and post-traumatic stress disorder in an urban population of young adults. *Archives of General Psychiatry, 48,* 216–222.

Brown, J. E. (1971). *The sacred pipe: Black Elk's account of the seven rites of the Oglala Sioux.* Baltimore: Penguin.

Calabrese, J. D. (1994). Reflexivity and transformation symbolism in the Navajo peyote meeting. *Ethos, 22*(4), 494–527.

Carter, J. (1982). Alcoholism in Black Vietnam veterans: Symptoms of post-traumatic stress disorder. *Journal of the National Medical Association, 74,* 655–660.

Chance, N. (1963). Conceptual and methodological problems in cross-cultural health research. *American Journal of Public Health, 52,* 410–417.

de Girolamo, G. (1993). International perspectives in the treatment and prevention of post traumatic stress. In J. P. Wilson & B. Raphael (Eds.), *International handbook of traumatic stress syndromes* (pp. 935–946). New York: Plenum Press.

Dressler, W. (1985). Extended family relationships, social support and mental health in a Southern black community. *Journal of Health and Social Behavior, 26,* 39–48.

Dressler, W. (1987). The stress process in a southern black community: Implications for prevention research. *Human Organization, 46,* 211–220.

Fabrega, H. (1987). Psychiatric diagnosis: A cultural perspective. *Journal of Nervous and Mental Disease, 175,* 383–394.

Farella, J. R. (1984). *The main stalk: A synthesis of Navajo philosophy.* Tucson: University of Arizona Press.

Freidenberg, J., Mulvihill, M., & Caraballo, L. R. (1993). From ethnography to survey: Some methodological issues in research on health seeking in East Harlem. *Human Organization, 52*(2), 151–161.

Friedman, M., & Jaranson, J. (1993). The applicability of the PTSD concept to refugees. In A. Marsella, T. Borneman, S. Ekblad, & J. Orley (Eds.), *Amidst peril and pain: The mental health and social well-being of the world's refugees* (pp. 207–228). Washington, DC: American Psychological Association Press.

Good, B. J., & Good, M. J. (1986). The cultural context of diagnosis and therapy: A view from medical anthropology. In M. Miranda & H. Kitano (Eds.), *Research and practice in minority communities* (pp. 36–43). Washington, DC: U.S. Government Printing Office.

Guarnaccia, P. J. (in press). Comments on culture and multiaxial diagnosis. In J. E. Mezzich, A. Kleinman, H. Fabrega, D. Parron, (Eds.), *Culture and psychiatric diagnosis*. Washington, DC: American Psychiatric Press.

Guarnaccia, P. J., Good, B. J., & Kleinman, A. (1990). A critical review of epidemiological studies of Puerto Rican mental health. *American Journal of Psychiatry, 147,* 1449–1456.

Holm, T. (1994). The National Survey of Indian Vietnam Veterans. *American Indian and Alaska Native Mental Health Research, 6*(1), 18–28.

Hughes, C. C. (1985). Culture-bound or construct-bound? In R. C. Simons & C. C. Hughes, (Eds.), *The culture bound syndromes* (pp. 3–41). Dordrecht, The Netherlands: Reidel.

Iwata, N., Okuyama, Y., Kawakami, Y., & Saito, K. (1989). Prevalence of depressive symptoms in a Japanese occupational setting: A preliminary study. *American Journal of Public Health, 70,* 1486–1489.

Jaranson, J. (1990). Mental health treatment of refugees and immigrants. In W. H. Holtzman & T. H. Borneman, (Eds.), *Mental health of immigrants and refugees* (pp. 207–215). Austin, TX: Hogg Foundation.

Jenkins, J. H. (1988). Conceptions of schizophrenia as a problem of nerves: A cross-cultural comparison of Mexican-Americans and Anglo-Americans. *Social Science and Medicine, 26*(2), 1233–1244.

Jones, E. E., & Thorne, A. (1987). Rediscovery of the subject: Intercultural approaches to clinical assessment. *Journal of Consulting and Clinical Psychology, 55,* 488–495.

Jordan, K., Schlenger, W., Hough, R., Kulka, R. A., Weiss, D., Fairbank, J. A., & Marmar, C. R. (1991). Lifetime and current prevalence of specific psychiatric disorders among Vietnam veterans and controls. *Archives of General Psychiatry, 48,* 205–215.

Kinzie, J. D. (1985). Cultural aspects of psychiatric treatment with Indochinese patients. *American Journal of Social Psychiatry, 1,* 47–53.

Kinzie, J. D., & Fleck, J. (1987). Psychotherapy with severely traumatized Cambodian refugees. *American Journal of Psychotherapy, 41,* 82–94.

Kinzie, J. D., Frederickson, R., Ben, R., Fleck, J., & Karls, W. (1984). Post-traumatic stress disorder among survivors of Cambodian concentration camps. *American Journal of Psychiatry, 141,* 645–650.

Kinzie, J. D., & Leung, P. (1989). Clonidine in Cambodian patients with PTSD. *Journal of Nervous and Mental Disease, 177,* 546–550.

Kinzie, J. D., Tran, K., Breckenridge, A., & Bloom, J. (1980). An Indochinese refugee clinic: Culturally accepted treatment approaches. *American Journal of Psychiatry, 137,* 1429–1432.

Kleinman, A. (1980). *Patients and healers in the context of culture: An exploration of the borderland between anthropology, medicine and psychiatry.* Berkeley: University of California Press.

Kleinman, A. (1988a). *The illness narratives: Suffering, healing and the human condition.* New York: Basic Books.

Kleinman, A. (1988b). *Rethinking psychiatry: From cultural category to personal experience.* New York: Free Press.

Kleinman, A., & Good, B. (Eds.). (1985). *Culture and depression.* Berkeley: University of California Press.

Kleinman, A., & Lin, T. Y. (1981). *Normal and abnormal psychology in Chinese culture.* Boston: Redeil.

Kluckhohn, C., & Leighton, D. (1974). *The Navaho* (rev ed.). Cambridge, MA: Harvard University Press.

Krippner, S., & Colodzin, B. (1989). Multicultural methods of treating Vietnam veterans with PTSD. *International Journal of Psychosomatics, 36,* 79–85.

Kulka, R. A., Schlenger, W. E., Fairbank, J. A., Hough, R. L., Jordan, B. K., Marmar, C. R., & Weiss, D. S. (1990). *Trauma and the Vietnam War generation: Report of findings from the National Vietnam Veterans Readjustment Study.* New York: Brunner/Mazel.

Lee, E., & Lu, F. (1989). Assessment and treatment of Asian-American survivors of mass violence. *Journal of Traumatic Stress, 2,* 93–120.

Manson, S. M. (1995). Culture and major depression: Current challenges in the diagnosis of mood disorders. *Psychiatric Clinics of North America, 18*(3), 487–501.

Manson, S. M., Beals, J., O'Nell, T., Piasecki, J., Bechtold, D. W., Keane, E., & Jones, M. (1996). Wounded spirits, ailing hearts: PTSD and related disorders among American Indians. In A. Marsella, M. Friedman, E., Gerrity, & R. M. Scurfield, (Eds.), *Ethnocultural variation in trauma and PTSD* (pp. 255–283). New York: American Psychological Association Press.

Manson, S. M., Shore, J. H., & Bloom, J. D. (1985). The depressive experience in American Indian communities: A challenge for psychiatric theory and diagnosis. In A. Kleinman & B. Good (Eds.), *Culture and depression* (pp. 331–368). Berkeley: University of California Press.

Marsella, A., Friedman, M., Gerrity, E., & Scurfield, R. (Eds.). (1996). *Ethnocultural variation in trauma and PTSD.* New York: American Psychological Association Press.

Marsella, A., Friedman, M. J., & Spain, E. H. (1993). Ethnocultural aspects of posttraumatic stress disorder. In J. M. Oldham, M. B. Riba, & A. Tasman (Eds.), *Review of Psychiatry,* (Vol. 12, pp. 157–182). Washington, DC: American Psychiatric Press.

Maypole, D., & Anderson, R. (1987). Culture-specific substance abuse prevention for blacks. *Community Mental Health Journal, 23,* 135–139.

McNabb, S. L. (1990a). The uses of "inaccurate" data: A methodological critique and applications of Alaska Native data. *American Anthropologist, 92,* 116–129.

McNabb, S. L. (1990b). Self-reports in cross-cultural contexts. *Human Organization, 49*(4), 291–299.

Mezzich, J. E. (1995). Cultural formulation and comprehensive diagnosis. *The Psychiatric Clinics of North America, 18*(3), 649–657.

Mollica, R., Caspi-Yavin, Y., Bollini, P., Truong, T., Tor, S., & Lavelle, J. (1992). The Harvard Trauma Questionnaire: Validating a cross-cultural instrument for measuring torture, trauma, and post-traumatic stress disorder in Indochinese refugees. *Journal of Nervous and Mental Disease, 180*(2), 110–115.

Mollica, R., & Lavelle, J. (1988). The trauma of mass violence and torture: An overview of psychiatric care of the Southeast Asian refugee. In L. Comas-Díaz & E. E. Griffith (Eds.), *Clinical guidelines in cross-cultural mental health* (pp. 262–304). New York: Wiley.

Moos, R. H. (1979). Social ecological perspectives on health. In G. C. Stone, F. Cohen,

& N. E. Adler (Eds.), *Health psychology: A handbook* (pp. 523–547). San Francisco: Jossey-Bass.

Murphy, J. M., & Hughes, C. C. (1965). The use of psychophysiological symptoms as indicators of disorder among Eskimos. In J. M. Murphy & A. H. Leighton (Eds.), *Approaches to cross-cultural psychiatry* (pp. 108–160). Ithaca: Cornell University Press.

Mezzich, J. E., Kirmayer, L. J., Kleinman, A., Fabrega, H., Parren, D., Good, B. J., Lin, K., & Manson, S. M. (1996). *The place of culture DSM-IV.* Manuscript submitted for publication.

Neighbors, H. W. (1990). The prevention of psychopathology in African Americans: An epidemiologic perspective. *Community Mental Health Journal, 26*(2), 167–179.

Neighbors, H. W., Jackson, J., Bowman, P., & Gurin, G. (1983). Stress, coping and black mental health: Preliminary findings from a national study. *Prevention in Human Services, 2,* 4–29.

Palinkas, L. A., Downs, M., Petterson, J. S., & Russell, J. (1993). Social, cultural, and psychological impacts of the *Exxon Valdez* oil spill. *Human Organization, 52*(1), 1–13.

Parson, E. (1985). Ethnicity and traumatic stress: The intersecting point in psychother-apy. In C. Figley (Ed.), *Trauma and its wake: The study of treatment of PTSD* (pp. 314–337). New York: Brunner/Mazel.

Parson, E. (1990). Post-traumatic psychocultural therapy (PTpsyCT): Integration of trauma and shattering social labels of the self. *Journal of Contemporary Psychothera-py, 20,* 237–258.

Penk, W., & Allen, I. (1991). Clinical assessment of post-traumatic stress disorder (PTSD) among American minorities who served in Vietnam. *Journal of Traumatic Stress, 4, 41*–66.

Robins, L. N. (1989). Cross-cultural differences in psychiatric disorder. *American Jour-nal of Public Health, 79*(11), 1479–1480.

Rogler, L. (1989). The meaning of culturally sensitive research in mental health. *Ameri-can Journal of Psychiatry, 146,* 296–303.

Rosser, R. (1986). Reality therapy with the Khmer refugees resettled in the United States. *Journal of Reality Therapy, 6,* 21–29.

Sandner, D. (1979). *Navajo symbols of healing: A Jungian exploration of ritual, image and medicine.* Rochester, VT: Healing Arts Press.

Scurfield, R. M. (1996). Healing the warrior: Admission of two American Indian war-veteran cohort groups to a specialized inpatient PTSD unit. *American Indian and Alaska Native Mental Health Research, 6*(3), 1–22.

Silver, S. (1994). Lessons from Child of Water. *American Indian and Alaska Native Men-tal Health Research, 6*(1), 4–17.

Silver, S., & Wilson, J. (1990). Native American healing and purification rituals for war stress. In J. Wilson, Z. Harel, & B. Kahana (Eds.), *Human adaptation to stress: From the Holocaust to Vietnam* (pp. 337–356). New York: Plenum Press.

Stokols, D. (1991). *Establishing and maintaining healthy environments: Toward a social ecol-ogy of health promotion* (Wellness Lecture Series). Berkeley, CA: University of California Press.

Strauss, J. S. (1991). A comprehensive approach to psychiatric diagnosis. *American Journal of Psychiatry, 132,* 1193–1197.

Wallace, A. F. C. (1966). *Religion: An anthropological view.* New York: Random House.

Westermeyer, J. (1989). Cross-cultural care of PTSD: Research, training, and service needs for the future. *Journal of Traumatic Stress, 2,* 515–536.

Westermeyer, J., & Wahmemholm, K. (1989). Assessing the victimized psychiatric patient: Special issues regarding violence, combat, terror and refuge seeking. *Hospital and Community Psychiatry, 3,* 245–249.

Wilson, J. (1988). Culture and trauma: The sacred pipe revisited. In J. Wilson, Z. Harel, & B. Kahana (Eds.), *Human adaptation to extreme stress: From holocaust to Vietnam* (pp. 38–71). New York: Plenum Press.

Wilson, J. (1989). *Trauma, transformation and healing.* New York: Brunner/Mazel.

Witherspoon, G. (1977). *Language and art in the Navajo universe.* Ann Arbor: University of Michigan Press.

CHAPTER 9

Assessment of Military-Related Posttraumatic Stress Disorder

TERENCE M. KEANE
ELANA NEWMAN
SUSAN M. ORSILLO

INTRODUCTION

Objective measurement of the psychological effects of combat and other military stressors has grown rapidly since the introduction of the third edition of the *Diagnostic and Statistical Manual of Mental Disorders* (DSM-III; American Psychiatric Association, 1980). Studies by Wilson (1979) and Egendorf, Kadushin, Laufer, Rothbart, and Sloan (1981) were among the first attempts to quantify the psychological effects of war as these investigators systematically examined American veterans from Vietnam. Early work by Grinker and Spiegel (1945), Gillespie, (1942), and Kardiner (1941) provided the clear precedent for measurement of the effects of war with veterans from other eras; however, it was 30 years or more before the current classification scheme was developed and conceptual models of the direct effects of overwhelming stressors gained widespread acceptance.

Over the past 15 years, growth in the quantity and quality of instruments to assess posttraumatic stress disorder (PTSD) and traumatic stress exposure can be characterized as exceptional. Initially driven by the demand for instruments to be used in clinic settings, this development has been maintained by studies funded in the public interest to estimate the prevalence of exposure to traumatic events and the development of PTSD in our society. With the recognition that many different types of traumatic experiences lead to PTSD, clinicians and researchers developed many instruments that tend to measure PTSD specifically as it pertains to these diverse life experiences.

This fact alone accounts for much of the proliferation of assessment instruments in the field.

One purpose of this chapter is to review the extant literature on the development and evaluation of instruments that measure combat and war-zone stressor exposure and attendant PTSD. A second purpose of this chapter is to present a method for the assessment of PTSD initially developed in our clinical–research program in Jackson, Mississippi (Keane, Fairbank, Caddell, Zimering, & Bender, 1985), and refined and enhanced in the National Center for PTSD–Boston. This method is premised upon the notion that all measures of a disorder are imperfectly related to the condition, and that multiple measures from different domains improve diagnostic accuracy and confidence. This multimethod approach to assessment of PTSD is valuable clinically, because it taps numerous domains of functioning and thus assists the clinician in identifying numerous targets for intervention. It is valuable in research because it increases the likelihood that patients classified as PTSD for research purposes are indeed PTSD.

A third purpose of this chapter is to recognize the changing nature of military activities in the post–Cold War era. As peacekeeping functions and humanitarian efforts increasingly become functions of military troops, they offer unique stressor experiences to which members of the military are exposed. Efforts to quantify these experiences require a specific methodology that will permit the stable measurement of the complex life events for those people who serve in these roles. We offer one possible methodology for clinicians and researchers to employ when confronted with measuring stressor exposure in a unique environment and setting.

Finally, military forces in the United States are becoming increasingly diverse. Racial and ethnic composition of the American military force is changing, and with more minorities involved in military actions, assessment measures must be developed that are culturally sensitive and broadly based to permit accurate evaluations and comparisons across minority groups. Similarly, women are represented in the military in greater numbers than they were historically, and their range of responsibilities and experiences has greatly expanded. Assessment instruments that are, at once, sensitive to different gender-based experiences in military assignments and also representative of women's unique responses to military stressors demand special consideration. The final purpose of this chapter is to focus upon strategies that will assist professionals in the successful development of instruments that meet these criteria.

MULTIMODAL ASSESSMENT

A comprehensive assessment of military-related PTSD requires a thorough evaluation of PTSD symptoms and stressors within a broad-based evaluation of general psychopathology (Keane, Wolfe, & Taylor, 1987). Typical parameters for assessment include the individual's level of functioning within developmental, social, familial, educational, vocational, medical, cognitive, interpersonal, behavioral, and emotional domains across the time periods prior to, during, and subsequent to military service. Such an approach provides an adequate foundation upon which to create accurate diagnostic and case formulations that account for the degree to which any pre- or post-war-zone experiences may contribute to the individual's current level of functioning.

Comprehensive PTSD assessment is best achieved through the use of multiple reliable and valid instruments, since every measure is associated with some degree of error (Keane et al., 1987). Therefore a multimethod approach, combining data derived from self-report measures, structured clinical interviews, and, when possible, psychophysiological assessment is recommended. Such multimodal assessment of PTSD combines each measure's relative strengths, minimizes the psychometric shortcomings of any one instrument, and maximizes correct diagnostic decisions. (See Weathers, Keane, King, & King, Chapter 4, this volume, for detailed information on psychometric theory and terms.)

In addition, the external validity of PTSD assessment can be enhanced by collecting information from multiple informants and available archives. Some individuals with PTSD may have difficulty specifying their symptoms, behaviors, and experiences due to denial, amnesia, avoidance, minimization, cognitive impairment, and/or motivational factors. Therefore, collateral reports from friends, neighbors, partners, family members, or health care providers can provide meaningful information to corroborate and clarify aspects of the individual's experiences. Any consistent patterns of discordance between informants can yield hypotheses about the individual's characteristic attributional style and/or the interpersonal consequences of the individual's behaviors. Similarly, consultation of all relevant archives (e.g., medical, legal, military, and educational records) may provide corroborative data to support and amplify self-reports.

Although comprehensive assessments require measures and methods that assess more than military-related experiences and distress, a review of all potential measures that could be used in multidimensional assessment is beyond the scope of this chapter. Our review will focus upon the most commonly used validated methods and measurement strategies applied specifically to the assessment of military-related PTSD, including measures of exposure, clinical interviews, self-report measures, and psychophysiological assessment. Given the chapter's emphasis on military-related PTSD, considerable weight will be placed on the assessment of exposure to potentially traumatic experiences that occur in the context of military duties. Several unpublished measures and not yet validated measures are included in this review if they have noteworthy features or historical relevance. Unless otherwise indicated, all data are derived from samples of U.S. male military personnel and based on DSM-III-R criteria for PTSD (American Psychiatric Association, 1987).

Evaluation of Exposure to Military-Related, Potentially Traumatic Events

Deployment in a war zone, combat duty or otherwise, does not in and of itself indicate that an individual has experienced a potentially traumatic event (PTE). In order to assess whether an individual was exposed to a PTE during a tour of duty, detailed descriptions of military duties and experiences must be obtained. Although examination of military records can be a helpful adjunct to this assessment, overreliance on these records is ill-advised, since there are often inaccuracies in these documents (e.g., Watson, Juba, & Anderson, 1989).

Although the assessment of military-related PTSD is well advanced scientifically, the assessment of stressor exposure in military and war settings is less well developed. For example, few measures of war-zone stressor exposure have undergone empirical validation, and only one study has compared the relative performance of the multiple combat exposure scales available (Watson et al., 1989). The following brief review identifies the four major conceptual approaches to measuring exposure to war-zone-related PTEs and describes the most popular validated measures within each of these domains. Table 9.1 provides a summary of the number of items, content areas covered, known internal consistency, and available convergence validity with PTSD and/or external corroboration (medals or assigned duty).

Many measures of combat-related PTSD exclusively focus upon detailing the intensity, frequency, and duration of traditional combat experiences involving threat of danger, loss of life, or severe physical injury (Green, 1993). Such exposure has been documented to be a risk factor for PTSD among Vietnam veterans (e.g., Kulka et al., 1990). Although many exposure scales have been developed, few have been empirically cross-validated, and the majority were derived based on experiences of Vietnam veterans. The two most widely used scales that focus exclusively on combat experiences are the 5-item Vietnam Veterans Combat Exposure Scale (Figley & Stretch, 1980) and the 7-item Combat Exposure Scale (Keane et al., 1989).

A second domain of military exposure that is related to PTSD symptoms includes those war-zone experiences outside the realm of traditional combat (e.g., Grady, Woolfolk, & Budney, 1989; Green, Grace, Lindy, & Gleser, 1990a; Yehuda, Southwick, & Giller, 1992). For example, in the context of combat-related activities, many Vietnam War veterans were confronted with guerrilla warfare that included exposure to grotesque death and mutilation, and many forms of abusive violence (e.g., Laufer, Gallops, & Frey-Wouters, 1984). Both the 6-item Military Stress Scale (Watson, Kucala, Manifold, Vassar, & Juba, 1988) and the 7-item Combat Exposure Index (Janes, Goldberg, Eisen, & True, 1991) include an assessment of exposure to such experiences. The 7-item Combat Exposure Scale (Lund, Foy, Sipprelle, & Strachan, 1984) and 10-item Combat Scale—Revised (Gallops, Laufer, & Yager, 1981) include one general item assessing "killing of civilians" that might potentially detect some forms of exposure to abusive violence. In addition, there are several psychometrically validated scales available that focus solely on the assessment of exposure to atrocities, such as the 6-item Atrocity Scale (Brett & Laufer, unpublished cited in Yehuda et al., 1992) and the 5-item Abusive Violence Scale (Hendrix & Schumm, 1990). The 4-item Objective Military Stress Scale (Solomon, Mikulincer, & Hobfoll, 1987), developed for Israeli soldiers during the Lebanon War, has one question regarding evacuation of dead soldiers. A 24-item Graves Registration Duty Scale, developed to assess aspects of handling human remains (e.g., matching or identifying body parts, transporting body parts), was recently validated on a primarily male sample of Persian Gulf Era troop members (Sutker, Uddo, Brailey, Vasterling, & Errera, 1994).

A third approach to assessing war-zone-related exposure to PTEs includes evaluating the many, generally unpleasant parameters of the military experience (e.g., bad environmental conditions; lack of military support; sleep, food, and water deprivation; harassment upon homecoming). Enduring such adversity was found to be a significant predictor of PTSD among both male and female Vietnam veterans (King, King, Gudanowski, & Vreven, 1995a). Wilson and Krause (1980) designed a 46-item "Specific Stressor In Vietnam" subscale in the Vietnam Era Stress Inventory (VESI) that included many items regarding exposure to ongoing harsh daily circumstances (Wilson & Krause, 1989). Despite the breadth and clinical acumen reflected in this scale, only three studies have examined its psychometric properties, and each was based on a modification of the measure (Green et al., 1990a; McFall, Smith, Mackay, & Tarver, 1990a; McFall, Smith, Roszell, Tarver, & Malais, 1990b; Wilson & Prabucki, 1989).

In the 100-item National Vietnam Veterans Readjustment Study (NVVRS) stressor measure (Kulka et al., 1990), several items assessed malevolent conditions related to deprivation and feeling removed from the world, in addition to combat, grotesque death, and abusive violence (Schlenger et al., 1992). Accordingly, a 72-item measure of combat exposure for both men and women was derived from the NVVRS stressor items that assessed perceived threat and malevolent environment in addition to traditional combat and exposure to atrocities (King et al., 1995a). Given that the environment in a war-zone differs substantially for males and females, Wolfe, Brown, Furey and Levin (1993a) developed the Wartime Stressor Scale for Women to assess the social and environmental context for women soldiers, including, for instance, questions about sexual discrimination as well as sexual assault.

The final approach to assessing exposure to military-related PTEs includes assessing the individual's emotional appraisal of events. Criterion A of the DSM-IV PTSD diagnosis (American Psychiatric Association, 1994) specifies that a traumatic event must involve actual or threatened injury to oneself or others (Criterion A1) and engender concomitant feelings of fear, helplessness, or horror (Criterion A2). Since the inclusion of Criterion A2 is a recent addition to the diagnostic nomenclature, none of the previously

TABLE 9.1. Self-Report Measures of Exposure to War-Zone-Related Trauma

Authors	Scale name	Items	Alpha	Relationship to measures of PTSD	Relationship to medals or specified duty	Handling bodies	Abusive violence items	Malevolent environment items
Keane et al. (1989)	Combat Exposure Scale	7	.85	.43 Mississippi Scale	—	0	0	0
Figley & Stretch (1981)	Vietnam Veterans Questionnaire Combat Exposure Scale	5	.93	+ but unspecified (Woolfolk & Grady, 1988)	Medals: $r = .42*$ Duty: $r = .40*$	0	0	0
Watson et al. (1988)	Military Stress Scale	6	—	.57 PTSD Interview	Medals: $r = .29$, ns Duty: $r = .40**$	0	1	0
Janes et al. (1991)	Combat Exposure Index	7	.84	—	***chi-squares for each type of medal noted	1	0	0
Lund et al. (1984); Foy et al. (1984)[a]	Combat Exposure Scale	7	CR = .93	.31 symptom intensity in a nonvalidated PTSD scale; Kendall's tau C	Medals: $r = .20$, ns duty: $r = .19$, ns $(43) = .64****$ for PTSD	0	1 possible item	0
Gallops, Laufer, & Yager (1981)	Combat Scale–Revised[b]	10	.84	—	Medals: $r = .42**$ Duty: $r = .40**$	0	1 possible	0
Solomon et al. (1987)	Objective Military Stress Scale	4	—	—	Medals: $r = .41*$ Duty: $r = .25$, ns	1	0	0

Brett & Laufer (unpublished)	Atrocity Scale	6		.70 Mississippi Scale, .39 Figley PTSD scale	—	—	6	—
Hendrix & Schumm (1990)	Abusive Violence Scale	5	.81	.28* IES intrusion scale .30 IES avoidance scale	—	—	5	—
Sutker et al. (1994)	Graves Registration Duty Scale	24	.88	.27* (number of SCID Criterion B symptoms)	—	24	—	—
Wilson & Krauss (1980)	VESI Stressor Scale	46	.87–.95 (Green et al., 1990a) .94 (McFall et al., 1990b)	Combat .23–.57*** (symptom clusters) Environment .25–.47* (symptom clusters)		1	5	19
Schlenger et al. (1992)	Exposure to War Zone NSVG	100	.74–.94 (median = .87)	18.4% higher rate among high vs. low exposed men; 13.2 for women	70% of men who received purple hearts reported high exposure	—	24—men, 10—women	12—men, 10—women
King et al. (1995)	War Zone Stress Index	72	.83–.94	—	—	0	9	18
Wolfe et al. (1993)	Wartime Stressor Scale for Women	27	.89	0.35 PK*** 0.43 Mississippi Scale***	—	1	0	9

Note. The Solomon scale is based on experiences of Israeli soldiers in the Lebanon War. All other scales are used on Vietnam veterans. Wolfe et al., King et al., and Schlenger et al. have female Vietnam veterans in their sample. — not available; CR, coefficient of reproducibility (reliability measure for a Guttman scale).

[a]This scale is often cited either way.

[b]The original scale was created in 1981 by Egendorf, Boulanger, Kadushin, Laufer, Sloan, and Smith as part of the study conducted by Egendorf, Kadushin, Laufer, Rothbart, and Sloan (1981). The scale is often referenced in three ways.

*$p < .05$; **$p < .01$; ***$p < .001$; ****$p < .0001$.

validated self-report measures includes assessment of all three specified emotional response domains. King et al. (1995a) derived a scale from items used in the NVVRS, which assessed an individual's appraisal of life threat, that can provide information about the respondent's level of fear. Two recently developed but nonvalidated exposure measures, the Potential Stressful Events Interview (Falsetti, Resnick, Kilpatrick, & Freedy, 1994), and the Evaluation of Lifetime Stressors (Krinsley et al., 1994) do have features that assess fear, horror, and helplessness. Both these measures, which include extensive structured interviews, assess lifetime exposure to all potentially traumatic events, including military-related experiences.

Evaluation of PTSD Symptoms among Military Personnel

Structured Clinical Interviews

Several structured interviews are available that have been developed for the assessment of PTSD as modules of comprehensive diagnostic assessment tools or as independent PTSD measures. Modules offer expediency in diagnosis but have typically yielded only dichotomous symptom ratings. Interviews focused solely on PTSD diagnostic criteria often require more time investment, but many yield evaluation of symptoms on a continuum. We will briefly present examples of each type of interview format that can be used to diagnose PTSD among military personnel. Notably, these interviews are all based on DSM-III-R criteria, and await updating to DSM-IV standards.

PTSD modules are available in the Diagnostic Interview Schedule (DIS; Robins, Helzer, Croughan, & Ratcliff, 1981a; Robins, Helzer, Croughan, Williams, & Spitzer, 1981b), the Structured Clinical Interview for DSM-III-R (SCID; Spitzer, Williams, Gibbon, & First, 1990), and the Anxiety Disorders Interview Schedule — Revised (ADIS-R; Blanchard, Gerardi, Kolb, & Barlow, 1986; DiNardo & Barlow, 1988). Of all these measures, the SCID has demonstrated high interrater reliability and is strongly correlated with other measures of PTSD. Although useful in clinical populations, questions about the diagnostic sensitivity of the DIS PTSD module, particularly in community samples (e.g., Keane & Penk, 1988; Kulka et al., 1990), suggest a need for additional psychometric evaluation in field studies.

PTSD structured interviews that have been used with veterans include the Clinician-Administered PTSD Scale (CAPS; Blake et al., 1990; Weathers & Litz, 1994), the PTSD Interview (PTSD-I; Watson, Juba, Manifold, Kucala, & Anderson, 1991), and the Structured Interview for PTSD (SI-PTSD; Davidson, Smith, & Kudler, 1989). Although all these measures performed well, the CAPS is extremely noteworthy; its strengths include good psychometrics (e.g., α coefficient = .94; sensitivity = .84; specificity = .95; κ coefficient = .78), clear behavioral anchors, a time frame concordant with that of DSM diagnostic criteria, and separate frequency and intensity ratings.

Self-Report Measures

Self-report checklists that provide information about PTSD symptomatology can be time- and cost-efficient tools in the multimethod assessment process. They can be combined to maximize efficiency, specificity, or sensitivity of the assessment battery. Many excellent self-report questionnaires are available to assess military-related PTSD; some solely assess diagnostic criteria, some correspond to the diagnostic criteria and their associated features, and other measures broadly sample the content of the disorder. We briefly review the measures that are commonly used in assessments of military personnel.

Several short scales have been developed that assess the 17 diagnostic symptoms of PTSD. Not surprisingly, they all have relatively comparable psychometric qualities, particularly internal consistency. The PTSD Checklist (PCL; Weathers, Litz, Herman, Huska, & Keane, 1993), available in both DSM-III-R and DSM-IV versions, has good sensitivity (.82) and specificity (.83), and is positively correlated with standard measures of PTSD (Mississippi Scale, $r = .93$; MMPI-2-PK Scale, $r = .77$; Impact of Event Scale, $r = .90$). The PTSD Inventory, used with Israeli soldiers deployed in the Lebanon War (I-PTSD; Solomon, 1993) and during the Yom Kippur War (Solomon et al., 1993), was originally validated using DSM-III criteria and has been updated to reflect DSM-III-R criteria. The current version has excellent internal consistency (Cronbach's α coefficient = .86), excellent specificity (.94 for both current and past PTSD), but weak sensitivity (current PTSD = .48, past PTSD = .48). The Purdue Post-Traumatic Stress Scale (Hendrix, Anelli, Gibbs, & Fournier, 1994) and the PTSD scale by Friedman and colleagues (Friedman, Schneiderman, West, & Corson, 1986) both demonstrate good psychometric properties, but are limited in their current applicability, since both are based on DSM-III criteria.

Several validated self-report instruments exist that include PTSD symptoms and diagnosis, and commonly associated features of the disorder. The Self-Rating Inventory for PTSD (SIP; Hovens et al., 1993; Hovens et al., 1994) consists of 47 items designed for use with Dutch World War II resistance fighters and is available in both English and Dutch. The SIP includes trauma-related symptoms such as those classified under the proposed Diagnosis of Extreme Stress Not Otherwise Specified classification (Herman, 1993). Relative to the CAPS, the SIP-PTSD subscale demonstrates excellent sensitivity (.92) and moderate specificity (.61) within a sample of civilian psychiatric outpatients and Dutch resistance fighters. The 43-item Los Angeles Symptom Checklist (LASC; King, King, Leskin, & Foy, 1995b) also appears to be a psychometrically sound measure of PTSD symptoms among Vietnam veterans (α coefficient = .91 for 17-item index and .94 for full index; test–retest reliability = .94 for the 17-item index and .90 for full index), although specificity and sensitivity data from military samples are still needed.

There are several measures that perform quite well in predicting PTSD diagnostic status that are not based directly on DSM diagnostic criteria. In fact, two of the primary self-report measures in the NVVRS, the Keane PTSD Scale of the MMPI (PK scale; Keane, Malloy, & Fairbank, 1984) and the Mississippi Scale for Combat-Related PTSD (Keane, Caddell, & Taylor, 1988) were designed to measure broadly the construct of PTSD. The 49-item MMPI-PK scale and the 46-item MMPI-2 PK have moderate or better psychometric performance, although the sensitivity and specificity of the PK scales have varied from study to study (e.g., Graham, 1993; Keane et al., 1984; Lyons & Keane, 1992; Query, Megran, & McDonald, 1986; Watson, 1990). In studies in which the diagnostic criterion is strongest (e.g., SCID or CAPS), the PK's performance is very good. When more questionable diagnostic criteria are employed (e.g., chart diagnosis), the PK has had more modest success. In addition, the MMPI-2-PK-scale has been shown to work as well when it is applied as a separate measure as it does when embedded within the full MMPI (Graham, 1993; Herman, Weathers, Litz, & Keane, in press; Litz et al., 1991; Lyons & Scotti, 1994).

The 35-item Mississippi Scale for Combat-Related PTSD (Keane et al., 1988), is one of the most widely used PTSD measures among veteran populations (e.g., Kulka et al., 1990; McFall et al., 1990a; Perconte et al., 1993), and is available in numerous languages (e.g., Dutch, Spanish). Three abbreviated versions of the scale also show promising correlations (.90–.96) with the original scale (Fontana & Rosenheck, 1994; Hyer, Davis, Boudewyns, & Woods, 1991; Wolfe, Keane, Kaloupek, Mora, & Wine, 1993c).

The 15-item Impact of Event Scale (IES; Horowitz, Wilner, & Alvarez, 1979; Zilberg, Weiss, & Horowitz, 1982), also used in the NVVRS preliminary validation trial (Kulka et al., 1991), was found to have less useful diagnostic utility than either the PK or Mississippi Scale, but nonetheless performed as a good indicator of PTSD status (sensitivity = .92; specificity = .62; correct classification = 81.6%). The IES has been translated widely and used with many different national military forces (e.g., Kulka et al., 1990; Schwarzwald, Solomon, Weisenberg, & Mikulincer, 1987).

More recently, two other promising scales were developed that broadly cover the domain of traumatic symptomatology. The 26-item Penn Inventory for Posttraumatic Stress (Hammarberg, 1992) contains questions that apply to all trauma types, making it useful for comparing military and civilian samples. It has similar sensitivity (.90), specificity (1.00), and overall efficiency (.94) to the Mississippi Scale.

Weathers and his colleagues (Weathers et al., 1996) derived a 25-item War-Zone-Related PTSD subscale (WZ-PTSD) that is embedded in the Symptom Checklist 90—Revised (SCL-90-R; Derogatis, 1977). In two different samples, this scale has demonstrated that the WZ-PTSD measure clearly outperforms the SCL-90-R Global Severity Index in identifying cases of PTSD.

Psychophysiological Assessment

Psychophysiological assessment can provide unique information on the extent of autonomic hyperarousal and exaggerated startle response in PTSD that is not solely reliant on self-report. In general, combat veterans with PTSD demonstrate significantly more psychophysiological reactivity to combat stimuli than such comparison groups as nonveterans with psychiatric disorders and combat veterans without psychiatric disorders (Prins, Kaloupek, & Keane, 1995), although the specificity of psychophysiological assessment exceeds its sensitivity. A psychophysiological assessment of PTSD usually involves presenting an individual with standardized stimuli (e.g., combat photos, noises, odors) or personalized cues (e.g., taped scripts of their traumatic experiences) of PTEs. Measurements are taken of one or more physiological indices, subjective appraisal (e.g., arousal and distress), and behavior (e.g., visible startle, crying, averting gaze). Psychophysiological indices that can be assessed include heart rate, blood pressure, muscle tension, skin conductance level and response, and peripheral temperature (e.g., Blanchard, Kolb, Pallmeyer, & Gerardi, 1982; Orr et al., 1990; Pitman, Orr, Forgue, de Jong, & Claiborn, 1987; Shalev, Orr, & Pitman, 1992, 1993). Again, since no one psychophysiological index is error free, convergent measures of psychophysiology are recommended. Although psychophysiological assessment once required elaborate and expensive laboratory equipment, portable systems have made this technique more feasible than ever before. Orr and Kaloupek (Chapter 3, this volume) provide a more thorough discussion of the findings from studies of the psychophysiological assessment of PTSD.

Interpretation of the Components of Multimodal Assessment

The ideal battery for the assessment of war-zone-related PTSD incorporates data derived from the multiple methods described earlier. However, inconsistency across these diverse domains is common in multimodal and multidimensional assessment and may result from either measurement artifacts or as manifestations of a varying presentation of the disorder. Distinguishing noise from signal among these multiple measures is a complex task that relies upon expertise in both clinical and empirical domains. Despite the wealth of psychometric data available regarding the performance of individual instruments, few studies are available that examine the relative contributions of particular instruments within a battery to the overall prediction of PTSD status. Two distinct strategies have evolved over time. In the NVVRS, a statistical algorithm was designed to approximate the process of clinical decision making and was used to reconcile cases in which disagreements occurred among various PTSD indicators (Kulka et al., 1991; Schlenger et al., 1992). This approach may be most useful in case determination for research and may provide data to inform clinical practice. Nonetheless, clinical judgment and expertise is also needed to interpret the qualitative contributions of particular measures and the manner in which individuals may minimize or distort their experiences. Thus, a fundamental general approach to interpretation incorporates a combination of good clinical skill and empirical knowledge about the relative psychometric qualities of each indicator. To facilitate the interpretation of multimodal data, Keane and his colleagues

(1987) suggested the use of consensus among clinical team members who represent expertise in different arenas. This approach ensures that all data are considered, that bias is minimized, and that empirical and psychometric concerns are appropriately evaluated so that the most accurate interpretation of the data can be attained.

NEW CHALLENGES TO MEASURING MILITARY-RELATED PTSD

New Issues in the Multidimensional Assessment of Exposure to Military-Related PTEs

With the end of the Cold War, the types of missions in which military personnel will participate will be markedly different from the conflicts of the past. As part of the construction of the new world order, it is likely that the U.S. armed forces, as well as multinational forces, will primarily engage in multilateral peacekeeping, humanitarian relief, and peace enforcement operations with the goal of confronting regional instabilities that threaten world interests (Henshaw, 1993). In an illustrative review, Moskos and Burk (1994) presented a sampling of the types of missions Western military forces have undertaken just since the end of the Gulf War in March 1991. Examples of such missions include: "Operation Provide Comfort" in Kurdistan, the goal of which was to supply relief to refugees; "Operation Sea Angel" in Bangladesh, where forces provided relief to victims of a flood; California "Joint Task Force Los Angeles," a domestic operation in which U.S. forces were called upon to restore order following riots; and "Operation Restore Hope," the purpose of which was to provide humanitarian aid and peacekeeping in Somalia. Although these operations differ in terms of the types of duties that military personnel were called upon to assume, they share a common theme of military "humanitarianism."

Preliminary data on the psychological adjustment of participants in the peace-enforcement mission in Somalia suggest that PTSD can develop as a result of the military-related stressors involved with this type of duty (Orsillo et al., 1994a). Although existing measures of military-related PTSD will most likely be appropriate for assessing symptom presentation, novel approaches to measuring exposure to PTEs must be developed to reflect the unique stressors that characterize these types of missions. There are many factors suggesting that as the issues surrounding military missions change, so too does the direction mental health professionals need to take in assessing exposure to PTEs.

For instance, one challenge inherent in the assessment of exposure to military-related PTEs among personnel engaged in these new military operations is the diversity in the nature and character of the missions. Although the vast majority of interventions can be described as peacekeeping or peace-making operations, the actual role of participants in these experiences may vary widely. On the one extreme are conventional observer missions, in which forces serve as impartial observers of a truce between two or more formerly warring parties (Henshaw, 1993). In this situation, the goal of the mission is usually short term and quite clear, and the presence of the troops is supported by all parties. However, peace operations can range in level of intervention to include missions that require a variety of activities that could potentially result in more direct exposure to PTEs, including the delivery of humanitarian assistance to poverty-stricken, starving people; disarmament of or preventive peacekeeping between potentially hostile forces; and activities involving conventional military capabilities, such as in the Gulf War (Eyre, Segal, & Segal, 1993; Henshaw, 1993).

A second task that evaluators may face in measuring exposure to PTEs during new military interventions is developing assessment instruments that account for the changing nature of the mission. For instance, the nature of the U.S. mission in Somalia changed after May 1993 from a humanitarian to a more traditional combat intervention (Michaelson, 1993). Data from over 3,000 active-duty personnel who served in Somalia, half of whom left Somalia before May 1993 and half of whom left after June, confirm significant differences between the groups regarding their exposure to high- and low-magnitude stressors (Orsillo et al., 1994b).

As we mentioned earlier, a multidimensional approach to the measurement of military-stressor exposure includes assessment of the general malevolency of the environment and individuals' subjective emotional response to traumatic events, in addition to an assessment of their participation in the types of military activities described earlier. Findings from a preliminary survey of individuals serving in Somalia support the notion that these separate components of exposure are independently associated with the development of PTSD among peace-enforcement participants (Orsillo et al., 1994a). Thus, it is important to consider these dimensions in the measurement of exposure within the new military missions as well.

Anecdotal reports from individuals who have served in peacemaking and peacekeeping operations suggest that a wide range of environmental stressors are often present. For instance, participants of the mission in Somalia were exposed to several noncombat-related stressors ranging from an adverse climate and contaminated food and water, to being confronted with armed locals who were not considered the "enemy," but who nonetheless posed a threat to their lives (Grinfeld, 1993). Soldiers who served in Haiti expressed distress over the quality of living conditions and the poverty with which they were confronted (Wilkinson, 1994).

Preliminary accounts also imply a wide range of subjective emotional responses among individuals who take part in these new types of military operations. Participants are often required to maintain the difficult balance of power with restraint in situations that could range in political climate from mildly confusing and disorganized to seriously and dangerously chaotic (Henshaw, 1993). Thus, peacekeepers may feel overwhelmed with the boredom, isolation, and cultural deprivation that often accompany the "observer" as compared to "intervener" role of their duties (Harris, Rothberg, Segal, & Segal, 1993), or they may become frustrated with the relatively inactive role they play in the peace process (Mortensen, 1990). Military personnel may also become disillusioned with their duties, since their role in the mission will not always result in an objectively defined success. Although the problems defined by the mission may be amenable to some degree of change, in many cases they may not always be resolvable (Henshaw, 1993).

Thus, multidimensional exposure scales may need to be tailored on a case-by-case basis to capture the full range of events included in each new military mission. In this next section, we will delineate the steps one can take to develop a clinically sensitive measure of exposure that can be used in this rapidly changing military environment. As issues of psychometric development are covered in another chapter in this book (Weathers, Keane, King, & King, Chapter 4, this volume), here we will focus solely on the generation of items that will effectively tap the construct of exposure.

Suggestions for the Development of Military-Related Exposure Scales

The first step an assessor must take in developing a measure of exposure is initial item selection (content validity). Items for a test are most often generated and chosen on the basis of their face validity in relation to a theoretical understanding of the concept to be measured (Nunally, 1973). This pool of initial items can be developed in several ways. If one does not have direct contact with participants in the mission, there are at least two alternative methods of obtaining content information. One approach is to survey a panel of experts in the field of military-related PTSD who can use their clinical expertise in the determination of appropriate items for an exposure scale. Another option is to gather descriptive information presented in media accounts of anecdotal reports by participants on the mission. Although these approaches can result in the development of face-valid items, the best manner in which to collect content information is to directly sample participants.

Information for item development can be directly collected from participants in many ways. One approach is to construct a scale based on the techniques described earlier, and then to derive feedback regarding the items from individuals who have served, or who are currently serving, in the mission. Another method involves incorporating descriptive data obtained through clinical interviewing or critical-incident debriefing into the development of items. Although both these approaches can be easily implemented, a potentially more effective and rigorous technique that can be used to collect this type of qualitative data for item generation is the use of focus group interviewing.

Focus group interviewing is a technique by which information about a novel content area can be quickly and inexpensively obtained by observing how participants interact with one another regarding a topic provided by the leader (Morgan, 1988). To use this methodology, an interested research-er would construct a focus group of participants who have been deployed to serve in the mission. Through directed group discussions about the na-ture of the duty, the unique stressors and conflicts that participants face should become readily apparent and can be incorporated into a measure of exposure.

The selection of focus group members will inevitably vary regarding the purpose of the assessment but should typically include and consider the ex-periences of a wide variety of participants. For instance, different gender or ethnic groups may encounter very different stressors in the military, so it may be important to create groups that accurately reflect the demograph-ics of the sample of interest. In addition, including participants of various branches and ranks of the military in a group, or running subgroups of spe-cial individuals (e.g., a "front line" Marine focus group) may be fruitful. For instance, it has been theorized that members of elite combat units who are self-selected and subsequently trained and socialized in traditional combat activities may have a more difficult adjustment to the types of duties required in peacemaking (Segal & Segal, 1993). Finally, sampling groups widely across the time period of the mission will help to elicit data regarding the chang-ing nature of the exposure variables.

In addition to content, another issue that needs to be addressed regard-ing item development is the format of the questions comprising the scale (Golden et al., 1984). Items can either be open-ended, allowing respondents to freely answer a question, including any information they feel is relevant and pertinent, or restricted, such as a forced choice (true–false) or multiple-choice item. Open-ended questions allow more personalized responses and may be helpful in providing detailed information about experiences in the war zone. However, these items are difficult to quantify and score. On the other hand, restricted items, although more standardized, are easier to in-terpret in a group or normative context. An assessment approach that in-cludes both types of items and thus combines nomothetic and ideographic methodologies may be the most flexible in allowing clinicians to better un-derstand exposure experiences.

Several surveys developed at the National Center for PTSD at the Boston VA Medical Center have successfully incorporated many of these methodo-logical nuances to instrument development. For instance, Wolfe, Brown, and Kelley (1993b) designed a survey to investigate the multidimensional com-ponents of exposure among individuals who served in the Gulf War. Items were generated both from previously validated exposure measures and feed-back from Operation Desert Storm (ODS) veterans, and the item format al-lowed for both fixed and open-ended responses. Litz and his colleagues (Litz, Moscowitz, Friedman, & Ehlich, 1995) designed a survey to evaluate the unique, long-term psychosocial sequelae that stem from participation in the peacemaking and peacekeeping mission in Somalia during Operation Restore Hope (ORH; later Operation Continue Hope, OCH). Items were generated based on anecdotal descriptions of events experienced by military personnel who were deployed to Somalia and qualitative information about the nature of the mission derived from debriefing groups. This survey also incorporated some open-ended questions to allow participants to report unique aspects of the stressors they faced. These efforts serve as models for the future development of psychometrically valid measures of exposure. In addition, both the Mississippi Scale and the Combat Exposure Scale were initially developed using this systematic approach.

Cultural Considerations in the Assessment of Military-Related PTSD

Another challenge to the assessment of military-related PTSD is the need to develop instruments that are culturally sensitive. Concurrent with changes in the function of the military, the demographic composition of the U.S. armed forces has also dramatically shifted. Over the last 20 years, the proportion of women in the armed forces has grown from less than 2% to more than 11%, and the percentage of African Americans serving has doubled from 10% to 20% (Binkin, 1993). This change in the demographics of the armed forces necessitates that cultural considerations be taken into account in the assessment of war-zone-related PTSD. Additionally, our sensitivity to cultural issues has increased, resulting in a growing emphasis on this important component of assessment (Keane, Kaloupek, & Weathers, 1996).

There are several clinical descriptions of ethnocultural-specific responses to traumatic events that underscore the importance of culturally sensitive instrumentation. Racial conflicts, discrimination, bicultural struggles, and identification with the "enemy" have all been cited as unique obstacles to readjustment commonly experienced by minority veterans (Kraft, 1993; Loo, 1994; Parson, 1985). In fact, differences in the level of exposure to war-zone-related stressors and the severity of PTSD symptoms experienced between ethnic minority and Caucasian veterans have been empirically documented (e.g., Green, Grace, Lindy, & Leonard, 1990b; Kulka et al., 1990). Unfortunately, it is very difficult to meaningfully interpret these group differences. Much of the research in this area is limited by the use of assessment instruments that are not culturally sensitive, and by the vast diversity among the cultural groups of interest (Marsella, Friedman, & Spain, 1993).

Guidelines to Ethnocultural Assessment

In an effort to improve the research on ethnocultural aspects of psychopathology, several writers have compiled guidelines for culturally sensitive assessment. First, an assessor should be clinically sensitive to ethnic issues and aware of his or her own prejudices and biases (Penk & Allen, 1991; Westermeyer, 1985). Second, researchers must go beyond comparing categories of ethnic groups as the sole means of understanding ethnocultural variability (Marsella et al., 1993; Penk & Allen, 1991). Moreover, the level of individuals' acculturation to the dominant culture must be assessed rather than assumed by their ethnic identity. Finally, it is key that instrumentation be developed that maintains equivalence across several different cultural groups.

Dimensions of Cultural Equivalence

Cultural equivalence in assessment is typically established within several different domains: content, semantic, technical, normative, and conceptual equivalence (Flaherty et al., 1988; Lonner, 1985; Marsella & Kameoka, 1988). First, it is important to ensure that the content being measured is relevant to the phenomena of each culture being studied. Second, semantic equivalence should be obtained ensuring, through translation and back-translation by bilingual experts, that the meaning of each item is the same in each culture. Measures are determined to be technically equivalent when the method of assessment (e.g., self-report, interview) results in comparable comfort and familiarity between cultures. For instance, it is important to note in developing a culturally sensitive assessment instrument that the variation in a Likert-type scale is meaningless to some ethnic groups (Flaskerud, 1988; Kinzie et al., 1982). Normative equivalence refers to the importance of using local norms to interpret findings. In many cases, because of cultural differences in definitions of problematic behavior, it may be inappropriate to use the criterion for caseness developed in one culture to determine the boundaries of pathology in another. Finally, it is crucial that conceptual equivalence be determined. This ensures that the instrument is measuring the same theoretical construct, such as shame or dependency, in each culture. Keane et al. (1996) provide a more thorough description of the process necessary for developing instruments necessary to appropriately and equivalently assess trauma across cultural and ethnic groups.

SUMMARY

Assessing traumatic life experiences and PTSD that occurs as a function of military service is conceptually and practically challenging. Military service varies from one action to the next, and in this post–Cold War era, clinicians and researchers will need to modify and alter their approaches to assessment in accordance with the particular details of the military activities involved. Moreover, the demographic composition of the forces is continuing to vary, and instruments need to be developed that are sensitive to the cultural nuances of the subcultures within our population. Efforts to ensure that minority populations are represented in all phases of instrument development are important to the ultimate utility of the assessment instruments, whether they be primarily for use in the clinic, or in field or laboratory research studies. Reliability and validity data for instruments are most informative if available on most, if not all, minority populations on which the instruments will be used.

Today there are many instruments available to assess war-zone stress exposure and military-related PTSD. These instruments have demonstrated utility in the clinic and in the laboratory. They are responsible for the great expansion of our knowledge since 1980 on the psychological, social, and physical effects of traumatic events. Our ability to appropriately assess both trauma exposure and PTSD has led to widespread recognition and acceptance of the central role that these phenomena play in the lives of individuals in society. Future research on trauma exposure and PTSD as it occurs following military actions will continue to figure prominently in the development of a humane and sensible public policy toward individuals who serve in the military. The development of assessment instruments and methods that are reliable and valid will assist immensely in that process.

REFERENCES

American Psychiatric Association. (1980). *Diagnostic and statistical manual of mental disorders.* Washington, DC: Author.

American Psychiatric Association. (1987). *Diagnostic and statistical manual of mental disorders* (3rd ed., rev.). Washington, DC: Author.

American Psychiatric Association. (1994). *Diagnostic and statistical manual of mental disorders* (4th ed.). Washington, DC: Author.

Binkin, M. (1993). *Who will fight the next war? The changing face of the American military.* Washington, DC: Brookings Institute.

Blake, D. D., Weathers, F. W., Nagy, L. N., Kaloupek, D. G., Klauminser, G., Charney, D. S., & Keane, T. M. (1990). A clinician rating scale for assessing current and lifetime PTSD: The CAPS-1. *Behavior Therapist, 18,* 187–188.

Blanchard, E. B., Gerardi, R. J., Kolb, L. C., & Barlow, D. H. (1986). The utility of the anxiety disorders interview schedule in the diagnosis of post-traumatic stress disorder (PTSD) in Vietnam veterans. *Behavior Research Therapy, 24,* 577–580.

Blanchard, E. B., Kolb, L. C., Pallmeyer, T. P., & Gerardi, R. (1982). A psychophysiological study of post traumatic stress disorder in Vietnam veterans. *Psychiatric Quarterly, 34,* 220–229.

Davidson, J. R. T., Smith, R. D., & Kudler, H. S. (1989). Validity and reliability of the DSM III criteria for posttraumatic stress disorder: Experience with a structured interview. *Journal of Nervous and Mental Disease, 177,* 336–341.

Derogatis, L. R. (1977). *The SCL-90 manual: 1. Scoring, administration and procedures for the SCL-90.* Baltimore: Johns Hopkins University School of Medicine, Clinical Psychometrics Unit.

DiNardo, P. A., & Barlow, D. H. (1988). *Anxiety Disorders Interview Scale – Revised.* Albany, NY: Center for Phobia and Anxiety Disorders.

Egendorf, A., Kadushin, C., Laufer, R. S., Rothbart, G., & Sloan, L. (1981). *Legacies of Vietnam: Comparative adjustment of veterans and their peers* (Vol. 3). New York: Center for Policy Research.

Eyre, D. P., Segal, D. R., & Segal, M. W. (1993). The social construction of peacekeeping. In D. R. Segal & M. W. Segal (Eds.), *Peacekeepers and their wives: American participation in the multinational force and observers* (pp. 42–55). Westport, CT: Greenwood Press.

Falsetti, S. A., Resnick, H. S., Kilpatrick, D. G., & Freedy, J. R. (1994). A review of the Potential Stressful Events Interview: A comprehensive assessment instrument of high and low magnitude stressors. *Behavior Therapist, 17,* 66–67.

Figley, C. R., & Stretch, R. H. (1980). Vietnam Veterans Questionnaire Combat Exposure Scale. In *Vietnam Veterans Questionnaire: Instrument development. Final Report.* West Lafayette, IN: Purdue University.

Flaherty, J. A., Gaviria, F. M., Pathak, D., Mitchell, T., Wintrob, R., Richman, J. A., & Birz, S. (1988). Developing instruments for cross-cultural psychiatric research. *Journal of Nervous and Mental Disease, 176,* 257–263.

Flaskerud, J. H. (1988). Is the Likert scale format culturally biased? *Nursing Research, 37,* 185–186.

Fontana, A., & Rosenheck, R. (1994). A short form of the Mississippi Scale for measuring change in combat related PTSD. *Journal of Traumatic Stress, 7,* 407–414.

Foy, D., Sipprelle, R. C., Rueger, D. B., & Carroll, E. (1984). Etiology of posttraumatic stress disorder in Vietnam veterans: Analysis of premilitary, military and combat exposure influences. *Journal of Consulting and Clinical Psychology, 52,* 79–87.

Friedman, M. J., Schneiderman, C. K., West, A. N., & Corson, J. A. (1986). Measurement of combat exposure, posttraumatic stress disorder, and life among Vietnam combat veterans. *American Journal of Psychiatry, 143,* 537–539.

Gallops, M., Laufer, R. S., & Yager, T. (1981). Revised combat scale. In R. S. Laufer & T. Yager (Eds.), *Legacies of Vietnam: Comparative adjustments of veterans and their peers* (Vol. 3, pp. 125–129). Washington, DC: U.S. Government Printing Office.

Gillespie, R. D. (1942) *Psychological effects of war on citizen and soldier.* New York: Norton.

Golden, C. J., Sawicki, R. S., & Franzen, M. D. (1984). Test construction. In G. Goldstein & M. Hersen (Eds.), *Handbook of psychological assessment* (pp. 19–37). New York: Pergamon Press.

Grady, D. A., Woolfolk, R. L., & Budney, A. J. (1989). Dimensions of war-zone stress: An empirical analysis. *Journal of Nervous and Mental Disease, 177,* 347–350.

Graham, J. R. (1993). *MMPI-2: Assessing personality and psychopathology.* New York: Oxford University Press.

Green, B. L. (1993). Identifying survivors at risk: Trauma and stressors across events. In J. P. Wilson & B. Raphael (Eds.), *International handbook of traumatic stress syndromes* (pp. 135–144). New York: Plenum Press.

Green, B. L., Grace, M. C., Lindy, J. D., & Gleser, G. G. (1990a). War stressors and symptom persistence in posttraumatic stress disorder. *Journal of Anxiety Disorders, 4,* 31–39.

Green, B. L., Grace, M. C., Lindy, J. D., & Leonard, A. C. (1990b). Race differences in response to combat stress. *Journal of Traumatic Stress, 3,* 379–393.

Grinfeld, M. J. (1993, February). U.S. troops to the rescue again: Soldiers' mental health now a serious priority for military leadership. *Psychiatric Times,* pp. 1, 6.

Grinker, R., & Spiegel, J. P. (1945). *Men under stress.* Philadelphia: Blakison.

Hammarberg, M. (1992). Penn Inventory for posttraumatic stress disorders: Psychometric properties. *Psychological Assessment: A Journal of Consulting and Clinical Psychology, 4,* 67–76.

Harris, J. J., Rothberg, J. M., Segal, D. R., & Segal, M. W. (1993). Paratroopers in the desert. In D. R. Segal & M. W. Segal (Eds.), *Peacekeepers and their wives: American participation in the multinational force and observers* (pp. 81–94). Westport, CT: Greenwood Press.

Hendrix, C. C., & Schumm, W. (1990). Reliability and validity of the Abusive Violence Scale. *Psychological Reports, 66,* 1251–1258.

Hendrix, C. C., Anelli, L. M., Gibbs, J. P., & Fournier, D. G. (1994). Validation of the Purdue Post-Traumatic Stress Scale on a sample of Vietnam veterans. *Journal of Traumatic Stress, 7,* 311–318.

Henshaw, J. H. (1993). Forces for peacekeeping, peace enforcement and humanitarian missions. In B. M. Blechman, W. J. Durch, D. R. Graham, J. H. Henshaw, P. L. Reed, V. A. Utgoff, & S. A. Wolfe (Eds.), *The American military in the twenty-first century* (pp. 397–430). New York: St. Martin's Press.

Herman, D. S., Weathers, F. W., Litz, B. T., & Keane, T. M. (in press). Keane PTSD scale of the MMPI-2: Reliability and validity of the embedded and stand-alone versions. *Assessment.*

Herman, J. L. (1993). Sequelae of prolonged and repeated trauma: Evidence for a complex posttraumatic stress disorder (DESNOS). In J. R. T. Davidson & E. B. Foa (Eds.), *Posttraumatic stress disorder: DSM-IV and beyond* (pp. 213–228). Washington, DC: American Psychiatric Press.

Horowitz, M. J., Wilner, N. R., & Alvarez, W. (1979). Impact of Event Scale: A measure of subjective distress. *Psychosomatic Medicine, 41,* 208–218.

Hovens, J. E., Falger, P. R. J., Op den Velde, W., Mweijer, P., de Grown, J. H. M., & van Duijn, H. (1993). A self-rating scale for the assessment of posttraumatic stress disorder in Dutch Resistance veterans of World War II. *Journal of Clinical Psychology, 49,* 196–203.

Hovens, J. E., van der Ploeg, H. M., Bramsen, I., Klaarenbeek, M. T. A., Schreuder, J. N., Rivero, V. V. (1994). The development of the Self-Rating Inventory for Posttraumatic Stress Disorder. *Acta Psychiatrica Scandinavica, 90,* 172–183.

Hyer, L., Davis, H., Boudewyns, P., & Woods, M. G. (1991). A short form of the Mississippi Scale for Combat-Related PTSD. *Journal of Clinical Psychology, 4,* 510–518.

Janes, G. R., Goldberg, J., Eisen, S. A., & True, W. R. (1991). Reliability and validity of a combat exposure index for Vietnam Era Veterans. *Journal of Clinical Psychology, 47,* 80–86.

Kardiner, A. (1941). *The traumatic neurosis of war.* New York: Paul B. Hoeber.

Keane, T. M., Caddell, J. M., & Taylor, K. L. (1988). Mississippi Scale for Combat-Related Posttraumatic Stress Disorder: Three studies in reliability and validity. *Journal of Consulting and Clinical Psychology, 56,* 85–90.

Keane, T. M., Fairbank, J. A., Caddell, J. M., Zimering, R. T., & Bender, M. (1985). A behavioral approach to assessing and treating PTSD in Vietnam veterans. In C. R. Figley (Ed.), *Trauma and its wake* (pp. 257–294). New York: Brunner/Mazel.

Keane, T. M., Fairbank, J. A., Caddell, J. M., Zimering, R. T., Taylor, K. L., & Mora, C.A. (1989). Clinical evaluation of a measure to assess combat exposure. *Psychological Assessment: A Journal of Consulting and Clinical Psychology, 1,* 53–55.

Keane, T. M., Kaloupek, D. G., & Weathers, F. W. (1996). Cross-cultural issues in the assessment of post-traumatic stress disorder. In A. J. Marsella, M. J. Friedman, E. Gerrity, & R. Scurfield (Eds.), *Ethnocultural aspects of post-traumatic stress disorder* (pp. 183–205). Washington DC: American Psychiatric Press.

Keane, T. M., Malloy, P. F., & Fairbank, J. A. (1984). Empirical development of an MMPI subscale for the assessment of combat-related posttraumatic stress disorder. *Journal of Consulting and Clinical Psychology, 52,* 888–891.

Keane, T. M., & Penk, W. (1988). The prevalence of post-traumatic stress disorder [Letter to the editor]. *New England Journal of Medicine, 318,* 1690–1691.

Keane, T. M., Wolfe, J., & Taylor, K. L. (1987). Post-traumatic stress disorder: Evidence for diagnostic validity and methods of psychological assessment. *Journal of Clinical Psychology, 43,* 32–43.

King, D. W., King, L. A., Gudanowski, D. M., & Vreven, D. L. (1995a). Alternative representation of war zone stressors: Relationships to posttraumatic stress disorder in male and female Vietnam veterans. *Journal of Abnormal Psychology, 104,* 184–196.

King, L. A., King, D. W., Leskin, G., & Foy, D. W. (1995b). The Los Angeles Symptom Checklist: A self-report measure of posttraumatic stress disorder. *Assessment, 2,* 1–17.

Kinzie, J. D., Manson, S. M., Vinh, D. T., Tolan, N. T., Anh, B., & Pho, T. N. (1982). Development and validation of a Vietnamese-language depression rating scale. *American Journal of Psychiatry, 138,* 1276–1281.

Kraft, S. (1993, January 30). Black like me: Troops in Somalia. *Los Angeles Times,* pp. 1, 13.

Krinsley, K., Weathers, F., Vielhauer, M., Newman, E., Walker, E., Young, L., & Kimerling, R. (1994). *Evaluation of Lifetime Stressors Questionnaire and Interview.* Unpublished measure.

Kulka, R. A., Schlenger, W. E., Fairbank, J. A., Jordan, B. K., Hough, R. L., Marmar, C. R., & Weiss, D. S. (1991). Assessment of posttraumatic stress disorder in the community: Prospects and pitfalls from recent studies of Vietnam veterans. *Psychological Assessment: A Journal of Consulting and Clinical Psychology, 3,* 547–560.

Kulka, R. A., Schlenger, W. E., Fairbank, J. A., Jordan, B. K., & Hough, R. L., Marmar, C. R., & Weiss, D. S. (1990). *Trauma and the Vietnam War generation: Report of findings from the National Vietnam Veterans Readjustment Study.* New York: Brunner/Mazel.

Laufer, R. S., Gallops, M. S., & Frey-Wouters, E. (1984). War stress and trauma: The Vietnam veteran experience. *Journal of Health and Social Behavior, 25,* 65–85.

Litz, B. T., Moscowitz, A., Friedman, M., & Ehlich, P. (1995). *Somalia Peacekeeping Survey.* Unpublished manuscript.

Litz, B. T., Penk, W., Walsh, S., Hyer, L., Blake, D. D., Marx, B., Keane, T. M., & Bitman, D. (1991). Similarities and differences between Minnesota Multiphasic Personality Inventory (MMPI) and MMPI-2 applications to the assessment of post-traumatic stress disorder. *Journal of Personality Assessment, 57,* 238–254.

Lonner, W. J. (1985). Issues in testing and assessment in cross-cultural counseling. *Counseling Psychologist, 13,* 599–614.

Loo, C. M. (1994). Race-related PTSD: The Asian American Vietnam veteran. *Journal of Traumatic Stress, 7,* 637–656.

Lund, M., Foy, D., Sipprelle, C., & Strachan, A. (1984). The Combat Exposure Scale: A systematic assessment of trauma in the Vietnam War. *Journal of Clinical Psychology, 6,* 1323–1328.

Lyons, J. A., & Keane, T. M. (1992). Keane PTSD scale: MMPI and MMPI-2 update. *Journal of Traumatic Stress, 5,* 111–117.

Lyons, J. A., & Scotti, J. R. (1994). Comparability of two administration formats of the Keane Posttraumatic Stress Disorder Scale. *Psychological Assessment, 6,* 209–211.

Marsella, A. J., Friedman, M. J., & Spain, E. H. (1993). Ethnocultural aspects of post-traumatic stress disorder. In J. M. Oldham, M. B. Riba, & A. Tasman (Eds.), *Review of psychiatry* (Vol. 12, pp. 157–181). Washington, DC: American Psychiatric Press.

Marsella, A. J., & Kameoka, V. A. (1988). Ethnocultural issues in the assessment of psychopathology. In S. Wetzler (Ed.), *Measuring mental illness: Psychometric assessment for clinicians* (pp. 231–256). Washington, DC: American Psychiatric Press.

McFall, M. E., Smith, D. E., Mackay, P. W., & Tarver, D. J. (1990a). Reliability and validity of Mississippi Scale for Combat-Related Posttraumatic Stress Disorder. *Psychological Assessment: A Journal of Consulting and Clinical Psychology, 2,* 114–121.

McFall, M. E., Smith, D. E., Roszell, D. K., Tarver, D. J., & Malais, K. L. (1990b). Convergent validity of measures of PTSD in Vietnam combat veterans. *American Journal of Psychiatry, 147,* 645–648.

Michaelson, M. (1993). Somalia: The painful road to reconciliation. *Africa Today, 12,* 53–73.

Morgan, D. L. (1988). Focus groups as qualitative research. *Sage University paper series on qualitative research methods* (Vol. 16). Beverly Hills, CA: Sage.

Mortensen, M. S. (1990, August). *The UN peacekeeper: A New Type of Soldier? Preliminary studies of professional roles in military forces.* Paper presented to the American Sociological Association Convention, Washington, DC.

Moskos, C. M., & Burk, J. (1994). The postmodern military. In J. Burk (Ed.), *The military in new times: Adapting armed forces to a turbulent world* (pp. 141–162). Boulder, CO: Westview Press.

Nunally, J. (1973). *Psychometric theory.* New York: McGraw-Hill.

Orr, S., Claiborn, J. M., Altman, B., Forgue, D. F., de Jong, J. B., Pitman, R. K., & Herz, L. R. (1990). Psychometric profile of PTSD, anxious and healthy Vietnam veterans: Correlations with psychophysiological responses. *Journal of Consulting and Clinical Psychology, 58,* 329–335.

Orsillo, S. M., Litz, B. T., Goebel, A. E., Friedman, M., Ehlich, P., & Bergman, E. D. (1994a, November). *An investigation of the psychological sequelae associated with peacemaking in Somalia.* Paper presented at the annual meeting of the Association for Advancement of Behavior Therapy, San Diego, CA.

Orsillo, S. M., Litz, B. T., Goebel, A. E., Friedman, M., Ehlich, P., & Bergman, E. D. (1994b, November). *Changes over time in the peacemaking mission in Somalia.* Paper presented at the annual meeting of the International Society for Traumatic Stress Studies, Chicago, IL.

Parson, E. R. (1985). The intercultural setting: Encountering black Viet Nam. In S. M. Sonnenberg, A. S. Blank, & J. A. Talbott (Eds.), *The trauma of war: Stress and recovery in Viet Nam veterans* (pp. 359–388). Washington, DC: American Psychiatric Press.

Penk, W. E., & Allen, I. M. (1991). Clinical assessment of post-traumatic stress disorder (PTSD) among American minorities who served in Vietnam. *Journal of Traumatic Stress, 4,* 41–66.

Perconte, S., Wilson, A., Pontius, E., Dietrick, A., Kirsch, C., & Sparacino, C. (1993). Unit-based intervention for Gulf War soldiers surviving a SCUD missile attack: Program description and preliminary findings. *Journal of Traumatic Stress, 6,* 225–238.

Pitman, R. K., Orr, S. P., Forgue, D. F., de Jong, J. B., & Claiborn, J. M. (1987). Psychophysiologic assessment of posttraumatic stress disorder imagery in Vietnam combat veterans. *Archives of General Psychiatry, 44,* 970–975.

Prins, A., Kaloupek, D., & Keane, T. M. (1995). Psychophysiological evidence for autonomic arousal and startle in traumatized adult populations. In M. J. Friedman, D. Charney, & A. Deutch (Eds.), *Neurobiological and clinical consequences of stress: From normal adaptation to PTSD.* New York: Raven Press.

Query, W. T., Megran, J., & McDonald, G. (1986). Applying posttraumatic stress disorder MMPI subscale to World War II POW veterans. *Journal of Clinical Psychology, 42,* 315–317.

Robins, L. N., Helzer, J. E., Croughan, J. L., & Ratcliff, K. S. (1981a). National Institute of Mental Health Diagnostic Interview Schedule: Its history, characteristics, and validity. *Archives of General Psychiatry, 38,* 381–389.

Robins, L. N., Helzer, J. E., Croughan, J. L., Williams, J. B. W., & Spitzer, R. L. (1981b). *NIMH Diagnostic Interview Schedule, Version III* (Publication No. ADM-T-42-3 [5-81,8-81]). Rockville, MD: NIMH, Public Health Service.

Schlenger, W. E., Kulka, R. A., Fairbank, J. A., Hough, R. L., Jordan, B. K., Marmar, C. R., & Weiss, D. S. (1992). The prevalence of post-traumatic stress disorder in the Vietnam generation: A multimodal, multisource assessment of psychiatric disorder. *Journal of Traumatic Stress, 5,* 333–363.

Schwarzwald, J., Solomon, Z., Weisenberg, M., & Mikulincer, M. (1987). Validation of the Impact of Event Scale for psychological sequelae of combat. *Journal of Consulting and Clinical Psychology, 55,* 251–256.

Segal, D. R., & Segal, M. W. (1993). Research on soldiers of the Sinai Multinational Force and Observers. In D. R. Segal & M. W. Segal (Eds.), *Peacekeepers and their wives: American participation in the multinational force and observers* (pp. 56–64). Westport, CT: Greenwood Press.

Shalev, A. Y., Orr, S. P., & Pitman, R. K. (1992). Psychophysiologic responses during script-driven imagery as an outcome measure in posttraumatic stress disorder. *Journal of Clinical Psychiatry, 532,* 324–326.

Shalev, A. Y., Orr, S. P., & Pitman, R. K. (1993). Psychophysiologic assessment of traumatic imagery in Israeli civilian patients with posttraumatic stress disorder. *American Journal of Psychiatry, 150,* 620–624.

Solomon, Z. (1993). *Combat stress reaction: The enduring toll of war.* New York: Plenum Press.

Solomon, Z., Mikulincer, M., & Hobfoll, S. E. (1987). Objective versus subjective measurement of stress and social support: Combat-related reactions. *Journal of Consulting and Clinical Psychology, 55,* 577–583.

Solomon, Z., Benbenishty, R., Neria, Y., Abramowitz, M., Ginzburg, K., & Ohry, A. (1993). Assessment of PTSD: Validation of the revised PTSD Inventory. *Israel Journal of Psychiatry and Related Sciences, 30,* 110–115.

Spitzer, R. L., Williams, J. B., Gibbon, M., & First, M. B. (1990). *Structured Clinical Interview for DSM-III-R — Patient edition (SCID-P).* New York: Biometrics Research Department, New York State Psychiatric Institute.

Sutker, P. B., Uddo, M., Brailey, K., Vasterling, J. J., & Errera, P. (1994). Psychopathology in war-zone deployed and nondeployed Operation Desert Storm troops assigned graves registration duties. *Journal of Abnormal Psychology, 103,* 383–390.

Watson, C. G. (1990). Psychometric posttraumatic stress disorder techniques: A review. *Psychological Assessment: A Journal of Consulting and Clinical Psychology, 2,* 460–469.

Watson, C. G., Juba, M. P., & Anderson, P. E. D. (1989). Validities of five combat scales. *Psychological Assessment: A Journal of Consulting and Clinical Psychology, 1,* 98–102.

Watson, C. G., Juba, M. P., Manifold, V., Kucala, T., & Anderson, P. E. D. (1991). The PTSD Interview: Rationale, descriptions, reliability, and concurrent validity of a DSM-III based technique. *Journal of Clinical Psychology, 47,* 179–188.

Watson, C. G., Kucala, T., & Manifold, V., Vassar, P., & Juba, M. (1988). Differences between post-traumatic stress disorder patients with delayed and undelayed onsets. *Journal of Nervous and Mental Disease, 176,* 568–572.

Weathers, F. W., & Litz, B. T. (1994). Psychometric properties of the Clinician-Administered PTSD Scale, CAPS-1. *PTSD Research Quarterly, 5,* 2–6.

Weathers, F. W., Litz, B. T., Herman, D. S., Huska, J. A., & Keane, T. M. (1993, October). *The PTSD Checklist: Reliability, validity, and diagnostic Utility.* Paper presented at the annual meeting of the International Society for Traumatic Stress Studies, San Antonio, TX.

Weathers, F. W., Litz, B. T., Keane, T. M., Herman, D. S., Steinberg, H. R., Huska, J. A., & Kraemer, H. C. (1996). The Utility of the SCL-90-R for the diagnosis of war-zone related post-traumatic stress disorder. *Journal of Traumatic Stress, 9,* 111–128.

Westermeyer, J. (1985). Psychiatric diagnosis across cultural boundaries. *American Journal of Psychiatry, 142,* 798–805.

Wilkinson, T. (1994, October, 21). GI suicides in Haiti alert army to the enemy within. *Los Angeles Times,* pp. 1, 8, 9.

Wilson, J. P. (1979). *The forgotten warrior project.* Cincinnati, OH: Disabled American Veterans.

Wilson, J. P., & Krause, G. E. (1980). *The Vietnam era stress inventory.* Cleveland, OH: Cleveland State University.

Wilson, J. P., & Krause, G. E. (1989). Vietnam Era Stress Inventory. In J. P. Wilson (Ed.), *Trauma transformation and healing* (pp. 265–308). New York: Brunner/Mazel.

Wilson, J. P., & Prabucki, K. (1989). Stress sensitivity and psychopathology. In J. P. Wilson (Ed.), *Trauma transformation and healing* (pp. 75–110). New York: Brunner/Mazel.

Wolfe, J., Brown, P. J., Furey, J., & Levin, K. B. (1993a). Development of a War-Time Stressor Scale for women. *Psychological Assessment, 5,* 330–335.

Wolfe, J., Brown, P. J., & Kelley, J. M. (1993b). Reassessing war stress: Exposure and the Persian Gulf War. *Journal of Social Issues, 49,* 15–31.

Wolfe, J., Keane, T. M., Kaloupek, D. G., Mora, C. A., & Wine, P. (1993c). Patterns of positive readjustment in Vietnam combat veterans. *Journal of Traumatic Stress, 6,* 179–193.

Yehuda, R., Southwick, S. M., & Giller, E. L. (1992). Exposure to atrocities and severity of chronic posttraumatic stress disorder in Vietnam combat veterans. *American Journal of Psychiatry, 149,* 333–336.

Zilberg, N. J., Weiss, D. S., & Horowitz, M. J. (1982). Impact of Event Scale: A cross-validation study and some empirical evidence supporting a conceptual model of stress responses syndromes. *Journal of Consulting and Clinical Psychology, 50,* 407–414.

Assessing Traumatic Experiences in Children

KATHLEEN O. NADER

INTRODUCTION

Prior to 1980, the assessment of childhood traumatic response was accomplished primarily through clinical case examination (Carey-Trefzer, 1949; Bloch, Silber, & Perry, 1956; Bergen, 1958; Lacey, 1972; Newman, 1976; Green, 1983) and/or review of case records (Levy, 1945). Clinicians most often reported case observations and parent or teacher report of children's reactions. Terr's examination of children following a school bus kidnapping (Terr, 1979, 1981, 1983) and other studies of children exposed to violence and disaster (Eth & Pynoos, 1985) demonstrated the effectiveness of interviewing children directly regarding their experiences and responses. However, the need for a more systematic statistical analysis of children's traumatic reactions resulted in the application of a number of research instruments. These instruments included measures of depression (e.g., Birleson Depression Inventory; Birleson, 1981), anxiety (e.g., Children's Manifest Anxiety Scale; Reynolds & Richmond, 1978), fear (e.g., Fear Survey Schedule for Children; Ollendick, 1983), "caseness" (Rutter's Scale; Rutter, 1967; Elander & Rutter, in press), and measures of trauma applying adult scales to children (e.g., Impact of Event Scale; Horowitz, Wilner, & Alvarez, 1979; see Weiss & Marmar, Chapter 13, this volume). After a sniper opened fire on a crowded elementary school playground in south-central Los Angeles in 1984, the necessity for an emergency revision of Calvin Frederick's 16-item Adult Posttraumatic Stress Reaction Index marked the emergence of PTSD scales for children (Frederick, 1985; Pynoos et al., 1987). Currently there are a number of instruments and subscales that measure children's posttraumatic reactions, and new instruments are developed frequently.

This chapter examines issues in the measurement of trauma in children. Several instruments that were available for review are discussed in the second section of this chapter: (1) instruments that directly measure childhood traumatic reactions include the Children's Posttraumatic Stress Reaction Index (CPTS-RI; Frederick, Pynoos, & Nader, 1992), the Child's Reaction to Traumatic Events Scale (CRTES; Jones, 1994), the Clinician-Administered PTSD Scale for Children (CAPS-C; Nader, Kriegler, Blake, & Pynoos, 1994b; Nader et al., 1996), My Worst Experience Survey and My Worst School Experience Survey (MWES, MWSES; Hyman, Zelikoff, & Clarke, 1988), and the When Bad Things Happen Scale (WBTH; Fletcher, 1991); (2) PTSD subscales within comprehensive diagnostic instruments include the Diagnostic Interview for Children and Adolescents—Revised (DICA-R; Reich, Shayka, & Taibleson, 1991) and the Diagnostic Interview Schedule for Children (DISC; Shaffer, Fisher, Piacentini, Schwab-Stone, & Wicks, 1992); and (3) instruments that assess symptoms or behaviors related to specific kinds or aspects of traumatic reactions include the Angie/Andy Child Rating Scale (A/A CRS; Praver, Pelcovitz, & DiGiuseppe, 1993), the Child Dissociative Checklist (CDC; Putnam, 1988, 1994), the Children's Impact of Traumatic Events Scale and the revised version (CITES; Wolfe, Wolfe, Gentile, & Larose, 1986; CITES-R; Wolfe & Gentile, 1991), the Children's Sexual Behavior Inventory (CSBI-3; Friedrich, 1995), and the Trauma Symptom Checklist for Children (TSCC; Briere, 1996a, 1996b).

THE NEED FOR ASSESSMENT

The potential results of unresolved traumatic response underscore the need for accurate assessment of childhood trauma. The extensive literature available on PTSD provides evidence that failure to resolve moderate to severe traumatic reactions may result in long-term consequences that interfere with the child's ability to engage, over time, in productive behaviors and to function adequately socially, academically, professionally, and personally (Wilson & Raphael, 1993). These long-term effects may include personal traits (e.g., lack of confidence, inhibitions, disruptions to moral development); disturbances in interpersonal functioning (e.g., loss of friends, irritability/bullying, withdrawal); cognitive dysfunction (e.g., memory and concentration problems, inhibited imagination); mental health disturbances (e.g., chronic and/or complicated posttraumatic stress disorder, PTSD; substance-related disorders; conduct, mood, anxiety, somatoform, eating, sleep, impulse control, personality, and/or dissociative disorders); attempts at numbing the emotions (e.g., drug abuse, alcoholism, overuse of medication); compulsive repetition of traumatic behaviors and sequences (e.g., promiscuity or prostitution after molestation); attempts at self-punishment or warding off (e.g., self-mutilation); and repetitive somatic complaints or general ill health (e.g., headaches, deficient immune response; Nader, 1996; Nader & Fairbanks, 1994; Nader & Pynoos, 1993a; Terr, 1991; van der Kolk & Saporta, 1991; Garbarino, Kostelny, & Dubrow, 1991; Herman, Perry, & van der Kolk, 1989; Pynoos & Nader, 1988; Pynoos et al., 1987; see reference list in Nader, Blake, & Kriegler, 1994a). In addition, there is a growing body of evidence that individuals who experience traumas are more likely to have children who experience traumas (Nader, in press-a).

When considering the assessment of PTSD in children, it should be recognized that the incidence of school and community violence has increased since the 1980s (Admundson, 1993). Unresolved traumatic exposure may perpetuate violent acts that result in trauma for others. Individual and/or intrafamilial violence has increased following violence or disaster, for example, in Kuwait after the Iraqi occupation (Ibrahim, 1992; Nader & Fairbanks, 1994) and in the midwestern United States following the floods (Kohly, 1994). In examining the psychological histories of those who commit acts that traumatize children, trauma or unresolved traumatic grief is sometimes a factor. Examples include the sniper who opened fire on a crowded elementary school playground in south-central Los Angeles in 1984 (Pynoos et al., 1987); the woman who took a fifth grade classroom hostage, nearly missed shooting a child, then shot herself in front of the children in 1987 (Nader, in press-b); and the young man who, in 1989, opened fire on an elementary school in Stockton, California. Thus, the accurate assessment and effective treatment of childhood trauma is important as one method of prevention of ongoing violence.

In situations in which the numbers of children affected prohibit the interview of the entire population (e.g., after war or large-scale violence/disaster), representative sampling with trauma, exposure, and history scales permits subsequent use of exposure and personal history questionnaires alone to identify children with risk factors. Additional risk and protective factors may be attained from parent interview or school records. Risk factors include, for example, personality characteristics, previous psychopathology, previous traumatic or loss experiences, family issues, relationship to deceased victims, and more (see Nader, 1996, in press-b).

Direct screening interviews with children exposed to traumatic events may have a therapeutic effect. Following a sniper attack in Los Angeles, some children were interviewed using the CPTS-RI (16-item original version) at 1 and 14 months following their experience, whereas others were interviewed at 14 months only. Those who were interviewed initially had significantly fewer symptoms than those with comparable exposures who were interviewed only at 14 months after the event (Nader, in press-b). Thus, early screening not only identifies the level of traumatic response, but also may be therapeutically beneficial.

ISSUES AFFECTING ACCURACY OF MEASUREMENT

There are a number of issues affecting the accuracy of assessment of children's posttraumatic reactions. Several of these issues are described here and include selection, preparation for, and method of measurement (e.g., training, interviewers, and interview style), trauma-intrinsic issues (e.g., briefing, phase of response), and child-intrinsic issues (e.g., culture, age).

The Nature of the Interview

Posttrauma screening instruments have been used in many settings and include (1) direct interviews with children by clinicians or researchers; (2) those that have been mailed or handed to children and adolescents to complete; and (3) those that have been distributed to groups of children to complete while a researcher reads the questions and explains their meaning, when needed. Using a semistructured interview method rather than having the child complete the instrument seems to increase the sensitivity of the measurement (Jones & Ribbe, 1991). In general, children and adolescents tend to answer more accurately when they can ask questions and when a skilled interviewer asks the appropriate probing questions. When questioned in a group, children tend to answer in the way they think that their peers will answer. During a study of children exposed to a disaster, it was observed that children filling out self-esteem questionnaires in a group tended to minimize their symptoms in order to look more normal. Both direct and group interviews were used in a study of children exposed to the Northridge, California earthquake in January 1994, conducted by Kelly Johnson, myself, and other researchers. Randomly selected children from each classroom were interviewed individually. On the first day of assessment, all of the children in the classroom were also subsequently interviewed in a group. Despite efforts to keep the children at a distance from one another and to have them answer honestly and without paying attention to their peers, it was apparent by the sounds and facial expressions the children made in response to questions that it was popular among the children to have symptoms as a result of the earthquake. Children who had appeared to answer thoughtfully and accurately in the one-to-one interviews increased the numbers and/or intensity of symptoms in the subsequent group situation. The greater effectiveness of direct interview in comparison to self-administered questionnaire is suggested by kappa levels on two different administrative techniques of the Diagnostic Interview for Children and Adolescents (see DICA and Reliability and Validity Measures, this chapter).

Interviewing children or adolescents by phone is another method of clinician-administered rating of children's symptoms. Reich and Earls (1990) found interviewing children by phone economical, saving both time and money, and permitting continued contact with respondents at a distance. However, when comparing matched groups of children interviewed by phone or in-person using the DICA, the telephone group as a whole reported fewer symptoms than the in person group. The need for privacy did not explain the differences in groups. Reich and Earls theorize that among the reasons for underreporting in the phone interviews may be the loss of nonverbal cues and the visible animation of both interviewer and respondent.

In situations involving trauma and disaster, instruments have been administered by researchers with varying degrees of clinical experience. It has been my observation—in the training and usage of more than one screening instrument—that when researchers, with and without clinical experience, are employed to interview children, children often report more of their symptoms to clinicians than to nonclinical researchers. Perhaps the more important variables affecting the success of the interview are the ability to establish rapport, attunement to nonverbal cues and contradictions in verbal report, perceived interest in the child and his or her emotional state, a thorough understanding of the meaning and nature of the specific posttrauma symptomatic reactions/questions, and issues of trust.

Training

Most of the authors of the instruments described here recommend some level of training before using the instruments. Although varying amounts of training have been recommended for the different instruments, in general, greater accuracy, better concordance with clinical diagnoses, and better therapeutic results have been reported for trained interviewers. Moreover, training in methods for screening children can be incorporated into a comprehensive program or may serve to increase the level of understanding of trauma for laypersons or clinical personnel (see Nader & Pynoos, 1993a).

Specialized methods are often required in interviewing victims of trauma. Health professionals in the former Yugoslavian Republics have reported a variety of harmful effects after survivors of rape have been interviewed by journalists, mental health professionals, and other personnel. These results have included suicides and suicide attempts, severe depressions, and acute psychotic episodes (Swiss & Giller, 1993).

Cultural beliefs may interact with traumatic reactions (to be discussed). Thus, training is important for accuracy and preventing harm in the process of assessing and treating trauma. For example, in Kuwait following the Gulf Crisis, adolescent girls were unwilling to admit a rape experience unless assured of confidentiality and separate record keeping. One member of the clergy explained that Arab women are considered tainted beyond repair if raped. He told the story of an adolescent relative who, after a year, worked up the courage to tell her family that she had been raped during the crisis. The next day, her brother killed her. Although some of the Kuwaiti male adolescents expressed outrage at the enemy for this atrocity (i.e., for the rape and abuse of their women) and felt protective toward the injured women, the danger and the need for silence still existed. Cultural views and reactions to the trauma, and to mental health intervention in general, vary across cultures. Understanding the beliefs and practices of the person being interviewed is crucial to assuring the collection of complete and accurate information and for the protection of those affected by the event.

Preliminary Briefing

Preliminary briefing is an essential part of preparation for assessment and/or intervention with children following traumatic events. Knowing the details of the traumatic event—including those identified by police, news, and eye-witness reports of the event—enables the researcher to recognize aspects of symptomatic response and variables affecting response. For example, following a hostage taking in which the assailant dictated a suicide note and then killed herself, the most severe responses were associated with children's worry about their peers; the woman had waved her guns around and had accidentally fired a shot, barely missing one child (Nader, in press-b). Therefore, questions regarding the child's sense of life threat and fear for others' safety were based on this knowledge. Similarly, following a tornado that knocked down a cafeteria wall and killed nine children, surviving children were capable of discussing their need to avoid reminders of the disaster when asked by interviewers about specific reminders such as rattling windows, sitting next to walls, and lasagna, the lunch served that day (see Nader, 1993; Nader & Pynoos, 1993a).

Having a clear understanding of the sequence and nature of the event provides the clinician with a sense of the child's accuracy of recall or distortion of events. For example, following a sniper attack, in their *initial* recall, children who were closest to the danger appeared to attempt to place distance between themselves and the danger, whereas children who were absent from school sometimes tried to bring themselves closer to the event. Yet, in their more thorough retelling of the event, they were able to be accurate in their specific memories of the sniper attack (Pynoos & Nader, 1989).

As mentioned, understanding cultural issues related to the affected population is essential to the accurate and ethical nature of the data-collection process. Specific procedures before, during and after data collection may assure ongoing accuracy as well as honor the beliefs of the affected population and lend assistance with the recovery process. Pat Busher, principal of Cleveland Elementary School in Stockton, California, had a large Southeast Asian population in her school community, including Cambodians, Vietnamese, Laotians, and others. Out of genuine interest and desire to work effectively with a mixed population, she engaged in formal and informal cross-cultural education, including reading, study of psychological issues, contacts in the community, and brought in experts to train her school staff. In January 1989, a young man opened fire on children on the Cleveland Elementary School grounds, killing 5 and injuring 29 children and 1 teacher. With an awareness of cultural beliefs and practices, Busher invited local clergy—including Cambodian and Vietnamese Buddhist monks, a Vietnamese Catholic priest, and Protestant ministers—to perform a blessing ceremony upon the school and school grounds. This included the exorcism of spirits, including the bad spirit of the man who killed the children and himself and the spirits of dead children, who might grab other children and take them into the next world. Children were given chants to use when frightened; children and adults were given factual information to dispel rumors and unfounded fears (Busher, personal communication, January 24 and 30, 1995). These sensitive, sensible, and respectful practices address fears and other arousal symptoms in the general population. Performing them effectively and appropriately can assist in separating fear-related arousal symptoms from ongoing traumatic reactions.

Translations of instruments may also be necessary for cultural adaptation. Karno, Burnam, Escobar, Hough, and Eaton (1983) recommend a system of translation and "back-translation" (to the original language) in developing an accurate translation of the instrument. Several back translations and retranslations may be necessary. The accuracy of the translation is then best confirmed by subsequent use of the instrument with children. For example, in this phase of translating an English instrument into German, a local German translator interprets both the German interviewer and the German child to an author or an authorized member of the translating team whose primary language is English. Moreover, it is of assistance to have someone who is not a mental health professional complete the back-translations. For example, in the translation process for one of the instruments to be described, in the second or third back-translation, the back-translated question still did not match the original item. Although a local psychologist dismissed this, saying the question was really okay, the problem was that the translator was a schoolteacher, and was not psychologically sophisticated; the general population, especially children and adolescents, are also unlikely to be sophisticated in psychological terminology. Having a translator who matches the target population's understanding of terminology is more informative in the back-translation process.

Phase of Response and Phase of Event

The phase of traumatic response is an additional factor influencing reactions and measurement. Although children may need and want to speak about their experiences, children may need family contact, some restoration of order, and/or time for initial recovery before they can give detailed answers regarding their reactions. Rumors are common, and fear is contagious in the aftermath of a traumatic event (Pynoos & Nader, 1988). Arousal symptoms may be common to the traumatized and untraumatized. Within the first 2–3 weeks following a catastrophic incident, some initial symptoms (e.g., bad dreams, fears) may disappear for those who are not traumatized. Moreover, the initial numbing and denial may decrease for children who are traumatized, so that assessment may be more accurate at 3–5 weeks following the event (Nader, in press-b).

For ongoing traumas, the phase of the event itself is important to recognize. For example, in 1991, after the Gulf War crisis was over, children in

Kuwait seemed to be in a different phase of their reactions than refugee children in Croatia in 1992, where the war continued (Nader, in press-b). Kuwaiti children had become focused upon the extent of the physical and psychological damage that had occurred, upon rebuilding, and upon issues of accountability. In contrast, Croatian children were still focused upon surviving the war and its horrors; they found watching the news and staying informed a useful coping mechanism. As the war was ongoing, numbing appeared to be prevalent. Symptoms appeared to be warded off or ignored, because there might be more to endure.

When the event is perceived to be over rather than ongoing, there will likely be reassessment of experience. For example, when asked if he had been injured during the war, one adolescent Croatian boy said, "No." Knowing that he had been captured and imprisoned for weeks, the interviewer pursued the issue. The boy admitted that he had been beaten daily while imprisoned. However, he told us, it was much worse for his defiant friend, who had been permanently crippled by his beatings. At this stage, the boy was more worried about his father, who was still imprisoned, and about the greater harm to his friends and others who had not as yet returned. From his current perspective, he could only consider his own injuries in comparison to the injuries of these others (Nader, in press-b).

Children suffering abuse with no end in sight and inner-city children enduring violence with no end in sight, like the Croatian children exposed to ongoing war, may of necessity ward off symptoms until "the war is over." When children exposed to single incidents of violence were compared to children exposed to ongoing, painful treatments for catastrophic illness (including bone-marrow transplantation, BMT), the most striking differences were the predominance of avoidance symptoms and the reduced number of arousal symptoms in the BMT patients (Nader & Stuber, 1992; see Nader, in press-b). From both a clinical and a research standpoint, the event phase will affect assessment of trauma symptoms and levels of severity of response over time.

Age

The instruments under review have been used effectively with children and adolescents. To address age differences, the DICA-R, for example, has a PTSD subscale for 6- to 12-year-olds and one for 13- to 17-year-olds. Limitations related to age have become apparent in the use of several of the instruments, and have resulted in the rewording of questions for better understanding, the breaking down of questions into simpler units for younger children, and the use of age-related answering systems. For example, children under the age of 8 may have difficulty with the concept of time, even when the time frame is narrowed to the preceding month. They may also have difficulty with the complexities of a 5-point scale. For the CAPS-C and the CPTS-RI, the 5-point scale has been used successfully with American children ages 8 and older.

Emotional sophistication or how "street-wise" the child is may also affect age cutoff levels. For example, the CPTS-RI has been successfully used without adaptation in wording with children ages 5 and older in south-central Los Angeles (Pynoos et al., 1987; Nader, Stuber, & Pynoos, 1991), with children ages 7 and older in rural New York (Nader & Pynoos, 1993a) and a translated version has been used with children ages 11 and older in Kuwait (Nader, Pynoos, Fairbanks, Al-Ajeel, & Al-Asfour, 1993). It was used as a yes–no questionnaire, with minor alterations in wording with children ages 5–7 in rural New York and for children ages 7–10 in the Middle East (see CPTS-RI, this chapter). A screening method for traumatic reactions in children ages 3–6 is under revision (Nader & Stuber, 1993; Nader et al., 1991). It has been used with Head Start children in south-central Los Angeles, children undergoing BMT (Stuber & Nader, 1995), and Head Start children exposed to Hurricane Hugo in Florida.

Wording of questions is particularly important for children. Children under age 5 have been best assessed by a combination of observation, questions during play, and supplemental information from caretaking adults (Nader et al., 1991). Depending on sophistication levels (language and emotional), children ages 5, 6, or 7 (or older in some cultures) may need simplification of terms and shortening of questions (Nader, 1993). Inasmuch as minor changes in wording can change the meaning of a question, it is important to use standard, recommended changes as suggested, for example, in the manuals provided for the instruments.

For children, differences in the wording of questions have resulted in the greater or lesser success of specific research questions. For example, it may be impossible for adults or children to avoid reminders in the aftermath of traumatic events. Although children may wish to avoid some reminders of the event, they may have even less control than an adult over the actual ability to avoid. Therefore, asking if a child stays away from reminders (e.g., CRTES) rather than if he or she wishes to avoid them (e.g., CPTS-RI and CAPS-C) may almost always elicit a negative response. This may explain why some studies have found high levels of intrusive reexperiencing symptoms and relatively few avoidance symptoms (see Jones, Frary, Cunningham, & Weddle, 1993). Similar wording difficulties exist for "survivor guilt." Asking children if they feel bad because someone else was hurt worse than they were (e.g., WBTH) is not likely to discriminate between traumatized and nontraumatized children, since most children feel bad that other children were hurt worse than they were. It may be of more interest to find out whether a child feels bad because he or she was not hurt as badly as others (Nader, 1993).

The order of questions/statements may be particularly significant for children and adolescents. Children have sometimes been found to be better at reporting their subjective symptoms than their overt, objectionable symptoms (see Parent, Teacher, or Child Interviews, this chapter). They exhibit concern regarding the judgment of their peers about their symptoms and symptom levels (see The Nature of the Interview, this chapter). Therefore, opening a symptom endorsement list with questions/statements about anger, impulsive acts, or other potentially socially undesirable feelings or behaviors may result in resistance. It may be of assistance to the accuracy of reporting to first ask the child about subjective symptoms that do not elicit defensiveness (e.g., the child's rating of the intensity of the event, reexperiencing symptoms; see CPTS-RI, CAPS-C, DICA-R-PTSD scale, DISC-PTSD scale). This also permits the child to discover that the interviewer is nonjudgmental about his or her answers before answering questions for which he or she fears judgment.

Children (especially young children) may respond to cues from the interviewer when answering questions. It is essential that the child sense a willingness to hear any answer and sense that there is no wrong answer. When there are open-ended questions or questions asking for a general list of results (e.g., "Has anything really bad ever happened to you?"), asking the open-ended question and waiting for an answer before giving specific examples or making specific probes can be informative (e.g., CPTS-RI; Nader, 1993).

In assessing symptoms endorsed by children, it is important to be cognizant of developmental issues. Some behaviors are common at specific phases of development and signal disturbances at other age levels. For example, when measuring dissociation, it is important to recognize that young children are often likely to exhibit forgetfulness, shifts in attention, and a variable sense of identity; that daydreaming may be a common behavior for youth; and that feeling unreal and detached from one's experience may be common for adolescents (Hornstein & Putnam, 1992; Putnam, 1993; Friedrich, Jaworski, Huxsahl, & Bengston, in press). Similarly, when measuring sexual concerns or behaviors, some thoughts or actions are common to an adolescent male (e.g., thinking about sex, having sexual feelings in the body, thinking about touching the opposite sex, and having difficulty stopping thinking about sex) and may be a sign of disturbance (e.g., sexual molestation) in an 8-year-old male (Friedrich et al., in press).

Interpreting Findings

In addition to age, there are other factors influencing the interpretation of symptom endorsement by children. The child's age, gender, life experiences, personality characteristics, health, and family circumstances must be taken into account. For example, some of the symptoms on the dissociation scales (e.g., feeling dizzy, forgetting things, having trouble remembering things, feeling like he or she is not in his or her body) may be common to other disorders (e.g., painful catastrophic ailment). Similarly, the number and nature of symptoms endorsed, for example, on a sexual behavior or sexual concerns inventory, may be influenced by life experiences, such as family nudity, children's witnessing of household sexual behaviors, types of television shows watched, children's access to magazines with nude pictures, and children's exposure to sexually reenacting traumatized children (see Friedrich, 1993b).

It is essential to examine the appropriate variables that may contribute to specific posttraumatic reactions in order to fully and accurately understand symptom endorsement and scale scores (see also Establishing Normative Data, this chapter). Some symptoms may appear only after prolonged or intense exposure. For example, dissociation has been found to be related to age, gender, and duration and severity of sexual abuse (Friedrich et al., in press). Since symptoms of dissociation have also been found in nonabused psychiatric patients, the other variables contributing to these symptoms must be identified. Symptoms such as intrusive reexperiencing may appear or increase in response to indirect witnessing as well as other variables. Children who have been exposed to traumatic events, or even children without direct exposure but who are very worried about a significant other during the event may have increased symptoms after seeing graphic media images (Nader, 1996; Nader et al., 1993). Moreover, it may be necessary to distinguish between symptoms associated with different variables. For example, are the symptoms related to loss or to trauma (e.g., trauma vs. grief dreams, trauma vs. grief play)? Are they associated with the fear that may initially affect the broader population or related to traumatic exposure and/or response?

Symptom Ratings

Scales that measure children's traumatic reactions have generally used one of three scoring systems: (1) measurement of the presence or absence of the symptom (e.g., DISC) or the degree of presence (e.g., CDC); (2) ratings of the frequency with which the symptom occurs (e.g., MWES/MWSES, CPTS-RI, DICA); or (3) both frequency and intensity ratings (e.g., CAPS-C, earlier versions of MWES/MWSES). Sometimes just asking about symptoms may produce them temporarily; specific symptoms may exist even in a healthy state or as a healthy temporary response to certain experiences. Additionally, in a study of a small sample of children exposed to a destructive wildfire, Jones, Ribbe, and Cunningham (1994) found that children reported fewer PTSD symptoms on the DICA-R than on Horowitz's Impact of Event Scale for Children (IES-C). They suggest that the measurement of intensity on the IES-C versus the measurement of presence or absence of symptoms on the DICA-R may account for the greater symptom report on the former. Thus, using both frequency and intensity ratings may permit a greater reporting of symptomatology and distinguish symptoms occurring in response to stress from symptoms resulting from traumatization.

In order to clearly establish the course and nature of childhood traumatic response, it may be necessary to rate duration and course of symptoms as well as frequency and/or intensity. Traumatic response may have an uneven course. Differences related to the nature of the experience may also be relevant to the accurate measurement of childhood traumatic reaction (see Long-Term versus Single-Incident Trauma, to follow). Very few scales include both a current and a lifetime rating, in order to document a more intense earlier reaction from the current level of symptoms (e.g., CAPS-C). In a study of Cambodian adolescents who had more than 10 years earlier been exposed to massive atrocities under the Pol Pot regime, Realmuto et al. (1992) suggested the need to study the differential course of symptoms in honor of the sometimes "cyclical nature of PTSD." They suggested devising developmentally relevant items, as well as duration and episode parameters, in order to record the changing pattern of symptom expression over time and distinguish chronic from acute traumatic response.

The manner in which children tend to answer questions may complicate the method by which "intensity" is measured. If the choices on the intensity scale include "none," "a little," "some," or "a lot," there may be great variations in what "a lot" means to different children and for different circumstances. Moreover, young children have learned to say "a lot" or "this big" with arms spread wide open as a fun response to adult inquiry. In working with preschool children, it became apparent that when we used hand measurements for the child to rate intensity of feelings, if having the hands all the way out was an option, most of the children would joyfully make that choice and giggle as though asked about something fun instead of about the trauma.

Qualitative differences in the meaning of scale ratings for different children again become relevant when determining which events are valid trauma precipitators. DSM-IV (American Psychiatric Association, 1994) Criterion A requires "actual or threatened death or serious injury, or a threat to the physical integrity of self or others" (p. 427) in addition to the experience of "intense fear, helplessness or horror" (p. 428) (or disorganized or agitated behavior in children). This definition of a trauma excludes events such as nonviolent divorce or being bullied at school without real threat of physical harm. Hyman (personal communication, May 1995) suggests that children exposed to these events meet symptom requirements of PTSD, and meeting the symptom criteria should be sufficient for the diagnosis. It has been my experience that, even though children with exposures to a variety of events may meet the criteria when the presence or absence of symptoms are measured, there are qualitative differences, for example, between the responses of children exposed to a sniper attack and those of children whose parents have divorced without preceding or current violence.

To some extent, these differences have been confirmed in comparing three different studies using the MWES: (1) children exposed to a hurricane (Goldwater, 1993), (2) children with clinical diagnosis of PTSD (Kohr, 1995); and (3) children from divorced or intact families (Berna, 1993). In fact, there are differences in the presentation and course for children with PTSD symptoms in response to different experiences. For example, there are differences between those children who are exposed to violence for which the life threat is external, visible, and menacing, and those children who have life-threatening ailments and undergo BMT, for which the life threat is a result of an invisible internal foe and the catastrophic attempts at cure (Nader &

Stuber, 1992). In order to accurately examine the differences in children's responses to a variety of events, it is essential that an intensity scale measure these qualitative differences in response and that such scale ratings include, for example, a clearly delineated definition of "a lot" (see CAPS-C intensity ratings).

Establishing Normative Data

There are important factors of which to be cognizant in reviewing normative data or in establishing norms. Differences in symptomatology by gender, ethnicity, socioeconomic status, and age are commonly distinguished in normative samples and analyses. Other groupings such as cognitive levels and regional factors may or may not be included. Young children and cognitively delayed children may be less able to provide detailed accounts of their symptoms and/or experiences (Elliott & Briere, 1994a). If exposure and preexisting conditions have not been measured, the normal population may include traumatized individuals, possibly raising the mean. Inquiry about the child's previous experiences has been employed in some studies or by some instruments (e.g., MWES; Nader, Pynoos, Fairbanks, & Frederick, 1990). Differences exist in exposures (Singer, Anglen, Song, & Lunghofer, 1995) and in symptom levels between children who live in large cities versus those who live in small cities and rural areas (Briere, 1996a; Richters & Martinez, 1991). Elliot and Briere (1994b) have found differences in symptom levels reported by children who deny the event and/or its symptoms. Normative samples may include individuals who deny trauma and who drastically underreport symptom levels, possibly lowering the mean (see TSCC-C, this chapter). It is generally expected that random selection and other statistical procedures take care of these difficulties; however, this assumes that the appropriate groupings have been identified (e.g., age, city vs. rural location); therefore, this area requires careful attention.

PARENT, TEACHER, OR CHILD INTERVIEWS

The importance of interviewing children regarding their psychological reactions has been well established (Terr, 1979; Lobovits & Handal, 1985; Reich & Earls, 1987; Nader & Pynoos, 1989; Weissman et al., 1987). As described earlier (Phases of Response and Training) interviewing children directly may be most effective 3–5 weeks after an event and when the interviewer is appropriately knowledgeable and deemed caring and trustworthy by the children. In addition to timing and method, avoidance of traumatic emotions and reminders may affect the accuracy of assessment.

Children may be traumatized by their experiences, yet may not report the full range of PTSD symptoms (Nader & Fairbanks, 1994). Elliot and Briere (1994b) found that sexually abused children who denied the abuse reported significantly fewer symptoms than nonabused children. Traumatized children who underreport may exhibit specific indicators of traumatic response. For example, there is some evidence that the suppression of reexperiencing phenomena in children with direct exposure to traumatic events may result in increased arousal symptoms such as increased difficulties with impulse control and somatic complaints (Nader & Fairbanks, 1994). McFarlane, Policansky, and Irwin (1987) found that anxiety and behavioral disturbance, observed at school but not observed by parents at 2 and 8 months following a destructive fire, were associated with posttraumatic phenomena at 26 months.

Issues regarding the concordance or discordance between parent and child reports of children's psychiatric symptoms have varied according to the nature of the symptoms and the disorder (Nader & Pynoos, 1989). Several researchers recommend using multiple sources of information in the assessment of children (e.g., children, parents, teachers, clinicians; Friedrich et al., in press; Reich & Earls, 1987; Briere, 1996b; Sternberg et al., 1993). Weissman et al. (1987) recommended that psychiatric status be based on independent assessment of both child and parent informants. In the event that one group must be chosen, they recommended interviewing the children.

For most psychiatric disorders, children generally report more symptoms for themselves than parents report for them (Lobovits & Handal, 1985). Some studies have found that children report more of all disorders for themselves (Weissman et al., 1987), whereas others have suggested variations by disorder, for example, that parents report more conduct disorders or objective behavioral symptoms (Herjanic & Reich, 1982). It has been suggested that as children grow older, they are better able to conceal their activities from their parents, and adolescents are therefore better reporters of their own conduct disturbances (Edelbrock, Costello, Dulcan, Conover, & Kala, 1986; Reich & Earls, 1987).

The question of parent–child concordance or discordance is important to the investigation of PTSD in children. Sternberg and her colleagues (1993) suggest that some parents may prefer not to recognize signs of the damage wrought by children's traumatic experiences, whereas some children may be biased defensively. They found fathers, in contrast to mothers, least likely to report problem behaviors in their children. Sternberg et al. offered several possible explanations for this: Fathers were not sufficiently familiar with their children's problems, were unused to describing them, mislabeled their children's behaviors, or had difficulty filling out standardized measures.

Clinical descriptive studies of children's postdisaster symptoms have suggested that parents may minimize the events impact on their children. Bloch et al. (1956) observed that after a tornado, some parents appeared to contend with anxiety through suppression or attempts to deny the event's impact. After a severe winter storm and flooding, Burke, Borus, Burns, Millstein, and Beasley (1982) suspected that children's symptoms were underestimated because of parents' denial of their children's problems. Following the Three Mile Island nuclear accident, children reported stronger and more symptomatic responses for themselves than parents reported for them (Handford et al., 1986). Kinzie, Sack, Angell, Manson, and Rath (1986) found that Cambodian children exposed to concentration-camp-like experiences were more anxious about schoolwork, more worried about friends, and complained of symptoms of depression at a higher rate than reported by their parents or guardians. In an acute-phase study of children exposed to a sniper attack (Pynoos et al., 1987), children reported more and different symptoms than parents reported for them (Nader & Pynoos, 1989). Parents reported more objective symptoms (e.g.,anxiety/arousal, bullying, rudeness, argumentativeness, irritability, and regression); children reported more subjective symptoms (e.g., intrusive thoughts and images, avoidance of feelings, sense of estrangement, impaired concentration, and sleep disturbance; Nader & Pynoos, 1989).

Parents who attend parent groups or training sessions have been observed to be better reporters of their children's reactions. This educational process has sometimes been assisted by a thorough parent interview (Nader & Pynoos, 1989). One year after a tornado, parents who had attended parent meetings with the consultant every 2 months were better reporters than their children of the children's ongoing traumatic reactions (symptoms were confirmed with the clinicians and teachers working with the children). Over time, children may minimize their symptoms, thinking that other children are no longer symptomatic, or that they should not be symptomatic after this much time has passed.

Although children are able to report symptoms that permit a diagnosis of PTSD and associated difficulties, there are some symptoms that are more effectively reported by parents or teachers. Parents have provided information regarding changes in behaviors at home and with peers (Reich & Earls, 1987; Nader & Pynoos, 1989). Reich and Earls (1987) found the reports of teachers to be particularly helpful in making behavioral diagnoses for a variety of disorders. Teachers are also of assistance in reporting visible symptoms of depression and anxiety, and marked changes in school performance or academic style.

It is important to keep in mind that parents' or teachers' own traumatic reaction may effect reporting. Parents under distress may minimize their children's reactions, or may consciously or unconsciously require the child to hide or bury symptoms. Teachers who are traumatized, or who feel guilty, may underreport children's symptoms (Pynoos & Nader, 1988) or become supersensitized to the children's symptoms (Nader & Pynoos, 1993a). Following a tornado, teachers reported fewer PTSD and reduced self-esteem symptoms for children than the children reported for themselves. In some circumstances, children may find it possible to suppress symptoms in the

classroom and focus on schoolwork. They may become quieter or more inhibited at school, a change in behavior that is sometimes appreciated in the
classroom. Ideally, the measurement of childhood PTSD includes the reports
of child, clinician, parent and teacher. In the absence of other reports, most
investigators suggest interviewing the child directly (Weissman et al., 1987;
Reich & Earls, 1987; Nader & Pynoos, 1989).

LONG-TERM VERSUS SINGLE-INCIDENT TRAUMA

Discussions of ongoing traumas versus single-incident traumas
(Nader & Stuber, 1992; Terr, 1991) have most often addressed the reactions
of abused and molested children. Clearly determining an accurate profile
for children exposed to ongoing versus single-incident experiences is complicated by differences in phase of response, phase of development, the nature of the traumatic event, relationship to the perpetrator, and other variables (Nader, in press-b). A number of symptoms have been identified that
occur most frequently if the trauma has been ongoing in nature and occurs
early in life (van der Kolk, Roth, Pelkovitz, & Mandel, 1993; Terr, 1991). These
symptoms have been observed in children who experienced ongoing traumas, dual or multiple unrelated traumas, or a single trauma combined with
previous loss (Nader, in press-b). Among the symptoms found in children following traumas that are not included in the DSM-IV PTSD diagnostic criteria
are affect dysregulation, somatization, loss of beliefs, dissociation, self-
destructive behaviors, loss of faith in authority or adults, and unrelenting
hopelessness. A number of these symptoms are addressed in the extended
questions on the CAPS-C, CITES-R, MWES/MWSES, WBTH, and the TSCC.

There is some indication that the long-term consequences of ongoing
traumas emphasize reexperiencing and avoidance. In a study of children
with catastrophic illness undergoing BMT, children showed fewer arousal
symptoms than children exposed to violence (Nader & Stuber, 1992). Similarly, Realmuto and his colleagues (1992) found a greater frequency of reexperiencing and avoidance symptoms and a lower frequency of arousal
symptoms in adolescents who had been exposed between 1975 and 1979 to
the wartime atrocities of the Pol Pot regime in Cambodia. They suggest the
possibility that massive trauma exposure in childhood might result in chronic
reexperiencing, avoidance, and vulnerability to arousal. Over time, intermittent hyperarousal episodes might be triggered by recent reminders, bio-
chemical factors, or current stress.

The theory that ongoing trauma may result in intermittent episodes
rather than chronic arousal is validated by my observation of Kuwaiti children and adults who had become accustomed to the sounds of war and were
able to discriminate benign from threatening sounds. In the first few months
after the war, periodic explosions represented a mine-cleaning sweep of the
beach areas. In contrast to visiting consultants who startled at every explo-

sion in their first few days in Kuwait, the Kuwaitis were unfazed by these explosions. The differences in symptom presentation over time and after ongoing exposure to trauma must be accounted for in the measurement of childhood trauma.

INSTRUMENTS DESIGNED TO MEASURE CHILDHOOD PTSD

Instruments designed to measure childhood trauma are described here. The instruments are listed in alphabetical order by their abbreviations. Their descriptions include a review of their use and content, the need for training, reliability and validity studies, translations and adaptations, and issues related to their usage. Measures of reliability may include examination of the instrument's reliability over time (test–retest), internal consistency, consistency between raters and/or interitem agreement between raters. Measures of validity include face validity (whether the scale appears to measure what it is intended to measure) and construct validity (whether the measure accurately reflects the construct or concept), including content (whether the test measures the appropriate behavior), convergent (whether there is correlation with characteristics similar to but not the same as those measured by the scale), discriminant (whether the behavior measured is due to another variable or the one measured) and criterion validity (predictive validity; correlation of the assessment device with the external behavior; Carver & Scheier, 1992).

Interviews with children continue to reveal the need to reword, arrange, and effectively present questions in order to best assess children and make the process easier for them. Moreover, we are still learning about children's responses to trauma. As a consequence, many of the instruments undergo periodic revisions and/or updates. Several of the instruments represented here were undergoing revision at the time of review.[1]

PTSD Scales

CAPS-C

The Clinician-Administered PTSD Scale for Children (CAPS-C; Nader et al., 1994b) is an instrument developed to measure cardinal and hypothesized signs and symptoms of PTSD in children and adolescents. This scale provides a method to evaluate the frequency and intensity of individual symptoms, the impact of symptoms on social and occupational functioning,

---

[1]The following write-ups were derived from review of the instruments, publications describing their use, assessments by users of the instruments, and input and feedback from instrument authors. Descriptions of some of these and other instruments not reviewed here, written solely by the instrument's author, can be found in Stamm (1996).

degree of improvement since an earlier rating, validity of ratings obtained, and overall intensity of symptoms. Whenever possible, it is recommended that the CAPS-C be used in conjunction with self-report, behavioral, and physiological measures.

CAPS-C is based upon DSM-IV diagnostic criteria for PTSD, and upon additional symptoms found in the literature for childhood PTSD, including those for complicated and ongoing traumas (Terr, 1991; van der Kolk et al., 1992). A form for evaluating the traumatic event's compliance with DSM-IV Criterion A precedes the symptom questionnaire. The initial 17 items are based upon Criteria B, C, and D (reexperiencing, numbing, and arousal symptoms) and includes one subquestion regarding regression, which was among the DSM-III-R criteria but was excluded from DSM-IV (it is not included in the rating of the presence of PTSD). Ratings for social and scholastic functioning (Criterion F) as well as overall severity and validity of reporting ratings follow. Nine additional questions measure symptoms found in the research literature regarding PTSD, and four questions measure independent variables. The instrument concludes with two coping questions aimed at transferring the child's focus from negative effects of traumatic experience to methods of coping with the event (Nader et al., 1994a).

Translations and Revisions. A 1996 revision of the CAPS-C and manual is in process (Nader et al., 1996). There are currently no language translations. Computer programs for use with the instrument are under development.

Reliability and Validity. Although psychometric testing is in the planning, it has not yet been conducted for this instrument. It has been used to measure childhood trauma in a clinical setting with success for children 8 years and older (Burgess, personal communication, December 1994; Baker, personal communication, July 1995; Friedrich, 1995).

Training. A training manual accompanies this instrument (Nader et al., 1994a). It is intended for use by mental health professionals. Training is available upon request.

Issues Related to Usage. The CAPS-C permits the assessment of DSM diagnostic criteria and includes additional questions regarding associated symptoms and exposure variables (including symptoms found for more complicated forms of PTSD; Terr, 1991; van der Kolk et al., 1993; Nader, in press-b). This is a new instrument that has as yet not undergone extensive use. It is differently worded than the adult CAPS and is applied to an untested population; new psychometric testing is necessary. Baker (personal communication, July 1995) found the 1994 instrument easiest to use when the trauma has been identified; she has used the scale successfully with sexually abused children. The children have done well with the PTSD questions;

the interview becomes a little long with the additional questions. Children under the age of 8 may have difficultly with the 5-point scales. In general, the rating scales employ a sophisticated format; there are aids for children's use of them. The 1996 version (Nader et al., 1996) will include the use of iconic representations of ratings (Newman & Ribbe, 1996). Although icons have been used successfully in depicting symptoms for children, the use of these somewhat playful icons in the rating scales may be ill-advised for several reasons, including the following: First, it is important for children to feel that it is okay to say or feel anything. Young children are easily focused upon one train of thought/emotion. These icons may set a more playful, less serious tone, and may subtly suggest that a lighter atmosphere is sought. Second, children below a certain age tend to take things literally and concretely; increased concreteness has been observed in trauma victims of all ages. Some of the icons locate stress in the stomach or place the occurrence of symptoms on specific days, which may elicit falsely low ratings for children who do not experience stress in the stomach or symptoms on those days. In the 1996 version, some of the clarifying/probe questions (asking for specific dates of onset or symptom descriptions) have been moved to precede the rating. This may result in some false low ratings for the younger children. Elementary-school-age children have often been able to say, for example, that they want to stay away from reminders or have repeated thoughts/images of the event on a daily basis. When asked to describe the things they want to avoid or the thoughts/images, and they cannot think of any, they sometimes decide that maybe they do not have these symptoms. The 1996 version has made some improvements over the original. For example, the additional questions have been reduced to those relevant to a DSM-IV acute distress disorder diagnosis, and important probe questions have been moved from the manual into the body of the CAPS-C.

CPTS-RI

The Child Posttraumatic Stress Reaction Index (CPTS-RI; Frederick, Pynoos, & Nader, 1992) is a 20-item scale used in direct, semistructured interview with children and adolescents. There is an associated training manual (Nader, 1993) that gives detailed instructions for its usage. CPTS-RI items include some of the DSM-IV PTSD symptoms from each of three main subscales and an associated feature. For the CPTS-RI, the DSM-IV Criterion B of reexperiencing trauma includes fear or upset in response to reminders, fear or upset with thoughts of the event, intrusive thoughts, intrusive images, traumatic or bad dreams, thinking there will be a recurrence of the event, and somatic symptoms. The DSM-IV Criterion C of numbing/avoidance includes numbing of affect, a sense of isolation, loss of interest in activities, avoidance of reminders (activities, places, people, thoughts, or conversations), and avoidance of feelings. The DSM-IV Criterion D for physiological arousal includes jumpiness, sleep disturbance, difficulty concentrating, and difficulties in impulse control.

The CPTS-RI has been used to assess specific posttraumatic stress symptoms after exposure to violence (Pynoos et al., 1987; Nader et al., 1990; Schwarz & Kowalski, 1991; Realmuto et al., 1992) and disaster (Pynoos et al., 1993; Nader & Pynoos, 1993a). Each child is interviewed about his or her individual response to the event. Only direct self-report of symptoms still present are recorded. The revised CPTS-RI includes a 5-point Likert frequency rating scale ranging from "none" (0) to "most of the time" (4) (Pynoos & Nader, 1988). Although the index does not provide a DSM PTSD diagnosis, there is a scoring system that establishes a level of "PTSD." Previous unpublished, empirical comparisons of CPTS-RI scores with clinical assessments for severity levels of PTSD have resulted in the following guidelines: a total score of 12–24 indicates a mild level of PTSD reaction; 25–39, a moderate level; 40–59, a severe level; > 60, a very severe reaction.

Translations and Revisions. The CPTS-RI has been translated into Cambodian (Realmuto et al., 1992), Arabic (one for 7- to 10-year-olds and one for 11- to 17-year-olds; Nader et al., 1993), Croatian (Nader, Vidovic, Anic, & Pynoss, 1992), Armenian (Pynoos et al., 1993), and Norwegian. The Croatian version of the Reaction Index has recently undergone a final back-translation and retranslation process with the author and a team of Croatian psychiatrists.

Two parent questionnaires have been used with the CPTS-RI. One of them is a more extensive clinical questionnaire used in semistructured interview with parents, permitting simultaneous education of parents and elicitation of premorbid personality and trauma-related information regarding their children (Nader, 1995). The others have been adapted to specific situations to match the CPTS-RI. Exposure questionnaires have been adapted to the specific traumatic situation and the traumatized culture for the English and other versions of the instrument. A war-exposure questionnaire accompanies the training manual (Nader, 1993) and is available in Arabic; a revised version of it (available in Croatian), with additional coping measures, is also available.

Reliability and Validity. A number of studies have demonstrated issues of reliability and validity for the CPTS-RI. In a study by the scale's coauthors and their colleagues of children exposed to a sniper attack, interrater reliability for this instrument was measured at .94, and interitem agreement by Cohen's kappa at .878 (Nader et al., 1990). In an as yet unpublished study of children exposed to a tornado, interrater reliability was established at .97. In a study of Kuwaiti children following the Gulf Crisis, internal consistency for this scale was established (Cronbach's α = .78), and 16 of the 20 items were significantly correlated with the total score at p < .01 (Nader & Fairbanks, 1994).

Using DSM-III-R criteria, the guidelines for severity levels of PTSD were empirically validated in a subsample of children from a study of the 1988 Spitak earthquake in Armenia (Pynoos et al., 1993). In this study, 43.6% of those with moderate reactions on the CPTS-RI, 89.3% of those rated severe, and 91.7% of those rated very severe on the CPTS-RI met the DSM-III-R criteria for PTSD. In an as yet unpublished study of children exposed to a tornado, in which clinicians underwent a week of thorough training (by this author) in the instrument's use prior to administration, children rating moderate to severe posttraumatic stress on the CPTS-RI were referred for treatment. All of the children who entered treatment following the tornado were independently diagnosed under the review of a New York State Mental Health psychiatrist. All of them met the criteria for PTSD.

Training. The CPTS-RI is accompanied by a training manual (Nader, 1993) and instructions for scoring. Training has improved the accuracy of the instrument's correlation with the clinical diagnosis of PTSD. Training is recommended and is available upon request. Training in the use of this instrument has also successfully assisted the training of psychologists, social workers, and psychiatrists in aspects of childhood traumatic response (Nader & Pynoos, 1993b).

Issues Related to Usage. The CPTS-RI has been successfully administered to a variety of populations. The 20-item index, with a few additional questions and exposure questions has taken from only 20–45 minutes with American children (usually depending on severity of response) and, of course, longer with added questions and an extensive exposure questionnaire. Children below 7 or 8 years of age may have difficulty with the 5-point scale and may require some minor rewording of terms. Some suggestions for rewording are provided in the training manual.

There have been two complaints by users of the CPTS-RI. First, it does not inquire about all of the DSM-III-R or DSM-IV symptoms (see Realmuto et al., 1992). Some of the DSM-IV items are omitted; others are asked more than once. Second, for research purposes, there are three questions that are asked regarding the presence of healthy conditions rather than the presence of symptoms (enjoyment of activities, sleep, and concentration). The scoring of these questions does not always clearly indicate the extent of the symptom. For this reason, the manual recommends making note of the level of symptomatic response for each of these questions, as well as making the positive rating on the scale. Since the scoring system was devised with the questions asked in this positive direction, changing them would impact scoring.

The CPTS-RI has been used most effectively in studies of children in the acute phase or first few years after an identified single-incident traumatic experience (Pynoos et al., 1987, 1993; Nader et al., 1990, 1993; Pynoos et al., 1993; Schwarz & Kowalski, 1991). For the accurate measurement of symptom levels of children years after an event or after prolonged exposure to trauma (e.g., adolescents previously exposed to war atrocities in Cambodia),

Realmuto et al. (1992) suggest that future revisions of the CPTS-RI include developmentally relevant items and episode and duration parameters.

CRTES

The Child's Reaction to Traumatic Events Scale (CRTES; Jones, 1994) is a revision of the Impact of Events Scale for Children (IES-C; modified for children by Jones [1992]). It is a 15-item self-report measure designed to assess psychological responses to stressful life events. It targets the Intrusion and Avoidance criteria of DSM-III-R and was derived from statements most frequently used by people to describe serious life events (Horowitz, Wilner, & Alvarez, 1979). It contains six of the original items from the Adult IES. A modified version of the IES has been used to study children exposed to catastrophic events (Malmquist, 1986; Yule & Williams, 1990; Cunningham, Jones, & Yang, 1994). The CRTES has been used with children exposed to fires (Jones & Ribbe, 1991; Jones, Ribbe, & Cunningham, 1994) and to a hurricane (Jones et al., 1993). There are 8 avoidance statements (3 avoidance of emotions, 2 of thoughts, 1 of conversations; 1 avoidance of reminders; 1 disavowal/dissociation) and 7 intrusion statements (4 of intrusive thoughts/images; 1 of dreams; 2 of feelings).

Like the IES, the CRTES uses a 4-point frequency rating scale: "not at all" (0), "rarely" (1), "sometimes" (3), and "often" (5). Horowitz et al. proposed cutoff scores using the summated scale scores. A low distress total score is less than 9; moderate distress 9–18; and high distress, 19 and over.

Translations and Revisions. The CRTES is a revision of the IES-C (Jones, 1992).

Reliability and Validity. Studies have demonstrated levels of reliability for an earlier version of the CRTES, the IES-C. In a study following Hurricane Andrew, tests of internal consistency have yielded Cronbach's alpha scores of .84, for the Intrusion subscale .72, for the Avoidance subscale, and .85 for the total scale (Jones et al., 1993). In a study of 71 African American children residing in a high-crime, low-income area (Cunningham et al., 1994), the tests of internal consistency for the CRTES yielded Cronbach's alphas of .73 for the total scale and .68 and .53, respectively, for the Intrusion and Avoidance subscales. For adolescent residents of a boarding school exposed to a dormitory fire (Jones & Ribbe, 1991), interviewers underwent 51 hours of training in the use of three instruments (DICA-6R-A; IES-C and the State–Trait Anxiety Index [STAI]). At the end of training, interrater reliability averaged .91.

In two studies of children exposed to fires, both the IES-C (an earlier version of the CRTES) and the DICA-R were used. These children and adolescents did not experience high levels of life threat. When the IES-C was used as a self-report measure, the DICA-6R-A (semistructured interviews) demonstrated greater differences between groups (Jones & Ribbe, 1991). When both measures were used in semistructured interviews, the IES-C revealed greater differences between the groups (Jones et al., 1994; see DICA, this chapter).

In a study of 213 elementary- and middle-school children exposed to Hurricane Andrew who were interviewed in small groups, Jones et al. (1993) found that appraisal (degree of perceived danger) best predicted level of distress. Life threat also predicted distress. Female elementary-school children demonstrated the most intrusive symptomatology. The avoidance subscale did not reveal significant differences in these children. The authors suggest a possible reason for the failure of the avoidance scale: Reminders remained rampant and pervasive in the environment. Inasmuch as children have reported significantly more avoidance of reminders and other avoidance symptoms in contrast to comparison-group children, during traumatic events in which reminders also remained rampant and pervasive (Pynoos et al., 1987), additional examination of this event (the group of children, the wording of questions, or the application of the questionnaire) must be examined.

Training. It is recommended that interviewers be trained by a clinician with a background in childhood psychopathology.

Issues Related to Usage. The CRTES is simply worded for children. It examines stress reactions based on common responses to stressful events as determined in the 1970s (Horowitz et al., 1979). The instrument requires a brief administration time of 3–5 minutes. It is easy to use.

The CRTES does not measure PTSD. Not all criteria or all categories of the two DSM-III-R or DSM-IV criteria addressed (Intrusion and Avoidance) are included in the instrument. There are multiple items for some of the DSM subcriteria. For example, there are four statements related to intrusive thoughts and images—Criterion B1—and six statements related to avoidance of thoughts, feelings or conversations—Criterion C1.

Since the measure is currently undergoing psychometric evaluation, the author requests that users share their results with his lab (Russell T. Jones, Ph. D., Associate Professor, Department of Psychology, Stress and Coping Lab, 4102 Derring Hall, Virginia Polytechnic Institute and State University, Blacksburg, VA 24060).

MWES and MWSES

My Worst Experience Survey and My Worst School Experience Survey (MWES and MWSES; National Center for Study of Corporal Punishment and Alternatives in the Schools [NCSCPAS], 1992; Hyman et al., 1988) assess the child's most stressful experience in general or at school and the associated thoughts, behaviors, and feelings related to the experience. The MWES consists of a preliminary inquiry about the worst experience and the child's rating of how upsetting it was, a page of possible worst experiences (e.g., abuse, death of significant other, disaster, personal or family problems, illness, divorce, robbery or kidnapping) and a 105-item list of possible responses to the experience endorsed by frequency of occurrence. The MWSES consists of a preliminary questionnaire and Parts I and II. The preliminary questionnaire is an inquiry about the worst experience and a few brief checklists regarding the circumstances of the event. Part I is a 39-item list of stressful experiences that might occur at school and is rated for frequency of occurrence. Part II is the 105-item endorsement checklist consisting of statements about thoughts, feelings, and behaviors since the experience. The instruments are self-report measures to be completed by children and adolescents, ages 8–17. The 105 items were selected based upon DSM-III-R and DSM-IV criteria for PTSD and research studies regarding traumatic stress in children (Berna, 1993; Kohr, 1995). The instrument has been administered in group settings, distributed for completion independently by children, and given in semistructured interviews. No studies have been done comparing these methods for the MWES.

The rating system for these instruments is a 5-point Likert scale ranging from "one time" (1) to "all of the time" (5). Scores range from 0 to 525. A study of 11- to 18-year-olds (Berna, 1993) has served as a comparison for other studies; his results have been used like population norms. Berna examined children from divorced and nondivorced parents. Mean scores for frequency of occurrence of symptoms measured on the MWES for the total group (n = 443) were 86.77 (9, or 2%, of children met PTSD criteria; intact families, n = 279, mean = 76.89; divorced families, n = 136, mean = 104.80). Although some of the children indicated previous traumatic experiences, the exact numbers and levels of traumatic exposure for these families (and subgroups) is unknown. Later studies with smaller samples have found that the scores of randomly selected subsamples of the children in Berna's study were significantly lower than those of children with exposures to traumatic events. For example, children with varying degrees of exposure to a hurricane (including those with and without life threat or witnessing of injury; Goldwater, 1993; n = 122) had a mean of 103.89 (10, or 8%, met PTSD criteria). Kohr (1995) compared a small group of children diagnosed with PTSD (n = 11) to comparable groups of children with other psychiatric disorders and a subsample from Berna's study. Group means were as follows: PTSD sample, 323.55; clinical sample, 139.55; Berna subsample, 87.27. Zahn (1994) compared 30 sexually abused children to an equivalent number of children from Berna's study and a subsample of emotionally disturbed children from a study by Rea (1994) and found significantly greater symptoms for the sexually abused children than for the other two groups (mean symptom frequency: sexually abused, 274.50; emotionally disturbed, 117.13; regular education group, 86.58).

Translations and Revisions. This survey is a revision of the School Trauma Survey (Hyman et al., 1988), which was used to assess the traumatic effects of severe corporal punishment of school-age children.

Reliability and Validity. Both parametric and nonparametric tests were used to evaluate the reliability and validity for the MWES. Test–retest reliability for the School Trauma Survey, on which the MWES was based, was established at .95, .97, and .94 (p < .05) respectively, for frequency, duration and intensity (Lambert, 1990). For 21 eighth-grade students (Berna, 1993), test–retest reliability has been established for the MWES with coefficients for symptom frequency, duration and intensity yielding Pearson product–moment correlations of .98, .96, and .99, respectively. Test–retest reliability was established for the MWSES with correlation coefficients of .87, .85, .69, and .82 (p < .003), respectively, for the frequency, duration, intensity, and total scores (Berna, 1993).

Validity of the MWES was established in several ways. Content validity was established by enlisting the aid of local and national professionals in the field of child trauma. The final version of the survey includes items endorsed by the professionals as relevant to the DSM-III-R diagnosis of PTSD. Face validity was established by the same professionals, who agreed that it appears to be assessing PTSD. Construct validity was established through use of a factor analysis that established seven factors: Depressed/Withdrawn, Oppositional/Defiant, Avoidant/Hypervigilant, Somatic, Reexperience/Intrusive Thoughts, Depressed/Hopeless/Suicidal, and Disturbing Dreams/Memories. The factors appear to cluster in a fashion reasonably consistent with DSM criteria groupings. Internal consistency was established for the MWES with Cronbach's coefficient alpha with factors ranging from .68 to .91 (Berna, 1993). Criterion validity was established in using a subsample of this study of 11- to 18-year-olds (Kohr, 1995). Control subjects were randomly selected from Berna's larger group of 443 children from three nonpublic high schools, who had completed the MWES for a previous study of children of divorced families versus children of intact families (Berna, 1993), and diagnostic groups were selected from the diagnosed patients of psychiatrists primarily in the Philadelphia area (n = 11 for each group): Subjects with psychiatric diagnosis of PTSD, subjects matched for age and sex as a control group, and subjects matched for age and sex with a psychiatric diagnosis other than PTSD. A one-way analysis of variance, multivariate analysis of variance (MANOVA), and Kruskal–Wallis analysis of variance indicated significant differences in MWES scores between groups for total score, frequency of symptoms, the seven factors, and the cluster scores. A Newman–Keuls test of the means and Mann–Whitney U test yielded a significant difference between the PTSD group and both other groups, but no significant difference between control and clinical groups. Similarly, in a study of sexually abused children (Zahn, 1994) compared to emotionally disturbed (Rea, 1994) and normal children (Berna, 1993), Zahn found significant differences between the sexually abused group and the other two groups for total frequency score and on each of the seven factors. The emotionally disturbed group was significantly higher on the Oppositional/Defiant Factor than the regular education group. When comparing diagnosis of PTSD by the MWES to diagnosis by psychiatric evaluation, the MWES diagnosed PTSD more frequently than did psychiatric evaluation (Zahn, 1994).

Training. Dr. Irwin Hyman of Temple University in Philadelphia provides 1–2 hours within a broader PTSD training workshop regarding the instruments and their usage. The instrument can be used by professionals and others. It is recommended, however, that a skilled clinician be available in case of any reactions to completing the survey. Score sheets are provided, which outline into which factor symptoms fall. Factors approximate DSM-IV criteria (Berna, 1993). A manual for the MWES and MWSES is in process and will be available before the end of 1996.

Issues Related to Usage. Small pilot samples of eighth graders (Berna, 1993) and adolescents (Curcio-Chilton, 1994) have endorsed the instrument's easy readability. The Flesch–Kincaid grade level established for the MWES was 5.4 (Zahn, 1994); the Fry Readability Formula places the survey at the third-grade level and the Readability Index places the survey at grades 1.8–3.2 (Kohr, 1995). Administration time is approximately 20–40 minutes.

As is true for most instruments written for children, there are some questions about wording and construction. For example, the reaction section begins with a statement regarding "unjustified anger." Opening with this question may elicit resistance from children and adolescents. On the MWSES, there is a list of possible persons involved in the worst school experience. Since this instrument was developed to measure stress symptoms perpetrated by educators, "other student" is not listed as one of the choices. For other traumatic or stress-inducing experiences, the MWES is generally used. For the MWES, a more extensive list of possible traumas (many traumas to which children are currently exposed are omitted) has been recommended (see Berna, 1993). Berna suggests that a better method of measuring multiple trauma be used in future revisions.

There have been some wording changes over time. It is important for the user to confirm which version of the instrument (there is no numerical distinction for minor changes in wording) was used before making comparisons to other studies (e.g., inclusion or omission of the word "very" has varied over time; comparing an endorsement of "angry" versus "very angry" or "upset" versus "very upset" may be expected to affect accuracy). Moreover, in assessing the results of a study using the instruments to measure PTSD, it must be remembered that the instruments include multiple questions for each of several DSM subcriteria (e.g., intrusive recollections, items 37 and 57; feelings of detachment, items 30, 42, 47, 74, 95, 97; see score sheets).

The score sheets are of assistance in examining issues rated by the survey. Survey items appear in three lists: (1) according to the seven factors found by Berna (1993), (2) by DSM-III-R criteria, and (3) by DSM-IV criteria. Means found in the survey of 443 school children (Berna, 1993) are included on the score sheets. The MWES has been used extensively with children for the purposes of dissertation studies. The doctoral candidates who have used it have found it to be an easy and effective method of measuring children's stress reactions.

WBTH

The When Bad Things Happen scale (WBTH; Fletcher, 1991) is a self-report measure that assesses DSM-IV PTSD, DSM-III-R PTSD, and additional trauma-related behaviors in children ages 8 and older. A tape is available to assist younger children in completing the instrument. The WBTH is given to children for completion. The instrument is accompanied by three other scales: (1) an interview with the child; (2) a parent interview; and (3) a parent questionnaire regarding the child. A fifth scale, Dimensions of Stressful Events (DOSE), measures exposure and result variables including, for example, number of traumas, relationship to perpetrator, sense of stigmatization, and moral and religious conflicts. It includes items related to child abuse. The World View Survey measures posttrauma beliefs in children age 12 and older.

The instrument has been used to measure childhood PTSD with Israeli children exposed to the Gulf Crisis (Moller-Thau & Fletcher, 1996) and by its author to measure a variety of childhood trauma exposures. It is currently being used to assess trauma in Armenia. Symptoms for PTSD are assessed by 67 questions. Symptoms are indicated by a "yes" answer on 47 of the questions and by a "no" on 20 items. Each DSM item is asked in two to six questions. Most of 10 associated symptoms are asked in two to five questions each. Symptoms are considered present if the child endorses the symptom on two or more questions. Frequency ratings include "never," "some," or "lots," rated 0, 1, and 2, respectively.

Translations and Revisions. The WBTH and accompanying instruments have been translated into Hebrew (Moller-Thau & Fletcher, 1996) and Armenian. Computer programs for scoring the first four of these scales are currently available for IBM-compatible computers. The programs work in conjunction with another program, EPI Info, which is distributed by the Centers for Disease Control (CDC) and the World Health Organization (WHO). Rudimentary data analysis is also possible. Programs can be obtained from Dr. Fletcher by sending three high-density 3.5-inch diskettes or four 5.25-inch diskettes.

Reliability and Validity. Collected data is currently undergoing analysis. In a pilot study of 15 children (Moller-Thau & Fletcher, 1996), the correlation between this instrument and the CPTS-RI was high and significant ($r = .84$; $p < .001$). A kappa statistic was measured at .67 when measuring agreement between the CPTS-RI and the WBTH with adolescents. The WBTH classified two children with PTSD that the CPTS-RI did not. For this small sample of children, the WBTH more often elicited responses that met Criteria A, B, and D and equally often found PTSD criterion met for Criterion C as the CPTS-RI. For Fletcher's current ongoing study ($n = 30$) of school-age children, internal consistency was demonstrated by Kuder–Richardson statistic for the dichotomous items in the two interviews at .90 for the child interview and .94 for the parent interview. Internal consistency was demonstrated by Cronbach's alpha at .92 for WBTH and .89 for the Parent's Report of Child's Reaction to Stress Scale. Cronbach's alpha for each DSM-IV Criterion subscale on the WBTH and Parent Report, respectively, were as follows: A, .70, .81; B, .89, .86; C, .70, .70; and D, .82, .81. Kuder–Richardson statistic for each Criterion subscale on the Child and Parent Interviews, respectively, were: A, .52,.60; B, .80, .86; C, .76, .86; and D, .78 and .83. All four PTSD measures significantly differentiated the 10 children seeking counseling for traumatic experiences from the 20 children recruited from the community. The severity scores on all of the questionnaires correlated significantly with a 20-item post hoc CBCL-PTSD scale.

Training. Familiarization with the scale and an understanding of DSM PTSD criteria is recommended.

Issues Related to Usage. The WBTH permits the assessment of DSM diagnostic criteria and includes questions regarding additional symptoms found for children following traumatic exposure. It asks about each symptom more than once permitting the endorsement of symptoms missed due to wording issues or state of mind. The questions are not asked equal numbers of times (e.g., some are asked two, others up to six ways), however, which must be taken into consideration when assessing results and comparing to results of other instruments. Some of the questions may be dropped in a future revision of the instrument.

As is true for all of the instruments for children, there are some wording issues. For example, some of the questions refer to the "bad thing." Careful consideration must be given to repeatedly labeling an event a "bad thing." There are upsetting or traumatic experiences that occur during good or desirable events, such as when family fun results in injury or death. Moreover, it may be psychologically important to actually name the event when inquiring about symptoms. In an instrument that is completed by the child, naming the event is only possible if the instrument has been adapted for the specific event prior to completion. Questions on child instruments sometimes benefit from alternative wordings (e.g., WBTH question 24 might read "Do you wish you could turn off [or stop] feelings that remind you of what happened?"). The question on survivor guilt may not discriminate between traumatized and nontraumatized children, since most children feel bad that other children were hurt worse than they were.

In general, the WBTH is worded simply for children. It has an easy format for children and adolescents. Concern for children is apparent in the wording and construction of the instrument. For example, in the introduction, the child is told that his or her answers "will help us to understand how you feel," and that there are no right or wrong answers. The child is thanked twice on the instrument.

PTSD Subscales

DICA-PTSD Scale

The Diagnostic Interview for Children and Adolescents—Revised (DICA-R; Reich et al., 1991) is an instrument designed for use in semistructured interview to assess common psychiatric diagnoses. It has been used widely in the United States and internationally (Earls, Reich, & Jung, 1988; Reich & Kaplan, 1994). It is based on the DSM and includes a PTSD scale (Jones & Ribbe, 1991; Jones et al., 1994); both DSM-III-R and DSM-IV diagnoses are possible. The interview inquires about trauma in language chosen to be easily understood by children and adolescents. There are separate questionnaires for children ages 6–12 and for adolescents ages 13–17.

The PTSD subscale consists of four initial questions to establish DSM Criterion A (Traumatic Experience), seven questions for Criterion B (Reexperiencing), nine questions for Criterion C (Numbing/Avoidance), and five questions for Criterion D (Arousal), with suggestions for appropriate probe questions. Criteria questions are followed by inquiries about duration (Criterion E) and intensity of the symptom complex and about intervention, parental concern, changes in interpersonal relationships, and changes at school (Criterion F). The rating scale is as follows: 1 = "no"; 2 = "rarely"; 3 = "sometimes or somewhat"; and 5 = "yes" (there is no 4 rating). Scores are added in order to determine the meeting of criteria for a diagnosis of PTSD using scoring sheet or computer program.

Translations and Revisions. The instrument has recently been revised to meet DSM-IV diagnostic criteria. It has reportedly worked equally well with Caucasian and African American children (Reich, personal communication, February 1994). The entire DICA-R has been translated into Spanish, and according to Reich, the PTSD scale has been used successfully with child victims of warfare in Ecuador. It has also been translated into Arabic for use in an ongoing study of Lebanese children.

Reliability and Validity. For the PTSD section of the DICA-R, in a test–retest of 90 children, Cohen's kappa was .79 (Reich, personal correspondence, February 1994). A computerized version of the DICA-R is a self-administered questionnaire. A study of the computerized version of the DICA-R resulted in the following kappa values for the subscales: Reexperiencing (x = .52); Avoidance/Numbing (x = .35); Arousal (x = .50). Kappa for the diagnosis for 6- to 12-year-olds was .35 and for 13- to 18-year-olds was .63 (Reich, personal communication, 1995). Kappas were generally lower than on the "in-person" interviews (Reich, Cottler, McCallum, Corwin, & VanEerdewegh, 1995).

For a study of adolescent residents of a boarding school exposed to a dormitory fire (Jones & Ribbe, 1991), interviewers underwent 51 hours of training in the use of three instruments (DICA-6R-A; IES-C and STAI). At the end of training, interrater reliability averaged .91. Although no significant difference was found between exposed and nonexposed residents in symptoms measured by the IES (as a self-report measure), significantly greater levels of PTSD symptomatology were found in residents as measured by the DICA-6R-A (in semistructured interview). There were not high levels of life threat for these adolescents. In contrast, for a group of children exposed to a destructive wildfire (Jones et al., 1994), the DICA-R did not distinguish the levels of PTSD symptoms between exposed and nonexposed children. There was, however, a difference in PTSD criteria met; victims met an average of 2.8 criteria, whereas controls met an average of 1.6 criteria. Both instruments were used in semistructured interview for these children. These children reported greater numbers of symptoms on the IES-C possibly related to the differences in rating method (see Symptom Ratings, already listed). They had significantly higher scores on the IES-C Avoidance subscale, which might suggest the underreporting of symptoms in general. These children did not experience high levels of life threat and may have been mirroring parental distress to resource loss (Ribbe, personal communication, May 1995).

Training. Training is required for the use of this instrument (Reich, personal communication, February 1994). Interviewers are taught to probe to ensure children's understanding and accuracy. Individuals administering the DICA-R need to have an understanding of the disorder and the precise nature of each symptom. Research assistants with bachelor's degrees can be trained to give the interview. The training is provided by Washington University. In addition, researchers have trained their own interviewers using the DICA-R manual.

Issues Related to Usage. The DICA-R permits the assessment of a number of diagnostic categories affecting children. Administered as a whole including the PTSD subscale, the DICA-R permits examination of associated disorders and their relationship to PTSD. It usually takes one to one-and-one-half hours to administer the entire DICA-R.

Some suggestions have been made by users of the DICA-R-PTSD subscale. As is generally true with instruments for children, there have been some concerns expressed regarding wording. Suggestions have been made regarding the use of negative contractions (e.g., using "was unable to" instead of "couldn't") and regarding the phrasing (e.g., making it clearer and less ambiguous). In an as yet unpublished study of children exposed to motor vehicle and bicycle accidents, Zink (personal communication, December 2, 1994) found that 7-year-olds had difficulty understanding the scale for 6- to 12-year-olds, and that rephrasing was necessary to enhance comprehension. Dr. Reich recommends training interviewers in methods of rewording for younger children (age 7 and under).

DISC-PTSD Module

The Diagnostic Interview Schedule for Children, Version 2.3 (Shaffer et al., 1992, in press) is a highly structured interview to assess common psychiatric disorders in children. It includes an optional PTSD module (Fisher et al., 1993). In a cooperative effort between Yale and Columbia Universities, it has been used in multisite, culturally diverse epidemiological surveys of children (Lahey et al., in press). The DISC and its PTSD subscale are designed for use with children ages 9–17 and for parents of 6- to 17-year-olds.

The DISC (and its PTSD module) has been undergoing revisions in wording for children. The scale has been updated for DSM-IV diagnostic criteria. The DISC-PTSD module generally asks one question for each of the subcriteria (two questions for two of the subcriteria). It permits the recording of a traumatic experience by three types of trauma (threat to a significant other, personal threat, and witnessing). It uses a time line of the past year (or shorter, if less time has passed) for rating the presence of symptoms.

The PTSD subscale asks three questions about the child's possible exposure to a traumatic event. As a part of the full diagnostic instrument, questioning is discontinued if the child does not endorse one of the exposures. There is a parent and a child version of the scale. A 3-point rating scale for presence or absence of symptoms includes "no" (0), "sometimes/somewhat" (1), and "yes" (2). The presence of symptoms in the last year and in the last month are measured.

Translations and Revisions. The DISC, including the PTSD module, is currently being updated to address DSM-IV criteria. The DISC-2.3-PTSD module has been translated into Spanish and Xhosa (South Africa). The DISC-IV will be translated into the following languages: Spanish, Icelandic, Chinese, Italian, and German. The English version of the interview should be available in the summer of 1996 (Fisher, personal communication, February 1996).

Reliability and Validity. In a study of a community probability sample of culturally diverse children using the PTSD module of the DISC based on DSM-III-R criteria, youths ages 9–17 ($n = 671$) and their parents who resided in randomly selected housing units were surveyed (Fisher et al., 1993; Lahey et al., in press). Based upon an algorithm combining information from parent and child, only 1.8% of the sample met full diagnostic criteria. There was little overlap between parent and child reports. Eight (1.2%) met criteria by child report and 4 (0.6%) met criteria by parent report. However, 21.2% (using combined algorithm) met two or more of the four diagnostic criteria for PTSD. There were strong associations between major depression, generalized anxiety disorder, conduct disorder, and substance-use disorder with increased risk of PTSD.

Training. It is recommended that interviewers be trained before administering the DISC. Training sessions usually take 3 days and are given at the DISC training center at Columbia University (contact person: Prudence Fisher). Sessions can also be arranged off-site. There is a fee for training.

Issues Related to Usage. When the DISC is administered as a whole, including the PTSD subscale, associated disorders and grief are also examined, and the analyses can distinguish between or control for those disorders. It takes, however, from 1 to 2½ hours to administer the entire instrument. Although traumatized children may become absorbed in a lengthy PTSD interview, they sometimes have become restless or agitated during the lengthy process of a multiple-disorder diagnostic instrument. The PTSD subscale is estimated by the authors to take approximately 6 minutes (30 seconds, if the child does not endorse a traumatic experience).

SPECIALIZED INSTRUMENTS

In addition to scales that measure general childhood trauma symptoms are scales that were constructed to assess specific kinds of trauma (e.g., physical or sexual abuse) or specific aspects of trauma (e.g., dissociation). Descriptions of four of these instruments follow. Most of the authors of these instruments suggest the use of multiple methods (e.g., medical exam, child report) and measures (e.g., including the Child Behavior Checklist [CBCL] Internalizing, Externalizing and Sexual Problems subscales) when assessing sexual abuse. Some of the following scales have been used in combination.

A/A CRS and CRS-EIA

The Child Rating Scales of Exposure to Interpersonal Abuse (CRS-EIA; Praver, 1994) and the Angie/Andy CRS (A/A CRS; Praver et al., 1993) are instruments in progress. The CRS-EIA assesses the frequency and severity of 6- to 11-year-old children's exposure to interpersonal abuse. The A/A CRS is a clinician-administered scale that consists of 105 items (99 of which are illustrated). It is based upon the Levonn (Richters & Martinez, 1990), which is a cartoon-based measure. In the Richters Scale, Levonn, the central character has been exposed to community violence. In the A/A CRS, either a girl (Angie) or a boy (Andy) has been exposed to four forms of violence: sexual abuse, physical abuse, witnessing family violence, and community violence. Cartoons created by Praver are accompanied by a two- to four-sentence scenario to illustrate vividly for the child specific posttraumatic symptoms. There is a corresponding parent questionnaire (A/A PRS), which refers to "some children" rather than Angie or Andy and does not employ the cartoons.

A/A CRS items were generated from a review of previous research on abuse and community violence and from the work of Pelcovitz et al. (in press) and Herman (1992a, 1992b), which includes a set of symptoms sometimes referred to as Complicated PTSD or Disorders of Extreme Stress Not Otherwise Specified (DESNOS). The instrument's primary aim is evaluating the latter rather than a PTSD diagnosis. The categories Regulation of Affect, Attention and Consciousness, Self-Perception, Relations with Others, Somatization, Systems of Meaning, and PTSD are compatible with previous findings regarding interpersonal abuse. The "scoring guide" at the end of the instrument consists of the assignment of questions to the seven categories.

The A/A CRS employs a 4-point thermometer rating scale, measuring "never" (1), "just a few times" (2), "some of the time" (3), and "a lot of the time" (4). The child is first presented with five sample cartoons depicting one of the four frequency ratings. Sample cartoons are repeated until the child responds correctly. A note in the introduction of the instrument suggests methods of checking to see if the child understands and of encouraging the child's responses. Sixteen reverse-positive items (positive psychological attributes marked by an R; e.g., 21R) were included in the original version in order to reduce negative valence and to act as a separate adaptive functioning scale. The instrument is undergoing revision and reduction in length.

Translations and Revisions. The A/A CRS has undergone previous revision after its review by five child psychology experts. Another revision is in process. The instrument is expected to be reduced to no more than 70 items.

Reliability and Validity. Item construction for the A/A CRS was reviewed by five child psychology experts. They reviewed the A/A CRS for grammar, accuracy, offensiveness, and appropriateness. Face validity was obtained by consensus of four of the experts.

Trained interviewers administered the A/A CRS to 208 children ages 6–11 from four hospital sites, the general population surrounding the hospital, and one school. Four groups included the following: (1) Intrafamilial Violence Group (IV: physical, sexual and/or witnessing spousal abuse; n = 32); (2) Extrafamilial Violence Group (EV: community violence or extrafamilial molestation; n = 46); (3) Combined Violence Trauma Group (CVT: combined IV and EV; n = 49); and (4) Nontrauma Group (NT; n = 65) (Praver, 1996). Internal consistency using coefficient alphas ranged from .70 to .95 (the latter for the Total Associated Symptoms Scale; .70–.88 for the six scales; .88–.95 for the three composite scales). Differences were found between socioeconomic status (SES) levels (Kruskal–Wallis; p = < .0019). Subsequent analyses controlled for SES. Construct validity was supported by the following findings: Using ANCOVA (analysis of covariance), IV, EV, and CV groups, each had significantly higher scores than the NT group on the six scales (the seven subscales excluding the PTSD scale), the composite, and the PTSD scales (p = .0001). As expected the NT group scored higher on the Adaptive Functioning scale than the IV or CV groups; NTs were not higher than the

EV group, however (possibly due to the tendency of traumatized children to answer in a socially acceptable manner to questions about positive attributes). Children in the CV group scored significantly higher on four of the six scales than children in the IV group, and higher on five of the six scales than the EV group.

Using discriminant function analysis, the six scales, the composite, and PTSD scales each significantly predicted membership in trauma and non-trauma groups ($p < .001$). The scales correctly classified between 76% and 90% of trauma and nontrauma groups. The PTSD scale correctly classified 72% of the trauma group and 94% of the nontrauma group. The Total Associated Symptoms Scale for the A/A CRS predicted 81% of trauma and 94% of nontrauma.

Convergent validity was supported by correlations between the A/A PRS and the Behavior Assessment System for Children–Parent Rating Scales (BASC-PRS; Reynolds & Kamphaus, 1992), ranging from .60 to .81. For the BASC-PRS, there were moderate correlations between the A/A-CRS-PTSD scale scores and the BASC-PRS composite scores ($r = .42$; $p = .0001$) and between the A/A CRS total and the BASC-PRS ($r = .54$; $p < .0001$). Scores on the A/A CRS were significantly higher than scores on the A/A PRS ($p \leq .0004$). With the exception of the Somatization Scale ($r = .12$; $p = .9$), correlations ranging from .26 to .47 for the subscales of the parent and child measures were significant ($p \leq .0002$).

Training. Training has been provided by Frances Praver and takes approximately 1 hour. The instrument has been administered by masters level mental health professionals without training.

Issues Related to Usage. The A/A CRS addresses a broad range of symptoms found for children following traumatic exposures, particularly ongoing traumas; it does not, however, include all of the DSM-IV subcriteria (this is likely to be remedied in the revised version). The instrument generally takes 30–45 minutes to administer; it has taken approximately 80 minutes for seriously disturbed children. The use of pictures in describing symptoms and emotions related to traumatic experience holds promise for use with elementary-school-age children.

Scoring for PTSD or DESNOS is not as yet described in the "Scoring Guide," which assigns questions to categories. Like many instruments measuring childhood trauma, the A/A CRS has more than one question for most symptoms and unequal numbers of questions per symptom. This fact must be considered in the process of analysis.

The instrument is in the process of change. Authors will want to consider some changes in wording and presentation in further adapting the instrument for this age group. For example, question 24 inquires about intrusive reexperiencing of thoughts by asking about how often "upsetting things" are remembered. The child may need assistance in focusing on trau-

matic events instead of the more general "upsetting things." A variety of images of upsetting things in pictures 8, 24, and 41 rather than only one, which
appears to depict assault, may also be helpful.

Responses to some of the questions may be affected by the child's age.
For example, picture 1 shows a child trying to reach for a cookie; question
1, which mentions the child trying to get the cookie, inquires about getting
upset and crying when unable to have or do something desired. The cookie
example may narrow the focus of the question for young children, who interpret information more literally and concretely. The age factor is important in the analysis of answers as well: Question 6 is about remembering
important things. Six- and 7-year-olds may be more prone than older children to forget things that adults consider important. Some behaviors such
as those measured by the first three questions (easy to tears/upset when frustrated, upset about little things, outbursts of aggression) are often more accurately observed by adults for elementary-school-age children. The PRS may
assist in these cases. A few of the pictures might benefit from revision. For
example, care must be taken that the combination of pictures and questions
does not suggest that upset occurs only in combination with destruction (e.g.,
question 16) or does not narrow the range of upsetting events (e.g., questions 8 and 24).

The A/A CRS is currently under revision and holds great promise for
use with -school-age children. The authors clearly attempt to gently assist
children in focusing upon emotions and responses, which may be more
difficult for young children to identify and express.

CDC

The Child Dissociative Checklist (CDC; Putnam, 1988, 1994) is largely derived from the prior childhood multiple personality disorder (MPD) predictor lists developed by Frank Putnam (in Elliot, 1982; Putnam, 1985) and has
been augmented by other predictor lists evaluating child maltreatment (Fagan & McMahon, 1984; Kluft, 1984, 1985). Questions were derived from clinical experience with children with dissociative disorders. The CDC is an
observer report measure to be completed by an adult who has observed the
child over the preceding 12-month period (Putnam, Helmers, & Trickett,
1993). It can take as little as 5 minutes to complete.

The measure is intended to be completed by someone who is familiar
with the child's behavior over a number of contexts. Responses require circling on a 3-point scale (2 = "very true"; 1 = "somewhat/sometimes true";
0 = "not true") the answer best describing the child's behavior over the past
12 months. It has been completed by parents, foster parents, teachers, and
other adults in close contact with the child, and has been successfully used
by staff on inpatient units, residential units, and in preschools (Putnam &
Peterson, 1994).

The current version is a 20-item instrument (version 3.0; 2/90). Items on the CDC measure several types of dissociative behavior including the following: (1) dissociative amnesias; (2) rapid shifts in: demeanor, access to information, knowledge, abilities and age appropriateness of behavior; (3) spontaneous trance states; (4) hallucinations; (5) alterations in identity; and (6) aggressive and sexual behavior (Putnam et al., 1993).

A CDC score of 12 or higher is highly suggestive of significant dissociative psychopathology (Putnam & Peterson, 1994; Putnam et al., 1993; Putnam, Helmers, Horowitz, & Trickett, 1995). Mean scores reported for sexually abused girls were established at 6 ± 6.4 and 2.3 ± 2.7 for comparison girls by Putnam et al. (1993). Similar scores were reported for a smaller sample of sexually abused and comparison girls ages 7–13 in 1991 (Malinosky-Rummel & Hoier, 1991): mean, 6.1 for abused girls and 1.6 for controls. Higher scores were found in a psychiatric inpatient population (Wherry, Jolly, Feldman, Adam, & Manjanatha, 1994) for children ages 4–12: mean, 16.13 ± 9.39 for sexually abused children and 10.44 ± 5.07 for non-sexually abused inpatient children. In a group of children with MPD, dissociative disorder of childhood (DDoC), and other dissociative disorders (ODD) for which clinicians completed the CDC (Putnam & Peterson, 1994), mean scores for MPD children were 23.6 ± 7.8, for DDoC children 19.8 ± 8.6, and for ODD children 16.1 ± 6.7.

Translations and Revisions. There have been three major revisions to the CDC (versions 1.2, 2.2, and 3.0; Putnam et al., 1993). The date is listed below the title of the instrument on all authorized versions. The first 16 items of the current version are identical to the original items of the earlier version (2.2, 2/88). Translations are in progress but not yet complete.

Reliability and Validity. Aspects of reliability and validity for this measure have been established in the following studies: Malinosky-Rummel and Hoier (1991), Wherry et al. (1994), Putnam et al. (1993), and Putnam and Peterson, 1994. The CDC has shown good internal consistency across a number of samples and has had good test–retest reliability, equal to or better than most parent report measures of children's behaviors (Putnam & Peterson, 1994).

In a study of sexually abused and comparison girls (Putnam et al., 1993), over a 1-year interval, Spearman test–retest reliability coefficients were ϱ = .69 (n = 73; p = .0001) for the total group and ϱ = .57 (p = .005) to ϱ = .92 (p = .0001) for individual items. The CDC was internally consistent across populations; Cronbach's alpha coefficient for the sample as a whole (n = 181) was .95, for control girls .73, for sexually abused girls .91, for children with dissociative disorder not otherwise specified (DDNOS) .64, and for children with MPD .80. Internal consistency was again measured by split-half reliability: whole sample (r = .88; p = .0001); controls (r = .71; p = .0001); sexually abused girls (r = .85; p = .0001); DDNOS (r = .69; p = .0001); and MPD (r = .73; p = .0001; Putnam et al., 1993). Similarly in a study by

Malinosky-Rummel and Hoier (1991), of 10 sexually assaulted girls and 50 controls, test–retest correlation was $r(60) = .732$ ($p < .001$) and Cronbach's alpha was .784 ($p < .001$). For a study in which clinicians reported on the items for children with MPD, DDoC and ODD (Putnam & Peterson, 1994), Cronbach's alpha was .86 and split-half reliability, .79.

Validity studies examined whether the CDC scores were accounted for by group membership or by other variables. In a study of control and sexually abused girls, age was negatively correlated with score for controls and abused girls ($n = 22$; $r = -.45$; $p = .034$) and not significantly correlated for DDNOS and MPD children. There were no significant correlations with socioeconomic status or ethnicity. Only the MPD and DDNOS groups included both boys and girls; there were no significant differences by gender. In a study of nonabused, suspected abused, and psychiatric inpatient nonabused and abused children (Friedrich et al., in press), which used several instruments, including the CDC, differences were found between nonabused children and psychiatric patients. Significant differences were not found, however, between nonabused and sexually abused inpatients.

Spearman rank-order correlations were calculated between each item and item-corrected CDC scores to establish partial construct validity of the scale. The coefficients ranged from $\varrho = .59$ to $\varrho = .79$, with a median coefficient of .73 (all correlations significant at $p < .0001$ or better). Criterion-referenced concurrent validity was tested with the Kruskal–Wallis to compare CDC scores across groups of children; $\chi^2 = 110.55$ ($n = 181$, $df = 3$; $p < .0001$). Pairwise comparisons were then performed with a Mann–Whitney U test, demonstrating differences between each group and all other groups (Putnam et al., 1993). For the study in which clinicians completed the CDC (Putnam & Peterson, 1994), Mann–Whitney U tests demonstrated that the CDC differentiated between cases of MPD and DDoC (tie-corrected Z score $= -1.98$, $p = .04$) but not between DDoC and ODD (tie-corrected Z score $= -1.61$, $p = .1$). When DDoC and ODD groups were combined (since both were based on proposed criteria), the CDC robustly distinguished the MPD cases from the combined pool of dissociative disorders not otherwise specified (DDNOS).

Training. No training is required for administering or completing the CDC.

Issues Related to Usage. The CDC is intended to provide a rapid, simple, cost-effective method of detecting pathological dissociation in children and adolescents. It may be administered serially to monitor treatment. It is a parent/adult report measure and, therefore, is susceptible to the inaccuracies common to such instruments. Parent report measures depend upon parental objectivity and accuracy. Mothers of sexually abused children have been found to vary widely in the accuracy with which they report their children's behaviors (Everson, Hunter, Runyon, Edelsohn, & Coulter, 1989; Friedrich, 1993b).

Several unauthorized versions with altered questions and/or answer formats are known to be in circulation (sometimes with the CDC author's name on them). Validity and reliability measures for the CDC do not apply to these unauthorized versions.

CITES-R

The Children's Impact of Traumatic Events Scale (CITES; Wolfe et al., 1986) is a measure of the impact of child sexual abuse. The CITES-R (Wolfe & Gentile, 1991) is a 78-item measure with 11 subscales based on factor analyses of the original 54-item scale. CITES-R subscales include four dimensions: PTSD (Intrusive Thoughts, Avoidance, Hyperarousal and Sexual Anxiety); Social Reactions (Negative Reactions from Others and Social support); Abuse Attributions (Self-Blame/Guilt, Empowerment, Vulnerability, and Dangerous World); and Eroticism (Wolfe, Gentile, Michienzi, Sas, & Wolfe, 1991). PTSD questions are patterned after the IES (Horowitz et al., 1979). Additional items including Hyperarousal and additional Avoidance questions have been added from DSM-III-R. The Guilt scale was derived from the concept of guilt in DSM-III. The Sexual Anxiety scale is comprised of items from a Finkelhor and Browne (1985) model of traumagenic factors including helplessness, betrayal, stigmatization, and traumatic sexualization. Items on the Abuse Attributions scale were patterned after the revised learned helplessness theory (Abramson, Seligman, & Teasdale, 1978; Peterson & Seligman, 1983) including internal versus external, stable versus unstable, and global versus specific. The CITES was developed for children ages 8–16. Although it is worded for children with good reading skills, it is recommended for use in a semistructured interview. The scale elicits answers on a 3-point scale from "not true" (0) to "very true" (2).

Translations and Revisions. The CITES-R (Wolfe & Gentile, 1991) is a revision of the original six-scale, 54-item CITES (Wolfe et al., 1986).

Reliability and Validity. In a study of two groups of children (from Family and Children's Services and Victim Witness Court cases from London, Ontario), Wolfe and her colleagues (1991) psychometrically examined the CITES. Principal component factor analysis using an eigenvalue cutoff of 1.00 resulted in 16 factors accounting for 71% of the variance. Twelve of the factors (accounting for 62% of the variance) had conceptual relevance for the measure. They included Intrusive Thoughts, Sexual Anxiety, Negative Reactions from Others, Self-Blame/Guilt, Dangerous World, Empowerment, Vulnerability/Self-Blame, Personal Vulnerability, and Eroticism. Using the factor analysis results and a refined conceptual framework, the CITES-R was developed as described earlier. Reliability analyses were conducted for the entire scale, the 4 dimensions and 10 subscales. Cronbach's alpha values were as follows: entire scale, .89; PTSD, .88; Social Reactions, .87; Attributions, .78; and Eroticism, .57. The alpha value for the six Intrusive Thoughts Items (four intrusive thoughts; one dreams; one reactivity to reminders) was .91. Based on DSM-III, a Play/Reenactment item was added. For the two Avoidance items based on the IES (avoidance of things, avoidance of thoughts) measured at initial assessment, 3-month and 9-month follow-up, alpha values were .39, .04, and .72, respectively. Six additional items were added based on DSM-III-R criteria (trouble remembering, reduced interest, three avoidance of thoughts items, difficulty feeling love). The Sexual Anxiety subscale consists of an original two Reexperiencing questions (fear and upset when thinking about sex), an additional two Avoidance items (never wanting to think about sex and wishing there was no such thing as sex) and the evaluation of sex as "dirty." Alpha values for the original two Sexual Anxiety items were .84. The new Hyperarousal scale includes difficulty concentrating, irritability, startle, restlessness/jumpiness and annoyance with others. The Social Reactions section includes the reactions of others often experienced by children exposed to a variety of traumatic experiences (e.g., two blame by others, being let down by trusted others, two rejection by others, two negative attributions by others, being made fun of by other children). The standardized alpha value for this scale was .80. The Social Support scale consisted of an original two items (being believed and most people are nice and understanding) which produced an alpha value of .57. Four items were added (having someone to talk to, feeling good about family response, protection by others, assistance from professionals). The Attributions subscale (four "my fault" items including culpability, badness, actions, and not smart enough to stop it; guilt feelings; perpetrator to blame; two victim not to blame, including no blame and too young; two feeling have caused others trouble; embarrassment when people know; feeling should be punished) yielded an alpha of .78. Three items suggesting a frequency of bad things happening to children comprised the original Dangerous World subscale; the alpha value was .68. Two new items include worry about other children being abused and adults must not be trusted by children. Issues of Empowerment originally consisted of five items ($\alpha = .67$; cannot prevent a repeat, cannot stop adults, now know what to do, this will not happen again, life will get better). Two items were added: know enough to protect self in future and family will protect. The Personal Vulnerability scale consisted of eight original ($\alpha = .57$) and two added items: five likelihood of repeat (the child's usual bad luck, cannot be stopped, normal frequency); discomfort being alone with males; was bad and needed to be punished; unlikely to repeat; fear of repeat; and difficulty trusting. The Eroticism scale contains two original items (more sexual feelings than friends and thinking of sex even when don't want to; $\alpha = .57$) and two additional items (sexual feelings when people kiss on TV and liking to look at images of naked people).

In the 1991 CITES study (Wolfe et al.), in order to assess convergent and discriminant validity and method variance, a multibehavior–multimethod matrix (MBMM; Campbell & Fiske, 1959) analysis was constructed.

Analysis of variance of the MBMM revealed significant convergent validity, significant discriminant validity and significant method variance (Wolfe et al., 1991). Convergent validity was evidenced in a significant correlation between the Sexual Abuse Fear Evaluation Subscale (SAFE; Wolfe & Wolfe, 1986), Sexual Fear scale scores with the CITES-PTSD Intrusive Thoughts ($r = .35$), and Sexual Anxiety ($r = .56$) scale scores. Scores from the Child Attitude Toward Father scale (Hudson, 1982) correlated significantly with the CITES Social Reactions, Negative Reactions by others scale ($r = .51$). Scores from the Child Attributional Questionnaire (also known as KASTAN; Seligman et al., 1984) overall positive scale scores correlated significantly negatively with the CITES-PTSD Avoidance Scale ($r = -.37$) and the CITES Social Reactions, Negative Reactions by others scale ($r = -.40$) and positively with the Attributional Style Self Blame/Guilt scores ($r = .54$; Wolfe et al., 1991).

Of concern is the magnitude of the error variance as compared to any of the effects; the scores on the tests are more subject to unknown sources of variance than they are to the recognized sources. This may be due to the relatively few items on the original CITES subscales or to the imprecise match between the CITES and the other scales (Wolfe et al., 1991). An analysis of the CITES-R 78-item measure and new factor analyses are needed and are underway. Psychometric testing and normative data from the new scale are in progress. Preliminary results based on a recent normative study using the CITES-R suggest the following alpha values: PTSD (21 items), .91; Intrusive Thoughts (7 items), .86; Avoidance (7 items), .71; Hyperarousal (6 items), .73; Sexual Anxiety (5 items), .86; Social Support (6 items), .81; Negative Reactions from others (9 items), .89; Self-blame/guilt (13 items), .84; Empowerment (6 items), .83; Dangerous World (4 items), .82; and Eroticism (5 items), .85. There are low but significant correlations between the CBCL PTSD scale and the CITES-R scales for Intrusive Thoughts ($r = -.28$; $p < .001$); Avoidance ($r = .17$; $p < .01$); Hyperarousal ($r = .28$; $p < .001$); Sexual Anxiety ($r = .20$; $p < .01$); Negative Reactions ($r = .18$; $p < .01$); Self-Blame/Guilt ($r = .22$; $p < .001$); Dangerous World ($r = .17$; $p < .01$); and Personal Vulnerability ($r = .24$; $p < .001$) (Wolfe & Birt, in press).

Training. It is recommended that the CITES-R be used by professionals trained in the field of trauma and in statistical methods for testing. A scoring program on diskette is available.

Issues Related to Usage. Although its intention (and some subscales) is to measure the impact of childhood sexual abuse, the CITES-R permits the examination of trauma factors, social reactions, and other subjective responses common to traumatized children in general.

The CITES-R takes 20–40 minutes to administer, depending on the child's tendency to elaborate answers. The CITES-R measures a broad range of symptoms that may be characteristic of sexually abused (as well as other traumatized) children. Like other sexual abuse scales, it does not include all of the DSM-IV PTSD symptoms. For example, the Intrusive Thought (IT) subscale does not include physiological reactivity to reminders; the Hyper-arousal subscale does not include sleep disturbance (sleep disturbance related to intrusive thoughts is a part of the IT scale), only addresses startle response as related to being surprised (not sounds), and measures fear in response to reminders rather than hypervigilance; detachment or estrangement from others is omitted from the Avoidance scale; and Criterion F is omitted. There are additional symptoms included in the PTSD scales that are not a part of DSM-IV (e.g., restlessness or jumpiness) and some DSM-IV items are asked several times over (e.g., several intrusive-thoughts and avoidance-of-thoughts questions). Since giving children an opportunity to endorse an item more than once gives the item more weight than other items, this must be taken into account when interpreting results. The multiple questions of the Dangerous World subscale may to some extent address Criterion C7, related to expectations of the future.

The CITES-R includes many questions that measure some of the additional symptoms of trauma (e.g., loss of friends, being made fun of by others, loss of faith in adults, distrust) endured by many traumatized children, including symptoms common to more complicated forms of PTSD. The latter have been found for prolonged or repeated traumas such as multiple sexual abuse. As intended, many of the additional symptom questions are worded specifically for sexual abuse. The scale is worded simply for children.

CSBI-3

The Children's Sexual Behavior Inventory 3 (CSBI-3, 1992; Friedrich, 1993b; Friedrich et al., 1992, in press) is the culmination of revisions of the CSBI and CSBI-R. It is a 36-item measure that permits parents or primary caregivers to rate sexual behavior in children ages 2–12 (Friedrich, 1993a, 1993b, 1995, personal communication, May 1995). The CSBI-3 assesses a wide variety of sexual behaviors related to sexual interest, self-stimulation, sexually intrusive behavior with other children and adults, gender-based behavior, and personal boundary permeability (36 items), and includes a number of validity and attitudinal items (Friedrich, 1995; Friedrich et al., 1992). The instrument begins with questions about demographic characteristics and interpersonal relationships.

The CSBI-3 uses a 4-point rating scale, indicating frequency of occurrence for the past 6 months: "never" (0), "less than once per month" (1), "one to three times per month" (2), and "at least once per week" (3). Total score is determined by summing all of the items less the validity items. Norms are based on the responses of exclusively female caregivers. Children who have no history of behavior problems and no history of sexual abuse rarely receive a total score higher than 5. For the CSBI-R, means are as follows: (1) sexually abused males ages 2–6: 15.3 (SD = 12.6); nonabused males ages 2–6: 3.1 (SD = 3.4); (2) sexually abused females ages 2–6: 14.1 (SD = 12.5); nonabused females ages 2–6: 2.5 (*SD* = 2.9); (3) sexually abused males ages 7–12: 11.9 (*SD* = 11.2); nonabused males ages 7–12: 1.8 (*SD* = 2.1); (4) sexually abused females ages 7–12: 7.3 (*SD* = 8.1); nonabused females ages 7–12: 1.6 (*SD* = 2.4; Friedrich, 1995).

Study of a large normative sample of children using the CSBI suggested that overall frequency of sexual behaviors rated decreased with age, particularly for girls (Friedrich et al., 1992). Sexually abused boys, however, tend toward broader and more aggressive sexual behaviors when they are older (Friedrich, 1995). Individual items differ by age and sex (Friedrich, 1993b). For example, 43.5% of nonabused 2- to 6-year-old boys and 48.8% of 2- to 6-year-old abused boys were reported as touching their mother's breasts. In the 7- to 12-year-old boys the levels had dropped to 11.7 and 22.9%, respectively (Friedrich, 1995).

CSBI-3 items have been reworded to read more simply (approximately an eighth-grade level). Validity items have been included to assess the parents' attention to each individual item (Friedrich, 1995). The children studied using the CSBI have been from clinical samples, therefore reducing the generalizability of the findings in relationship to nonclinically referred sexually abused children (Friedrich, 1993b). A comprehensive multisite normative sample is underway. It will include a significant subset of children with pediatric evaluations for sexual abuse, and will address family stress levels, exposure to sexuality in the home, and parental attitudes toward sexuality in children. Initial evaluation of CSBI-3 data indicate that psychiatric outpatients and inpatients without a history of sexual abuse exhibit significantly more sexual behavior than the normative nonpsychiatric sample. As a group, however, they exhibit fewer behaviors at lower frequency than sexually abused children. In an ongoing study of children with attention-deficit/hyperactivity disorder (ADHD), for example, parents frequently report problems of masturbation and problems with interpersonal boundaries. As a group, however, they exhibit less sexual interest and less sexual aggression than sexually abused children (Friedrich, 1995).

Translations and Revisions. There have been two revisions of the CSBI (Friedrich, 1990): CSBI-R (Friedrich, 1993b) and CSBI-3 (1995). The CSBI has been translated into French, Spanish, German, and Swedish.

Reliability and Validity. In a sample of 880 normal and 276 clinical (confirmed history of sexual abuse, often seeking treatment) children ages 2–12 (Friedrich et al., 1992), reliability of the 35-item unrevised CSBI was established with an alpha coefficient of .82 for the normative sample and .93 for the clinical sample. Test–retest reliability was calculated using 70 children from the normative sample, with a correlation of .85. Three-month test–retest reliability of 24 sexually abused children benefiting from weekly therapy resulted in a significant correlation of .47 ($p < .02$). Using both principal components and maximum-likelihood factor analysis, single, similar, and large primary factors emerged accounting for 40–53% of the total variance in the normal and clinical samples (Friedrich et al., 1992). Correlations between parent and teacher report were significant but low ($r = .3$).

For the normative sample described earlier (Friedrich et al., 1992), validity measures included comparison of normative and abused samples of children for which 27 of 35 items differed significantly ($p < .05$). Differences were found for age (2–6 vs. 7–12 years) and sex. Age, family income, and maternal education were not significantly associated with CSBI scores for children ages 2–6. Sexually abused children had higher stressful life events scores than nonabused children and life-events intensity was related to CSBI total score for boys and girls in each of the age groups. This suggests that family distress is of central importance in those variables that differentiate sexually abused from nonabused children. Friedrich et al. (1992) suggest that abuse and events may compound each other and be related to greater sexualization overall. Analyses of ROC (Receiver Operating Characteristics), a measure of discriminant analysis, indicated that the CSBI total score would accurately identify most children in each group. The greatest sensitivity was for 2- to 6-year-old boys (.92), and the lowest overall sensitivity was for 7- to 12-year-old girls (.70; females ages 2–6: .85; males ages 7–12: .90).

The CSBI was compared to the Child Behavior Checklist (CBC; Achenbach & Edelbrock, 1983). Sexual behavior was found to be directly related to the internalizing and externalizing behavior problems on the CBC (Friedrich et al., 1992). Friedrich and his colleagues found both the sensitivity and the specificity of the CSBI to be better overall than the CBC in discriminating sexually abused children from those non-sexually abused. In a recent study, the CSBI did not discriminate between sexually abused and nonsexually abused children ages 3 and under. A number of these children were involved in custody disputes; several of the highest scores were for children who were most likely not sexually abused (Hewitt, Friedrich, & Allen, 1994).

As a result of findings in the preceding study, 27 of the original 35 items in the CSBI were retained; six items were dropped, three rewritten and six new items were included in the CSBI-R. The CSBI-R was used with a new normative sample of 141 children and a clinical sample of 133 children with a confirmed history of sexual abuse. Sexually abused children were distinguished from nonabused children by increased scores on 30 of the 36 items (the other 6 items: dresses like the opposite sex; touches sex parts in public; touches women's breasts; stands too close to people; tries to look at people undressing; and touches sex parts at home). There was a significant difference between groups on 35 of the 36 items (Friedrich, 1993b). CSBI-3 items are face-valid. For the CSBI-3, correlations between parent and psychiatric nurse reports were significant but low ($r = .4$; Friedrich, 1995).

Training. This is a clearly and simply worded parent-report measure to be administered by mental health professionals. Training is needed in order to interpret scoring.

Issues Related to Usage. Sexually abused children exhibit more sexual behavior than nonsexually abused children (e.g., engage in sexual behaviors toward others, draw more genitalia, and interact sexually with anatomically correct dolls more; Deblinger, McLeer, Atkins, Ralphe, & Foa, 1989; Gale, Thompson, Moran, & Sack, 1988; Goldston, Turnquist, & Knutson, 1989; Kolko, Moser, & Weldy, 1988; Yates, Beutler, & Crago, 1985; Jampole & Weber, 1987). Therefore, measuring the frequency of children's sexual behaviors may help to distinguish sexually abused from non-sexually abused children (Friedrich et al., 1992; Friedrich, 1993b). It may be difficult for a parent to answer the question, "Is your child exhibiting sexual behavior?" The CSBI-3 permits caregivers to think about the frequency of specific behaviors (Friedrich, 1993b). Friedrich also suggests that the CSBI-3 enables therapists and parents to target specific behaviors for treatment. Some physicians have used the CSBI-3 to reassure parents that their children's behaviors are within normative levels (e.g., a 5-year-old boy touching himself; Friedrich, 1995).

There is no item or group of items that, without fail, indicate sexual abuse. Developmental level, setting, and history of the child are important in the interpretation of individual behaviors (e.g., a 5-year-old masturbating at home in bed compared to a 9-year-old masturbating in public). Additional variables may affect the frequency of sexual behaviors (e.g., the level of family nudity, witnessing of intercourse, psychiatric history, family stress, and exposure to television nudity; Friedrich, Grambsch, Broughton, Kuiper, & Beilke, 1991) and the parent's report of sexual behaviors (e.g., child's developmental level and attitudes toward childhood sexuality; Friedrich, 1995). Factors such as number of perpetrators, frequency, and/or duration of sexual abuse, use of force, and/or severity of abuse, have been found to increase sexual behavior scores (Friedrich, 1993b). Additionally, not all children who are abused exhibit sexual behaviors. Inhibition and withdrawal are also reactions to trauma (Friedrich, 1993b; Pynoos & Nader, 1988). Particularly, older females with better social skills are more likely to inhibit inappropriate behavior. There is some evidence that children removed from abusive environments exhibit lower levels of sexual behavior unless the behaviors are triggered by a stressor such as renewed visits with family. On the other hand, some of the sexual behaviors in the CSBI-R are commonly seen in nonabused children as well (Friedrich, 1993b).

Friedrich (1995) points out that the wording of some of the CSBI-3 items is confusing or misleading. For example, when parents endorse that their children insert objects into the vagina or rectum, they often mean insertion into the labia. This and other items of concern (e.g., "makes sexual sounds" and "knows more about sex than other children their age") continue to have discriminant validity.

CSBI-3 items are face-valid; parents can deny or exaggerate children's sexual behaviors (Friedrich, 1993b). Parent-report measures depend upon parental objectivity and accuracy. Although mothers have been found to be more accurate reporters of their children's behavior problems (Friedrich, 1995), mothers of sexually abused children have been found to vary widely in the accuracy with which they report their children's behaviors (Everson et al., 1989; Friedrich, 1993b). Consequently, using more than one reporter regarding children's sexual behaviors, and confirming the existence of sexual abuse with other measures and methods are recommended. Friedrich (1993b, 1995) suggests that the CSBI-3 is best used as a part of a comprehensive evaluation of children for sexual abuse, with careful clinical interviewing and assessment of other behavior problems (e.g., on the CBC).

TSCC

The Trauma Symptom Checklist for Children (TSCC; Briere, 1996a, 1996b) is a child self-report measure developed to assess the affects of trauma and child abuse in 8- to 16-year-olds. It is a 54-item scale with six subscales: Anger (9 items), Anxiety (9), Depression (9), Dissociation (10), Posttraumatic Stress (10) and Sexual Concerns (10). Some symptoms overlap subscales (e.g., Item 11: PTS and Dissociation; Items 24 and 25: PTS and Anxiety). Subscales are not intended to provide a diagnosis of specific disorders (e.g., PTSD or dissociative disorder). The TSCC has two validity scales, one that taps a tendency to deny any symptomatology, and one that indexes a tendency to overrespond to symptom items. The instrument has been used to assess the level of symptoms for children exposed to child abuse and other violence (Singer et al., 1995) and to assess the outcome of therapy for sexually abused children (Lanktree & Briere, 1995; Cohen & Mannarino, 1992). The scale is rated on a 4-point Likert-type frequency format ranging from "never" (0) to "almost all of the time" (3). Scores are cumulative for each subscale.

Normative studies totaling 3,008 children are currently in process (Singer et al., 1995; Evans & Briere, 1994; Friedrich et al., in press). Preliminary findings suggest differences by age, sex, and environment (urban, suburban, and rural environments; Briere, personal communication, October 1995; 1996b). The TSCC yields T-scores for age and sex combinations. In a study of 399 children ages 8–15 (Elliot & Briere, 1994b), children who were nonabused ($n = 72$), sexually abused disclosing (Group 1, $n = 60$, partially credible and Group 2, $n = 149$, credible), and sexually abused nondisclosing (Group 1, $n = 19$, children with evidence of abuse who did not admit abuse; Group 2, $n = 20$, children with evidence of abuse who admitted at first then recanted) were compared. Sexually abused nondisclosing children reported the lowest scores with the exception of depression for the nondisclosing recanters, whose scores were higher than those of the nonabused children but lower than abused-disclosing children's scores (raw mean scores, Group 1, 2: Anger, 2.25, 5.59; Anxiety, 4.45, 5.31; Depression, 4.47, 7.47; Dissociation, 4.41, 5.61; Posttraumatic Stress, 4.71; 5.62; and Sexual Concerns, 2.08, 3.10). Nonabused children had middle scores (raw mean scores: Anger, 6.88;

Anxiety, 6.24; Depression, 6.20; Dissociation, 6.13; Posttraumatic Stress, 6.89; and Sexual Concerns, 3.41). Sexually abused disclosing children who were credible had the highest scores, and those who were partially credible had scores just below theirs (raw mean scores: Anger, 7.47, 7.21; Anxiety, 10.47, 9.77; Depression, 9.28, 8.45; Dissociation, 8.54, 8.07; Posttraumatic Stress, 12.72, 11.23; and Sexual Concerns, 5.69, 5.33). Children with nonsupportive mothers were more likely to recant their original disclosures of sexual abuse than children with supportive parents. Twenty-two percent of the children in this study could not be placed in any of the groups; abuse remained unclear, and the children were eliminated from the study. The larger normative study ($n = 3,008$) described in the manual will provide a more definitive estimate of normal scores.

Translations and Revisions. There is a Cambodian translation in progress.

Reliability and Validity. A number of studies (Evans & Briere, 1994; Friedrich, 1993b; Lanktree & Briere, 1993; Elliott & Briere, 1994b) have demonstrated aspects of reliability for the TSCC. Lanktree, Briere, and Hernandez (1991) found internal consistency for the instrument measured by Cronbach's alpha for the total TSCC (.96) and for each of the subscales: Anxiety, .85; Depression, .89; Posttraumatic Stress, .86; Dissociation, .83; Anger, .84; and Sexual Concerns, .68. Internal consistency was again demonstrated by Singer et al. (1995) for the total scale (Cronbach's $\alpha = .95$) and the subscales (Cronbach's α ratings): Anxiety, .82; Depression, .86; Posttraumatic Stress, .87; Dissociation, .83; Anger, .89 (Sexual Concerns, omitted by request of school administrators). The TSCC Sexual Concerns and Dissociation subscales were used in a study of nonabused comparison children, nonabused psychiatric inpatients, and sexually abused psychiatric inpatients (Friedrich et al., in press). Reliability tests resulted in Cronbach's alpha of .84 and .89, respectively.

Based upon samples of sexually abused children, the TSCC subscales correlate significantly with the Child Behavior Checklist for Children (mean $r = .67$) (Lanktree et al., 1991; Achenbach, 1991) and with the Children's Depression Inventory (mean $r = .53$) (Lanktree, Briere, Boggiano, & Barrett, 1993; Kovacs & Beck, 1977) demonstrating concurrent validity. The Sexual Concerns subscale was significantly correlated with the sex content on the Rorschach and the CBC internalizing and externalizing scores. The Dissociation subscale was significantly correlated with Minnesota Multiphasic Personality Inventory (MMPI) Scale 8, CDC total score, CBC internalizing and externalizing scores, but not with Rorschach sex and morbid content scores (Friedrich et al., in press).

A number of studies have demonstrated the use of the TSCC in discriminating between groups. In a study of 3,735 high-school students (Singer et al., 1995), a significant amount of the variance (29%) in symptoms as measured by the TSCC was explained by exposure to violence. In a study of 157 females and 49 males (Elliott & Briere, 1994a), the Anxiety, Depression, Dissociation, Posttraumatic Stress, and Sexual Concerns scales distinguished sexually abused from nonabused females. Only the Anxiety and Posttraumatic Stress scales were predictive of sexual victimization for the smaller number of males. Using the Sexual Concerns and Dissociation subscales in the study of four groups of children (nonpsychiatric patient, nonabused comparison children; nonabused psychiatric inpatients; suspected abused children; and sexually abused psychiatric inpatients) by three age groups (Friedrich et al., in press), control-group children were least likely and older children most likely to endorse Sexual Concerns and Dissociation symptoms. No differences were found, however, between the three clinical groups. Although the scales did not distinguish nonabused psychiatric inpatients from abused inpatients, sexually abused children were more likely to endorse the following six of eight items on the Sexual Concerns scale: "touching my private parts too much," "thinking about sex when I don't want to," "not trusting people because they might want sex," "getting scared or upset when I think about sex," "can't stop thinking about sex," "getting upset when people talk about sex." They were also more likely to endorse 6 of 10 Dissociation items: "pretending I'm someone else," "feeling dizzy," "forgetting things, can't remember things," "feeling like I'm not in my body," "pretending I'm somewhere else," and "trying not to have any feelings."

Training. The TSCC has a simple and easy-to-follow format. It is completed by children and adolescents without training. Professional manual and test booklets can be obtained from Psychological Assessment Resources Inc. (1-800-331-TEST).

Issues Related to Usage. This scale allows measurement of several trauma-relevant domains without asking the number of questions usually indicated in the more thorough scales. Subscales do not measure the full range of symptoms, for example, of PTSD or Dissociation; they have been compared psychometrically to corresponding scales (e.g., CDI, CBCL, MMPI 8). Its users have found TSCC to have predictive validity with reference to child sexual abuse. The instrument is worded simply for children and appears easy to administer. It takes approximately 10–20 minutes to complete unless the child is traumatized or clinically impaired. It can be scored and profiled in 10 minutes. Subject protection committees are sometimes not allowing the Sexual Concerns scales. A 44-item alternative version (excluding Sexual Concerns) is available.

It is important to remember that there are some overlapping symptoms between the Posttraumatic Stress and other subscales, which would effect correlations between the scales. As with other scales written for children, issues of wording come into question (i.e., wording appropriately for children and still eliciting an answer regarding the intended symptom/item). For example, items 24 and 25, "feeling scared of men" and "feeling scared of women" serve as a PTSD item related to reactivity to reminders (as well as serving as indicators of anxiety). They, of course, do not cover the full range of reminders or of possible reactions. For example, item 5, "pretending I am someone else" is an item on the Dissociation scale. Pretending is a very common behavior at some ages.

Some of the wording/content issues have been addressed by creating subscales. For example, because some items may involve fantasy or role playing more than classic dissociation, two subscales were created: Overt Dissociation (DIS-O) and Fantasy (DIS-F). Similarly, the Sexual Concerns subscales measure sexual distress (SC-D) and sexual preoccupation (SC-P). Some SC items tap sexual thoughts or feelings that are not symptomatic per se (e.g., "thinking about having sex" and "having sex feelings in my body") but are atypical earlier in development or when present with greater than normal intensity. Other items tap unwanted sexual responses or conflicts (e.g., "thinking about sex when I don't want to"), negative responses to sexual stimuli (e.g., "getting upset when people talk about sex"), or fear of being sexually exploited (e.g., "not trusting people because they might want sex"; Briere, 1996a, 1996b).

The TSCC is an easy and cost-effective method of interviewing children. With some of the other scales, researchers have found a greater accuracy in face-to-face interview rather than in giving children scales to complete. There are as yet no data available comparing the TSCC used in face-to-face interview with the child-completion method.

CONCLUSIONS

New scales for the measurement of trauma in children and adolescents emerge frequently as researchers explore the most effective wording and construction to accurately assess children. As described in this chapter, a number of successful scales are currently available to measure PTSD and associated reactions. With continued learning about childhood PTSD and about wording and methods of assessment from child interviews, periodic revisions are necessary.

The accurate measurement of PTSD in children may serve diagnostic, preventive, and therapeutic purposes. Risk factors found in a representative sample of children can assist in determining interventions for the affected population as a whole. A number of issues affect the accuracy of measurement with child and adolescent samples. These include the following: (1) method of interview (e.g., personal, phone, group, or unmonitored paper-and-pencil completion); (2) the experience and style of the interviewer; (3) the child's understanding and perception of the interviewer and the questions asked; (4) wording and placement of questions; and (5) corroborating interviews/data. Training, thorough preliminary briefing, an understanding of the phase of the event, and an understanding of the specific family and/or population under study may improve accuracy. Accurate translations, especially those that have undergone more than one back-translation and have been reviewed by the author(s) of the instruments, are essential. For comparison's sake, specific relevant factors such as geographical location (e.g., city vs. rural) must be taken into account.

Age factors become important in the effective screening of children for trauma-related symptoms. These include issues related to wording (e.g., cognitive and language levels, phase-related meaning of events to children, differences in children's ability to choose specific behaviors, children's expectations or lack of understanding of symptoms, course, and other trauma-related phenomena), rating methods, and the order of questions (e.g., placement of questions that may elicit defensiveness).

In general, it is important to interview children directly regarding their traumatic reactions. Most researchers suggest that, when possible, supplemental information be obtained from parents, teachers, and clinicians. It is especially important when establishing child sexual abuse to use corroborating information and a number of scales. In addition, using both frequency and intensity ratings may permit a greater reporting of symptomatology and distinguish stress-related symptoms from trauma-related symptoms.

The instruments described in this chapter have been useful in a variety of situations. Most instruments are undergoing, in need of, or have recently undergone some wording changes. The CPTS-RI and the CRTES have provided a fairly quick and easy method of assessing stress following single-incident traumatic events. Neither provides a PTSD diagnosis or for the more complicated symptoms associated with repeated or long-term trauma or more complicated traumatic response. Other instruments, such as the MWES and WBTH, although longer, permit a PTSD diagnosis and measure additional symptoms. The CAPS-C, DICA-PTSD Scale, and DISC-PTSD Scale provide specific DSM-IV diagnosis, criterion by criterion. The A/A CRS includes the slightly different and more extensive list of symptoms that are described for DESNOS or Complicated PTSD (Pelcovitz et al., 1993; Herman, 1992a, 1992b). The CAPS-C permits the measurement of both frequency and intensity of symptoms as well as the measurement of symptoms at an additional, difficult time period. Its format, however, is somewhat sophisticated, and the clinician may need to assist the child through the rating scale with some of the questions.

It is expected that we as clinicians and researchers will, over time, alter and improve our methods of assessing children's reactions to traumatic events. A growing body of literature, increased experience in interviewing children directly, and ongoing systematic assessment continue to add to our ability to do so accurately.

REFERENCES

Abramson, L. Y., Seligman, M. E. P., & Teasdale, J. D. (1978). Learned helplessness in humans: Critique and reformulation. *Journal of Abnormal Psychology, 57*, 49–74.

Achenbach, T. M. (1991). *Manual for the Child Behavior Checklist/4–18*. Burlington: University of Vermont Department of Psychiatry.

Achenbach, T. M., & Edelbrock, C. (1983). *Manual for the Child Behavior Checklist and the Revised Child Behavior Profile*. Burlington: University of Vermont.

Admundson, K. J. (1993). *Violence in the schools: How America's school boards are safeguarding your children*. Alexandria, VA: National School Boards Association.

American Psychiatric Association. (1994). *Diagnostic and statistical manual of mental disorders* (4th ed.). Washington, DC: Author.

Bergen, M. (1958). The effect of severe trauma on a four-year-old child. *Psychoanalytic Study of the Child, 23*, 407–429.

Berna, J. M. (1993). *The worst experiences of adolescents from divorced and separated parents and the stress responses to those experiences*. Dissertation submitted to Temple University Graduate Board, Philadelphia, PA.

Birleson, P. (1981). The validity of depressive disorder in childhood and the development of a self-rating scale: A research report. *Journal of Child Psychology and Psychiatry, 22*, 73–88.

Bloch, D., Silber, E., & Perry, S. (1956). Some factors in the emotional reaction of children to disaster. *American Journal of Psychiatry, 113*, 416–422.

Briere, J. (1996a). *Trauma Symptom Checklist for Children (TSCC)*. Odessa, FL: Psychological Assessment Resources.

Briere, J. (1996b). *Trauma Symptom Checklist for Children (TSCC) professional manual*. Odessa, FL: Psychological Assessment Resources.

Burke, J., Borus, J., Burns, B., Millstein, K., & Beasley, M. (1982). Changes in children's behavior after a natural disaster. *American Journal of Psychiatry, 139*(8), 1010–1014.

Campbell, D. T., & Fiske, D. W. (1959). Convergent and discriminant validation by the multi-trait-multimethod-matrix. *Psychological Bulletin, 56*, 81–105.

Carey-Trefzer, C. (1949). The results of a clinical study of war-damaged children who attended the Child Guidance Clinic, the hospital for sick children, Great Ormond Street, London. *Journal of Mental Science, 95*, 535–559.

Carver, C. S., & Scheier, M. F. (1992). *Perspectives on personality* (2nd ed.). Boston: Allyn & Bacon.

Cohen, J. A., & Mannarino, A. P. (1992, November). *The effectiveness of short-term structured group psychotherapy for sexually abused girls: A pilot study*. Paper presented at the University of Pittsburgh School of Medicine, as part of lecture series "Therapy for Sexually Abused Children," Pittsburgh, PA.

Cunningham, P. B., Jones, R. T., & Yang, B. (1994). *Impact of community violence on African American children and adolescents in high violent crime neighborhoods: Preliminary findings*. Poster presented at 7th Annual Research Conference, "A System of Care for Children's Mental Health: Expanding the Research Base," Tampa, FL.

Curcio-Chilton, K. (1994). *Stress symptoms of adolescents diagnosed with conduct disorder*. Unpublished doctoral dissertation, Temple University, Philadelphia, PA.

Deblinger, E., McLeer, S. V., Atkins, M. S., Ralphe, D., & Foa, E. (1989). Posttraumatic stress in sexually abused girls. *Child Abuse and Neglect, 13*, 403–408.

Earls, F., Reich, W., & Jung, K. G. (1988). Psychopathology in children of alcoholic and antisocial parents. *Alcohol Clinical Experimental Research, 12*, 481–487.

Edelbrock, C., Costello, A., Dulcan, M. K., Conover, N. C., & Kala, R. (1986). Parent–child agreement on child psychiatric symptoms assessed via structured interview. *Journal of Child Psychology and Psychiatry, 27,* 181–190.

Elander, J., & Rutter, M. (in press). Use and development of the Rutter Parents' and Teachers' Scales. *International Journal of Methods in Psychiatric Research.*

Elliott, D. (1982). State intervention and childhood multiple personality disorder. *Journal of Psychiatry and the Law, 10,* 441–456.

Elliott, D., & Briere, J. (1994a). *The Trauma Symptoms Checklist for Children: Validation data from a child abuse evaluation center.* Unpublished manuscript, UCLA School of Medicine, Los Angeles, CA.

Elliott, D., & Briere, J. (1994b). Forensic sexual abuse evaluations of older children: Disclosures and symptomatology. *Behavioral Sciences and the Law, 12,* 261–277.

Eth, S., & Pynoos, R. (1985). Developmental perspectives on psychic trauma in childhood. In C. Figley (Ed.), *Trauma and its wake* (pp. 36–52). New York: Brunner/Mazel.

Evans, J. J., & Briere, J. (1994, January 24–28). *Reliability and validity of the trauma symptoms checklist for children in a normal sample.* Paper presented at the 1994 San Diego Conference on Child Maltreatment, San Diego, CA.

Everson, M. D., Hunter, W. M., Runyon, D. K., Edelsohn, G. A., & Coulter, M. L. (1989). Maternal support following disclosure of incest. *American Journal of Orthopsychiatry, 59*(2), 197–207.

Fagan, J., & McMahon, P. P. (1984). Incipient multiple personality in children: Four cases. *Journal of Nervous and Mental Disease, 172,* 26–36.

Finkelhor, D., & Browne, A. (1985). The traumatic impact of child sexual abuse: A conceptualization. *American Journal of Orthopsychiatry, 55,* 536–541.

Fisher, P., Hoven, C. W., Moore, R. E., Bird, H., Chiang, P., Lichtman, J., & Schwab-Stone, M. (1993, October). *Evaluation of a method to assess PTSD in children and adolescents.* Poster presented at the APHA meeting.

Fletcher, K. (1991). *When Bad Things Happen Scale.* (Available from the author, University of Massachusetts Medical Center, Dept. of Psychiatry, 55 Lake Avenue North, Worcester, MA 01655)

Frederick, C. (1985). Selected foci in the spectrum of posttraumatic stress disorders. In J. Laube & S. A. Murphy (Eds.), *Perspectives on disaster recovery* (pp. 110–130). East Norwalk, CT: Appleton-Century-Crofts.

Frederick, C., Pynoos, R., & Nader, K. (1992). *Childhood PTS Reaction Index (CPTS-RI).* (Available from Frederick and Pynoos, 760 Westwood Plaza, Los Angeles, CA 90024; or Nader, P.O. Box 2251, Laguna Hills, CA 92654)

Friedrich, W. (1990). Children's Sexual Behavior Inventory: An adult report measure. (Available from the author, Mayo Clinic Psychology Dept., 200 First Street, S.W., Rochester, MN 55905)

Friedrich, W. (1993a). Sexual victimization and sexual behavior in children: A review of recent literature. *Child Abuse and Neglect, 17,* 59–66.

Friedrich, W. (1993b). Sexual behavior in sexually abused children. *Violence Update, 3*(5), 6–11.

Friedrich, W. (1995). Evaluation and treatment: The clinical use of the Child Sexual Behavior Inventory: Commonly asked questions. *American Professional Society on the Abuse of Children (APSAC) Advisor, 8*(1), 1, 17–20.

Friedrich, W., Grambsch, P., Broughton, D., Kuiper, J., & Beilke, R. L. (1991). Normative sexual behavior in children. *Pediatrics, 88*(3), 456–462.

Friedrich, W., Grambsch, P., Damon, L., Hewitt, S. K., Koverola, C., Lang, R. A., Wolfe,

V., & Broughton, D. (1992). Child Sexual Behavior Inventory: Normative and clinical comparisons. *Psychological Assessment, 4*(3), 303–311.

Friedrich, W., Jaworski, T. M., Huxsahl, J. E., & Bengtson, B. S. (in press). Dissociative and sexual behaviors in children and adolescents with sexual abuse and psychiatric histories. *Journal of Interpersonal Violence.*

Gale, J., Thompson, R. J., Moran, T., & Sack, W. H. (1988). Sexual abuse in young children: Its clinical presentation and characteristic patterns. *Child Abuse and Neglect, 12,* 163–170.

Garbarino, J., Kostelny, K., & Dubrow, N. (1991). What children can tell us about living in danger. *American Psychologist, 46*(4), 376–383.

Goldston, D. B., Turnquist, D. C., & Knutson, J. F. (1989). Presenting problems of sexually abused girls receiving psychiatric services. *Journal of Abnormal Psychology, 98,* 314–317.

Goldwater, A. (1993). *Attributional styles of child victims of natural disasters.* Dissertation submitted to Temple University Graduate Board, Philadelphia, PA.

Green, A. (1983). Dimensions of psychological trauma in abused children. *Journal of the American Academy of Child Psychiatry, 22,* 231–237.

Handford, H. A., Mayes, S., Mattison, R., Humphrey, F., Bagnato, S., Bixler, E., & Kales, J. (1986). Child and parent reaction to the Three Mile Island nuclear accident. *Journal of the American Academy of Child and Adolescent Psychiatry, 25,* 346–356.

Herjanic, B., & Reich, W. (1982). Development of a structured psychiatric interview for children: Agreement between child and parent on individual symptoms. *Journal of Abnormal Child Psychology, 10*(3), 307–324.

Herman, J. L. (1992a). Complex PTSD: A syndrome in survivors of prolonged and repeated trauma. *Journal of Traumatic Stress, 5*(3), 377–391.

Herman, J. L. (1992b). A new diagnosis. In J. L. Herman (Ed.), *Trauma and recovery* (pp. 115–127). New York: Basic Books.

Herman, J. L., Perry, J. C., & van der Kolk, B. A. (1989). Childhood trauma in borderline personality disorder. *American Journal of Psychiatry, 146*(4), 490–495.

Hewitt, S. K., Friedrich, W. N., & Allen, J. (1994, January). *Assessment of very young children with suspected sexual abuse.* Paper presented at the annual Responding to Child Maltreatment Conference, San Diego, CA.

Hornstein, N. L., & Putnam, F. W. (1992). Clinical phenomenology of child and adolescent dissociative disorders. *Journal of the American Academy of Child and Adolescent Psychiatry, 31,* 1077–1085.

Horowitz, M., Wilner, N., & Alvarez, W. (1979). Impact of Event Scale: A measure of subjective stress. *Psychosomatic Medicine, 41,* 209–218.

Hudson, W. W. (1982). *One clinical measurement package: A field manual.* Homewood, IL: Dorsey Press.

Hyman, I., Zelikoff, W., & Clarke, J. (1988). *School Trauma Survey—Student Form.* Philadelphia, PA: National Center for the Study of Corporal Punishment and Alternatives in the Schools (NCSCPAS), Temple University.

Ibrahim, Y. M. (1992, August 4). Iraqis left coarse scars on the psyche of Kuwait. *New York Times,* p. A3.

Jampole, L., & Weber, M. K. (1987). An assessment of the behavior of sexually abused and nonabused children with anatomically current dolls. *Child Abuse and Neglect, 11,* 187–192.

Jones, R. T. (1992). *Impact of Event Scale for Children.* (Available from the author, Dept. of Psychology, Stress and Coping Lab, 4102 Derring Hall, Virginia Polytechnic Institute and State University, Blacksburg, VA 24060)

Jones, R. T. (1994). *Child's Reaction to Traumatic Events Scale (CRTES): A self report traumatic stress measure.* (Available from the author, Dept. of Psychology, Stress and Coping Lab, 4102 Derring Hall, Virginia Polytechnic Institute and State University, Blacksburg, VA 24060)

Jones, R. T., Frary, B., Cunningham, P. B., & Weddle, D. (1993, August). *Predictors of child and adolescent functioning following trauma-related events.* Paper presented at a symposium "Children's Responses to Natural Disasters," at the annual meeting of the American Psychological Association Convention, Toronto, Ontario, Canada.

Jones, R. T., & Ribbe, D. P. (1991). Child, adolescent and adult victims of residential fire. *Behavior Modification, 15(4),* 560–580.

Jones, R. T., Ribbe, D. P., & Cunningham, P. B. (1994). Psychosocial correlates of fire disaster among children and adolescents. *Journal of Traumatic Stress, 7*(1), 117–122.

Karno, M., Burnam, A., Escobar, J. I., Hough, R. L., & Eaton, W. W. (1983). Development of the Spanish-language version of the National Institute of Mental Health Diagnostic Interview Schedule. *Archives of General Psychiatry, 40,* 1183–1188.

Kinzie, J. D., Sack, W. H., Angell, R. H., Manson, S., & Rath, B. (1986). The psychiatric effects of massive trauma on Cambodian children: I. The children. *Journal of the American Academy of Child Psychiatry, 25*(3), 370–376.

Kluft, R. P. (1984). Multiple personality in childhood. *Psychiatric Clinics of North America, 7,* 121–134.

Kluft, R. P. (1985). Childhood multiple personality disorder: Predictors, clinical findings and treatment results. In R. P. Kluft (Ed.), *Childhood antecedents of multiple personality* (pp. 167–196). Washington, DC: American Psychiatric Association Press.

Kohly, M. (1994). *Reported child abuse and neglect victims during the flood months of 1993.* Missouri Department of Social Services, Division of Family Services, Research and Development Unit, St. Louis, MO.

Kohr, M. (1995). *Validation of the My Worst Experience Survey.* Unpublished doctoral dissertation, Temple University, Philadelphia, PA.

Kolko, D. J., Moser, J. T., & Weldy, S. R. (1988). Behavioral/emotional indicators of sexual abuse in child psychiatric inpatients: Controlled comparison with physical abuse. *Child Abuse and Neglect, 12,* 529–541.

Kovacs, M., & Beck, A. T. (1977). An empirical clinical approach toward a definition of childhood depression. In J. G. Shchulterbrandt & A. Raskin (Eds.), *Depression in childhood: Diagnosis, treatment and conceptual models* (pp. 43–57). New York: Raven Press.

Lacey, G. N. (1972). Observations on Aberfan. *Journal of Psychosomatic Research, 16,* 257–260.

Lahey, B., Flagg, E., Bird, H., Schwab-Stone, M., Canino, G., Dulcan, M., Leaf, P., Davies, M., Brogan, D., Bourdone, D. K., Horwitz, S., Rubio-Stipec, M., Freeman, D., Lichtman, J., Shaffer, D., Goodman, S., Narrow W., Weissman, M., Kandel, D., Jensen, P., Richter, J., & Regier, D. (in press). The NIMH Methods for the Epidemiology of Child and Adolescent Mental Disorders (MECA) study: Background and methodology. *Journal of the American Academy of Child and Adolescent Psychiatry.*

Lambert, C. J. (1990). *The fractional structure and reliability of a scale measuring stress responses as a result of maltreatment in the schools.* Unpublished doctoral dissertation, Temple University, Philadelphia, PA.

Lanktree, C. B., & Briere, J. (1993, August). *Effectiveness of therapy for sexual abuse trauma in children.* Paper presented at the annual meeting of the American Psychological Association, Toronto, Canada.

Lanktree, C. B., & Briere, J. (1995). Outcome of therapy for sexually abused children: A repeated measures study. *Child Abuse and Neglect, 19,* 1145–1155.

Lanktree, C. B., Briere, J., Boggiano, A. K., Barrett, M. (1993, August). *Effectiveness of therapy for sexually abused children: Changes in Trauma Symptom Checklist for Children scores.* Paper presented at the annual meeting of the American Psychological Association, Toronto, Ontario, Canada.

Lanktree, C. B., Briere, J., & Hernandez, P. (1991, August). *Further data on the Trauma Symptom Checklist for Children (TSC-C): Reliability, validity, and sensitivity to treatment.* Paper presented at the annual meeting of the American Psychological Association, San Francisco, CA.

Levy, D. M. (1945). Psychic trauma of operations in children. *American Journal of Diseases of Children, 69,* 7–25.

Lobovits, D. A., & Handal, P. J. (1985). Childhood depression: Prevalence using DSM-III criteria and validity of parent and child depression scales. *Journal of Pediatric Psychology, 10,* 45–54.

Malinosky-Rummel, R. R., & Hoier, T. S. (1991). Validating measures of dissociation in sexually abused and a nonabused children. *Behavioral Assessment, 13,* 341–357.

Malmquist, C. P. (1986). Children who witness parental murder: Posttraumatic aspects. *Journal of the American Academy of Child Psychiatry, 25*(3), 320–325.

McFarlane, A. C., Policansky, S. K., & Irwin, C. (1987). A longitudinal study of the psychological morbidity in children due to natural disaster. *Psychological Medicine, 17,* 727–738.

Moller-Thau, D., & Fletcher, K. E. (1996). *Diagnosing child PTSD with two self-report measures: The Childhood PTSD Reaction Index and the When Bad Things Happen Scale.* Manuscript in preparation.

Nader, K. (1993). *Instruction manual, Childhood PTSD Reaction Index* (rev. English version). (Available from the author, P.O. Box 2251, Laguna Hills, CA 92654)

Nader, K. (1995). *Childhood Post-traumatic Stress Disorder (PTSD): Parent Inventory.* (Available from the author, P.O. Box 2251, Laguna Hills, CA 92654)

Nader, K. (1996). Children's exposure to violence and disaster in the community. In C. Corr & D. Corr (Eds.), *Helping children cope with death and bereavement* (pp. 201–220). New York: Springer.

Nader, K. (in press-a). Violence: Effects of a parent's previous trauma on currently traumatized children. In Y. Danieli (Ed.), *International handbook of multigenerational legacies of trauma.* New York: Plenum Press.

Nader, K. (in press-b). Treating traumatic grief In systems. In C. R. Figley, B. E. Bride, & N. Mazza (Eds.), *Death and trauma: The traumatology of surviving.* London: Taylor and Francis.

Nader, K. O., Blake, D. D., & Kriegler, J. A. (1994a). *Instruction Manual: Clinician-Administered PTSD Scale, Child and Adolescent Version (CAPS-C).* White River Junction, VT: National Center for PTSD.

Nader, K., & Fairbanks, L. (1994). The suppression of reexperiencing: Impulse control and somatic symptoms in children following traumatic exposure, *Anxiety, Stress and Coping: An International Journal, 7,* 229–239.

Nader, K. O., Kriegler, J. A., Blake, D. D., & Pynoos, R. S. (1994b). *Clinician Administered PTSD Scale, Child and Adolescent Version (CAPS-C).* White River Junction, VT: National Center for PTSD.

Nader, K. O., Kriegler, J. A., Blake, D. D., Pynoos, R. S., Newman, E., & Weather, F. (1996). *Clinician Administered PTSD Scale, Child and Adolescent Version (CAPS-C).* White River Junction, VT: National Center for PTSD.

Nader, K., & Pynoos, R. S. (1989). *Child Posttraumatic Stress Disorder Inventory: Parent Interview.* Unpublished manuscript, University of California at Los Angeles.

Nader, K., & Pynoos, R. (1993a). School disaster: Planning and initial interventions. *Journal of Social Behavior and Personality, 8*(5), 299–320.

Nader, K., & Pynoos, R. S. (1993b). The children of Kuwait following the Gulf Crisis. In L. Lewis & N. Fox (Eds.), *Effects of war and violence in children* (pp. 181–195). Hillsdale, NJ: Erlbaum.

Nader, K., Pynoos, R., Fairbanks, L., Al-Ajeel, M., & Al-Asfour, A. (1993). Acute post-traumatic stress reactions among Kuwait children following the Gulf Crisis. *British Journal of Clinical Psychology, 32,* 407–416.

Nader, K., Pynoos, R., Fairbanks, L., & Frederick, C. (1990). Children's PTSD reactions one year after a sniper attack at their school. *American Journal of Psychiatry, 147,* 1526–1530.

Nader, K., & Stuber, M. (1992, October 23). *Catastrophic events vs. catastrophic illness: A comparison of traumatized children.* A workshop presented at the annual meeting of the International Society for Traumatic Stress Studies, Los Angeles, CA.

Nader, K., & Stuber, M. (1993). *3–5 year old Child Trauma Checklist.* (Available from Nader, P.O. Box 2251, Laguna Hills, CA 92654; or Stuber, 760 Westwood Plaza, Los Angeles, CA 90024)

Nader, K., Stuber, M., & Pynoos, R. (1991). Post-traumatic stress reactions in preschool children with catastrophic illness: Assessment needs. *Comprehensive Mental Health Care, 1*(3), 223–239.

Nader, K., Vidovic, V., Anic, N., & Pynoos, R. (1992). *In the midst of war: Refugee children in Croatia.* Manuscript in preparation, University of California, Los Angeles.

National Center for Study of Corporal Punishment and Alternatives in Schools. (1992). *My Worst Experience Survey.* Philadelphia, PA: Temple University Press.

Newman, C. J. (1976). Children of disaster: Clinical observations at Buffalo Creek. *American Journal Psychiatry, 133,* 306–312.

Newman, E., & Ribbe, D. (1996). Review of The Clinician Administered PTSD Scale for Children. In B. H. Stamm (Ed.), *Measurement of stress, trauma, and adaptation.* Lutherville, MD: Sidran Press.

Ollendick, T. H. (1983). Reliability and validity of the revised fear survey schedule for children (FSSC-R), *Behaviour Research and Therapy, 21,* 685–692.

Pelcovitz, D., van der Kolk, B., Roth, S., Kaplan, S., Mandel, F., & Resick, P. (in press). Development and validation of the structured interview for measurement of complex PTSD. *Journal of Traumatic Stress.*

Peterson, C., & Seligman, M. E. P. (1983). Learned helplessness and victimization. *Journal of Social Issues, 39,* 103–116.

Praver, F. (1994). *Child Rating Scales — Exposure to Interpersonal Abuse.* Unpublished copyrighted instrument.

Praver, F. (1996). *Validation of a Child Measure for Post-Traumatic Stress Responses to Interpersonal Abuse.* Unpublished dissertation, St. John's University, Jamaica, NY.

Praver, F., Pelcovitz, D., & DiGiuseppe, R. (1994). *The Angie/Andy Child Rating Scales.* (Available from Praver, 5 Marseilles Drive, Locust Valley, NY 11560; Pelcovitz, Dept. of Psychiatry, 400 Community Drive, Manhasset, NY 11030; or DiGiuseppe, Psychology Dept., St. John's University, Grand Central and Utopia Parkways, Jamaica, NY 11439)

Putnam, F. W. (1985). Pieces of the mind: Recognizing the psychological effects of abuse. *Justice for Children, 1,* 6–7.

Putnam, F. W. (1988). *Child Dissociative Checklist.* (Available from the author at National Institute of Mental Health, Building 15K, 9000 Rockville Pike, Bethesda, MD 20892-2668)

Putnam, F. W. (1993). Dissociative disorders in children: Behavioral profiles and problems. *Child Abuse and Neglect, 17,* 39–45.

Putnam, F. W. (1994). *Child Dissociative Checklist.* (Available from the author at National Institute of Mental Health, Building 15K, 9000 Rockville Pike, Bethesda, MD 20892-2668)

Putnam, F. W., Helmers, K., & Trickett, P. K. (1993). Development, reliability and validity of a child dissociation scale. *Child Abuse and Neglect, 17,* 731–741.

Putnam, F. W., Helmers, K., Horowitz, L. A., & Trickett, P. K. (1995). Hypnotizability and dissociativity in sexually abused girls. *Child Abuse and Neglect, 19*(5), 645–655.

Putnam, F. W., & Peterson, G. (1994). Further validation of the Child Dissociative Checklist. *Dissociation, 7*(4), 204–211.

Pynoos, R., Frederick, C., Nader, K., Arroyo, W., Eth, S., Nunez, W., Steinberg, A., & Fairbanks, L. (1987). Life threat and posttraumatic stress in school age children, *Archives of General Psychiatry, 44,* 1057–1063.

Pynoos, R. S., Goenjian, A., Tashjian, M., Karakashian, M., Manjikian, R., Manoukian, G., Steinberg, A., & Fairbanks, L. A. (1993). Post-traumatic stress reactions in children after the 1988 Armenian earthquake. *British Journal of Psychiatry, 163,* 239–247.

Pynoos, R., & Nader, K. (1988). Psychological first aid and treatment approach for children exposed to community violence: Research implications. *Journal of Traumatic Stress, 1*(4), 445–473.

Pynoos, R. S., & Nader, K. (1989). Children's memory and proximity to violence. *Journal of the American Academy of Child and Adolescent Psychiatry, 28*(2), 236–241.

Rea, C. D. (1994). *Comparisons of patterns of traumatic stress symptoms in adolescents with and without overt behavior difficulties.* Unpublished doctoral dissertation submitted to Temple University Graduate Board, Philadelphia, PA.

Realmuto, G. M., Masten, A., Carole, L. F., Hubbard, J., Groteluschen, A., & Chun, B. (1992). Adolescent survivors of massive childhood trauma in Cambodia: Life events and current symptoms. *Journal of Traumatic Stress, 5*(4), 589–599.

Reich, W., Cottler, L., McCallum, K., Corwin, D., & VanEerdewegh, M. (1995). Computerized interviews as a method of assessing psychopathology in children. *Comprehensive Psychiatry, 36*(1), 40–45.

Reich, W., & Earls, F. (1987). Rules for making psychiatric diagnoses in children on the basis of multiple sources of information: Preliminary strategies. *Journal of Abnormal Child Psychology, 15*(4), 601–616.

Reich, W., & Earls, F. (1990). Interviewing children by telephone: Preliminary results. *Comprehensive Psychiatry, 31*(3), 211–215.

Reich, W., & Kaplan, L. (1994). The effects of psychiatric and psychosocial interviews on children. *Comprehensive Psychiatry, 3,* 50–53.

Reich, W., Shayka, J. J., & Taibleson, C. (1991). *Diagnostic Interview for Children and Adolescents (DICA).* St. Louis, MO: Washington University.

Reynolds, C. R., & Kamphaus, R. W. (1992). *Behavior assessment system for children.* A manual. Circle Pines, MN: American Guidance Service.

Reynolds, C. R., & Richmond, B. O. (1978). What I Think and Feel: A revised measure of children's manifest anxiety. *Journal of Abnormal Child Psychology, 6*(2), 271–280.

Richters, J. E., & Martinez, P. (1990). *Things I have seen and heard.* Unpublished structured interview for assessing young children's violence exposure, National Institute of Mental Health, Rockville, MD.

Richters, J. E., & Martinez, P. (1991). Community violence project: Children as victims or witnesses to violence. *Psychiatry, 56,* 7–21.

Rutter, M. (1967). A children behavior questionnaire for completion by teachers: Preliminary findings. *Journal of Child Psychology and Psychiatry, 8,* 1–11.

Schwarz, E. D., & Kowalski, J. M. (1991). Malignant memories: PTSD in children and adults after a school shooting. *Journal of the American Academy of Child and Adolescent Psychiatry, 30*(6), 936–944.

Seligman, M. E. P., Peterson, C., Kaslow, N. J., Tannenbaum, R. L., Alloy, L. B., & Abramson, L. Y. (1984). Attributional style and depressive symptoms among children. *Journal of Abnormal Psychology, 93,* 235–238.

Shaffer, D., Fisher, P., Dulcan, M., Davies, M., Piacentini, J., Schwab-Stone, M., Lahey, B. B., Bourdon, K., Jensen, P., Bird, H., Canino, G., & Regier, D. (in press). The NIMH Diagnostic Interview Schedule for Children (DISC-2.3): Description, acceptability, prevalences, and performance in the MECA study. *Journal of the American Academy of Child and Adolescent Psychiatry.*

Shaffer, D., Fisher, P., Piacentini, J., Schwab-Stone, M., & Wicks, J. (1992). *The Diagnostic Interview Schedule for Children* (DISC). (Available from the authors, Columbia NIMH DISC Training Center, Division of Child and Adolescent Psychiatry–Unit 78, New York State Psychiatric Institute, 722 West 168th Street, New York, NY 10032)

Singer, M. I., Anglen, T. M., Song, L. Y., & Lunghofer, L. (1995). Adolescents' exposure to violence and associated symptoms of psychological trauma. *Journal of American Medical Association, 273*(6), 477–482.

Stamm, B. H. (Ed.). (1996). *Measurement of stress, trauma and adaptation.* Lutherville, MD: Sidran Press.

Sternberg, K. J., Lamb, M. E., Greenbaum, C., Cicchetti, D., Dawud, S., Cortes, R. M., Krispin, O., & Lorey, F. (1993). Effects of domestic violence on children's behavior problems and depression. *Developmental Psychology, 29*(1), 44–52.

Stuber, M., & Nader, K. (1995). Psychiatric sequelae in adolescent bone-marrow transplant survivors: Implications for psychotherapy. *Journal of Psychotherapy Practice and Research, 4*(1), 30–41.

Swiss, S., & Giller, J. E. (1993). Rape as a crime of war: A medical perspective. *Journal of the American Medical Association, 270*(5), 612–615.

Terr, L. (1979). Children of Chowchilla: Study of psychic trauma. *Psychoanalytic Study of the Child, 34,* 547–623.

Terr, L. (1981). Psychic trauma in children: Observations following the Chowchilla schoolbus kidnapping. *American Journal of Psychiatry, 138*(1), 14–19.

Terr, L. (1983). Chowchilla revisited: The effects of psychic trauma four years after a schoolbus kidnapping. *American Journal of Psychiatry, 140,* 1542–1550.

Terr, L. C. (1991). Childhood traumas: An outline and overview. *American Journal of Psychiatry, 148*(1), 10–20.

van der Kolk, B. A., Roth, S., Pelcovitz, D., & Mandel, F. S. (1992). *Disorders of extreme stress: Results from the DSM-IV field trials for PTSD.* Unpublished manuscript.

van der Kolk, B., & Saporta, J. (1991). The biological response to psychic trauma: Mechanisms and treatment of intrusion and numbing. *Anxiety Research, 4,* 199–212.

Weissman, M., Wichkramaratne, P., Warner, V., John, K., Prusoff, B., Merikangas, K.,

& Gammon, D. (1987). Assessing psychiatric disorders in children. *Archives of General Psychiatry, 44,* 747–753.

Wherry, J. N., Jolly, J. B., Feldman, J., Adam, B., & Manjanatha, S. (1994). The Child Dissociative Checklist: Preliminary findings of a screening instrument. *Child Abuse and Neglect, 3,* 51–66.

Wilson, J., & Raphael, B. (Eds.). (1993). *International handbook of traumatic stress syndromes,* New York: Plenum Press.

Wolfe, V. V., & Birt, J. (in press). Child sexual abuse. In E. J. Mash & L. G. Terdal (Eds.), *Behavioral assessment of childhood disorders* (3rd ed.). New York: Guilford Press.

Wolfe, V. V., & Gentile, C. (1991). *Children's Impact of Traumatic Events Scale—Revised (CITES-R).* (Available from Wolfe, Dept. of Psychology, London Health Sciences Center, 800 Commissioners Road East, London, Ontario N6A4G5)

Wolfe, V. V., Gentile, C., Michienzi, T., Sas, L., & Wolfe, D. A. (1991). The Children's Impact of Traumatic Events Scale: A measure of post-sexual-abuse PTSD symptoms. *Behavioral Assessment, 13*(4), 359–383.

Wolfe, D. A., Wolfe, V. V., & Best, C. L. (1988). Child victims of sexual abuse. In V. B. Van Hasselt (Ed.), *Handbook of family violence* (pp. 157–185). New York: Plenum Press.

Wolfe, V. V., Wolfe, D. A., Gentile, C., & Larose, L. (1986). *Children's Impact of Traumatic Events Scale (CITES).* (Available from Wolfe, Dept. of Psychology, London Health Sciences Center, 800 Commissioners Road East, London, Ontario N6A4G5)

Yates, A., Beutler, L. E., & Crago, M. (1985). Drawings by child victims of incest. *Child Abuse and Neglect, 9,* 183–189.

Yule, W., & Williams, R. M. (1990). Post-traumatic stress reactions in children. *Journal of Traumatic Stress, 3*(2), 279–295.

Zahn, B. S. (1994). *Stress symptoms in 11–16 year old victims of child sexual abuse.* Dissertation submitted to Temple University Graduate Board, Philadelphia, PA.

CHAPTER 11

Assessing Posttraumatic Stress Disorder in Couples and Families

JOHN P. WILSON
ROBERT R. KURTZ

INTRODUCTION

The rapid growth in research on posttraumatic stress disorder (PTSD) has led to many new avenues of application of theory and clinical practice (Wilson & Raphael, 1993). To date, posttraumatic stress reactions have been studied and conceptualized as individual attempts at adaptation following a disaster or traumatic event (Green, 1993; Green et al., 1990). Posttraumatic family stress theory, on the other hand, represents an attempt to describe and predict the entire family's response to trauma and extreme stress. Research on this topic has had a long and fruitful history that predates PTSD as a diagnostic category in DSM-III (American Psychiatric Association, 1980) and its subsequent revisions (e.g., Hansen & Hill, 1964; Boss, 1987). Events that are experienced as so stressful that they produce dramatic changes in the family organization and behavior are often traumatic in their consequences to families as well as individuals (Figley, 1983, 1985, 1988, 1989b). To date, however, there have been only a few, but influential, attempts to construct an integrative theory of how trauma and the development of PTSD influence family functioning or to define posttraumatic family therapy (Stanton & Figley, 1978; Figley, 1983, 1985, 1988, 1989b; McCubbin & McCubbin, 1989; Craine, Hanks, & Stevens, 1992).

When evaluating the relationship of trauma and its impact to families, several assumptions underlie much of the family stress literature: (1) Stresses and even crises are normative events in the history of the family; (2) stress places extreme demands upon individuals and families; (3) most families adapt reasonably well to stress; and (4) if the initial attempts at adaptation fail, the family will experience additional negative stressors (Hobfoll & Spielberger, 1992). Viewed from the perspective of dynamic systems theory, a traumatic experience by an individual family member or an entire family unit will cause disequilibrium to the existing family structure and may lead to crises of coping and adaptation (Lewis, 1986; Figley, 1989b).

The challenge to the researcher and clinician alike is to understand how families cope with extreme stress and the presence of PTSD, and to identify those processes that foster recovery from traumatic events (Figley, 1985, 1988). However, the needs and roles of the researcher and the clinician are different. The family therapist cannot wait for conceptual clarity to be achieved before intervening and providing care. He or she must understand family dynamics resulting from trauma and determine what interventions might foster adaptive family responses. The clinician usually needs a pragmatic, holistic, and integrated theory in order to guide his or her work. Additionally, clinicians often search for theories that will bridge conceptual knowledge to the demands for help wanted by traumatized clients and their families because of the inherent challenges to treatment posed by the complexity of family systems.

The purpose of this chapter is to review some of the major theoretical orientations of traumatic stress in relation to its potential and differential impact on families. Issues of therapeutic importance will be highlighted, as will specific techniques of assessing traumatic impacts to family systems. We will also attempt to integrate the tenets of family stress theory into a broader perspective of family systems theory as it pertains specifically to traumatic events and PTSD within family units.

ORIENTATION TO THE CHAPTER STRUCTURE

Since individual assessment of PTSD has already been discussed in the present volume, we will limit our discussion to marital and family process measures. The chapter will also be limited to those instruments or observation techniques that appear relevant for treating families suffering from PTSD rather than for research purposes (see Jacob, 1987, for a review of research instruments).

The goals of family assessment within the clinical context differ somewhat from the goals of scientific inquiry. The functions of assessing PTSD in a clinical setting with families are as follows: (1) screening and initial evaluation; (2) definition of the client's problem, which may include diagnosis, labeling, or quantification of its severity; (3) planning or establishing treatment goals; (4) monitoring treatment progress; and (5) evaluation of treatment outcome (Carlson, 1989; Jacob & Tennenbaum, 1988). Of these core objectives, planning treatment, monitoring progress, and evaluation of interventions appear to be most useful for the practitioner.

In general, a family evaluation will be more useful if it is explicitly guided by theory and research (Grotevant, 1989). Therefore, we will provide a brief review of the clinical research findings on families and PTSD, which is followed by a discussion of family assessment issues and techniques. More specifically, we will review how families appear to respond to trauma when: (1) one of the marital partners shows symptoms of PTSD; (2) the entire family experiences a traumatic event; (3) PTSD in children and adolescents exists; and (4) there are effects of transgenerational transmission of trauma. We will review those family processes that are affected by PTSD and patterns of family interaction that are adversely impacted by traumatic events.

CLINICAL RESEARCH FINDINGS ON MARITAL SUBSYSTEMS

In the broadest overview of the literature on PTSD and families, it is clear that the study of Vietnam veterans was seminal in the earlier research studies that began to study how PTSD symptoms affect marriage and families (Carroll, Foy, Cannon, & Zwler, 1991; Harkness, 1993; Wilson & Raphael, 1993). For example, the most frequently identified *marital problems* associated with PTSD symptoms of Vietnam War veterans were (1) constricted intimacy and expressiveness, marked by limited affective expression of emotions and a lack of self-disclosure (Carroll et al., 1991); (2) overt hostility in the form of unpredictable outbursts of verbal and physical aggression; and (3) global maladjustment, characterized by general dissatisfaction and recurrent crises (Carroll, Rueger, Foy, & Donahue, 1985; Silver & Iacono, 1986; Roberts et al., 1982; Solomon, Mikulincer, Fried, & Wosner, 1987).

These findings strongly indicated that the existence of PTSD had negative consequences to intimate bonding within a marital relationship. An important question confronting the clinician is whether the characteristics found in the research findings are specific to the Vietnam War veteran population or generalize to other trauma populations. For example, is hostility characteristic of all PTSD victims in the context of interpersonal relationships? Or more generally, what are the specific manifestations of affective dysregulation on relationships, especially in complex family systems?

The growing literature on rape trauma also illustrates the high risk potential for negative consequences within dyadic relationships. Although few controlled studies have been reported in this area, descriptive studies have identified a common pattern of distress (Miller, Williams, & Bernstein, 1982; Ochberg, 1988). In the wake of rape trauma, couples generally reported difficulties in affective expression, commitment, emotional support, sexual relations, and communication. Couples in which there was a history of rape trauma were described by their therapists as presenting with poor communication skills, excessive dependency, and lack of trust. The limited data available suggest that rape trauma appears to have an impact upon many of the areas that are typically assessed in treatment, which include (1) expression of affect, (2) decision making, (3) personal commitment, (4) perceptions of emotional distance and closeness, (5) worldview, (6) self-esteem, and (7) cultural schemata of meaning (see Wolfe & Kimerling, Chapter 7, this volume, for a discussion).

In general, the research literature on trauma consistently supports the idea that PTSD has a significant impact upon the marital relationship. Trauma affects the core tasks of establishing good communication, expressing support and caring, commitment to others, and the resolution of conflict (Nichols, 1988). Family stress theory (e.g., Boss, 1987) states that traumatic stress leads to role ambiguity between spouses. Role ambiguity, in turn, may create dysfunctional behavior in the marriage and the family. According to Hansen and Johnson (1979), ambiguity has been identified "as a fundamental and pervasive quality of stress conditions that makes the definitional aspect of family interaction especially problematic" (p. 570). Stated simply, stress changes peoples' expectations and performance of marital roles. In addition, since a major symptom of PTSD is *affective dysregulation,* the communication of both positive and negative feelings is likely to be adversely impacted. As noted in the massive literature on marital systems, the communication of feelings plays a central role in couple satisfaction (e.g., Greenberg & Johnson, 1988; Gottman, 1991). When communication quality is diminished, the regulation of roles and expectations is harder to maintain, which may contribute to reoccurring patterns of conflict, detachment, isolation, and withdrawal so characteristic of avoidance and numbing patterns in PTSD. When an unstable relationship is created, it may cause negative socioemotional reactions in the partners such as hostility, confusion, irritability, withdrawal, explosive outbursts, detachment, and so forth, which may alternate with needs for nurturance, affection, protection, and dependency. *Thus, it is our view that cyclical patterns of instability and role dysregulation are quite typical in families or relationships impacted by PTSD and its associated features, such as alcohol abuse, depression, and hyperaroused states of coping.*

MARITAL ASSESSMENT AND PTSD

Before an assessment of a marital relationship is attempted, several issues must be addressed. First, a psychosocial history of the couple should be established. We recommend taking a relationship history *after* the couple has had a chance to describe the impact of the trauma to their lives in detail. Second, clinical experience suggests that considerable variance can exist in marital dynamics before a stressful life event. Research indicates that these differences exist to the degree that the couple has been able to successfully negotiate issues of emotional commitment, interpersonal closeness and distance, and decision making (Lewis, 1986). The impact of trauma on a recently formed relationship is likely to differ from that in a marriage with a long history and well-established patterns of relating. Stress theory states that couples initially rely on well established patterns to maintain a sense of "normality" during stressful transition periods (e.g., Lewis, 1986; Boss,

1987). Thus, if a couple has established *dysfunctional patterns* of relating *prior* to the trauma, then those patterns are likely to amplify and contribute to additional stress in the posttrauma period of coping and readjustment (e.g., McCubbin & Patterson, 1983). A third assessment issue concerns the *severity* of the victim's trauma reaction and the subsequent meaning it has to the couple. For example, unexplained and poorly understood outbursts of hostility can lead to estrangement, fear, and anxiety in the nontraumatized spouse (e.g., Carroll et al., 1985). Similarly, episodes of depression, detachment, loss of sex drive and appetite, emotional constriction, psychic numbing, dissociation, flashback experiences and unusual behaviors, and so on, may be confusing and a source of great distress to the partner, especially one who is unfamiliar with PTSD syndromes (Waysman, Mikulincer, Solomon, & Weisenberg, 1993).

MEASURES OF MARITAL ADJUSTMENT AND COPING

As the practitioner considers treatment options, it should be noted that there are numerous marital adjustment measures available. Among the various reference sources, *Measures for Clinical Practice* (Fischer & Corcoran, 1994) lists over 30 self-report instruments. Although it is beyond the scope of this chapter to review all assessment instruments for couples and marital units, we will select several that have special relevance for PTSD assessment. Some of the scales are single-variable instruments that are excellent for research purposes but of limited use in clinical practice. Nevertheless, as aids in diagnosis and treatment, self-report instruments may provide useful information that cannot be obtained through interviewing the couple.

Marital Adjustment Test and Dyadic Adjustment Scale

Marital satisfaction is a construct with a long history in family systems research (Heyman, Sayers, & Bellack, 1994). The Marital Adjustment Test (MAT; Locke & Wallace, 1959) and its updated cousin, the Dyadic Adjustment Scale (DAS; Spanier, 1976), are widely used instruments with excellent psychometric properties. The DAS has been used in over 1,000 studies as of 1989. The measure consists of 32 questions concerning overall happiness and satisfaction, consensus between partners on various issues, and dyadic cohesion. Ratings are typically scored on a 6-point scale of agreement and scores can range from 0 to 151. The instrument is typically used as a measure of global marital satisfaction, and the wording is also appropriate for cohabiting couples. Moreover, four subscales of the measure have been defined by factor-analytic studies conducted by Spanier (1976): (1) *dyadic consensus* (13 items), (2) *affective expression* (4 items), (3) *dyadic satisfaction* (10 items), and (4) *dyadic cohesion* (5 items). Thus, the scale is capable of yielding five scores: one for total adjustment and four derived from the subscales. A number of studies have shown that the scale discriminates quite readily between distressed and nondistressed couples (Weiss, Hops, & Patterson, 1973). As a cautionary note, we believe that assessment would be more useful for planning therapy if additional items were included on the affective expression subscale, since research on traumatized families (e.g., Figley, 1986) shows that the modulation of affect is a core symptom of PTSD associated with marital difficulties. In addition, the DAS appears to confuse *marital satisfaction* with the construct of *marital adjustment* (Heyman et al., 1994). This confusion stems procedurally from the DAS combining items of interactional processing (e.g., disagreeing) with subjective ratings of happiness (Norton, 1983). Nevertheless, the DAS is a valid scale that can provide a quick index of the level of distress present in a relationship in which one or both partners suffer from PTSD.

Personal Assessment of Intimacy in Relationships

The Personal Assessment of Intimacy in Relationships (PAIRS) is another potentially useful questionnaire to assess the impact of PTSD on couples. This questionnaire is a 36-item instrument designed to measure "intimacy" (Schaeffer & Olson, 1981). The client rates statements about his or her relationship on a 5-point scale of agreement/disagreement. The items describe activities, feelings, and attitudes that reflect degrees of intimacy in the relationship. The scores can range from 0 to 150. The original 75-item scale was factor analyzed in a series of studies with couples participating in a marital enrichment program resulting in the 36-item scale. Five subdimensions of intimacy were identified: emotional, sexual, intellectual, and recreational. The reliability and validity testing on the PAIRS instrument appears adequate with a Cronbach's alpha coefficient of .70 for the subscales. In addition, the PAIRS instrument correlates in expected directions with the Family Environment Scale (Moos & Moos, 1981) on many of the same variables. Since intimacy is an aspect of relationships adversely impacted by the presence of PTSD, the PAIRS is a potential assessment tool to evaluate this dimension of interpersonal functioning.

Marital Satisfaction Inventory

The Marital Satisfaction Inventory (MSI) is another scale that was developed to provide a multidimensional self-report of marital interaction (Snyder, 1979). The MSI was designed to provide information about more specific aspects of the marital relationship (Jacob & Tennenbaum, 1988). To meet this goal, 11 subscales on the MSI were developed from the 280-item measure of marital satisfaction (see Table 11.1). The true–false response format usually takes approximately 30–45 minutes to complete.

The test–retest reliability of all scales over a 6-week interval was a mean

TABLE 11.1. Marital Satisfaction Inventory Subscales

Subscale	Abbreviation	Number of items
Conventionalism	CNV	21
Global Distress	GDS	43
Affective Communication	AFC	26
Problem-Solving Communication	PSC	38
Time Together	TTO	20
Disagreement about Finances	FIN	22
Sexual Dissatisfaction	SEX	29
Role Orientation	ROR	25
Family History of Distress	FAM	15
Dissatisfaction with Children	DSC	22
Conflict over Childrearing	CCR	19

of .89 (Snyder, Wills, & Keiser, 1981). The MSI has been used to discriminate between distressed couples in marital therapy and couples from the general population. The scales correlate with structured clinical ratings of couples entering therapy (Snyder et al., 1981). Factor analysis suggests that the affectively loaded scales (Global Distress [GDS], Affective Communication [AFC], Problem-Solving Communication [PSC], Time Together [TTO]) influence the major results on the MSI.

TRAUMATIC EVENTS AND FAMILY EXPOSURE

There are very few studies of family functioning under extreme conditions. A recent study, however, examined how family members reacted to the threat of a SCUD missile attack during the Persian Gulf War of 1991 (Ben-David & Levee, 1992). The authors interviewed 66 families regarding their reactions shortly after being sealed in rooms while subjected to the SCUD missile attacks. The results indicate that three major dimensions of family dynamics appear to be affected by the threat to the family: emotional atmosphere, family modes of organization (e.g., roles), and style of interaction among family members.

In the study, "emotional atmosphere" referred to the amount of emotion that was expressed. Some families, for example, expressed such high amounts of fear and anxiety that other family functions became subordinate to the fear. Similarly, "family modes of organization" referred to the clarity of role assignment. Some families were characterized by having clear and defined roles about which family member was to perform certain functions, whereas other families manifested less organizational clarity and effective functioning. "Interactional style" referred to the amount and tone of the communication between family members. The results indicate that there was a wide range of positive and negative affect manifest in the families studied, as well as different coping styles.

Beyond war trauma, there are, of course, many other traumatic events that can impact on family functioning. For example, Baum, Gatchel, and Schaeffer (1983) have examined families exposed to toxic chemical and hazardous disasters. As noted by Wilson and Raphael (1993), disasters can be subdivided into those that are natural, such as earthquakes, and those that are technological, such as toxic spills and plane crashes (Smith & North, 1993). Family members exposed to these types of stressors expressed feelings of loss of control, helplessness, and powerlessness (Baum et al., 1983). In a major review of disaster studies (Wilson & Raphael, 1993), it was found that family members showed elevated levels of psychological distress and psychosocial disruption. More specifically, high levels of demoralization, depression, and anxiety were found among family members, along with symptoms of PTSD (Wilson & Raphael, 1993). Thus, in general, when a family is exposed to extreme threat, the family system often experiences affective dysregulation in terms of interpersonal reactions and the capacity to bind anxiety and emotions stimulated by the trauma.

As noted by Smith and North (1993), the rate of diagnosable *disorders* following disasters is extremely variable, but *symptoms* of Axis I anxiety and depressive disorders are quite high. In general, the rates of PTSD *symptoms* reported were higher for studies of technological disasters than for natural disasters. However, what is important for the practitioner is to discern the *specific stressor experiences* of the individual family members during the traumatic event, their role in the event, and types of coping behavior utilized after the trauma.

Family stress theory, like individual stress appraisal, emphasizes that the family's perception of trauma is an important determinant of posttraumatic adaptation. As with individuals exposed to trauma, families may seek to increase cohesiveness and unity or, alternately, separate and turn outward from the primary unit. For example, families may respond with more anger and externalize reactions rather than attending to each other's needs. Ben-David and Levee (1992) suggest that some families adopt a style of attributing "blame" to a stressor event, and that family members may or may not communicate these perceptions to one another. Alternatively, members blame one another for putting themselves in harm's way. Nevertheless, the primary concern among exposed groups is the physical health of family members, especially young children. These findings appear consistent with previous research within families containing a member with PTSD. Studies reviewed by Carroll et al. (1991) present a picture of family life marked by minimal communication, overt hostility, and difficulties with emotional support.

In a parallel way, family systems theory has long been able to identify patterns that weaken families, diminish the quality of daily life, and impede individual growth (Jacob, 1987; Walsh, 1993). Family stress theory emphasizes family resources as well as family perceptions of which factors will help them. Angell's (1936) classic study of families coping with the Great Depression of the 1930s, identifies family adaptability and integration as resources. Family integration refers to unifying forces in family life, such as affection and support. Family adaptability refers to the family's ability to vary its responses. These two dimensions identified how adaptation affected all later attempts to define family resources (Karpel, 1986). Therapeutically, assessment of family resources becomes as important as identification of dysfunction (Walsh, 1993).

Research has shown that among the best predictors of PTSD is the severity of the trauma to which individuals are exposed (Pynoos, Frederick, & Nader, 1987; Green, 1993; Wilson & Raphael, 1993). All things being equal, the severity of threat to self or others has a high risk consequence to individuals and families.

Although there are many instruments designed to assess the severity of the trauma, we have found that subjective family perceptions appear to have an even stronger impact than "objective criteria." Most families will share their perceptions of the severity of a traumatic event, although they may disagree about the emotional impact to themselves.

Standardized instruments to assess PTSD such as the Impact of Event Scale (IES) permit comparisons between groups with PTSD and normative groups (see Weiss & Marmar, Chapter 13, this volume). Typically, families wonder whether their behaviors are "normal" in response to a trauma (Horowitz, Wilner, & Alvarez, 1979). Individual assessments such as the Structured Clinical Interview for DSM-IV (SCID-PTSD) Module (Weiss, 1993) or the Symptom Checklist 90 — Revised (SCL-90-R; Derogatis, 1983) cannot be compared to instruments tailored to assess family functioning. Therefore, McCubbin and his associates created a series of instruments to measure the stresses that affect the entire family (Olson et al., 1989). The Family Inventory of Life Events (FILE; McCubbin, Patterson, & Wilson, 1983) is one example of such an instrument. The inventory is designed to measure individual perceptions of stressful events that a family may have been exposed to during the last 12 months. On the other hand, Reiss and Oliveri (1991) developed a new approach to the assessment of family stress. Their approach is different from previous methods in four respects: (1) They developed a systematic set of items that would most likely be stressful to the family as a group rather than to individuals; (2) the families were asked to rate the amount of stress perceived as a group rather than as individuals; (3) families were asked how accountable they felt they were for the event in the first place; and (4) they used a variant of a *Q*-sort methodology.

In Reiss and Oliveri's procedure, stressors are explored in separate areas of family life which includes health, jobs, family activities, extended family life, and the family's neighborhood. The clients' answers are classified in four categories: (1) events perceived as having high impact on the family but for which they are not held accountable (e.g., natural disasters); (2) high-impact events for which the family is held accountable (e.g., child drops out of school, or family member attempts suicide); (3) low impact events for which the family is held accountable; and (4) situations that do not pertain to the family. We believe that this approach holds much promise but is still in the research and development stage. Reiss and Oliveri hypothesize that family crises will result when the event has *high impact*: The family is perceived to be *accountable* for the traumatic event, and the family members act ineffectively in terms of coping with the crises.

Another assessment instrument for consideration is the Family Crises-Oriented Personal Evaluation Scale (F-COPES). It is a self-report inventory that measures internal and external family strategies for coping with traumatic events (McCubbin, Cauble, & Patterson, 1982). The 29-item instrument is answered on a 5-point Likert-type scale.

The inventory contains five subscales: (1) *acquiring social support* (9 items), (2) *reframing* (8 items), (3) *seeking spiritual support* (4 items), (4) *mobilizing family to acquire help* (4 items), (5) *passive appraisal* (4 items).

The internal consistency–reliability estimates ranged from .63 to .86 for the full scale. Stability estimate of the F-COPES scores after 4 weeks was .61–.95. (McCubbin & Thompson, 1991).

In our view, the instruments described here have the advantage of directly assessing the family's responses to stressful events. They are short and easy to administer. Clinically, we have found it more useful to employ instruments that assess numerous relevant variables to family functioning, rather than single variables of only a few areas of adaptation. In this regard, family assessment methods can be differentiated broadly by the *frame of reference* of the rater (insider or outsider), and by the *type of data* collected (subjective or objective; Cromwell, Olson, & Fournier, 1976). The "insider frame" refers to family members' ratings of family functioning. The "outsider frame" refers to clinical rating scales and judgments based upon observations of family interaction. Studies that have compared different models of family functioning through insider and outsider perspectives have reported *low convergence* between views (Hampson, Beavers, & Hulgus, 1989). Similarly, in a study on *client-based* descriptions of family therapy, Kuehl, Newfield, and Joanning (1990) found that families were more likely to drop out of treatment if their perceptions appeared too discrepant from those of the therapist. Therefore, it appears that early in treatment, clinicians should refrain from imposing "objective views" upon the family in crisis in order to reduce the risk of treatment failure.

The difference between subjective and objective measures of family functioning is based upon the amount of emotional reactivity rated. "Objective means that what is being defined belongs to the object of perception or thought and is not affected by personal feelings or prejudice. Subjective means that what is being defined belongs to the thinking subject rather than the object of thought, and it is relied on one's personal feelings or opinions" (Kerr & Bowen, 1988, p. 18). The subjective–objective frame can be seen as a continuous dimension, therefore, rather than a dichotomous one. Using this definition, the family members, the clinician, and the researcher may be either more subjective or more objective in their assessments. It would be expected that family members coming for treatment for emotional reactions to trauma would be highly subjective in their perceptions.

In summary, the research reviewed suggests that if one or more family members show symptoms of PTSD, the family as a unit will be affected. These observations support family stress theory (e.g., Boss, 1987) and family systems theory (e.g., Steinglass, 1987). More specifically, families may experience changes in expression of affect, organization, daily interaction (process), and orientation (beliefs). These broad categories were proposed in an early generic model of family assessment by Fisher (1976), who identified four categories of family constructs that should be assessed by the practitioner. The four categories are as follows:

1. *Family structure:* Organization of the family. Roles and expectations as well as patterns of task and social functions.
2. *Process:* Actions and activities within the family which including control, regulatory, and communication functions.
3. *Affective expression:* Patterns of affect regulation.
4. *Orientation:* The family's attitudes and beliefs about the family unit, especially in terms of its competency and its relations with the outside world.

These general categories appear to be applicable to a family's responses to traumatic stress. In a critique of assessment techniques, Grotevant and Carlson (1989) found that only 3 of 17 instruments of global family functioning assess all four categories in the framework. The three assessment instruments were (1) the *Beavers Systems Model* (Beavers & Hampson, 1990, 1993); (2) the *Circumplex Model* (Olson, Russell, & Sprenkle, 1983; Olson et. al, 1989); and (3) the *McMaster Family Assessment Device* (Epstein, Bishop, Ryan, Miller, & Keitner, 1993). All three instruments have both "insider" and "outsider scales" that assess the same variables (see Walsh, 1993, for reviews).

ASSESSING WHOLE FAMILY FUNCTIONING

Family Environment Scale

The Family Environment Scale (FES; Moos & Moos, 1981) was one of the first instruments developed specifically for family assessments. The instrument is composed of 10 rationally derived subscales assessing three broad areas: the interpersonal relationships among family members, personal growth characteristics emphasized by the family, and the system organizational features of the family (see Table 11.2).

Currently, the FES can be used in three different forms: the Real form (Form R), the Ideal form (Form I), and the Expectations form (Form E). All

TABLE 11.2. Family Environment Subscales

Dimension	Subscale	Description
Relationship	Cohesion	Degree of commitment, help, and support
	Expressiveness	Encouragement of open expression of feelings
	Conflict	Amount of openly expressed anger, aggression, and conflict
Personal growth	Independence	Amount of self-sufficiency, assertiveness, making own decisions
	Achievement orientation	Achievement-oriented or competitiveness framework
	Intellectual	Interest in politics, intellectual, social, and cultural activities
	Active recreational orientation	Participation in social or recreational activities
	Moral–religious emphasis	Emphasis on ethical and religious issues
System maintenance	Organization	Clarity of organization in planning family activities and responsibilities
	Control	Extent to which set rules and procedures are used to run family life

forms consist of 90 true–false statements. The FES can be completed in about 15–20 minutes and is easy to score. The internal consistency reliability estimates for the 10 subscales varied between .61 for independence to .78 for cohesion. Test–retest reliability estimates for 8 weeks varied, but ranged from between .68 and .86.

Clearly, some of the family dimensions on the FES may be more affected by PTSD than others. The relationship dimensions of Cohesiveness, Expressiveness, and Conflict are likely to change along with some of the System Maintenance Dimensions. One of the shortcomings of this instrument is that no "outsider" rating form is available on the same variables. Oliveri and Reiss (1984) found that the FES does not correlate with rated dimensions in the expected directions in terms of construct validity.

Circumplex Model of Marital and Family Systems

The Circumplex Model of Marital and Family Assessment attempts to bridge the gap between research, theory, and practice (Olson, 1993). Several self-report instruments are available in the Circumplex Assessment Package, all based on measuring the dimensions of Cohesion, Adaptability, and Communication. For clinical work with premarital and married couples, there are two comprehensive inventories called PREPARE and ENRICH. PREPARE, for premarital couples, has been found to predict with 80–85% accuracy which couples will divorce. ENRICH is designed for married couples and is able to discriminate with 90% accuracy couples who are satisfied from clinically impaired couples. Both instruments are computer scored and have norms based on over 100,000 couples.

Olson and his colleagues at the University of Minnesota also developed an acronym for the Family Adaptability and Cohesive Evaluation Scale (FACES III) and the Marital Adaptability and Cohesiveness Evaluation Scale (MACES III). The three dimensions of Cohesion, Flexibility, and Communication were merged from conceptual clustering of over 50 concepts developed to describe marital and family dynamics. The study of how different families cope effectively with stress (Olson et al., 1989) has been a part of this large-scale research program.

In a similar vein, the Clinical Rating Scale (CRS) was developed by Olson (1990) in order to do clinical assessment on the same dimensions as FACES III. Among the Dimensions that are measured on the Circumplex Model are (1) Family Cohesion, (2) Parent–Child Relationship, (3) Internal and External Bonding, (4) Family Flexibility, (5) Leadership, (6) Discipline, and (7) Communication Patterns.

The Circumplex Model of Marriage and Family Systems is an evolving assessment procedure. The system has changed over the years as a result of input from research (e.g., Olson, 1986, 1993). For example, the most recent revision of FACES III makes the model more similar to the Beavers System Model (Beavers & Hampson, 1993) and the McMaster Family Model (Olson, 1993). The circumplex model has been used in research in family stress as well as in numerous other studies of family processes (e.g., Walsh & Olson, 1989; Ben-David & Levee, 1992; Craine et al., 1992), and therefore has good research support and norms.

Beavers Systems Model

The Beavers Model of family assessment emphasizes family competence. Family competence, which is considered a continuous dimension, is defined as how well a family unit performs the necessary and nurturing tasks of organizing and managing itself (Beavers & Hampson, 1993). The Beavers System employs both a self-report inventory (Beavers, Hampson, & Hulgus, 1985) and an external observation measure, the Beavers Interactional Competence Scale (BICS; Beavers & Hampson, 1990, 1993).

Both the self-report instrument and the observation scale assess the same dimensions, which allows for comparison of "insider" and "outsider" ratings (Hampson et al., 1989). The system also rates families on both style and competence, with less competent families rigidly adhering to one style (centrifugal or centripetal). The Beavers Scales generate the following subcategories:

I. Structure
   A. Overt power: chaos to egalitarian
   B. Parental coalitions: parent–child coalition to strong parental coalition
   C. Closeness: indistinct boundaries to closeness with clear boundaries
II. Mythology: degrees of congruence in role function
III. Goal: directed negotiations; problem solving
IV. Autonomy
   A. Clarity of expression
   B. Responsibility for behavior
   C. Permeability: degree of openness
V. Family affect
   A. Range of feelings: wide range to restricted
   B. Mood and tone: warm and affectionate to cynical, pessimistic
   C. Unresolved conflict
   D. Empathy
VI. Global health pathology

The continuum of family competence assessed by the Beavers System moves from extremely chaotic and noninteractive through marked dominance–submission patterns, to greater capacity for egalitarian and successful families. At the most *dysfunctional end* of the competence dimension are seen the most extreme and inflexible family styles. The empirical studies support the findings (Beavers & Hampson, 1993, p. 77) that system rigidity is pathogenic. The research found that families who were most successful at coping with stress demands were those who were able to express a wide range of feelings, including frustration and joy, and in fact, the presence of the stressful situation may have even contributed to their support of one another (Beavers, Hampson, & Hulgus, 1985; Hampson, Beavers, & Hulgus, 1988). In the more dysfunctional families, there was less expression of affect and greater emotional constriction. Thus, for families with PTSD, the effects of trauma will likely accentuate the preexisting organization and role structures.

A major advantage with using either the Olson or Beavers instruments is the way theory, research, and clinical practice are integrated. The results of the assessments are easily understood and can provide goal setting with families. Beavers and his colleagues (e.g., Beavers & Hampson, 1990) provide useful descriptions of how therapy can attain modest goals to help families cope with both normative and situational stress and, by implication, traumatic stress.

McMaster Model

The McMaster Model of Family Functioning has evolved over a period of more than 25 years (Epstein, Baldwin, & Bishop, 1983). The assessment system does not cover all aspects of family functioning but does focus on the dimensions seen as having the most impact on the emotional and physical health or problems of family members. Similar to the Beavers Systems Model, the dimensions of family functioning are assessed on a continuum from dysfunctional to optimal.

The self-report instrument for the McMaster Model is called the Family Assessment Device (FAD; Epstein et al., 1983). The 60-item questionnaire is scored on a 4-point scale from *strongly agree* to *strongly disagree*. From the responses, the questionnaire generates six scales:

1. *Problem solving:* the ability to solve family problems
2. *Communication:* the information exchange among family members
3. *Roles:* clear and accepted assignment of tasks and their completion
4. *Affective responsiveness:* ability to express appropriate emotions
5. *Affective involvement:* the value place on the family member's concerns
6. *Behavior control:* the way the family maintained behavior standards

Another scale measures global functioning. The internal consistency reliabilities for the six subscales vary from .72 to .83, with the general functioning scale's reliability at .92. The FAD scores were able to distinguish between individuals who are college students and individuals who have siblings, spouses, parents, or children in a psychiatric hospital.

One of the chief advantages to the McMaster Model is its face validity. The concepts are described in clear, understandable dimensions that allow for ease of goal setting in family therapy. Setting clear and attainable goals seems to have the therapeutic impact of lowering family anxiety and inspiring a sense of hope (e.g., Epstein & Bishop, 1981) that family problems will be resolved.

In summary, we recommend that practitioners consider using at least one "whole-family" inventory when assessing the impact of PTSD on the family. The family instruments appear to assess the variables most often reported to be affected in the clinical research literature. The potential impact of PTSD symptoms, including the numbing of responsiveness, withdrawal, and affective dysregulation, are generally included in the assessment models (see Table 11.2).

The Circumplex Model, the Beavers Systems Model, and the McMaster Model include both "insider" (self-report) and "outsider" (rated observation) perspectives on the same family dimensions. This permits clinicians to compare their observations with the family members' own views of their family functioning. In the early phases of treatment, clinicians need to be sensitive to discrepancies between these views, because the family members may feel misunderstood and disrespected if clinicians impose their discrepant observation upon them (Griffith & Griffith, 1994).

In addition to the potentially dysfunctional reactions to PTSD in the family, the instruments also identify family resources or processes attributed to healthy family functioning. We believe that these processes, such as "connectedness" and "acceptance of feelings," can contribute to a supportive environment toward recovery from trauma (e.g., Figley, 1989a). Therefore, assessment devices that identify resources as well as dysfunction may be more useful in therapy. Family therapy research indicates that families need a balance between stability and flexibility for continuity and change (e.g., Olson, 1993). Similarly, needs for connectedness and togetherness must be balanced with individual autonomy and separateness (e.g., Beavers & Hampson, 1993; Kerr & Bowen, 1988). PTSD in one or more family members appears to create enough stress within many families to disrupt the balance of these normal family functions.

PTSD IN CHILDREN AND ADOLESCENTS

Children and adolescents respond to trauma in similar ways to adults (see Nader, Chapter 10, this volume). The classic symptoms of reexperiencing, avoidance, and increased arousal must be viewed from the developmental perspective when assessing children. A review of the literature indicates that developmental issues influence the children's perceptions, symptomatic presentation, course of recovery, and behavior in treatment (Pynoos & Nader, 1993). For example, in the Buffalo Creek Dam disaster, young children were less severely affected than were adolescents, due to their inability to fully understand the magnitude and implications of the disaster (Gleser, Green, & Winget, 1981).

In recent years, a number of excellent measures designed to assess behavioral problems in children have been developed. Since these measures are described in a previous chapter (see Nader, Chapter 10, this volume), we will not review child and adolescent measures in this chapter.

TRANSGENERATIONAL EFFECTS OF TRAUMA ON FAMILIES

Studies of children of Holocaust survivors have found that the effect of trauma on parents may have a negative impact upon their children (e.g., Krystal, 1968; Rakoff, Segal, & Epstein, 1965; Segal, Silver, & Rakoff, 1973; Danieli, 1993). Early studies suggested that separation–individuation difficulties became prominent in such families when the children reached adolescents (e.g., Baracos & Baracos, 1973; Phillips, 1978). More recent

Holocaust survivor studies are not reporting significant differences between control groups and children from survivor families in the incidence of pathology (e.g., Leon, Butcher, Kleinman, Goldberg, & Almagot, 1981; Rose & Garseke, 1987; Klein-Parker, 1988).

The mixed findings in the research have created theoretical debates over whether transgenerational effects of trauma are passed on and how these influences are generated. Studies reviewed by Harkness (1993) suggest that children of Vietnam War veterans with PTSD are identifiable as high-risk children, especially if their fathers are violent. The children of Vietnam War veterans with PTSD often show symptom constellations similar to those exhibited by fathers, such as depression, anxiety, low frustration tolerance, and outbursts of anger (Figley & Sprenkle, 1978). This research tends to support a major theoretical assumption of transgenerational family therapy, which is that the effects of traumatic stress are passed down through at least three generations. More specifically, traumatic stress affects the generations by affecting (1) family organization or structure (Lewis, 1986); (2) family life cycle development (Carter & McGoldrick, 1989); and (3) relational patterns within the family, such as intimacy, control, and conflict (e.g., Kerr & Bowen, 1988).In other words, children in families of an adult trauma survivor can be affected either directly or indirectly by parents with PTSD. For example, the child could become the target of the parent's related hostility and aggression, or the child could be influenced less directly by parental neglect or disengagement from parental roles.

Assessment of Transgenerational Influences of Trauma

Since transgenerational family theory assumes that the effects of past trauma may take years to develop, the clinician must gather data not only of the immediate nuclear family but also of former generations. It would be important to know, for example, whether a Vietnam War veteran suffering form PTSD had a father who served in World War II or the Korean Conflict and something about the father's reactions to those experiences.

When assessing a family's history transgenerationally, many clinicians use family genograms (McGoldrick & Gerson, 1985; Danieli, 1993). A family genogram is an assessment device that visually depicts a family genealogy or family tree. The device records information about members of a nuclear and extended family, and their interrelationships. Genograms were pioneered by Murray Bowen and colleagues (Bowen, 1978) and are used by clinicians in both social and biological sciences. Genograms allow the transgenerational family therapist to create a chronological "map" of a family's structure and history of interrelationships over generations of critical life cycle events such as marriages, births, deaths, separations, and so on, which are listed by date. When constructing a family genogram for potential effects of traumatic events, a therapist should focus on attention to those events in a family history that might have stimulated extreme stress.

Attention would be given to potentially traumatic events in the family history, which are listed by date. Carter and McGoldrick (1989) write that families transmit anxiety or stress along two axes. There is a "vertical" flow of stress that has to do with behavioral patterns handed down through generations of the family. There is also a "horizontal" flow of stress, which refers to a family's difficulties in negotiating life circumstances, such as unfortunate events. Genograms contain information about stressors on both horizontal and vertical axes. McGoldrick and Gerson (1989) theorize that repetitive patterns of marital and family behavior, as well as prescribed roles, values, religious and personal beliefs, and other "unwritten rules" of a family, are evolved through the generations by interaction into how the family appears today (Roberto, 1992; Danieli, 1993).

At the most basic level, a clinician must focus on organizational information about the family. Who is in a family household, and how are the roles and authority lines organized? The clinician also needs to know the family's stage in its life cycle and the life cycle stages of its individual members, since stress has differential effects on people depending upon developmental level (Wilson & Raphael, 1993). Another area that the clinician must assess via the genogram is the pattern of relational patterns and behaviors. How close or distant have family members been? How have they handled crises in the past? Have certain family members taken leadership when crises and transitions have appeared?

Recent writings in family therapy have emphasized "solution-oriented," collaborative approaches to working with families in crises (e.g., de Shazer, 1985, 1988; O'Hanlon & Weiner-Davis, 1989; White & Epston, 1990). Drawing from systemic–constructivist philosophies, the approaches share similar assumptions. Like most therapies, a core objective of solution-oriented intervention is to provide families with increased response flexibility. This is accomplished by highlighting helpful responses or resources that might not have been noticed by clients in their attempts to cope with trauma.

In a thought-provoking and clinically useful article, Kuehl (1995) described how genograms can be used with these "emergent models" of the 1990s (Nichols & Schwartz, 1995) in family therapy. By asking a variety of questions while taking a family history, the therapist helps the family identify effective coping among their kin. For example, a question such as "Who in the family seems to be handling this situation well?" followed by "And what are they doing that is different?" is designed to focus on strengths and future responses rather than on weakness and past (limited) response patterns.

Solution-oriented therapists accept the family's definition of the problem and through careful questioning and using the genogram, elicit resources, strengths, and exceptions to the distress (e.g., O'Hanlon & Weiner-Davis, 1989; White & Epston, 1990). This strategy often gives the family a sense of hope that they can cope with traumatic events. The genogram is a flexible assessment tool, and Kuehl (1995) describes how it can be used in the newest therapeutic formats.

SUMMARY

When a family member experiences a traumatic event of sufficient magnitude to induce the symptoms of PTSD, the research suggests that the entire family will experience an increase in tension. Family systems theory (e.g., Kerr & Bowen, 1988) postulates that a family can respond to this increased distress in one of four ways: (1) They can distance from each other; (2) one person can accommodate his or her own functioning to preserve relationship harmony; (3) they can engage in conflict; or (4) the couple can band together over a common cause (triangulate). Since these reactive patterns have been reported in the literature, these factors should be assessed when treating a family with PTSD. Moreover, which pattern of coping the family adopts is largely dependent upon the amount of distress experienced, the family resources, the family belief system, the family structure or organizational patterns, and patterns of posttraumatic coping. Clearly, some of these phases are not easily assessed and thus have to be evaluated indirectly or by someone outside the family system. Therapeutically, making family resources explicit appears to have been helpful in aiding families to resolve problems (e.g., Nichols & Schwartz, 1995; Rolland, 1994). In addition, the family's background of coping with previous stressors must be assessed (e.g., Harkness, 1993; Rolland, 1994).

The whole-family assessment instruments recommended in this chapter appear to assess some of the more important variables of a family's responses to PTSD. Family cohesion or distance and the amount of family conflict are two dimensions that the research literature suggests are affected by high amounts of stress and the presence of PTSD. In addition, family interactions around roles, rules, and responsibilities regarding dealing with problems and interpersonal issues generated by PTSD appear to be affected.

Careful family evaluations help the clinician focus and set up mutually achievable goals for family intervention. Research has shown that in this way, family interventions have a higher probability of success (Wilson & Raphael, 1993).

REFERENCES

American Psychiatric Association. (1980). *Diagnostic and statistical manual of mental disorders* (3rd ed.). Washington, DC: Author.

Angell, R. C. (1936). *The family encounters the depression.* New York: Scribner's.

Baracos, H., & Baracos, C. (1973). Manifestation of concentration effects on the second generation. *American Journal of Psychiatry, 130*(7), 820–821.

Baum, A. B., Fleming, R., & Singer, J. E. (1983). Coping with victimization by technological disaster. *Journal of Social Issues, 39*(2), 117–138.

Baum, A. B., Gatchel, R. J., & Schaeffer, M. A. (1983). Emotional, behavioral, and physiological effects of chronic stress at Three Mile Island. *Journal of Consulting and Clinical Psychology, 51*, 565–572.

Beavers, W. R., & Hampson, R. B. (1990). *Successful families: Assessment and intervention.* New York: Norton.

Beavers, W. R., & Hampson, R. B. (1993). Measuring family competence: The Beavers Systems model. In F. Walsh (Ed.), *Normal family processes* (2nd ed., pp. 73–103). New York: Guilford Press.

Beavers, W. R., Hampson, R. B., & Hulgus, Y. F. (1985). The Beavers Systems approach to family assessment. *Family Process, 24,* 398–405.

Ben-David, A., & Levee, Y. (1992). Families in the sealed room: Interaction patterns of Israeli families during SCUD missile attacks. *Family Process, 31,* 35–44.

Boss, P. G. (1987). Family stress. In M. B. Sussman & S. Steinmetz (Eds.), *Handbook of marriage and the family* (pp. 695–721). New York: Plenum Press.

Bowen, M. (1978). Family reaction to death. In M. Bowen (Ed.), *Family therapy in clinical practice* (pp. 321–337). New York: Jason Aronson.

Carlson, C. I. (1989). Criteria for family assessment. *Journal of Family Psychology, 3*(2), 158–177.

Carroll, E. M., Foy, D. W., Cannon, B. J., & Zwler, G. (1991). Assessment issues involving families of trauma victims. *Journal of Traumatic Stress, 4*(1), 25–35.

Carroll, E. M., Rueger, D. B., Foy, D. W., & Donahue, C. P. (1985). Vietnam combat veterans with posttraumatic stress disorder: Analysis of marital and cohabiting adjustment. *Journal of Abnormal Psychology, 94,* 329–337.

Carter, B., & McGoldrick, M. (1989). *The changing family life cycle: A framework for family therapy* (2nd ed.). Boston: Allyn & Bacon.

Craine, M. H., Hanks, R., & Stevens, H. (1992). Mapping family stress. *American Journal of Family, 20*(3), 195.

Cromwell, R. E., Olson, D. H., & Fournier, D. G. (1976). Tools and techniques for diagnosis and evaluation in marital and family therapy. *Family Process, 15,* 1–33.

Danieli, Y. (1993). Diagnostic and therapeutic use of the multigenerational family tree in working with survivors of the Nazi Holocaust. In J. P. Wilson & B. Raphael (Eds.), *International handbook of traumatic stress syndromes* (pp. 889–899). New York: Plenum Press.

Derogatis, L. R. (1983). *SCL-90-R: Administration, scoring, and procedures manual.* Baltimore, MD: Clinical Psychometric Research.

deShazer, S. (1985). *Keys to solution in brief therapy.* New York: Norton.

deShazer, S. (1988). *Clues and investigating solutions in brief therapy.* New York: Norton.

Epstein, N. B., Baldwin, L. M., & Bishop, D. S. (1983). The McMaster Family Assessment device. *Journal of Marital and Family Therapy, 9*(2), 171–180.

Epstein, N. B., & Bishop, D. S. (1981). Problem centered system therapy of the family. In A. S. Gurman & D. P. Kniskern (Eds.), *Handbook of family therapy.* New York: Brunner/Mazel.

Epstein, N. B., Bishop, D. S., Ryan, C., Miller, I., & Keitner, G. (1993). The McMaster Model view of health family functioning. In F. Walsh (Ed.), *Normal family processes* (2nd ed., pp. 138–161). New York: Guilford Press.

Figley, C. R. (1983). Catastrophes: An overview of family reactions. In C. R. Figley & H. I. McCubbin (Eds.), *Stress in the family: Vol. 2. Coping with catastrophes* (pp. 3–20). New York: Brunner/Mazel.

Figley, C. R. (1985). *Trauma and its wake: The study and treatment of post-traumatic stress disorder.* New York: Brunner/Mazel.

Figley, C. R. (Ed.). (1986). *Trauma and its wake: Vol. II. Traumatic stress theory, research and intervention.* New York: Brunner/Mazel.

Figley, C. R. (1988). Post-traumatic family therapy. In F. M. Ochberg (Ed.), *Post-traumatic therapy and victims of violence* (pp. 83–109). New York: Brunner/Mazel.

Figley, C. R. (1989a). *Helping traumatized families.* San Francisco: Jossey-Bass.

Figley, C. R. (Ed.). (1989b). *Treating stress in families.* New York: Brunner/Mazel.

Figley, C. R., & Sprenkle, D. H. (1978). Delayed stress response syndrome: Family therapy indications. *Journal of Marriage and Family Counseling, 4,* 53–60.

Fischer, J., & Corcoran, K. (1994). *Measures for clinical practice: A sourcebook. Vol. 1: Couples, families, and children* (2nd ed.). New York: Free Press.

Fisher, L. (1976). Dimensions of family assessment: A critical review. *Journal of Marriage and Family Counseling,* 367–382.

Gleser, G. C., Green, B. L. H., & Winget, C. N. (1981). *Prolonged effects of disasters: A study of Buffalo Creek.* New York: Academic Press.

Gottman, J. M. (1991). Predicting the longitudinal course of marriages. *Journal of Marital and Family Therapy, 17,* 3–7.

Green, B. L. (1993). Identifying survivors at risk: Trauma and stressors across events. In J. P. Wilson & B. Raphael (Eds.), *International handbook of traumatic stress syndromes* (pp. 135–145). New York: Plenum Press.

Green, B. L., Lindy, J. D., Grace, M. C., Gleser, G. C., Leonard, A. C., Korol, M., & Wenget, C. (1990). Buffalo Creek survivors in the second decade: Stability of stress symptoms. *American Journal of Orthopsychiatry, 60,* 43–54.

Greenberg, L. S., & Johnson, S. M. (1988). *Emotionally focused therapy for couples.* New York: Guilford Press.

Griffith, J. L., & Griffith, M. E. (1994). *The body speaks: Therapeutic dialogues for mind–body problems.* New York: Basic Books.

Grotevant, H. D. (1989). The role of theory in guiding Family assessment. *Journal of Family Psychology, 3*(2), 104–118.

Grotevant, H. D., & Carlson, C. I. (Eds.). (1989). *Family assessment: A guide to methods and measures.* New York: Guilford Press.

Hampson, R. B., Beavers, W. R., & Hulgus, Y. (1988). Comparing Beavers and circumplex models of family functioning. *Family Process, 27,* 85–92.

Hampson, R. B., Beavers, W. R., & Hulgus, Y. (1989). Insiders and outsiders views of family. *Journal of Family Psychology, 3*(2), 118–137.

Hansen, D., & Hill, R. (1964). Families under stress. In H. T. Christensen (Ed.), *Handbook of marriage and the family.* Chicago: Rand McNally.

Hansen, D., & Johnson, V. (1979). Rethinking family stress theory: Defunctional aspects. In W. Burr, R. Hell, F. Nye, & I. Reiss (Eds.), *Contemporary theories about the family* (Vol. 1). New York: Free Press.

Harkness, L. L. (1993). Transgenerational transmission of war-related trauma. In J. P. Wilson & B. Raphael (Eds.), *Handbook of traumatic stress syndromes* (pp. 635–645). New York: Plenum Press.

Heyman, R. E., Sayers, S. L., & Bellack, A. S. (1994). Global marital satisfaction versus marital adjustment: An empirical comparison of three measures. *Journal of Family Psychology, 8*(4), 432–447.

Hobfoll, S. E., & Spielberger, C. D. (1992). Family stress: Integrating theory and measurement. *Journal of Family Psychology, 6*(2), 99–112.

Horowitz, M. J. (1976). *Stress response syndromes.* New York: Jason Aronson.

Horowitz, M. J., Wilner, N., & Alvarez, W. (1979). Impact of Event Scale: A measure of subjective distress. *Psychosomatic Medicine, 41,* 209–218.

Jacob, T. (Ed.). (1987). *Family interaction and psychopathology.* New York: Plenum Press.

Jacob, T., & Tennenbaum, D. L. (1988). *Family assessment: Rationale, methods, and future directions.* New York: Plenum Press.

Karpel, M. A. (1986). *Family resources: The hidden partner in family therapy.* New York: Guilford Press.

Kerr, M. E., & Bowen, M. (1988). *Family evaluations.* New York: Norton.

Klein-Parker, F. (1988). Dominant attitudes of adult children of Holocaust survivors toward their parents. In J. P. Wilson, Z. Harel, & B. Kahana (Eds.), *Human adaptation to extreme stress* (pp. 193–218). New York: Plenum Press.

Krystal, H. (1968). *Massive psychic trauma.* New York: International Universities Press.

Kuehl, B. P. (1995). The solution oriented genogram: A collaborative approach. *Journal of Marital and Family Therapy, 21*(3), 239–250.

Kuehl, B. P., Newfield, N. H., & Joanning, H. (1990). A client-based description of family therapy. *Journal of Family Psychology, 3*(3), 310–321.

Leon, G., Butcher, J., Kleinman, M., Goldberg. J., & Almagot, M. (1981). Survivors of the Holocaust and their children. *Journal of Personal Social Psychology, 41,* 503–516.

Levine, A. G. (1982). *Love Canal: Science, politics, and people.* Lexington, MA: Lexington Books.

Lewis, J. (1986). Family structure and stress. *Family Process, 25,* 235–247.

Locke, H. J., & Wallace, K. M. (1959). Short marital adjustment and prediction tests: Their reliability and validity. *Marriage and Family Living, 21,* 251–255.

McCubbin, H. I., Cauble, A. E., & Patterson, J. M. (Eds.). (1982). *Family stress, coping, and social support.* Springfield, IL: Thomas.

McCubbin, H. I., & Patterson, J. (1983). Family stress adaptation to crisis: A double ABCX model of family behavior. In H. I. McCubbin, M. Sussman, & J. Patterson (Eds.), *Advances in family stress theory and research.* New York: Haworth Press.

McCubbin, H. I., Patterson, J. M., & Wilson, L. (1983). *FILE—Family Inventory of Life Events.* Madison: University of Wisconsin Press.

McCubbin, H. I., & Thompson, A. (Eds.). (1991). *Family assessment inventories for research and practice* (2nd ed.). Madison: University of Wisconsin Press.

McCubbin, M. A., & McCubbin, H. I. (1989). Theoretical orientations to family stress and coping. In C. R. Figley (Ed.), *Treating stress in families.* New York: Brunner/Mazel.

McGoldrick, M., & Gerson, R. (1985). *Genograms of family assessment.* New York: Norton.

McGoldrick, M., & Gerson, R. (1989). Genograms and the family life cycle. In B. Carter & M. McGoldrick (Eds.), *The changing family life cycle* (2nd ed., pp. 164–186). Boston: Allyn & Bacon.

Miller, W., Williams, A., & Bernstein, M. (1982). The effects of rape in marital and sexual adjustment. *American Journal of Family Therapy, 10,* 51–58.

Moos, R. H., & Moos, B. S. (1981). *Family Environment Scale manual.* Palo Alto, CA: Consulting Psychologists Press.

Nichols, W. C. (1988). *Marital therapy: An integrative approach.* New York: Guilford Press.

Nichols, W. C., & Schwartz, R. C. (1995). *Family therapy: Concepts and methods* (3rd ed.). Boston: Allyn & Bacon.

Norton, R. (1983). Measuring marital quality—A critical look at the dependent variable. *Journal of Marriage and the Family, 45,* 141–151.

Ochberg, F. M. (1988). *Post-traumatic therapy and victims of violence.* New York: Brunner/Mazel.

Ochberg, F. M. (1993). Post-traumatic therapy. In J. P. Wilson & B. Raphael (Eds.), *International handbook of traumatic stress syndromes.* New York: Plenum Press.

O'Hanlon, W. H., & Weiner-Davis, M. (1989). *In search of solutions.* New York: Norton.

Oliveri, M. E., & Reiss, D. (1984). Family concepts and their measurement: Things are seldom what they seem. *Family Process, 23*(1), 33–48.

Olson, D. H. (1986). Circumplex model VII: Validation studies and FACES III. *Family Process, 25*, 337–35.

Olson, D. H. (1990). *Clinical rating scale for the Circumplex Model.* St. Paul: Family Social Science, University of Minnesota.

Olson, D. H. (1993). Circumplex model of marital and family systems: Assessing family functioning. In F. Walsh (Ed.), *Normal family processes* (2nd ed., pp. 104–138). New York: Guilford Press.

Olson, D. H., McCubbin, H. I., Barnes, H. A., Larsen, A., Muxen, M., & Wilson, M. (1989). *Families: What makes them work* (2nd ed.). Newbury Park, CA: Sage.

Olson, D. H., McCubbin, H. I., Barnes, H. A., Muxen, M., & Wilson M. (Eds.). (1986). *Family inventories: Inventories used in a national survey of families across the family life cycle.* St. Paul: Family Social Science, University of Minnesota.

Olson, D., Russell, C., & Sprenkle, D. (1983). Circumplex Model IV: Theoretical update. *Family Process, 22*, 69–83.

Phillips, R. D. (1978). Impact of Nazi Holocaust on children of survivors. *American Journal of Psychotherapy, 32*, 370–378.

Pynoos, R. S., Frederick, C., & Nader, K. (1987). Life threat and post-traumatic stress in school age children. *Archives of General Psychiatry, 44*, 1057–1063.

Pynoos, R. S., & Nader, K. (1993). Issues in the treatment of post-traumatic stress in children and adolescents. In J. P. Wilson & B. Raphael (Eds.), *International handbook of traumatic stress syndromes* (pp. 535–551). New York: Plenum Press.

Raphael, B. (1986). *When disaster strikes.* New York: Basic Books.

Rakoff, V., Sigal, J., & Epstein, N. (1965). Children and families of concentration camp survivors. *Canada's Mental Health, 14*, 24–26.

Reiss, D., & Oliveri, M. E. (1991). The family's conception of accountability and competence: A new assessment of family stress. *Family Process, 30*, 193–214.

Roberto, G. G. (1992). *Transgenerational family therapies.* New York: Guilford Press.

Roberts, W. F., Penk, W. E., Gearing, M. L., Rabenowitz, R., Dolan, M. P., & Patterson, E. T. (1982). Interpersonal problems of Vietnam combat veterans with symptoms of post-traumatic stress disorder. *Journal of Abnormal Psychology, 71*, 444–450.

Rolland, J. S. (1994). *Family illness and disability: An integrative treatment model.* New York: Basic Books.

Rose, S. L., & Garseke, J. (1987). Family environment, adjustment, and coping among children of Holocaust survivors. *American Journal of Orthopsychiatry, 57*(3), 332–344.

Schaeffer, M. T., & Olson, D. H. (1981). Assessing intimacy: The PAIR inventory. *Marital and Family Therapy, 7*(1), 47–60.

Segal, J., Silver, D., & Rakoff, F. (1973). Some second generation effects of survival of the Nazi persecution. *American Journal of Orthopsychiatry, 43*, 320–327.

Silver, S. M., & Iacono, C. (1986). Symptom groups and family patterns of Vietnam veterans with post-traumatic stress disorder. In C. R. Figley (Ed.), *Trauma and its wake: Vol. II. Traumatic stress theory, research and intervention.* New York: Brunner/Mazel.

Smith, E. M., & North, C. S. (1993). Posttraumatic stress disorder in natural disasters and technological accidents. In J. P. Wilson & B. Raphael (Eds.), *Instructional handbook of traumatic stress syndromes.* New York: Plenum Press.

Snyder, D. K. (1979). Multidimensional assessment of marital satisfaction. *Journal of Marriage and the Family, 41*, 813–823.

Snyder, D. K., Wills, R. M., & Keiser, T. W. (1984). Empirical validation of the marital satisfaction inventory: An actuarial approach. *Journal of Consulting and Clinical Psychology, 49,* 262–268.

Solomon, Z., Mikulincer, M., Fried, B., & Wosner, Y. (1987). Family characteristics and posttraumatic stress disorder: A follow-up of Israel combat stress reaction casualties. *Family Process, 26*(3), 383–394.

Spanier, G. B. (1976). Measuring dyadic adjustment: New scales for assessing the quality of marriage and similar dyads. *Journal of Marriage and Family, 38,* 15–28.

Spanier, G. B. (1989). Assessing the strengths of the Dyadic Adjustment Scale. *Journal of Family Psychology, 59,* 146–149.

Spanier, G. B., & Thompson, L. (1982). A confirmatory analysis of the Dyadic Adjustment Scale. *Journal of Marriage and the Family, 44,* 731–738.

Stanton, M. D., & Figley, C. (1978). Treating the Vietnam veteran within the family system. In C. R. Figley (Ed.), *Stress disorders among Vietnam veterans.* New York: Brunner/Mazel.

Steinglass, P. (1987). A systems view of family interaction and psychotherapy. In T. Jacob (Ed.), *Family interaction and psychopathology* (pp. 25–63). New York: Plenum Press.

Walsh, F. (1993). *Normal family processes* (2nd ed.). New York: Guilford Press.

Walsh, F., & Olson, D. H. (1989). Utility of the Circumplex Model with severely dysfunctional family systems. In D. H. Olson, C. S. Russell, & H. D. Sprenkle (Eds.), *Circumplex Model: Systematic assessment and treatment of families* (2nd ed.). New York: Haworth.

Waysman, M., Mikulincer, M., Solomon, Z., & Weisenberg, M. (1993). Secondary traumatization among wives of posttraumatic combat veterans: A family typology. *Journal of Family Psychology, 7*(1), 104–119.

Weiss, D. S. (1993). Structured clinical interview techniques. In J. P. Wilson & B. Raphael (Eds.), *International handbook of traumatic stress syndromes* (pp. 165–178). New York: Plenum Press.

Weiss, R., Hops, H., & Patterson, G. R. (1973). A framework for conceptualizing marital conflict, technology for altering it, some data for evaluating it. In L. A. Marsh & E. J. Hardy (Eds.), *Behavior change: Methodology, concepts, and practice.* Champaign, IL: Research Press.

White, M., & Epston, D. (1990). *Narrative means to therapeutic ends.* New York: Norton.

Wilson, J. P., & Raphael, B. (Eds.). (1993). *International handbook of traumatic stress syndromes.* New York: Plenum Press.

CHAPTER 12

Assessing Traumatic Bereavement and Posttraumatic Stress Disorder

BEVERLEY RAPHAEL
NADA MARTINEK

INTRODUCTION

Many people die quietly at the end of life, perhaps after prolonged illness, and perhaps with suffering, or "in their sleep." Their deaths may be "unexpected" at the time they happen, but anticipated because they have reached the natural ending of the lifespan. But other deaths, by their very nature, are not gentle and timely encounters with death. Traumatic bereavements include those that encompass the additional element of sudden, perhaps horrific, shocking encounters with death and trauma, with the death of a loved one. This may be exemplified in a range of settings of personal or community violence or catastrophe. Parents bereaved by sudden infant death syndrome (SIDS), for instance, vividly describe the shocking nature of their experience and the horror of the images haunting them. The families of murder victims similarly describe the horrific nature of their bereavement. This may also apply to other deaths resulting from personal violence or in massive incidents, for instance the Oklahoma City bombing. These descriptions of "traumatic" bereavements stand in stark contrast to the experiences of quiet death in the home, without mutilation, bodily distortion, shock, threat, horror, and helplessness.

That reactions might be different has been recognized in a number of reports studying community populations and identifying complications of "grief." For instance, Raphael and Maddison (1976) described the "traumatic circumstances" of deaths, how these predicted more adverse health outcomes for bereaved widows, and that they were possibly linked to the development of a "traumatic neurosis" related to these circumstances, which interfered with the grieving process.

The picture of grief or bereavement reactions and trauma was inevitably complicated by Lindemann's (1944) classic clinical description of the symptomatology and management of acute grief. This was derived from his work with the bereaved survivors of the Cocoanut Grove nightclub fire in Boston, and many of those people had themselves not only been bereaved, but also severely traumatized. Lindemann made no effort to dissect out these separate phenomena.

Horowitz's (1976) original conceptualization of traumatic stressor experiences also included loss of a loved one as a trauma. His cognitive processing model, with its alternating intrusive/reexperiencing and avoidant/numbing responses suggested a framework that did not fit with classic descriptions of acute grief, for instance, the empirical data of Parkes's model available at that time (Parkes, 1971), although both indicated processes of intense preoccupation and periods of numbness.

An important development arising from this conceptualization of trauma was the Impact of Event Scale (IES; Horowitz, Wilner, & Alvarez, 1979), which measured these intrusive and avoidant phenomena. This identified reexperiencing items such as preoccupations and images, recurrent dreams, as well as distress at reminders. Avoidant phenomena included feelings of numbness and avoidance of, or attempts to shut out, reminders. It might be suggested that these phenomena are, when considered broadly, not dissimilar to the preoccupations and numbing of acute grief. As will be discussed, there are substantial differences in the phenomenology of the acute reactions to traumatic stressors such as confrontation with life threat and death, and to the loss of a loved one. Different adaptations are required to these different stressors, although both may challenge the assumptive worlds of those affected. In traumatic bereavements, these two may occur together, through particularly traumatic circumstances of the death, so that both elements of psychological stress must be dealt with simultaneously: Adaptive processes are thus likely to be more complex.

This separation of trauma and loss stressors was also considered by Green, Grace, and Gleser (1985) in their study of the Beverly Hills Supper Club fire, where they assessed the impact of bereavement, life threat, and other stressors to do with the disaster experience. Further reports by this group indicate that in psychotherapy with survivors, they found traumatic stress and bereavement effects to operate separately. Both had to be dealt with, although they suggested, as has been the experience of other workers, that the trauma effects had to be dealt with first, before the grief could be worked with (Lindy, Green, Grace, & Tichener, 1983). Similar assessments of trauma and loss stressors were carried out by McFarlane in his studies following the Australian bushfire disasters (McFarlane, 1988a, 1988b).

Further attention to these issues also appeared in the report of Wilson, Smith, and Johnson (1985) where, in their study of a number of different survivor groups, they clearly differentiated out loss and life threat as different stressor experiences with potentially different correlates.

Extension of these conceptualizations was most clearly defined by Pynoos's group. They systematically studied a group of school-age children following a sniper attack at a school, using two measures to specifically investigate loss (a Grief Reaction Inventory of 9 items) and traumatic stress (a PTSD Reactions Index of 16 items), and the symptoms that followed. They showed the validity of these measures in that the severity of exposure to life threat correlated with a high symptom level (> 12 of 16) on the PTSD scale, and closeness of acquaintance to the child who died correlated with scores on the Grief index. They reported further that sometimes grief and traumatic stress were manifested independently, and at other times there appeared to be an interplay between them. It is also of interest to note that life threat correlated most with the onset of PTSD, loss of a significant other with the onset of a single depressive episode or adjustment reaction, and worry about or sudden separation from a significant other (such as a sibling) with persistent anxiety about such separation (Pynoos et al., 1987a; Pynoos, Nader, Frederick, Gonda, & Stuber, 1987b).

More recently, workers in the bereavement field have attempted to examine further the interactions of trauma and grief. Schut, Keijser, Van Den Bout, and Dijhuis (1991) looked at posttraumatic symptomatology in a population of bereaved people to examine the relationship between bereavement and posttraumatic phenomena. Although only 9% of the population met diagnostic criteria for PTSD at all time periods throughout the study of 25 months, symptomatic levels were at 20–31% and mostly appeared to relate to more shocking circumstances of death. However, these authors did not dissect out separate phenomenological approaches to assessment.

Other bereavement research, for instance with SIDS and other deaths (e.g., Dyregov & Mattheisen, 1987a, 1987b, 1987c) showed high levels of intrusive and avoidant symptomatology using the IES. These workers found, too, that those bereaved in this way had more adverse outcomes compared to stillbirth and neonatal deaths, indicating these were more traumatic bereavements. Other workers and clinicians (e.g., L'Hoir, 1992; Raphael, 1992) indicate the high levels of preoccupation and intrusive images of the dead baby, psychophysiological reactivity, and avoidance and numbing associated with reminders.

These studies and other clinical reports highlight the problems of current conceptualizations and measures.

CONCEPTUALIZATIONS OF TRAUMATIC STRESS, GRIEF, AND TRAUMATIC BEREAVEMENT

Freud's original conceptualizations of traumatic stress and grief show that, in terms of his observations, he saw these as separate entities involving different psychological processes.

He suggested that "such an event as an external trauma is bound to provoke a disturbance on a large scale" and lead to the mental apparatus being "flooded with large amounts of stimulus" which have "broken through the protective shield of the ego." He goes on to relate these to accidents and events that threaten the individual's life. Later these might lead to the "traumatic neuroses," with fixation to the trauma and repetitions (Freud, 1920/1959).

On the other hand his conceptionalization of the processes of grief in *Mourning and Melancholia* (1917) is quite different. He speaks of a loss of interest in the outside world "in so far as it does not recall the dead one" and a "turning away from every effort that is not connected with thoughts of the dead" (p. 153). He also goes on to describe the processes of internalization, preoccupation with thoughts of the dead person, the review of memories, and the withdrawal, bit by bit, of bonds to the deceased.

In an effort to dissect out the phenomena of grief and trauma, and thus to provide a model that might be the basis for assessment, the following comparisons and contrasts are put forward on a basis of current research and clinical understandings in the field of bereavement (Parkes, 1972; Parkes & Weiss, 1983; Raphael, 1983; Zisook & Schuchter, 1991; Stroebe, Stroebe, & Hansson, 1993; Jacobs, 1993; Byrne & Raphael, 1994) and traumatic stress (Wilson & Raphael, 1993).

Cognitions and Related Affective Phenomena

The preoccupations with traumatic stress are those of the scene of the trauma, the traumatic encounter with death. They may be of the gruesome, dead body. These images are associated with anxiety, intense distress that is a repetition of the shock, horror, and fear associated with the trauma. Memories, even if in different perceptual modalities, are of the traumatic event or scene and circumstances associated with this: the image of a mutilated face, the affect of terror, the smell of blood, the sound of sirens. The reexperiencing is of the traumatic aspect of the event.

The preoccupations of the bereaved are images of the lost person. These come to mind also as unbidden and intrusive. But whereas there may be images of the dead person, especially if the death has been horrific, there is more frequently an intense preoccupation with images and memories of the lost person, alive. The affects associated with these images are those of yearning and longing, and the distress is related to the absence of the lost person. It is that they are not there; that is the source of affective distress, and the memory is painful, in that it is a reminder of their absence. Memories and cognitions of the lost person may be associated with a range of other affective reactions, for instance, anger, sadness, longing. Reexperiencing phenomena may include a sense of the person's presence, which is usually reassuring and not linked to fear, unless there are associated, additional traumatic components. The distress is separation distress and not fear of threat.

Dreams, too, are further indications of cognitive processes that may differ. In traumatized populations, they are usually intense and often involve direct reexperiencing, with associated affect (fear) and physiological reactivity associated with waking, and are described as "nightmares."

In bereaved populations the content (unless associated with trauma) frequently reflects longing for the lost persons with dreams of them as though alive, and often a sense of loss on waking and finding they are not there. There is more frequently symbolic or latent content to these dreams.

Both types of dreams may lessen and change progressively over time, representing resolution. Although there is a lack of studies of sleep architecture in acute situations, there is much to suggest that this is normal for the bereaved, and that the dreams of the traumatized may impact differently. However, as most findings for trauma are from studies carried out on populations with PTSD, it is difficult to conclude from these that the reported changes also apply to the acute, "reactive" phenomena that settle over time and do not lead to disorder.

A range of affects may, of course, arise with these cognitions. But it is safe to conclude that anxiety-like states in relation to traumatic stressors are anxiety/fear reactions to threat and danger, or to reminders of this, whereas anxiety in the bereavement reaction is specific and generated by separation from the lost person and imagined futures without that person, and precipitated by his or her failure to return. Yearning is specific for bereavement in terms of yearning for the lost person to return, although it is possible that the traumatized person will yearn for a return of times before the trauma, for it not to have happened. These phenomena may seem similar if it is considered that they both reflect the longing for things to be as they were, but here, as earlier, the *specific content* is different. Sadness is much more commonly linked to loss reactions and may be difficult to differentiate from the depressions of bereavement. Sadness is not typically associated with the traumatic stressor experience apart from any concomitant loss.

These cognitive and related processes are summarized in Table 12.1.

Avoidance Phenomena

Initial reactions of shock or numbness, disbelief, and denial are described for both traumatic stressor events and loss. However, substantial differences appear when the two areas are considered separately.

The traumatically stressed person wishes to avoid reminders of the event, including places, discussion, similar situations or other cues, and attempts to dampen affects that arise in association with such reminders.

The bereaved, on the other hand, may search for or actually seek out places of familiarity and links to and reminders of the lost person. Avoidance is more in this instance for reminders of the *absence* of the lost person. Although bereaved people may attempt to mitigate the pangs of grief, this is usually only temporarily, for the bereaved experience serves, even though it is painful, as a normal and necessary tribute to the deceased.

TABLE 12.1. Cognitions and Related Affective Phenomena

Posttraumatic reactions	Bereavement reactions
Cognitive processes	

• Intrusions of *scene of trauma* (e.g., death)
  Not associated with yearning or longing
  Associated with distress, anxiety at image
	• Image of *lost person* constantly comes to mind (unbidden or bidden)
	  Associated with yearning or longing
	  Distress that person is not there

• Preoccupation with the *traumatic event* and circumstances of it	• Preoccupation with the *lost person* and loved images of him or her
• *Memories* usually of the *traumatic* scene	• *Memories of person* associated with affect relevant to memory (often positive)
• Reexperiencing of threatening aspects of the event	• Reexperiencing of *person's presence*, as though he or she were still there (e.g., hallucinations of sound, touch, sight)
Affective reactions	

Anxiety
• Anxiety is the principal affect
  And is *general* and generated by threat
  Fearful of *threat/danger*
  Precipitated by *reminders, intrusions*
	• Anxiety, when present, is *separation* anxiety
	  Is specific and generated by separation from lost person
	  Is generated by imagined futures without lost person
	  Is precipitated by his or her *failure to return*

Yearning/longing
• These are not prominent features
  Not person oriented; if occurs, is for things to have been as they were before—for the return of "innocence of death" and the sense of personal invulnerability
	• Yearning for lost person
	  Is intense, painful, profound
	  Is triggered by reminders of him or her
	  Yearning for him or her to return, to be there

Sadness • Sadness not commonly described • Nostalgia for event not described	• Sadness frequent and profound • Feelings of nostalgia common and persistent

The traumatically stressed person may wish to talk of the experience, but often wishes to avoid doing so, withdraws, and avoids discussion with significant others, for fear this will bring back painful reexperiencing. On the other hand, the bereaved is usually very driven to talk of the lost relationship and the lost person.

Both may use social support and interactions in the resolution process, and there may also be gender and culture-based patterns of coping, which lead to a greater use of these processes, as reported in the bereaved (usually studies on populations of widows) as opposed to populations of the trauma-tized (which are usually men).

These phenomena are summarized in Table 12.2.

Arousal Phenomena

Both bereaved and traumatized populations are likely to experience high levels of arousal, which, unless pathological response supervenes, will progressively diminish over time from the event.

In traumatic stress, arousal mechanisms are oriented to threat and danger, to a return of the threatening stressor or similar threat. There is a general scanning of the environment, an alertness to danger, and a general arousal. There is an exaggerated response to threat or other sudden stimuli, particularly those in any way symbolic of, or linked to, the traumatic experience.

On the other hand, the arousal of the bereaved is focused on the lost person, generates a scanning of the environment for the lost person or cues of them, and may generate actual searching behaviors. This hyperalertness does not lead to an overreaction to threat stimuli, but to stimuli related to the lost person, perhaps, for example, to cues of their presence.

These areas are summarized in Table 12.3.

Other Phenomena

Clarification of other phenomena is lacking, because most studies deal with clinical populations already suffering from some complications of trauma,

TABLE 12.2. Avoidance Phenomena

Posttraumatic reactions	Bereavement reactions
• *Avoids* reminders of event, including places	• May search for and *seek out* places of familiarity, *treasured objects* (e.g., linking objects, photos and images) • May try to *avoid reminders of the absence* of the lost person
• Attempts to lessen affect; numbing, lessened feelings generally	• May try to *mitigate* pangs of grief but only temporarily, including distracting, but also seeks to express grief as normal
• May have great difficulty talking of event during avoidance times, although at others may be powerfully driven to talk of experience (but not person)	• May be very driven to talk of lost relationship and lost person
• Withdrawal from others (protective of self)	• May seek others for support, or to talk of deceased

TABLE 12.3. Arousal Phenomena

Posttraumatic reactions	Bereavement reactions
• *Oriented to threat* and danger	• *Oriented to lost person*
• General *scanning* and *alertness* to *danger,* fearfulness	• Generates *scanning* of *environment for lost one or cues* of them
• Exaggerated *startle* response (i.e., response to minimal threat) and	• Generates *searching* behavior and
• Overresponse to cues of trauma	• Overresponse to cues of lost person

grief, a combination of these, and/or other disorders. Of interest however will be further studies on the following:

• *Psychophysiological reactions.* These tend to show for instance, increased reactivity of blood pressure, pulse, and electromyogram (EMG) or skin conductance (SC) responses to narratives or reminders relevant to specific traumatic stimuli (Orr, 1994).

• *Dexamethasone suppression test (DST).* Studies correlate changes with separation anxiety rather than depression in acutely bereaved populations (Schuchter, Zisook, Kirkorowicz, & Risch, 1986), and changes have not been studied in acutely traumatized populations.

• Variable urinary cortisol, plasma growth hormone, and other responses in traumatized and bereaved populations (Jacobs, 1993).

• *Cardiovascular response and differentiation of response in different emotional states.* These have been studied in relation to sadness associated with grief (Sinha, Lovallo, & Parsons, 1992). Another study by Brown, Sirota, Niaura, and Engebretson (1993) concluded that elation and sadness are associated with endocrine concomitants. Whether such research will distill into the basis for physiological measures remains to be seen.

• *Decreased natural-killer cell activity in bereavement* (Bartrop, Luckhurst, Lazarus, Kiloh, & Penny, 1977). This has been found by Bartrop et al. and replicated by others.

• *Sleep architecture.* Although there are studies in acutely bereaved populations (Reynolds et al., 1992), there are no comparable studies in acutely traumatized populations.

• *Animal models of the neurobiology of trauma* (Bremner, Southwick, & Charney, 1991) *and loss* (Laudenslager, 1988).

• *Dissociative phenomena.* Recent work has identified the importance of dissociative phenomena in response to traumatic stressors and how these may be associated with outcome (Spiegel, 1994). Similar studies of the bereaved's reaction to loss have yet to be carried out, although there are certainly some clinical reports of such dissociative experiences.

Facial Expression

There has been no systematic study of this area with respect to trauma and loss, although new computerized technologies and other methods provide a framework that could facilitate such research. However Darwin's classic observations in *The Expression of Emotion in Man and Animals* clearly differentiate basic and different responses to trauma and grief (Darwin, 1872).

These observations are summarized in Table 12.4.

TIME COURSE OF TRAUMA AND BEREAVEMENT REACTIONS

The time course of reactive processes, and when they merge into patterns or levels of phenomena that may be seen as pathologies of trauma or grief, is an area that is relatively poorly studied in terms of any comparison of both groups of phenomena and related conditions.

Davidson and Foa (1993), in their review of field studies for DSM-IV, outline support for diagnostic categorization of PTSD at 1 month of ongoing symptomatology meeting the specific criteria in reexperiencing, avoidance, and arousal domains. They have also indicated that when these symptoms persist for 3–4 months, chronicity is likely (Blank, 1993), although a fluctuating course and delayed onset are well established (e.g., McFarlane, 1988a, 1988b).

Middleton, Burnett, Raphael, and Martinek (1996) have explored the phenomenology of normal bereavement in community populations. There

TABLE 12.4. Signs of Reactive Process: Facial Expression

Posttraumatic reactions	Bereavement reactions

• Occur upon witnessing something horrific, torture, etc., fear and threat
• "... probably that horror would generally be accompanied by *strong contraction of the brow,* but as far as fear is one of the elements, the *eyes and mouth* would be *opened,* and the *eyebrows raised*—as far as antagonistic action of the corregations permitted this movement" (pp. 322–323)
• "*Contraction of platysma* does add greatly to the expression of fear" (p. 317)
• Eyes somewhat staring
• Pupils may be dilated
	• "Contraction of the grief muscles ...appears to be common to all the races of mankind
	• *Obliquity of the eyebrows* contraction of central fascia of frontal muscle
	    Inner ends of eyebrows (p. 188) puckered into bunch
	    Transverse furrows across the middle part of the forehead
	• *Depression of corners of mouth*
	    Mouth closed
	    Corners drawn downward and outward (pp. 201–202)
	    Curved mouth concavely downward

Note. Page numbers are from Darwin (1872).

are as yet no diagnostic criteria for normal grief, or for bereavement pathologies, although these have been proposed (Raphael, 1989). Nevertheless recent explorations have indicated general agreement also for concepts of "chronic," "delayed," and "absent" grief (Middleton, Moylan, Raphael, Burnett, & Martinek, 1993).

PTSD, in essence, with its current criteria, represents a continuation of the phenomenology of acute reaction to trauma, but with ongoing high intensity and severity reflecting a failure of resolution and an intensity like that which first occurred. Levels of PTSD as the chronic condition following traumatic stressors vary enormously, and it is beyond the scope of this chapter to review this. Suffice it to say the more severe the stressor, other factors being equal, the more likely PTSD will evolve.

"Chronic grief" might be seen as a similar set of phenomena, in that it represents an ongoing and intensive experience of grief at a level that is much the same as for the acute experience. Evidence from Middleton's studies (1995) suggests that the major decline in bereavement phenomenology occurs between weeks 4–6 and 10–13; that is, like trauma reactions, intense grief persisting longer than 3–4 months is likely to be chronic grief (9.2%). These findings are further replicated by Byrne and Raphael's (1994) study of elderly bereaved widowers in which 8.8% exhibited chronic grief.

Although other comorbidities may occur in both instances, particularly anxiety, depression, and substance abuse, and there may be significant functional impairments, these basic phenomena define these conditions.

TRAUMATIC BEREAVEMENTS, THEIR PHENOMENA, AND COURSE

Studies of what might be considered to be traumatic bereavements, and the interfaces of trauma and grief are in their infancy. Only the work of Pynoos et al. (1987a, 1987b) has attempted to provide systematic formulations in community-based studies. Although these point to directions, they do not provide for detailed longitudinal examination of groups and phenomena over time, or their interactions.

Traumatic bereavements are described by Rynearson (1984) in a range of his studies dealing with those bereaved by murder. In these, he clearly describes the presence of phenomena of reexperiencing cognitions of trauma and the preoccupations of bereavement. This may occur even where the bereaved was not present and did not see or directly, personally experience the life threat. The avoidance phenomenology of trauma and of bereavement, and the arousal, as well as other areas representing a complex overlay of symptoms, are also present. Suicidal bereavements may have similar phenomenology. Bereaved persons may be tormented by the images of the deceased, especially if they found them, perhaps after hanging or shooting themselves. Their bereavements may be difficult to resolve because of incapacity to move on through grief processes and ongoing preoccupation with the trauma.

Parents of SIDS babies also describe the ongoing cognitions that may block grieving because of preoccupation with images of the baby's "dead, cold face."

Disaster bereavement, such as that following natural (earthquakes) or man-made disasters (e.g., rail crash) also give evidence of the cognitive preoccupation with the traumatic event, overlying the capacity to grieve for the lost person (Raphael, 1986).

Outcomes are likely to be more adverse after traumatic bereavements (e.g., Lundin, 1984), and this may be related to the double psychological burden of dealing with both psychological processes. Effective interventions for both have been described, although evidence is stronger for intervention with the bereaved (Raphael, 1977) than with the traumatized, and perhaps only partially successful where there is traumatic bereavement (Kleber & Brom, 1987).

CLINICAL ASSESSMENTS OF TRAUMA, GRIEF, AND TRAUMATIC BEREAVEMENTS

Clinical assessments involve taking a careful clinical history of the experience of trauma and/or loss, the surrounding events, previous and lifetime experiences of trauma and loss, the presence of other stressors (e.g., dislocation; Raphael, 1986) and life events, and other factors that may influence the response to, and processing of, these experiences. These include stage of development, relationships, personal characteristics and qualities, and reactions of others to the event and the person experiencing it.

A focus on the phenomenology, as identified earlier, can allow assessment of each of the relevant areas of reaction and as well their interrelationships, the alternation of their patterns, and their subsequent time course. Furthermore, the presence of functional impairments and ongoing high intensity of reaction may enable those assessing the clinical reaction to determine whether pathology is likely.

Cognitive Processes and Related Affective Trauma

Here, inquiry needs to determine the nature of the preoccupations and associated affects, particularly those related to the scene of the death or its gruesomeness, as opposed to nostalgic images of the deceased, alive. The nature of reminders and the reactions they trigger, and the particular nature of dreams, will be relevant in this context (see Table 12.1).

Avoidant Phenomena

Here, the exploration is of what is avoided, and what affects are triggered if avoidance fails; the nature of cutting off and numbing, as opposed to the yearning for return and searching; and the holding of reminders of the bereaved (see Table 12.2).

Arousal Phenomena

Assessment of the sources of arousal and its focus, either on threat, or for the lost person, can help to differentiate and identify these separate reactive processes (see Table 12.3).

Changes over Time

It is clear from clinical and theoretical experience, as indicated earlier, that traumatic and bereavement phenomena may interweave, and that time courses may be different. An initial clinical assessment may indicate, for instance, that traumatic stress phenomena may predominate, but as time progresses, more grieving profiles will appear, or the trauma affects may reappear, or the person may be locked into the trauma and unable to grieve at all. There is no simple formula or detailed knowledge of likely courses, but the clinician's therapeutic approach may need to be sensitive and flexible to encompass these separate affects. Therapy may need to facilitate the working through of both the trauma and grief, building on what is known and established to be effective in achieving such aims (Parkes, 1980; Raphael, 1977; Kleber & Brom, 1987; Marmar, Horowitz, Weiss, Wilner, & Kaltreider, 1988).

SYSTEMATIC MEASURES OF BEREAVEMENT AND TRAUMA

It is beyond the scope of this chapter to deal with all the measures and assessments of traumatic stress reaction, for the majority of chapters of this book deal with these in great depth. In this section, however, some of the aspects relevant to measuring the phenomenology of bereavement, systematically and over time, will be addressed, and how they may relate to, or be used in association with, systematic assessments of traumatic stress reactions and traumatic bereavements.

The measure most widely used to assess bereavement has been the Texas Inventory of Grief (TIG) and its revised form, the Texas Revised Inventory of Grief (TRIG; Faschingbauer, Zisook, & DeVaul, 1987). This latter measure examines an 8-item scale focused on "past life disruption" and a 13-item scale encompassing "present emotion of grief." However, Burnett, Middleton, Raphael, and Martinek (in press) point out that this grief measure does not really allow the respondent to grade either the frequency or the severity of a particular symptom behavior or emotion; that is, it may remain completely true throughout that a person "at times" still "feels the need to cry for the person who died."

Another significant measure is the Grief Experience Inventory (GEI; Sanders, 1979, 1980), which was developed systematically and used to compare groups with different bereavements (e.g., parent, adult child, and spouse). The domains covered by this measure are despair, anger, guilt, social isolation, loss of control, rumination, depersonalization, somatization, and deep anxiety, as well as some additional scales of denial, social disability, atypical response, and "research scales." The report dealt with cross-sectional data for these groups, finding that the deaths of children led to more intense grief reactions. The issue of trauma was not dealt with as a possible explanatory factor.

Zisook and Shuchter (1985) have also systematically explored bereavement phenomena over time, using a range of measures, including the TGI and specifically defined questionnaires. Zisook, Schuchter, and Lyons (1987) and Zisook and Shuchter (1991) also report on a widowhood questionnaire used 7, 13, 19, and 21 months after death in a prospective study. This has provided interesting information on phenomena over time in a number of domains, including preoccupation with the lost person, although the validity of the findings must be in some question because of low sample response, high dropout rates, and pooling of data.

Jacobs et al. (1987a) have also been involved in systematic measurement of bereavement phenomena, defining dimensions of numbness, separation anxiety, depression, and depressive-type symptoms (mourning dimensions), and showing the gradual diminution of symptoms over time, as well as correlates with pathology.

Vargas, Loya, and Hodde-Vargas (1989) also explored the multidimensional aspects of grief reactions and suggest that certain features that have been associated mostly with pathological grief (e.g., difficulty relinguishing the lost object) may be present in many, if not most, bereaved people, and that pathology may best be determined by measuring the frequency and intensity of these features.

There have also been a number of scales developed to deal with particular areas of grief, for instance, perinatal grief (Toedter, Lasker, & Alhadeft, 1988) and suicidal bereavement (Barrett & Scott, 1989).

Problems with many of the aforementioned measures are the difficulties of identifying the specific core phenomena of grief/bereavement and the relationship of these to other groupings of phenomena, such as posttraumatic stress reactions, anxiety, depression, and so forth. The development of measures that will be useful across the age span is also problematic, for instance, in childhood. Although a number of systematic studies have been carried out with children, prospectively and repeatedly over time, in recent years, the studies of Pynoos et al. (1987a, 1987b) are among the few reporting a bereavement measure, and a trauma measure and the differentiating of these two sets of phenomena in children.

The main studies are summarized in Table 12.5.

There have been significant problems with these measures in that their

TABLE 12.5. Systematic Measures of Bereavement and Trauma

Study	Bereaved subjects	Measure	Dimensions
Lindemann (1944)	Bereaved disaster victims (Cocoanut Grove fire)	Interview	"Somatic distress; preoccupation with the image of the deceased; guilt; loss of warmth to others plus some irritability and anger; loss of usual behavior patterns"
Parkes (1971)	Widows	Interview	"Numbness and separation anxiety; pining and yearning for the lost person; and searching behaviors"
Faschingbauer et al. (1977, 1987)	Bereaved patient population	Texas Grief Inventory (TGI); Texas Revised Grief Inventory (TRIG)	"Present emotion of grief"; "past life disruption"
Zisook & Schuchter (1985)	Widows	Widowhood Questionnaire	"Acceptance of loss; continuous relationship with the lost person; anger and guilt; different affects"
Sanders (1979, 1980)	Bereaved individuals— spouse, child, and parent	Grief Experience Inventory (GEI)	"Despair; anger; guilt; social isolation; loss of control; rumination; depersonalization; somatization and deep anxiety"
Jacobs et al. (1987a)	Acutely bereaved widows and widowers	Grief measures; adapted CES Depression Scale (CES-D)	"Numbness and disbelief"; "separation anxiety"; "sadness and despair"
Vargas et al. (1989)	Relatives and close friends of victims of accidental deaths, suicides, homicides, and sudden natural deaths	Grief Reaction Measure	"Depressive symptoms; preservation of the lost object; suicidal ideation and decedent-directed anger"
Toedter et al. (1988)	Women who experienced pregnancy loss and their spouses or partners	Perinatal Grief Scale	"Active grief"; "difficulty coping"; "despair"
Barrett & Scott (1989)	Suicide survivors	Grief Experience Questionnaire (GEQ) to measure suicide bereavement	"Somatic reactions; general grief reactions; search for explanation; loss of social support; stigmatization; guilt; responsibility; shame; rejection; self-destructive behavior; and reactions to a unique form of death"

reliability and validity across different bereavements and times have not been clearly established. Furthermore, many have not provided measures that have been developed and tested on populations of "normally" bereaved people in the community.

Middleton's group (1996) has explored the development of such a measure of core bereavement phenomena and has developed two conceptually overlapping scales. The Core Bereavement Items (CBI; a 17-item measure) was developed by the utilization of a very extensive bereavement questionnaire derived from currently available information on bereavement phenomena, from which the "best" items were derived by a factoring methodology. Those with adequate factor loadings produced seven scales of three to seven items. Three of these scales had the highest correlation coefficients and constituted the CBI. A fourth dealt with a generic group of questions measuring what appeared to be personal resolution.

The major dimensions of phenomena in the CBI are in three factors: *Images and Thoughts,* with seven items of cognitions about the person who is lost; *Acute Separation,* with five items, including yearning and focusing on the lost person (or arousal oriented to them and searching); and *Grief,* with five items of affective response to reminders of the lost person, including sadness. The other scales are Sense of Presence; Dreams about the Deceased; Nonresolution; Personal Resolution. The related scale of the Bereavement Phenomenology Measure (BPM) was part of the development of this measure and used in the above and related studies (Byrne & Raphael, 1994; Baume, 1996).

These measures are presented below in Table 12.6.

These measures have been shown to have high reliability and validity and to discriminate between different groups of bereaved people and show identifiable change over time following the loss. They provide systematic measures to assess acute and chronic reactions to loss. These phenomena may then be measured alongside the measurement of traumatic stress phenomena, with measures such as the IES and a range of other systematic assessment formats in self-report measures. Traumatic bereavement will then encompass using both measures and distilling out the relevant patterns of each over time. These formulations will not only extend scientific understanding, but also potentially contribute to a basis for clinical decision making and treatment monitoring.

The further importance of these systematic measures for assessing bereavement over time and across groups is that they allow for the details of bereavement phenomena to now be systematically assessed and examined alongside those of trauma.

Although these studies did not specifically examine traumatic bereavements, those bereavements related to the loss of a child had the highest levels of symptomatic distress, and more detailed examination of the profiles should indicate those phenomena that might correlate most clearly with trauma in bereavement— X's death. However the use of this bereavement-specific measure with measures of traumatic stress in cross-sectional studies over time

Table 12.6. Measures of Core Bereavement Phenomena

CBI (17 items)[a]	BPM (20 items)[b]

A: Images and thoughts

CBI (17 items)[a]	BPM (20 items)[b]
1. Images of events surrounding X's death?	1. Thoughts of X coming to mind?
2. Thoughts of X coming to mind?	2. Distress at thoughts of X?
3. Distress at thoughts of X?	3. Preoccupation with images/memories of X?
4. Think about X?	4. Feel as though seen/heard/touched X?
5. Images of X cause distress?	5. Feel as if X present?
6. Preoccupation with images/memories of X?	6. When dreaming, feel as if X alive?
7. Thinking of reunion with X?	7. Pining/yearning for X?

B: Acute separation

CBI (17 items)[a]	BPM (20 items)[b]
8. Missing X?	8. Looking for X in familiar places?
9. Reminded of X by familiar objects?.	9. Distress when faced with reminders of X?
10. Pining/yearning for X?	10. General present feelings of sadness?
11. Looking for X in familiar places?	11. General present feelings of unreality?
12. Distress/pain when confronted with X not present/returning?	12. General present feelings of anger?

C: Grief

CBI (17 items)[a]	BPM (20 items)[b]
13. Reminders causing—Longing for X?	13. General present feelings of guilt?
14. Reminders causing—Loneliness?	14. General present feelings of nostalgia?
15. Reminders causing—Crying about X?	15. General present feelings of anxiety?
16. Reminders causing—Sadness?	16. General present feelings of depression?
17. Reminders causing—Loss of enjoyment?	17. In general, crying about X?
	18. Acting as though X is alive?
Alpha = .91	19. Spontaneously mentioning X to others?
	20. Able to organize life since X's death?
	Alpha = 85

[a]Middleton (1995).
[b]Middleton (1995); Byrne and Raphael (1994).

will allow for the better understanding of traumatic bereavements per se and their differentiation from both normal bereavements and PTSD.

THERAPEUTIC ASSESSMENT OF TRAUMA, LOSS, AND TRAUMATIC BEREAVEMENTS

Ultimately, of course, assessment must encompass a careful clinical exploration, as well as any systematic questionnaires and measures. Such an assessment must be based on a full understanding of each individual's experience, and must be set in the context of current experiences, as well as past, and how they are perceived by the individual subject to these experiences. Although the measures delineated earlier represent a significant improvement, there is still a need for further refinement. This is well exemplified in attempts to assess lifetime experience of bereavement and traumatic stressors.

The actual occurrence of the experience, its timing, and reactions to it at the time, may be selectively recalled, depending on current mental state. Accuracy of recall, even for clear-cut events such as the death of a family member, is open to question, as is the experience of trauma. Attributional needs may highlight some aspects rather than others, perhaps more negative outcomes than positive. A child who loses a parent in childhood may be unclear on date and time, especially if young, and subsequent outcomes may be governed more by family disruption, chaos, and breakdown or denial, than by the specific impact of grief. The phenomenology of childhood bereavement has recently been systematically studied (e.g., Weller, Weller, Fristad, & Bowes, 1991; Silverman & Worden, 1992) but the work of the Pynoos group, with the two briefer measures outlined, provides the best basis for realistic assessment of populations of bereaved and traumatized children, as well as individual clinical instances.

Furthermore, a later loss may lead to renewal of previous grief and/or traumatic stressor effects that may cloud or intensify the current phenomenology.

Assessing the Stressor Experience

Another issue in assessment is the clear delineation of the stressor experience and its various components. It is only through gaining a careful description of the experience itself that the stressor nature of that experience can be identified. This might also require an assessment of the context. Thus the details of a death, for instance, will need to be explored, bit by bit. For instance the statement "death by suicide" or "death by accident" may encompass many different levels of experience. A father spoke of his horrific images of his son's "purple face" when he hung himself and he (the father) found him, cut him down, and tried, unsuccessfully, to resuscitate him. A young woman spoke of her horror at the motor vehicle accident in which she was trapped and injured and her mother beside her died before she could help. A young mother spoke with horror of her baby's coldness and stillness in the middle of the night.

Although questionnaires can be used to rate death (i.e., who died, degree of warning and cause of death, or perceived severity), as they might with a traumatic encounter with death, the actual nature of the experience may only be defined by hearing the "trauma story" in the case of trauma, or the "story of the death/loss" and its circumstances in the case of bereavement.

A man involved in a rescue team in a major disaster risked his own life to rescue a victim who turned out to be his closest friend. A woman, a senior health worker in a remote rural area, was called to a motor vehicle accident in the absence of other emergency staff, to find the victim, whose life she struggled to save, was her only child. In each of these instances, there is a victim of trauma and loss, but the details and nature of these complex stressors and the factors or events surrounding them, and how they are perceived and experienced as stressors, may only be apparent after very careful assessment. There is also the need to take into account any dissociative phenomena that may well hide the intensity of the impact by distancing and dampening of affect. Furthermore, the readiness of the individual to disclose the nature and extent of his or her experience may be influenced by its severity and meaning. Thus, the survivor of a concentration camp, the ex-prisoner of war, the combat soldier, the woman surviving domestic assault, and the refugee who has suffered torture, may have many levels of stories of loss and grief, as well as trauma and posttraumatic stress reactions. These may only be disclosed after the establishment of trust, after a period of time, and at a time of some security, bit by bit (i.e., in a relationship that is based on therapeutic components).

Another matter that may affect the capacity to disclose adequately the experience of trauma, loss, or traumatic bereavement is the struggle the person has for his or her own physical or psychological survival. He or she may then be unable, or unwilling, to provide such information.

Thus assessments of the nature of the trauma and the loss are critical and must be linked to subsequent assessments of the phenomena of these reactive processes over time. But both the nature of the experiences themselves, and the painful reactive processes associated with them, mean that the assessment process itself is sensitive, stressful, and may have significant effects. The assessment may be helpful or "therapeutic," facilitating adaptive and resolution processes, or a source of further distress and perhaps secondary traumatization, and thus disruptive to adaptation and resolution. In this context, then, it is essential that assessment processes be optimal and "therapeutic" wherever possible.

A Format for Therapeutic Assessment

Whenever there is a framework of assessment for those traumatically bereaved (and also for nontraumatic bereavements), and for those exposed to traumatic stress effects, it is useful in either clinical settings or research studies to consider formats that are more "therapeutic" than not. This has been proposed in a model put in place following a rail disaster (Raphael, 1979–1980) in which those bereaved suffered traumatic bereavements, as is the case in most disasters.

The therapeutic nature of the assessment of the acutely and traumatically bereaved includes the following:

- Establishment of rapport and providing necessary reassurance and comfort.

- Exploration of what has happened, circumstances of the death and life threat, and the nature of the bereaved's experience, including the details of the day, warning, shock, horror, separation from loved ones, helplessness, degree of uncertainty about the death, threat to the bereaved personally, damage, mutilation or circumstances of particular suffering or horror. This is likely to take a substantial period of time, with the bereaved resting and dealing with affects in "doses," and with pressure for avoidance in terms of the traumatic intrusion and memories.

- Exploration of what has happened since and the bereaved's reactive processes, affects, cognitions, arousal, and reactions to the "recovery" environment, both supportive and nonsupportive.

- Exploration of the lost relationship, which means taking a history of the relationship with the lost person and providing a way of reviewing the lost relationship and possibly helping start some of the grieving processes. This may only be carried out very tentatively if the trauma and loss are still very acute.

- Closure of the assessment process, for the occasion of assessment may require allowing the traumatically bereaved person to regather defenses and control, and move away from more traumatic and painful aspects. Options for further support, care, and guidance are likely to be necessary for closure, either until treatment commences, or there is return to a supportive environment, or the next contact. This component may also need to ensure the presence of active practical and emotional support and provision of relevant information.

This concept of "therapeutic" assessment must be emphasized. It is repeatedly suggested that the bereaved and traumatized will benefit from "getting it all out," without recognition of the many different ways in which both loss and trauma are resolved. There are potential differing phenomena, time courses, and needs in acute, subacute, and longer-term phases. Although there is profound social belief in the value of catharsis, its timing and nature may be open to question. Recent reviews of the increasingly popular process of psychological debriefing, applied to a wide range of traumatic experiences, including traumatic bereavements, call for caution (Raphael, Meldrum, & McFarlane, 1995). This "quick fix" has *not* been established to be effective for traumatic stress situations and may be counterproductive in some instances, even though perceived so positively. Those suffering the double impact of loss and trauma may *not* benefit automatically from reviewing their experience at a time determined by a researcher, yet may be so affected as to require the outreach of a clinician. It is thus essential that they are protected from converging researchers in the ever-widening field of trauma studies, and are at least offered, both clinically and in terms of research participation, a skilled, soundly based, and sensitive assessor who is cognizant of the differing reactive processes, the sensitivity of the time, and the very individual nature and timing of response.

CONCLUSIONS

The phenomena of trauma and loss differ in important ways. The reactive processes following the trauma of encounter with death and/or life threat may lead to traumatic stress reaction and perhaps the development of PTSD. The reactive processes following the loss of a loved one lead to grief and perhaps chronic grief disorder. Refinements of clinical skills and systematic measures make it possible to assess the two sets of phenomena and their interaction in traumatic bereavement. Further empirical studies are needed to extend these theoretical and scientific understandings. This is even more true, because assessment of these reactions to external agents may give important clues to the aetiology of evolving disorders and their prevention. But in the acute situation at least, assessment, be it by interview, clinical appraisal, or questionnaire, is likely to deal with very sensitive matters. To this end, it must also be compassionate, empathetic, and wherever possible, therapeutic.

REFERENCES

Barrett, T. W., & Scott, T. B. (1989). Development of the grief experience questionnaire. *Suicide and Life-Threatening Behavior, 19,* 201–215.

Bartrop, R. W., Luckhurst, E., Lazarus, L., Kiloh, L. G., & Penny, R. (1977). Depressed lymphocyte function after bereavement. *Lancet, 97,* 834–836.

Baume, P. (1996). *The effects of youth suicide on the family: A study of parent survivors.* Ph.D. thesis, University of Queensland.

Blank, A. S. (1993). The longitudinal course of posttraumatic stress disorder. In J. R. T. Davidson & E. B. Foa (Eds.), *Posttraumatic stress disorder: DSM-IV and beyond* (pp. 3–23). Washington, DC: American Psychiatric Press.

Bremner, J. D., Southwick, S. M., & Charney, D. S. (1991). Animal models for the neurobiology of trauma. *PTSD Research Quarterly, 2*(4), 1–3.

Brown, W. A., Sirota, A. D., Niaura, R. T., & Engebretson, T. (1993). Endocrine correlates of sadness and elation. *Psychosomatic Medicine, 55,* 458–467.

Burnett, P., Middleton, W., Raphael, B., & Martinek, N. (in press). Measuring core bereavement phenomena. *Psychological Medicine.*

Byrne, G. J. A., & Raphael, B. (1994). A longitudinal study of bereavement phenomena in recently widowed elderly men. *Psychological Medicine, 24,* 411–421.

Darwin, C. (1872). *The expression of emotion in men and animals.* London: Murray.

Davidson, J. T., & Foa, E. B. (Eds.). (1993). *Posttraumatic stress disorder: DSM-IV and beyond.* Washington DC: American Psychiatric Press.

Dyregov, A., & Mattheisen, S. B. (1987a). Similarities and differences in mothers' and fathers' grief following the death of an infant. *Scandanavian Journal of Psychology, 28,* 1–15.

Dyregov, A., & Mattheisen, S. B. (1987b). Anxiety and vulnerability in parents follow-ing the death of an infant. *Scandinavian Journal of Psychology, 28,* 16–25.

Dyregov, A., & Mattheisen, S. B. (1987c). Stillbirth neonatal death and sudden infant death (SIDS): Parental reactions. *Scandanavian Journal of Psychology, 28,* 104–114.

Faschingbauer, T. R., DeVaul, R. A., & Zisook, S. (1977). Development of the Texas Inventory of Grief. *American Journal of Psychiatry, 134,* 696–698.

Faschingbauer, T. R., Zisook, S., & DeVaul, R. A. (1987). The Texas Revised Invento-ry of Grief. In S. Zisook (Ed.), *Biopsychosocial aspects of bereavement.* Washington, DC: American Psychiatric Press.

Freud, S. (1917). Mourning and melancholia. In *Collected papers* (Vol. 4). New York: Basic Books.

Freud, S. (1959). *Beyond the pleasure principle.* New York: Bantam. (Original work pub-lished 1920)

Green, B. L., Grace, M. C., & Gleser, G. L. (1985). Identifying survivors at risk: Long-term impairment following the Beverley Hills Supper Club fire. *Journal of Con-sulting and Clinical Psychology, 53,* 672–678.

Horowitz, M. A. (1976). *Stress response syndromes.* New York: Jason Aronson.

Horowitz, M. A., Wilner, N., & Alvarez, W. (1979). Impact of Event Scale: A measure of subjective stress. *Psychosomatic Medicine, 41*(3), 209–218.

Jacobs, S. C. (1993). *Pathologic grief: Maladaptation to loss.* Washington, DC: American Psychiatric Press.

Jacobs, S. C., Kasl, S. V., Ostfeld, A. M., Berkman, L., Kosten, T. R., & Charpentier, P. (1987a). The measurement of grief: Bereaved versus non-bereaved. *Hospice Jour-nal, 2,* 21–36.

Kleber, R. J., & Brom, D. (1987). Psychotherapy and pathological grief: Controlled outcome study. *Israeli Journal of Psychiatry Related Sciences, 24,* 99–109.

Laudenslager, M. L. (1988). The psychobiology of loss: Lessons from human and non-human primates. *Journal of Social Issues, 44,* 19–36.

L'Hoir, M. (1992, February 12–16). *Psychological aspects of SIDS: Post-traumatic stress dis-orders?* Paper presented at the second SIDS Family International Conference, Holmes Building, University of Sydney. (Published in Proceedings)

Lindemann, E. (1944). Symptomatology and management of acute grief. *American Jour-nal of Psychiatry, 101,* 141–148.

Lindy, J. D., Green, B. L., Grace, M., & Tichener, J. (1983). Psychotherapy with sur-vivors of the Beverly Hills Supper Club fire. *American Journal of Psychotherapy, 37,* 593–610.

Lundin, T. (1984). Morbidity following sudden and unexpected bereavement. *British Journal of Psychiatry, 144,* 84–88.

Marmar, C. R., Horowitz, M. J., Weiss, D. S., Wilner, N. R., & Kaltreider, N. B. (1988). A controlled trial of brief psychotherapy and mutual-help group treatment of conjugal bereavement. *American Journal of Psychiatry, 145,* 203–209.

McFarlane, A. C. (1988a). The aetiology of post-traumatic stress disorders following a national disaster. *British Journal of Psychiatry, 152,* 116–121.

McFarlane, A. C. (1988b). The longitudinal course of post-traumatic morbidity: The range of outcomes and their predictors. *Journal of Nervous and Mental Disease, 176*(1), 30–39.

Middleton, W. (1995). *Bereavement phenomenology and the processes of resolution.* M.D. Thesis, University of Queensland, Australia.

Middleton, W., Moylan, A., Raphael, B., Burnett, P. & Martinek, N. (1993). An international perspective on bereavement related concepts. *Australian and New Zealand Journal of Psychiatry, 27,* 457–463.

Middleton, W., Burnett, P., Raphael, B., & Martinek, N. (1996). *A longitudinal study comparing bereavement phenomena in recently bereaved spouses, adult children and parents.* Manuscript submitted for publication, Department of Psychiatry, University of Queensland, Australia.

Orr, S. P. (1994). An overview of psychophysiological studies of PTSD. *PTSD Research Quarterly, 5,* 1.

Parkes, C. M. (1971). The first year of bereavement: A longitudinal study of the reaction of London widows to the death of their husbands. *Psychiatry, 33,* 444–466.

Parkes, C. M. (1972). *Bereavement: Studies of grief in adult life.* New York: International Universities Press.

Parkes, C. M. (1980). Bereavement counselling: Does it work? *British Medical Journal, 281,* 3–10.

Parkes, C. M., & Weiss R. S. (1983). *Recovery from bereavement.* New York: Basic Books.

Pynoos, R. S., Frederick, C., Nader, K., Arroyo, W., Steinberg, A., Eth, S., Nunez, F., & Fairbanks, L. (1987a). Life threat and post-traumatic stress in school-age children. *Archives of General Psychiatry, 44,* 1057–1063.

Pynoos, R. S., Nader, K., Frederick, C., Gonda, L., & Stuber, M. (1987b). Grief reactions in school-age children following a sniper attack at school. *Israeli Journal of Psychiatry and Related Sciences, 24,* 53–63.

Raphael, B. (1977). Preventive intervention with the recently bereaved. *Archives of General Psychiatry, 34*(12), 1450–1454.

Raphael, B. (1979–1980). A primary prevention action program: Psychiatric involvement following a major rail disaster. *Omega, 10*(3), 211–226.

Raphael, B. (1983). *The anatomy of bereavement.* New York: Basic Books.

Raphael, B. (1986). *When disaster strikes.* New York: Basic Books.

Raphael, B. (1989, May). *Diagnostic criteria for bereavement reactions.* Paper presented at International Symposium on Pathological Bereavement, Seattle, WA.

Raphael, B. (1992, February 12–16). *Traumatic stress and SIDS.* Paper presented at the second SIDS Family International Conference, Holmes Building, University of Sydney. (Published in Proceedings)

Raphael, B., & Maddison, D. C. (1976). The care of bereaved adults. In O. W. Hill (Ed.), *Modern trends in psychosomatic medicine.* London: Butterworth.

Raphael, B., Meldrum, L., & McFarlane, A. C. (1995). Does debriefing after psychological trauma work? *British Medical Journal, 310,* 1479–1480.

Reynolds, C. F., Hoch, C. C., Buysse, D. J., et al. (1992). Electroencephalographic sleep in spousal bereavement and bereavement related depression in late life. *Biological Psychiatry, 31,* 69–82.

Rynearson, E. K. (1984). Bereavement after homicide: A descriptive study. *American Journal of Psychiatry, 141,* 1452–1454.

Sanders, C. M. (1979). The use of the MMPI in assessing bereavement outcome. In C. S. Newmark (Ed.), *MMPI: Clinical and research trends* (pp. 223–247). New York: Praeger.

Sanders, C. M. (1980). A comparison of adult bereavement in the death of a spouse, child and parent. *Omega, 10,* 303–322.

Schuchter, S. R., Zisook, S., Kirkorowicz, C., & Risch, C. (1986). The dexamethasone test in acute grief. *American Journal of Psychiatry, 143,* 879–881.

Schut, H. A. W., Keijser, J. D., Van Den Bout, J., & Dijhuis, J. H. (1991). Post-traumatic stress symptoms in the first years of conjugal bereavement. *Anxiety Research, 4,* 225–234.

Silverman, P. R., & Worden, J. W. (1992). Children's reactions in the early months after the death of a parent. *American Journal of Orthopsychiatry, 62,* 93–104.

Sinha, R., Lovallo, W. R., & Parsons, O. A. (1992). Cardiovascular differentiation of emotions. *Psychosomatic Medicine, 54,* 422–435.

Spiegel, D. (Ed.). (1994). *Dissociation — Culture, mind, and body.* Washington, DC: American Psychiatric Press.

Stroebe, M. S., Stroebe, W., & Hansson, R. O. (Eds.). (1993). *Handbook of bereavement: Theory, research, and intervention.* New York: Cambridge University Press.

Toedter, L. J., Lasker, J. N., & Alhadeft, J. M. (1988). The perinatal grief scale: Development and initial validation. *American Journal of Orthopsychiatry, 58,* 435–449.

Vargas, L. A., Loya, F., & Hodde-Vargas, J. (1989). Exploring the multidimensional aspects of grief reactions. *American Journal of Psychiatry, 146,* 1484–1488.

Weller, R. A., Weller, M. D., Fristad, M. A., & Bowes, J. M. (1991). Depression in recently bereaved prepubertal children. *American Journal of Psychiatry, 148,* 1536–1540.

Wilson, J. P., & Raphael, B. (Eds.). (1993). *International handbook of traumatic stress syndromes.* New York: Plenum Press.

Wilson, J. P., Smith, W. K., & Johnson, S. K. (1985). A comparative analysis among various survivor groups. In C. R. Figley (Ed.), *Trauma and its wake: The study and treatment of post-traumatic stress disorder.* New York: Brunner/Mazel.

Zisook, S., & Schuchter, S. R. (1985). Time course of spousal bereavement. *General Hospital Psychiatry, 7,* 95–100.

Zisook, S., & Schuchter, S. R. (1991). Depression through the first year after the death of a spouse. *American Journal of Psychiatry, 148,* 1346–1352.

Zisook, S., Schuchter, S. R., & Lyons, L. E. (1987). Adjustment to widowhood. In S. Zisook (Ed.), *Biopsychosocial aspects of bereavement* (pp. 49–74). Washington, DC: American Psychiatric Press.

ASSESSING TRAUMATIC REACTIONS, DISSOCIATION, AND POSTTRAUMATIC STRESS DISORDER

CHAPTER 13

The Impact of Event Scale — Revised

DANIEL S. WEISS
CHARLES R. MARMAR

INITIAL STUDIES OF THE ORIGINAL IMPACT OF EVENT SCALE

In 1979 Horowitz and colleagues (Horowitz, Wilner, & Alvarez, 1979) published a short self-report measure for capturing the level of symptomatic response to specific traumatic stressors as it was manifest in the previous 7 days; it was modestly titled the "Impact of Event Scale" (IES). Based on his views of the response to traumatic stressors, Horowitz (1976) identified responses in the realm of intrusion and avoidance as the primary domains of measurement. Building on the link between traumatic life events and subsequent psychological symptoms that had long been observed (Breuer & Freud, 1895/1955; Charcot, 1887), Horowitz and colleagues noted that measurement of this response had primarily been confined either to experimental physiological measures such as galvanic skin responses or to self-report on more general measures of anxiety, such as the Taylor Manifest Anxiety Scale (Taylor, 1953).

The advance introduced by Horowitz and colleagues with the publication of the IES was a self-report measure that could be anchored to any specific life event, and that tapped two of the most commonly reported specific categories of experiences in response to traumatic life events: intrusive symptoms comprising nightmares, intrusive thoughts or images or feelings, and avoidance symptoms comprising attempts to dampen or avoid experiences associated with the traumatic event and the associated numbing of responsiveness. It is well to recall that the publication of the IES predated the publication of the third edition of the *Diagnostic and Statistical Manual of Mental Disorders* (DSM-III; American Psychiatric Association, 1980) and the official adoption of "posttraumatic stress disorder" (PTSD) in the nomenclature. In some ways, it can be argued that the IES and the data collected on it were evidence that bolstered the case for PTSD as a diagnostic entity.

The original IES tapped the B and C Criteria of the diagnosis of PTSD, the signs and symptoms of intrusive cognitions and affects together or oscillating with periods of avoidance, denial, or blocking of thoughts and images. In the initial report of the measure (Horowitz et al., 1979), cluster analysis of the responses of 66 individuals, admitted to an outpatient clinic for the treatment of stress response syndromes in response to one of a variety of traumatic life events, supported the existence of homogeneous clusters of items characterized by intrusion and avoidance (Cronbach's α for intrusion = .79, for avoidance = .82). The correlations between subscales of .42 was small enough to allow for substantial independence of the item subscales while indicating some covariation. The test–retest reliability in the original study was satisfactory, with coefficients of .87 for intrusion and .79 for avoidance. Its sensitivity to change was supported by indications of change in a population in which clinical impressions by experienced clinicians suggested such movement, as well as relevant differences in the response to traumatic events of varying severity.

Zilberg, Weiss, and Horowitz (1982) conducted an in depth replication and cross-validation of the psychometric characteristics of the IES and the accompanying conceptual model of responses to traumatic stress that had given rise to the development of the initial scale. They studied 35 outpatients with pathological grief and compared them to 37 field subject volunteers who had also experienced the death of a parent but had not sought treatment for the impact of the loss (Horowitz et al., 1984). Both groups were evaluated at three time points. For the patients these time points were (1) at entry into the study before their course of treatment began; (2) 4 months after the termination of treatment; and (3) 12 months after the termination of the time-limited psychotherapy. The field subjects were assessed along a similar 3-point time line: (1) at entry into the study, which was designed to occur 2 months postbereavement; (2) 7 months after the event; and (3) 13 months after the event.

The results of that study demonstrated that all items were endorsed frequently, with a range from 44% to 89% of the pooled sample. This replicated the high relevance of the item pool for responses to traumatic stress. The rank order of items based on frequency of endorsement in the parental-bereavement patient groups was compared with the rank order reported in the initial publication of the IES. A Spearman rank correlation of .86 ($p <$ .001) was obtained. This result suggested that the content of experience following traumatic events, as represented in the IES item pool, was similar across types of events and patient versus nonpatient populations.

A factor analysis was undertaken to assess the validity of the item assignments to the Intrusion and Avoidance subscales. Two factors were extracted using a principal factors procedure with a varimax rotation. The avoidance items were loaded on the first factor, with coefficients ranging from .39 to .86; the intrusion items produced coefficients ranging from .09

to .34. The second factor was clearly defined by the intrusion items, with loadings from .58 to .75, while the avoidance items produced coefficients ranging from .11 to .35. In the case of all items, the loading on the hypothesized factor was higher than it was on the other factor. This was taken as strong evidence of the coherence of the two subscale item sets.

Reliability data were also reported in this cross-validation study. Coefficients of internal consistency were reported for both subscales for all three time points for the two groups, both separately and combined. These coefficients ranged from .79 to .92.

Zilberg et al. (1982) also reported on the sensitivity of the IES to distinguish between patient and control groups. Eleven of the 15 items showed a significant difference in mean endorsement at the first evaluation. This strong discrimination was achieved in the expected direction, with the patients having a significantly higher magnitude of response on both the subscales and all items, although only 11 showed a strong enough effect to be detected with these relatively small samples. Another index of sensitivity was the ability of the subscales to detect change in clinical status over time. Correlated *t*-tests were performed. The results revealed that the IES was sensitive to change not only over the period between the first and third evaluation, but also over the shorter period between the first and second assessments, and the second and third periods. These changes were evident in both patients and field subjects, indicating that some parallel processes exist in response to traumatic stress in both pathological and normal contexts (Weiss, 1993).

This study carefully examined the structure of the relationship between the intrusion and avoidance subscales, in order to clarify whether a total score or the reporting of subscale scores was preferable. The authors argued that if the data had produced correlations of the order of .40–.60 in all six of the time-by-group conditions, then it would have been difficult to maintain separate subscale scoring solely on empirical grounds. The empirical findings and a conceptual rationale converged to suggest that separate scores be retained. In five of the six conditions, the subscales were substantially correlated, ranging from .57 to .78. There was one striking exception; the patient sample at the pretherapy evaluation point produced a coefficient of only .15. This is a time when the subjects as a group were presenting a well-defined syndrome, but this syndrome could be any among three. First, a group of patients frozen in avoidance would yield high-avoidance and low-intrusion scores; a group stuck in undercontrolled intrusion would demonstrate high intrusion and low avoidance; finally, a group that was oscillating over the 1-week period covered by the IES would show similar level ratings of intrusion and avoidance in the medium or high range. The first two groups would contribute to an overall negative correlation, whereas the third group would contribute to a positive one. Overall, one might expect a mildly positive correlation. This was what was obtained.

LITERATURE USING THE ORIGINAL IES

The results of the Zilberg et al. study, as well as a plethora of studies conducted since that time using the IES, have demonstrated the worth of this instrument. There has been research on simulation on the IES (Lees-Haley, 1990; Perkins & Tebes, 1984) and a series of validation studies. These studies were conducted with Vietnam War veterans (Hendrix, Jurich, & Schumm, 1994), Israeli combat soldiers (Schwarzwald, Solomon, Weisenberg, & Mikulincer, 1987; Solomon, 1989), and mixed samples (e.g., Neal et al., 1994).

Natural disasters are among the traumatic events that have been studied using the IES. Studies of earthquakes (Anderson & Manuel, 1994; Carr, Lewin, Carter, & Webster, 1992; Kaltreider, Gracie, & LeBreck, 1992; Lundin & Bodegard, 1993; Paton, 1990), firestorms (Koopman, Classen, & Spiegel, 1994; Maida, Gordon, Steinberg, & Gordon, 1989; McFarlane, 1988), floods (Green et al., 1994), and hurricanes (Waters, Selander, & Stuart, 1992) have all employed the IES with consistent findings as to its utility and integrity to document response to life events, to partially predict who will experience distress over time, and to monitor change over time in the response to traumatic exposures.

There is also a literature using the IES in criminal victimization and accident situations. Railway accidents have been examined in several studies (Andersen, Christensen, & Petersen, 1991; Malt et al., 1993) using the IES, and this measure of response to traumatic events has been among the most sensitive indices of tracking intrusive and avoidant symptoms. There is a literature involving other transportation accidents. Yule and Udwin (1991), for instance, studied the response of 24 girls after a cruise ship sinking and found that the IES completed at 10-days postaccident could forecast help-seeking behavior over the following months.

The IES has been employed in a variety of studies involving criminal victimization (Arata, Saunders, & Kilpatrick, 1991) and the impact on family members of people who had been victims of homicide (Amick-McMullan, Kilpatrick, Veronen, & Smith, 1989). Girelli, Resick, Marhoefer-Dvorak, and Hutter (1986) studied the reactions to rape using, among other measures, the IES. They found that the avoidance subscale was an important variable in the models they tested.

Studies of adults sexually abused as children (Alexander, 1993; Murphy, Kilpatrick, Amick-McMullan, & Veronen, 1988) and adults whose children had been sexually abused (Kelley, 1990) have also employed the IES.

The IES has been used to document the psychological response in life-threatening medical circumstances, for instance, cancer (Cella, Mahon, & Donovan, 1990). These investigators found that the impact of recurrence was more problematic than initial diagnosis.

The IES has also been used as an outcome measure in treatment studies. Davidson and colleagues (1993) examined the response to the tricyclic amitriptyline using the IES, among other measures. Eye movement desensitization has been examined using the IES (Renfrey & Spates, 1994). Frank, Kosten, Giller, and Elisheva (1988) used the IES as a key outcome measure in their randomized study of phenelzine and imipramine in their study of Vietnam combat theater veterans. In a comparative outcome study of behavioral group therapy for sexual assault victims, the IES was one of several outcome variables (Resick, Jordan, Girelli, & Hutter, 1988).

Studies using the IES to investigate the impact on emergency services workers have also been conducted. Fullerton, McCarroll, Ursano, and Wright (1992) used the IES to help understand the factors that mitigate the response experienced by firefighters. McCarroll, Ursano, and Fullerton (1995) used the IES to show that those who handled human remains during the Gulf War were more likely to be symptomatic at 1 year than those who did not.

In summary, there is a large literature using the original IES and documenting its usefulness, validity, reliability, and its centrality in the measurement armamentarium for researchers interested in tracking psychological response to traumatic events. This literature notwithstanding, we concluded that the IES could be made even more useful if it had the capacity to track not only the intrusive and avoidant symptoms of PTSD and the response to traumatic stressors, but also the hyperarousal symptoms that are part of the DSM-IV diagnostic criteria and are an integral part of the psychological response to traumatic events. Thus, we undertook a revision of the original IES and presented the measure and psychometric data regarding its use.

DEVELOPMENT OF THE IMPACT OF EVENT SCALE—REVISED

Despite the usefulness of the original IES, complete assessment of the response to traumatic events required tracking of response in the domain of hyperarousal symptoms. For a longitudinal study of the response of emergency services personnel to traumatic events, including the Loma Prieta earthquake (Marmar et al., 1996; Weiss, Marmar, Metzler, & Ronfeldt, 1995), we developed a set of seven additional items, with six to tap the domain of hyperarousal, and one to parallel the then DSM-III-R and now DSM-IV diagnostic criteria. These additional seven items were randomly interspersed with the existing seven intrusion and eight avoidance items of the original IES. The Impact of Event Scale—Revised (IES-R) comprises these 22 items.

An important consideration in the construction of the IES-R was to maintain comparability with the original version of the measure as much as possible. Consequently, we did not alter the 1-week time frame to which the instructions refer in measuring symptomatic response, nor did we initially alter Horowitz's original scoring scheme of 0, 1, 3, and 5 for the responses of "not at all," "rarely," "sometimes," and "often" to the frequency response directions. The only modification to the original items that was made was to change the item "I had trouble falling asleep or staying asleep" from its double-barreled status into two separate items. The first is simply "I had trouble staying asleep," and because of a somewhat higher correlation between it and the remaining intrusion items, we assigned it to represent the original item in the Intrusion subscale. The second item, "I had trouble falling asleep," was assigned to the new Hyperarousal subscale because of its somewhat higher correlation with the other hyperarousal items, its somewhat lower correlation with the intrusion items, and its more apparent link with hyperarousal than with intrusion. With the exception of this minor modification in that item, and the addition of an item tapping flashback-like reexperiencing, the Intrusion and Avoidance subscales of the IES-R remain the same as in the original IES.

These decisions allow the user of the IES-R to substantially compare results on the Intrusion and Avoidance subscales with the original IES, assuming that the revised order of the items, the bifurcated-sleep-problems item, and the addition of the six hyperarousal items and one intrusion item exert a minimal to nonexistent effect on the items' responses to the core set of 15 items. Such an assumption is typically made in psychological assessment, and there appears to be little research that counters the safety of that assumption.

The six new hyperarousal items target the following domains: anger and irritability; jumpiness and exaggerated startle response; trouble concentrating; psychophysiological arousal upon exposure to reminders; and hypervigilance. As mentioned earlier, the one new intrusion item taps the dissociative-like reexperiencing captured in true flashback-like experiences. The complete set of items, instructions, and scoring scheme appear in the Appendix.

PSYCHOMETRIC PROPERTIES OF THE IES-R

Data were collected on the IES-R from subjects in two different studies. The first was a study of four broad categories of emergency personnel: police, firefighters, paramedics and emergency medical technicians, and California highway department workers (Caltrans). Subjects were recruited from three sites: (1) those who worked the I–880 freeway collapse that occurred during the 1989 Loma Prieta earthquake; (2) those who lived and worked in the San Francisco Bay Area the day of the earthquake, but were not assigned to I–880 duty; (3) emergency personnel from the San Diego area.

Very detailed information about the subject sample can be found elsewhere (Marmar et al., 1996). All subjects provided written, informed consent for participation in the study. The complete sample comprised 189 subjects from the I–880 site, 140 Bay Area control (BAC) subjects, and 101

San Diego (SDC) controls. For all subjects, a subset of the measures was completed in regard to a specific critical incident. For the I–880 subjects, the freeway collapse rescue operation was the designated incident. For the counterpart replication group, each worker selected a critical incident that was the most distressing for him or her, with the proviso that the incident was neither a mass disaster nor one in which the worker was the victim of an assault. The average time elapsed since the incident for the I–880 group was 1.5 years, for the BAC, 3.3 years, and for the SDC, 4.1 years. Subjects in this study were assessed twice. Data on the IES-R come from both assessments.

The second group of subjects comprised those who experienced the 1994 Northridge earthquake in the Los Angeles area. There was a total of 206 workers from two insurance companies who were affected by the quake in terms of both home and workplace. For 64 of them from one company, initial data were collected approximately 6 weeks after the earthquake, following a 2.5-hour group debriefing session. The remaining 146 subjects, from another company, completed a set of questionnaires regarding the impact of the earthquake in approximately the same time frame as the subjects from the first company. The subjects were followed up with a second set of questionnaires approximately 6 months after the initial assessment. This allowed for the calculation of long-term estimates of stability.

A variety of analyses were conducted using these data to document the basic psychometric properties of the IES-R. Analyses of internal consistency, item-to-scale correlations both across and within subscales, and test–retest reliability analyses were performed. The results of these analyses are presented here.

Data from the first wave of the Northridge data were collapsed across subjects from both companies. This yielded a sample of 197 subjects on whom estimates of internal consistency using coefficient alpha for the Intrusion, Avoidance, and Hyperarousal subscales could be calculated. The results of these analyses produced the following coefficients for the Time 1 data: Intrusion alpha = .91, Avoidance alpha = .84, and Hyperarousal alpha = .90. These data are evidence of highly internally consistent subscales.

Data from the first wave of the I–880 study were also collapsed across subjects from all three study groups. This yielded a sample of 429 subjects on whom complete data were available. The results of these analyses produced the following coefficients for the Time 1 data: Intrusion alpha = .87, Avoidance alpha = .85, and Hyperarousal alpha = .79. These data are also evidence of highly internally consistent subscales.

The comparable data from the second wave of the I–880 study produced 317 subjects on whom the following estimates of internal consistency were calculated: Intrusion alpha = .87, Avoidance alpha = .86, and Hyperarousal alpha = .79. These results are virtually identical to the Time 1 data and are consistent with internally consistent subscales. The Wave 2 data from the Northridge sample comprised 175 subjects. Their responses to the IES-R produced the following estimates of internal consistency: Intrusion alpha = .92, Avoidance alpha = .85, and Hyperarousal alpha = .89.

A summary of the four sets of estimates of internal consistency shows that the internal consistency of the three subscales is very high, and that in none of the 12 sets of data is a single item not positively correlated with its assigned subscale.

A second question for basic reliability has to do with the stability of the variables over time. There were test–retest data available both for the I-880 samples and the Northridge earthquake samples. The I-880 data yielded the following test–retest correlation coefficients: Intrusion = .57, Avoidance = .51, Hyperarousal = .59. For the Northridge earthquake samples, the test–retest correlation coefficients were considerably higher: Intrusion = .94, Avoidance = .89, Hyperarousal = .92. It is likely that both the shorter interval between assessments and the greater recency of the traumatic event for the Northridge sample contributed to the higher coefficients of stability.

These initial data are reassuring concerning the basic psychometric properties of the IES-R. There are a number of subsidiary questions, however, about the alignment of items to subscales, that are helpful to examine to bolster the case for the scoring of the subscales.

Using the Time 1 Northridge data, each item was examined to determine if its correlation with its assigned subscale was greater than its correlation with the other two subscales. Because of obvious part–whole problems, the standard Pearson product–moment correlation coefficient for an item with its assigned subscale was not appropriate for the within-subscale correlations. To remedy this confound, we utilized the item-to-subscale correlation with that item removed from the subscale generated by the standard alpha coefficient analyses, and compared these to the cross-subscale Pearson correlations. This analysis provided 22 chances for the assignment of items to be investigated.

The results of this analysis demonstrated that only 1 of these 22 items showed a stronger relationship between it and a different subscale. This was Item 15—"I had trouble falling asleep." The corrected correlation of this item with its assigned hyperarousal subscale was .71; its correlation with the intrusion subscale was .79. Of the remaining 21 items, 19 showed a correlation with their assigned subscale that was higher than that with the other two subscales, and 2 showed a correlation that was equal. One of those was Item 2—"I had trouble staying asleep," and the other was Item 5—"I avoided letting myself get upset when I thought about it or was reminded of it."

The explanation of these results appears to be that the two sleep items are very highly correlated and tend to drive a relationship between them in terms of intrusion and hyperarousal. Future data may suggest a modification of the assignment of these items, and may suggest that the inclusion of the double-barreled aspect of the sleep item in the original IES was partially responsible for its relationship with the original intrusion items. The equal relationship of the avoidance item with Avoidance and Intrusion subscales may be due to the fact that in order to acknowledge not dealing with feelings of which the subject is aware, the presentation of feelings invokes intrusion, and not dealing with it invokes avoidance.

A final comment about these data is that the sample studied was not a clinical sample seeking treatment for well-established PTSD. As Zilberg et al. (1982) argued, the composition of the sample may affect the interrelationship of the items, and if data were collected on a sample, all of whom had current PTSD, the assignment of items to subscales might be even stronger than the already-strong results demonstrated in the Northridge data.

A second kind of evidence regarding the IES-R has to do with the relationship among the three subscales. A principal factors factor analysis with varimax rotation on the Northridge Time 1 data set yielded a strong, single factor that accounted for 49% of the variance. This result may also be due to the fact that not all subjects in this sample described medium or high levels of symptoms. The subscale correlations for these data were .74 for intrusion with avoidance, .87 for intrusion with hyperarousal, and .74 for avoidance and hyperarousal. These coefficients echo the results of the factor analysis, and illustrate that although the DSM-IV criteria are organized into the three domains of intrusion, avoidance, and hyperarousal, the empirical support of this organization of symptoms in studies of both scales and diagnostic interviews remains to be more carefully elucidated and documented.

RECOMMENDATIONS FOR FURTHER USE AND RESEARCH

Based on the data reported in this chapter, careful analysis of archival, original IES data, and preliminary data we have begun to collect, we are recommending to the field two changes for the utilization of the IES-R. These changes are reflected in the Appendix, where the scale appears. First, we are recommending that the directions be modified so that the respondent is not asked about the frequency of symptoms in the past 7 days but is asked to report the degree of distress of the symptom in the past 7 days. Second, we are recommending that the response format be modified to a 0–4 response format with equal intervals, rather than the unequal intervals originally adopted by Horowitz et al. (1979). Because we are also recommending that the subscale scoring be modified to the mean of the nonmissing items, these changes bring the IES-R closer in format to the Symptom Checklist 90 — Revised (SCL-90-R; Derogatis, 1994) and allow for comparison of symptom levels across these two instruments. The gain in comparability across these two widely used measures, and the clarification of the frequency versus intensity response format, seem to be modifications that will enhance the validity and usefulness of the IES-R.

The analyses of the item data of the Time 1 Northridge data suggest that further attention be paid to the clustering of items, both in terms of the psychometric properties of the IES-R and other instruments such as the Clinician-Administered PTSD Scale (Blake et al., 1995), or the Stress Response Rating Scale (Weiss, Horowitz, & Wilner, 1984), as well as the implication that such results have for the understanding of the diagnostic criteria for PTSD. These issues also raise the question of the natural history of responses to traumatic stress (Weiss, 1993) and the pattern of response in those who are following a normal course of recovery of psychological equilibrium in the months following exposure to a traumatic stressor. The pattern of symptoms and the homogeneity of intrusion, avoidance, and hyperarousal, as opposed to the differentiation of response in these three domains, is clearly an area in which much more detailed and careful work is required. Investigations that use measures of severity of exposure, recency of exposure, and other potentially mediating variables, such as peritraumatic dissociation (see Marmar, Weiss, & Metzler, Chapter 14, this volume) to further illuminate the patterns of response in both normal recovery and the derailing of normal recovery into disorder are sorely needed.

APPENDIX: IMPACT OF EVENT SCALE—REVISED

Instructions: The following is a list of difficulties people sometimes have after stressful life events. Please read each item, and then indicate how distressing each difficulty has been for you *during the past 7 days* with respect to _____. How much were you distressed or bothered by these difficulties?

	Not at all	A little bit	Moderately	Quite a bit	Extremely
1. Any reminder brought back feelings about it.	0	1	2	3	4
2. I had trouble staying asleep.	0	1	2	3	4
3. Other things kept making me think about it.	0	1	2	3	4
4. I felt irritable and angry.	0	1	2	3	4
5. I avoided letting myself get upset when I thought about it or was reminded of it.	0	1	2	3	4
6. I thought about it when I didn't mean to.	0	1	2	3	4
7. I felt as if it hadn't happened or wasn't real.	0	1	2	3	4
8. I stayed away from reminders about it.	0	1	2	3	4
9. Pictures about it popped into my mind.	0	1	2	3	4
10. I was jumpy and easily startled.	0	1	2	3	4

11. I tried not to think about it.	0	1	2	3	4
12. I was aware that I still had a lot of feelings about it, but I didn't deal with them.	0	1	2	3	4
13. My feelings about it were kind of numb.	0	1	2	3	4
14. I found myself acting or feeling like I was back at that time.	0	1	2	3	4
15. I had trouble falling asleep.	0	1	2	3	4
16. I had waves of strong feelings about it.	0	1	2	3	4
17. I tried to remove it from my memory.	0	1	2	3	4
18. I had trouble concentrating.	0	1	2	3	4
19. Reminders of it caused me to have physical reactions, such as sweating, trouble breathing, nausea, or a pounding heart.	0	1	2	3	4
20. I had dreams about it.	0	1	2	3	4
21. I felt watchful and on guard.	0	1	2	3	4
22. I tried not to talk about it.	0	1	2	3	4

REFERENCES

Alexander, P. (1993). The differential effects of abuse characteristics and attachment in the prediction of long-term effects of sexual abuse. *Journal of Interpersonal Violence, 8,* 346–362.

American Psychiatric Association. (1980). *Diagnostic and statistical manual of mental disorders* (3rd ed.). Washington, DC: Author.

Amick-McMullan, A., Kilpatrick, D. G., Veronen, L. J., & Smith, S. (1989). Family survivors of homicide victims: Theoretical perspectives and an exploratory study. *Journal of Traumatic Stress, 2,* 21–35.

Andersen, H. S., Christensen, A. K., & Petersen, G. O. (1991). Post-traumatic stress reactions amongst rescue workers after a major rail accident. *Anxiety Research, 4,* 245–251.

Anderson, K. M., & Manuel, G. (1994). Gender differences in reported stress response to the Loma Prieta earthquake. *Sex Roles, 30,* 725–733.

Arata, C. M., Saunders, B. E., & Kilpatrick, D. G. (1991). Concurrent validity of a crime-related post-traumatic stress disorder scale for women with the Symptom Checklist-90—Revised. *Violence and Victims, 6,* 191–199.

Blake, D. D., Weathers, F. W., Nagy, L. M., Kaloupek, D. G., Gusman, F. D., Charney, D. S., & Keane, T. M. (1995). The development of a clinician-administered PTSD scale. *Journal of Traumatic Stress, 8,* 75–90.

Breuer, J., & Freud, S. (1955). Studies on hysteria. In J. Strachey (Ed. and Trans.), *The standard edition of the complete psychological works of Sigmund Freud* (Vol. 2). London: Hogarth Press. (Original work published 1895)

Carr, V. J., Lewin, T. J., Carter, G. L., & Webster, R. A. (1992). Patterns of service utilisation following the 1989 Newcastle earthquake: Findings from Phase 1 of the Quake Impact study. *Australian Journal of Public Health, 16,* 360–369.

Cella, D. F., Mahon, S. M., & Donovan, M. I. (1990). Cancer recurrence as a traumatic event. *Behavioral Medicine, 16,* 15–22.

Charcot, J. M. (1887). *Leçons sur les maladies du système nerveux faites á la Salpêtiére.* Paris: Progrès Medical, Delahaye and Lecroisne.

Davidson, J. R., Kudler, H. S., Saunders, W. B., Erickson, L., Smith, R. D., Stein, R. M., Lipper, S., Hammett, E. B., Mahorney, S. L., & Cavenar, J. O., Jr. (1993). Predicting the response to amitriptyline in posttraumatic stress disorder. *American Journal of Psychiatry, 150,* 1024–1029.

Derogatis, L. R. (1994). *SCL-90-R administration, scoring, and procedures manual* (3rd ed.). Minneapolis: National Computer Systems.

Frank, J. B., Kosten, T. R., Giller, E. L., & Elisheva, D. (1988). A randomized clinical trial of phenelzine and imipramine for posttraumatic stress disorder. *American Journal of Psychiatry, 145,* 1289–1291.

Fullerton, C. S., McCarroll, J. E., Ursano, R. J., & Wright, K. M. (1992). Psychological responses of rescue workers: Fire fighters and trauma. *American Journal of Orthopsychiatry, 62,* 371–378.

Girelli, S. A., Resick, P. A., Marhoefer-Dvorak, S., & Hutter, C. K. (1986). Subjective distress and violence during rape: Their effects on long-term fear. *Violence and Victims, 1,* 35–46.

Green, B. L., Grace, M. C., Vary, M. G., Kramer, T. L., Gleser, G. C., & Leonard, A. C. (1994). Children of disaster in the second decade: A 17-year follow-up of Buffalo Creek survivors. *Journal of the American Academy of Child and Adolescent Psychiatry, 33,* 71–79.

Hendrix, C. C., Jurich, A. P., & Schumm, W. R. (1994). Validation of the Impact of Event Scale on a sample of American Vietnam veterans. *Psychological Reports, 75,* 321–322.

Horowitz, M. J. (1976). *Stress response syndromes.* New York: Jason Aronson.

Horowitz, M. J., Weiss, D. S., Kaltreider, N. B., Krupnick, J., Wilner, N., Marmar, C. R., & DeWitt, K. N. (1984). Reactions to the death of a parent: Results from patients and field subjects. *Journal of Nervous and Mental Disease, 172,* 383–392.

Horowitz, M. J., Wilner, N., & Alvarez, W. (1979). Impact of Event Scale: A measure of subjective stress. *Psychosomatic Medicine, 41,* 209–218.

Kaltreider, N. B., Gracie, C., & LeBreck, D. (1992). The psychological impact of the Bay Area earthquake on health professionals. *Journal of the American Medical Women's Association, 47,* 21–24.

Kelley, S. J. (1990). Parental stress response to sexual abuse and ritualistic abuse of children in day-care centers. *Nursing Research, 39,* 25–29.

Koopman, C., Classen, C., & Spiegel, D. (1994). Predictors of posttraumatic stress symptoms among survivors of the Oakland/Berkeley, Calif., firestorm. *American Journal of Psychiatry, 151,* 888–894.

Lees-Haley, P. R. (1990). Malingering mental disorder on the Impact of Event Scale (IES): Toxic exposure and cancerphobia. *Journal of Traumatic Stress, 3,* 315–321.

Lundin, T., & Bodegard, M. (1993). The psychological impact of an earthquake on rescue workers: A follow-up study of the Swedish group of rescue workers in Armenia, 1988. *Journal of Traumatic Stress, 6,* 129–139.

Maida, C. A., Gordon, N. S., Steinberg, A., & Gordon, G. (1989). Psychosocial impact of disasters: Victims of the Baldwin Hills fire. *Journal of Traumatic Stress, 2,* 37–48.

Malt, U. F., Karlehagen, S., Hoff, H., Herstromer, U., Hildingson, K., Tibell, E., & Leymann, H. (1993). The effect of major railway accidents on the psychological health of train drivers: I. Acute psychological responses to accident. *Journal of Psychosomatic Research, 37,* 793–805.

Marmar, C. R., Weiss, D. S., Metzler, T., Ronfeldt, H., & Foreman, C. (1996). Stress responses of emergency services personnel to the Loma Prieta earthquake Interstate 880 freeway collapse and control traumatic incidents. *Journal of Traumatic Stress, 9,* 63–85.

McCarroll, J. E., Ursano, R. J., & Fullerton, C. S. (1995). Symptoms of PTSD following recovery of war dead: 13–15-month follow-up. *American Journal of Psychiatry, 152,* 939–41.

McFarlane, A. C. (1988). Relationship between psychiatric impairment and a natural disaster: The role of distress. *Psychological Medicine, 18,* 129–139.

Murphy, S. M., Kilpatrick, D. G., Amick-McMullan, A., & Veronen, L. J. (1988). Current psychological functioning of child sexual assault survivors: A community study. *Journal of Interpersonal Violence, 3,* 55–79.

Neal, L. A., Busuttil, W., Rollins, J., Herepath, R., Strike, P., & Turnbull, G. (1994). Convergent validity of measures of post-traumatic stress disorder in a mixed military and civilian population. *Journal of Traumatic Stress, 7,* 447–455.

Paton, D. (1990). Assessing the impact of disasters on helpers. *Counseling Psychology Quarterly, 3,* 149–152.

Perkins, D. V., & Tebes, J. A. (1984). Genuine versus simulated responses on the Impact of Event scale. *Psychological Reports, 54,* 575–578.

Renfrey, G., & Spates, C. R. (1994). Eye movement desensitization: A partial dismantling study. *Journal of Behavior Therapy and Experimental Psychiatry, 25,* 231–239.

Resick, P. A., Jordan, C. G., Girelli, S. A., & Hutter, C. K. (1988). A comparative outcome study of behavioral group therapy for sexual assault victims. *Behavior Therapy, 19,* 385–401.

Schwarzwald, J., Solomon, Z., Weisenberg, M., & Mikulincer, M. (1987). Validation of the Impact of Event Scale for psychological sequelae of combat. *Journal of Consulting and Clinical Psychology, 55,* 251–256.

Solomon, Z. (1989). Psychological sequelae of war: A 3-year prospective study of Israeli combat stress reactions. *Journal of Nervous and Mental Disease, 177,* 342–346.

Taylor, J. A. (1953). A personality scale of manifest anxiety. *Journal of Abnormal and Social Psychology, 48,* 285–290.

Waters, K. A., Selander, J., & Stuart, G. W. (1992). Psychological adaptation of nurses post-disaster. *Issues in Mental Health Nursing, 13,* 177–190.

Weiss, D. S. (1993). Psychological processes in traumatic stress. *Journal of Social Behavior and Personality, 8,* 3–28.

Weiss, D. S., Horowitz, M. J., & Wilner, N. (1984). The Stress Response Rating Scale: A clinician's measure for rating the response to serious life events. *British Journal of Clinical Psychology, 23,* 202–215.

Weiss, D. S., Marmar, C. R., Metzler, T., & Ronfeldt, H. (1995). Predicting symptomatic distress in emergency services personnel. *Journal of Consulting and Clinical Psychology, 63,* 361–368.

Yule, W., & Udwin, O. (1991). Screening child survivors for post-traumatic stress disorders: Experiences from the "Jupiter" sinking. *British Journal of Clinical Psychology, 30,* 131–138.

Zilberg, N. J., Weiss, D. S., & Horowitz, M. J. (1982). Impact of Event Scale: A cross-validation study and some empirical evidence supporting a conceptual model of stress response syndromes. *Journal of Consulting and Clinical Psychology, 50,* 407–414.

CHAPTER 14

The Peritraumatic Dissociative Experiences Questionnaire

CHARLES R. MARMAR
DANIEL S. WEISS
THOMAS J. METZLER

EMPIRICAL STUDIES OF TRAUMA AND DISSOCIATION: A BRIEF OVERVIEW

The past decade has witnessed an intense reawakening of interest in the study of trauma and dissociation. In particular, the contributions of Janet, which had been largely eclipsed by developments within modern ego psychology, have enjoyed a resurgence of interest. Putnam (1989a), and van der Kolk and van der Hart (1989a, 1989b) have provided a contemporary reinterpretation of the contributions of Janet to the understanding of traumatic stress and dissociation.

Paralleling the resurgence of interest in theoretical studies of trauma and dissociation, there has been a proliferation of research studies addressing the relationship of trauma and general dissociative tendencies. Hilgard (1970) observed that students rated as highly hypnotizable reported more frequent histories of childhood punishment than their low-hypnotizability peers. She speculated that a heightened hypnotic capacity might confer protection against reexperiencing painful childhood memories. Chu and Dill (1990) reported that psychiatric patients with a history of childhood abuse reported higher levels of dissociative symptoms than those without histories of childhood abuse. Carlson and Rosser-Hogan (1991), in a study of Cambodian refugees, reported a strong relationship between the amount of trauma the refugees had experienced and the severity of both traumatic stress response and dissociative reactions. Spiegel and Cardeña (1991) reviewed studies linking traumatic stress response and general dissociative tendencies, and reported the following:

1. Retrospective studies support a strong relationship between early physical or sexual abuse and later dissociative phenomenology.
2. Repeated and severe childhood abuse is more strongly associated with adult dissociative phenomena than are isolated instances of abuse.
3. Dissociation at the time of childhood trauma may be a mechanism to cope with overwhelming traumatic events.
4. Adults with posttraumatic stress disorder (PTSD) have higher levels of hypnotizability than adults patients without PTSD.

Following on Hilgard's original observations concerning trauma and hypnotizability, Stutman and Bliss (1985) reported in a nonpatient population that veterans who had high levels of PTSD symptoms were more hypnotizable than their counterpart veterans who were low in PTSD symptoms. Spiegel, Hunt, and Dondershine (1988) compared the hypnotizability of Vietnam combat veterans with PTSD to patients with generalized anxiety disorders, affective disorders, and schizophrenia, as well as to a normal comparison group. The group with PTSD was found to have hypnotizability scores that were higher than both the psychopathological and normal controls. Hypnotizability scores in childhood have been shown to have stable trait-like characteristics, raising the possibility that traumatized individuals with higher levels of pretrauma-exposure hypnotizability may be more prone to developing PTSD. It is also possible that chronic PTSD results in changes in level of hypnotizability. Prospective studies are required to disentangle these possibilities.

Recent empirical studies have supported a strong relationship among trauma, dissociation, and personality disturbances. Herman, Perry, and van der Kolk (1989) found a high prevalence of traumatic histories in patients with borderline personality disorder. Level of adult dissociative symptoms was better predicted by childhood traumatic history than even the borderline diagnostic status. Ogata et al. (1990), in a study of trauma and dissociation in borderline personality disorder, found a higher frequency of childhood abuse in borderline personality disorder subjects than in depressed controls.

A profound relationship has been reported for childhood trauma and multiple personality disorder (MPD). In discussing the causes of MPD, Kluft (1993) proposes a four-factor theory: (1) inherent capacity to dissociate, (2) traumatic life experiences that overwhelm the adaptational capacities of the child to utilize nondissociative defenses, (3) the role of the environment in shaping the development of fragmented aspects of personality development, and (4) an inadequate availability of restorative experiences by protective others. Kluft proposes that the dissociative processes that underlie multiple personality development continue to serve a defensive function for individuals who have neither the external or internal resources to cope with traumatic experiences. Coons and Milstein (1986) reported that 85% of a series of 20 MPD patients had documented allegations of childhood abuse. Similar observations have been made by Frischolz (1985) and Putnam, Guroff, Silberman, Barban, and Post (1986), who reported rates of severe childhood abuse as high as 90% in patients with MPD. The nature of the childhood trauma in many of these cases is notable for its severity, multiple elements of physical and sexual abuse, threats to life, bizarre elements, and profound rupture of the sense of safely and trust when the perpetrator is a primary caretaker or other close relationship.

PERITRAUMATIC DISSOCIATION: ACUTE DISSOCIATIVE RESPONSES TO TRAUMA

The studies reviewed clearly demonstrate the relationship between traumatic life experience and general dissociative response. One fundamental aspect of the dissociative response to trauma concerns immediate dissociation *at the time the traumatic event is unfolding*. Trauma victims, not uncommonly, will report alterations in the experience of time, place, and person, which confer a sense of unreality to the event as it is occurring. Dissociation during trauma may take the form of altered time sense, with time being experienced as slowing down or rapidly accelerated; profound feelings of unreality that the event is occurring, or that the individual is the victim of the event; experiences of depersonalization; out-of-body experiences; bewilderment, confusion, and disorientation; altered pain perception; altered body image or feelings of disconnection from one's body; tunnel vision; and other experiences reflecting immediate dissociative responses to trauma. We have designated these acute dissociative responses to trauma as peritraumatic dissociation (Marmar et al., 1994b; Marmar, Weiss, Metzler, Ronfeldt, & Foreman, 1996b; Weiss, Marmar, Metzler, & Ronfeldt, 1995).

Although actual clinical reports of peritraumatic dissociation date back nearly a century, systematic investigation has occurred more recently. Spiegel (1993) reviewed studies of detachment experiences at the time of trauma, one feature of peritraumatic dissociation. Noyes and Kletti (1977) surveyed 101 survivors of automobile accidents and physical assault. They reported feelings of unreality and altered experience of the passage of time during the event in 72% of participants, automatic movement in 57%, sense of detachment in 52%, depersonalization in 56%, reported detachment from the body in 34%, and derealization in 30%. Hillman (1981) reported on the experiences of 14 correctional officers held hostage during a violent prison riot. The hostage victims described employing dissociative perceptual alterations to cope with the terror and pain of their experience, including time distortion and psychogenic anesthesia to protect against overwhelming pain. Wilkinson (1983) investigated the psychological responses of survivors of the Hyatt Regency Hotel skywalk collapse in which 114 people died and 200 were injured. Survivors commonly reported depersonalization and derealization experiences at the time of the structural collapse. Siegel (1984) studied 31 kidnapping and terrorist hostages, and reported that during the hostage experience, 25.8% experienced alterations in body imagery and sensations, depersonalization, and disorientation, and 12.9% experienced out-of-body experiences.

Holen (1993), in a long-term prospective study of survivors of a North Sea oil rig disaster, found that the level of reported dissociation during the trauma was a predictor of subsequent PTSD. Cardeña and Spiegel (1993) reported on the responses of 100 graduate students from two different institutions in the Bay Area following the 1989 Loma Prieta earthquake. At the time the earthquake was occurring, the participants reported experiencing derealization and depersonalization; time distortion; and alterations in cognition, memory, and somatic sensations. These results suggest that among nonclinical populations, exposure to catastrophic stress may trigger *transient dissociative phenomena*. Koopman, Classen, and Spiegel (1994) investigated predictors of posttraumatic stress symptoms among survivors of the 1991 Oakland Hills fire storm. In a study of 187 participants, dissociative symptoms at the time the firestorm was occurring more strongly predicted subsequent posttraumatic symptoms than did anxiety and the subjective experience of loss of personal autonomy.

These independently replicated clinical and research findings point toward an important vulnerability role for *peritraumatic dissociation* as a risk factor for subsequent PTSD. These findings were at first surprising, given the prevailing clinical belief that dissociative responses to trauma at the time of occurrence of life-threatening or otherwise terrifying events conferred a sense of distance and safety to the victim. For example, an adult survivor of childhood incest reported that during the experience of being sexually abused, she would leave her body and view the assault from above, with a feeling of detachment and compassion for the helpless little child who was being sexually assaulted. Although the use of out-of-body and other peritraumatic dissociative responses at the time of traumatic stress occurrence may defend against even more catastrophic states of helplessness and terror, dissociation at the time of trauma is one of the most important risk factors for the subsequent development of chronic PTSD. Possible causal relationships between peritraumatic dissociation and the heightened risk for PTSD are discussed in the section of this chapter addressing mechanisms underlying peritraumatic dissociation.

THE PERITRAUMATIC DISSOCIATIVE EXPERIENCES QUESTIONNAIRE: A PROPOSED MEASURE OF ACUTE DISSOCIATIVE RESPONSES TO TRAUMA

Based on the important clinical and early research observations on peritraumatic dissociation as a risk factor for chronic PTSD, we embarked on a series of studies to develop a reliable and valid measure of peritraumatic dissociation. We designate this measure the Peritraumatic Dissociative Experiences Questionnaire (PDEQ; Marmar, Weiss, Metzler, & Delucchi, 1996b). The first version of the PDEQ was a rater version, consisting of nine items addressing dissociative experiences *at the time the traumatic event was occurring:* (1) moments of losing track or blanking out; (2) finding the self acting on "automatic pilot"; (3) a sense of time changing during the event; (4) the event seeming unreal, as in a dream or play; (5) feeling as if floating above the scene; (6) feeling disconnected from body or body distortion; (7) confusion as to what was happening to the self and others; (8) not being aware of things that happened during the event that normally would have been noticed; and (9) not feeling pain associated with physical injury.

In a first study with the PDEQ, the relationship of peritraumatic dissociation and posttraumatic stress was investigated in male Vietnam theater veterans (Marmar et al., 1994b). Two hundred and fifty-one male Vietnam theater veterans from the Clinical Examination Component of the National Vietnam Veterans Readjustment Study were examined to determine the relationship of war-zone stress exposure, retrospective reports of dissociation during the most disturbing combat trauma events, and general dissociative tendencies with PTSD case determination. Peritraumatic dissociation was assessed with a rater version of the PDEQ. Total score on the PDEQ was strongly associated with level of posttraumatic stress symptoms, level of stress exposure, and general dissociative tendencies.

Total PDEQ score was weakly associated with general psychopathology as assessed by the 10 clinical scales of the MMPI-2. Logistical regression analyses supported the incremental value of dissociation during trauma, over and above the contributions of level of war-zone stress exposure and general dissociative tendencies, in accounting for PTSD case determination. These results provided initial support for the reliability and validity of the rater version of the PDEQ, and for a trauma–dissociation linkage hypothesis: The greater the dissociation during traumatic stress exposure, the greater the likelihood of meeting criteria for current PTSD.

In a first replication of this finding, the relationship of peritraumatic dissociation with symptomatic distress was determined in emergency services personnel exposed to traumatic critical incidents (Weiss, Marmar, Metzler, & Ronfeldt, in press; Marmar et al., 1996b). A total of 367 emergency services personnel who had responded to either a large-scale mass disaster operation or smaller critical incident were investigated, including police, firefighters, EMT/paramedics, and California Department of Transportation workers. One hundred and fifty-four of the EMS workers had been involved in the 1989 Interstate–880 Nimitz Freeway collapse that occurred during the Loma Prieta earthquake. A variety of predictors of current symptomatic distress were measured, including level of critical-incident exposure, social support, psychological traits, locus of control, general dissociative tendencies, and peritraumatic dissociation. Findings demonstrated that level of current symptomatic distress were positively associated with degree of exposure to the critical incident, and negatively associated with level of adjustment. After controlling for both exposure and adjustment, symptomatic distress could still for the most part be predicted by social support, experience on the job, locus of control, general dissociative tendencies, and dissociative experiences at the time of the critical incident. The two dissociative variables, total score on the Dissociative Experience Scale (DES; Bernstein & Putnam, 1986), and total score on the PDEQ, were strongly predictive of symptomatic response, even after controlling for exposure, adjustment, and the three other predictors. This study added further support to the growing body of literature linking dissociative tendencies and experiences to distress as a result of exposure to traumatic stressors.

In a second replication, the relationship of peritraumatic dissociation and posttraumatic stress was investigated in female Vietnam theater veterans (Tichenor, Marmar, Weiss, Metzler, & Ronfeldt, 1994). Part of the impetus for this study was to assess the relationship of peritraumatic dissociation with posttraumatic stress response in a female sample, as the two earlier studies focused primarily on male participants. Seventy-seven female Vietnam theater veterans were investigated using the rater version of the PDEQ. Total score on the PDEQ was found to be associated strongly with posttraumatic stress symptomatology, as measured by the Impact of Event Scale, and also positively associated with level of stress exposure and general dissociative tendencies, the latter measured by the DES. Scores on the PDEQ were unassociated with general psychiatric symptomatology, as assessed by the 10 clinical scales of the MMPI-2. As in the two earlier studies, PDEQ scores were predictive of posttraumatic stress symptoms above and beyond the level of stress exposure and general dissociative tendencies. The findings provide further support for the reliability and validity of the PDEQ, and provide additional support for a linkage between trauma and dissociation, replicating the earlier findings with male Vietnam War veterans and emergency services personnel.

Most recently we have investigated the relationship of peritraumatic dissociation with current posttraumatic stress response in participants exposed to the 1994 Los Angeles area Northridge earthquake (Marmar, Weiss, Metzler, & Ronfeldt, 1994a). The sample comprised 60 adult men and women who had lived close to the epicenter of the earthquake and were working for a large private insurance company. A self-report version of the PDEQ was used to assess dissociation at the time of the earthquake occurrence. As in the earlier studies with male and female veterans and emergency services personnel, reports of dissociation at the time of the traumatic event were predictive of current posttraumatic stress response symptoms, after controlling for the level of exposure.

Across the four studies, the PDEQ has been demonstrated to be internally consistent, strongly associated with measures of traumatic stress response, strongly associated with a measure of general dissociative tendencies, strongly associated with level of stress exposure, and unassociated with measures of general psychopathology. These studies support the reliability and convergent, discriminant, and predictive validity of the PDEQ. Strengthening these findings are two independent studies utilizing the PDEQ by investigators in other PTSD research programs. Bremner and colleagues (1992), utilizing selective items from the PDEQ as part of a measure of peritraumatic dissociation, reported a strong relationship of peritraumatic dissociation with posttraumatic stress response in an independent sample of Vietnam War veterans. In the first prospective study with the PDEQ, Shalev, Peri, Schreiber, and Caneti (1996) examined the relationship of PDEQ ratings gathered in the first week following trauma exposure with posttraumatic stress symptomatology at 5 months. In this study of acute-physical-trauma victims admitted to an Israeli teaching hospital emergency room, PDEQ ratings at 1 week predicted stress symptomatology at 5 months, over and above exposure levels, social supports, and Impact of Event Scale scores in the first week. This study is noteworthy in that it is the first finding with the PDEQ in which ratings were gathered prospectively. Retrospective ratings of peritraumatic dissociation months, years, or decades after the occurrence of traumatic events are subject to the bias that greater current distress may result in greater recollection of dissociation at the time of traumatic stress occurrence. Shalev and colleagues' findings are therefore important in supporting the use of retrospective ratings of peritraumatic dissociation.

MECHANISMS FOR PERITRAUMATIC DISSOCIATION: PSYCHOBIOLOGICAL DYNAMICS

The strong, replicated findings relating peritraumatic dissociation with subsequent PTSD raise theoretically important questions concerning the mechanisms that underlie peritraumatic dissociation. Speculation concerning psychological factors underlying trauma-related dissociation date back to the early contributions of Breuer and Freud (1895/1955). In their formulation, traumatic events are actively split off from conscious experience but return in the disguised form of symptoms. The dissociated complexes have an underground psychological life, causing hysterics to "suffer mainly from reminiscences." Janet (1889) proposed that trauma-related dissociation occurred in individuals with a fundamental constitutional defect in psychological functioning, which he designated *la misère psychologique*. Janet proposed that normal individuals have sufficient psychological energy to bind together their mental experiences, including the memories, cognitions, sensations, feelings, and volition, into an integrated synthetic whole under the control of a single personal self with access to conscious experience (Nemiah, in press). From Janet's perspective, peritraumatic dissociation resulted in the coexistence within a single individual of two or more discrete, dissociative streams of consciousness, each existing independently from the others, each with rich mental contents, including feelings, memories, and bodily sensations, and each with access to conscious experience at different times.

Contemporary psychological studies of peritraumatic dissociation have focused on individual differences in the threshold for dissociation. Adult trauma victims who dissociate during their trauma may have experienced childhood or adolescent traumatic events that lower their threshold for dissociation. It is also possible that the threshold for peritraumatic dissociation or generalized dissociative vulnerability is a hereditable trait, aggravated by early trauma exposure and correlated with hypnotizability, as suggested by Spiegel and colleagues (1988). Hypnosis has been conceptualized as a structured and controlled form of dissociation (Nemiah, 1985; Spiegel & Spiegel, 1978). Three critical elements to the hypnotic experience—absorption, compartmentalization of experience, and suggestibility—share much in common with the clinical phenomena of trauma-related dissociation. Further supporting the linkage between hypnotizability and trauma-related dissociation are the findings of Stutman and Bliss (1985), who found greater hypnotizability in nonpatient veterans who were high in PTSD symptoms when compared with nonpatient veterans who were low in PTSD symptoms. Spiegel and colleagues (1988) compared patients with schizophrenia, generalized anxiety disorder, affective disorders, and PTSD, and found that the PTSD group had higher hypnotizability scores than those of the other groups and normal controls. In a recent investigation of hypnotizability, clinical dissociation, and trauma in sexually abused girls and control subjects, Putnam, Helmers, Horowitz, and Trickett (1995) reported a positive association of hypnotizability and clinical dissociation in the trauma victims but not in the control subjects. This study suggests that high hypnotizability alone, in the absence of trauma, is not a sufficient condition for high levels of dissociation. Taken together, the studies on trauma, dissociation, and hypnotizability suggest that individuals who are constitutionally predisposed to be highly hypnotizable and additionally experience trauma early in life are those with greatest vulnerability to subsequent dissociation at the time of threat. Further research is required to determine whether Janet's speculation of a genetically determined weakness in the capacity to bind and integrate psychological information may be related to a genetically determined increase in hypnotizability.

A second line of investigation concerning the underlying mechanisms for peritraumatic dissociation focuses on the neurobiology and neuropharmacology of anxiety. A study by Southwick and colleagues (1993) with yohimbine challenges suggests that in individuals with traumatic stress disorder flashbacks occur in the context of high-threat arousal states. It is also significant that panic-disordered patients frequently report dissociative reactions at the height of their anxiety attacks (Krystal, Woods, Hill, & Charney, 1991). The effects of yohimbine in triggering flashbacks in PTSD patients and panic attacks in patients with panic disorder is mediated by a central catecholamine mechanism, as yohimbine serves as an alpha-adrenergic receptor antagonist, resulting in increased firing of locus ceruleus neurons. These observations suggest that the relationship between peritraumatic dissociation and PTSD may, for some individuals, be mediated by high levels of anxiety during the trauma. The possibility that panic-level states of anxious arousal may trigger dissociation in some individuals is consistent with the Moleman, van der Hart, and van der Kolk (1992) report on the general relationship of high arousal and dissociation.

Marmar et al. (1996a) reported on individual differences in the level of peritraumatic dissociation during critical-incident exposure in emergency services personnel. They found the following factors to be associated with greater levels of peritraumatic dissociation: younger age; higher levels of exposure during critical incident; greater subjective perceived threat at the time of critical incident; poorer general psychological adjustment; poorer identity formation; lower levels of ambition and prudence, as defined by the Hogan Personality Inventory; greater external locus of control; and greater use of escape/avoidance and emotional self-control coping. Taken together these findings suggest that emergency services personnel with less work experience, more vulnerable personality structures, higher subjective levels of perceived threat and anxiety at the time of incidence occurrence, greater reliance on the external world for an internal sense of safety and security, and greater use of maladaptive coping strategies are more vulnerable to peritraumatic dissociation.

In order to disentangle cause-and-effect relations in trauma–dissociation linkage, future studies are required that *prospectively* examine dissociative tendencies in populations that are subsequently exposed to trauma. In addition, family history, twin studies, cross-fostering studies, and biological marker studies will be required to determine if peritraumatic and general dissociative tendencies are characteristics that are inherited or learned early in life. Alternatively, it remains to be demonstrated whether trauma determines greater vulnerability to dissociative responses, both generally and specifically, with respect to peritraumatic responses. It will also be of interest to determine what factors protect against peritraumatic dissociation and determine prospectively if such resilience factors reduce the risk of developing subsequent PTSD.

TREATMENT OF TRAUMA-RELATED DISSOCIATION

To date, no controlled clinical trials have been reported of psychosocial or pharmacological intervention specifically targeting trauma-related dissociation. Kluft (1993), in an overview of clinical reports on treatment approaches for trauma-related dissociation, recommends individual, supportive–expressive psychodynamic psychotherapy, augmented as needed with hypnosis or drug-facilitated interviews. For the treatment of the most severe form of trauma-related dissociation, multiple personality disorder, Kluft

(1993), drawing on the work of Braun (1986) and Putnam (1989b), outlines nine stages of a supportive–expressive, psychodynamically informed treatment:

1. Establishing a therapeutic alliance involving the creation of a safe atmosphere and a secure treatment frame to establish trust and realistic optimism.
2. Preliminary interventions designed to gain access to the more readily reached dissociative aspects of personality, including the establishment of agreements with the alters against terminating treatment abruptly, self-harm, or other self-defeating behaviors.
3. History gathering and mapping of the nature and relationship among alters to define the constellation of personalities.
4. Metabolism of the trauma, which includes the access to and processing of traumatic events related to the development of MPD.
5. Movements toward integration and resolution across the alters by facilitating cooperation, communication, and mutual awareness.
6. Integration–resolution, involving a smooth collaboration among the alters.
7. Learning new coping skills to manage stress without resorting to dissociation.
8. Solidification of gains in working through in the transference, including the management of anxiety related to conflicted sexual, aggressive, and dependency issues as they arise in the relationship with the therapist.
9. Follow-up to assess the stability of the outcome and address new layers of personality that have not emerged in the prior treatment.

Spiegel (1993) proposes eight "C" principles for the psychotherapy of individuals experiencing acute traumatic–dissociative reactions:

1. *Confrontation* with the trauma to counter depersonalization and derealization.
2. *Condensation* of the traumatic experience in the form of the reconstruction of the memory of the traumatic event, including the technical use of hypnosis to relive the experiences and address psychogenic amnesia.
3. *Confession* to address shame and guilt.
4. *Consolation,* an appropriate expression of sympathy for the tragic circumstances that the patient has experienced.
5. *Consciousness,* the bringing into conscious awareness, without dissociation, of the traumatic memories and associated feelings.
6. *Concentration,* the use of hypnosis and self-hypnosis to help the patient gain conscious control over disturbing memories.
7. *Control,* the further management of memories and associated affects

through flexible experiencing and suppression of traumatic memories rather than dissociation.

8. *Congruence,* the integration of traumatic memories into preexisting self-concepts.

A number of investigators have advocated the use of hypnosis as adjunct to the treatment of trauma related dissociation. In 1993, van der Hart and Spiegel advocated the use of hypnosis as a way of creating a safe, calm mental state in which the patient has control over traumatic memories, as an approach to the treatment of trauma-induced dissociative states presenting as hysterical psychosis. Batson (1994), in the treatment of MPD, advocated the use of hypnosis to create a safe retreat from the terrifying circumstances surrounding trauma. Under hypnosis, the patient can go back to a childhood environment that was associated with safety and security, and utilize this safe haven as a nucleus around which to build and integrate previously dissociative aspects of the self. Batson, in agreement with Spiegel and Kluft, emphasized the patients' growing control over the transitions in their dissociative mental states, allowing for retreat from terror and gradual integration.

Contemporary psychodynamic approaches to the treatment of trauma-related dissociation emphasize the establishment of the therapeutic alliance, reconstruction of traumatic memories, working through of problematic weak and strong self-concepts activated by the trauma, and transference interpretation aimed at helping the patient process perceived threats in the relationship with the therapist without resorting to dissociation (Horowitz, 1986; Marmar, 1991; Steinman, 1994). Contemporary psychoanalytic theory emphasizes the complementarity of traumatic and structural models (Nemiah, in press). The traumatic model addresses the fractionation of the ego into multiple dissociative elements, the pathological use of dissociation as a defense, and the abreaction and integration of dissociated traumatic memories. As the previously dissociative elements are brought in to a more coherent self, Gabbard (1994) advocates the further use of traditional psychodynamic psychotherapy to solidify gains, mourn losses, and resolve conflicts trough interpretation.

FUTURE RESEARCH DIRECTIONS AND PRACTICAL CLINICAL APPLICATIONS OF THE PDEQ

Future research will clarify the relationship among subjective threat appraisal, emotional distress at the time of trauma occurrence, peritraumatic dissociation, activation of central nervous system structures that regulate threat arousal, and psychophysiological arousal in the peripheral nervous system. Trauma victims can be challenged by reminders of their traumatic events and assessed for level of peritraumatic dissociation and changes in central nervous system activity, determined with brain imaging procedures; event-related potential; and peripheral psychophysiological assessment.

Specific treatment interventions for peritraumatic dissociation, and dissociative responses that occur in the course of uncovering traumatic memories, will depend upon rapid identification of those experiencing peritraumatic dissociation and advances in the understanding of the psychological and neurobiological factors underlying trauma-related dissociation. The PDEQ can be used to screen for acute dissociative responses at the time of traumatic stress exposure. From a neuropharmacological point of view, Pitman (personal communication, 1994) has advocated the use of medications to lower threat arousal levels at the time of traumatic occurrence. Alpha^2-adrenergic agonists, beta-blockers, or other nonsedating, antiarousal agents could be provided to emergency services personnel to aid in the modulation of arousal responses to life-threatening or gruesome exposure. Advances in critical-incident stress-debriefing procedures may lead to psychological interventions that lower immediate threat appraisal and consequently reduce the likelihood of sustained peritraumatic dissociation. The PDEQ can be used to determine the effectiveness of novel pharmacological or psychotherapeutic interventions in reducing acute dissociative response to trauma.

The PDEQ can additionally be used as part of a standard assessment battery for individuals presenting with acute or chronic PTSD symptoms. Higher PDEQ scores in acute trauma victims support the need for active intervention. Higher PDEQ scores in those individuals presenting years to decades following traumatic exposure support the validity of subjective complaints of PTSD, and also alert the clinician to the risks for reentry into dissociative states during the uncovering phase of psychotherapy. The current 10-item self-report and clinician versions of the PDEQ are included as appendices to this chapter.

APPENDIX A: PERITRAUMATIC DISSOCIATIVE EXPERIENCES QUESTIONNAIRE— SELF-REPORT VERSION

Instructions: Please complete the items below by circling the choice that best describes your experiences and reactions *during the* _____ *and immediately afterward.* If an item does not apply to your experience, please circle "Not at all true."

1. I had moments of losing track of what was going on—I "blanked out" or "spaced out" or in some way felt that I was not part of what was going on.

1	2	3	4	5
Not at all true	Slightly true	Somewhat true	Very true	Extremely true

2. I found that I was on "automatic pilot"—I ended up doing things that I later realized I hadn't actively decided to do.

1	2	3	4	5
Not at all true	Slightly true	Somewhat true	Very true	Extremely true

3. My sense of time changed—things seemed to be happening in slow motion.

1	2	3	4	5
Not at all true	Slightly true	Somewhat true	Very true	Extremely true

4. What was happening seemed unreal to me, like I was in a dream or watching a movie or play.

1	2	3	4	5
Not at all true	Slightly true	Somewhat true	Very true	Extremely true

5. I felt as though I were a spectator watching what was happening to me, as if I were floating above the scene or observing it as an outsider.

1	2	3	4	5
Not at all true	Slightly true	Somewhat true	Very true	Extremely true

6. There were moments when my sense of my own body seemed distorted or changed. I felt disconnected from my own body, or that it was unusually large or small.

1	2	3	4	5
Not at all true	Slightly true	Somewhat true	Very true	Extremely true

7. I felt as though things that were actually happening to others were happening to me—like I was being trapped when I really wasn't.

1	2	3	4	5
Not at all true	Slightly true	Somewhat true	Very true	Extremely true

8. I was surprised to find out afterward that a lot of things had happened at the time that I was not aware of, especially things I ordinarily would have noticed.

1	2	3	4	5
Not at all true	Slightly true	Somewhat true	Very true	Extremely true

9. I felt confused; that is, there were moments when I had difficulty making sense of what was happening.

1	2	3	4	5
Not at all true	Slightly true	Somewhat true	Very true	Extremely true

10. I felt disoriented; that is, there were moments when I felt uncertain about where I was or what time it was.

1	2	3	4	5
Not at all true	Slightly true	Somewhat true	Very true	Extremely true

APPENDIX B: PERITRAUMATIC DISSOCIATIVE EXPERIENCES QUESTIONNAIRE—RATER VERSION

Instructions: I'd like you to try to recall as best you can how you felt and what you experienced at the time [most upsetting event] happened, including how you felt the few minutes just before. Now, I'm going to ask you some specific questions about how you felt *at that time*.

[*Note.* DK = Don't know, 01 = Absent or false, 02 = Subthreshold, 03 = Threshold.]

1. (At that time) Did you have moments of losing track of what was going on: that is, did you "blank out," "space out," or in some other way not feel that you were part of the experience?   DK 01 02 03

2. (At that time) Did you find yourself going on "automatic pilot," that is, doing something that you later realized you had done but hadn't actively decided to do?   DK 01 02 03

3. (At that time) Did your sense of time change during the event; that is, did things seem unusually speeded up or slowed down?   DK 01 02 03

4. (At that time) Did what was happening seem unreal to you, as though you were in a dream or watching a movie or a play?   DK 01 02 03

5. (At that time) Were there moments when you felt as though you were a spectator watching what was happening to you—for example, did you feel as if you were floating above the scene or observing it as an outsider?   DK 01 02 03

6. (At that time) Were there moments when your sense of your own body seemed distorted or changed—that is, did you feel yourself to be unusually large or small, or did you feel disconnected from your body?   DK 01 02 03

7. (At that time) Did you get the feeling that something that was happening to someone else was happening to you? For example, if you saw someone being injured, did you feel as though you were the one being injured, even though that was not the case?   DK 01 02 03

8. Were you surprised to find out after the event that a   DK   01   02   03
lot of things had happened at the time that you were
not aware of, especially things that you felt you ordinarily would have noticed?

9. (At that time) Were there moments when you had dif-   DK   01   02   03
ficulty making sense of what was happening?

10. (At that time) Did you feel disoriented, that is, were there   DK   01   02   03
moments when you felt uncertain about where you were
or what time it was?

REFERENCES

Braun, B. G. (1986). Issues in the psychotherapy of multiple personality. In B. G. Braun (Ed.), *Treatment of multiple personality disorder* (pp. 1–28). Washington, DC: American Psychiatric Press.

Batson, R. (1994, November). *Treatment of trauma related dissociation.* Paper presented at the 10th annual meeting of the International Society for Traumatic Stress Studies, Chicago, IL.

Bernstein, E. M., & Putnam, F. W. (1986). Development, reliability, and validity of a dissociation scale. *Journal of Nervous and Mental Diseases, 174,* 727–735.

Bremner, J. D., Southwick, S., Brett, E., Fontana, A., Rosenheck, R., & Charney, D. S. (1992). Dissociation and posttraumatic stress disorder in Vietnam combat veterans. *American Journal of Psychiatry, 149,* 328–332.

Breuer, J., & Freud, S. (1955). Studies on hysteria. In J. Strachey (Ed. and Trans.), *The standard edition of the complete psychological works of Sigmund Freud* (Vol. 2). London: Hogarth Press. (Original work published 1895)

Cardeña, E., & Spiegel, D. (1993). Dissociative reactions to the San Francisco Bay Area Earthquake of 1989. *American Journal of Psychiatry, 150,* 474–478.

Carlson, E. B., & Rosser-Hogan, R. (1991). Trauma experiences, posttraumatic stress, dissociation, and depression in Cambodian refugees. *American Journal of Psychiatry, 148,* 1548–1551.

Chu, J. A., & Dill, D. L. (1990). Dissociative symptoms in relation to childhood physical and sexual abuse. *American Journal of Psychiatry, 147,* 887–892.

Coons, P. M., & Milstein, V. (1986). Psychosexual disturbances in multiple personality. *Journal of Nervous and Mental Disease, 47,* 106–110.

Frischolz, E. J. (1985). The relationship among dissociation, hypnosis, and child abuse in the development of multiple personality disorder. In R. P. Kluft (Ed.), *Childhood antecedents of multiple personality* (pp. 99–126). Washington, DC: American Psychiatric Press.

Gabbard, G. O. (1994). *Psychodynamic psychiatry in clinical practice: The DSM-IV edition.* Washington, DC: American Psychiatric Press.

Herman, J. L., Perry, J. C., & van der Kolk, B. A. (1989). Childhood trauma in borderline personality disorder. *American Journal of Psychiatry, 146,* 490–495.

Hilgard, E. R. (1970). *Personality and hypnosis: A study of imaginative involvement.* Chicago: University of Chicago Press.

Hillman, R. G. (1981). The psychopathology of being held hostage. *American Journal of Psychiatry, 138,* 1193–1197.

Holen, A. (1993). The North Sea Oil Rig Disaster. In J. P. Wilson & B. Raphael (Eds.), *International handbook of traumatic stress syndromes*. New York: Plenum Press.

Horowitz, M. J. (1986). *Stress response syndromes* (2nd ed.). Northvale, NJ: Jason Aronson.

Janet, P. (1889). *L'automatisme psychologique*. Paris: Ballière.

Kluft, R. P. (1993). Multiple personality disorder. In D. Spiegel, R. P. Kluft, M. D. Loewenstein, J. C. Nemiah, F. W. Putnam, & M. Steinberg (Eds.), *Dissociative disorders: A clinical review*. Lutherville, MD: Sidran Press.

Koopman, C., Classen, C., & Spiegel, D. (1994). Predictors of posttraumatic stress symptoms among survivors of the Oakland/Berkeley, California, Firestorm. *American Journal of Psychiatry, 151, 888*–894.

Krystal, J., Woods, S., Hill, C., & Charney, D. S. (1991). Characteristics of panic attack subtypes: Assessment of spontaneous panic, situational panic, sleep panic, and limited symptom attacks. *Comparative Psychiatry, 32,* 474–480.

Marmar, C. R. (1991). Brief dynamic psychotherapy of post-traumatic stress disorder. *Psychiatric Annals, 21,* 404–414.

Marmar, C. R., Weiss, D. S., Metzler, T. J., & Delucchi, K. (1996a). Characteristics of emergency services personnel related to peritraumatic dissociation during critical incident exposure. *American Journal of Psychiatry, 153,* 94–102.

Marmar, C. R., Weiss, D. S., Metzler, T. J., & Ronfeldt, H. M. (1994a, January). *Peritraumatic dissociation and posttraumatic stress after the Northridge earthquake.* Paper presented at the Anxiety Disorders of America annual meeting, Santa Monica, CA.

Marmar, C. R., Weiss, D. S., Metzler, T. J., Ronfeldt, H. M., & Foreman, C. (1996b). Stress responses of emergency services personnel to the Loma Prieta earthquake Interstate 880 freeway collapse and control traumatic incidents. *Journal of Traumatic Stress, 9,* 63–85.

Marmar, C. R., Weiss, D. S., Schlenger, W. E., Fairbank, J. A., Jordan, B. K., Kulka, R. A., & Hough, R. L. (1994b). Peritraumatic dissociation and posttraumatic stress in male Vietnam theater veterans. *American Journal of Psychiatry, 151,* 902–907.

Moleman, N., van der Hart, O., & van der Kolk, B. A. (1992). Dissociation and hypnotizability in posttraumatic stress disorder. *Journal of Nervous and Mental Disease, 180,* 271–272.

Nemiah, J. C. (1985). Dissociative disorders. In H. I. Kaplan & B. J. Sadock (Eds.), *Comprehensive textbook of psychiatry* (4th ed., pp. 942–957). Baltimore: Williams & Wilkins.

Nemiah, J. C. (in press). Early concepts of trauma, dissociation, and the unconscious: Their history and current implications. In D. Bremner & C. R. Marmar (Eds.), *Trauma, memory, and dissociation.*

Noyes, R., & Kletti, R. (1977). Depersonalization in response to life-threatening danger. *Comparative Psychiatry, 18,* 375–384.

Ogata, S. N., Silk, K. R., Goodrich, S., Lohr, N. E., Westen, D., & Hill, E. M. (1990). Childhood sexual and physical abuse in adult patients with borderline personality disorder. *American Journal of Psychiatry, 147,* 1008–1013.

Putnam, F. W. (1989a). Pierre Janet and modern views of dissociation. *Journal of Traumatic Stress, 2,* 413–429.

Putnam, F. W. (1989b). *The diagnosis and treatment of multiple personality disorder.* New York: Guilford Press.

Putnam, F. W., Batson, R., van der Kolk, B., Fine, C., & Marmar, C. M. (1994, November). *Treatment of PTSD: Implications of working with dissociative phenomena in the treat-*

ment of PTSD. Plenary symposium conducted at the Meeting of the International Society for Traumatic Stress Studies Chicago, IL.

Putnam, F. W., Guroff, J. J., Silberman, E. K., Barban, L., & Post, R. M. (1986). The clinical phenomenology of multiple personality disorder: Review of 100 recent cases. *Journal of Clinical Psychiatry, 47,* 285–293.

Putnam, F. W., Helmers, K., Horowitz, L.A., & Trickett, P. K. (1995). Hypnotizability and dissociativity in sexually abused girls. *Child Abuse and Neglect, 19,* 645–655.

Shalev, A., Peri, T., Schreiber, S., & Caneti, L. (1996). Predictors of PTSD in injured trauma survivors: A prospective study. *American Journal of Psychiatry, 153,* 219–225.

Siegel, R. K. (1984). Hostage hallucinations. *Journal of Nervous and Mental Disease, 172,* 264–272.

Southwick, S. M., Krystal, J. H., Morgan, C. A., Johnson, D., Nagy, L. M., Niculaou, A., Heninger, G. R., & Charney, D. S. (1993). Abnormal noradrenergic function in posttraumatic stress disorder. *Archives of General Psychiatry, 50,* 266–274.

Spiegel, D. (1993). Dissociation and trauma. In D. Spiegel (Ed.), *Dissociative disorders: A clinical review.* Lutherville, MD: Sidran Press.

Spiegel, D., & Cardeña, E. (1991). Disintegrated experience: The dissociative disorders revisited. *Journal of Abnormal Psychology, 100,* 366–378.

Spiegel, D., Hunt, T., & Dondershine, H. E. (1988). Dissociation and hypnotizability in posttraumatic stress disorder. *American Journal of Psychiatry, 145,* 301–305.

Spiegel, H., & Spiegel, D. (1978). *Trance and treatment: Clinical uses of hypnosis.* New York: Basic Books.

Steinman, I. (1994, November). *Psychodynamic treatment of multiple personality disorder.* Paper presented at the 10th annual meeting of the International Society for Traumatic Stress Studies, Chicago, IL.

Stutman, R. K., & Bliss, E. L. (1985). Posttraumatic stress disorder, hypnotizability, and imagery. *American Journal of Psychiatry, 142,* 741–743.

Tichenor, V., Marmar, C. R., Weiss, D. S., Metzler, T. J., & Ronfeldt, H. M. (in press). The relationship of peritraumatic dissociation and posttraumatic stress: Findings in female Vietnam theater veterans. *Journal of Consulting and Clinical Psychology.*

van der Hart, O., & Spiegel, D. (1993). Hypnotic assessment and treatment of trauma-induced psychoses: The early psychotherapy of H. Breukink and modern views. *International Journal of Clinical and Experimental Hypnosis, 41,* 191–209.

van der Kolk, B. A., & van der Hart, O. (1989a). Pierre Janet on posttraumatic stress. *Journal of Traumatic Stress, 2,* 265–378.

van der Kolk, B. A., & van der Hart, O. (1989b). Pierre Janet and the breakdown of adaptation in psychological trauma. *American Journal of Psychiatry, 146,* 1530–1540.

Weiss, D. S., Marmar, C. R., Metzler, T. J., & Ronfeldt, H. M. (1995). Predicting symptomatic distress in emergency services personnel. *Journal of Consulting and Clinical Psychology, 63*(3), 361–368.

Wilkinson, C. B. (1983). Aftermath of a disaster: The collapse of the Hyatt Regency Hotel skywalks. *American Journal of Psychiatry, 140,* 1134–1139.

CHAPTER 15

Assessing Posttraumatic Dissociation with the Structured Clinical Interview for DSM-IV Dissociative Disorders

MARLENE STEINBERG

INTRODUCTION

Advances in the systematic assessment of dissociative symptoms and disorders have facilitated new research into these disorders and their relationship to posttraumatic stress disorder (PTSD). This development should be situated within the context of changes in diagnostic taxonomy and nomenclature. For over a century, both the dissociative disorders and PTSD have been recognized as posttraumatic syndromes but have been codified under different psychiatric classification since the first edition of the *Diagnostic and Statistical Manual of Mental Disorders* (DSM-I; American Psychiatric Association, 1952). From a historical perspective, the dissociative disorders and PTSD are syndromes that share a common sociotemporal context as well as overlapping symptomatology. In the classificatory schemes of the earliest diagnostic manuals, the dissociative disorders were lumped together under the rubric of "hysteria." With respect to PTSD, the early editions of DSM tended to regard what was then termed "gross stress reaction" as implying a premorbid condition in the patient. It was not until the social upheavals of the early 1970s that PTSD and the dissociative disorders emerged as fields of new interest and concern. The present edition of DSM (DSM-IV; American Psychiatric Association, 1994) has assigned a separate section to the dissociative disorders, while classifying PTSD and acute stress disorder as anxiety disorders. What is not clear from the present classificatory arrangement is the overlap in symptomatology and etiology.

As both the dissociative disorders and PTSD are posttraumatic syndromes, they have a number of features in common. The first is etiological. Patients diagnosed with PTSD or a dissociative disorder have histories of severe trauma. In the case of persons with dissociative identity disorder (MPD) the abuse is usually more chronic and repetitive. Second, both syndromes are marked by persistent time distortions; patients typically report disturbances of memory and temporal continuity. They may be amnesic for certain aspects of the trauma and hypermnesic for others. Alternately, they may have illusory versions or wishful fantasies of the past. Flashbacks, in which the patient relives the past trauma as if it were present reality, are a common form of temporal confusion in both patient populations (Steinberg, 1995). Third, the pacing of therapy for trauma survivors requires sensitive treatment of both cognitive and affective distortions. Many patients suffering from PTSD or a dissociative disorder have histories of dysfunction in both employment situations and interpersonal relationships because of their distorted cognitive skills and their emotional hyperreactivity. Kluft (1994) has described the result as "entrapment in a vicious cycle of maladaptive responses and behaviors" (p. 122).

Understandably, these common elements have led some researchers to propose that the dissociative disorders and PTSD belong in a common diagnostic category, or to postulate an integrative theory that would account for both syndromes. Some have hypothesized that PTSD and the dissociative disorders should be categorized as acute forms of pathological posttrauma adaptations (Wilson, 1994). Others have considered the possibility that PTSD is fundamentally a dissociative disturbance (Steinberg, 1995; DSM-III-R Work Group for the Dissociative Disorders).

PTSD AND DISSOCIATION

The link between trauma and dissociative symptoms has been noted by a number of researchers (Braun, 1990; Coons, Cole, Pellow, & Milstein, 1990; Fine, 1990; Kluft, 1988; Putnam, 1985; Spiegel, 1991; Steinberg, 1995; Terr, 1991). In fact, DSM-IV specifies dissociative symptoms within the criteria for both PTSD and acute stress disorder, a new diagnostic category also grouped with the anxiety disorders. In the case of acute stress disorder, Criterion B states that "the individual has at least three of the following dissociative symptoms: a subjective sense of numbing, detachment, or absence of emotional responsiveness; a reduction in awareness of his or her surroundings; derealization; depersonalization; or dissociative amnesia" (p. 429). For PTSD, Criterion B-3 stipulates that "the traumatic event is persistently reexperienced . . . [by] acting or feeling as if the traumatic event were recurring (includes a sense of reliving the experience, illusions, hallucinations, and dissociative flashback episodes, including those that occur on awakening or when intoxicated)" (p. 428). Criterion C-3 includes "persistent avoidance of stimuli associated with the trauma. . . . [including] inability to recall an important aspect of the trauma" (p. 428).

With respect to the dissociative disorders, chronic or repetitive trauma, usually inflicted in childhood, is implicated in the development of these syndromes. Kluft's (1984) four-factor theory holds that dissociative identity disorder (DID) develops in persons with (1) a biological capacity to dissociate; (2) overwhelming childhood experiences that cause their dissociative potential to evolve into an entrenched defensive process; (3) a number of normal or abnormal intrapsychic structures that incorporate dissociative processes in the formation of alter personalities; (4) an absence of countervailing protective, nurturing, or healing experiences with significant others. Also, it appears that the dissociative disorders, particularly DID and dissociative disorder not otherwise specified (DDNOS), represent profound changes in the patient's childhood self-structure, whereas PTSD does not invariably have such an impact (Wilson, 1994). This difference appears to be connected to the childhood origin of dissociative disturbances. Although Kluft (1985) has also noted that initial dissociative splits in the personality may be precipitated by extrafamilial or nonabusive trauma (e.g., severe illness, death of parent, war), the most common form of overwhelming stress in childhood is intrafamilial abuse.

On the other hand, PTSD may be produced by a wider variety of traumatic experiences. DSM-IV indicates that PTSD "can develop in individuals without any predisposing conditions, particularly if the stressor is especially extreme" (p. 427). For example, one study of Desert Storm veterans found that exposure to death and the handling of human remains may traumatize "psychologically robust persons" (Sutker, Uddo, Brailey, Allain, & Errara, 1994). It has also been observed that persons vary in their response to traumatic stressors, depending on a number of psychological, social, and situational variables, and that some individuals appear to be more vulnerable than others, either to traumatic experiences in general or to specific trauma. In addition, PTSD patients in the early stages of recovery are at risk for developing severe and chronic PTSD if they are subjected to additional or chronic stressors during this period.

In terms of diagnostic assessment, patients suffering from DID often have delayed diagnosis and/or previous misdiagnosis as compared to patients with PTSD. It has been estimated that patients suffering from dissociative disorders spend an average of 6.8 years in the mental health care system prior to receiving a correct diagnosis, and receive an average of 3.6 previous diagnoses (Putnam, Guroff, Silberman, Barban, & Post, 1986). The long time gap between onset and diagnosis in the dissociative disorders, appear to be by-products of a combination of social as well as clinical factors. Many of the stressors that are implicated in PTSD are matters of public knowledge or awareness (e.g., wars, natural disasters, transportation accidents, crime, etc.), such that disclosure on the patient's part is not as likely to be a source of shame. On the other hand, timely identification of DID requires specialized interviews, which are not yet routinely performed in trauma survivors (Steinberg, 1994b, 1995). In the case of DID, the intrafamilial abuse that is involved in the majority of cases typically occurs in the privacy of the home and is kept secret from the outside world. As a result, survivors of family abuse may fail to draw connections between present symptoms and past traumas, or they may hesitate to disclose either their symptoms or their history. In these situations, accurate differential diagnosis requires systematic assessment of patients' dissociative symptoms, in addition to their trauma history.

POPULATIONS AT RISK FOR DISSOCIATIVE SYMPTOMS AND DISORDERS

Persons with Known Histories of Trauma

Given increased professional awareness of both the incidence of trauma in the general population and the variety of stressors that can affect people's lives, clinicians have begun to recognize the importance of taking trauma histories. Even in circumstances involving public or collective disasters of one kind or another, such as natural disasters, transportation accidents, or acts of terrorism, a thorough history of patients' experiences is necessary.

Mental health professionals working in facilities with survivors of traumas such as the following should routinely screen their patient populations for dissociative symptoms:

- VA or military hospitals
- Rape crisis units
- Trauma centers
- Shelters for battered women
- Emergency responders (e.g., police, fire, paramedics)
- Disaster workers
- Social service agencies and mental health clinics

Persons with Covert Histories of Trauma

Clinicians should also note that there are patient populations who do not present with overt histories of trauma, or who may not be perceived to be at risk for PTSD or dissociative disorders. These groups include the following:

Persons with Histories of Amnesia for Their Past, Including Traumatic Events

Research using the Structured Clinical Interview for DSM-IV Dissociative Disorders (SCID-D; Steinberg, 1994a) indicates that amnesia may be regarded as the "gateway" symptom of the five core dissociative symptoms, in that it affects patients' recall of dissociative episodes as well as of the narrative of their life history (Steinberg, 1995). Ironically, individuals with severe amnesia will sometimes comment that they cannot remember how much they have forgotten. Moreover, patients with dissociative disorders will frequently report amnesia for large portions of their later childhood and adolescence, in addition to normal amnesia of early childhood.

Patients with dissociative disorders who have covert histories of trauma are often polysymptomatic in their presentation and/or comorbid with other disorders (Coons, 1980; Kluft, 1991; Putnam et al., 1986; Steinberg, 1994b; Steinberg, 1995; Torem, 1990). It is advisable for clinicians to take comprehensive histories of dissociation in patients who fall into the following categories that are often comorbid with the dissociative disorders:

- Patients previously diagnosed as having "atypical" or "NOS (not otherwise specified)" disorders.
- Patients with a history of eating disorders, or recurrent or atypical depression.
- Patients who have been diagnosed with borderline personality disorder.
- Patients who have been diagnosed with PTSD.
- Patients who have been diagnosed with impulse control disorders.
- Patients who have substance abuse disorders.
- Patients who fall into one or more of the following categories:
  1. Meet criteria for more than two psychiatric diagnoses, or have a history of fluctuating symptoms leading to a variety of diagnoses.
  2. Endorse hearing voices but are otherwise without symptoms of psychosis.
  3. Have difficulty recalling symptom histories.
  4. Have a history of unsuccessful treatments with a series of therapists.
- Patients who are nonresponsive to treatment.

Vicariously Traumatized Persons

It has recently been recognized that persons may manifest symptoms of PTSD through secondhand exposure to the trauma histories of others (Terr, 1990, 1991). Such cases include Holocaust survivors and their children (Danieli, 1982, 1985; Krystal, 1988), intimates of rape victims (Kelly, 1988), and mental health professionals who work with trauma survivors (Lindy & Wilson, 1994). Hodgkinson and Shepherd (1994) report that disaster workers not only experience high levels of stress at the time of the traumatic event, but that these elevated levels are still present at 12-month follow-up. Detection of vicarious traumatization may require taking a history of traumatic events that may have affected other family members as well as exposure to trauma through one's employment.

ORGANIZING AND ASSESSING DISSOCIATION: FIVE MEASURABLE COMPONENTS

Definitions of dissociation include those by Nemiah (1991): "the exclusion from consciousness and the inaccessibility of voluntary recall of mental events . . . such as memories, sensations, feelings, fantasies and attitudes"; and DSM-IV: "disruption in the usually integrated functions of consciousness, memory, identity, or perception of the environment" (American Psychiatric Association, 1994, p. 477). Although these and other definitions may appear overly broad (Frankel, 1990), the complex nature of dissociation can be organized into five core dissociative symptoms: amnesia, depersonalization, derealization, identity confusion, and identity alteration (Steinberg, 1994a, 1994b; Steinberg, Rounsaville & Cicchetti, 1990). The SCID-D (Steinberg, 1994a) allows for clinical investigations of the phenomenology and prevalence of these five core dissociative symptoms and has improved diagnostic accuracy with regard to dissociative disorders. This chapter will focus on the assessment of posttraumatic dissociative symptoms and syndromes using the SCID-D.

The Structured Clinical Interview for DSM-IV Dissociative Disorders

The SCID-D is the first diagnostic tool developed for assessing the severity of dissociative symptoms as well as for the diagnosis of dissociative disorders (Steinberg, 1993a, 1994a; Steinberg et al., 1990). The SCID-D has undergone extensive NIMH funded field-testing for reliability and validity (Steinberg, Cicchetti, Buchanan, Hall, & Roundsaville, 1989–1992). Good-excellent reliability for each of the five dissociative symptoms and disorders have been noted in several investigations (Goff, Olin, Jenike, Baer, & Buttolph, 1992; Steinberg et al., 1989–1992, 1989–1993, 1990). This semistructured clinical interview comprehensively assesses five core dissociative symptoms (amnesia, depersonalization, derealization, identity confusion, and identity alteration) and makes diagnoses of the dissociative disorders based on DSM-IV criteria. The SCID-D uses open-ended questions and embeds DSM-IV criteria throughout the interview. Although the SCID-D is not a trauma questionnaire, its ability to elicit spontaneous descriptions of trauma and dissociation from patients without the use of leading questions makes it a valuable instrument for diagnosis, as well as symptom documentation for psychological and forensic evaluations. Guidelines for the administration, scoring, and interpretation of the SCID-D are described in the *Interviewer's Guide to the SCID-D* (Steinberg, 1994b).

The SCID-D allows a trained interviewer to make DSM-IV diagnoses of dissociative amnesia, dissociative fugue, depersonalization disorder, DID (MPD), and DDNOS. Disorders newly proposed in DSM-IV consisting of predominantly dissociative symptoms, including possession trance disorder (in the DSM-IV appendix) and acute stress disorder, can also be assessed with the SCID-D (Steinberg, 1994b, 1995).

Assessing the Five Core Dissociative Symptoms

Systematic review of the five dissociative symptoms assessed with the SCID-D are presented here. Excerpts from a SCID-D interview of a patient who shall be referred to here as "Terri," diagnosed initially as having PTSD, are included to illustrate the varied manifestations of dissociation. Terri was referred for evaluation of her dissociative symptoms and to rule out the presence of a dissociative disorder. She is a middle-aged Caucasian woman, married for 15 years but childless. At present she is unemployed because of the dysfunction caused by her dissociative symptoms. She is, however, attending college part-time in order to complete requirements for a bachelor's degree. She initially presented with symptoms of severe age regression.

Assessing Amnesia with the SCID-D

Amnesia is usually described as "gaps" in the patient's memory, ranging from minutes to years, and sometimes referred to as "lost time." Patients with severe amnesia are often unable to recall the frequency or duration of their amnestic episodes. In addition, they may "come to themselves" away from home, unable to remember how they got there; or have trouble remembering their name, age, or other personal information (Steinberg, 1994b, 1995, 1996).

The SCID-D is divided into five major sections, one for each of the five dissociative symptoms. When the history taking is completed, the interviewer proceeds with the SCID-D questions concerning the symptom of amnesia. Terri describes having had recurrent gaps in her memory, as well as significant distress in connection with her amnesia. She uses the term "panic" to describe her reactions to the discovery that one of her time gaps was connected to a spending binge:

INTERVIEWER: What is your experience of a time gap like?

PATIENT: I panic. I get real nervous. Like Saturday. I don't know all of what happened on Saturday. Till a lot of the day was over. And where was I? And how come I have $5,000 on my credit cards? And all that kind of stuff.

I: What is the longest period of time you've ever lost?

P: Maybe an afternoon. Are you talking about blocks of time, like my not remembering my childhood? Years, if that's what you mean.

Given the high frequency, duration, and distress caused by Terri's amnesic episodes, she receives a rating of "severe" for this symptom.

Assessing Depersonalization with the SCID-D

Depersonalization is a symptom that manifests in a variety of ways in trauma survivors. This may happen because the symptom is initially frightening to many people who experience it; patients describe depersonalization in terms of feeling detached from the self, feeling that the self is strange or unreal, feeling physically separated from part(s) of one's body, or detached from one's emotions (Steinberg 1994b, 1995, 1996).

On the depersonalization section of the SCID-D, Terri indicates that she experiences several forms of this symptom, including out-of-body experiences. In one example, Terri describes an episode of depersonalization in which different parts of her body felt as if they were not under her control and were numb.

I: Can you describe that feeling of unreality more precisely?

P: It's weird. It's *really* weird. . . . All of a sudden I just got—it's like my legs couldn't move, you know what I mean? And it was like I was real cold, and part of me was real hot, and I couldn't feel—like my head was real dizzy and stuff. And my body was split into sections. It was like this part from here up [gestures, pointing to waist] was hot, and my legs were ice cold. And they were numb. They just weren't *there*.

I: How often has that happened to you?

P: A lot. (*smiles and giggles*) Monthly.

Again, Terri's depersonalization receives a rating of "severe," given its frequency and the resultant dysfunction.

Assessing Derealization with the SCID-D

Just as with depersonalization, the symptom of derealization is common in patients with histories of severe trauma. Derealization in particular includes feelings of estrangement or detachment from the environment, or a sense that the environment is unreal. Patients who have experienced recurrent emotional, physical, and/or sexual abuse frequently endorse derealization episodes in which close relatives or their own home seem unreal or foreign to them. These feelings are often associated with traumatic memories of childhood events that patients may spontaneously share when describing intense derealization experiences (Steinberg, 1995).

Clinicians involved with the assessment of trauma survivors should note that both depersonalization and derealization are included in the diagnostic criteria for acute stress disorder and PTSD. Patients with histories of extrafamilial trauma also may present flashbacks and age-regressed states, in which the contemporary environment becomes unreal while a past experience is relived.

Terri indicates that her experiences of derealization usually consist of familiar places appearing unfamiliar or unreal. Like many patients endorsing this symptom, she finds it difficult to verbalize or describe.

I: Have you ever felt as if familiar surroundings or people you knew seemed unfamiliar or unreal?

P: Yes.

I: Can you describe that?

P: I think that places I should know sometimes look different. Like certain parts of Boston. Or when I go for a walk near my house sometimes. Sometimes I worry that I might be crazy. Like I don't remember ever being in the parking lot where I go to school, even though I drive there several times a week.

The frequency of Terri's experiences of derealization, as well as their impact on her life, led the interviewer to rate this symptom as "severe."

Assessing Identity Confusion with the SCID-D

The remaining two core symptoms assessed by the SCID-D concern the disturbances in personal identity that characterize patients suffering from dissociative disorders. Identity confusion and identity alteration may be distinguished as follows: Identity confusion refers to an internal fragmentation of the self that is not ordinarily perceptible to others (Steinberg, 1994b, 1995, 1996). The person suffering from identity confusion typically describes experiences of inner warfare or conflict, which generate a subjective feeling of incoherence or instability in the sense of self. The SCID-D's definition of identity confusion (Steinberg 1994a, 1994b) should be distinguished from Erikson's (1968) usage, in which the term refers to weaknesses in the sense of self related to developmental issues in adolescence and early adulthood.

Identity alteration on the SCID-D refers to external behavioral manifestations of personality transformation objectively perceptible to others (Steinberg, 1994b). Unlike identity confusion, it is not a primarily subjective experience. Although some patients suffering from identity alteration may be conscious of their switching, others become aware of it through physical evidence (purchases, documents, etc.) or interpersonal feedback. In addition, identity alteration represents a change from a specific personality or ego state to another, as distinct from a sense of inner incoherence or struggle.

In terms of identity confusion, the patient in our case study experiences the symptom as an inner fight.

I: Have you ever felt as if there was a struggle going on inside of you as to who you really are?

P: Oh, God. Yes. That's like daily, hourly. I feel like an amoeba with fifteen thousand different ideas about where it wants to go. And it's like literally being pulled in every direction possible until there's nothing left, and it's like split in half. That's a constant battle.

Assessing Identity Alteration with the SCID-D

The fifth dissociative symptom assessed by the SCID-D, identity alteration, has been previously defined as a person's shift in role or identity, which is observable by others through changes in the person's behaviors (Steinberg, 1994b). Manifestations of identity alteration include the use of different names, the possession of a learned skill for which one cannot account, and the discovery of strange or unfamiliar personal items in one's possession. These transitions in role or behavior may be connected with amnesic episodes, in which a person is unable to remember events that occurred while experiencing altered identity. Identity alteration in DID is characterized by its complexity, distinctness, the ability of alters to take control of behavior, and the interconnection with other dissociative symptoms (Steinberg, 1995).

Identity alteration is the dissociative symptom most likely to be noticed by others in the patient's home or workplace environment because of its behavioral manifestations. This symptom often causes the patient significant distress or anxiety because of its actual or potential effects on employment and interpersonal relationships. Terri described serious disturbances in adult functioning that were related to her childlike behavior:

I: Have you ever felt as if, or found yourself acting as if, you were still a child?

P: Yes.

I: What is that experience like?

P: Well, it's scary. It's scary for me sometimes, but at least I can play.

I: Do you picture the child part in any particular way?

P: Yeah, she's about 4. She's scared a lot, though. But she goes into Dana's office, and then she feels safe. And when she gets scared, she goes onto a big red chair with a teddy bear, and I tell her it's okay. Dana's there. So, she feels good.

I: Dana is your therapist?

P: Umhmm.

I: How often does that occur?

P: That T. J. comes out? We call her "T. J.," for "Terri junior." She comes out a lot . . . maybe daily now.

Due to the complexity and subtlety of dissociative identity disturbances, they are further assessed in follow-up sections on identity confusion and alteration. These are sections, one or two of which may be administered at the interviewer's discretion, for further assessment of DID. They are usually omitted when the patient does not appear to suffer from a dissociative disorder. A series of questions assesses the degree of volition and distinctness of personality states, drawing on patients' own terminology for their altered state(s) of identity. In order to confirm the impression that Terri's "parts" are "distinct identities or personality states" (American Psychiatric Association, 1994, p. 487), the interviewer administered one of the nine optional follow-up modules of the SCID-D. In this instance, Terri's interviewer uses the module on "Different Names," because the patient had mentioned having different parts with distinctive personal characteristics and different names.

I: Earlier you mentioned having used other names; you mentioned "T. J." Are there any other names?

P: Yes.

I: What are the other names?

P: (*giggles*) Well, there's Vicki. Vicki's the cool one, an adolescent, 16 or 17. Then there's "The Bad Dude." He's got *good* moves. Then there's Terry with the *y*. She's depressed and suicidal. She's about 11. Then there's a little baby, that doesn't talk. I just call her "Sweetie." And then there's a boy who cuts, but I don't know how old.

I: When were you first aware of using these names?

P: In the hospital, a long time ago, when I was 11. I had an emergency operation. And they said that I kept saying that my name was "Vicki." What did I know? I was only 11.

I: How often does that occur, that you refer to yourself by different names?

P: Um, daily.

Terri then goes on to describe the problems created for her by her different parts. The frequent emergence of "T. J." at her workplace cost her her last job. "The Bad Dude" engages in minor lawbreaking. One of the other children emerged one day while Terri was driving a van full of passengers over one of the most congested stretches of highway in the Northeast. When asked, Terri affirms that she has clear visual images of these internal "parts," they recurrently control her behavior, and she has ongoing dialogues with them. Terri appears to suffer from identity alteration at a high level of severity.

Assessing Intrainterview Dissociative Cues

Intrainterview dissociative cues are monitored throughout the interview to supplement the patient's verbal information. The SCID-D includes a postinterview assessment of these intrainterview dissociative cues. These cues include a number of verbal and nonverbal behaviors, such as alteration in demeanor, spontaneous age regression, trancelike appearance, and so on, which are suggestive of the presence of dissociative symptoms and/or disorders. The interviewer is to note the presence of these cues during the course of the interview and rate them afterward. Terri's manifestation of intrainterview age regression was observed throughout the interview. In addition, the interviewer noted that Terri appeared to undergo rapid shifts in her demeanor at least twice during the interview, changing from a very childish personality to a somewhat more mature persona.

Severity Ratings

After the interview, the rater records the five symptom severities and dissociative disorder diagnosis on the summary score sheet, which records this summary information in a visually concise form.

Severity rating definitions are provided in the *Interviewer's Guide to the SCID-D* (Steinberg, 1994b), and allow the interviewer to determine symptom severity based on the subject's responses to each section of the SCID-D. The severity of each dissociative symptom is assessed through questions concerning the frequency, duration, distress, and dysfunction associated with each dissociative experience (see Table 15.1) . These symptom profiles can be represented iconically in a SCID-D symptom profile graph, as demonstrated by the characteristic profiles of patients with dissociative and nondissociative disorders, respectively (see Figure 15.1).

Diagnostic Assessment

The constellation of Terri's symptoms meets DSM-IV criteria for a diagnosis of dissociative identity disorder. This case study concludes with a sample diagnostic evaluation report, suitable for inclusion in the patient's records and psychological reports.

Sample SCID-D Evaluation Report

Summary of Evaluation: Terri Miller

Date(s) of evaluation: 4/20/94

Referral source: Dana Jones, M.D. (present therapist)

Reason for referral: Present therapist suspects presence of underlying dissociative disorder.

Information obtained from: Patient and present therapist.

Brief summary: The patient is a 44-year-old female Caucasian junior college graduate, presently unemployed. She is married and lives with her husband; the couple is childless. Ms. Miller has been in outpatient therapy for the past 4 years due to a history of depression, eating disorders, and severe panic attacks. Her referring clinician's diagnosis is PTSD. She reports an unstable employment history, and once

TABLE 15.1. Severity Rating Definitions of Depersonalization

Depersonalization—Detachment from one's self, for example,
a sense of looking at one's self as if one is an outsider

Severity	SCID-D items
A. Mild	
• Single episode or rare (total of 1–4) episodes of depersonalization which are brief (less than 4 hours), and are usually associated with stress or fatigue.	38–47, 54, 55, 64
B. Moderate (one of the following):	
• Recurrent (more than 4) episodes of depersonalization (may be brief or prolonged; may be precipitated by stress).	38–47, 54, 55, 64
• Episodes (1–4) of depersonalization which (one of the following):	
• Produce impairment in social or occupational functioning.	63
• Are not precipitated by stress.	64
• Are prolonged (over 4 hours).	55
• Are associated with dysphoria.	65
C. Severe (one of the following):	
• Persistent episodes of depersonalization (24 hours and longer).	38–47, 55
• Episodes of depersonalization occur daily or weekly. May be brief or prolonged.	38–47, 54
• Frequent (more than 4) episodes of depersonalization that (one of the following):	
• Produce impairment in social or occupational functioning.	63
• Do not appear to be precipitated by stress.	64
• Are prolonged (over 4 hours).	55
• Are associated with dysphoria.	65

Note. The severity rating definitions are not an inclusive list. The purpose of these definitions is to give the rater a general description of the parameters of the spectrum of dissociative symptoms and their severity. From Steinberg (1994a).

required inpatient treatment. The patient reported no major medical problems, but has a history of alcohol abuse. Her referring therapist has prescribed an antianxiety agent for her occasional panic attacks.

Family history: The patient states that her parents were undiagnosed depressives, and that her father was an alcoholic who never sought treatment. She married her present husband when she was 29; it was the first marriage for both spouses. They are presently in couple therapy because of the stresses on the marriage caused by Terri's symptoms. Terri is not particularly close to any members of her family of origin.

SCID-D evaluation summary: In addition to performing a routine diagnostic evaluation, I administered the SCID-D (Steinberg, 1994a), in order to systematically evaluate posttraumatic dissociative symptoms and the dissociative disorders. Scoring and interpretation of the SCID-D were performed according to the guidelines described

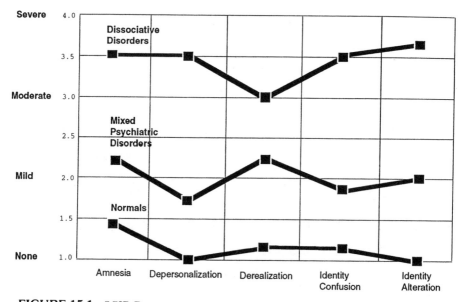

FIGURE 15.1. SCID-D symptom profiles in psychiatric patients and normal controls. Data derived from Steinberg et al. (1990).

in the *Interviewer's Guide to the SCID-D* (Steinberg, 1994b). A review of the significant findings from the SCID-D includes:

Ms. Miller endorsed *amnesia* covering a period of years in her later childhood and adolescence. She also reported frequent amnesia for recent conversations, together with time gaps lasting several hours. With respect to *depersonalization,* she mentioned recurrent out-of-body experiences during medical or dental procedures, as well as "splits" in her body in which her extremities feel numb, or different body parts feel different degrees of heat or cold. On the *derealization* section of the interview, Ms. Miller remarked that she feels that places she should know seem unfamiliar, even when they are locations that she visits in the course of daily routine. She endorsed a high level of *identity confusion,* stating that she experiences it as "constant battle," on a daily basis. Her remarks about "feeling stupid" and "having no opinions" appear to reflect a belief that she has no consistent personal center. In terms of *identity alteration,* the patient reported that her husband has commented that she often acts like a different person, and that she was fired from her last job because of episodes of spontaneous age regression. In addition, she endorsed the use of different names for her different personalities as well as visual images associated with each name. The different personalities included a frightened child of about 4, who emerged inappropriately in her workplace, a "cool" teenage female, a tough male adolescent who engages in various acts of delinquency, another self-cutting male of uncertain age, a depressed and suicidal 11-year-old female who tends to emerge when the patient is driving, and a preverbal infant. The patient maintained that these personalities engaged in internal dialogues with one another, and that most of them had spoken to her therapist.

In addition, I observed two intrainterview dissociative cues during the administration of the interview. Throughout the interview, Ms. Miller appeared to be age regressed. She spoke in a high-pitched, childlike voice. She twice underwent rapid shifts in her demeanor with no apparent external cause, changing from a very childish personality to a more mature one within the space of about 10 seconds.

Mental status exam: The patient came to the interview casually dressed and was calm and cooperative. She spoke fluently and answered most questions with relevant replies. At two points she went off on conversational tangents. Her affect was not always appropriate to the situations she described; for example, at one point she giggled while describing a fugue episode in which she had a highway accident. However, she denied the presence of psychotic symptoms; likewise she denied suicidal or homicidal ideation.

Assessment: On the basis of this evaluation, Ms. Miller's symptoms and history are consistent with a primary diagnosis of a dissociative disorder. She suffers from chronic amnesia, depersonalization, derealization, identity confusion, and identity alteration, all at a high level of severity Her "parts" appear to be sufficiently distinct to meet DSM-IV Criterion A for dissociative identity disorder. These findings are consistent with a diagnosis of dissociative identity disorder.

Recommendation: I would recommend individual psychotherapy aimed at reducing the patient's baseline level of amnesia, as well as fostering greater awareness of and cooperation between her internal personalities. The use of an antianxiety agent as needed may assist in relieving the patient's occasional panic attacks.

DIRECTIONS FOR FUTURE RESEARCH IN THE DISSOCIATIVE DISORDERS AND PTSD USING THE SCID-D

The SCID-D is a tool with numerous applications for researchers as well as clinicians. In terms of future research, the use of the SCID-D should open up a number of new avenues of investigation:

1. *Outcome studies:* Researchers interested in pharmacological treatments of the dissociative disorders, as well as researchers conducting comparative studies of pharmacotherapy and the psychotherapies can use the SCID-D to record and monitor changes in patients' symptom severity levels. At present, no controlled double-blind studies have been done comparing either the relative efficacy of pharmacotherapy and psychotherapy in the treatment of dissociation, or the relative efficacy of different forms of psychotherapy. Because the SCID-D summary score sheet can be used to record the severity as well as the presence of dissociative symptoms, it is an effective tool for the establishment of patients' baselines prior to medication trials, as well as facilitating the matching of patient groups for comparative studies.

2. *Reassessment of DSM diagnostic categories:* Increasing recognition of the prevalence of the dissociative disorders and the high level of misdiagnosis of patients has led a number of researchers to speculate that dissociation

may be a more inclusive concept than was previously thought. In particular, the inclusion of three dissociative symptoms (amnesia, depersonalization, and derealization) among the criteria for acute stress disorder and PTSD suggests the wisdom of greater cooperation between specialists in PTSD and researchers in the field of dissociation.

3. *Cost–benefit analysis in the managed care era:* The study of cost–benefit analysis in the mental health care field is still in its early stages. However, the coming of managed care has increased pressure on psychotherapists to demonstrate the effectiveness of specific treatments as well as cost control. Given researchers' findings that an average of 7 to 10 years elapses between initial assessment of patients with undetected dissociative disorders and proper diagnosis (Coons, Bowman, & Milstein, 1988; Kluft 1991; Putnam et al., 1986), routine screening of patients from populations known to be at risk for the dissociative disorders, such as trauma survivors, is highly cost-effective. The costs of SCID-D administration are minor in comparison to the systemic costs of misdiagnosis and misdirected treatment. Moreover, patients typically find that the open-ended format of the SCID-D represents the beginning of the actual therapeutic process for them, as well as the establishment of their correct diagnosis; thus their recovery period *after* diagnosis may be effectively shortened as well.

SUMMARY AND CONCLUSION

Because the dissociative disorders are posttraumatic in etiology and frequently misdiagnosed, it is essential that clinicians use specific interview strategies to rule out dissociative disorders in patients with histories of trauma or PTSD. Routine administration of the SCID-D, a clinical diagnostic interview, allows the clinician to evaluate the severity of dissociative symptoms and the presence of dissociative disorders. Because accurate diagnostic assessment of patients with posttraumatic syndromes is essential to the implementation of appropriate therapy, it is recommended that use of the SCID-D be part of the clinical training of all professionals (e.g., clinical/counseling psychology, psychiatric residencies, psychiatric nurses, social service, etc.) involved in the assessment of trauma survivors. Social workers and clergy with graduate training in pastoral psychology should also be encouraged to learn to administer, score, and interpret the SCID-D, in that members of both professions frequently encounter persons suffering from posttraumatic syndromes. Workshops in SCID-D administration and interpretation are offered several times each year at different sites in the United States and abroad.

With respect to differential diagnosis of the posttraumatic syndromes, SCID-D research indicates that a subset of patients diagnosed with chronic PTSD suffer from undetected DID or DDNOS. To date, virtually identical dissociative symptom profiles have been found using the SCID-D in patients with PTSD as compared to patients with DID and DDNOS (Steinberg et al.,

1989-1992). As researchers in PTSD and the dissociative disorders continue to study the long-term effects of childhood trauma as well as the precise relationship between PTSD and dissociation, the SCID-D provides a cost-effective instrument for accurate diagnosis, symptom documentation, treatment planning, and long-term follow-up care. Given the high costs of misdiagnosis, health insurers would be wise to cover the relatively minor expense of administering the SCID-D interview as part of the diagnostic evaluation process. It is recommended that assessment of the five dissociative symptoms, as described in the SCID-D and *Interviewer's Guide to the SCID-D* (Steinberg, 1994a, 1994b), be included in evaluations of all patients with dissociative symptoms or suspected/documented histories of trauma.

ACKNOWLEDGMENT

Supported by NIMH First Independent Research Support and Transition Award MH-43352 and RO1-43352 to Marlene Steinberg.

REFERENCES

American Psychiatric Association. (1952). *Diagnostic and statistical manual of mental disorders.* Washington, DC: Author.

American Psychiatric Association. (1994). *Diagnostic and statistical manual of mental disorders* (4th ed.). Washington, DC: Author.

Braun, B. G. (1990). Dissociative disorders as sequelae to incest. In R. P. Kluft (Ed.), *Incest-related syndromes of adult psychopathology* (pp. 227–246). Washington, DC: American Psychiatric Press.

Coons, P. M. (1980). Multiple personality: Diagnostic considerations. *Journal of Clinical Psychiatry, 41,* 330–336.

Coons, P. M., Bowman, E. S., & Milstein, V. (1988). Multiple personality disorder: A clinical investigation of 50 cases. *Journal of Nervous and Mental Disease, 176*(5), 519–527.

Coons, P. M., Cole, C., Pellow, T., & Milstein, V. (1990). Symptoms of posttraumatic stress and dissociation in women victims of abuse. In R. P. Kluft (Ed.), *Incest-related syndromes of adult psychopathology* (pp. 205–226). Washington, DC: American Psychiatric Press.

Danieli, Y. (1982). *Therapists' difficulties in treating survivors of the Nazi Holocaust and their children.* Unpublished doctoral dissertation, New York University.

Danieli, Y. (1985). The treatment and prevention of long-term effects and intergenerational transmission of victimization: A lesson from Holocaust survivors and their children. In C. R. Figley (Ed.), *Trauma and its wake* (pp. 278–294). New York: Brunner/Mazel.

Erikson, E. H. (1968). *Identity: Youth and crisis.* New York: Norton.

Fine, C. G. (1990). The cognitive sequelae of incest. In R. P. Kluft (Ed.), *Incest-related syndromes of adult psychopathology* (pp. 161–182). Washington, DC: American Psychiatric Press.

Frankel, F. H. (1990). Hypnotizability and dissociation. *American Journal of Psychiatry, 147*(7), 823–829.

Goff, D. C., Olin, J. A., Jenike, M. A., Baer, L., & Buttolph, M. L. (1992). Dissociative symptoms in patients with obsessive–compulsive disorder. *Journal of Nervous and Mental Disease, 180*(5), 332–337.

Hodgkinson, P. E., & Shepherd, M. A. (1994). The impact of disaster support work. *Journal of Traumatic Stress, 7*(4), 587–600.

Kelly, L. (1988). *Surviving sexual violence.* Minneapolis: University of Minnesota Press.

Kluft, R. P. (1984). Multiple personality in childhood. *Psychiatric Clinics of North America, 7*(1), 121–134.

Kluft, R. P. (1985). Childhood multiple personality disorder: Predictors, clinical findings and treatment results. In R. P. Kluft (Ed.), *Childhood antecedents of multiple personality.* Washington, DC: American Psychiatric Press.

Kluft, R. P. (1988). The dissociative disorders. In J. Talbott, R. Hales, & S. Yudofsky (Eds.), *American Psychiatric Press textbook of psychiatry* (pp. 557–585). Washington, DC: American Psychiatric Press.

Kluft, R. P. (1991). Multiple personality disorder. In A. Tasman & S. Goldfinger (Eds.), *Psychiatric update* (Vol. 10). Washington, DC: American Psychiatric Press.

Kluft, R. P. (1994). Countertransference in the treatment of multiple personality disorder. In J. P. Wilson & J. D. Lindy (Eds.), *Countertransference in the treatment of PTSD* (pp. 122–150). New York: Guilford Press.

Krystal, H. (1988). *Integration and self-healing: Affect, trauma, alexithymia.* Hillsdale, NJ: Analytic Press.

Lindy, J. D., & Wilson, J. P. (1994). Empathic strain and countertransference roles: Case illustrations. In J. P. Wilson & J. D. Lindy (Eds.), *Countertransference in the treatment of PTSD* (pp. 62–82). New York: Guilford Press.

Nemiah, J. C. (1991). Dissociation, conversion, and somatization. In A. Tasman & S. Goldfinger (Eds.), *American Psychiatric Press review of psychiatry* (Vol. 10). Washington, DC: American Psychiatric Press.

Putnam, F. W. (1985). Dissociation as a response to extreme trauma. In R. P. Kluft (Ed.), *Childhood antecedents of multiple personality* (pp. 65–97). Washington, DC: American Psychiatric Press.

Putnam, F. W., Guroff, J. J., Silberman, E. K., Barban, L., & Post, R. M. (1986). The clinical phenomenology of multiple personality disorder: 100 recent cases. *Journal of Clinical Psychiatry, 47,* 285–293.

Spiegel, D. (1991). Dissociation and trauma. In A. Tasman & S. Goldfinger (Eds.), *American Psychiatric Press review of psychiatry* (Vol. 10, pp. 261–275). Washington, DC: American Psychiatric Press.

Steinberg, M. (1993). *Structured Clinical Interview for DSM-IV Dissociative Disorders (SCID-D).* Washington, DC: American Psychiatric Press.

Steinberg, M. (1994a). *Structured Clinical Interview for DSM-IV Dissociative Disorders— Revised (SCID-D-R).* Washington, DC: American Psychiatric Press.

Steinberg, M. (1994b). *Interviewer's Guide to the Structured Clinical Interview for DSM-IV Dissociative Disorders—Revised (SCID-D-R).* Washington, DC: American Psychiatric Press.

Steinberg, M. (1995). *Handbook for the assessment of dissociation: A clinical guide.* Washington, DC: American Psychiatric Press.

Steinberg, M. (1996). *The clinician's guide to the assessment of dissociative symptoms and disorders* [audiotape]. N. Tonawanda, NY: Multi-Health Systems.

Steinberg, M., Cicchetti, D. V., Buchanan, J., Hall, P. E., & Rounsaville, B. J. (1989–1992). *NIMH field trials of the Structured Clinical Interview for DSM-IV Dissociative Disorders (SCID-D).* New Haven, CT: Yale University School of Medicine.

Steinberg, M., Kluft, R. P., Coons, P. M., Bowman, E. S., Fine, C. G., Fink, D. L., Hall, P. E., Rounsaville, B. J., & Cicchetti, D. V. (1989–1993). *Multicenter field trials of the Structured Clinical Interview for DSM-IV Dissociative Disorders (SCID-D).* New Haven, CT: Yale University School of Medicine.

Steinberg, M., Rounsaville, B. J., & Cicchetti, D. V. (1990). The Structured Clinical Interview for DSM-III-R Dissociative Disorders: Preliminary report on a new diagnostic instrument. *American Journal of Psychiatry, 147*(1), 76–82.

Sutker, P. B., Uddo, M., Brailey, K., Allain, A. N., & Errera, P. (1994). Psychological symptoms and psychiatric diagnoses in Operation Desert Storm troops serving graves registration duty. *Journal of Traumatic Stress, 7*(2), 159–171.

Terr, L. C. (1990). *Too scared to cry: Psychic trauma in childhood.* New York: Harper & Row.

Terr, L. C. (1991). Childhood traumas: An outline and overview. *American Journal of Psychiatry, 148*(1), 10–20.

Torem, M. S. (1990). Covert multiple personality underlying eating disorders. *American Journal of Psychotherapy, 65*(3), 357–368.

Wilson, J. P. (1994). The need for an integrative theory of post-traumatic stress disorder. In M. B. Williams (Eds.), *Handbook of PTSD therapy.* New York: Greenwood.

Neuropsychological Assessment in Posttraumatic Stress Disorder

Jeffrey A. Knight

INTRODUCTION

Reviewing and discussing the neuropsychological assessment of posttraumatic stress disorder (PTSD) is a challenge for a number of reasons. As a recent inclusion in the *Diagnostic and Statistical Manual of Mental Disorders* (i.e., appearing in DSM-III; American Psychiatric Association, 1980), comparatively little has been written to date on PTSD from a neuropsychological perspective. Major emphases early in the development of the PTSD literature centered around defining the set of primary PTSD criteria and associated features, debating the validity of its status as a unique anxiety disorder, developing reliable diagnostic interviews and psychological methods for measuring PTSD, expanding conceptualizations of the role of trauma in the production of PTSD in various populations, and exploring psychological and pharmacological treatments. The PTSD criteria have remained relatively stable across revisions of the DSM, and diagnostic interviews for PTSD have been created to classify cases in clinical and research protocols. Over the past 15 years, developments in these areas have established a firm foundation for now focusing on etiological questions.

Another reason for the relative dearth of formal neuropsychological study of PTSD may be that, at this point in time, few clinical neuropsychologists have been trained directly to study trauma, and few traumatologists are trained in the systematic study of brain–behavior relationships. Clinical neuropsychologists have traditionally focused on the evaluation and treatment of identifiable neurological conditions of the central nervous system that produced disruptions in cognitive functioning and whose presence could be corroborated by other diagnostic methods, for example, autopsy, electroencephalogram (EEG), angiography, computed tomography (CT) scan, magnetic resonance imaging (MRI), serum assays, and cerebrospinal fluid (CSF) analysis. Psychiatric disorders were not as readily characterized by these methods, and psychiatric conditions, historically, might have been invoked to explain symptoms when no classic neurological explanation emerged. Psychiatric disorders now represent an ever increasing portion of the neuropsychological literature as the roots of disordered emotion, behavior, and information-processing are conceptualized from a brain-based, biological–psychiatric perspective. Clinical neuropsychology has long been the nexus between brain function and dysfunction, affect, and behavior and cognition; and it will continue in this role for future study of trauma effects on the brain.

Considering the potential physical and neurological damage that often accompanies psychologically traumatic events, relatively little of the trauma literature addresses these aspects in depth. Traumatologists as a group view PTSD largely from either the perspective of psychological constructs indexed to behavioral observations, self-reports, and psychophysiological responding, or from biopsychological perspectives indexed to psychopharmacological studies. Explanations for PTSD symptom development, maintenance, alteration, and remission involve mainly operant and classical conditioning processes, psychodynamic formulations, and models of neurotransmitter system functioning. Traumatologists and clinical neuropsychologists would most likely agree in principle that familiarity with each others' perspectives is important for understanding the complexities of PTSD, but cross-reading two extensive literatures has practical limits, and applying the synthesis of these perspectives to actual cases or research designs is a larger challenge needing a framework and guidance.

To facilitate the synthesis and application process, this chapter will focus on the status of neuropsychological contributions to understanding the neurocognitive concomitants of PTSD symptoms. The main goals are (1) to introduce trauma clinicians and researchers to brain-based views that are important to consider in their work, and (2) to familiarize neuropsychologists with PTSD-related factors that may not be typically considered or addressed during evaluations and case formulations. Content sections of this chapter will (1) review the relevant literature on neuropsychological evaluation to date, (2) present general assessment issues related to trauma populations and specific considerations in conducting neuropsychological evaluations with PTSD patients, and (3) conclude with a discussion of future directions and issues of central concern given the emergent status of empirical research and model development in this area.

BRAIN-BASED CORRELATES OF PTSD

The degree to which PTSD coexists with, is caused by, or is the cause of neurocognitive problems is a critical issue needing conceptualization and systematic study. At issue is not just the task of specifying additional methods to identify cases of PTSD, but also the pursuit of variables that inform us about why PTSD develops in some trauma-exposed individuals and not others, as well as the factors that modulate the severity of symptom manifestation following exposure to trauma. The findings from the National Vietnam Veterans Readjustment Study (NVVRS; Kulka et al., 1990) suggest that alternatives in addition to traumatic exposure need to be considered as determinants of PTSD.

The NVVRS found prevalence rates of 30.9% for male combat veterans meeting diagnostic criteria for lifetime PTSD, and another 22.5% who developed partial PTSD after the military. Of these, 15.2% had symptoms at levels sufficient to meet the requirements for current PTSD at the time of the study. Comparisons among prevalence rates for lifetime and current PTSD show that about 49% of the male theater veterans who ever exhibited symptoms continued to have symptoms, supporting the contention that PTSD is a chronic disorder. The overall rates were higher among Black and Hispanic veterans and among those experiencing heavy combat. From an absolute perspective, the current PTSD group is a large number of afflicted individuals, but it is a relative minority of the sample.

Various psychosocial factors from the NVVRS were analyzed to investigate potential predisposing factors. Statistical adjustment for predisposing factors had the most impact on reducing prevalence rates for combat theater veterans. The variables found to contribute consistently to the predisposition adjustment models were having drug abuse or dependence before the military, being raised in a family that had a hard time making ends meet, having had symptoms of an affective disorder before going to Vietnam, and exhibiting problem behaviors in childhood. Although not an established relationship in the NVVRS, these variables could reflect patterns of adjustment to preexisting trauma, developmental conditions such as learning disabilities and attention deficit disorder, or other neurological problems. It may also be the case that a coexisting neurobiological condition contributes to the development and maintenance of chronic PTSD symptoms in this minority portion of the sample. A role for nontrauma exposure variables is suggested by structural equation modeling of the NVVRS data conducted by King and King (1995), who concluded that the effects of combat exposure were mediated by the outcome of cognitive processing of perceived threat. Schlenger (personal communication, 1995) found a correlation of .24 between the continuous version of the NVVRS global war zone stress exposure index and the probability of developing PTSD for Vietnam theater veterans. The small amount of variance attributable to this relationship combined with the minority percentage prevalence rates suggests that those who develop chronic PTSD may have a particular response to trauma possibly based on constitutional variables. To advance beyond psychological and diagnostic studies of PTSD, neuropsychological aspects of constitutional variables should be investigated by trauma researchers for their causal relationship to clinical symptom development and maintenance.

More is hypothesized and less is known about the relationship between enduring neurocognitive changes and the corresponding neurobiological mechanisms underlying the brain's response to trauma. Although models are emerging, at present there is no well-formulated consensus model that can be used to guide neuropsychological investigations. Assessing PTSD neuropsychologically involves some a priori assumptions about the relationship between traumatic experiences and brain functioning, which also require further elaboration and refinement. In the absence of a dominant neuropsychological model to serve as a guide, hypothesized neurobiological systems, logical extensions from knowledge of related disorders, and patterns among clinical features must serve the purpose. In attempting to apply neuropsychological methods to clinical evaluations and research protocols, two considerations are of clear importance: (1) What is the relationship between the traumatic event, PTSD development, and the neurocognitive impairments observed; and (2) what underlying brain systems are related to the patterns of cognitive symptoms that manifest clinically?

As with psychiatric disorders in general, PTSD does not conform to classic neurological lesion analysis. Unlike a tumor, stroke, aneurysm, or multiple sclerosis, psychiatric disorders often have few or no corresponding neuroanatomical correlates that are pathognomonic and identifiable via autopsy, CT scan, or MRI scan (Raz, 1989). When findings are present, they may not reliably correlate with the level of functional deficits or symptom severity (Devous, 1989, p. 219). However, advances in the behavioral neurosciences, electrophysiological measurement (quantitative EEG, evoked potential mapping), and functional neuroimaging techniques, such as positive emission topography (PET), single-photon emission computed tomography (SPECT), and functional MRI, show promise as a basis for possible development of nonpsychological models of functional disorders (Andreasen, 1989; McGuire, Shah, & Murray, 1993) and can provide appropriate correlative methods for studying psychiatric disorders by noninvasively measuring metabolic functioning of the living brain as it actively processes information. Thus far, studies employing these methods have primarily focused on schizophrenic disorders and mood disorders followed by some of the anxiety disorders such as obsessive–compulsive disorder and panic disorder (Orsillo & McCaffrey, 1992). The logical extension for studying anxiety disorders is the application of these methods to PTSD.

Some recent articles have suggested neurobiological aspects of brain functioning that might be involved in the development of PTSD symptoms. Watson, Hoffman, and Wilson (1988) postulated neurochemical changes in the locus coeruleus and amygdala following exposure to uncontrolled stress. Kolb (1989) hypothesized that changes at synaptic levels of cortical neurons in PTSD patients result from protracted and excessive sensitizing stimulation, eventually producing alteration in habituation learning. Other investigators have more specifically focused on *activation of the beta-adrenergic stress hormone systems in response to emotional experiences* (Cahill, Prins, Weber, & McGaugh, 1994), the central role of *abnormal noradrenergic function in the pathophysiology of PTSD* (Krystal et al., 1989; Southwick et al., 1993); and *altered functioning of brainstem catecholaminergic systems in childhood PTSD* (Perry, 1994; cf. Charney, Deutch, Krystal, Southwick, & Davis, 1993, for a review of the psychobiological mechanisms of PTSD). Some of the neurobiological formulations are extrapolations from preclinical studies, and others follow from investigations with human subjects. These neurobiological perspectives suggest mechanisms for some PTSD symptoms but only more generally posit the impact of trauma on complex mental processes and higher cortical functioning.

Regional brain areas previously hypothesized as responsible for PTSD symptoms, including the locus coeruleus, hippocampus, and septo-amygdalar complex continue to be studied. Bremner and coinvestigators (1995) found that the mean right hippocampal volume from 26 MRI scans of combat-PTSD subjects was 8% smaller than for control subjects. No differences were found in volume for other brain regions. Using PET to measure regional brain function, Semple, Goyers, McCormick, and Morris (1993) reported regional blood flow differences between control subjects and PTSD males with substance abuse histories in the areas of the hippocampus, parietal lobes (decreased flow), and orbito-frontal complex (increased flow). Ito, Teicher, Glod, and Harper (1993) employed neuroimaging, neuropsychological, and electrophysiological methods to investigate the association between abuse histories and neurological abnormalities in 104 child and adolescent inpatients. Physically and/or sexually abused subjects showed increased abnormalities in left frontal, temporal, or anterior regions, while those experiencing primarily neglect or psychological abuse showed only left temporal abnormalities. To date, no consensus functional scanning correlates of PTSD have been established; yet, the findings in the aforementioned studies point to the presence of alterations in brain areas associated with neuropsychological deficits in other related disorders.

Various brain regions have been associated with clinical symptoms in other disorders that share features with PTSD. Disorders of arousal and attention have been generally associated with frontal system dysfunction (Stuss & Benson, 1984) and fronto-subcortical pathology (Damasio, 1985). Orsillo and McCaffrey (1992) described findings suggesting that temporal lobe epilepsy and trauma to the temporal area results in symptoms similar to those seen in anxiety disorders. Alternative models and hypotheses suggest a relationship between left frontal lobe and left temporal lobe dysfunction in panic disorder and obsessive–compulsive disorder (Volkow, Harper, & Swann, 1986). Uddo, Vasterling, Brailey, and Sutker (1993) studied memory problems in PTSD veterans and noted that investigations into the pathogenesis of PTSD implicate brain structures involved in memory, such as the limbic system and septo-hippocampal-amygdalar complex. Brende (1982) conducted a study of lateralized electrodermal responding (EDRs) in six trauma-exposed subjects, and found that (1) peripheral EDRs reflected activity of the contralateral hemisphere, (2) left hemisphere functioning was associated with hypervigilance symptoms, and (3) right hemisphere functioning was associated with emotions and imagery. Finding multiple cortical and subcortical regions via neuroimaging protocols and other methods that are linked to symptoms is consistent with the varied clinical presentations of PTSD patients, who often also exhibit psychiatric features of depression, panic, generalized anxiety, and obsessive–compulsive disorders. Multiple, relevant brain regions may also reflect the influence of neurological conditions existing comorbidly with PTSD.

NEUROPSYCHOLOGICAL COMORBIDITY AND PTSD

The comorbidity of PTSD symptoms with those of assorted psychiatric disorders compounds the task of defining and studying the range of traumatized samples seeking treatment. As complexity of the clinical presentation increases, attributing causality to any given variable correspondingly increases in difficulty. Beyond diagnostic comorbidity, other factors influence the complex manifestations of PTSD, including the spectrum of possible traumatogenic events previously experienced by trauma survivors, the range of trauma-specific parameters determining the severity of the trauma experiences, and the individual coping responses exhibited by diverse populations exposed to trauma. Along with other neurologically related factors, these factors likewise contribute to the difficulty in studying the neuropsychological concomitants of PTSD. Unless it is assumed that all of these factors are equipotent for producing neurocognitive changes, clinical and research protocols must systematically consider their impact singularly and in concert (Merskey, 1992). The discussion that follows addresses the multiply determined clinical presentations that are more common in chronic PTSD cases.

Sources of Neuropsychogenic Trauma

Many types of potentially traumatizing experiences are found across clinical PTSD samples. For traumatic events involving physical injury, traumatologists will collect specifics about the incidents and build a model to describe the socioemotional effects of the experience on the individual and related others. Neuropsychologists will gather information about the same events and focus on neurobehavioral consequences that will impact the individual. Many events that threaten the physical integrity of the person and result in the production of PTSD symptoms also have associated effects on brain functioning. Examples of traumatizing events particularly relevant to neuropsychological formulations span a range of categories. Depending on the level of injury to the brain, either cumulative or from a single episode, all of the following could be sources of neuropsychogenic trauma:

- *Interpersonal violence:* beatings from family members, beatings from strangers, near-death experiences from stabbing, shootings, strangulation, rape.
- *Motor vehicle accidents:* as a driver, passenger, witness, or pedestrian.
- *Natural disasters:* physical injury from floods, flying debris in high winds, collapsing structures.
- *Other threat to life and health:* from falls, physical punishment, electrocution, suffocation, high-risk sports.
- *Industrial/occupational accidents:* falls, electrocution, fires causing anoxia, equipment malfunctions causing head injury.
- *Military-related injuries* (combat and noncombat):
  Head wounds: stabbings, low- and high-velocity missile wounds.
  Concussions from direct explosions: land mines, hand grenades, bombs, rockets, mortars, or from firing large-scale artillery weapons.
  Falls: from training equipment, from air transportation, trees, rocks, cliffs, bridges, buildings, moving armored vehicles, personnel carriers, or jeeps.
  Torture as prisoners of war: nutritional deprivation, beatings, electrocution.
  Exposure to neurotoxins and noxious gases.
- *Other civilian punishment and torture conditions:* can involve starvation (Gurvit, 1993; Sutker, Allain, & Winstead, 1987; Sutker, Galina, West, & Allain, 1990), high levels of induced pain, and electrocution (Cooper & Milroy, 1994; Daniel, Haban, Hutcherson, Botter, & Long, 1985; Hopewell, 1983; Mellen, Weedn, & Kao, 1992; Millen, 1993).

These potentially traumatic experiences carry varying degrees of risk for associated neurocognitive problems. Some of these conditions and neuropsychologically relevant variables will be discussed in greater detail.

PTSD and Developmentally Based Neurocognitive Problems

Learning disabilities and attention deficit disorder have been recently investigated as comorbid conditions with PTSD. Adults with developmental disorders, which in clinical PTSD populations may not have been previously diagnosed, carry a set of behavioral and learning problems in verbal and nonverbal modalities that can preexist or are coincident with life events that would include traumatic experiences (Gaddes, 1985; Rourke, 1985; Spreen, 1988). Learning disabilities and attention deficit disorder may occur separately or in conjunction with each other, and concurrently with anxiety and depression (Biederman, Newcorn, & Sprich, 1991; Bigler, 1990). Children with some types of behavioral problems may be at higher risk for acquired injuries. Hyperactive children in households of irritable, intolerant, and violent caretakers may be subjected to physical punishment and may engage in play that results in injuries (Cuffe, McCullough, & Pumariega, 1994;

Famularo, Kinscherff, & Fenton, 1992a). Histories of academic difficulties, and the development or exacerbation of family and social problems for these individuals, may have been noted from interview data to have a correlated onset that closely postdates an injury or follows a series of subclinical events. Although clinical correlations have been observed for these conditions, the exact role of learning disabilities and attention deficit disorder in the development and maintenance of PTSD is unknown. However, establishing the history of these conditions in patients undergoing neuropsychological evaluations is important for accurately interpreting test findings.

PTSD Resulting from Neurological Conditions and Neurological Trauma

Clinical and research protocols should include assessments of pretrauma, trauma-indexed, and posttrauma neurological factors capable of producing neuropsychological deficits. Although the presence of these factors complicates causal models and interpretation, ignoring them increases the risk of misattributing the sources of impaired test performances.

Traumatic Head Injury

Penetrating head injury (PHI) and closed head injury (CHI) — major and minor — can coexist with psychological trauma. Penetrating head injury constitute 2–6% of all head injuries, and can include open head wounds from knives, sharp or blunt objects; skull fractures associated with falls, beatings, crush injures; or, missile wounds from gunshots, shrapnel, and other projectiles. Military combat, crime episodes, and miscellaneous accidents are the most common sources of PHI (Kampen & Grafman, 1989). Amount of damage depends on the velocity of the object and the cavitation surrounding the track of the object. Hemorrhaging occurs locally and throughout the brain. High-velocity wounds are frequently fatal, whereas low-velocity wounds such as stabbings produce local damage. Changes in behavior, affect, and cognition will be a product of the tissue damage and the resulting alteration in regional brain metabolism. PHI will always be obvious and assessable by patient report and documented medical history; however, reports of CHI events may be more variable, especially if no treatment was received.

In severe CHI, gross acceleration–deceleration movements of the brain within the skull produce widespread diffuse damage due to axonal shearing and concussive damage to the surface of the cortex in orbito-frontal, anterior and inferior temporal regions of the brain (Davidoff, Kessler, Laibstain, & Mark, 1988; McAllister, 1992). For minor head injury, movement effects are less pronounced and result in more circumscribed deficits related to abilities mediated by the anterior cortex, such as memory, attention and concentration, judgment, and abstract reasoning (Barth et al., 1983; Bigler & Synder, 1995; Kwentus, Hart, Peck, & Kornstein, 1985). Even in cases of common whiplash injuries in which no head contact or loss of consciousness is reported, complex attentional processing can be impaired (Radanov, Stefano, Schnidrig, Sturzenegger, & Augustiny, 1993).

Segalowitz, Lawson, and Berge (1993) reported an incident rate of 30% for head injuries occurring in a general population of 3,961 people sampled from high schools, university psychology classes, and general physicians offices. Reporting a head injury was significantly related to other reports of hyperactivity, sleep disturbance, depression, and problems with social functioning. Levin (1985) noted that in some patients with minor CHI, residual deficits might be manifested only under conditions of stress. Neurobehavioral effects of CHI can overlap with symptoms of anxiety, depression, manic behavior, or organic personality disorder (McAllister, 1992), and confound the differentiation between associated features of PTSD. Rattok and Ross (1993) assessed for PTSD in a traumatically head-injured population and found that 18% met criteria for PTSD. The PTSD symptoms existed independently of cognitive deficits.

Although some sources of traumatic psychological stress mentioned previously are capable of producing multiple neurological problems, the following need to be considered in particular for their concomitant head-injury potential: random physical assaults (Shepard, Quercohi, & Preston, 1990), torture (Rassmussen, 1990), domestic violence, falls from high places, sports and sports accidents (Roberts, Allsop, & Barton, 1990), industrial accidents, domestic accidents, airplane accidents, and motor vehicle accidents (MVAs).

For MVAs, a wide range of head and body injuries can be sustained by drivers, passengers, and pedestrians, with attendant psychological adjustment problems for loss of function from residual chronic symptoms (Kuch, Evans, & Watson, 1991). When the effects of the injury are combined with the symptoms of PTSD from the life-threatening event and mood disorder secondary to the PTSD, the task of attributing the relative contribution of any given factor to the cognitive changes reported by the patient and formulating a treatment plan becomes more difficult. Horton (1993) reported a case study of concurrent PTSD and head injury following a MVA that illustrates the point. As part of a multicar accident, the patient witnessed the death of the driver of another car, who fell asleep at the wheel, producing the crash that demolished the patient's car. PTSD symptoms and cognitive problems were reported. Within 3 months of treatment with behavioral techniques, the PTSD symptoms abated, but memory problems at work remained. Neuropsychological testing found mild to moderate impairments in pattern consistent with mild CHI. The treatment approach was augmented as a result of the test findings to include instruction in compensatory memory methods and organizational strategies.

PTSD can develop in cases of head trauma when no memory or only sparse memory exists for the event. A multisystems theory of memory was advanced by Layton and Wardi-Zonna (1994) to account for PTSD reactions in patients with head injuries and no recall of the traumatic accident that caused their injury. Two cases of PTSD with concurrent neurogenic amnesia for the traumatic event were presented to illustrate the dilemma of assigning a diagnosis in the absence of conscious memory for the experience. They argued against the notion that neurogenic amnesia functions protectively to prevent posttraumatic emotional reactions. Aspects of the traumatic experience appear to become sufficiently encoded to produce reexperiencing symptoms.

Watson (1990) notes that symptoms of head injury and PTSD overlap in two cases of MVA survivors who suffered severe concussive injuries producing amnesia for the event. Reexperiencing of the event took the form of specific pain and other physical symptoms. Baggaley and Rose (1990) also reported a clinical case involving a soldier who was in a vehicle that exploded, killing eight other passengers. Coma lasted 36 hours, with a posttraumatic amnesia lasting 72 hours. While recovering physically, he developed PTSD without intrusive recall, and with nightmares characterized by unretrievable content. The phobic avoidance was consistent with specific trauma cues and was treated successfully with *in vivo* exposure methods.

McMillan (1991) described a case of severe head injury, amnesia for the event, and PTSD following a traffic accident. Despite absence of memory for the trauma, the patient experienced intrusive thoughts about the other passenger who had died, as well as avoidance of cognitive and physical events associated with consequences of the accident. Neuropsychological testing results (test battery not reported) were interpreted as revealing a moderate degree of general impairment that improved modestly on repeat testing 7 months later. Treatment using behavioral intervention was successful. PTSD clearly developed, even with loss of consciousness and organic amnesia for the event and its immediate consequences. The direct sequelae of the traumatic event and the head injury can each produce disruptions to interpersonal and intrapersonal domains of functioning for the trauma survivor.

Neurotoxic Exposure

Neurotoxic exposure can accompany traumatic events that occurred in military combat, industrial accidents, environmental accidents, suicide attempts, and intentional or accidental poisonings. The negative effects of toxin exposure on neurocognitive abilities, affect, and personality have been well described (Hartman, 1988, 1992; White, Feldman, & Proctor, 1992). Schottenfeld and Cullen (1985) reported finding that PTSD developed frequently in workers who were acutely or chronically exposed to toxins.

Hypoxic/Anoxia Episodes

Psychological traumas involving suicide attempts via carbon monoxide poisoning, respiratory-suppressing drug overdoses, near drownings (accidents, floods, storms), fires, chest injuries affecting circulation (crush injuries, stab wounds, shooting wounds), toxic spills and acute exposures, and electrocution can produce neurological damage that may have an acute and chronic impact on cognitive abilities. A variety of neuropsychological deficits have been noted to occur from the nonspecific neuropathological changes following anoxia, including dysfunctional memory attributed to reductions in hippocampal volume (Hopkins, Weaver, & Kesner, 1994; Hopkins et al., 1995).

Preexisting PTSD Exacerbated by the Onset of a Neurological Condition

These patients may present with increased PTSD symptoms following the development of a neurological disorder or onset of an acute condition. The exacerbation may result from the added effects of the neurological condition to existing trauma symptoms, direct triggering of trauma content, or indirectly as a threat to health that having the disease implies. Alternatively, the disease process may diminish the patient's capabilities for suppressing negatively valenced memories and affect. Chemtob and Herriott (1994) report a case of PTSD as a sequela of severe Guillain–Barré syndrome in a 24-year-old female. Cassidy and Lyons (1992) reported on the case of a 63-year-old, World War II male combat veteran who experienced increased dissociative episodes of hand-to-hand combat, intrusive recall of traumatic memories, and avoidance of reminders of the war after surviving a cerebral vascular accident (CVA). Clinically, the disinhibiting sequelae of CVA in the previous example above have also been observed with head injury occurring at some interval posttrauma that produced increased levels of hypervigilance, daytime flashbacks, intrusive memories, with decreased control over rage episodes, and decreased ability to override persistent physical reactions after being startled.

Neurological Factors Increasing Risk for Experiencing Trauma and Developing PTSD

Having a neurological condition can affect areas of higher cognitive processing involved in learning and memory, attention, planning, reasoning, judgment, monitoring of the environment, awareness of consequences, volition, sequencing abilities, controlling impulsivity, integration of complex information, and self-regulation (Brooks, 1989; Lezak, 1989). The psychosocial impact of impairments in these areas may increase the risk of incurring a trauma. Alterations in judgment and decreased appreciation of behavioral consequences may result in various kinds of accidents, beatings, or assaults.

Neuropsychological Effects of Substance Abuse in PTSD–Chronic Alcoholism

Alcohol is frequently abused by individuals with PTSD as an agent for regulating physiological arousal, promoting sleep, decreasing pain, and numbing responsiveness (Keane & Wolfe, 1990). Drinking occurs at varying rates and intervals. As a result, the potential neuropsychological effects are salient for PTSD patients. Harper, Kril, and Daly (1987) noted that radiological evidence indicating cortical atrophy in chronic alcoholics and in heavy social drinkers showed correlations with clinical and neuropsychological deficits. Their neuropathological studies revealed reduced brain weights and increased pericerebral space attributed to loss of white matter, particularly neuronal cell death and axonal degeneration in the anterior frontal lobe (superior frontal gyrus).

Parsons (1987) described negative cognitive effects of alcohol abuse. Neuropsychological deficits are predicted by frequency of drinking occasions and maximum quantity consumed each time. By their self-appraisal, alcoholics rate themselves as having reduced efficiency for common tasks requiring memory, problem-solving, perceptual–motor functioning, language, and communication. As duration of drinking increases, impairment scores approach those of brain-damaged patients. Much variability has been observed in the degree of deficits exhibited by alcohol abusers, as well as in recovery of function rates once abstinent. Alcohol impacts individual cognitive abilities, mood, behavior, and social functioning.

Gill and Sparadeo (1988) noted that 50–70% of all head-injury patients who were injured in MVAs had been drinking. The presence of alcohol can exacerbate the short-term neurobehavioral effects of head injury and delay or complicate recovery. Edna (1982) reported that injured patients having alcohol in the bloodstream had lower levels of consciousness when admitted and longer duration of coma not accounted for by other factors like skull fractures and hematomas. As a readily available substance that can be effective in modulating the affective states associated with PTSD, the impact of alcohol abuse on cognitive processes needs to be given serious consideration in formulations of neuropsychological status in trauma patients.

Neuropsychological Effects of Substance Abuse in PTSD–Chronic Stimulant Abuse

The effects of chronic cocaine use on neuropsychological functioning including new learning and memory, have been documented (Ardila, Roselli, & Strumwasser, 1990; Uddo & Gouvier, 1990). Hoff, Riordan, Alpert, and Volkow (1991) found impaired performances on the Wisconsin Card sorting Test and the an abbreviated Booklet Categories Test for a group of 20 cocaine abusers compared to 20 controls. Baxter and colleagues (1988) employed PET to study cerebral glucose metabolic rates of cocaine abusers in recent withdrawal. Previous studies in the literature had found decreases in anterior cortex, particularly in prefrontal and left-anterior temporal regions. However, when controlling for depression via the inclusion criteria, the findings of previous studies were not replicated. Azrin, Millsaps, Burton, and Mittenberg (1992) concluded that detrimental cognitive effects found for cocaine abusers were significantly related to length of abstinence and were reversible within 6 months of abstinence. As cocaine has been found to be an actively abused drug of choice among clinical PTSD patients (Cottler, Compton, Mager, Spitznagel, & Janca, 1992; Famularo, Kinscherff, & Fenton, 1992b; Fullilove, Lown, & Fullilove, 1992; Hamner, 1993; MacKay, Meyerhoff, Dillon, Weiner, & Fein, 1993), current use or recent abstinence needs to be considered as a confound when interpreting test performances.

Multiple Comorbidities

In clinical settings treating chronic PTSD, many more comorbid conditions can be present (Sierles, Chen, McFarland, & Taylor, 1983), and complex manifestations may be common. For instance, it may be the case that a patient reports being in a relationship involving repeated physical battering; has a childhood history of physical and sexual abuse, possibly from multiple perpetrators; and has developed a substance abuse problem. The substance abuse problem may be severe enough to produce MVAs while intoxicated (Hillbom & Holm, 1986). In constructing the DSM-IV profile, the symptoms may meet criteria for an Axis I diagnoses of PTSD, major depression, substance abuse disorder, panic disorder, and an Axis II personality disorder. This clinical presentation can be straight forwardly conceptualized from the trauma perspective, with the clinical symptoms explained psychologically. Yet, depending on the extent and severity of head injury from the beatings and MVAs, a neuropsychological explanation could be advanced for the role of organic factors that might produce the mood and panic disorder symptoms. Both perspectives contribute to the process of understanding a complex symptom presentation.

Although populations, types of traumas, and comorbidity have thus far received separate discussion, the previous hypothetical case description illustrates how these factors may commonly combine with each other. In practice, clinicians and researchers assess and treat the aggregate effects of these multiple comorbidities, thus reducing somewhat the utility of addressing them in isolation. Instead of disentangling the effects, considering them as bundled for both research and clinical purposes may be more prudent. As more research focuses on the shared symptoms and etiologies of trauma-related and neurological conditions, descriptive models will evolve into more comprehensive formulations, including brain-function bases for symptoms of overlapping disorders.

EXISTING LITERATURE ON
THE NEUROPSYCHOLOGICAL EVALUATION OF PTSD

The published studies examining neuropsychological test performances from PTSD patients to date are few and vary in format from single clinical case to small group designs. As a group, these studies utilize a range of PTSD samples and administer both standard and nonstandard test batteries. Although existing studies have reported variability in cognitive problems among trauma samples, clinical observations suggest that PTSD symptoms show the most overlap with the neurocognitive domains of attention, memory, and executive functioning. Tests assessing some or all of these domains are included in the studies reviewed here. Selected relevant studies have been divided into combat trauma and noncombat trauma groups and reviewed briefly. A general discussion of points common to the group of studies follows at the end of this section.

Studies with Combat Veteran Populations

Gil, Calev, Greenberg, Kugelmass, and Lerer (1990) noted that empirical data on memory and cognition in PTSD were lacking, but reports from clinical studies document deficits in these domains across PTSD groups and across time (Archibald & Tuddenham, 1965; Burstein, 1984, 1985; Bleich, Seigel, Garb, & Lerer, 1986). In a review of studies employing the Luria–Nebraska Neuropsychological Battery (LNNB) to assess psychiatric patients, Moses and Maruish (1988) reported on results from a group of 36 POW survivors of the Bataan Death March during World War II. Findings from the LNNB were in the normal performance range for their age and education levels. Although several of the subjects were noted to exhibit a variant of PTSD, no diagnostic information was given, and the extent of PTSD in the group is unknown.

Gurvits and coinvestigators (1993) studied 27 medication-free PTSD Vietnam veterans and 15 non-PTSD combat controls via neuropsychological testing, neurological examination, and sleep-deprived EEG methods. All subjects were without substance abuse or dependence during the previous year. Although the PTSD group showed more neurological soft signs (NSS) than non-PTSD subjects, neuropsychological testing revealed few differences, and obtained differences between groups did not fall into the impaired range. Nine of the neuropsychological tests were significantly correlated (using Bonferroni-corrected *p*-values) with presence of NSS.

Uddo et al. (1993) compared 16 outpatient male, PTSD veterans with 15 National Guard enlistees on a battery of verbal memory, visual memory, and attention/concentration measures, including the Auditory Verbal Learning Test, Rey–Osterrieth Complex Figure Test (ROCF), Controlled Oral Word Association Test (Verbal Fluency), and the Digit Span and Visual Span subtests from the Wechsler Memory Scale—Revised. The PTSD group scored significantly lower than controls on measures of new learning, immediate recall, and delayed recall in verbal and visual modalities. No differences were found for Digit Span and Verbal Fluency. The pattern of performance characteristics was noted to be similar to patients with identified fronto-subcortical pathology. The findings could not be attributed to comorbid neurological disorders, because these conditions were excluded from the study.

Sutker, Allain, and Johnson (1993) employed twin-study methodology to investigate the effects of differential exposure to war trauma on psychological complaints and cognitive functioning in a twin pair of Army pilots from World War II, one of whom was shot down and captured as a POW. Measures of cognitive functioning included the Wechsler Memory Scale—Revised, the Wechsler Adult Intelligence Scale—Revised (WAIS-R), Categories Test, Wisconsin Card sorting Test, Porteus Maze Test, Trailmaking Test, and the modified Rey Auditory Verbal Learning Test. The POW twin was described as meeting lifetime PTSD criteria, but not current PTSD; the control twin had never experienced PTSD symptoms. The test performances of the POW twin were characterized as showing deficits compared to his brother and to education-matched norms on arithmetic calculations, visuospatial analysis, organization and manipulation, memory for visual material, planning and inhibition of impulsivity; and complex concept formation, conceptual shifting and cognitive flexibility. Considered within the context of his WAIS-R Full-Scale IQ of 118, the POW twin's scores were relatively lower than what would have been expected given demographic factors and his brother's scores. The findings were hypothesized to reflect an acquired dysfunction involving the frontal lobes.

McNally and Shin (1995) examined 105 Vietnam combat veterans using the Shipley Institute of Living Scale (SILS) to compute WAIS-R Full Scale IQ estimates. Multiple regression analyses showed that IQ predicted 3% more of the variance in PTSD symptoms beyond variance attributable to combat exposure and years of education. The authors also reported that the lower a subject's intelligence quotient, the more severe the PTSD symptoms. Although the regression analyses were statistically significant, the actual benefit may not manifest clinically considering the multifactorial nature of IQ. The SILS is a completely verbal measure from which an IQ estimate that has a reasonably good correlation with WAIS-R Full-Scale IQ scores can be derived. In PTSD samples with learning disabilities that produce significant splits between Verbal IQ and Performance IQ scores, the SILS-IQ estimate will likely correlate less well. The protective influences of IQ in PTSD populations needs further elaboration.

Dalton, Pederson, and Ryan (1987) conducted neuropsychological testing on 100 male Vietnam veteran inpatients being treated in a specialized PTSD unit. All veterans received the Information, Arithmetic, Similarities, Picture Completion, Picture Arrangement, and Block Design subtests of the WAIS-R; 51 received the remaining subtest for a complete WAIS-R administration. Additional tests in the battery included the Rey Auditory Verbal Learning Test, Temporal Orientation, Serial Digit Learning, Trailmaking Test—Parts A and B, the Stroop Color–Word Naming Test, and the SILS. Few deficit performances were detected in this sample, with most mean test values being comparable to scores from normal, nonclinical samples. Only Trails B, Benton Visual Retention Test, and the Stroop Color–Word Naming Test showed slightly reduced group performances, and these findings were interpreted as reflecting mild anxiety effects, as would be expected in psychiatric inpatient samples.

Gil et al. (1990) evaluated the neuropsychological test performances of 12 PTSD, 12 matched psychiatric controls, and 12 normal controls. The PTSD sample was drawn from the Jerusalem Mental Health Center outpatient clinic and had traumatic histories involving battles, terrorists attacks, and car accidents. The test battery consisted of the WAIS, the Bender–Gestalt test, Benton Visual Retention Test, the Mental Control and Paired Associate items from the Wechsler Memory Scale, a Hebrew version of the verbal fluency test, the ROCF, and the Continuous Performance Test. PTSD patients showed significant impairment relative to controls, but at similar levels of impairment to the matched psychiatric controls on all tests. The pattern of findings reflected a meaningful decrease compared to premorbid abilities, and the decrease could not be attributed to acquired neurological injury or substance abuse because these conditions were excluded from the study. The authors interpreted the findings as supporting the hypothesis of a general cognitive dysfunction, rather than a PTSD-specific dysfunction.

Everly and Horton (1989) reported pilot data on 14 patients administered one test — the Four-Word Short-Term Memory Test, which is a modification of the Peterson Paradigm. No sample demographics were provided, and no information on type of trauma was given. Potential age effects were disconfirmed by an age-split analysis of the scores. Results indicated that 12 of the 14 subjects showed short-term memory deficits.

Studies with Noncombat Trauma Populations

Literature on trauma in noncombat populations mostly includes experiencing or witnessing accidents, natural disasters, interpersonal violence, and the various forms of child abuse. Tarter, Hegedus, Winsten, and Alterman (1984) examined 101 delinquent adolescents referred by juvenile court for neuropsychiatric assessment, which involved structured cognitive testing, and compared the physically abused delinquents to nonabused delinquents. The abused delinquents had significantly greater histories of paternal and maternal alcoholism, parental criminality, physical abuse, and temporary foster home placement. Although no differences were found due to gender and race, the abused delinquents obtained statistically lower scores on an auditory attention span test for words, Trails A, Purdue Pegboard — nondominant hand, PIAT Reading Comprehension, WISC-R/WAIS Full-Scale IQ, Verbal IQ, three Verbal subtests — Vocabulary, Comprehension, Similarities, and the Arithmetic subtest. These findings reflected primary difficulties in verbal or linguistic processing realms.

Dinklage and Grodzinsky (1993) investigated the hypothesis that excessive, repetitive trauma can produce alterations in synaptic sensitivity, eventually producing depression of synaptic habituation and discrimination, neuronal changes, and possibly neuronal death. To examine this hypothesis, 10 chronically traumatized children ages 8–15 were compared with 10 gender-, age-, and IQ-matched controls on neuropsychological tests, including WISC-R, Continuous Performance Test, Story Memory, Sentence Repetition, and the ROCF. Results showed that relative to the matched psychiatric controls, the group of abused children had higher levels of inattentiveness, poorer impulse control, and below-average verbal memory. These finding were not apparent from the standard IQ measures. Of particular note was the fragmented production style demonstrated on the ROCF, which is a complex stimulus. The piecemeal approach suggests difficulty in either perceiving the larger basic structure separately from the details, imposing an organizing structure when reproducing the whole figure, or both. A similar limitation working with visuospatial stimulus configurations has been observed for adult borderline personality disorder patients.

The effects of severe abuse during early childhood on personality formation and brain development are unknown, but of increasing interest to researchers who observe correlations with *PTSD* (Famularo, Kinscherff, & Fenton, 1991; Kiser, Heston, Millsap, & Pruitt, 1991; Rowan & Foy, 1993), *borderline personality disorder (BPD), multiple personality disorder (MPD),* and *potential neuropsychological deficits* (Andrulonis, Gluck, Stroebel, & Vogel, 1982; Glod, 1993; Knoll, 1993; O'Leary, Browers, Gardner, & Cowdry, 1991; O'Leary and Cowdry, 1994; Silk, Lee, Hill, & Lohr, 1995; Teicher, Ito, Glod, Schiffer, & Gelbard, 1994). Swirsky-Sacchetti and colleagues (1993) compared neuropsychological test performances of 10 female BPD patients to 10 age- and education-matched nonpatient controls. The BPD group obtained lower WAIS-R Full-Scale, Verbal, and Performance IQ scores, plus demonstrated impairments in motor skills, figural memory, complex visuomotor integration, and freedom from distractibility. The results were interpreted as reflecting dysfunction in fronto-temporal regions.

O'Leary and Cowdry (1994) reviewed findings across four studies presenting neuropsychological test data on BPD subjects and concluded that as a population, no obvious impairments in verbal skills or reasoning were present. However, when performances were compared with matched healthy controls, the visuospatial skills and memory of BPD subjects were impaired relative to their education levels, IQ, and general neuropsychological functioning. The visuospatial deficits were interpreted as revealing problems with inhibiting attention to irrelevant information and selecting visual details from a complex configuration. Memory deficits were not sufficiently explained by immediate versus delayed recall, or deliberate versus incidental memory dimensions. Deficits also were not confined to emotion-laden material and suggested broader memory problems. No localizing pattern emerged, although fronto-temporal involvement was suggested by the findings. Etiological factors for possible underlying organic determinants were not posited.

Rosenstein (1994) reviewed the literature on neurophysiological correlates in MPD and presented corresponding neuropsychological data from two clinical cases. Test findings for the MPD patients were interpreted as showing above-average overall intelligence scores with significant WAIS-R Verbal–Performance IQ differentials (> 23 points), and impaired free recall on memory tests. Severe depression and mildly abnormal EEGs were also present. Stringer and Cooley (1994) presented cognitive testing data from a case study of an MPD female with 2 female and 6 male alternate personalities. Two of the "adult personalities" each received a separate administration of the 20 subtests of Comprehensive Ability Battery (CAB) on different days. In addition, experimental attention measures, including visual digit span and the digit–consonant divided attention task, were administered to the personalities under separate (only one of the two personalities present), and "copresent" conditions (both personalities reported as simultaneously present in consciousness). Thus, each of the two "personalities" was administered three trials. The three trials consisted of one in which visual digits were monitored, one in which auditory consonants were monitored, and one in which both stimulus sources were monitored simultaneously. The expected decrement in tracking accuracy under the dual-stimulation condition is assessed against the baseline for single-stimulus presentation trials. For the "copresent" condition, in which dual stimuli were presented simultaneously, one personality was instructed to monitor presentation of the visual digits and the other personality instructed to monitor auditory consonants. The results showed individual variation across the 20 subtests of the CAB for the two personalities, but they were generally in the average-to-superior range on most tests except spatial ability, perceptual speed, and accuracy, which were low-average to below-average. Findings for the divided-attention task when only one personality was present showed the expected performances decrement for the dual-stimulus presentation condition. However, performances under the "copresent" condition showed no decrement in tracking performances compared against baseline, single-task performances. Assuming that two personalities present accounted for the performance, the findings suggest the possibility of a cognitive superiority for divided attention when the copresent personalities each monitored one component of the simultaneously presented dual stimulus, much like reciprocally aware, parallel processors consciously attending to the environment.

Summary Discussion of Studies

Overall, the findings in these studies are inconsistent regarding the presence and extent of neuropsychological impairments in PTSD and trauma-related disorders. Symptom complaints from PTSD patients usually include attention/concentration, memory, and some executive dysfunction. Although various studies detected these problems, as a group the studies reviewed did not consistently find impairments in these domains. However, drawing general conclusions from across the group of studies is problematic, because many of studies reviewed here are descriptive or uncontrolled case studies. The impact of the studies as a group is affected by methodological and sampling issues, the limits of the case-study format, and problems with the group designs. In general, the reporting of basic information was variable. Specifics about PTSD diagnostic procedures, trauma-history evaluation methods, and testing protocols ranged from missing or sparse to incomplete. Studies often noted that patients or subjects had PTSD without reporting specific PTSD symptoms or other general trauma-history variables to describe the subjects, such as presence of multiple traumas; chronicity of symptoms; or severity, as defined by frequency, duration, and magnitude of the stressors. Findings were often not interpreted relative to a conceptual model. The clinical case studies typified uncontrolled investigations suffering from the typical threats to internal and external validity (Campbell & Stanley, 1963). Their main contribution is the demonstration of neuropsychological assessment of comorbid conditions and PTSD that suggest further issues to explore.

Conclusions derived from the factorial designs are variously constrained due to design and methodological limitations, including (1) small sample sizes; (2) poorly specified inclusion and exclusion criteria, if present at all; (3) inadequate matching of the control group on relevant variables such as gender, age, education, type, and severity of psychiatric disorder; substance abuse parameters—drug type, pattern of drug use, duration and severity of use, time since start of sobriety (if sober); and (4) nonequivalence on cohort factors such as service era and military experience, medical health status, and comorbid neurological status. Some studies reduced the need to match on these variables by employing a priori exclusion criteria.

Generalization across group studies is limited due to discrepancies in findings possibly related to nonequivalence of samples for the aforementioned reasons, and parameters of the traumatizing event(s), which are not addressed sufficiently in standard neuropsychological protocols. To increase rigor in the group designs, matching must occur for the relevant variables, and these variables will be both trauma- and neuropsychologically based when studying cognitive problems of PTSD. Group studies that blend the variants together, disregarding appropriate matching factors, may obscure the differences within their sample that truly represent trauma effects on cognitive abilities.

None of the studies reviewed reported methods to account for potential reactivity to the testing process, or whether reactivity was measured in their studies. For some of the studies reviewed, it is possible that findings reflect altered engagement with the tasks during the data collection (cf. section on reactivity to the testing process for examples). Manifestations of reactivity to the testing process may vary widely across diverse groups, such as accident and crime survivors, combat veterans, and MPD patients. In studies where deficits in attention and memory were detected, it is unclear whether a true deficit was found or whether competition for attentional resources due to reactivity interfered with memory. Determining the difference is important for addressing the issue of stability of the impairments detected. On short-interval retesting, deficits caused by reactivity should reverse unless identical reactivity is elicited again.

In the research studies with identified, comorbid neurological conditions, the designs limited the ability to demonstrate an incremental effect for PTSD above the effects known to result from the neurological condition alone. Test batteries varied in composition, and the absence of standardization restricts comparisons across studies. Some greater degree of standardization needs to be developed without impeding the discovery of the unique contributions of trauma effects to the neuropsychological test results. Clinical protocols striving only to determine if cognitive processing problems exist may be secondarily concerned with incremental validity, but this is of greater concern for defining the components of a model.

The studies reviewed represent initial attempts to understand the functional impact of PTSD on brain–behavior correlates. Although the collective findings present a mixed picture at this point in time regarding consensus effects of trauma, they highlight the need for conceptual and methodological refinements that will shape future studies. Addressing these aspects will produce parallel benefits for practical issues surrounding test interpretation.

TEST INTERPRETATION ISSUES

Previous discussion related to types of comorbidity and neurobiological substrates is germane to the interpretation of test data, because these factors form a significant part of the context for determining presence and absence of deficits, for analyzing variations in test performances, and for developing conclusions and recommendations. The bulk of the interpretive context is derived from the history provided by the patient, collateral interviews, and the medical record. Obtaining a good neuropsychological history cannot be stressed enough. Although emphasizing solid history taking is not novel, suggesting that neuropsychologists include trauma histories and traumatologists include neurological factors to increase comprehensiveness may be a new perspective. For neuropsychologists who administer a standard battery each time, the additional history will primarily assist during the interpretation process. For those who employ a flexible battery approach, the comorbidity information may influence initial test selection as the test battery is composed.

Preinterpretation Considerations

Some general points, commonly understood to be important for neuropsychological test interpretation, have increased significance when testing PTSD patients in clinical settings.

1. *Recent sleep quality and sleep patterns should be assessed.* Chronic sleep problems are often present in PTSD patients (Woodward, 1993), including sleep apnea (Boza, Trujillo, Millares, & Liggett, 1984) and REM sleep behavior disorder (Lapierre & Montplaisir, 1992). Neuropsychological deficits resulting from hypoxia secondary to sleep apnea range from global, diffuse cognitive dysfunction to isolated memory problems (Greenberg, Watson, & Deptual, 1987; Martzke & Steenhuis, 1993). Other sleep problems are due to increased sleep onset latencies and midsleep awakenings from regularly occurring nightmares. Alcohol and drugs may be taken in extreme amounts to promote sleep. In some, the emotional aftereffects of the trauma-related nightmare persist into the next day and may result in sustained increases in hyperarousal, hypervigilance, and flashbacks. Daytime naps may be substituted to compensate for lost nighttime sleep, thus affecting circadian rhythms and potentially the fatigability during the test battery.

2. *Residual effects of peripheral physical damage as a result of the traumatic experience should be systematically reviewed* (e.g., motor vehicle accidents; torture survivors—ears, eyes, fingers; and military veterans—damage from explosions, booby traps).

3. *Medication and psychoactive substance use should be assessed as well for pattern of usage and any recent change (increases or decreases).* Fluctuations in usage patterns may parallel phasic changes in PTSD symptoms or be related to anticipatory anxiety about the testing process. For some, the increased medication or psychoactive substance use may facilitate test performances by reducing anxiety, whereas in others, excessive use detracts from test performances.

4. *The role of compensation-seeking, litigation, and secondary gain needs to be considered.* PTSD is a compensable disorder in the VA system, in workers' compensation claims, and in lawsuits. Recent controversies over PTSD in the courtroom and false memory syndrome in childhood sexual abuse cases could focus added attention on nontest aspects of the neuropsychological assessment process in forensic cases. In VA settings, receiving compensation is associated with service and monetary support. Veterans are often vigilant for any possible evaluations suggesting a positive change in their disability status that might become part of their official charts and jeopardize their compensation rating. Including neuropsychological measures of malingering in the test battery will assist in evaluating suspected, intentionally manipulated performances.

5. *Particular emphasis needs to be applied to evaluating attentional problems.* Systematic investigation of attentional functions is generally required to establish the patient's ability to engage the tests. Intact attentional abilities are the foundation for higher cognitive information-processing abilities, including memory and language (Mirsky, Fantie, & Tatman, 1995). As attention is not a unitary construct, specific measures of multiple modes should be included in test batteries. This recommendation is of particular importance with PTSD patients who experience hypervigilance, intrusive recollections,

hyperarousal, and dissociation that have a high potential for disrupting engagement with the testing process. These considerations and the discussion points in the section describing reactivity to the testing process should be used to answer the following questions: Was the patient distraction-free when instructions were given, so that all task requirements, not just the gist of the instructions, were fully understood before the test began? Were all facets of attention adequately engaged during testing? Was adequate attention applied to each test?

In addition to the standard data analysis and test interpretation process, the neuropsychological evaluation should ultimately address these fundamental questions. First, *do any deficits exist?* This can be addressed by comparing the test performances to age- and education-matched normative values when available.

Second, *when deficits are present, what is the pattern?* The pattern of deficits can first be described as lateralized, localized, or diffuse relative to normal population values. Qualitative performance features can be characterized in a similar manner, and when available, evaluated against normative values. Once performance levels for each test are established, levels within and across tests can be compared for patterns of relative strengths and weaknesses in the neurocognitive domains sampled.

Third, *is the pattern of deficits similar to other disorders, and is this pattern typical of PTSD populations?* Obtained patterns of deficits can be analyzed against other known disorders; but given the high incidence of observed comorbidity, this exercise may have less utility in chronic PTSD samples. Unless a suitable set of comorbid comparison groups is available, determining whether the pattern is typical of PTSD will be more complicated. Based on absence of consistent findings from the review of literature in the previous section, deciding which variables or test patterns to use in the process is open to debate. Comparing findings across studies is difficult at present because of the lack of standardization of diagnostic methods; variability in sample demographics and characteristics, in testing environments, and in the batteries of tests administered. An insufficient amount of study has been conducted that controls for these relevant variables across various types of traumas and populations. Individual settings need to establish local normative values based on comparisons of PTSD versus relevant non-PTSD control samples of clinical interest. This approach creates comparison groups of regionally similar, neurologically normal samples, in addition to the typical neurological, psychiatric, medical, and non-PTSD samples.

Fourth, *was the clinical testing process free from the effects of unintended affective priming?* If present, did the priming produce a main effect across tests, or interact with various components of the test battery to produce differential responding? Although relevant clinical considerations for neuropsychological testing are presented in the section reactivity to the testing process, previous investigation by Zimering, Caddell, Fairbank, and Keane (1993) demonstrated the effects of affective priming on task performance using an experimental paradigm. Exposure to auditory combat sounds produced subsequent decrements in performance on a motor steadiness task and letter vigilance during a continuous performance task. Corresponding increases in frightening and violent intrusive thoughts were also reported during the postprime intervals.

Fifth, *when present, do cognitive problems at the time of testing represent an exacerbation of existing symptoms typical of the phasic variation of PTSD, or a stable level of symptoms for the PTSD patient?* Do the observed cognitive problems covary with general level of distress and symptom severity; or, is there an interaction pattern among subsets of symptoms, with some deficits remaining relatively stable and others showing variation that is correlated with PTSD reexperiencing symptoms? Answering this question is a clinical consideration based on the history of symptom fluctuations. Symptom pattern variations serve as the context for integrating test findings during the formulation of clinical recommendations. For example, PTSD veterans can experience cyclical variation in symptoms related to seasons of the year, anniversary reactions, and publicly celebrated holidays. Variations in medical and psychological symptoms may prompt compensatory changes in medication use and substance abuse to modulate effects. The effects of an alcohol-abuse lifestyle can lead to traumatic brain injuries (TBIs) of varying severity from fights or motor vehicle accidents. TBIs are known to produce short- and long-term increases in depression and anxiety, confusion, social withdrawal, as well as cognitive function changes. Thus, the level of test performances for any given administration could represent cyclical variation in symptoms that may regress to the mean on retesting, or alternatively, test performances that are influenced by recent, minor TBI. Neither may be reported spontaneously by the patient.

PTSD Status and Reactivity to the Testing Process

One of the underlying assumptions for validity of neuropsychological test interpretations is that maximal performances were obtained during data collection so that decrements in performance levels relative to comparison norms would be associated with brain-related conditions. Methods for determining the role of confounding factors that attenuate performance must be systematically employed by the evaluator. Standardizing the test administration procedures, creating a conducive testing environment, and minimizing error due to nontest-related factors are some methods commonly incorporated for optimizing validity of the data collected. Psychiatric disorders, and PTSD in particular, require that additional considerations be addressed. For neurological disorders and syndromes in which the lesion is static or progressive, variations in the pattern of test performances are assumed to be attributable to the underlying lesion. In psychiatric samples with distorted reality testing, skewed information-processing tendencies, and disturbances of mood, neuropsychological test performances can more proportionately reflect psychiatric status. With PTSD, where reactivity to environmental cues characterizes the condition, the neuropsychological testing process can interact with the patient's trauma history, resulting in performance levels that inaccurately represent true cognitive functioning. The literature to date has not adequately addressed the range of reactivity to the testing process that can exist when assessing PTSD patients.

Interaction of Trauma Histories and Administrator Characteristics

Where PTSD Criterion A traumatic events occurred within an interpersonal context such as physical violence, rape, or threat to life by another person, patients will report both general and specific characteristics of the perpetrator or assailant. These details and general descriptions constitute cues that function to evoke physiological arousal and memories of the trauma when encountered in the everyday environment. The interpersonal context for testing is often a small office where the patient meets with the test administrator, who by virtue of gender or race alone may be a triggering stimulus for recall of traumatic experiences (e.g., Asians—for Vietnam veterans, or males—for sexual assault survivors).

Beyond general characteristics, trauma survivors may remember small details about the perpetrator that have become associated with threat or may have served as warning signals cuing escape/avoidance in the past. For instance, incest survivors who were abused when the perpetrator was intoxicated may have learned the connection between the bloodshot eyes associated with drinking and an increased probability of molestation. Should a test examiner's eyes resemble the perpetrator's (i.e., bloodshot, possibly due to allergies or wearing contact lenses), intrusive memories or dissociative episodes of varying lengths may be unintentionally triggered. Smells and odors can also function as powerful memory retrieval cues for trauma survivors. What would, under usual circumstances, be benign characteristics of the examiner may become significant in the testing process. This scenario could apply to men and women who might have been incest victims during childhood and to military veterans who experienced sexual assaults in the service. Although sexual assault is more commonly considered an act perpetrated by men toward women and girls, reports of mother–son, older females–younger boys, and men assaulting men in the military are reported in clinical populations. Without knowledge of the history of sexual assault, the stimulus value of the test administrator and the examinee's subsequent reactivity during testing may be undetected or, if detected, misattributed. Disengagement with the testing process by the examinee may be as subtle as a focused stare at the test stimuli and increased latencies to respond during the task to a full dissociation or panic attack.

Interaction of Trauma Histories and Testing Environment

In other instances, a number of features in the testing environment combine to produce a disruption in the examinee's level of task engagement. For example, if a trauma such as being a prisoner of war, an elevator accident, a car accident, or sexual assault involved being in a confined space, the combination of a small testing room and features of the test administrator may elicit a range of reactions, including intrusive memories, increased physiological reactivity, and dissociation. Adequacy of the neuropsychological testing environment on a number of levels is always an issue needing attention. Room space for clinical activities in most settings is limited, and assessments are often conducted in rooms not specifically designed for testing. The features of the room space can be very important for PTSD patients. If the room is not sound-isolated, noise in the hallway or adjoining rooms may repeatedly draw the attention of the hypervigilant patient. Spurious noise problems are frequently addressed by masking them with white-noise generators or small fan devices in the room. Although successful in blocking other noises, the constant low-level din emitted from the masking device can resemble the characteristics of background noise from past traumas and may trigger memories for patients who were in chaotic combat, accidents, or natural disasters. Combat veterans exposed to the concussive effects of artillery explosions and torture survivors may have chronic tinnitus that is compounded by the masking devices (Graessner, 1993).

Chronic PTSD patients who have developed a pattern of attending to stimuli around them and then escaping cognitively from triggered intrusive images may automatically engage in these monitoring processes and escape strategies during testing without reporting them. Depending on the test being administered at the moment, the effects on performance could include slower reaction times, longer times to completion, interference with storage during memory tasks, incomplete processing of instructions for the task, the appearance of inconsistent responding, or premature discontinuation of the task by the patient, which might look like "giving up." Examiners should be aware of these instances, but, unless reported freely by the patient or when prompted, they may go undetected.

Another aspect of the testing environment that might interact with trauma histories is silence. For a portion of trauma survivors, a conditioned emotional response may be elicited by silence. For these individuals, silence or hiding in silence may have followed or preceded the onset of a traumatic experience. Combat veterans who waited in silence while setting an ambush, or ones who noticed the silence before being ambushed on patrol, may become more agitated by quiet in sound-reduced testing rooms. Incest and crime victims who hid in silence may have similar reactions. Silence is also an environmental condition that offers nothing for the PTSD patient to monitor, and without a stimulus present to capture attention, unwanted thoughts of the trauma may intrude. To prevent silences, patients may talk at fairly continuous rates and provide overdetailed answers to free-response sections of tests.

Interaction of Trauma Histories with Test Features and Task Requirements

Reactivity in this category is not necessarily intuitive if the test behavior of neurological patients is the primary comparison sample. Patients with dementias, cerebral vascular accidents, and neoplasms will infrequently have direct traumatic associations with features of the test stimuli or the task. Frustration and some catastrophic reactions can be observed when these patients notice poor performances, but idiosyncratic associations are more rare. In PTSD patients, however, a generalization gradient may have developed from a specific trauma-event cue or set of cues to broader classes of stimuli. The neuropsychological test examiner may encounter unexpected reactions to the test materials that are associated with traumatic experiences. A case example of a military combat veteran illustrates how test characteristics interact with patient history.

During administration of the test battery, a veteran whose trauma involved a near-death experience from artillery fire had a series of responses to the neuropsychological tests that culminated in discontinuation of the testing because of the level of distraction he experienced. During a computerized administration of a Continuous Performance Task—which requires sustained monitoring for, and response to, the appearance of an X in one condition, or an X which was preceded by an A in another condition—he developed heightened levels of physiological arousal because the colored, letter stimuli of the task in his view "exploded" onto the screen. His vigilance became heightened, and memories of the shelling he experienced were evoked. Once primed by these memories, subsequent testing was affected. During the Visual Span task from the Wechsler Memory Scale—Revised, he again experienced an intrusive recall of his traumatic experience. This test, which is a visual analog of the Digit Span task, required the patient to observe and reproduce a sequence that is finger tapped by the administrator on small, colored squares printed on a stimulus card. The Forward Span test uses a card with green squares and the Backward Span task uses one with red squares. The process of reproducing the tapped sequence on the red squares reminded him of red tracers from small arms and artillery fire. During motor speed testing for the Finger Tapping test, his association was to past experiences of squeezing the trigger to fire a machine gun while on guard duty. During this association, he raised his head, looked out the window and had a momentary flashback of the landscape around his guard post. The effects of these experiences lingered and manifested during the Sensory–Perceptual Examination, producing sensory errors that were inconsistent ipsilaterally and contralaterally. Subsequent retesting of sensory–perceptual functions on another day produced a within-normal-limits performance. Had he not provided the information on the distracting intrusions he experienced, the inconsistency in his performance could possibly have been misconstrued as motivational problems or malingering.

Computerized tasks, such as the Continuous Performance Test, that present stimuli at short, repeating intervals may elicit a dissociation in patients who are prone to this experience. Explanations for this are unclear, but this response during testing is an acute, reactive state that limits the potential of patients to generate their best performance. It may be that if targets are presented at a rate that is too fast, the patient may feel unable to process the information, producing feelings of failure, inadequacy, and helplessness, which may be associated with past trauma. Alternatively, the dissociative experience may be a manifestation of a photosensitive seizure or a reflex epilepsy. Photosensitive seizures can result from the presentation of synchronized visual stimuli such as a flickering light in specific frequency ranges. Monochromatic red light has been shown to be more potent than other colors (Engel, 1989). Complex reflex epilepsies are elicited by very specific stimuli or stimulus conditions that frequently involve some level of cognitive or emotional appreciation of the stimulus (Forster, 1977).

The previous discussion illustrated how the visually oriented test stimuli can elicit reactions; not being able to see can be equally distressing. Neuropsychological procedures that require wearing a blindfold (e.g., Tactual Performance Test) may be problematic for survivors of nighttime physical or sexual assault, or for veterans with combat experiences such as being ambushed in the dark, being assigned to explore enemy tunnels in Vietnam, being blindfolded and tortured as prisoners, or having temporary loss of sight from explosions or concussions. More generally, wearing a blindfold increases feelings of vulnerability by reducing patients' ability to be vigilant of the environment, and these feelings in turn may exacerbate PTSD symptoms during testing.

Thematic Associations Cued by Testing

The testing process may activate a variety of thematic associations with traumatic experiences in PTSD patients. Conceptual themes involving the absence of prediction and control may be aroused during assessment and manifest as overt discomfort and agitation when faced with ambiguity. It is not uncommon for PTSD veterans to report anticipatory anxiety beginning days before an appointment in which a new procedure or an anticipated negative experience is expected. Their distress related to these themes can often be traced to past anticipation of engaging the enemy and the need for information to maximize prediction and increase the likelihood of survival. Anticipation can prompt a search for information that may increase distractibility and confound performances on the initial tests in the neuropsychological battery. Alternatively, a proportion of veteran samples also report that they become less anxious and very focused once the objectives of a task or situation are clear, similar to battle conditions in which their attention became acutely focused once the fighting had begun. These individuals may show greater freedom from distractibility on portions of the testing.

Themes related to survivor guilt, acts of commission and omission (atrocities committed or witnessed and not prevented), trauma contexts, and low self-worth may trigger further associations with more specific memories. Poor test performance can activate cognitive schemas surrounding feelings of guilt associated with responsibility for the consequences of underperforming in the past (e.g., negative consequences to others, or when lives were at stake). If patients notice that their performance is flagging, followed by feelings of "failure" that cue recall, then trauma memories may intrude during task execution. Low self-esteem and feelings of low self-worth may interact with the intrusive memory to further depress or interrupt test performances. As an example, after fairly easily completing the Vocabulary section of the SILS, then experiencing much difficulty on the Abstract Reasoning section, a combat veteran was overcome by visual and verbal intrusions of leading his men in a failed mission. Feeling failure on the test cued the intrusions during the SILS; some of the intrusions were auditory, such as "Don't fail; don't let the men down."

Performance anxiety can also induce physiological arousal, and these states can subsequently trigger intrusions during testing. During traumatic experiences, physiological reactions can be a very prominent aspect of the experience (e.g., feeling or hearing their heartbeat in their ears may have been paired with the silence of sitting still and keeping quiet during an ambush in Vietnam, or with hiding from sexual abuse perpetrator). If an error-free performance, defined as either exhibiting or inhibiting an action, was linked to survival in the past, the similarity of task requirements during testing may activate this schema. This possible interaction should be considered for tasks in which exhibition and inhibition of specified responses are tested (e.g., motor Go/No-Go tests), and for procedures in which direct feedback in the form of correct–incorrect is standard during the task (e.g., the Wisconsin Card Sorting Test, the Categories Test).

Single words may be sufficient to cue a theme. Previous findings using the Stroop paradigm (Litz & Herman, 1993; McNally, Kaspi, Riemann, & Zeitlin, 1990) have shown increased latencies for color naming of trauma-relevant words in combat veterans. These findings have been interpreted as representing not only past exposure to trauma, but also the severity of intrusive symptoms during the task (McNally, 1995). Language assessment tasks may inadvertently trigger associations. For the Controlled Oral Word Association procedure, which measures verbal fluency by asking patients to produce as many words as possible starting with a target letter, traumatized patients may generate words directly related to their trauma that prime affect- and cue-intrusive recollections (e.g., words beginning with "S" for combat veterans: shrapnel, shelling, sharpshooter, sniping).

Idiosyncratic responses to other tests have been observed in combat veterans. Items in Subtests IV, V, and VI of the Categories Test include configurations that can resemble defensive physical perimeters of military compounds as viewed from aerial maps. Establishing defensive perimeters and planning missions that targeted enemy positions often involved detection of pattern configurations. To some, Mesulum's Letter and Shape Cancellation task resembles a schematic of a minefield. The recall trials of the ROCF and the Visual Reproduction of the Wechsler Memory Scale can remind some of diagrammatic renderings of enemy compounds. Spacial associations, linked to visual memory, may rapidly induce intrusions.

Receiving instructions for completing neuropsychological tests has been reported by some veterans as feeling like being briefed for an upcoming mission. As they listen to the instructions from the examiner, their attentional focus narrows so that the objectives would be clear. In some this narrowing of focus leads to an intense engagement with the task, and they may overly associate the moment with past military experiences. In others, if closely associated with a trauma experience, it may subsequently be distracting. Using the computerized Continuous Performance Test (visual X/A–X version) again as an example, a veteran reported that listening to instructions elicited a "mission-mode" in him as he prepared to engage the task. Task instructions that required him to respond to target letters as quickly as possible on the screen paralleled mission requirements to quickly spot an enemy soldier in the bushes/jungle and shoot before being shot ("It was like shooting at something coming out of the dark"). Pressing the computer key on this task was analogous to pulling the trigger. Assuming a *mission mentality* produces a narrowed focus of attention that either facilitates or impairs test performances. Shorter latency commission errors can increase from too rapidly responding to *any* on-screen stimulus change (the "shoot-first" strategy); while omissions errors ("missed targets") can distressingly induce feelings of being vulnerable because of poor vigilance (symbolically shot by the enemy).

In hospital settings where PTSD patients with medical problems are being tested, feelings of vulnerability resulting from having a serious illness can induce increased reexperiencing and generalized arousal that may be present during testing. In the hospital context, patients may be shuffled through clinics and receive procedures with little explanation and little feedback about test results. If prediction and control are reduced, a decreased sense of rapport with the care providers can result in a distrust in the process. Feelings of vulnerability can be heightened in the absence of trust. For trauma survivors whose traumatic events involved violations of interpersonal trust, or those who have become highly distrustful subsequent to the trauma, the testing process may evoke emotional reactions. Abused children may distrust adults, and adult trauma survivors may distrust authority figures, government, institutions, hospitals, and staff affiliated with medical centers.

Impersonal treatment, which can be part of the patient experience in large institutions, often inflames existing agitations. Military veterans are known to express feeling of being experimented upon, and some have documentation of their military treatment (e.g., radiation exposure from being placed in open trenches during nuclear bomb testing). The word "testing," in neuropsychological testing can elicit reactions, because it seems like a direct challenge, or something that must be endured. General negative associations with testing may be present for many patients who had poor academic histories or aversive experiences taking tests in school, and may be particularly true of trauma survivors with learning disabilities. Strategic attention applied to developing good examiner–patient rapport is central for reducing potential arousal that accompanies feeling of vulnerability from these factors.

Whereas the types of themes discussed here may be shared to a degree by many patients as reactions to illness or as part of normal life, for traumatized patients they may be more readily activated because of their past connection with life-threatening events producing traumatic stress reactions. Chronic PTSD patients may not necessarily be aware of the relationship between past experiences, cue-evoked themes, and the impact on their neurocognitive abilities when themes are cued during interviews or testing. Although awareness of some impact may occur if physiological arousal or feelings of discomfort increase, the patient may causally attribute these reactions to the testing process rather than past trauma experiences.

Accounting for the Potential Process Confounds

The degree to which these parameters alter neuropsychological test results is not well researched, although general performance enhancement is an unlikely outcome. The process of conducting neuropsychological testing with PTSD populations for clinical or research purposes should include mechanisms for addressing the presence of altered states of engagement with the testing. The test administrator needs to be clinically aware of the general range of potential reactions from traumatized populations, and be informed of the specific types of reactions the individual patient might exhibit during the course of testing, based on an understanding of their trauma experiences. Testing may need to be tailored accordingly. Although some patients with PTSD have levels of hypervigilance requiring a clear view of exits—examiner's back to the door, others may need a physical arrangement of the furniture that allows them the perception of clear egress if necessary—patient's back to the side wall.

Levels of arousal need to be carefully observed as signs that attention may be shifting internally to intrusions or externally as an increase in hypervigilance. Preparing patients for testing by providing a thorough explanation of the upcoming test procedures facilitates them in predicting the experience and may reduce the anticipatory anxiety. Eliciting their participation in reporting attentional shifts to the examiner increases the likelihood of detecting shifts. Succeeding here may be a challenge that depends in good measure on rapport with the test administrator, assessment team, or primary referral source. One salient feature of PTSD patients is avoidance of stimuli and circumstances that arouse memories and physiological reactivity. Self-observation of, and comfort talking about, their symptoms may not be a well-developed part of their behavioral repertoire, especially if increased anxiety results from monitoring and disclosure. To ensure the validity of test interpretations, process checks should be included with data collection so that patterns of deficits can be correctly attributed to reactivity when present, rather than to underlying lesions.

Patients may not be able to tolerate a lengthy battery of tests. A common consideration for geriatric populations and others with fatigue-prone disorders, PTSD patients should be monitored for fatigue levels as well. Veteran populations have been described as "commonly reporting fatigue, concentration difficulties, somatic distress, and other complaints that impair capacity to endure lengthy testing sessions" (Dalton et al., 1986, 1989). Monitoring for fatigue is a good assessment practice in general. For the more chronic groups of PTSD patients with greater symptom severity, the cognitive demand of sustained, focused, mental activity may produce fatigue, accompanied by increased hypervigilance and vulnerability to intrusive recollections as their cognitive capacity to inhibit these reactions wanes.

To minimize fatigue for clinical evaluations, long batteries can be divided into shorter sessions. Although this assists in maintaining peak performance for each session, it complicates the correlation of test findings across sessions, because the patient is open to effects of environmental events that may exacerbate symptoms and alter mood states. In controlled settings, acute shifts in clinical presentation will primarily result from sleep disturbance, nightmares, flashbacks, increased intrusions, carryover effects of therapy groups, and interactions with visitors. For outpatients, similar factors may be influential, with the added effects of substance abuse and increased use of prescription medication to control symptom escalation.

Blind interpretation of testing data from PTSD protocols can be confounded, because transient alterations in attention from intrusions or dissociations are difficult to rule in or rule out by examining the pattern among test performances. Attentional measures within the neuropsychological test battery are often examined to make a judgment about examinees' ability to concentrate, and if they fall within expected ranges, a generalized assumption of adequate attention across the test battery may be inferred. However, the transient nature of these alternations in attention and their occurrence as a result of specific cuing during testing makes this practice potentially problematic for establishing the validity of the whole test battery. To facilitate the data interpretation by the neuropsychologist, clinical psychometrists, trainees, and neuropsychological research technicians need to have structured-process recording forms available for recording their observations during testing, and they should also be trained in observing the many diverse reactions demonstrated by PTSD patients.

FUTURE DIRECTIONS

With each advance in behavioral neuroscience methods, the potential for discovering psychopathological etiologies improves. Correlative measurement of cortical functioning via structured neuropsychological testing, electrophysiological assessments, and noninvasive scanning techniques offers opportunities for understanding the cortical activity of PTSD patients as they process information. Functional neuroimaging methods also provide a comparative standard against which functional neuropsychological deficits can be indexed. These methods all complement information obtained from psychological evaluations, structural neuroanatomical scans, and neurochemical assays.

In recent years, psychiatric disorders have been increasingly conceptualized as manifestations of brain dysfunction. PTSD may constitute a unique opportunity to investigate the effects of the interaction of environment and brain functioning on development of psychopathology. Unlike most other disorders in the DSM, the Criterion A component of the PTSD diagnosis explicitly implicates environmental experiences as causal agents in the symptom development process. The human brain as repository of past experience, primary processor of present experience, and architect of planned future experience is the wellspring of PTSD symptoms. Although current technologies and methodologies may limit the depths to which precise causal mechanisms can be probed in research protocols, many potential empirical investigations can be initiated to continue advancing our understanding of the complexities of PTSD's neurocognitive concomitants.

Different research goals may need to be defined, based on the intended applications of findings from the neuropsychological studies. If the goal is to identify the unique contributions of a single traumatic experience in determining the cognitive impairments associated with PTSD symptoms, then a relatively pure — unconfounded, noncomorbid — sample of trauma survivors needs to be studied. This sample should contain patients who meet Criterion A, are beyond the acute stress disorder stage, have developed sufficient PTSD symptoms to meet diagnostic criteria but have not yet begun a pattern of negative coping behaviors that would confound interpretations of the data, and are free of preexisting neurological problems and prior trauma. Findings here would conceivably add to our understanding of the cognitive effects of trauma in isolation. However, findings and models developed subsequently from this method of study may not generalize to typical clinical samples that are characterized by complicated symptom presentations. Alternatively, if comorbidity is presumed to occur at rates high enough to be considered inherently associated with PTSD, especially in the case of chronic PTSD, then generalizability of the developed models will be enhanced by studying samples that also contain the comorbid characteristics of interest. Experimental designs that account for confounds by blocking them as levels of the independent variable or multivariate statistical techniques will need to be employed in these studies to disentangle relative causal influences of the target variables.

Model Development

A neuropsychological model of PTSD is needed to guide research investigations and clinical process. Future research into the origins of the current PTSD symptom clusters will likely find that they reflect dynamic patterns of whole-brain activity. What remains unclear is the balance between cortical and subcortical contributions to observed or reported PTSD symptoms. Having a well-defined model that attributes symptoms to hypothesized brain regions or brain systems would assist in focusing investigations, developing measures, and refining the assessment process. Neuropsychological tests, generally regarded as more sensitive to cortical brain activity, should be indirectly affected by the subcortical activity that may underlie the form and expression of some clusters of PTSD symptoms. Nightmares and triggered symptoms such as exaggerated startle response and physiological reactivity to reminders of the trauma are likely to be primarily associated with subcortical origins compared to conscious, effortful avoidance of thoughts, feelings, and circumstances reminiscent of the trauma, sense of foreshortened future, and concentration difficulties. However, if existing neurobiological models of PTSD are accurate (Kolb, 1987, 1988, 1989; Pitman, 1989a, 1989b), then the effects of the postulated neural hypersensitization process from traumatic stress exposure should influence multiple brain systems and be detectable across many levels of functional testing.

The challenge for developing a neuropsychological model of PTSD is defining the assumptions upon which hypotheses can be formulated. The relationship of test responses to the phenomenon of interest is only as valid as the established correspondence to brain functioning. Current conceptualizations of brain-function correlates of PTSD produce more questions than answers. Neuropsychological approaches will be influenced by developments in molecular and neurobiology that contribute to answering questions about the mechanisms of trauma's impact on the brain, affecting cognitive functions and altering the manner in which information is subsequently processed. If mechanisms can be discovered, then cortical status can be included as one of the preexisting vulnerabilities that may determine whether PTSD develops after exposure to a potentially traumatizing event.

A comprehensive formulation of the neuropsychology of PTSD would need to include the following to be viable as a heuristic for guiding research into the next century:

1. The model needs to address possible differences in neuropsychological test performances as a function of basic demographic characteristics such as age, gender, and developmental level (in children).

2. The interactions of demographic factors with the type and severity of trauma experienced may create unique subtypes that need to be predicted. Trauma researchers are currently struggling with the challenge of how best to specify the psychological effects for the complex combinations of frequency, intensity, and duration of trauma exposure. Adopting the most effective procedures for classification of trauma experiences will be important for constructing representative groups against which neuropsychological test findings can be indexed.

3. While current clinical research strives to define the distributed effects of trauma on psychological functioning for adults and children, the same process must be extended to neuropsychological functioning in PTSD. It is conceivable that early traumatic experiences affect the overall organization of the brain, producing deficits in processing some types of information, and possibly a corresponding superiority for other types of information. A very extreme example of this organization can be seen for idiot savants, whose severe limitations in overall intellectual development are matched by an equally extreme untrained, native ability in some circumscribed activity such as mental calculations, or playing a musical instrument. Stringer and Cooley's (1994) demonstration of superior divided-attention performances for copresent multiple personalities may be one example of distributed processing abilities resulting from a trauma-influenced cortical organization. If this type of organizational process occurs along multiple continua, then many potential versions of PTSD-related cognitive patterns might emerge on testing.

4. Clinical samples have repeatedly shown that PTSD symptoms do not exist in isolation; as such, the high rates of comorbidity must be explained, not just viewed as a nuisance variable. A salient issue in this regard is the contribution of preexisting factors and posttrauma adaptation to the PTSD symptom presentation. For example, preexisting factors may promote acute stress responses, whereas posttrauma adaptations can produce chronic, maladaptive coping patterns manifesting as substance abuse as a method of managing the hyperarousal and reexperiencing. Having a current substance abuse lifestyle alone can produce cognitive changes independent of any hypothesized effects from trauma (Ardila et al., 1990; Mittenberg & Motta, 1993; Parsons, 1987), which highlights the point of studying symptom aggregates. Moreover, the various combinations of factors closely represent the actual patients who seek treatment, and whose cognitive functioning is affected by a composite of their symptoms.

5. The level of general psychopathology must be considered, especially as a function of the effects of chronicity on cognitive abilities. Predictions here will need to account for cognitive effects of chronicity from trauma acquired as an adult and during development as a child. Chronicity is reflect-

ed separately by DSM Axis I and DSM Axis II disorders and by the interactions between these axes. In addition to possibly altering information-processing abilities, early traumatic experiences may affect the course of cortical development in children in a manner that consequently shapes the development of a trauma-adapted personality, manifesting as BPD and MPD, and other syndromes such as attention deficit disorder and learning disabilities. Emerging findings point to an overlap among these syndromes, suggesting the effects of trauma as the common denominator.

6. Can existing neurological disorders and syndromes be employed as models of anatomical substrates to explain the expression of some PTSD symptoms (e.g., fugue states, reduplicative paramnesias, temporo-limbic epilepsy, Capgras syndrome)?

7. Does clear neurological disease overshadow the psychiatric effects of PTSD, or when comorbidly present, do the two interact to create a clinical hybrid?

8. Can a "pure" PTSD lesion be acquired in the absence of biological predisposition, or does PTSD develop because of preexisting vulnerabilities that might include residual brain effects from earlier traumas or acquired injuries?

Once a theoretical model is specified, practical issues will remain for testing its postulates. Some considerations include the following:

1. Can a representative PTSD group be defined for studying the isolated effects of trauma on cognitive variables that is without pretrauma and posttrauma confounds?

2. Would findings from studying this group be meaningful and generalize to the type of chronic PTSD patient commonly presenting for treatment?

3. What are the best methods for interpreting how much of the neuropsychological test performances are a reflection of PTSD versus the plethora of comorbid psychiatric, medical, and neurological conditions?

4. Are the psychological effects of trauma established sufficiently and the investigation methods advanced enough for use in examining which of the parameters of the traumatic experience predicts patterns of neurocognitive processing?

5. If early trauma is implicated as a determining factor in shaping neurocognitive functioning, then what factors are most critical for defining control- and target-study groups?

6. If the effects of trauma on neuropsychological functioning are hypothesized to be different for adults than for children and adolescents with developing brains, then what are the most sensitive measures to select for each population—clinical neuropsychological or experimental neuropsychological measures? Very basic knowledge of neuropsychological performances in PTSD populations has yet to be established. At this point in time, the

sensitivity of these instruments for measuring the neurocognitive aspects of PTSD has not been established, nor has it been disconfirmed. It is unclear which test instruments are most sensitive, or if clinical neuropsychological measures are best suited for assessing the cognitive problems accompanying PTSD. Clinical neuropsychological tasks that are useful for examining the effects of neurological disorders on cognitive functioning may prove too prone to ceiling effects in traumatized patients, especially younger adult samples.

7. What are the optimal administration procedures for sampling the neurocognitive effects of PTSD, given available measures? Using tests with established literatures to study PTSD is a reasonable starting strategy, but if future studies that are better controlled find few deficits, then the overall composition of test batteries will need to be reconsidered, and testing procedures may need to be modified. Given that PTSD presents clinically with static and phasic components, the combination of history-collection procedures, tests selected, and the administration methods employed should adequately sample the variation. To increase sensitivity to the cognitive problems reported by patients, research protocols may need to test PTSD patients in affectively primed and unprimed states as an analog that mimics information-processing conditions in everyday settings.

Answers to these questions will dictate study designs, sampling strategies, and the search for methods most sensitive to the corresponding cognitive dysfunctions.

Treatment Integration

Functional recommendations from neuropsychological evaluations will need to be integrated more effectively with clinical treatment protocols. At present, if impairments are detected, typical test findings are less likely to be interpreted from a PTSD framework and more likely summarized as performances showing a diffuse patterns of neurocognitive deficits, ranging in severity from mild to moderate, similar to organic-psychiatric or general-psychiatric groups. As noted previously, some samples, and some individuals within PTSD samples, will exhibit greater degrees of functional impairment in cognitive domains resembling other brain syndromes because of coexisting closed head injuries, learning disabilities, attention deficit disorder, seizure disorders, medical problems, and substance abuse. In chronic clinical PTSD samples with coexisting mood disorders, the effects of depression will likely be evident in the test findings as well.

To increase the utility of the testing process and the findings obtained, results need to be more closely linked to clinical behavioral problems experienced by the patient. For instance, do PTSD patients with anger-control problems and rage episodes demonstrate patterns of deficits on tests that are affected by frontal lobe dysfunction? Are scanning and tracking errors on testing correlated with clinical hypervigilance, or does the presence of hypervigilance result in better performances on these tests? Do the type of amnestic problems defined for neurological disorders manifest similarly on testing for PTSD patients with psychogenic amnesia? Can levels of PTSD symptom severity be explained by decreased overall cognitive capacity as demonstrated across a battery of tests requiring sustained mental activity? Answering these questions would add to practical impact of the testing results.

Although greater integration of neuropsychological assessment can occur in the future, current application can reap immediate benefits. Presently, in many settings, PTSD patients may be placed into treatment protocols that implicitly require certain levels of sustained attention and concentration focus, plus minimum capacities for verbal abstraction and memory (e.g., various forms of group and process-oriented individual therapy). Neuropsychological test findings can assist in matching patients to treatment with greater accuracy than a simple mental status examination. Neuropsychological testing can also be used when explaining to patients that portions of their reactions and internal experiences may be a product of brain injury. For example, a veteran undergoing an evaluation reported being overwhelmed with guilt feeling surrounding the responsibility he felt for the death of close friends in a combat firefight. He also experienced 30 days of coma from a closed head injury and subsequently began hearing auditory hallucinations of his friends' voices, telling him that he was at fault for their deaths. He concluded that he caused the voices as a way to punish himself for surviving the battle when they had died; the combination of hallucinations and attributions invariably produced episodes of deep depression and suicidal ideation. In this case,in which anatomical lesions were present and documented in the medical record (e.g., diffuse abnormalities on the MRI scan from the previous closed head injury), feedback about the effects of brain damage as a possible cause of the voices was very useful in modifying his attribution that they were self-caused as punishment. This information, combined with his neuropsychological findings, provided the foundation of an alternative explanation for his symptoms and subsequently reduced for him the sustained discomfort that typically had continued after each hallucinatory episode.

Observing the PTSD patient's overall response to a battery of tests provides additional clinical benefit. The amount of effort required by the patient to sustain concentration and complete a neuropsychological test battery can inform clinicians about patient fatigability and the likely emergence or change in symptoms resulting from sustained mental exertion. As the previous section on reactivity to the testing process showed, patients can exhibit reactions during testing that are not necessarily elicited during the interview process. These reactions during structured testing may be analogous to the types of responses that develop when faced with daily challenges.

In conclusion, state-of-the-art neuropsychological assessment of PTSD relies mainly on methods developed in previous decades, before the official PTSD diagnosis was formalized in the DSM-III. The adequacy of conceptual models and testing methods needs to evaluated to determine appropriateness for examining cognitive dysfunction in PTSD. Expanded application of new imaging techniques and the introduction of computer-based testing protocols will augment the available non-self-report methods for examining PTSD cognitive processes. Advances in our understanding of the effects on neurocognitive functioning resulting from traumatic experiences will occur in conjunction with ongoing theorizing and the many parallel lines of investigation from all sectors of trauma study. Although trauma investigators with diverse perspectives on causality may depend upon levels of analysis that assume different degrees of parsimony, each contributes a complementary piece to the conceptual puzzle. Future developments will continue to define the role of neuropsychological approaches as the intermediary between the psychological and neurobiological investigations of trauma.

REFERENCES

American Psychiatric Association. (1980). *Diagnostic and statistical manual of mental disorders* (3rd ed.). Washington, DC: Author.

Andreasen, N. C. (1989). *Brain imaging applications in psychiatry.* Washington, DC: American Psychiatric Press.

Andrulonis, P. A., Glueck, B. C., Stroebel, C. F., & Vogel, N. G. (1982). Borderline personality subcategories. *Journal of Nervous and Mental Disease, 170,* 670–679.

Archibald, H. C., & Tuddenham, R. D. (1965). Resistant stress reaction after combat: A 20-year follow-up. *Archives of General Psychiatry, 12,* 475–481.

Ardila, A., Roselli, M., & Strumwasser, S. (1990). Neuropsychological deficits in chronic cocaine abusers. *International Journal of Neuroscience, 57,* 73–79.

Azrin, R. L., Millsaps, C. L., Burton, D. B., & Mittenberg, W. (1992). Recovery of memory and intelligence following chronic cocaine abuse. *The Clinical Neuropsychologist, 6*(3), 344.

Baggaley, M. R., & Rose, J. (1990). Post-traumatic stress disorder [Correspondence to the editor]. *British Journal of Psychiatry, 156,* 911.

Barth, J., Macciocchi, S., Giordani, B., Rimel, R., Jane, J., & Boll, T. (1983). Neuropsychological sequelae of minor head injury. *Neurosurgery, 13,* 529–533.

Baxter, L. R., Schwartz, J. M., Phelps, M. E., Mazziotta, J. C., Barrio, J., Rawson, R. A., Engel, J., Guze, B. H., Selin, C., & Sumida, R. (1988). Localization of neurochemical effects of cocaine and other stimulants in the human brain. *Journal of Clinical Psychiatry, 49*(2), 23–26.

Biederman, J., Newcorn, J., & Sprich, S. (1991). Comorbidity of attention deficit hyperactivity disorder, with conduct, depressive, anxiety and other disorders. *American Journal of Psychiatry, 148*(5), 564–577.

Bigler, E. D. (1990). The neurobiology and neuropsychology of adult learning disorders. *Journal of Learning Disabilities, 25*(8), 488–506.

Bigler, E. D., & Snyder, J. L. (1995). Neuropsychological outcome and quantitative neuroimaging in mild head injury. *Archives of Clinical Neuropsychology, 10*(2), 159–174.

Bleich, A., Seigel, B., Garb, R., & Lerer, B. (1986). Post-features and psychopharmacological treatment. *British Journal of Psychiatry, 149,* 365–369.

Boza, R. A., Trujillo, M., Millares, S., & Liggett, S. B. (1984, August). Sleep apnea and associated neuropsychiatric symptoms. *VA Practitioner,* 43–45.

Brende, J. O. (1982). Electrodermal responses in post-traumatic stress disorder: A pilot study of cerebral hemisphere functioning in Vietnam veterans. *Journal of Nervous and Mental Disease, 170*(6), 352–361.

Bremner, J. D., Randall, R., Scott, T. M., Bronen, R. A., Seibyl, J. P., Southwick, S. M., Delaney, R. C., McCarthy, G., Charney, D. S., & Innis, R. B. (1995). MRI-based measurement of hippocampal volume in patients with combat-related posttraumatic stress disorder. *American Journal of Psychiatry, 152*(7), 973–981.

Brennen, J. D., Scott, T. M., Delaney, R. C., Southwick, S. W., Mason, J. W., Johnson, D. R., Innis, R. B., McCarthy, G., & Charney, D. S. (1993). Deficits in short-term memory in post-traumatic stress disorder. *American Journal of Psychiatry, 150*(7), 1015–1019.

Brooks, N. (1989). Closed head trauma: Assessing the common cognitive problems. In M. D. Lezak (Ed.), *Assessment of the behavioral consequences of head trauma.* New York: Alan Liss.

Burstein, A. (1984). Treatment of post-traumatic stress disorder with imipramine. *Psychosomatics, 25,* 683–687.

Burstein, A. (1985). Post-traumatic flashbacks, dream disturbances, and mental imaging. *Journal of Clinical Psychiatry, 46,* 374–378.

Cahill, L., Prins, B., Weber, M., & McGaugh, J. L. (1994). Beta-adrenergic activation and memory for emotional events. *Nature, 371,* 702–704.

Campbell, D. T., & Stanley, J. C. (1963). *Experimental and quasi-experimental design for research.* Chicago: Rand-McNally College.

Cassidy, K. L., & Lyons, J. A. (1992). Recall of traumatic memories following cerebral vascular accident. *Journal of Traumatic Stress, 5*(4), 627–631.

Charney, D. S., Deutch, A. Y., Krystal, J. H., Southwick, S. S., & Davis, M. (1993). Psychobiologic mechanisms of post-traumatic stress disorder. *Archives of General Psychiatry, 50*(4), 294–305.

Chemtob, C. M., & Herriott, M. G. (1994). Post-traumatic stress disorder as a sequela of Guillain-Barré syndrome. *Journal of Traumatic Stress, 7*(4), 705–711.

Cooper, P. N., & Milroy, C. M. (1994). Violent suicide in South Yorkshire, England. *Journal of Forensic Sciences, 39*(3), 657–667.

Cottler, L. B., Compton, W. M., Mager, D., Spitznagel, E. L., & Janca, A. (1992). Post-traumatic stress disorder among substance users from the general population. *American Journal of Psychiatry, 149,*(5), 664–670.

Cuffe, S. P., McCullough, E. L., & Pumariega, A. J. (1994). Comorbidity of attention-deficit hyperactivity disorder and post-traumatic stress disorder. *Journal of Child and Family Studies, 3*(3), 327–336.

Dalton, J. E., Pederson, S. L., Blum, B. B., & Besynen, J. K. (1986). Neuropsychological screening for Vietnam veterans with PTSD. *VA Practitioner, 3*(7), 37–47.

Dalton, J. E., Pederson, S. L., & Ryan J. J. (1989). Effects of post-traumatic stress disorder on neuropsychological test performances. *International Journal of Clinical Neuropsychology, 11*(3), 121–124.

Damasio, A. R. (1985). The frontal lobes. In K. M. Heilamn & E. Valentein (Eds.), *Clinical neuropsychology* (2nd ed.). New York: Oxford University Press.

Daniel, M., Haban, G. F., Hutcherson, W. L., Botter, J., & Long, C. (1985). Neuropsychological and emotional consequences of accidental, high-voltage shock. *International Journal of Clinical Neuropsychology, 7*, 102–106.

Davidoff, D. A., Kessler, H. R., Laibstain, D. F., & Mark, V. H. (1988). Neurobehavioral consequence of minor head injury: A consideration of post-concussive versus post-traumatic stress disorder. *Cognitive Rehabilitation, 6,*(2), 8–13.

Devous, M. D., Sr. (1989). Imaging brain function by single-photon emission computer tomography. In N. C. Andreasen (Ed.), *Brain imaging applications in psychiatry.* Washington, DC: American Psychiatric Press.

Dinklage, D., & Grodzinsky, G. M. (1993, February). *Neuropsychological deficits in severely sexually abused children.* Paper presented at the annual meeting of the International Neuropsychological Society, Galveston, TX.

Edna, T. (1982). Alcohol influence and head injury. *ACTA Chirurgica Scandinavia, 148,* 209–212.

Engel, J., Jr. (1989). *Seizures and epilepsy.* Philadelphia: F. A. Davis.

Everly, G. S., & Horton, A. M., Jr. (1989). Neuropsychology of post-traumatic stress disorder: A pilot study. *Perceptual and Motor Skills, 68,* 807–810.

Famularo, R., Kinscherff, R., & Fenton, T. (1991). Posttraumatic stress disorder among children clinically diagnosed as borderline personality disorder. *Journal of Nervous and Mental Disease, 179,* 428–431.

Famularo, R., Kinscherff, R., & Fenton, T. (1992a). Psychiatric diagnoses of maltreated children: Preliminary findings. *Journal of the American Academy of Child and Adolescent Psychiatry, 31*(5), 863–867.

Famularo, R., Kinscherff, R., & Fenton, T. (1992b). Psychiatric diagnoses of abusive mothers: A preliminary report. *Journal of Nervous and Mental Disease, 180*(10), 658–661.

Forster, F. M. (1977). *Reflex epilepsy, behavioral therapy and conditioned reflexes.* Springfield, IL: Thomas.

Fullilove, M. T., Lown, E. A., & Fullilove, R. E. (1992). Crack 'hos and skeezers: Traumatic experiences of women crack users. *Journal of Sex Research, 29*(2), 275–287.

Gaddes, W. H. (1985). *Learning disabilities and brain function: A neuropsychological approach* (2nd ed.). New York: Springer-Verlag.

Gil, T., & Calev, A., Greenberg, D., Kugelmass, S., & Lerer, B. (1990). Cognitive functioning in post-traumatic stress disorder. *Journal of Traumatic Stress, 3*(1), 29–45.

Gill, D., & Sparadeo, F. (1988, August). *Neurobehavioral complications from alcohol use prior to head injury.* Paper presented at the annual meeting of the American Psychological Association, Atlanta, GA.

Glod, C. A. (1993). Long-term consequences of childhood physical and sexual abuse. *Archives of Psychiatric Nursing, 7*(3), 163–173.

Graessner, S. (1993). Tinnitus in torture survivors. *Torture, 3*(2), 47.

Greenberg, G. D., Watson, R. K., & Deptual, D. (1987). Neuropsychological dysfunction in sleep apnea. *Sleep, 10,* 254–262.

Gurvit, I. H. (1993). Neurological complications of repeated hunger strikes. *Torture, 3*(2), 47.

Gurvits, T. V., Lasko, N. B., Schachter, S. C., Kutine, A. A., Orr, S. P., & Pitman, R. K.

(1993). Neurological status of Vietnam veterans with chronic post-traumatic stress disorder. *Journal of Neuropsychiatry and Clinical Neurosciences, 5*(2), 183–188.

Hamner, M. B. (1993). PTSD and cocaine abuse. *Hospital and Community Psychiatry, 44*(6), 591–592.

Harper, C., Kril, J., & Daly, J. (1987). Are we drinking our neurones away? *British Medical Journal, 294,* 534–536.

Hartman, D. E. (1988). *Neuropsychological toxicology: Identification and assessment of human neurotoxic syndromes.* Oxford, UK: Pergamon Press.

Hartman, D. E. (1992). Neuropsychological toxicology. In A. E. Puente, & R. J. McCaffrey, III (Eds.), *Handbook of neuropsychological assessment: A biopsychosocial perspective. Critical issues in neuropsychology* (pp. 485–507). New York: Plenum Press.

Hillbom, M., & Holm, L. (1986). Contributions of traumatic head injuries to neuropsychological deficits in alcoholics. *Journal of Neurology, Neurosurgery, and Psychiatry, 49,* 1348–1353.

Hoff, A. L., Riordan, H., Alpert, R., & Volkow, N. (1991, February). *Cognitive function in chronic cocaine abusers.* Paper presented at the annual meeting of the International Neuropsychological Society, San Antonio, TX.

Hopewell, C. A. (1983). Serial neuropsychological assessment in a case of reversible electrocution encephalopathy. *Clinical Neuropsychology, 5*(2), 61–65.

Hopkins, R. O., Gale, S. D., Johnson, S. C., Anderson, C. V., Bigler, E. D., Blatter, D. D., & Weaver, L. K. (1995). Severe anoxia with and without concomitant brain atrophy and neuropsychological impairments. *Journal of the International Neuropsychological Society, 1*(5), 501–509.

Hopkins, R. O., Weaver, L. K., & Kesner, R. P. (1994, May). *Qualitative MRI analysis of the hippocampus correspondus with persistent memory impairments in carbon monoxide poisoned subjects.* Paper presented at Tennet V: Theoretical and Experimental Neuropsychology Meeting, Montreal, Quebec, Canada.

Horton, A. M., Jr. (1993). Post traumatic stress disorder and mild head trauma: Follow-up of a case study. *Perceptual and Motor Skills, 76,* 243–246.

Ito, Y., Teicher, M. H., Glod, C. A., & Harper, D. (1993). Increased prevalence of electrophysiological abnormalities in children with psychological, physical, and sexual abuse. *Journal of Neuropsychiatry and Clinical Neurosciences, 5*(4), 401–408.

Kampen, D. L., & Grafman, J. (1989). Neuropsychological evaluation of penetrating head injury. In M. D. Lezak (Ed.), *Assessment of the behavioral consequences of head trauma* (pp. 49–60). New York: Alan Liss.

Keane, T. M., & Wolfe, J. (1990). Comorbidity in post-traumatic stress disorder: An analysis of community and clinical studies. *Journal of Applied Social Psychology, 20*(21), 1776–1788.

King, D. W., & King, L. A. (1995). Alternative representations of war zone stressors: Relationships to posttraumatic stress disorder in male and female Vietnam veterans. *Journal of Abnormal Psychology, 104*(1), 184–196.

Kiser, L. J., Heston, J., Millsap, P. A., & Pruitt, D. B. (1991). Physical and sexual abuse in childhood: Relationship with post-traumatic stress disorder. *Journal of the American Academy of Child and Adolescent Psychiatry, 30,* 776–783.

Knoll, J. (1993). *PTSD/Borderlines in therapy.* New York: Norton.

Kolb, L. C. (1987). A neuropsychological hypothesis explaining post-traumatic stress disorder. *American Journal of Psychiatry, 144*(8), 989–995.

Kolb, L. C. (1988). A critical survey of hypotheses regarding post-traumatic stress disorder in light of recent research findings. *Journal of Traumatic Stress, 1*(3), 291–304.

Kolb, L. C. (1989). Chronic post-traumatic stress disorder: Implications of recent epidemiological and neuropsychological studies. *Psychological Medicine, 19,* 821–824.

Krystal, J. H., Kosten, T. R., Southwick, S. M., Mason, J. W., Perry, B. D., & Giller, E. L. (1989). Neurobiological aspects of PTSD: Review of clinical and preclinical studies. *Behavior Therapy, 20*(2), 177–198.

Kuch, K., Evans, R., & Watson, C. P. N. (1991). Accidents and chronic myofascial pain. *Pain Clinic, 4,* 79–86.

Kulka, R. A., Schlenger, W. E., Fairbank, J. A., Hough, R. L., Jordan, B. K., Marmar, C. R., & Weiss, D. S. (1990). *Trauma and the Vietnam War generation.* New York: Brunner/Mazel.

Kwentus, J., Hart, R., Peck, E., & Kornstein, S. (1985). Psychiatric complications of closed head trauma. *Psychosomatics, 26,* 8–17.

Lapierre, O., & Montplaisir, J. (1992). Polysomnographic features of REM sleep behavior disorder: Development of a scoring method. *Neurology, 42*(7), 1371–1374.

Layton, B. S., & Wardi-Zonna, K. (1994, February). *Post-traumatic stress disorder with neurogenic amnesia for the traumatic event.* Paper presented at the annual meeting of the International Neuropsychological Society, Cincinnati, OH.

Levin, H. (1985). Neurobehavioral recovery. In D. P. Becker & J. T. Povlishock (Eds.), *Central nervous system status report* (pp. 281–299). Washington, DC: NINCDS/NIH.

Lezak, M. D. (1989). Assessment of psychosocial dysfunctions resulting from head trauma. In M. D. Lezak (Ed.), *Assessment of the behavioral consequences of head trauma* (pp. 113–144). New York: Alan Liss.

Litz, B. T., & Herman, D. S. (1993, October). The parameters of selective-attention in combat-related PTSD. In P. Resnick (Chair), *The role of cognition in PTSD.* Symposium presented at the meeting of the International Society for Traumatic Stress Studies, San Antonio, TX.

MacKay, S., Meyerhoff, D. J., & Dillon, W. P., Weiner, M. W., Fein, C. (1993). Alteration of brain phospholipid metabolites in cocaine-dependent polysubstance abusers. *Biological Psychiatry, 34*(4), 261–264.

Martzke, J. S., & Steenhuis, R. E. (1993). *Isolated memory disturbance in the absence of global dysfunction in patients with sleep apnea.* Paper presented at the annual meeting of the International Neuropsychological Society, Galveston, TX.

McAllister, T. W. (1992). Neuropsychiatric sequelae of head injuries. *Psychiatric Clinics of North America, 15*(2), 395–413.

McCarthy, R. A., & Warrington, E. K. (1990). *Cognitive neuropsychology: A clinical introduction.* New York: Academic Press.

McCordie, W. R. (1994, August). Clinical neuropsychology in the Veterans Administration. *VA Practitioner,* pp. 61–66.

McGuire, P. K., Shah, G. M. S., & Murray, R. M. (1993). Increased blood flow in Broca's area during auditory hallucinations in schizophrenia. *Lancet, 342,* 703–706.

McMillan, T. M. (1991). Post-traumatic stress disorder and severe head injury. *British Journal of Psychiatry, 159,* 431–433.

McNally, R. J. (1995). Cognitive processing of trauma-relevant information in PTSD. *PTSD Research Quarterly, 6*(2), 1–6.

McNally, R. J., Kaspi, S. P., Riemann, B. C., & Zeitlin, S. B. (1990). Selective processing of threat cues in posttraumatic stress disorder. *Journal of Abnormal Psychology, 99,* 398–402.

McNally, R. J., & Shin, L. M. (1995). Association of intelligence with severity of posttraumatic stress disorder symptoms in Vietnam combat veterans. *American Journal of Psychiatry, 152*(6), 936–938.

Mellen, P. F., Weedn, V. W., & Kao, G. (1992). Electrocution: A review of 155 cases with emphasis on human factors. *Journal of Forensic Sciences, 37*(4), 1016–1022.

Merskey, H. (1992). Psychiatric aspects of the neurology of trauma. *Neurology Clinics, 10*(4), 895–905.

Millen, L. (1993). Toxic tests: Clinical, neuropsychological, and forensic aspects of clinical and electrical injuries. *Journal of Cognitive Rehabilitation, 11*(1), 6–18.

Mirsky, A. F., Fantie, B. D., & Tatman, J. E. (1995). Assessment of attention across the lifespan. In R. L. Mapou & J. Spector (Eds.), *Clinical neuropsychological assessment: A cognitive approach*. New York: Plenum Press.

Mittenberg, W., & Motta, S. (1993). Effects of chronic cocaine abuse on memory and learning. *Archives of Clinical Neuropsychology, 8*(6), 477–488.

Moses, J. A., Jr., & Maruish, M. E. (1988). A critical review of the Luria–Nebraska neuropsychological battery literature: V. Cognitive deficit in miscellaneous psychiatric disorders. *International Journal of Clinical Neuropsychology, 60*(2), 63–73.

O'Leary, K. M., Browers, P., Gardner, D. L., & Cowdry, R. W. (1991). Neuropsychological testing of patients with borderline personality disorder. *American Journal of Psychiatry, 148,* 106–111.

O'Leary, K. M., & Cowdry, R. W. (1994). Neuropsychological testing results in borderline personality disorder. In K. R. Silk (Ed.), *Biological and neurobehavioral studies of borderline personality disorder* (pp. 127–158). Washington, DC: American Psychatric Press.

Orsillo, S. M., & McCaffrey, R. J. (1992). Anxiety disorders. In A. E. Puente & R. J. McCaffrey (Eds.), *Handbook of neuropsychological assessment: A biological perspective* (pp. 215–261). New York: Plenum Press.

Parsons, O. A. (1987). Neuropsychological consequences of alcohol abuse: Many questions—some answers. In O. A. Parsons, N. Butlers, & P. E. Nathan (Eds.), *Neuropsychology of alcoholism: Implications for diagnosis and treatment* (pp. 153–175). New York: Guilford Press.

Perry, B. D. (1994). Neurobiological sequelae of childhood trauma: PTSD in children. In M. M. Murburg (Ed.), *Catecholamine function in posttraumatic stress disorder: Emerging concepts* (pp. 233–255). Washington, DC: American Psychiatric Press.

Pitman, R. (1989a). Post-traumatic stress disorder, conditioning and network theory. *Psychiatric Annuals, 18,* 182–189.

Pitman, R. (1989b). Post-traumatic stress disorder, hormones, and memory. *Biological Psychiatry, 26,* 221–223.

Radanov, B. P., Stefano, G. D., Schnidrig, A., Sturzenegger, M., & Augustiny, K. F. (1993). Cognitive functioning after whiplash. *Archives of Neurology, 50,* 87–91.

Rassmussen, O. V. (1990). Medical aspects of torture. *Danish Bulletin of Medicine, 33,* 1–88.

Rattok, J., & Ross, B. P. (1993, June). *Posttraumatic stress disorder in the traumatically head injured.* Paper presented at the 15th European Conference of the International Neuropsychological Society, Funchal, Maderia, Portugal.

Raz, S. (1989). Structural brain abnormalities in the major psychoses. In E. D. Bigler, R. A. Yeo, & E. Turkheimer (Eds.), *Neuropsychological function and brain imaging* (pp. 245–267). New York: Plenum Press.

Roberts, G. W., Allsop, D., & Barton, C. J. (1990). The occult aftermath of boxing. *Journal of Neurology, Neurosurgery, and Psychiatry, 53*(5), 373–378.

Rosenstein, L. D. (1994). Potential neuropsychological and neurophysiologic correlates of multiple personality disorder. *Neuropsychiatry, Neuropsychology, and Behavioral Neurology, 7*(3), 215–229.

Rourke, B. P. (1985). Overview of learning disability subtypes. In B. P. Rourke (Ed.), *Neuropsychology of learning disabilities* (pp. 3–14). New York: Guilford Press.

Rowan, A. B., & Foy, D. W. (1993). Post-traumatic stress disorder in child sexual abuse survivors: A literature review. *Journal of Traumatic Stress, 6,* 3–20.

Schlenger, W. E. (1995). Personal communication regarding analyses of the NVVRS dataset.

Schottenfeld, R. S., & Cullen, M. R. (1985). Occupation-induced posttraumatic stress disorders. *American Journal of Psychiatry, 142,* 2, 198–202.

Segalowitz, S. J., Lawson, S. M., & Berge, B. E. (1993, February). *Unreported head injury in the general population: subtle residual effects.* Paper presented at the annual meeting of the International Neuropsychological Society, Galveston, TX.

Semple, W. E., Goyers, P., Mccormick, R., & Morris, E. (1993). Preliminary report: Brain blood flow using PET in patients with posttraumatic stress disorder and substance abuse histories. *Biological Psychiatry, 34,* 115–118.

Shepard, J. P., Quercohi, R., & Preston, M. S. (1990). Psychological distress after assaults and accidents. *British Medical Journal, 301,* 849–856.

Sierles, F. S., Chen, J. J., McFarland, R. E., & Taylor, M. A. (1983). Post-traumatic stress disorder and concurrent psychiatric illness: A preliminary report. *American Journal of Psychiatry, 140,* 1177–1179.

Silk, K. R., Lee, S., Hill, E. M., & Lohr, N. E. (1995). Borderline personality disorder symptoms and severity of sexual abuse. *American Journal of Psychiatry, 152*(7), 1059–1064.

Southwick, S. M., Krystal, J. H., Morgan, C. A., Johnson, D. R., Nagy, L. M., Nicolaou, A., Heninger, G. R., & Charney, D. S. (1993). Abnormal noradrenergic function in posttraumatic stress disorder. *Archives of General Psychiatry, 50*(4), 266–274.

Spreen, O. (1988). *Learning disabled children growing up: A follow-up into adulthood.* New York: Oxford University Press.

Stringer, A. Y., & Cooley, E. L. (1994). Divided attention performance in multiple personality disorder. *Neuropsychiatry, Neuropsychology, and Behavioral Neurology, 7*(1), 51–56.

Stuss, D. T., & Benson, D. F. (1984). Neuropsychological studies of the frontal lobes. *Psychological Bulletin, 95,* 3–28.

Sutker, P. B., Allain, A. N., & Johnson, J. L. (1993). Clinical assessment of long-term cognitive and emotional sequelae to World War II prisoner-of-war confinement: Comparison of pilot twins. *Psychological Assessment, 5*(1), 3–10.

Sutker, P. B., Allain, A. N., & Winstead, D. K. (1987). Cognitive performances in former WWII and Korean-Conflict POWs. *VA Practitioner, 4*(6), 77–85.

Sutker, P. B., Galina, Z. H., West, J. A., & Allain, A. N. (1990). Trauma-induced weight loss and cognitive deficits among former prisoners of war. *Journal of Consulting and Clinical Psychology, 58,* 323–335.

Swirsky-Sachetti, T., Gorton, G., Samuel, S., Sobol, R., Genetta-Wasley, A., & Burleigh, B. (1993). Neuropsychological function in borderline personality disorder. *Journal of Clinical Psychology, 49*(3), 385–396.

Tarter, R. E., Hegedus, A. M., Winsten, N. E., & Alterman, A. I. (1984). Neuropsychological, personality and familial characteristics of physically abused delinquents. *Journal of the American Academy of Child Psychiatry, 23*(6), 668–674.

Teicher, M. H., Ito, Y., Glod, C. A., Schiffer, F., & Gelbard, H. A. (1994). Early abuse, limbic system dysfunction, and borderline personality disorder. In K. R. Silk (Ed.), *Biological and neurobehavioral studies of borderline personality disorder: Progress in psychiatry, No. 45* (pp. 177–207). Washington, DC: American Psychiatric Press.

Uddo, M., & Gouvier, W. D. (1990, August). *Effects of chronic cocaine use on new learning and memory.* Paper presented at the annual meeting of the American Psychological Association, Boston, MA.

Uddo, M., Vasterling, J. J., Brailey, K., & Sutker, P. (1993). Memory and attention in combat-related PTSD. *Journal of Psychopathology and Behavioral Assessment, 15,* 43–52.

Volkow, N. D., Harper, A., & Swann, A. C. (1986). Temporal lobe abnormalities and panic attacks. *American Journal of Psychiatry, 143*(11), 1484–1485.

Watson, P. B. (1990). Post-traumatic stress disorder [Correspondence to the editor]. *British Journal of Psychiatry, 156,* 910–911.

Watson, P. B., Hoffman, L., & Wilson, G. V. (1988). The neuropsychiatry of post-traumatic stress disorder. *British Journal of Psychiatry, 152,* 164–173.

White, R. F., Feldman, G. G., & Proctor, S. P. (1992). Neurobehavioral effects of toxic exposures. In R. F. White (Ed.), *Clinical syndromes in adult neuropsychology: The practitioner's handbook* (pp. 1–52). Amsterdam: Elsevier Press.

Woodward, S. H. (1993). Sleep disturbance in post-traumatic stress disorder. *PTSD Research Quarterly, 4*(1), 4–7.

Zimering, R. T., Caddell, J. M., Fairbank, J. A., & Keane, T. M. (1993). Post-traumatic stress disorder in Vietnam veterans: An experimental validation of the DSM-III diagnostic criteria. *Journal of Traumatic Stress, 6*(3), 327–342.

CHAPTER 17

Structured Clinical Interview Techniques

DANIEL S. WEISS

INTRODUCTION

Since a previous discussion of structured clinical interview techniques appeared (Weiss, 1993), considerable activity has occurred in the area of non-self-report measures of posttraumatic stress disorder (PTSD) and posttraumatic stress symptoms. This chapter presents a discussion of the context into which structured clinical interviews fall, some general considerations, a description of current techniques, and some implications and summary comments.

HISTORICAL CONTEXT

The assessment of the impact of exposure to traumatic stress can occur directly from the person exposed or through the mediating information channel of a clinician. Although it is arguable whether the diagnosis of PTSD is best conceptualized in terms of the criteria that appeared in the DSM-III (American Psychiatric Association, 1980), or the DSM-III-R (American Psychiatric Association, 1987), or the DSM-IV (American Psychiatric Association, 1994), whichever combination of signs and symptoms is ultimately adopted or shown to have the greatest validity and generalizability will require procedures to measure and document their presentation. It has partially been through the use of structured clinical interview techniques that the diagnostic criteria have evolved over the 15 years since their appearance in 1980.

The use of such interview techniques did not begin with the diagnosis of PTSD; in fact, specific, structured techniques aimed solely at PTSD followed the development and initial use of such techniques with other psychiatric illnesses. Publication of the Research Diagnostic Criteria (e.g., Williams & Spitzer, 1982) illustrated a growing emphasis by researchers in the field of psychological and psychiatric disorder that standard instruments and standard methods for assessment (e.g., Endicott & Spitzer, 1978; Wing, Cooper, & Sartorius, 1974) were needed to further the ends of a cumulative knowledge base for psychiatric disorders. This activity eventually was incorporated into research on PTSD.

A structured clinical interview technique is a formalized interview process or procedure that has internally logical or consistent rules that govern the content of questions asked of an interviewee, the order in which the topics are covered, and the specific kind of information sought. Usually practices are also developed that govern the making of diagnostic decisions. Moreover, structured clinical interview techniques are designed to be administered by individuals with clinical training and experience — consequently they can be differentiated from other diagnostic interview schedules designed to be administered by nonclinically trained personnel. A key feature of this distinction regarding the interviewer is the format in which the questions are posed and the responses are elicited. In structured clinical interviews, the questions asked are not always required to be responded to by a "yes" or a "no." In some cases, however, that type of closed question is most fitting. The key feature that differentiates those interviews that are structured clinical interview techniques designed to be used by nonclinicians from those that are designed to be used by clinicians is that the former have been developed in the context of epidemiological studies in which the major goal has been to make estimates of incidence and prevalence, rather than to make careful decisions about each and every individual interviewed.

The most well-studied method designed for nonclinicians is the National Institute of Mental Health (NIMH) Diagnostic Interview Schedule (Robins, Helzer, Croughan, & Ratcliff, 1981; Robins, Helzer, Croughan, Williams, & Spitzer, 1981). This interview protocol was constructed so that it could be administered by trained, nonclinician interviewers. Additionally, it was designed so that a computer algorithm could be applied to the respondent's "yes" or "no" answers to the questions and the output of that program be diagnostic decisions based on the DSM decision rules. In these respects, therefore, it is not identical to the structured clinical interview definition that we have used in this chapter. Nevertheless, it is included here because of its widespread use, its important role in contributing to prevalence estimates of PTSD and other comorbid diagnoses, and its potential for use where skilled clinicians are either too expensive to use in a widespread fashion or are unavailable. As a caveat, however, it should be stated that the intention of its designers was that no interpretation would be required by interviewers to make diagnostic decisions regarding the presence or absence of symptoms.

GENERAL CONSIDERATIONS

Indications for Use

The decision to use a structured clinical interview in working with individuals who have been exposed to a traumatic stressor is contingent on several considerations. If the clinical interview is undertaken in the context of systematic empirical research, then the use of a structured clinical interview is the state of the art, and its absence would be seen as a significant flaw in that research. If the interview is being done strictly in the context of treatment, one can still argue that a structured interview in an intake or evaluation interview is good practice. Employing a structured clinical interview will enable the clinician to have high quality, but need not prevent interviewees from presenting their story in their own words, a highly important aspect of clinical work with traumatic stress (Agger & Jensen, 1990).

Another reason for employing a structured clinical interview as a part of an initial or follow-up evaluation is that the structured protocol, when used correctly, will ensure thorough examination of the complete set of signs and symptoms of PTSD. A variety of archival studies in which clinical interviews were conducted absent a structured protocol to provide primary data about PTSD are handicapped by the fact that certain items were not the object of inquiry. Obviously, using a structured clinical interview will protect against this problem.

In some structured clinical interviews, an option to "skip out" exists. In the DSM-IV, for example, PTSD cannot be considered if there is not a qualifying event to fulfill Criterion A. A structured clinical interview that follows the DSM-IV will allow the rest of the protocol to be skipped out because PTSD cannot be diagnosed. But because there may be disagreement about whether a particular event qualifies, the absence of any further symptom information may be a distinct loss. The pros and cons of allowing a complete interview to occur, even when the typical instructions indicate a skip out, will depend upon the reason the interview is being conducted and how likely the absence or presence of such information will be salient at a later point. If the focus of attention is almost exclusively on responses to traumatic stress, then the decision to skip out with a potentially questionable event would not be warranted, but the decision to skip out the section on panic disorder or social phobia would make sense if the respondent does not meet the initial inclusion criteria. Although the structured interviews provide rules about these decisions, the interviewer, especially one who is working with individuals exposed to traumatic stress, must be responsive and alert to the burden put on the interviewee by an extended inquiry. Clinical judgment is typically the best guide when flexibility is available.

Dimensional versus Diagnostic Issues

A provocative issue in the wide area of the relationship between diagnostic criteria, diagnoses, and level of severity of symptoms is that a categorical nomenclature does not easily accommodate indices of severity and/or the duration of signs and symptoms. These issues are especially important in the realm of PTSD, as treatment outcome studies are likely to be more informative if outcome is assessed not only from the perspective of the number of persons who no longer meet the criteria for PTSD, but also if the degree of diminution of severity of symptoms can be quantified. Generally, rating scales are used for this purpose; however, some structured interviews have attempted to incorporate ratings of severity of symptoms as well.

Even though it might appear to be self-evident, the decision as to what level of severity of a symptom counts as evidence of having that symptom for purposes of making a diagnostic decision has not been systematically specified, nor has it been carefully studied empirically. Dysfunction and disability in psychological capacities are considerably harder to quantify than, for example, objective medical findings. It would be helpful to have available explicit criteria as to what was a "severe" level of numbing of responsiveness, or a "mild" level of nightmares. Scales for grading the level of coma exist in neurology, and these are tied to easily observable and reliable criteria. In PTSD, there are measures of overall severity of symptoms: the Mississippi Scale for Combat-Related PTSD (Keane, Caddell, & Taylor, 1988) and the Impact of Event Scale—Revised (see Weiss & Marmar, Chapter 13, this volume). Nonetheless, the relationship between scores on these measures and membership or not in the diagnostic class are not straightforward. It varies from study to study, and from trauma to trauma. It may depend upon the base rate of severe symptoms in the various groups, individual differences among the patients being studied, the amount of time elapsed since the traumatic event, as well as the criteria used to decide who is, and who is not, a case (for a succinct but penetrating discussion of this issue, the reader is referred to Kendell, 1988). Even the advent of the Clinician-Administered PTSD Scale (CAPS; Blake et al., 1995), which will be discussed more thoroughly subsequently, has not completely addressed this issue. Yet it is probably safe to conclude that the use of structured clinical interview techniques adds important clinical information to any study, whether the techniques are used to their fullest to make diagnostic decisions or merely to help navigate the interview itself.

STRUCTURED CLINICAL INTERVIEW FOR DSM-III-R (IV)

The most widely used, at this point in time, and the most thoroughly research clinical interview is the Structured Clinical Interview for DSM-III-R (SCID; Spitzer, Williams, Gibbon, & First, 1990). At this writing, work is ongoing to revise the SCID to align with the DSM-IV, just as the SCID based on DSM-III was revised to the current version, aligned with the DSM-III-R. Unlike the other structured interviews designed for use by clinicians discussed in this chapter, the SCID covers more than just PTSD, and more than just the anxiety disorders. This feature may or may not be desirable contingent on why a structured clinical interview is to be employed. All other things being equal, which they frequently are not, an appropriate recommendation is to use a comprehensive structured clinical interview such as the SCID to collect information about comorbidity and to have the option to discover other co-occurring symptoms following exposure to traumatic stress that are not currently included in the diagnostic criteria for PTSD.

The SCID has been under continual development and refinement by Spitzer's group at the New York State Psychiatric Institute. For Axis I disorders, there are currently three versions of the SCID: the SCID-P (patient edition), which is designed for use with those groups in which differential diagnosis with psychotic disorders is not likely; the SCID-P with Psychotic Screen; and the SCID-NP (nonpatient edition), which is designed for use with groups in which interviewees are not necessarily identified as psychiatric patients. The SCID's user's guide is extensive and gives practice guidelines, extensive do's and don'ts, and other important information. Its review and study are essential for proper use of the technique.

The SCID comprises modules for each disorder included. These are presented after an initial, open-ended narrative that includes identifying information, demographics, and a history of the present illness in the patient versions, or a history of the periods of greatest emotional distress in the nonpatient version. This feature of the SCID is crucial, in that it is the opportunity to establish rapport and set the tone for an interview that is smooth, empathic, and concerned versus one that is choppy, insensitive, and treats the interviewee as merely an object of study. The introductory module informs the interviewee as well that the inquiry will be aimed at current status as well as lifetime status. For the PTSD module, an additional introductory narrative may well be warranted, particularly for subjects known to have been exposed to particular traumas.

To illustrate this point, our use of the SCID in the National Vietnam Veterans Readjustment Study (NVVRS; Kulka et al., 1990) included such an open-ended narrative by interviewees, during which they had the opportunity to relate their experiences of traumatic exposure, whether in combat or otherwise, as the initiation of the inquiry prior to more specific and thorough exploration following the SCID protocol using the PTSD module. The use of the SCID-PTSD module in the NVVRS also deviated from usual practice, in that all items were administered to all respondents, even if the interviewer judged that the traumatic event would not ultimately qualify for Criterion A of the diagnostic criteria. The goal of this deviation was to be able to investigate symptom patterns over and above the need to make reliable and valid diagnoses for the estimate of prevalence. In the SCID currently, the PTSD module is a special addition and not included in the published version. Whether this will change in the DSM-IV edition could not be determined at the time this volume went to press.

The PTSD Module and Interview Criteria

The SCID furnishes the clinician with the chance to assess the occurrence or absence of each one of the criteria that comprise the diagnosis of PTSD according to the DSM criteria for both current status and lifetime status. Accordingly, meeting the diagnostic criteria can be established for both time frames. In assessing the presence or absence of any sign or symptom, the clinician is instructed by the SCID user's guide to indicate whether the presentation of the criterion item is absent, present, or subthreshold. This is defined as "the threshold for the criterion item is almost met." Such a provision is also afforded for the diagnosis itself: "The full criteria are not quite met but clinically the disorder seems likely." This may be especially true with PTSD, in which, for example three avoidance symptoms are required, but survivors may clearly manifest only one or two. In fact, it was just such a subthreshold presentation that was described as partial PTSD in the NVVRS (Weiss et al., 1992).

Because of the possibility of partial presentations or subthreshold diagnoses, to the degree that it is possible to clarify what goes into the decision-making process about the presence or absence of a criterion symptom, this should be done. A complete exposition of this issue is the heart of cross-method studies of reliability and validity. Materials for these decisions are presented here for the SCID-PTSD module. Similar materials should be developed for any structured interview technique. The CAPS (Blake et al., 1995) has also carefully tackled this requirement.

The NVVRS clinical research team prepared materials for its clinical interviewers illustrating what clinical phenomena were appropriately coded for each item. These materials were integrated previously (Weiss, 1993) and are presented here again to demonstrate what counts as an instance of a symptom being present for the SCID-PTSD module items. Also presented are exemplars of clinical phenomena that do not meet the criterion.

Recurrent and Intrusive Distressing Recollections of the Event

In order to be coded present, the recollections must be recurrent, intrusive, and distressing. These recollections are typically characterized as spontaneous and uncontrollable, and seem to have a "life of their own." They are unbidden, unwelcome, and unable to be easily stopped once started. Examples that meet this criterion would include a veteran driving along in a car, not focusing on any particular thoughts, who has a sudden and distressing memory of placing mutilated corpses in body bags after a rocket attack (referring to a specific wartime experience). Another example would be a victim of an earthquake who is reading a novel and suddenly has the interfering thought, "If only I had checked the foundation of the house and had it reinforced—I could have prevented the damage and destruction," during which the memory of the house inspection is recalled.

Clinical phenomena that do not meet the criterion for intrusive recollections include the repeated ruminative thoughts of the severely depressed individual who thinks "I am worthless" outside the context of a traumatic event, the ruminative and obsessive thoughts of the individual who feels "I am sinful," or the intrusive thoughts of an individual with social fears who thinks "I will make a fool of myself in front of all these people." These are three related examples of intrusive thoughts that do not relate to traumatic life events but are specific for other disorders. Another example of a phenomenon that does not meet this criterion is the combat veteran who frequently thinks of his Vietnam experiences and may be saddened by the memories, but does so volitionally, without a sense of intrusion to the experience of the remembering.

Recurrent and Distressing Dreams of the Event

Dreams must be recurrent and distressing. Night terrors, if present, indicate presence of this symptom, and the content of the dream should align with the traumatic exposure. The content of trauma-related nightmares may consist of relatively straightforward dreams of aspects of the event(s) (e.g., repetitive dreams of specific firefights for a veteran) or symbolic representations with some form of trauma-relevant combat theme (e.g., running in terror through a jungle with one's spouse and children while trying to escape an unseen assailant).

Clinical phenomena that do not meet the criterion include dreams or recurrent nightmares of falling off a cliff, which are of a fantasy nature and not linked to traumatic experiences. In addition, dreams of monsters or other threatening fantasy figures, or anxiety dreams related to conflicts or fears involving daily living rather than traumatic exposure, do not satisfy this criterion.

Sudden Acting or Feeling as If the Traumatic Event Were Recurring

This criterion taps the phenomenon of a sense of sudden reliving of the experience. Included in this are illusions, pseudohallucination, and dissociative episodes (e.g., flashbacks), even those that occur upon awakening or when intoxicated. The consequential distinction is between an intrusive memory—in which people perceive themselves to be remembering the event—and a feeling as if the event were happening again. During this experience, the individual loses the ability to distinguish the past from the present. Behavior during reliving experiences is dissociative-like, and sometimes is unknown to the subject until described by another person who has observed the behavior (often a spouse or close friend). Phenomena that signify the presence of this item include the case of a war veteran who hears a car backfire, hits the dirt, and sees a battle scene pass before his eyes with the dissociative quality of reliving the experience. Reliving experiences can frequently be set off by the sight of blood, or a dead, mutilated animal at the side of the road, or another stimulus reminiscent of the trauma. Another example would be someone who was subjected to severe shaking in an earthquake, who relives the earthquake experience, including the sense of distorted time and terror about safety after a heavy truck passing by shakes the building.

Intense Psychological Distress at Exposure to Cues of the Event

The focus here is on psychological distress—fear, anxiety, anger, sense of impending doom—in the face of a representation that symbolizes or resembles an aspect of the traumatic event. The representation can be external, such as anniversaries, or it can be internal, such as anticipating having to approach a feared location. A classic example of this phenomenon is the assault victim who becomes fearful and anxious whenever approaching the scene of the attack. Another example is a survivor of torture with electrodes who needs to have an electrocardiogram. Being unable to face certain situations or continue with the ordinary course of daily activities because of the possibility of reminders or reexposure is the feature. The female survivor of a tornado is unable to step inside a mobile home, because it was inside such a structure that she witnessed her child being killed.

Phenomena that do not meet the criterion for distress upon reexposure are the sad feeling experienced at anniversaries of a trauma, but ones that do not impede ongoing functioning.

Physiological Reactivity on Exposure to Cues of the Event

The clinical phenomenon here includes reactivity expressed in a variety of ways: heavy or irregular breathing, lightheadedness, tingling in the extremities, tightness in the chest, knot in the stomach, damp or cold palms or feet, and other indicators of arousal. Frequently occurring in conjunction with attempts at avoidance of stimuli reminiscent of the traumatic event (e.g., a woman who was raped in an elevator breaks out in a sweat when entering an elevator), these episodes can be extremely distressing and approach a level of arousal that is exhausting.

Efforts to Avoid Thoughts, Feelings, or Conversations Associated with the Event

Intentional efforts to avoid thoughts or feelings, or deliberate efforts to avoid activities or situations that arouse recollections of the event must have been made, but need not have been successful. Nonetheless, in instances in which avoidance has been attempted but did not succeed, there should be indications that distress has occurred. Avoidance strategies may vary on several dimensions. They may be obvious or subtle, relatively adaptive or manifestly maladaptive. Obvious forms of avoidance include the refusal to discuss or talk about the trauma, and the use of alcohol or drugs to cloud memories. Overworking is also a strategy used to avoid thoughts and feelings about trauma. Sometimes the interviewee is self-aware of these strategies; other times, the phenomena are clinically more subtle.

Phenomena that do not meet criterion for avoidance include the inability to remember aspects of the event, depressive social withdrawal, and overall loss of interest in things.

Efforts to Avoid Activities, Places, or People That Arouse Recollections of the Event

The avoidance of places, people, or things that are a reminder of the trauma, and that evoke significant distress, include certain locales that are associated with the trauma. Examples include avoiding crossing a certain bridge because it failed in an earthquake or a flood. Like avoidance of thoughts or feelings, avoidance of people, places, or activities, may not be successful in reducing distress; in any case, evidence of distress is required for the avoidant activities to be meaningful expressions of the symptom.

Avoidance of social situations or people that provoke anxiety unrelated to a traumatic event (declining to give sales presentations) is an example of a phenomenon that does not meet the criteria.

Inability to Recall an Important Aspect of the Event

The clinical phenomenon here is also referred to as "psychogenic amnesia"; this is not merely that the person could not keep track of everything that happened, but rather that the individual is aware of important details that cannot be remembered; that is, there are gaps and holes in the story as it is remembered and told. Psychogenic amnesia may be either partial or complete. High levels of distress often accompany descriptions of events in which the respondent is unable to recall important details, and this distress is usually expected to accompany this symptom.

Examples that are instances of the phenomenon include the combat veteran who cannot remember an episode in which a buddy was killed or how he survived; another is the automobile accident victim whose wife was killed, and who cannot remember being told that his spouse died. Phenomena that do not meet the criterion for psychogenic amnesia include forgetting minor details, or a victim with head injury, alcohol-induced "blackouts," or other neurological memory failures.

Markedly Diminished Interest in Significant Activities

The essential feature here is a change in level of interest subsequent to the trauma or the onset of symptoms. Activities in which interest is lost must have been meaningful to the respondent prior to the trauma, as evidenced by continued interest or focus on the activity. Developmental changes must be ruled out in assessing this item.

Examples that fit this phenomenon include the athletically active woman who gives up all physical fitness activities after a scarring train accident; the witness to a shooting who abandons a lifelong passion for duck hunting; or the volunteer paramedic who no longer teaches CPR after having failed to revive a clearly moribund victim after a disaster. Examples that do not meet the criterion are changes in activity due to physical limitations, or the severe anhedonia of depression. Thus, if both PTSD and major depression are present, a clinical determination must be made of whether the loss of interest is clearly tied to response to the trauma.

Feelings of Detachment or Estrangement from Others

Here, too, the essential aspect is change after the trauma. The phenomenon is common in psychological disturbance, but the key feature here is a marked increase in feelings of distance and detachment. An example is a parent, an active churchgoer, whose child is abducted: The parent continues to participate in the church, but feels alone and alienated, receives no comfort, and feels that faith has betrayed him or her. An example that is not scored as present would be the emergency/disaster worker who feels that civilians cannot appreciate what he or she has been through but does not feel socially isolated from others who have not had similar experiences.

Restricted Range of Affect

The restriction of affect or psychic numbing is relative to the range available to the trauma. The phenomenon is often recognized by people who are unable to have loving feelings; they are numb and do not have feelings they think they should. An example would be an earthquake survivor whose coworker was killed, and who does not feel choked up, or moved, or sad about the lost coworker and continues to function in a mechanical, lifeless, business-only manner.

Sense of a Foreshortened Future

Examples that fit this phenomenon would be a child who does not expect to have a career, marriage, children, or a long life. Other examples include the hurricane survivor who does nothing to prepare for future emergencies because he "won't be around, anyway," and the combat veterans who drifts in and out of employment, because he does not have a sense of a job history or the implications of this for any future opportunities. This symptom is to be distinguished from a chronic lack of regard for future consequences from someone with antisocial personality disorder, for example.

Difficulty Falling or Staying Asleep

This item is self-evident, although the patterns of sleep disturbance themselves may be of both clinical and research interest.

Irritability or Outbursts of Anger

This phenomenon is often observed by the interviewee with some chagrin and an apology. There is a sense of loss of control, sometimes coupled with fear of even greater expression of anger or hostility. Examples include the supervisor at work, having been robbed at gunpoint, who angrily explodes at a subordinate for having thoughtlessly told a joke about mugging. This item needs to be understood in relation to the level of pretrauma anger expressivity.

Difficulty Concentrating

Trauma survivors very frequently report difficulties concentrating in both the acute and chronic phases of response. For example, a combat veteran might report that he or she found it difficult to concentrate on classroom lectures and assigned reading materials, whereas a sexual assault victim may find that he or she is no longer able to concentrate on the computational and accounting tasks of employment. The report of difficulty concentrating is to some extent a function of intrusive images and thoughts that may interfere with cognitive tasks that allow attention to wander, such as reading or mental arithmetic.

Hypervigilance

This phenomenon represents excessive attention to external stimuli beyond that called for a given realistic appraisal of the level of external threat. This symptom can often be observed during the interview, especially if the situation may have reminders of the trauma (e.g., a victim of falling books and furniture during an earthquake will not sit near the clinician's books). This item is to be differentiated from the generalized suspiciousness in a person with longstanding paranoid trends or paranoid personality disorder. Another example would be of the assault victim who continually looks over his or her should when walking down streets and in stairwells.

Exaggerated Startle Response

This phenomenon must not predate the trauma and can sometimes be witnessed during the interview if a sudden noise or movement occurs, and the individual exhibits a startle response out of line with both the stimulus and what would typically be expected.

NVVRS Research with the SCID

The NVVRS used the SCID in two ways. First, a pretest validation study aimed at selecting measures for diagnosing PTSD to be used in the household survey was undertaken. The set of survey-based measures was administered to 243 Vietnam theater veterans in treatment for PTSD or other psychiatric disorders at VA Medical Centers or Vet Centers, as well as to veterans without psychiatric disorder. Eight sites across the country were employed, and subjects' diagnoses had to be double determined to be used in this phase; that is, the chart diagnosis had to agree with the diagnosis made by an independent, expert clinician who had administered the SCID and was blind to the chart diagnosis.

The results of that study suggested that a survey interview measure that was similar to the Diagnostic Interview Schedule (DIS) and the Mississippi scale (Keane et al., 1988) was the best candidate, yielding kappa coefficients of .71 and .75, respectively, when scored as scales with a cutoff. The DIS-type diagnostic measure yielded a coefficient of .64 when scored using DSM-III-R algorithm rules. In this study, the SCID was used as one part of a "gold standard."

The second study utilized the clinical examination component of the NVVRS. It provided a second validity check on the household survey measures of PTSD. Over 300 theater veterans and 100 era veterans were selected to undergo a follow-up clinical interview with one of 29 expert, mental health clinicians using the SCID. Participants were selected to include all those who appeared on the basis of the National Survey of the Vietnam Generation data to be current cases, and a sample of those whose results indicated they were not cases. A second constraint on participants was that they lived within 28 areas.

All 440 SCID-PTSD modules were reviewed (via audiotape) for accuracy, completeness, and clinical veracity by one of five study expert clinicians. Additional scrutiny was given to those cases in which a subthreshold diagnostic decision was made, or in which the review indicated an additional opinion was needed for a two-clinician review of any change. The quality review of the 440 cases results in major changes in the initial interviewer's diagnosis of either or both lifetime or current PTSD in only 11 cases. For current PTSD, three were changed from negative to subthreshold or partial, and four were changed from positive to negative. For the lifetime SCID-PTSD diagnosis, one case was changed from negative to subthreshold or partial, five cases from negative to positive, one case from positive to partial, and one case from positive to negative.

A blind interrater reliability study on 15 randomly selected PTSD subthreshold or absent cases was conducted, with each of the three clinical coprincipal investigators rereviewing 10 of the cases subject only to the constraint that the case was not reviewed in the prior quality review procedure. Kappa coefficients (Cohen, 1960) were computed between the blind reviewer's diagnosis and the initial interviewer's diagnosis before quality review for both lifetime and current PTSD in the sample of 30 cases. The coefficient for lifetime PTSD was .94 and for current PTSD, .87. Although this study cannot be considered a full-scale reliability study, the results do suggest that the SCID can produce reliable diagnoses of both lifetime and current PTSD.

OTHER STRUCTURED INTERVIEWS

There are a variety of other structured interviews that can be used in the PTSD diagnostic process. Most are focused solely on PTSD, although several have broader applications.

Diagnostic Interview Schedule

The background, history, and findings of the NIMH-DIS have been chronicled extensively and in many different forums (e.g., Regier et al., 1988). The logic and background of the DIS and the goals and objectives of its use and relationship to operationalizing the diagnostic criteria formulated in various nomenclatures are very thoroughly and compellingly presented by Robins (1989). Despite its development and use in epidemiological context, many of the reliability and validity studies of the DIS have included use of other structured clinical interviews.

In an important study, Anthony et al. (1985) reported results of the DIS that were not encouraging. Kappa coefficients ranged from − .02 to .35 for a variety of disorders, none of them PTSD. In this study, a clinical reappraisal of all DIS positives and a sample of DIS negatives from the Baltimore Epidemiologic Catchment Area (Regier et al., 1988) site was conducted using an interview based on the Present State Examination (Wing et al., 1974) but modified to obtain DSM-III diagnoses. After examining the bulk of the reports, Burke (1986) concluded that the DIS works reasonably well for alcohol abuse and major depression, but that it may have significant difficulty in other disorders.

With respect to PTSD, initially the DIS did not contain a module for PTSD. The NVVRS utilized a form of the DIS that had included items relevant for the diagnosis of PTSD, and, subsequently, other data about PTSD have been reported (Centers for Disease Control, 1988; Helzer, Robins, & McEvoy, 1987). Nevertheless, the NVVRS data probably provide the best estimate of the validity of the diagnosis of PTSD.

A comparison of the diagnostic decisions based on the DIS survey data with those from the clinician's SCID diagnosis indicated that although the DIS had performed acceptably in the preliminary validation study, in the full sample it did not perform acceptably. For the 440 cases in the clinical examination component, the DIS-PTSD module achieved a sensitivity of only 21.5, a specificity of 97.9, and a kappa of .26. Thus, the DIS-PTSD module with lay interviewers appears to have had problems that do not yet appear to have been addressed.

Anxiety Disorders Interview Schedule—Revised

The Anxiety Disorders Interview Schedule—Revised (ADIS-R; DiNardo & Barlow, 1985) was developed to be able to cover in considerable detail the class of anxiety disorders. The original ADIS (DiNardo, O'Brien, Barlow, Waddell, & Blanchard, 1983) did not contain PTSD as one of the anxiety disorders; the only published study located that examined PTSD was conducted on male Vietnam War veterans (Blanchard, Gerardi, Kolb, & Barlow, 1986). The ADIS skips out for PTSD if Criterion A is not fulfilled.

The results of the diagnostic study were promising, yielding a kappa coefficient of .86. Nevertheless, the patients were all VA patients, and there was not a look at reliability when both raters were using the ADIS-R. If PTSD is the major emphasis, the ADIS-R may not be the best choice; if differential diagnosis in the anxiety disorders is the focus, the ADIS-R is likely a reasonable selection.

Structured Interview for PTSD

The Structured Interview for PTSD (SI-PTSD) was introduced in 1989 by Davidson and colleagues (Davidson, Smith, & Kudler, 1989). It is now one of several structured interviews focused exclusively on PTSD. It is designed to elicit information not only about the presence or absence of symptoms, but also attempts to scale the severity of the experience of each of the symptom categories. The SI-PTSD is designed to provide both lifetime and current diagnostic decisions. The 1989 study made diagnoses using DSM-III criteria; however, a newer, unpublished version is linked to the DSM-III-R criteria (Davidson, Kudler, & Smith, 1990). It is not clear at this time how the SI-PTSD will respond to the change to DSM-IV.

The original publication included data from 116 veterans of the Vietnam, Korean, and Second World Wars, all of whom were in treatment. In a subsample of 41 patients, the SCID for DSM-III was administered by a separate interviewer. Thirty-seven of 41 diagnoses were in agreement, yielding a kappa coefficient of .79.

A second goal of the SI-PTSD appears to be to combine the dimensional and diagnostic approach to PTSD. The diagnostic decisions are made based on the interviewer's assessment that the symptom severity is at least a 2 on a 0–4 scale, where a 2 means "moderate." The items comprising the syndrome can then be summed and used as a continuous variable.

The authors note that, so far, this measure has been limited in use to combat veterans, presumably all male. Nonetheless, the SI-PTSD has had a promising beginning.

PTSD Interview

The PTSD Interview (PTSD-I; Watson, Juba, Manifold, Kucala, & Anderson, 1991) is based on DSM-III-R diagnostic criteria. The format is on a 1–7 response format, where 1 is "never" and 7 is "always." Consequently, the PTSD-I is also able to provide both dichotomous diagnostic decisions and continuous data for the set of symptoms. Watson suggests that a rating of 4 on the 1–7 scale, corresponding to a self-rating of "somewhat" or "commonly" be used to indicate presence of a symptom. It does not appear that this decision has been subjected to empirical analysis. In this approach, however, it is the patient not the interviewer that makes the severity ratings, and this may dilute the power of the clinician's input.

The interview inquires as to the presence of current symptomatology, but the approach to the presence of the disorder on a lifetime basis is less than ideal. Watson et al. (1991) reported high internal consistency and good test–retest reliability, although these indices refer more to the scale version than to the diagnostic interview approach. In the latter format, data were reported for 61 Vietnam War veterans, 53 patients, and 8 staff members at the author's institution. When the data were analyzed from the perspective of specificity, sensitivity, and concordance, coefficients of .89, .94 and .84 were obtained, respectively. A modification of the DIS-PTSD module was used in this study as the "gold standard."

The PTSD-I has not been reported to be used in any other patient group outside of Vietnam War veterans. This is a distinct limitation of this instrument, as is the fact that it cannot produce valid, lifetime diagnosis rates. Finally, it is not clear how the PTSD-I will align with the DSM-IV.

Clinician-Administered PTSD Scale

A new entry into the arena of PTSD measurement in structured interview is the Clinician-Administered PTSD Scale (CAPS-1; Blake et al., 1995). Designed to fulfill a number of criteria, the CAPS-1 is explicitly targeted to be used by nonclinicians as well as clinicians. In this way it resembles the DIS more than the SCID. The CAPS-1 also provides both a dimensional and categorical approach to PTSD and explicitly separates out frequency of symptomatic experiences from intensity of the symptomatic experience.

In addition to the 17 symptoms in the DSM-III-R and DSM-IV-PTSD criteria, the CAPS-1 contains eight additional items: guilt over acts committed or omitted, survivor guilt, homocidality, disillusionment with authority, feelings of hopelessness, memory impairment, sadness and depression, and feelings of being overwhelmed.

The CAPS-1 provides standard, prompt questions for both the intensity and frequency response domains, and detailed instructions are contained in an Instruction Manual. The CAPS-1 inquires first about current symptom status and then about the lifetime status. The CAPS-1 indicates that a frequency rating of at least 1 on a 0–4 scale ("once or twice within the past month") and a severity rating of at least 2 on a 0–4 scale ("moderate") will qualify for the presence of the symptom for diagnostic purposes. In the reports of the CAPS-1, Blake et al. (1995) acknowledge that this decision rule is rationally derived. Moreover, Weathers (1993) suggests that these decision rules may overestimate PTSD symptomatology. It may be that in trying to be more precise about frequency and intensity, their separation creates an artifact rather than adding clarifying information.

Data in the initial study were presented on 60 combat veterans who were administered the CAPS-1 on two different occasions, with an interval of 2–3 days separating the administrations. These interviews were administered by different clinicians. A group of 63 additional veterans was administered the CAPS-1 by a single rater. All 123 subjects were also administered the SCID-PTSD module, which served as the "gold standard."

Test–retest reliability ranged from .90 to .98 across the 17 items for the different sets of rater pairs. Internal consistency was .94. The kappa coefficient for the CAPS-1 was .78, a very encouraging result.

The CAPS-1 authors indicate that the explicit anchors and behavioral referents for guiding ratings is an important advance of this measure. It is likely this will increase reliability, without a consequent cost in validity.

Like the PTSD-I, the CAPS-1 published information is so far limited to male Vietnam War veterans, although it appears that the measure is being used in other studies. Early informal communication suggests that the administration of both frequency and intensity for both current and lifetime diagnoses is laborious, and it may be that for just a diagnosis, the extra information that the CAPS-1 gathers is extraneous. The CAPS-1 format presumes a traumatic event, rather than eliciting it. Finally, it is not clear to what end the additional eight items of the CAPS-1 will be put, and what impact there would be of deleting these items on the CAPS-1 protocol.

SUMMARY AND RECOMMENDATIONS

This chapter has described a variety of structured interviews, some more "clinical" than others, some more focused exclusively on PTSD than others. An attempt was made to clarify the range of coverage, the samples on which studies have occurred, whether the measures were designed to be used by clinicians or nonclinicians, and whether merely categorical or dimensional and categorical outcomes are produced.

An inherent difficulty is that the measurement armamentarium for making diagnoses of PTSD, or any other diagnosis, always lags behind the promulgation of the diagnostic criteria. Just as the research literature is beginning to accumulate findings using a particular structured interview technique, a modification in the diagnostic criteria seems to appear. This has been true between 1980 and 1987, and between 1987 and 1994, with the conversion from DSM-III to DSM-III-R to DSM-IV. It seems as if this state of affairs will continue to characterize this domain of the interface between research and clinical practice.

One clear observation is that most structured interviews appear in the literature with data from just one victim group, and frequently just one sample at that. It is desirable that data from another group besides Vietnam War veterans be presented quickly for those diagnostic instruments to be used for PTSD. This is still a limitation of this area of work.

The choice of which interview to use, whether to use a technique that permits nonclinicians to be involved, or a protocol that covers more than PTSD, will be dictated by the goals and circumstances under which the assessment is being conducted. Nonetheless, the regular use of standard structured interviews ought to be a regular activity for those who work with survivors of trauma, regardless of whether this is in the context of research. The increase in precision is well worth the added time. The choice of the particular technique will vary with preference, time, training, and research evidence.

Issues that require further empirical attention are those of the relationship between dimensional and categorical approaches, especially the issues raised in the study by Weathers (1993) about the impact on diagnostic rates by the setting of cutting scores on a response scheme that is dimensional. A second area that requires more attention is the impact on diagnostic reliability of whether the interviewer is a clinician or a paraprofessional. Despite the continued work with the DIS and the next generation of that measure, the Composite International Diagnostic Interview (CIDI; Wittchen, 1994) and its clinician-administered companion, the Schedules for Clinical Assessment in Neuropsychiatry (SCAN; Janca, Ustun, & Sartorius, 1994), the issue of the reliability of diagnoses made by nonclinicians continues to be of importance.

The ability of some measures, such as the CAPS-1, to approximate a diagnostic decision based on a dimensional score may not be as advantageous as it first seems, as high scores can be obtained by severe levels of symptoms in some domains, with below-threshold levels in others. Further work in this area is definitely required.

REFERENCES

Agger, I., & Jensen, S. B. (1990). Testimony as ritual and evidence in psychotherapy for political refugees. *Journal of Traumatic Stress, 3,* 115–130.

American Psychiatric Association. (1980). *Diagnostic and statistical manual of mental disorders* (3rd ed.). Washington, DC: Author.

American Psychiatric Association. (1987). *Diagnostic and statistical manual of mental disorders* (3rd ed., rev.). Washington, DC: Author.

American Psychiatric Association. (1994). *Diagnostic and statistical manual of mental disorders* (4th ed.). Washington, DC: Author.

Anthony, J. C., Folstein, M., Romanoski, A. J., Vonkorff, M. R., Nestadt, G. R., Chahal, R., Merchant, A., Brown, C. H., Shaprio, S., Kramer, M., & Gruenberg, E. M. (1985). Comparison of lay Diagnostic Interview Schedule and a standardized psychiatric diagnosis. *Archives of General Psychiatry, 42,* 667–676.

Blake, D. D., Weathers, F. W., Nagy, L. M., Kaloupek, D. G., Gusman, F. D., Charney,

D. S., & Keane, T. M. (1995). The development of a clinician-administered PTSD scale. *Journal of Traumatic Stress, 8,* 75–90.

Blanchard, E. B., Gerardi, R. J., Kolb, L. C., & Barlow, D. H. (1986). The utility of the Anxiety Disorders Interview Schedule (ADIS) in the diagnosis of post-traumatic stress disorder (PTSD) in Vietnam veterans. *Behaviour Research and Therapy, 24,* 557–580.

Burke, J., Jr. (1986). Diagnostic categorization by the Diagnostic Interview Schedule (DIS): A comparison with other measures of assessment. In J. E. Barrett & R. M. Rose (Eds.), *Mental disorder in the community: Progress and challenge* (pp. 255–285). New York: Guilford Press.

Centers for Disease Control, Vietnam Experience Study (CDC). (1988). Health status of Vietnam veterans I: Psychosocial characteristics. *Journal of the American Medical Association, 259,* 2701–2702.

Cohen, J. (1960). A. coefficient of agreement for nominal scales. *Educational and Psychological Measurement, 20,* 37–46.

Davidson, J., Kudler, H., & Smith, R. (1990). *The Structured Interview for PTSD (SI-PTSD).* Unpublished manuscript, Department of Psychiatry, Duke University, Durham, NC.

Davidson, J., Smith, R., & Kudler, H. (1989). Validity and reliability of the DSM-III criteria for posttraumatic stress disorder: Experience with a structured interview. *Journal of Nervous and Mental Disease, 177,* 336–341.

DiNardo, P. A., & Barlow, D. H. (1985). *Anxiety Disorders Interview Schedule—Revised (ADIS-R).* Albany, NY: Phobia and Anxiety Disorders Clinic, State University of New York at Albany.

DiNardo, P. A., O'Brien, G. T., Barlow, D. H., Waddell, M. T., & Blanchard, E. B. (1983). Reliability of DSM-III anxiety disorder categories using a new structured interview. *Archives of General Psychiatry, 40,* 1070–1074.

Endicott, J., & Spitzer, R. L. (1978). A diagnostic interview: A schedule for affective disorder and schizophrenia. *Archives of General Psychiatry, 35,* 837–844.

Helzer, J. E., Robins, L. N., & McEvoy, L. (1987). Post-traumatic stress disorder in the general population. *New England Journal of Medicine, 317,* 1630–1634.

Janca, A., Ustun, T. B., & Sartorius, N. (1994). New version of World Health Organization instruments for the assessment of mental disorders. *Acta Psychiatrica Scandinavica, 90,* 73–83.

Keane, T. M., Caddell, J. M., & Taylor, K. L. (1988). Mississippi scale for combat-related posttraumatic stress disorder: Three studies in reliability and validity. *Journal of Consulting and Clinical Psychology, 56,* 85–90.

Kendell, R. E. (1988). What is a case? Food for thought for epidemiologists. *Archives of General Psychiatry, 45,* 374–376.

Kulka, R. A., Schlenger, W. E., Fairbank, J. A., Hough, R. L., Jordan, B. K., Marmar, C. R., & Weiss, D. S. (1990). *Trauma and the Vietnam war generation: Report of the findings from the National Vietnam Veterans Readjustment Study.* New York: Brunner/Mazel.

Regier, D. A., Body, J. H., Burke, J. D., Race, D. S., Myers, J. K., Kramer, M., Robins, L. N., George, L. K., Karno, M., & Locke, B. Z. (1988) One-month prevalence of mental disorders in the United States. *Archives of General Psychiatry, 42,* 918–924.

Robins, L. N. (1989). Diagnostic grammar and assessment: Translating criteria into questions. *Psychological Medicine, 19,* 57–68.

Robins, L. N., Helzer, J. E., Croughan, J., & Ratcliff, K. S. (1981). National Institute of Mental Health Diagnostic Interview Schedule: Its history, characteristics, and validity. *Archives of General Psychiatry, 38,* 318–389.

Robins, L. N., Helzer, J. E., Croughan, J., Williams, J. B. W., & Spitzer, R. L. (1981). *NIMH Diagnostic Interview Schedule: Version III-A (May, 1981).* Rockville, MD: National Institute of Mental Health.

Spitzer, R. L., Williams, J. B. W., Gibbon, M., & First, M. B. (1990). *User's guide for the Structured Clinical Interview for DSM-III-R.* Washington, DC: American Psychiatric Press.

Watson, C. G., Juba, M. P., Manifold, V., Kucala, T., & Anderson, P. E. D. (1991). The PTSD Interview: Rationale, description, reliability, and concurrent validity of a DSM-III based technique. *Journal of Clinical Psychology, 47,* 179–188.

Weathers, F. W. (1993). *Rational and empirical scoring rules for the Clinician-Administered PTSD Scale.* Unpublished manuscript.

Weiss, D. S. (1993). Structured clinical interview techniques. In J. Wilson & B. Raphael (Eds.), *International handbook of traumatic stress syndromes* (pp. 179–187). New York: Plenum Press.

Weiss, D. S., Marmar, C. R., Fairbank, J. A., Schlenger, W. E., Kulka, R. A., Hough, R. L., & Jordan, B. K. (1992). The prevalence of lifetime and partial post-traumatic stress disorder in Vietnam veterans. *Journal of Traumatic Stress, 5,* 365–376.

Williams, J. B. W., & Spitzer, R. L. (1982). Research diagnostic criteria and the DSM-III: An annotated comparison. *Archives of General Psychiatry, 39,* 1283–1289.

Wing, J. K., Cooper, J. E., & Sartorius, N. (1974). *The description and classification of psychiatric symptoms: An instruction manual for the PSE and CATEGO systems.* London: Cambridge University Press.

Wittchen, H. U. (1994). Reliability and validity studies of the WHO—Composite International Diagnostic Interview (CIDI): A critical review. *Journal of Psychiatric Research, 28,* 57–84.

Thematic Assessment of Posttraumatic Stress Reactions

SUSAN ROTH
LESLIE LEBOWITZ
RUTH R. DEROSA

INTRODUCTION

It is currently not very controversial to argue, as a social scientist, that people actively construct their experience, and that this complex process results in representations of both the self and the world. It is also well accepted among the community of scholars who study people exposed to traumatic events that such exposure is an extraordinary experience that challenges the representational process, disorganizing personality in the worst case, and routinely demanding an integration of emotionally intense meanings. At the most basic level, the construction of experience is essential for psychological well-being, in the way Lifton (1979) discusses a psychic death that follows from the failure to engage in the ongoing process of symbolizing experience in a meaningful way. Beyond the basic level, meanings become more specific and classifiable as markers of the individual's construction of the traumatic experience. It is these meanings that are the topic of this chapter, and it is these meanings that researchers have tried to measure as a way of representing the effects of trauma, as a way of tapping into a clinically significant traumatic process, and as a way of allowing for the articulation of targets of therapeutic change separate from symptoms of disorder. To say it in another way, it is with the victim's goal of symbolizing experience in a meaningful way that particular "traumatic" meanings, or constructions of traumatic experience, evolve over time, characterizing a dynamic adaptation that is a critical focus for trauma scholars and clinicians.

In the current chapter, we will begin with a description of Seymour Epstein's (1994) cognitive–experiential self-theory (CEST) as a way of grounding or contextualizing the empirical work on traumatic meanings. This theoretical perspective has been applied by Epstein to the understanding of post-traumatic stress reactions, and the description of his self-theory will serve the additional purpose of introducing many of the critical concepts of other theorists who have focused on the psychological meaning of traumatic exposure.

The empirical work on traumatic meanings and their assessment, what we refer to as *thematic assessment,* is broken up into two major sections. In the first section, we review three clusters of research that can be characterized as (1) studies that are driven by a particular theoretical model; (2) studies that focus on the measurement of a particular traumatic theme; and (3) studies that evaluate survivors' narrative accounts of the traumatic experience. Some of the research to date that falls into each of these three clusters is illustrated in Table 18.1. The last grouping of studies includes our own work at Duke University over the past 10 years, which we will devote the second of the two major sections on empirical work to describing in some detail. It is in the context of our own work that we hope to make a strong argument for the value of a narrative methodology.

The thematic assessment of posttraumatic stress reactions is a type of assessment that has been steadily increasing in popularity in recent years as the field of traumatic stress matures, leaving time and space for an emphasis on what are often more complex and consequently more "difficult to measure" aspects of traumatic experiences. In our discussion of the theoretical and empirical contributions to date, we intend to draw out the implications of our current knowledge base for both future research and clinical practice.

COGNITIVE-EXPERIENTIAL SELF-THEORY

A number of different traditions within psychology and psychiatry have converged on the same perspective, which is that the essence of the traumatic process lies in the recovery from an invalidation or preemption of healthy fundamental beliefs or schemas (Epstein, 1991, 1994; Horowitz, 1986, 1991; Janoff-Bulman, 1992; McCann & Pearlman, 1990). We have chosen to focus our discussion on Epstein's articulation of this point of view, because central aspects of his orientation are most consistent with our own orientation, research findings, and clinical experience. Although there are multiple levels of consciousness considered in Epstein's theory, there is an emphasis on the preconscious, on an experiential system that is no less wise nor adaptive than the rational mind, and on an emotional system that is neither subsumed under rational, cognitive constructions, nor separate from cognitive processes.

Epstein (1994) presents compelling evidence that people apprehend reality in two fundamentally different ways—one intuitive, narrative, experiential; the other analytical, deliberate, and rational. His CEST argues for the

TABLE 18.1. Empirical Research on Traumatic Meaning

Theoretically driven studies	Single-theme studies	Studies approaching a narrative methodology
Dutton et al. (1994)	Fontana, Rosenheck, & Brett (1992)	Dansky (1991)
Janoff-Bulman (1989, 1992)	Frazier & Schauben (1994)	Dansky, Roth, & Kronenberger (1990)
McCann et al. (1988)	Joseph, Yule, & Williams (1993)	DeRosa, Fischer, & Roth (1995)
McCann & Pearlman (1990)	Kubany (1994)	DeRosa et al. (1995)
Norris & Kaniasty (1991)	Kubany et al. (1994)	Krupnick & Horowitz (1981)
Resick (1993)	Riggs et al. (1992)	Lebowitz & Roth (1994)
	Wong & Cook (1992)	Newman (1992)
		Newman & Roth (1994)
		Roth & Lebowitz (1988)
		Roth & Newman (1991, 1992)
		Schwartzberg (1993)
		Scurfield et al. (1984)

existence of two major adaptive systems, an experiential system and a rational system, both of which organize experience and direct behavior. It is the experiential system that is assumed to be associated with affect, and thus with a different mode of processing information or of knowing than the rational system. Epstein describes the experiential system, for example, as "experienced passively and preconsciously: we are seized by our emotions," in contrast to the rational system as "experienced actively and consciously: we are in control of our thoughts" (1994, p. 711). Likewise, the experiential system is "self-evidently valid: experiencing is believing," whereas the rational system "requires justification via logic and evidence" (p. 711). Important for our purpose of considering thematic assessment, the experiential system encodes reality in metaphors and narratives, and derives knowledge that is often more compelling and more likely to influence behavior.

According to CEST, people have constructs about the self and the world in both the experiential and rational systems. In contrast to *beliefs* in the rational system, there are implicit beliefs or schemas in the experiential system that include generalizations from emotionally significant past experiences, which are organized into an overall system, and which are subject to disorganization following unassimilable emotional experiences. Generalizations and abstractions in the experiential system result from the use of prototypes, metaphors, scripts, and narratives. Although the experiential and rational systems are reciprocally influential, the experiential system is assumed to be dominant over the rational system, because it is less effortful, likely to be experienced as more compelling because of its association with affect, and difficult to control because its influence is usually outside of awareness.

Thus, generalizations from past experiences, implicit schemas that are organized in the experiential system, are threatened by exposure to trauma; the meaning of the traumatic experience subsequently has the power to influence the survivor's behavior.

According to CEST (Epstein, 1991, 1994), a preconscious theory of reality determines to a large extent how a person perceives, thinks, feels, and behaves. Unconscious and conscious processes exert less influence on everyday behavior. Behavior is determined by the joint influence of the need to maximize pleasure and minimize pain, the need to maintain a coherent and stable conceptual system, the need for relatedness, and the need to enhance self-esteem. Associated with these needs or basic functions of a personal theory of reality are four basic beliefs: (1) a belief regarding the benevolence of the world; (2) a belief that the world is meaningful; (3) a belief that people are trustworthy and worth relating to; and (4) a belief that the self is worthy. As a result of exposure to traumatic events, the basic constructs or beliefs about self and world are threatened at a deep, experiential level, and the individual must reestablish stability by allowing fundamental beliefs to account for the traumatic experience. By the processes of assimilation and/or accommodation, the meaning attributed to the traumatic event and the nature of the fundamental belief system is brought in line to establish consistency.

In summary, Epstein presents a theory that argues for two adaptive systems that organize experience and direct behavior. The experiential system encodes reality in prototypes, metaphors, scripts, and narratives, and derives knowledge that is often more compelling and more likely to influence behavior. The experiential system is compelling because of its association with affect, and relatively powerful, also, because its influence is usually outside of awareness. The organization of experience into constructs or beliefs about the self and world are associated with needs or basic functions of a personal theory of reality, and are subject to disorganization upon exposure to traumatic events.

Empirical work on the assessment of traumatic meanings must attempt to tap meanings as they are represented in the experiential system, and as they intersect with pretrauma construction of a personal reality. Assessments must allow for the uncovering of preconscious meanings and the decoding of metaphors and scripts, and recognize the importance of accounting for emotions. Researchers and clinicians evaluating traumatic meanings must access the wise and adaptive part of the victim's mind that is holding the trauma in anticipation of finding a place for it to rest in peace.

THEMATIC ASSESSMENT

The empirical work on traumatic meanings is not at present a clearly unified and coherent body of literature, reflecting a relatively early phase in the research process. It is possible, however, to organize the existing studies into three reasonably cohesive groupings that characterize the work to date. In all cases, the research has focused on the relationship between exposure variables and traumatic meanings, and/or between traumatic meanings and posttraumatic stress reactions and disorder. This represents an agreement, at least in regard to the central role of the person's construction of experience, in understanding the relationship between traumatic exposure and psychological sequelae.

Theoretically Driven Studies

There are two groups of studies that have evaluated traumatic schemas that are defined a priori by a particular theoretical model. One group of studies represents the work of Ronnie Janoff-Bulman and her colleagues (Janoff-Bulman, 1989, 1992), and compares trauma survivors to nontrauma survivors, as well as different survivor populations, on Janoff-Bulman's self-report World Assumptions Scale. Janoff-Bulman's model specifies three categories of assumptions that are posited to be core elements of our basic conceptual system, and that are potentially shattered by exposure to traumatic events: the benevolence of the world (including the benevolence of people); the meaningfulness of the world (involving peoples' beliefs about the distribution of outcomes, e.g., beliefs about justice); and the worthiness of self. In a long-standing research program described in her recent book (1992), Janoff-Bulman found in a number of samples that the assumptive world of trauma victims differs from that of nonvictims in the expected direction, and that some victimizations are more likely to affect particular assumptions than others.

Although the World Assumptions Scale was published in 1989 and carries with it initial reliability and validity studies, it has not yet established itself as a measure of choice for trauma researchers, even for those who rely on a self-report methodology. In fact, the traumatic schemas deriving from the work of McCann and Pearlman and colleagues (McCann, Sakheim, & Abrahamson, 1988; McCann & Pearlman, 1990) have been evaluated more broadly across research sites, perhaps because of their greater clinical grounding and complexity. Unfortunately, these schemas proposed by McCann and Pearlman have not been consensually defined. Preliminary unpublished work on the development of self-report measures in this domain is available from both Pearlman and colleagues at the Traumatic Stress Institute (personal communication, November 1995) and Resick (reported in Resick, 1993). In addition, there are two published studies on the mediating role of the McCann et al. schemas, which assess these schemas in yet two different ways. Although there is consistent support for the importance of assessing traumatic schemas within the McCann–Pearlman framework, consensus has not yet been reached about the measure of choice. This is partly a function of the stage of development of this research agenda. Certainly a consensus measure would facilitate our accumulation of knowledge about the psychological accommodation to traumatic meaning.

In a recently published study, Mary Ann Dutton and her colleagues (Dutton, Burghardt, Perrin, Chrestman, & Halle, 1994) examined battered women's cognitive schemas in relation to, on the one hand, (1) childhood victimization history, (2) sexual abuse within the battering relationship, and (3) their interpretation of the violence from their intimate partner, and in relation to, on the other hand, posttraumatic stress reactions. Battered women from a specialized family violence outpatient clinic were evaluated with an earlier version of the current Belief Scale from the Traumatic Stress Institute (Pearlman). Results supported the general conclusion that the meaning attached to violence from an intimate partner relates to negative cognitive schemas, and more specifically that the expectation of some form of violence in the future, and self-blame for prior violence, were two of the most important variables. In addition, negative cognitive schemas were found to co-occur with measures of posttraumatic stress symptoms, supporting the role of generalized constructions of traumatic experiences in adaptation to traumatic events.

In an early study of the mediating role of beliefs in explaining the distress of victims, Norris and Kaniasty (1991) borrowed from McCann et al.'s framework in evaluating, by self-report, sets of beliefs about safety, esteem, and trust in a large, statewide sample that was composed of representative subsamples of violent crime victims, property crime victims, and nonvictims. The three groups were defined according to recent victimizations (past 6 months, 3 months on the average). For violent crime, negative schemas in all three domains were related to victimization severity and to distress. For property crime, only beliefs in the safety domain were affected by victimization, although beliefs in all domains related to distress.

This study provides support for the notion that changes in beliefs are central to the experience of crime, and is interesting also in bringing forward the fact that there are at times more than shades of difference across studies in the definition and/or measurement of constructs originating in the same framework. Trust, for example, is defined by McCann et al. as both the belief and expectancy that one can trust or rely upon one's own perceptions and judgment, as well as the belief or expectancy that others are trustworthy. For Norris and Kaniasty, beliefs in the trust domain were evaluated by measures of cynicism and pessimism adapted from an anomia scale, in which "anomia" was defined as an individual's generalized, pervasive sense of social malintegration or alienation. Items such as "hardly fair to bring children into the world" and "public officials not interested in the problems of the average person" have a totally different sense than, for example, Pearlman's "I feel uncertain about my ability to make decisions," or "People shouldn't place too much trust in their friends." Clearly, even researchers who agree at a certain level of abstraction about what are important constructs to measure do not necessarily have the same idea about how to oper-ationalize these constructs. This is actually not all that surprising, given the complexity of victim experience that we are trying to capture. Although researchers in this area have, in one or another context, taken the time to understand the phenomenology of victims, and although researchers' own construction of victims' experience are going to come into play one way or another, perhaps the voice of victims just needs to be louder and more defining in terms of what we attempt to assess. We will return to this point later.

Single-Theme Studies

There is a significant amount of research dealing with a variety of trauma populations on issues relating broadly to cognitive or subjective appraisal of traumatic exposure. What follows is not intended in any way to be an exhaustive review of this body of literature, but rather a sampling of proto-types that have been published in the last few years and focus on a particu-lar aspect of the meaning or construction of traumatic experience. As a group, these studies again point clearly to the importance of the personal meaning of trauma in accounting for posttrauma adaptation. As individual works of scholarship, they range from the more paradigmatic research models to the more narrative, from the purely cognitive to a cognitive–affective integra-tion, and from an assessment of more straightforward, isolated meanings to more complex, dynamic, multifaceted ones.

In a recent study by Frazier and Schauben (1994), one main focus was on the relationship between characterological and behavioral self-blame and adjustment to extreme stress, a research question that has received consider-able attention. In a presentation of their findings on rape victims in the con-text of previous research, the authors make a convincing argument that self-blame (of any kind) is not adaptive and, in fact, is associated with great-er symptomatology *and* disruptions of beliefs (again, an earlier, but differ-ent, version of the Belief Scale from the Traumatic Stress Institute). We do not mean to minimize the importance of self-blame for rape or other vic-tims as a trauma theme demanding investigation. We do intend, however, to be critical of the assumption that a victim's experience of blame can neces-sarily be captured by experimenter-generated, a priori constructions or categorizations of that experience. It seems that there is sufficient evidence at this point that the distinction between the two kinds of blame, charac-terological and behavioral, although logically coherent, is not experiential-ly relevant, for the most part, at least for rape victims. We are sounding here a caution in general about trying to fit square pegs into round holes. This caution extends to the paradigmatic study of causal attributions and attribu-tional style as mediators of response to trauma. Although some of this work

is clearly productive (e.g., Joseph, Yule, & Williams, 1993), the standard attributional dimensions (i.e., internal, stable, global, controllable) seem too
confining with respect to the understanding of how individuals explain to
themselves the occurrence of a traumatic event.

Some investigators, looking at individual trauma themes in relation to
Posttraumatic Stress Disorder (PTSD) and/or trauma characteristics, have focused on individual affects such as guilt, anger, and shame (e.g., Kubany,
1994; Kubany, Gino, Denny, & Torigoe, 1994; Riggs, Dancu, Gershuny, Greenberg, & Foa, 1992; Wong & Cook, 1992). Work by Kubany and his colleagues
is particularly interesting, in our view, in that their themes have both an affective and cognitive component. In the Kubany et al. hostility study, for
example, the investigators use the Cook–Medley Hostility Scale, which they
describe as a measure of cynical hostility, centering around *beliefs that reflect*
an absence of interpersonal trust and doubts about the basic goodness of other people.
Obviously, the same basic assumptions or beliefs keep popping up, one way
or the other, particularly in the work that is more phenomenologically based.
The confusion seems to be about how best to section and name what seem
to be some commonly understood experiences of trauma survivors as they
try to make sense of what happened to them.

The potential complexity of this undertaking is illustrated in Kubany's
(1994) article on guilt, in which he describes various attempts to classify and
characterize types of guilt reactions experienced by male combat veterans.
Kubany's work is clearly grounded in the victims' phenomenology, which
he nicely illustrates with narrative examples. Nevertheless, his focus on identifying false assumptions and faulty logic, on which dysfunctional guilt is
often based, has straightforward implications for the alleviation of guilt, and
involves the veteran's ability to find new meaning in his behavior in the traumatic situation.

The suggestion of the need for a broader range of therapeutic interventions than ones that simply focus on PTSD is highlighted in a very creative study by Fontana, Rosenheck, and Brett (1992). Their argument is that
different subjective experiences critical to the traumatic process are legitimate and important targets of therapeutic change. In their study of Vietnam theater veterans, they identified experiences that Vietnam combat
veterans have frequently reported as traumatic. They focused on a major
dimension of psychological meaning: the degree of personal responsibility
for death and destruction. The assumption was that different roles represented experiences with different meaning regarding responsibility. The experiences were organized in terms of four roles that veterans played in the
initiation of death and injury: (1) target of killing; (2) observer of killing;
(3) agent of killing; and (4) failure at preventing killing. These subjective
variables significantly increased the power to account for psychiatric symptomatology over the objective variables of combat exposure, witnessing abusive violence, and participating in abusive violence.

Studies Approaching a Narrative Methodology

Traumatic experiences demand the integration of emotionally intense meanings that evolve over time in interaction with each other and with preexisting schemas. These meanings are often encoded metaphorically, experienced preconsciously, and are generally complex. This complexity has led to a lack of consensus about how to define and measure this realm of traumatic experience. Nevertheless, the research on thematic assessment has consistently supported the central role of traumatic meanings in understanding posttraumatic sequelae, and has heralded the value of targeting these meanings in treatment. Furthermore, we would argue that those approaches that most creatively represent the voice of the victim, in as much complexity as possible, will be most likely to inform us about that which we are trying to understand.

The following are examples of studies that come closest to focusing on a constellation of dynamic, emotionally connected meanings whose definitions have emerged from listening to victims describe their experience. Unfortunately, this type of research is still in its infancy, as indicated once again by an absence of investigators building on one another's accumulated knowledge. Although our own work falls in this category, we will devote the next section to describing it in more detail.

One of the early, now classic, studies in this "narrative" category is by Krupnick and Horowitz (1981). They were interested in recurrent themes, consisting of memories, ideas, and feelings evoked by highly stressful events. The assumption in their work, as in the work previously described, is that failure to adequately confront and work through these themes can lead to a prolonged posttraumatic reaction. They argue that awareness of common themes provides a therapeutic framework for understanding the patient's difficulties and suggests a therapeutic focus.

Krupnick and Horowitz defined their common themes on the basis of clinical literature that indicated a consensus about the importance of certain thematic contents in diverse populations with stress-related disorders. On the basis of a coding manual that operationalized the themes, clinical data from evaluation and therapy interviews of 30 patients with PTSD (15 after bereavement and 15 after personal injury) were rated to determine whether themes could be reliably identified, and to assess their frequency in each subgroup. The results of the study suggested the general viability of this approach to the study of trauma themes.

The themes identified by these investigators focus upon major negative emotional states evoked by trauma (fear, anger, guilt, shame, and grief), which are assumed to be mediated by underlying ideas and attitudes. This cognitive core complicates the characterization of the themes and leaves more room for the researchers' theoretical perspective to overlay the subject's phenomenology. In this case, the interpretive framework is psychoanalytic, which obviously impacts on how victim experience or narrative is taken to a higher level of abstraction. Again, we are sensitive to the issue of the potential for muffling the victim's voice, even if the process of hearing it is highly valued. On the other hand, at the other end of the road is the risk of a lack of any organizing principles in a group of themes. This is a criticism we feel it is fair to levy against another early study involving a thematic analysis of therapy sessions with Vietnam veterans (Scurfield, Corker, Gongla, & Hough, 1984). Issues such as anger, guilt, alienation, and power, among many others, were rated along with "therapeutic themes" such as "restoring self-pride" and "reducing stigma and shame." The most prominent themes were then defined on the basis of descriptions of group content, with virtually no interpretive frame.

A recent study by Schwartzberg (1993) impressively combines phenomenological research methodology with an organizing theoretical perspective in an attempt to understand how HIV-positive gay men have found meaning in, or made sense of, AIDS. Each subject participated in an intensive, semistructured clinical interview, dealing with such issues as gay identity, relationships, psychosocial adaptation to HIV, mortality, and spirituality.

Data analysis involved two distinct phases. In the first phase, the interest was in the particular ideas men held about the impact of HIV and AIDS. In the author's words, "What were the metaphors they used, images they conjured, associations they made, and tacit beliefs they revealed about what AIDS and HIV meant to them?" (p. 484). The result of systematically analyzing interview transcripts resulted in 10 distinct categories of representations, including, for example, "HIV as catalyst for personal growth," "HIV as belonging," "HIV as inescapable loss," "HIV as punishment," and "HIV as a contamination of one's self."

In the second phase of data analysis, the interview data were reexamined to explore whether men were able to integrate HIV and AIDS into a more encompassing, coherent framework for reascribing meaning to life. What emerged from the data were four general patterns that typified subjects' abilities to integrate HIV into an overall framework for ascribing meaning to the world: high meaning, defensive meaning, shattered meaning, and irrelevant meaning.

This study is, in our view, an exemplary example of the investigation of psychological meaning in response to trauma. The organization of narrative material without imposition of a priori categorizations, the attention to metaphors and images in the language of participants, the incorporation of information pertaining to the interaction of representations that emerged in the first level of analysis, the description of themes as emotional–cognitive complexes, the recognition that meanings evolve over time, the attempt to decipher the relationship between traumatic meanings and a more encompassing psychological framework of participants, are all represented in this work. After reading just this one article on HIV-positive gay men, one has a more than superficial understanding of what the experience of this existential and medical crisis must be like.

WORK FROM THE DUKE GROUP
ON THE PROCESS OF COPING WITH TRAUMA

Feminists and other social scientists working to expand our current knowledge base have put forward compelling arguments for the methodological importance of open and semistructured interviews and narrative/thematic analysis (Anderson & Jack, 1992; Anderson, Armitage, Jack, & Wittner, 1990; Mishler, 1986; Reinharz, 1992; Westkott, 1990). The belief that interviewing and the analysis of narrative is central to creating new bodies of more inclusive and accurate information is so fundamental to radical social scientists that it cuts across disciplinary lines and is gaining momentum and power more generally as a legitimate methodology.

The use of this narrative methodology is valued for the following reasons:

1. It focuses on the meanings that people give their lives and the ways in which they actively and privately construct their experience.
2. It is an ideal methodology for gathering information that expands or alters existing paradigms.
3. It facilitates finding out information that is less readily accessible (i.e., less conscious or less socially supported).
4. It is uniquely responsive to the emergence of new information and allows the process of inquiry to shape the inquiry itself. In other words, by being able to follow up on interesting things, or introduce new questions because of compelling information, the research endeavor is more fluid and responsive to the implications of the emerging data.
5. It is empowering, because it offers a voice to traditionally silenced people, and because the dialectical nature of an unstructured interview equalizes the power hierarchy between researcher and respondent.
6. Meaning can only be discerned when adequately contextualized. The open-ended interview process and narrative analysis most closely approximates normal modes of discourse that, in turn, provide the greatest and most meaningful context for communication.

Furthermore, to organize experience in narrative form is one of the central ways that people naturally make sense of and give meaning to their experience.

Our work at Duke University on the process of coping with trauma has centered upon the use of a narrative methodology. Although we aspire to high standards of methodological rigor, we also find notions of experiential knowledge and the value of narrative analysis compelling. In addition to Lebowitz and DeRosa, many other students at Duke have, over the years, contributed to the efforts reported here. The most notable contributions have been made by Elana Newman, currently at the University of Tulsa, whose tireless efforts enabled the development of a complex coding manual for our themes and contributed greatly to the productivity of the research endeavor more generally. The most recent work on our coding manual is represented in this volume by Lifton, Newman, Lebowitz, and Roth. We hope that our work will ultimately allow us to abstract, from victims' narratives, templates of psychological dynamics with threads of interwoven meanings that capture the experience of the adaptations individuals make to intolerable experiences.

Coping with Sexual Trauma

All but the most recent (1994 and on) work is summarized in a paper by Roth and Newman (1993) on coping with sexual trauma. Our research program on thematic issues in recovery began in earnest with the work described in Roth and Lebowitz (1988), which was based on unstructured interviews with treatment-seeking survivors of a variety of different sexual traumas (e.g., date rape, stranger rape, childhood incest). Subjects were asked to present their story of what had happened, and what it had meant to them, and from these data, themes relating to difficulties in coping were abstracted and organized into conceptually coherent and clinically meaningful categories.

These themes have since been studied with narrative material in a variety of different contexts (Dansky, 1991; Newman, 1992; Roth & Batson, 1993; Roth & Newman, 1991, 1992), with the goal of understanding how they evolve over time, as individuals move toward resolution of traumatic meanings. Our coding system is complex and difficult to learn (see Roth & Newman, 1993, for a summary of reliability and validity studies), but early evidence for the utility of our themes in capturing the complex coping process we had hoped to characterize was extremely encouraging. In our work prior to 1994, we devoted considerable effort to building rich, descriptive accounts, with the narrative material obtained in our interviews, of how our subjects were processing traumatic material over time (see, e.g., Roth & Newman, 1992). Our validity studies were primarily clinical case studies. An initial attempt to translate our knowledge into a self-report instrument (Dansky, Roth, & Kronenberger, 1990) to measure our themes turned sour for us when the instrument appeared not to have the necessary correspondence to our manual-rated themes in two separate investigations (Dansky, 1991; Newman, 1992).

The actual content of our themes would not surprise anyone reading this chapter at this point, or perhaps anyone treating sexual trauma survivors. The themes are helplessness, rage, fear, loss, shame, guilt, and schemas about the self, others, and the world, such as self-blame, alienation, and trust. Although we have previously referred to our themes as schemas and affects, we believe, in fact, that they all are more accurately represented as cognitive–affective complexes. And although we have, with one exception (Roth & Newman, 1992), represented the themes as if they operated independently from one another, we actually believe that they form a network that defines a traumatic dynamic, which drives behavior, and becomes an important target of therapeutic change. Understanding the nature of the dynamic in individual cases, and abstracting common dynamics, is a central challenge for the future.

Recent Theme Work

Recent narrative work on sexual trauma themes (Lebowitz & Roth, 1994) has illuminated how cultural beliefs or constructions about women, sexuality, and rape influence how women survivors of rape make sense of their traumatic experience. Women's descriptions of their cultural beliefs and their impact on their experience of rape fell into four categories: (1) The rape illuminated aspects of the sociocultural context which was previously unnoticed; (2) women incorporated culturally generated constructions of femaleness, sexuality, and the meaning of rape into their descriptions of how they experienced the rape, thereby highlighting the nature of these embedded constructs; (3) women spontaneously described more general aspects of what it means to be socialized as a woman in this society, and these were linked to the experience of being raped; and (4) some women talked about how they believed rape functions as a form of social control. In addition to providing knowledge of the importance of the cultural context of rape in recovery from sexual trauma, this study is more generally illuminating in regard to the nature of the relationship between traumatic meaning and the broader-based personal theory of reality. This work has also led to the development of a Cultural Messages Scale (Lebowitz & Kiely, in press), designed to evaluate both familiarity with and endorsement of a broad domain of cultural messages about women and sexuality.

Another recent focus in our work has been the relationship between our trauma themes and psychological symptomatology in both sexual trauma and other survivor groups. Newman, Riggs, and Roth (in press) studied the relationship between the resolution of our trauma themes and PTSD, as well as its DSM-IV-associated features (Complex PTSD). Results indicated that among sexual trauma survivors, and also among a heterogeneous group of survivors, variables quantifying thematic resolution were significant predictors of posttraumatic symptomatology. Likewise, DeRosa et al. (1996b) evaluated our trauma themes in people exposed to the Hamlet chicken plant fire, in which 25 employees were killed and many more injured. The only significant predictor of chronic PTSD was the number of unresolved trauma themes. Both of these studies provide important quantitative support for the validity of our method of coding trauma themes.

One final examination of data from the Hamlet sample represents a critical step toward the goal of understanding the dynamic interplay among trauma themes (DeRosa, Fischer, & Roth, 1996a). Exploratory cluster analyses were conducted to examine the nature of the *patterns* of theme resolution that may be similar across subjects. Meaningful clusters emerged and significantly differentiated groups on PTSD symptomatology. Individuals in one group had resolved most of their themes and were described as feeling empowered to effect change and interact with others without self-reproach. The second group included individuals who were struggling with maladaptive themes across the board, and who had the most difficulty with rage, trust, and loss. The third group was described as having rage coupled with empowerment. Finally, the fourth group, while also struggling with rage, had resolved themes dealing with interpersonal relationships. Results indicated that the groups (first and third) with the ability to feel empowered are the only clusters that include individuals who never had PTSD, or who experienced only an acute or brief episode of PTSD. Although many subjects in the "rage and empowerment" group were still struggling to cope with many of the thematic issues, fewer individuals were diagnosed with chronic PTSD. These data are consistent with our previous argument (Roth & Newman, 1992) that mastery of helplessness is a central theme in recovery:

> Working through the overwhelming experience of helplessness allows the victim to experience rage and fear, let go of feelings of guilt and shame about the abuse, face and grieve loss, and incorporate the experience into more adaptive schemas of self, others and the world. By recognizing one's helplessness, one often recognizes the fear and loss surrounding the trauma as well as the responsibility of others, and the courage in self. (p. 222)

SUMMARY AND CONCLUSIONS

As we have tried to keep a running summary going throughout this chapter, we believe we have the luxury of bringing home, in another way, the most important message about thematic assessment we have tried to give in this chapter. We would like to end the chapter with a poem of a client of Roth, written while participating in a comprehensive treatment program designed by Roth and Ronald Batson for incest survivors (see Roth, DeRosa, & Turner, 1996). After a description by the client of intolerable behavior by her father, the client was asked several times in different ways by Roth in the context of group therapy whether she was angry at her father. After evading the question for some time, the client somewhat impatiently pulled the following poem from her purse and read it aloud. We believe if you study it, you will see our major conclusions come to life.

DAMN
Your god and my god are different.
Your god spits gold, counts heads, keeps tabs
while my god sits and worries.
Your god justifies your wrath,

enables your rages,
cleans up your messes.
A wife in flowing robes,
a mother with a white beard,
an ever-indulging, never questioning Santa Claus.
Everything you ever wanted for free, and you are
always right.
My god holds my hand while i walk away.
My god keeps me from killing you.

REFERENCES

Anderson, K., Armitage, S., Jack, D. C., & Wittner, J. (1990). Beginning where we are: Feminist methodology in oral history. In J. M. Nielsen (Ed.), *Feminist research methods.* Boulder, CO: Westview Press.

Anderson, K., & Jack, D. C. (1991). Learning to listen: Interview techniques and analyses. In S. B. Gluck & D. Patai (Eds.), *Women's words: The feminist practice of oral history.* New York & London: Routledge.

Dansky, B. S. (1991). *Recovery from sexual trauma: The influence of coping, social support, affect, and cognitive schemata on psychological well-being.* Unpublished doctoral dissertation, Duke University, Durham, NC.

Dansky, B. S., Roth, S., & Kronenberger, W. G. (1990). The trauma constellation identification scale: A measure of the psychological impact of a stressful life event. *Journal of Traumatic Stress 3,* 557–573.

DeRosa, R. R., Fischer, K., & Roth, S. (1996a). *Post-traumatic stress disorder and alterations in cognitive schemas and affects after disaster.* Manuscript submitted for publication.

DeRosa, R. R., Roth, S., Caddell, J. M., Schlenger, W. E., Fairbank, J. A., & Davidson, J. (1996b). *Disaster and the meaning of the traumatic experience: Implications for the development and maintenance of PTSD.* Manuscript submitted for publication.

Dutton, M. A., Burghardt, K. J., Perrin, S. G., Chrestman, K. R., & Halle, P. M. (1994). Battered women's cognitive schemata. *Journal of Traumatic Stress, 7,* 237–257.

Epstein, S. (1991). The self-concept, the traumatic neurosis, and the structure of personality. In D. Ozer, J. M. Healy, Jr., & A. J. Stewart (Eds.), *Perspectives in personality.* London: Jessica Kingsley.

Epstein, S. (1994). Integration of the cognitive and the psychodynamic unconscious. *American Psychologist, 49,* 709–725.

Fontana, A., Rosenheck, R., & Brett, E. (1992). War zone traumas and posttraumatic stress disorder symptomatology. *Journal of Nervous and Mental Disease, 180,* 748–755.

Frazier, P., & Schauben, L. (1994). Causal attributions and recovery from rape and other stressful life events. *Journal of Social and Clinical Psychology, 31,* 1–14.

Horowitz, M. J. (1986). *Stress response syndromes.* Northvale, NJ: Jason Aronson.

Horowitz, M. J. (Ed.). (1991). *Person schemas and maladaptive interpersonal patterns.* Chicago: University of Chicago Press.

Janoff-Bulman, R. (1989). Assumptive worlds and the stress of traumatic events: Applications of the schema construct. *Social Cognition, 7,* 113–136.

Janoff-Bulman, R. (1992). *Shattered assumptions: Toward a new psychology of trauma.* New York: Free Press.

Joseph, S., Yule, W., & Williams, R. (1993). Post-traumatic stress: Attributional aspects. *Journal of Traumatic Stress, 6,* 501–515.

Krupnick, J. L., & Horowitz, M. J. (1981). Stress response syndromes: Recurrent themes. *Archives of General Psychiatry, 38,* 428–435.

Kubany, E. S. (1994). A cognitive model of guilt typology in combat-related PTSD. *Journal of Traumatic Stress, 7,* 3–21.

Kubany, E. S., Gino, A., Denny, N. R., & Torigoe, R. Y. (1994). Relationship of cynical hostility and PTSD among Vietnam veterans. *Journal of Traumatic Stress, 7,* 21–33.

Lebowitz, L., & Kiely, M. (in press). Psychometric review of the Cultural Messages Scale. In B. H. Stamm (Ed.), *Measurement of stress, trauma, and adaptation.* Lutherville, MD: Sidran Press.

Lebowitz, L., & Roth, S. (1994). "I felt like a slut": The cultural context and women's response to being raped. *Journal of Traumatic Stress, 7,* 363–391.

Lifton, R. J. (1979). *The broken connection: On death and the continuity of life.* New York: Simon & Schuster.

McCann, I. L., & Pearlman, L. A. (1990). *Psychological trauma and the adult survivor: Theory, therapy and transformation.* New York: Brunner/Mazel.

McCann, I. L., Sakheim, D. K., & Abrahamson, D. J. (1988). Trauma and victimization: A model of psychological adaptation. *Counseling Psychologist, 16,* 532–594.

Mishler, E. G. (1986). *Research interviewing, context, and narrative.* Cambridge, MA: Harvard University Press.

Newman, E. (1992). *The process of recovery in adult female survivors of childhood sexual abuse: Schema, affect and symptom change.* Unpublished doctoral dissertation, Duke University, Durham, NC.

Newman, E., Riggs, D., & Roth, S. (in press). Thematic resolution and PTSD: An empirical investigation of the relationship between meaning and trauma-related diagnoses. *Journal of Traumatic Stress.*

Norris, F. H., & Kaniasty, K. (1991). The psychological experience of crime: A test of the mediating role of beliefs in explaining the distress of victims. *Journal of Social and Clinical Psychology, 10,* 239–261.

Reinharz, S. (1992). *Feminist methods in social research.* New York & Oxford: Oxford University Press.

Resick, P. A. (1993). The psychological impact of rape. *Journal of Interpersonal Violence, 8,* 223–255.

Riggs, D. S., Dancu, C. V., Gershuny, B. S., Greenberg, D., & Foa, E. B. (1992). Anger and post-traumatic stress disorder in female crime victims. *Journal of Traumatic Stress, 5,* 613–627.

Roth, S., & Batson, R. (1993). The creative balance: The therapeutic relationship and thematic issues in trauma resolution. *Journal of Traumatic Stress, 6,* 159–277.

Roth, S., DeRosa, R. R., & Turner, K. (1996). Cognitive-behavioral interventions for posttraumatic stress disorder. In E. Giller, Jr. & L. Weisaeth (Eds.), *Clinical psychiatry: International practice and research: Posttraumatic stress disorder* (Vol. 2, No. 2, pp. 281–296). London: Bailliere Tindall.

Roth, S., & Lebowitz, L. (1988). The experience of sexual trauma. *Journal of Traumatic Stress, 1,* 79–107.

Roth, S., & Newman, E. (1991). The process of coping with sexual trauma. *Journal of Traumatic Stress, 4,* 279–297.

Roth, S., & Newman, E. (1992). The role of helplessness in the recovery process for sexual trauma survivors. *Canadian Journal of Behavioral Science, 24,* 220–232.

Roth, S., & Newman, E. (1993). The process of coping with incest for adult survivors: Measurement and implications for treatment and research. *Journal of Interpersonal Violence, 8,* 363–377.

Schwartzberg, S. S. (1993). Struggling for meaning: How HIV-positive gay men make sense of AIDS. *Professional Psychology: Research and Practice, 24,* 483–490.

Scurfield, R. M., Corker, T. M., Gongla, P. A., & Hough, R. L. (1984). Three post-Vietnam rap/therapy groups: An analysis. *Group, 8,* 3–21.

Westkott, M. (1990). Feminist criticism of the social sciences. In J. McCarl Nielsen (Ed.), *Feminist research methods.* Boulder, CO: Westview Press.

Wong, M. R., & Cook, D. (1992). Shame and its contribution to PTSD. *Journal of Traumatic Stress, 5,* 557–562.

CHAPTER 19

Use of the Rorschach in Assessing Trauma

PATTI LEVIN
BRUCE REIS

INTRODUCTION

The psychological symptoms of trauma are varied and complex. Within the same individual, symptoms may appear florid and acute, while at another point in time, the individual may appear symptom free. In our clinical experience, psychological sequelae of trauma are often dissociated from cognitive connection to the traumatic precipitants. This split often occurs in cases of posttraumatic stress disorder (PTSD) reactions, months or years following the stressor event. For these reasons, the cognitive, affective, and relational sequelae of trauma, and particularly the etiological component(s), can be missed and misdiagnosed during the traditional evaluation of traumatized patients.

Although anxious affect often accompanies the presentation of a PTSD, we do not regard PTSD as an anxiety disorder, per se. Rather, we conceptualize the PTSD diagnosis as a complex cluster of anxious, dissociative, depressive, and other elements.

The symptomatology of traumatic stress reactions includes emotional constriction or numbing, hyperarousal and hypervigilance, memory processing difficulties, feelings of helplessness, depression, problems in anger modulation, difficulties in object relations, and somatization (Horowitz, 1976; van der Kolk, 1987; van der Kolk & van der Hart, 1989; Wilson & Walker, 1990). Several major PTSD/trauma subgroups exist, and research continues to contribute meaningful data (Kardiner, 1941; Krystal & Niederland, 1968; Burgess & Holmstrom, 1974; Keane, Malloy, & Fairbank, 1984; Horowitz, 1976; Sales, Baum, & Shore, 1984; Lindy, 1985; Green, Lindy, & Grace, 1985; Wilson, Harel, & Kahana, 1988). Major issues in differential diagnosis confront the evaluating clinician: PTSD versus psychosis, comorbidity with Axis II disorders, and the complex picture of the dissociative disorders.

OVERVIEW OF THE RORSCHACH

The Rorschach Inkblot Test consists of 10 standard ink blots and was developed in 1921 by a Swiss psychiatrist, Hermann Rorschach. In 1925, it began to be systematized by five psychologists in the United States: Beck, Klopfer, Piotrowski, Hertz, and Rappaport (with Shafer, Gill, and Holt). Each of the five developed separate scoring and interpretative systems with different theoretical frameworks. Because of the lack of agreement among the different systems, the Rorschach was subject to much criticism and suffered a lack of face validity. In 1974, Exner created the first standardized system, which includes objective criteria for scoring, administration, and interpretation. His Comprehensive System is based on discussions with the four systematizers still living, three surveys of over 1,000 clinical psychologists, and a thorough review, analysis, and replication of all existing studies (over 4,000 articles and 30 books) in an attempt to consolidate the most valid and reliable parts of the existing systems. Exner created a major database of normative samples for nonpatients, as well as several categories of psychiatric populations, with which protocols can be compared. The Comprehensive System, continually updated through ongoing research, provides construct validity and reliability, and has put the Rorschach on solid psychometric ground (Parker, 1983).

Each response from the 10 cards is coded systematically, then calculated into ratios and percentages in the Structural Summary, which provides the groundwork for the interpretation of the subject's reality testing, thinking, mediational processes, affect, controls, self-perception, and object relations, along with other important information about the process and content of perception. Results are compared to sample norms and standard deviations. Exner's system (1986, 1990, 1991) is data based and atheoretical: Empirically defensible elements form the structural aspects of the Comprehensive System. An ideographic interpretation of content and pattern fleshes out the nomothetic structural analysis.

RORSCHACH INVESTIGATIONS OF TRAUMA-SEQUELAE DISORDERS

The Rorschach has been used as an assessment and research instrument in the evaluation of trauma-sequelae disorders. To date, there are over 20 published studies that have investigated the utility of the Rorschach in traumatized populations. Although no single psychological test is valid on its own, the Rorschach has a unique contribution in the assessment of psychological trauma as a wideband instrument with both ideographic and nomothetic strengths. The projective assessment of trauma-sequelae disorders by the Rorschach test may provide essential information not always tapped by self-report measures. "Emotional constriction may well be the most common expression of PTSD, and the diagnosis is likely to be missed during this phase" (van der Kolk & Ducey, 1989; p. 271). Most victims of trauma are ambivalent about discussing their experiences in their attempts to avoid the associated affect, particularly in the early phase of therapy or evaluation, before enough trust has developed. Such avoidance, denial, and guardedness, as well as the complex nature of the symptomatology, can complicate diagnosis and subsequent appropriate treatment.

In a brief review, Frank (1992) noted that only six published studies have been conducted on the Rorschach performance of Vietnam combat veterans with PTSD. Levin's (1990) study of the use of the Rorschach with 27 civilian trauma survivors included a review of eight Rorschach articles on Vietnam combat veterans and five Rorschach articles on other (civilian) trauma survivors. Armstrong (1991) used the Rorschach with subjects diagnosed with multiple personality disorder or severe dissociative disorders and reviewed several similar reports. This chapter attempts to consolidate findings of Rorschach investigations of traumatized adults in order to illustrate typical patterns of responding and profiles of symptomatology.

Noncivilian Populations

The first reported study of the use of the Rorschach to assess the psychological impact of environmental stressors was done in 1965 by Shalit. Rorschachs were administered to 20 servicemen in the Israeli navy in the 10th hour of a severe storm at sea. Results were compared to Rorschachs previously administered in the routine selection process. Human movement (M) had been hypothesized to remain consistent as a basic personality-trait representation, but inanimate movement (m) would increase due to the subjective experience, or state reaction, of helplessness in the face of intense situational stress. The hypotheses were confirmed.

The first study with the Rorschach on Vietnam combat veterans with the newly created diagnosis of PTSD was by van der Kolk and Ducey (1984, 1989). They interpreted the four severely constricted records among the 14 in their study as evidence of psychic numbing, and therefore the apparent inability to use fantasy or thought as an experimental action. Eight subjects with markedly extratensive Experience Balance (EB) styles and less than normative human movement responses (M) demonstrated "extensive use of unstructured color (CF and pure C), and diminished ego functions," viewed as the intrusive phase of PTSD. These authors additionally found an unusually elevated number of inanimate movement responses (m), indicating "the perception of threatening forces beyond one's control" and a subjective sense of helplessness. Subjects in this study were found to perceive extensive concrete, uncensored percepts of traumatic war events, including numerous blood and anatomy responses. These traumatic percepts were similar to a previous analysis of the Rorschach content of two Vietnam combat veterans with PTSD by Bersoff (1970), who described responses replete with direct and symbolic trauma content "to the almost exclusion of previous, more time spanning, characterological concerns" (p. 200).

Single-subject investigations of the patterns of Rorschach responding in traumatized individuals include Salley and Teiling's (1984) study, which reported the Rorschach responses of a Vietnam combat veteran who experienced dissociated rage attacks. The authors noted the overabundance of divider themes in the content, such as subground explosions, interpreted as the patient's need to wall off, or dissociate, certain aspects of his inner experience. There was a preoccupation with morbid subjects (e.g., wounded people, body parts, and blood), particularly on the chromatic cards. No psychotic thought process was evident. A review of the authors' scoring found a number of errors, including missed inanimate movement (m) scores, which would have corroborated other studies. They did, however, note an elevation in diffuse shading determinants (Y). Both of these indices tap feelings of helplessness, anxiety, and a sense of being out of control of one's environment. Carr (1984) commented on Sally and Teiling's study with his observation of the similarity of several of his own traumatized patients' Rorschachs. Trauma-related percepts underscored the "essence of PTSD . . . the concretization of very specific stimuli that have served to precipitate anxiety around a trauma not yet appropriately integrated" (p. 420). Kowitt (1985) and Carr (1985) exchanged comments about theoretical vantage points regarding "unconscious fantasies and conflicts . . . concealed within the traumatic imagery" (Kowitt, 1985, p. 21).

Souffrant (1987) used the Rorschach to differentiate the presence or absence of PTSD in 60 Vietnam combat veterans. Two hypothesized predictors were significant discriminators between the cohorts: an elevation in inanimate movement (m), and the FC:CF + C ratio, weighted in the direction of unstructured color. The statistically significant elevation in inanimate movement scores indicated an inability to integrate intrusive recollections, as well as evidence of psychic numbing, resulting from severe situational stress. Although both cohorts showed an inability to modulate affect, represented by the predominance of unstructured color responses (CF and C), prediction of PTSD was heightened by the combination with inanimate movement.

Hartman et al. (1990) published Rorschach data from 41 inpatient Vietnam combat veterans with PTSD. The authors referred to their subjects' "tenuous and precarious reality testing," citing an elevated X−% indicative of severe perceptual distortions and bizarre percepts. Ineffective coping strategies (almost half were ambitents), combined with elevated schizophrenia indexes, led the authors to conclude that their sample was similar to Exner's (1986) character-disordered patients. The authors also suggested that subjects' high Lambda scores were possibly a correlate of emotional numbing. However, their assumption was actually further corroborated by the study's mean affective ratio (Afr = .45), which more significantly reflects attempts at avoiding affect.

In contrast, Swanson, Blount, and Bruno (1990), in their study of 50 Vietnam combat veterans with PSTD, linked the low affective ratios with the tendency to "avoid emotionally laden situations." Other results supported Hartman et al.'s findings and indicated impaired reality testing, low stress tolerance, elevated inanimate movement, and unmodulated affect (FC:CF + C = .86:2.16). Subjects engaged in passive ideation and were passive–dependent. They experienced painful, negative introspection (elevated V). (See Table 19.1, below.)

In 1991, Cohen and de Ruiter critiqued the van der Kolk and Ducey study based on conceptual and methodological problems related to non-Exnerian formulations. Ducey and van der Kolk (1991) responded with a discussion of the usefulness of supplementing Exner's classifications for heuristic purposes.

Acute posttraumatic stress among Gulf War veterans was measured by the Rorschach in a 1995 study by Sloan, Arsenault, Hilsenroth, Harvill, and Handler. Thirty Marines, tested soon after 3 months of active duty, experienced acute situational stress and a vulnerability to loss of controls (D = −3.67 and m = 2.74). Difficulty in coping with their high stress levels was related to the overrepresentation of ambient EB scores (43%).

Civilian Populations

In a 1967 study, Modlin reported that in 40 subjects demonstrating a "post-accident anxiety syndrome," total responses to the 10 Rorschach cards averaged between eight and nine. Although Exner's (1990) Comprehensive System subsequently regards records of 14 or fewer answers to be invalid, Modlin related his findings to the premorbid characteristics of a particularly homogeneous sample: "simple, literal, unimaginative ... stoic ... conventional," with limited and constricted capacity for emotional expression. This result was viewed as evidence of vulnerability to the syndrome, as opposed to an indication of the effects of the traumatic events. No other Rorschach variables were discussed.

Nichols and Czirr (1986) recommended the use of the Rorschach test in the differential diagnosis of elderly patients suspected of having PTSD. Elders often present with depressive symptomatology, physical complaints, and occasionally psychotic conditions. The authors found that "while PTSD patients often show depressive indications and color stress [on the Rorschach], form level is generally good and bizarre responses tend to be related to actual experiences" (p. 424).

Cerney (1990) reported results from a Rorschach study of 48 inpatient subjects suffering from traumatic loss, including victims of various types of serious abuse, witnesses of violence, and those having experienced the death or serious injury of a relative or friend. There was no mention of a systematized diagnosis. Cerney noted two distinct modes among women victims of sexual and/or physical abuse: either constricted or absent use of color determinants, with minimal, if any, content of a markedly aggressive nature, versus a cohort with color-dominated responses and numerous primitive and aggressive percepts. Though Cerney did not make the link, this pattern appears consistent with the phasic aspects of hyperarousal and numbing in PTSD.

Levin (1990, 1993) compared Rorschach protocols of adults diagnosed with PTSD (and no previous Axis I or Axis II diagnoses prior to the trauma) with Exner's (1990) nonpatient norms. Subjects with histories of childhood trauma were purposely not selected for inclusion. The 27 subjects in this study experienced various traumatic events after the age of 18, including rape, violent assaults, electrical and chemical accidents, bombings, fires, and other major accidents. The current sample has been expanded to 36 subjects (P. Levin, personal communication, February 19, 1994) and replicates Levin's previous study. Levin found FC:CF + C to be significantly weighted in the direction of unstructured color (77%), indicating that affect was discharged with little or no cognitive mediation or modulation. At the same time, subjects had significantly low affective ratios, indicative of an avoidance of affectively provocative situations. The positive hypervigilance indices, elevated perseveration scores, and concrete trauma-related percepts provide a picture of psychological preparedness, guardedness, and preoccupation with traumatic themes. This study replicated the consistent findings in the literature of elevated inanimate movement (m) and diffuse shading (Y). In addition, there was considerable negative introspection (V) focused on painful self-aspects. I.B. Weiner (personal communication, April, 21, 1995) suggests that Vista responses are not necessarily a stable, trait-type variable, other than the fact that most people have none. When it appears, it may be in response to situational variables. Reality testing, similarly, was significantly impaired. Level 2 fabulized combinations (FABCOM 2) were the only indication of cognitive slippage, a metaphor for the implausibility of the traumatic experience. Subjects used passive ideation and were passive–dependent, likely to prefer drifting off into their own world to replace the noxious experiences from real life (J. E. Exner, personal communication, April 25, 1995). Forty-seven percent of the sample had ambitent EB scores, indicative of vulnerability to stress due to an ineffective coping strategy. Levin noted that problems in emotional control, as well as fixation on the trauma, had a disorganizing effect on cognitive processing.

Kaser-Boyd (1993) examined the Rorschach protocols of 28 battered women, all of whom later went on to murder their battering spouses. Unlike other traumatized samples, Kaser-Boyd's sample produced low numbers of shading (Y and V) and form dimension responses, findings that may have related to the noted general constriction of these women's records. The overall pattern of Rorschach scores, however, resembled in several ways the patterns seen from other traumatized subjects. Kaser-Boyd notes, for instance, that the primary defense of the women in her sample to the experience of strong emotion was to back away, as indicated by high lambdas and low affective ratios. She understood this coping pattern to be consistent with the constricted and overcontrolled phase of the biphasic response that other authors (van der Kolk & Ducey, 1984) have noted in Rorschachs of traumatized combat veterans. Many of the findings from the battered women's records strongly resembled the Rorschach findings from the Vietnam combat veteran studies (cited earlier). Like the male veterans studied by Swanson et al. (1990), and Hartman et al. (1990), these female spousal-abuse victims viewed reality in an unconventional, but not psychotic manner, with severe perceptual distortions (15% of the sample) and bizarre percepts, but with no parallel increase in special scores as might have been expected in a true process thought disorder. Similar to the veterans, these women took an oversimplified approach to their environment (high Lambda), tended to use an ambitent style with passive ideation in problem solving, avoided emotionally laden situations (low Afr), and tended to act on, rather than cognitively modulate, affect when stressed (CF + C > FC). Comparing the findings of the veteran studies with those from her own sample, Kaser-Boyd suggested "that there is something common to the experience of inescapable violence and . . . further, that this can be detected in the processing of Rorschach stimuli" (p. 468).

Other Civilian Populations by Specific Diagnosis

Similarities between borderline personality disorder (BPD) and posttraumatic stress disorder (PTSD), as manifested in veteran populations, have been noted in the literature (Brende, 1983; Parson, 1984). Hartman et al. (1990) noted the similarities between their Rorschach study of Vietnam veterans and Exner's character-disordered subjects' normative data (1990). Other authors (e.g., Herman & van der Kolk, 1987) have noted clinical similarities between those patients diagnosed with BPD and a pattern of posttraumatic adaptations evidenced in trauma survivors. Similar to combat trauma, childhood sexual abuse appears to lead to clinical syndromes that may often closely resemble BPD. Indeed, some research suggests that childhood abuse experiences are an etiological factor in the genesis of BPD (Herman, Perry, & van der Kolk, 1989).

The psychoanalytically oriented research in the 1980s into Rorschach patterns of patients with BPD (e.g., Kwawer, Lerner, Lerner, & Sugarman, 1980) underscored a number of frequently noted responses taken to be characteristic of borderline psychopathology. These responses include a preponderance of unstructured color (FC < CF + C); moderately severe thought disorder scores with a preponderance of fabulized combinations; and frequent breakthroughs of aggressive and/or sexual (primary process) content, often associated with unusual or poor form quality. In the 1990s, a different perspective has been applied to the Rorschachs of BPD patients, informed by trauma studies.

For example, Saunders's (1991) Rorschach investigation illustrated the areas of overlap between trauma-induced symptoms and BPD. Thirty-three subjects diagnosed with BPD, and with histories of extended childhood sexual abuse, were found to produce more color-dominated (CF + C) responses, more "primary process breakthroughs connected with sexual and aggressive content" (p. 62), and disturbances in thought processes and movement scores than in the 29 BPD subjects without such a history. Rappaport's system was used in this study.

Meyers (1988) identified many of the same Rorschach trauma indicators in her sample of 10 outpatient women with childhood (latency-age) incest histories. These records were scored using Piotrowski's system. Meyers found difficulty with affect and impulse controls, feelings of helplessness, and dissociative reactions, as indicated by high numbers of inanimate movement scores.

Rorschach Patterns in Dissociative Disorders

The diagnosis of adult dissociative identity disorder (DID; formerly called multiple personality disorder, MPD) is widely regarded as causally linked to childhood experiences of chronic and severe physical and sexual abuse (Putnam, 1989). It has been suggested that the disorder be renamed posttraumatic multiple personality disorder in order to illustrate this etiological factor (Spiegel, 1984).

A number of Rorschach investigations of dissociative disordered patients have been conducted (Wagner & Heise, 1974; Lovitt & Lefkof, 1985; Armstrong, 1991; Labott, Leavitt, Braun, & Sachs, 1992). Armstrong's (1991) original study of 14 subjects diagnosed with MPD or severe dissociative disorders has been recently enlarged to a sample of 119 (J. Armstrong, personal communication, December 14, 1994). Armstrong's administration includes a pretest invitation to the patient "to express all self-aspects in testing" (1993a, 1993b). The larger sample has essentially replicated her original findings: significantly introversive EB styles (53% introversive and 32% superintroversive), with unusual complexity of organization (low lambda and high number of blends); high number of form dimension responses, indicative of the ability to distance and detach when looking inward; the tendency to back away from affect (low Afr); atypical reality testing; and the presence of concrete trauma-related percepts, defined as a combination of Morbid (MOR), Aggressive (AG), blood (Bl), sex (Sx), and anatomy (An) contents. Subjects were found to have highly ideational, intellectual, and complex coping styles. Armstrong noted that "while they have many [Rorschach] points in common with PTSD patients, they retain an ability to access fantasy that is unusual in a traumatized population" (1993a; see Table 19.1, below).

Lovitt and Lefkof (1985) studied 3 female patients diagnosed with MPD (2 adults and 1 adolescent). The Rorschach was repeated two to three times in order to test predetermined secondary personalities. All of the main (host) personalities had ambient EB styles, while two of the three secondary personalities in each of the two adult patients had superintroversive EB styles, similar to Armstrong's (1991) findings. Seven of the eight secondary personalities of the two adults had a constriction of color responses, which responses were nevertheless predominantly unstructured. The most significant finding was the wide variability among the alters in the numerous scoring categories.

In contrast, Labott et al. (1992) used the Piotrowski scoring method for comparison with a previous study by Wagner, Allison, and Wagner (1983) on a sample of 16 female inpatients diagnosed with MPD, and 16 psychiatric controls. The host personality was asked to remain present throughout the testing. The study raised questions about the validity of the Wagner signs as reliable indicators of MPD. No determinants were given that might have allowed for specific structural comparison with other Rorschach studies.

SUMMARY AND CONCLUSIONS

A clear first step in improving the database of Rorschachs of trauma survivors is the standardization of administration and scoring practices. As seen in the earlier review of studies, investigations have used Piotrowski's, Rappaport's, and Exner's systems. We recommend the future exclusive use, for both research and clinical purposes, of Exner's Comprehensive System, for reasons of its statistical robustness, normative databases, standardized administration and scoring, and psychometric reliability and validity.

We also recommend an increase in sample sizes for more powerful generalization. To date, with the exception of Armstrong's most current and ongoing research, sample sizes have not exceeded 50 subjects. Attempts to define Rorschach trauma patterns are contingent upon large-scale studies. Too, in reporting the results of future studies, tabular presentation of all indices and ratios, rather than selected ones, will allow for a more full comparison and highlight differences among traumatized groups.

The presentation of single-subject Rorschach protocols remains a valuable and necessary idiographic tool. Content analysis, as suggested in this chapter, may provide concrete reference points to unassimilated traumatic material and can be used in conjunction with the presentation of structural summary data.

Although the studies cited here suggest the emergence of possible trauma profiles, convergent validity studies are needed. Future investigations might correlate selected Rorschach variables with reliable and valid measures of dissociation, such as the Dissociative Experience Scale (DES; Bernstein & Putnam, 1986) and/or other measures of PTSD. Such correlative data will add confidence that we are indeed measuring what we believe ourselves to be measuring. Rorschach studies of specific trauma populations (e.g., rape victims, automobile accident survivors, survivors of natural vs manmade disasters) could help clarify if there might be any differences in trauma sequelae based on type of traumatic stressor.

Rorschach investigations of traumatized populations are a relatively new area of research. Despite the use of divergent administration and scoring systems, difficulties of construct validity in defining "trauma," and generally small sample sizes, as well as other methodological problems, commonalities across traumatized groups do emerge. A number of determinants appear to be consistently elevated, which displays the psychological mechanisms of the sequelae to traumatic stressors (see Table 19.1).

The single, most consistent finding across Rorschach studies of various traumatized populations, regardless of the Rorschach scoring system, is the presence of elevations in the number of inanimate movement responses (m). Where the mean number of such responses for nonpatient adults is approximately 1.0, the presence of elevations in inanimate movement has been associated with subjects' responses to a specific environmental stressor. Elevated inanimate movement has been interpreted in a number of essentially similar ways. In the earliest study by Shalit (1965), these elevations were viewed as reflecting a sense of disruption and fear of disintegration of controls, suggesting that elevations in inanimate movement relate directly to the individual's perception of helplessness or lack of control in situations of extreme stress. Too, such disruption in one's sense of control negatively affects attention and concentration (J. E. Exner, personal communication, April 26, 1995), a common symptom seen by clinicians.

Inanimate movement responses are considered by some to be related to dissociative processes. Schachtel (1966) characterized the inanimate movement response as the "attitude of the impotent spectator," an expression that describes unintegrated thoughts during extreme threat in which the individual's sense of helplessness precludes other coping strategies. Similarly, another determinant that is consistently elevated across subject groups is diffuse shading (Y), which taps feelings of anxiety and helplessness. In addition, consistent with both clinical descriptions and recent psychobiological research (van der Kolk, 1994), traumatized populations often evidence raw, unmodulated affect, which is seen on the Rorschach in the predominant use of unstructured color (FC < CF + C), except when the patient is so numbed and avoidant that the protocol appears barren, constricted, and often devoid of any color responses—a denial of affect. The expressions of affective overwhelming of cognitive controls have been interpreted via traditional psychoanalytic Rorschach analysis as reflecting primary process breakthroughs and have played a part in leading other researchers to diagnose borderline personality. We believe that there is compelling evidence, particularly from the field of psychobiological investigation of PTSD (for a review, see van der Kolk, 1994), that argues for understanding the presence of unmodulated, unassimilated affect as relating to failures in particular neurotransmitter actions within the limbic system. Such research suggests that intense

TABLE 19.1. Descriptive Statistics on Rorschach Variables for "Pure Trauma" Adults, Vietnam Combat Veterans and Dissociative Disordered Adults

	"Pure trauma"[a]		Vets[b]		DID[c]	
	M	SD	M	SD	M	SD
m	3.53	2.48	1.06	1.03	2.36	2.11
Y	2.36	1.74	0.54	1.21	2.30	2.65
M	4.36	2.78	1.54	1.17	4.83	2.93
FC	1.81	1.86	0.40	0.60	1.79	1.49
CF	2.03	1.58	0.52	0.85	1.53	1.59
C	0.81	1.19	0.22	0.46	0.45	0.74
WSumC	4.14	2.75	2.79	2.26	3.09	2.12
Afr	0.45	0.23	0.49	0.15	0.47	0.17
X + %	0.59	0.11	0.46	0.15	0.43	0.15
X − %	0.15	0.08	0.29	0.15	0.15	0.11
Populars	6.78	2.20	4.72	2.13	4.89	1.68
FD	0.97	0.91	0.32	0.61	2.40	2.25
V	0.69	0.89	0.86	1.70	0.98	1.47
D Score	− 1.42	1.98	− 1.82	1.97	− 1.17	2.20
Adj D	− 0.14	1.48	− 0.82	1.41	− 0.16	1.40
Lambda	0.53	0.43	1.28	1.59	0.42	0.34
Zf	13.67	5.62	11.76	5.09	11.74	4.17
Blends	6.00	2.84	4.28	3.31	6.62	3.92
FABCOM	0.52	1.06	0.56	0.83	0.40	0.69
WSum6	4.33	5.09	6.56	7.52	19.73	21.96
MOR	1.61	1.76	2.68	2.82	3.84	2.77
AG	1.14	1.29	1.58	1.88	1.61	1.85
Bl	0.75	1.16	0.48	0.90	0.98	1.38
Sx	0.81	1.26	0.14	0.49	1.37	1.79
An	1.08	1.59	1.42	1.81	1.20	1.22

[a]"Pure trauma" adults; $n = 36$ (P. Levin, personal communication, February 19, 1994).
[b]Vietnam combat veterans; $n = 50$ (Swanson et al. 1990).
[c]Dissociative disordered adults; $n = 119$ (J. Armstrong, personal communication, December 14, 1994).

emotional memories of trauma are processed through the hippocampally mediated memory system and are difficult to extinguish due to permanent brain alterations over time.

Fixation on the trauma was first noted in 1888 by Pierre Janet, who also observed traumatic memory to be stored as visceral sensations or visceral images. Rorschach studies (Carr 1984; van der Kolk & Ducey, 1989; Armstrong, 1991; Levin, 1993) across traumatized populations consistently have found references to highly personalized images and memory fragments that relate directly to aspects of the trauma experienced by the subject. Our experience has been that this press to relive, in Rorschach traumatic themes related to the individual's previous exposure, often supersedes otherwise intact reality testing functions, resulting in a preponderance of aggressive and morbid themes, often involving contents of blood, damaged anatomy, and sexual percepts. We do not, however, view these responses and accompanying perceptual distortions to be indicative of a formal thought disorder so much as the "undigested reliving similar, but not identical to a flashback" (Levin, 1993). Armstrong (1991) has taken a similar view, suggesting "that patients' morbid, brutal and sadistically sexual projective test associations may not be evidence of psychological regression but rather reflect their understanding of an external world that has behaved in an aggressive 'primitive' fashion toward them" (p. 542).

Trauma sequelae, as described by Rorschach studies, may serve an adaptive, defensive function, seen in the attempt to limit affective involvement as a safeguard to the flooded affect and precarious controls that predominate. A mantle of interpersonal distance, guardedness, and hypervigilance to further feared threat are all defensive protections that may serve the trauma survivor in the struggle to regain equilibrium.

The Rorschach profiles that have emerged through the data, gleaned from the studies reviewed, validate clinical observation and experience. In Table 19.2, proposed Rorschach indices are linked with DSM-IV criteria to provide clinicians with a heuristically meaningful opportunity to correlate Rorschach data with specific symptoms. Furthermore, the Rorschach can pro-

TABLE 19.2. Comparison of DSM-IV Categories and Rorschach Variables

DSM-IV category of PTSD	Proposed Rorschach variables
B. Reexperiencing symptoms	
1. Intrusions	M−; CF + C > FC; m&Y; HVI; PSV; Sx&Bl; V; X − %; An; MOR; low M
2. Dreams	Indices not available
3. Dissociative symptoms	Pure C; m; M−; M no form; FAB2; X − %; FD
4. Psychological distress at triggers	m&Y; Pure C; D score; V; AG; MOR
5. Physiological reactivity at triggers	HVI; ?Pure C; Y
C. Avoidance symptoms	
1. Avoid thoughts/feelings	Afr; Lambda; low M; WSumC; Lambda
2. Avoid situations	Afr; HVI; Mp > Ma; Isolation index
3. Amnesia	Indices not available
4. Diminished interest	Afr; Lambda; HVI
5. Detachment	M no form; Afr; m; HVI; T = 0; FD; Mp
6. Foreshortened future	MOR
D. Arousal symptoms	
1. Sleep difficulties	Indices not available
2. Irritability/anger	m&Y; AG; S; ?Pure C
3. Poor concentration	m; Mp > Ma
4. Hypervigilance	HVI
5. Startle	?Pure C; HVI

vide a rich and unique elaboration, clarification, and integration of the complex symptom picture of the disorders that are causally related to trauma.

REFERENCES

Armstrong, J. (1991). The psychological organization of multiple personality disordered patients as revealed in psychological testing. *Psychiatric Clinics of North America, 14,* 533–546.

Armstrong, J. (1993a). Psychological assessment of multiple personality disorder. *Society for Personality Assessment Exchange, 3*(2), 4–5, 10.

Armstrong, J. (1993b). A method for assessing multiple personality disorder through psychological testing. In M. Cohen & J. Turkus (Eds.), *Multiple personality disorder: Continuum of care.* Northvale, NJ: Jason Aronson.

Bernstein, E., & Putnam, F. (1986). Development, reliability, and validity of a dissociation scale. *Journal of Nervous and Mental Disease, 174,* 727–735.

Bersoff, S. (1970). Rorschach correlates of traumatic neurosis of war. *Journal of Projective Techniques and Personality Assessment, 34*(3), 194–200.

Brende, J. (1983). A psychodynamic view of character pathology in combat veterans. *Bulletin of the Menninger Clinic, 47,* 197–216.

Burgess, A., & Holmstrom, R. (1974). Rape trauma syndrome. *American Journal of Psychiatry, 131,* 981–985.

Carr, A. (1984). Content interpretation re: Salley and Teiling's "Dissociated rage attacks in a Vietnam veteran: A Rorschach study." *Journal of Personality Assessment, 48*(4), 420–421.

Carr, A. (1985). Rorschach content interpretation in post-traumatic stress disorders: A reply to Kowitt. *Journal of Personality Assessment, 49*(1), 25.

Cerney, M. (1990). The Rorschach and traumatic loss: Can the presence of traumatic loss be detected from the Rorschach? *Journal of Personality Assessment, 55*(3–4), 781–789.

Cohen, L., & de Ruiter, C. (1991). The Rorschach and PTSD revisited: Critique of van der Kolk and Ducey (1989). *Journal of Traumatic Stress, 4,* 407–417.

Ducey, C., & van der Kolk, B. (1991). The psychological processing of traumatic experience: Reply to Cohen and de Ruiter. *Journal of Traumatic Stress, 4,* 425–432.

Exner, J. (1986). *The Rorschach: A comprehensive system: Vol. I. Basic foundations* (2nd ed.). New York: Rorschach Workshops.

Exner, J. (1990). *A Rorschach workbook for the comprehensive system* (3rd ed.). Asheville, NC: Rorschach Workshops.

Exner, J. (1991). *The Rorschach: A comprehensive system: Vol. 2. Interpretation* (2nd ed.). New York: Wiley.

Frank, G. (1992). On the use of the Rorschach in the study of PTSD. *Journal of Personality Assessment, 59*(3), 641–643.

Green, B., Lindy, J., & Grace, M. (1985). Posttraumatic stress disorder: Toward DSM-IV. *Journal of Nervous and Mental Disease, 173*(7), 406–411.

Hartman, W., Clark, M., Morgan, M., Dunn, V., Fine, A., Perry, G., & Winsch, D. (1990). Rorschach structure of a hospitalized sample of Vietnam veterans with PTSD. *Journal of Personality Assessment, 54*(1–2), 149–159.

Herman, J., Perry, J. C., & van der Kolk, B. (1989). Childhood trauma in borderline personality disorder. *American Journal of Psychiatry, 146,* 490–495.

Herman, J., & van der Kolk, B. (1987). Traumatic antecedents of borderline personality disorder. In B. A. van der Kolk (Ed.), *Post-traumatic stress disorder: Psychological and biological sequelae.* Washington, DC: American Psychiatric Press.

Horowitz, M. (1976). *Stress response syndromes.* Northvale, NJ: Jason Aronson.

Janet, P. (1889). *L'automatisme psychologique.* Paris: Ballière.

Kardiner, A. (1941). *The traumatic neuroses of war.* New York: Hoeber.

Kaser-Boyd, N. (1993). Rorschachs of women who commit homicide. *Journal of Personality Assessment, 60*(3), 458–470.

Keane, T., Malloy, P., & Fairbank J. (1984). Empirical development of an MMPI subscale for the assessment of combat-related posttraumatic stress disorder. *Journal of Consulting and Clinical Psychology, 52*(5), 888–891.

Kowitt, M. (1985). Rorschach content interpretation in posttraumatic stress disorders: A reply to Carr. *Journal of Personality Assessment, 49*(1), 21–24.

Krystal, H., & Niederland, W. (1968). Clinical observations on the survivor syndrome. In H. Krystal (Ed.), *Massive psychic trauma.* New York: International Universities Press.

Kwawer J., Lerner, H., Lerner, P., & Sugarman, A. (Eds.). (1985). *Borderline phenomena and the Rorschach test.* New York: International Universities Press.

Labott, S., Leavitt, F., Braun, B., & Sachs, R. (1992). Rorschach indicators of multiple personality disorder. *Perceptual and Motor Skills, 75,* 147–158.

Levin, P. (1990). A normative study of the Rorschach and post-traumatic stress disorder (Doctoral dissertation, Massachusetts School of Professional Psychology, 1990). *Dissertation Abstracts International, 51,* 08-B, 4057.

Levin, P. (1993). Assessing PTSD with the Rorschach projective technique. In J. Wilson & B. Raphael (Eds.), *International handbook of traumatic stress syndromes.* New York: Plenum Press.

Lindy, J. (1985). The trauma membrane and other clinical concepts derived from psychotherapeutic work with survivors of natural disasters. *Psychiatric Annals, 15*(3) 153–160.

Lovitt, R., & Lefkof, G. (1985). Understanding multiple personality disorder with the comprehensive Rorschach system. *Journal of Personality Assessment, 59,* 289–294.

Meyers, J. (1988). The Rorschach as a tool in understanding the dynamics of women with histories of incest. In H. Lerner & P. Lerner (Eds.), *Primitive mental states and the Rorschach.* Madison, CT: International Universities Press.

Modlin, H. (1967). A post accident anxiety syndrome: Psychosocial aspects. *American Journal of Psychiatry, 123*(8), 1008–1012.

Nichols, B., & Czirr, R. (1986). Post-traumatic stress disorder: Hidden syndrome in elders. *Clinical Gerontologist, 5*(3–4), 417–433.

Parker, K. (1983). A meta-analysis of the reliability and validity of the Rorschach. *Journal of Personality Assessment, 47*(3), 227–231.

Parson, E. (1984). The reparation of the self: Clinical and theoretical dimensions in the treatment of the Vietnam combat veteran. *Journal of Contemporary Psychotherapy, 14,* 4–56.

Putnam, F. (1989). *Diagnosis and treatment of multiple personality disorder.* New York: Guilford Press.

Sales, E., Baum, M., & Shore, R. (1984). Victim readjustment following assault. *Journal of Personality Assessment, 48*(1), 98–104.

Salley, R., & Teiling, P. (1984). Dissociated rage attacks in a Vietnam veteran: A Rorschach study. *Journal of Personality Assessment, 48*(1), 98–104.

Saunders, E. (1991). Rorschach indicators of chronic childhood sexual abuse in female borderline inpatients. *Bulletin of the Menninger Clinic, 55,* 48–70.

Schachtel, E. (1966). *Experiential foundations of Rorschach's test.* New York: Basic Books.

Shalit, B. (1965). Effects of environmental stimulation on the M, FM and m responses in the Rorschach. *Journal of Projective Techniques and Personality Assessment, 29,* 228–231.

Sloan, P., Arsenault, L., Hilsenroth, M., Harvill, L., & Handler, L. (1995). Rorschach measures of posttraumatic stress in Persian Gulf war veterans. *Journal of Personality Assessment, 64*(3), 397–414.

Souffrant, E. (1987). The use of the Rorschach in the assessment of post traumatic stress disorder among Vietnam combat veterans (Doctoral dissertation, Temple University, 1987). *Dissertation Abstracts International, 48,* 04B.

Spiegel, D. (1984). Multiple personality disorder as a posttraumatic stress disorder. *Psychiatric Clinics of North America, 7,* 101–110.

Swanson, G., Blount, J., & Bruno, R. (1990). Comprehensive system Rorschach data on Vietnam combat veterans. *Journal of Personality Assessment, 54*(1–2), 160–169.

van der Kolk, B. (1987). The psychological consequences of overwhelming life experiences. In B. van der Kolk (Ed.), *Psychological trauma.* Washington, DC: American Psychiatric Press.

van der Kolk, B. (1994, January/February). The body keeps the score: Memory and the evolving psychobiology of posttraumatic stress. *Harvard Review of Psychiatry,* pp. 253–265.

van der Kolk, B., & Ducey, C. (1984). Clinical implications of the Rorschach in posttraumatic stress disorder. In B. A. van der Kolk (Ed.), *Post-traumatic stress disorder: Psychological and biological sequelae.* Washington, DC: American Psychiatric Press.

van der Kolk, B., & Ducey, C. (1989). The psychological processing of traumatic experience: Rorschach patterns in post traumatic stress disorder. *Journal of Traumatic Stress, 2*(3), 259–274.

van der Kolk, B., & van der Hart, O. (1989). Pierre Janet and the rediscovery of psychological trauma. *American Journal of Psychiatry, 146*(12), 1530–1540.

Wagner, E., Allison, R., & Wagner, C. (1983). Diagnosing multiple personalities with the Rorschach: A confirmation. *Journal of Personality Assessment, 47,* 143–149.

Wagner, E., & Heise, M. (1974). A comparison of Rorschach protocols of three multiple personalities. *Journal of Personality Assessment, 38,* 308–331.

Wilson, J., Harel, Z., & Kahana, B. (Eds.). (1988). *Human adaptation to extreme stress: From the Holocaust to Vietnam.* New York: Plenum Press.

Wilson, J., & Walker, A. (1990). Toward an MMPI trauma profile. *Journal of Traumatic Stress, 3*(1), 151–168.

Author Index

Subject Index

ACN2079